# THE PATH TO PARALYSIS

# THE PATH TO PARALYSIS

How American Politics Became
Nasty, Dysfunctional, and
a Threat to the Republic

DONALD G. NIEMAN

ANTHEM PRESS

Anthem Press
An imprint of Wimbledon Publishing Company
www.anthempress.com

This edition first published in UK and USA 2025
by ANTHEM PRESS
75–76 Blackfriars Road, London SE1 8HA, UK
or PO Box 9779, London SW19 7ZG, UK
and
244 Madison Ave #116, New York, NY 10016, USA

© Donald G. Nieman 2025

The author asserts the moral right to be identified as the author of this work.

All rights reserved. Without limiting the rights under copyright reserved above,
no part of this publication may be reproduced, stored or introduced into
a retrieval system, or transmitted, in any form or by any means
(electronic, mechanical, photocopying, recording or otherwise),
without the prior written permission of both the copyright
owner and the above publisher of this book.

*British Library Cataloguing-in-Publication Data*
A catalogue record for this book is available from the British Library.

*Library of Congress Cataloging-in-Publication Data*
A catalog record for this book has been requested.
2024938956

ISBN-13: 978-1-83999-276-6 (Pbk)
ISBN-10: 1-83999-276-X (Pbk)

Cover Credit: A crowd-erected gallows hangs near the United States Capitol during
the 2021 storming of the United States Capitol @ wikimedia commons

This title is also available as an e-book.

For
Leigh Ann
Whose love, ideas, and partnership enrich my life
Brady
Whose commitment to a better world and ideas about politics inspired me
And
Binghamton Students in the Wheeler-Nieman Modern U.S.
History Survey, 2011–2020
Whose questions and ideas challenged us and made us dig deeper

# CONTENTS

*Acknowledgments* ix
*Introduction* xiii

**CHAPTER 1** 1964 — 1
**CHAPTER 2** The Liberal Consensus Under Fire, 1965–1969 — 29
**CHAPTER 3** Conflict, Crisis, and Continuity, 1969–1976 — 69
**CHAPTER 4** A New Right Emerges, 1972–1980 — 97
**CHAPTER 5** Reagan: The Revolution That Wasn't—and Was, 1980–1988 — 127
**CHAPTER 6** Conservatives at the Crossroads, 1988–1992 — 161
**CHAPTER 7** Ideological Convergence and Political Polarization, 1992–2000 — 183
**CHAPTER 8** The Lost Opportunity, 2000–2008 — 225
**CHAPTER 9** The Tipping Point, 2008–2012 — 265
**CHAPTER 10** Reaping the Whirlwind, 2013–2016 — 305
**CHAPTER 11** American Carnage, 2016–2020 — 335
**CHAPTER 12** "A republic, if you can keep it" — 373

*Conclusion* 405
*Bibliographical Essay* 411
*Index* 421

# ACKNOWLEDGMENTS

The idea for this book originated in History 104: Modern America, a course I co-taught at Binghamton University for a decade with my wife, Professor Leigh Ann Wheeler. The 250–300 students, mostly freshmen in need of general education credits, who filed into Lecture Hall 1 or 2 got a bit of a surprise. Two for the price of one, a husband and wife teaching a course together. Leigh Ann and I love teaching, although she's better at it than I am. Teaching together was an especially rich intellectual and personal experience. We planned every session together, debated what should be included, found new angles to pursue and fresh questions to ask, shared our perspectives with our students, sometimes disagreed, and occasionally finished one another's sentences. It was a true family affair; on snow days, our son Brady was often there. Students responded positively to our interpretive disagreements and modeling of history as a conversation about the past. The questions they asked and observations they made pushed us to be better teachers and historians. Years later, students who took the class— including one Brady and I encountered in Istanbul—tell us it was a memorable experience. Leigh Ann and I no longer teach the course, thanks to departmental policies aimed at standardization. Nevertheless, the insights we developed together teaching the last section of the course made me want to write this book, and they inform every page. I asked Leigh Ann to be a co-author. She declined to focus on her biography of Anne Moody, which has been a heroic undertaking. It will appear soon and be a major contribution to African American, civil rights, and women's history. In a sense, though, she is my co-author because the book's inspiration and many of its insights come from her.

 I began work on the project as I prepared to leave my position as provost of Binghamton University, a job I held from 2012 to 2022. I wrote much of it during the leave the University generously granted in 2022–2023, before I returned to full-time teaching. After 22 years as a dean of arts & sciences and then a provost, the leave was a blessing, an opportunity to read, write, think, and re-engage the world of scholarship. I want to thank President Harvey Stenger for providing the leave and for being such a wonderful boss and good friend over the course of a decade in which we did our best to make a great university better. I also want to thank staff in the Provost's Office, including Don Loewen, Michael McGoff, Susan Strehle, John Cordi, James Pitarresi, Katharine Krebs, Madhu Govindaraju, Hari Srihari, Daryl Santos, and Vicki Griffin, whose hard work, collegiality, efficiency, and friendship made it possible for me to teach the modern U.S. history course on a regular basis. Especially Vicki, whose efficiency, professionalism, and constant good humor made everything run like clockwork. Dean Celia Klin, who has made support for faculty a priority, deserves a shout out as well. Generous financial assistance from the Harpur College Faculty Research Fund, which she has worked tirelessly to build, provided support for publication.

Management, editors, and staff at Anthem Press have been all any author could ask. Tej P. J. Sood, the Publisher and Managing Director, believed in an unusual project and had good ideas for bringing it to life. Ponni Brinda has managed the project from the time I submitted the proposal and helped it through the peer review and editorial processes with efficiency, professionalism, and good humor. Jebaslin Hephzibah and Balaji Devadoss ensured that design and production proceeded professionally and smoothly. Swetha Babuji has brought her keen eye as an expert copyeditor to the project.

I have benefitted from thoughtful, knowledgeable critiques by four anonymous readers, two recruited by Anthem Press and two by Oxford University Press, whose offer to proceed with publication I regretfully declined. All four readers made me believe in the project at a time when I had doubts. Their comments helped me rethink parts of the book, incorporate the findings of scholarship I had neglected, clarify my arguments, and correct embarrassing errors. They also reminded me of the generosity and collegiality of academics whose uncompensated labor helps others make their work better and elevates the standards of scholarship. I don't know who you are, but you have my sincere thanks and gratitude.

Many other people have provided ideas, critiques, and suggestions that have improved the manuscript. My son, Brady Wheeler-Nieman, got me interested in the topic of political polarization through a paper he wrote as a high school junior on George W. Bush and the War on Terror. Discussions with him over the years have helped me better understand U.S. politics and especially to see it through the eyes of Gen Z. Members of Binghamton University's Modern U.S. History Workshop—created and led with aplomb by Professors Leigh Ann Wheeler and Wendy Wall—read and commented on Chapters 1 and 4; their questions and suggestions caused me to rethink aspects of those chapters. I am especially grateful to Kevin Boyle of Northwestern University and Alison Kibler of Franklin and Marshall College, who served as commentators for the workshop sessions on those chapters. My friend Andy Schocket read the manuscript and offered his usual mix of good questions and well-informed observations punctuated with one-liners Groucho Marx would appreciate. In addition to her contributions to the conceptualization of the book through our co-teaching, Leigh Ann Wheeler has read significant chunks of the manuscript, even as she was busy with her Anne Moody biography. As always, her comments and questions made me think more deeply, write more clearly, avoid many errors, and enjoy the process. She is the best editor I have ever had and anyone could ask for, as her many doctoral students will attest.

My mother-in-law Shirley Hoden, and brother-in-law Todd Wheeler didn't read or comment on the manuscript. But they have been an important part of my life for 25 years, adding joy, laughter, and love to holidays and special family occasions. I treasure our early morning conversations when they visit because I always come away from them with a positive outlook on our messy world and something new to think about. Our dear friend and colleague, Jean Quataert, might have read the manuscript had she not passed in May 2021. She was an integral part of our family, including our spirited conversations about politics. Her passion for justice, understanding of the possibilities and limits of politics, outrageous sense of humor, and salty language made the time we spent together memorable as well as fun. All of us miss her and think of her often.

Writing a book is always a joy. Sharing the process with Leigh Ann and Brady has made it even more special. They keep me grounded, make me laugh, ensure that there are plenty of dogs in my life, share the things that are truly important (like Yankees' baseball, Cape May Point, music, family memories, and hope for the future), and make my life far richer than I deserve. It is to them that I dedicate this book with deep love, many fond memories, and hope for making many more memories together.

DGN

Cape May Point, New Jersey

March 2024

# INTRODUCTION

Some historic events are seared into our collective memory. We can bring to mind where we were, what we were doing, and who was with us when we heard the news. Like the Kennedy Assassination or 9–11, the Capitol Insurrection is one of those events. Few will forget where they were when they learned— from a text, a phone call, the Internet, Instagram, Facebook, or television— that angry mobs had stormed the Capitol and stopped Congress from counting electoral votes in the 2020 presidential election. Horrific scenes were played over and over on television and the Internet. They showed angry men and women breaking through doors and windows, trampling and beating Capitol Police officers, shouting "Hang Mike Pence," waving the Confederate flag, rifling through House Speaker Nancy Pelosi's desk, and more. Americans were shocked, incredulous. Things like that happened in banana republics, not in the U.S. For over 230 years, presidential elections had taken place every four years, during peace and war. Political parties had battled one another for power, and the contests had always been spirited, sometimes bitter. But ballots, not mobs, determined the outcome—with one crucial exception. In 1861, 11 states withdrew from the Union rather than accepting the election of a Republican president, plunging the nation into civil war. Watching the chaos on January 6, 2021, many feared we were headed there again.

The Capitol Insurrection came in the wake of decades of intensifying political division, hyper-partisanship, and bitter conflict. Presidential candidates—and presidents—had been charged with supporting policies that enabled baby killers, establishing "death panels" to determine whether the elderly would receive medical care, gutting social safety net programs that supported the impoverished and the elderly, taking guns away from law-abiding citizens, paroling convicted Black murderers who used their freedom to commit rape, and more. One president, opponents charged, wasn't qualified to hold office because he hadn't been born in the U.S. Since 1998, two presidents had been impeached (but not convicted), one of them twice. They were the first presidential impeachments since Reconstruction. Politics had become downright nasty, and every election cycle provided evidence that politicians would sink to new lows in attacking their enemies. The 2020 election provided confirmation: a sitting president refused to accept the outcome and incited his followers to storm the Capitol.

Recrimination, character assassination, and no-holds-barred political warfare made governing difficult and produced years of gridlock on matters the public cared about like gun violence, immigration, climate change, the deficit, childhood poverty, and Social Security and Medicare reform. On some issues, like climate, the parties couldn't agree that there was a problem, even though almost all scientists assured them that there was. Disagreement over the very existence of an existential problem prevented serious debate about the best solutions, not to mention the give and take necessary to forge policy. Americans occupied different political universes. They recognized different facts, and they could avoid views—and facts—that challenged their beliefs. Intensifying conflict made some more passionate about and deeply engaged in politics. Many focused on a single issue—guns, abortion, immigration, and climate to name a few—and supported politicians who took their side, even when they violated basic norms of decency. For many others, partisanship was motivated as much by the desire to defeat a despised enemy as to achieve particular policy outcomes.

Many Americans, however, disengaged. They were confused by changes they didn't fully understand. But they knew that large budget deficits weren't sustainable, gun violence was out of control, the social safety network needed mending, too few people benefitted when the economy boomed, and too many suffered when decisions made by those who benefitted the most led to recession. They were disgusted by a dysfunctional political process that failed to address the issues and politicians who seemed more interested in exploiting division than solving problems. They were frustrated by gridlock perpetuated by politicians who seemed more interested in denying their opponents victories than governing.

How did we get to this sorry, scary place? That is what this book seeks to explain. Donald Trump disrupted American political norms. The forces he channeled to gain power and the way he exercised it are critical in explaining January 6 and the fraught state of American politics today. But there's much more to the story than Trump and the eight chaotic years of his presidency and post-presidency. While he certainly influenced events, he was also the product of a political system and a society, culture, and economy that had experienced wrenching changes over the previous half-century. His success lay in the con man's ability to exploit the frustration, resentment, confusion, and anger produced by those changes. Explaining why American politics is dysfunctional and a threat to the republic, therefore, requires that we take the long view, the perspective provided by history.

There are many points where we could begin. But I believe the best place is 1964. It was a pivotal moment that stands in sharp contrast to what followed and, certainly, where we are today. The country still reeled from John Kennedy's assassination, was beset by racial conflict, feared nuclear Armageddon, and confronted a norm-busting presidential candidate. But it was high noon in the American Century. Americans were bombarded with messages assuring them that their nation—the leader of the free world—was a place where opportunity was open to all without regard to race, color, or creed; labor and management cooperated to assure broadly shared prosperity; and politicians worked together to achieve sensible solutions to problems. Many even believed these things, or at least thought they were more true than not.

And why not? The country's economy was booming, real income was growing, the gap between rich and poor was shrinking, Jim Crow was on the run, young people were attending college in astonishing numbers, and no one expected the party to end. Americans trusted their leaders, and they believed that the government could make things better as it had through the GI Bill, the interstate highway system, and Social Security. They rewarded a president who supported civil rights, declared war on poverty, and promised to build a Great Society with a landslide victory over a challenger who equated Social Security with socialism.

Lyndon Johnson was a liberal. He was a devotee of Franklin Roosevelt's New Deal and was committed to use the power of the federal government to expand social, economic, and racial equity. Like most postwar liberals, he believed the U.S. must defend democracy and free markets by standing firm against Communism. However, Johnson didn't win because of his liberalism. Few Americans considered themselves liberals; a Lou Harris Poll conducted in November 1964 revealed that 20% of Americans described themselves as liberal while 35% identified as conservatives and 44% said they were "middle of the road." Voters supported Johnson's ambitious agenda because they were optimistic and believed the Cold War shibboleths that proclaimed the U.S. a land of liberty and justice for all. Were there naysayers? Of course. After all, almost 40% of voters cast their ballot for Barry Goldwater. But most Americans faced the future with confidence and thought there were no limits to what a rich, innovative, powerful, and principled nation that had liberated Europe and Asia from fascist tyranny could accomplish.

That soon changed, in part because of decisions made by political leaders like Lyndon Johnson and Richard Nixon, but also in response to wrenching social, cultural, and economic changes that were underway. Taken together, decisions by leaders and changing circumstances gradually dimmed the sunny potential of 1964, began a realignment of American politics, and created new, even toxic disagreements among Americans that would fester for decades and make political conflict increasingly bitter and dysfunctional. Vietnam, Watergate, and stagflation knocked political leaders from their pedestals and created deep cynicism about politics and politicians. The nation's economy remained strong, but as Europe and Japan recovered from the devastation of World War II, they became formidable competitors in basic industries like automobiles and steel as well as areas of innovation like electronics. Then there was the oil shock of the 1970s, a product of rising demand and conflict in the Middle East that led to dramatic increases in the price of crude oil that hit the entire economy like a hurricane. The U.S. experienced runaway inflation, began shifting from an industrial to a knowledge economy, and saw jobs disappear and factories close in once prosperous industrial cities from the Northeast through the Midwest.

Many Americans suffered, saw their communities wither, and lost faith in government's ability to make their lives better. Too many politicians, like Nixon, were self-serving and corrupt. Even well-intentioned leaders like Gerald Ford and Jimmy Carter seemed incapable of solving the problems that confronted Americans who lost their jobs, waited hours in line to buy gas, and struggled to keep up with escalating prices. As cynicism grew and optimism shrank, generosity declined. The war on poverty had cost billions but many concluded that poverty won. With so many people economically pinched, uncertain about their future, fearful the nation was in economic decline, and disillusioned about government, support for public expenditures to help the disadvantaged plummeted.

Sharp conflict over race, culture, values, and identity also emerged in the 1970s. It would shape American politics for the next 50 years. Race had long been a flashpoint in American politics and culture, and it intensified in the 1970s. Conflict over Black rights in the South had generated significant sympathy for the cause among White northerners in the mid-1960s. But as the movement headed North, many northern Whites had second thoughts. When LBJ told his aide Bill Moyers that passage of the Civil Rights Act would cost Democrats the South for a generation, he thought he was being facetious.[1] What he didn't anticipate was that his civil rights policies would erode support among Whites

---

1 Charles Kaiser, "'We may have lost the South:' what LBJ really said about Democrats in 1964," *The Guardian*, January 23, 2023 https://www.theguardian.com/books/2023/jan/22/we-may-have-lost-the-south-lbj-democrats-civil-rights-act-1964-bill-moyers (accessed February 11, 2023).

generally, including many northern working-class Whites who formed the core of the New Deal coalition. Race also fed opposition to anti-poverty programs. Many Whites came to see them as giveaways that coddled lazy Blacks who refused to work and had "illegitimate" children they couldn't support.

New battlegrounds also emerged. Second-wave feminism brought demands for women's rights and opened opportunities long the preserve of men. It also generated a backlash from men and many women who rejected the Equal Rights Amendment and defended traditional gender roles. They charged that feminists were trading the privileges and protections women enjoyed for a false promise of equality that would sow discord, undermine the family, and make women more vulnerable. Evangelical Christians also found their voices. Long disengaged from politics, they rallied against what they saw as feminists' assault on the family, liberal abortion laws, Supreme Court decisions that sanctioned the slaughter of hundreds of thousands of unborn every year, and a gay and lesbian rights movement that was turning the country against God's design. Race, gender, the family, abortion, and homosexuality combined to trigger heated moral disagreements that no amount of data would resolve and that wouldn't go away. Politicians were only too happy to exploit them.

In this environment, American politics shifted right. It shouldn't have come as a surprise. During the 1950s, after all, Americans had twice elected Dwight Eisenhower president, and in 1960, his vice president, Richard Nixon, lost to John Kennedy by the narrowest of margins. The U.S. was a center-right nation, and a majority of Americans hadn't embraced liberalism. However, prosperity, giddy optimism, Cold War verities depicting the U.S. as the land of equality and opportunity, and trust in government persuaded Americans to elect LBJ in a landslide and support his bold vision for a Great Society. That and a choice between Johnson and an opponent who seemed to be an unbalanced extremist who tried to persuade Americans that things were going to hell in a handbasket at a time most were upbeat. As optimism and trust evaporated and prosperity dimmed, however, conservatives found a receptive audience. Republicans had just the man to work the audience—one who had been doing it for years. Ronald Reagan combined a conservative vision with an avuncular demeanor and reassurance that a return to conservative fundamentals would restore the American Dream. He was Goldwater without the strident, scary edge, and he was seeking election at a time Americans weren't happy. Reagan not only won two terms as president, he changed the national conversation. Ultimately, his success forced Democrats like Bill Clinton to alter their party's message, accepting greater limits on government's reach and acknowledging some of the virtues of the market.

The country's shift to the right produced sharply different policies but not political dysfunction. The conflict was bitter; liberal Democrats attacked Reagan and his allies as greedy, heartless champions of a new Social Darwinism. Their policies, Democrats charged, were designed to help the rich become richer while making the lives of the poor even more precarious. Ideological differences were stark, and the parties disagreed fundamentally about the role of government in a free society—at least until the late 1980s, when Sunbelt Democrats like Bill Clinton moved the Democratic party to the center. Even in the midst of sharp ideological conflict, however, stuff got done, even if many considered it bad stuff. Bipartisanship was taken for granted and compromises necessary to govern were routine if hard fought. Deal-making was, in part, the product of parties that competed for a large number of swing states across the country and were themselves ideologically diverse. There was still a healthy bloc of moderate Republicans and an influential group of conservative Blue Dog Democrats in Congress, making negotiations between parties easier and compromises more likely, despite sharp conflict over policy.

Social and cultural issues certainly made the political discussion more heated. Beginning with Richard Nixon's efforts to exploit crime and White grievance, Republicans courted conservative voters disenchanted with social and cultural change. The strategy made for strange bedfellows, bringing more working-class Whites, White evangelicals, and Catholics into a party that had long been associated with big business and the country club set. But Republican strategists knew that addition was the key to success, and by appealing to social conservatives they could bring new voters into the GOP. In the 1970s and 1980s, however, social conservatives weren't the tail that wagged the dog. Their positions were recognized on Republican platforms, and Reagan delivered his lines supporting their views so effectively that he might have won an Oscar for his performance. But they didn't define the party—there were still Republicans who supported rights to abortion, gay rights, and affirmative action. Republicans continued to talk the social conservatives' talk, but when push came to shove, they didn't prioritize their policies. Cutting taxes, reducing the size of government, and stopping Soviet expansion were what mattered. Nevertheless, a fateful alliance had been forged, and because social conservatives delivered support that was too important to sacrifice, their influence in Republican ranks would grow.

As Republicans took positions designed to please social conservatives, Democrats attacked them as racist, sexist defenders of corporate privilege. It was a message designed to appeal to minorities and women—newer constituencies—while maintaining the loyalty of working-class Whites. Tensions among these groups caused strains within the party. Nevertheless, the appeal to identity issues—especially race and gender—became central to Democratic rhetoric and strategy.

The late 1980s and 1990s saw important changes in the political landscape. Democrats adapted and moved to the center, making it harder for Republicans to caricature them as tax-and-spend liberals out of touch with mainstream American values. The collapse of the Iron Curtain and, then, of the Soviet Union, deprived Republicans of another tried and true line of attack—charging Democrats with being too soft on Communism to defend the nation from the Soviet menace. By 1992, Republicans also carried baggage from 12 years in power—the Savings and Loan fiasco, the Iran-Contra scandal, and a nasty recession. As a result, Democrats became more competitive, and elections more closely contested, with power shifting back and forth at a rate not seen since the Gilded Age. In the 32 years since 1992, Democrats have occupied the White House for 20 years, and Republicans 12. In Congress, Republicans have commanded a House majority for 22 years and controlled the Senate for 16.

Republicans could no longer cruise to victory over hapless opponents like Jimmy Carter, Walter Mondale, and Michael Dukakis. They had to fight for victories, and social and cultural issues were potent weapons. The parties still differed on political economy. Democrats accepted a more circumscribed role for government and acknowledged that the market was a powerful force that could be harnessed to produce positive results. But they also insisted on government's responsibility to ensure a level playing field, creating conditions in which everyone who was willing to work hard could get ahead and make investments essential to protect the planet and help the nation compete in a global knowledge economy. But the differences had narrowed. Faced with the need to distinguish themselves, put the enemy on the defensive, and generate enthusiasm among voters who had become part of the party's base, Republicans increasingly prioritized social and cultural issues. Democrats responded in kind, charging their opponents with defending racism, sexism, homophobia, and greed.

Changes within the parties, but especially within the Republican Party, facilitated this shift. While both parties were becoming more ideologically homogenous, Republicans were achieving a remarkable ideological coherence for a major party in a two-party system that theoretically, at least, rewarded those who built a big tent. In 1994, as Republicans captured the House for the first time in 40 years, they made their biggest gains in the South. Indeed, when Congress convened in 1995, a majority of southern senators and representatives were Republicans for the first time in more than 100 years. Their number would continue to grow, giving them greater influence within the party and the party itself a decidedly more conservative cast, especially on social and cultural issues.

Liberal Republicans had become extinct, and moderates were on borrowed time. As the spectrum of views within the Republican Party narrowed, so did the possibility of compromise with Democrats. The range of views among Democrats also narrowed as the conservative contingent from the South dwindled, but the party retained a strong group of moderates who balanced the weight of liberals.

As the margins in elections narrowed, political tactics and discourse also shifted. One might have expected that close competition would have persuaded Republicans to seek the support of independent voters in the center. Instead, they chose to appeal to social conservatives and to employ scorched earth tactics designed to define Democrats as immoral, self-serving, and beholden to special interests like Blacks, feminists, gays and lesbians, treehuggers, and assorted others. They weren't real Americans, some Republicans openly charged. Stirring rage seemed to work for talk radio hosts like Rush Limbaugh and TV shows like the McLaughlin Group; they got high ratings by airing political food fights. So why wouldn't outrage, name-calling, and character assassination work in the political arena? In the early 1990s, Bill Clinton, the centrist New Democrat president, became a test case. Conservatives ruthlessly attacked him and his wife, Hillary. They were children of the 1960s bent on destroying traditional values, they charged, and crafty, self-dealing, unprincipled liars who stopped at nothing to get what they wanted. They even ordered a close friend who knew too much about their shenanigans murdered.

A Republican House back-bencher from Georgia named Newt Gingrich had deployed a variation of this strategy on Capitol Hill in the late 1980s. He hurled invective and charges of corruption against Democrats in speeches on C-SPAN and encouraged colleagues to do the same—to "talk like Newt." In 1989, Gingrich targeted House Speaker Jim Wright, burying him in a cascade of unsubstantiated charges of corruption that, while never proven, brought down one of the most powerful Democrats in Washington. When Gingrich deployed the same scorched earth tactics to help Republicans win control of the House in 1994, they elected him speaker, and he used his confrontational style on Clinton, who was already the subject of withering conservative attacks. His tactics—which included shutting down the government—backfired politically, but they succeeded in making politics nastier and bipartisanship seem like a quaint relic of the past.

Paralleling the growth of vicious hyper-partisanship—and contributing to it—was a growing geographical divide between the two major parties. During the 1990s, both believed there were relatively few states where they couldn't compete, and the presidential election map showed chunks of red and blue in most regions of the country, although Democrats were developing dominance in the Northeast and West Coast. That changed in the early 2000s, in part because of the role cultural issues came to play in defining the two parties. Democrats continued to dominate the coasts, leaving the remainder of the country deep red, with a few blue outposts in the industrial Midwest and the Mountain West. In 2008, Barack Obama significantly increased the number of those outposts. But he had the advantage of a major recession that most voters blamed on the Republicans to help him. By the end of his presidency, the country's interior was becoming redder, a trend that has continued. The parties' regional strengths sharpened their ideological homogeneity and gave them strikingly different identities, largely defined by their positions on social issues—and on whom they were for and whom they were against. There were few swing states, and within states, election outcomes in House, Senate, and gubernatorial races aligned with presidential elections. It was once common to have a U.S. Senator represent a state carried by a presidential candidate of the opposing party, but now it was almost unheard of. As a result, the parties had less reason to craft messages that appealed to all regions of the country, further reinforcing their insularity and ideological purity.

These developments intensified partisan conflict and made it even more vicious. Republicans cast Democrats as coastal college-educated, tree-hugging elites who supported same-sex marriage, abortion, feminism, open borders, and gun control and pandered to minorities who provided the votes to keep them in power. Democrats returned the favor, characterizing Republicans as benighted, Bible-thumping rubes who lived in flyover country, were poorly educated, trafficked in conspiracy theories, defended White supremacy, wanted to keep women in the kitchen, and were too dumb to understand that their leaders were using them to support an agenda that privileged the wealthy. These stereotypes inflamed political discourse, shut down conversation, and made bipartisanship even more difficult. Voters in each party's base equated compromise with capitulation and were likely to turn on those who consorted with the enemy. It was no idle threat. In many if not most districts, primary challengers posed a greater threat to incumbents than candidates of the opposing party they would face in the general election. Republicans were most likely to be primaried if they veered from the party line, but it sometimes happened to Democrats, even though their party continued to accommodate a wider range of perspectives. Partisans might revel in the fight, but many voters were turned off and tuned out, concluding that politicians were more interested in skewering enemies than solving their problems.

Perhaps the most dramatic changes in the late twentieth and early twenty-first centuries occurred in communications, including political communications.

Cable news, cell phones with video cameras, email, the Internet, and social media transformed politics as dramatically as conflict over social issues had done. They shaped, reinforced, and exacerbated hyper-partisanship and made bipartisanship more elusive. Broadcasting became narrowcasting as most news providers sought to win the loyalty of particular groups rather than attract a broad cross section of the public. There were exceptions, of course. Network news continued to play it down the middle but claimed a smaller share of viewers. Many news providers blurred—even erased—the lines between news and opinion. They created echo chambers where the views of one party or one segment of a party reverberated and kept dissenting views from challenging the preconceptions of their audience. The news was also democratized. Anyone who created a website, had proficiency with social media, or knew how to use email could become a journalist, and they needn't be bothered by standards professionals used to ensure accuracy. With so many news outlets, many of them blatantly partisan, and a 24-7 news cycle, politicians found it easier to get the public's attention—or at least that segment of the public that they cared about. Many used it to disseminate vicious attacks, half-truths, lies, and conspiracies because it endeared them to their base, helped them raise money, and made them famous or at least notorious. In the quest for air time, campaign contributions, and advancement, being sober, measured, and nuanced made you just one of the pack—indistinguishable, unremarkable, and invisible.

When the country elected its first Black president and confronted the worst economic collapse since the Great Depression, the elements of a toxic mix converged. Barack Obama confronted a party that was on the defense and feared for its future. But its leaders knew that the best defense was an aggressive, relentless offense and that they needn't be constrained by truth in mounting it. They deployed the tools they had inherited from Richard Nixon, Newt Gingrich, and the Bushes, exploiting divisive cultural issues, forsaking governance in favor of political theater, and using populist appeals to deep divisions in American society. In doing so, they became a prisoner of the toxicity they deployed. The genie was out of the bottle, and confrontation, disinformation, and vilification became systemic.

Political parties are by definition partisan. They have different visions, compete for power, and often engage in attacks on opponents to win elections. Negative campaigning works. Fear of what an opponent will do if victorious is generally more powerful in motivating supporters than hope that their candidate will, if elected, enact policies to make things better. Compromise is always difficult because it means sacrificing some of what you want and abandoning some ideas you've promised supporters you'd fight for. That American politics was divisive, partisan, and contentious, and that compromise was difficult was normal. Hyper-partisanship, vicious attacks without end, bald-faced lies, denial of basic facts, and wild conspiracy theories were not. Neither were conscious decisions to shut down government, risk default on the nation's debt, create gridlock to prevent an opponent from achieving a victory, charge that your opponent had stolen an election, or incite a mob to storm the Capitol to prevent recognition of a lawfully elected president.

Sadly, though, that's where we are. This book examines decisions made by political leaders and dramatic changes in U.S. politics since the mid-1960s to explain how we got here. Retracing the path doesn't provide easy answers about how to fix a broken system. History rarely works that way. However, by understanding the critical choices individuals have made, the consequences of changes in demography, technology, the economy, and culture, and roads not taken, history reveals something quite scary. Hyper-partisan, win-at-any-cost politics have become systemic, so the challenge of reclaiming a more functional, constructive politics and preserving democracy is enormous. That's not good news, but if we don't recognize the depth of the ditch we have dug, we won't have the hard discussions—including with those whom we have written off as "deplorables"—necessary to ensure the republic doesn't die in it. So, let's take a look at how our politics became systemically dysfunctional, and how we dug the ditch.

# CHAPTER 1

# 1964

## A Time of Innocence

In September 1964, a grainy black and white campaign ad for President Lyndon Johnson rolled across television screens. It featured the faces of children—girls and boys, Black and White. They conveyed despair, not joy, and they were clearly poor. "Poverty is not a trait of character," an authoritative voice began. "It is created anew in each generation not by heredity but by circumstances." Noting that "today millions of American families are caught in circumstances beyond their control," the narrator warned that "their children will be compelled to live lives of poverty unless the cycle is broken." Fortunately, hope was at hand. President Johnson's War on Poverty would "provide everyone a chance to grow and make his own way. A chance at education […] a chance at a fruitful life." "For the first time in American history," poverty could be vanquished if the nation rallied behind the President. "Vote for President Johnson on November 3," the narrator commanded. "The stakes are too high for you to stay home."[1]

Viewed from the perspective of the third decade of the twenty-first century, the ad seems odd. A candidate running for president proclaiming that poverty was caused by social and economic circumstances rather than character flaws and highlighting innocent children as its victims. A politician intent on winning election asserting that visionary presidential leadership and the power of the national government could create opportunity for all and end poverty—which even the Bible said would always be with us. But the ad was unremarkable. The year was 1964, and

---

1 https://video.search.yahoo.com/yhs/search?fr=yhs-mnet-001&ei=UTF-8&hsimp=yhs-001&hspart=mnet&param1=796&param2=84469&p=lbj+poverty+ad+1964&type=type9043493-spa-796-84469#id=1&vid=6064582f2dcff1189f7d64972336f816&action=click (accessed November 6, 2022).

in the nine months since he had succeeded John Kennedy, Lyndon Baines Johnson (LBJ) had secured passage of landmark civil rights legislation, challenged Congress to join him in a War on Poverty, and won legislation that initiated the assault. LBJ was simply running on his record.

The ad was one of many the Johnson campaign ran, and it was by no means the most frequently aired. Indeed, most of the campaign's ads sought to sow doubts—indeed, fear—about the Republican candidate, Senator Barry M. Goldwater of Arizona. Nevertheless, the poverty ad is striking, and it speaks volumes about the distance we have traveled in the past six decades. When my co-instructor (and wife, Leigh Ann Wheeler) and I ask twenty-first century students at a highly selective, generally liberal public university in the Northeast if a candidate would air such an ad today, their emphatic response is, "No way!" Even though many of them support policies designed to ease disparities, promote equity, and attack poverty, they believe that such a straightforward, empathic appeal to action on behalf of the poor would alienate more voters than it would attract. The ad's implicit faith in government's ability to solve complex problems sounds naïve, and the assumption that there could be agreement on such an ambitious program in a political system that is bitterly divided and perpetually gridlocked seems preposterous.

## An Age of Anxiety

Of course, they're right. The America of Lyndon Johnson and Barry Goldwater and the America of Donald Trump and Joe Biden are light years apart. For starters, Goldwater's extremism made him a pariah, while Trump's won him election in 2016. Nor does the difference lie in the severity of the problems the country faces or even the anxiety Americans feel about them. As the 1964 presidential campaign began, Americans had much to worry about. They were still reeling from the assassination of President Kennedy eight months earlier. While there was no internet or social media to spread them, conspiracy theories abounded. Federal, state, and local investigators quickly concluded that a lone gunman, Lee Harvey Oswald, fired the shots that killed the President. Even though the mainstream media accepted these conclusions, conspiracy theories spread, claiming that dark forces on the right or the left were responsible. A week after the assassination, polling revealed that only 29% of Americans believed that Oswald acted alone,[2] prompting President Johnson to appoint a bipartisan commission, led by Chief Justice Earl Warren, to investigate.

---

2 Peter Knight, *The Kennedy Assassination* (Edinburgh, UK, 2007), 76.

"Out of the nation's suspicions, out of the need for facts," LBJ later wrote, "the Warren Commission was born."[3]

The commission's 26-volume report, released in September 1964, supported the lone shooter theory and reassured most Americans[4] that neither the Soviets nor Castro were involved. Nevertheless, there was a lot to worry about. Tensions between the U.S. and the Soviet Union and fear of nuclear war remained front-of-mind for most Americans. The two nations maintained huge stockpiles of nuclear weapons that could be delivered by missiles, long-range bombers, and submarines, and they continued to expand their arsenals. U.S. and Soviet leaders counted on a strategy known as mutually assured destruction (MAD) to keep the peace. It *was* mad, and scary, too.

The Cuban missile crisis was still fresh in the minds of Americans. For 13 days in October 1962, the U.S. and the Soviets stood at the precipice of war when the U.S. demanded that the Soviet Union remove missiles—recently discovered by surveillance flights—from Cuba. After Kennedy imposed a naval blockade of Cuba and threatened to fire on Soviet ships that attempted to breach it, Soviet leaders agreed to remove the missiles. Nevertheless, the showdown reminded Americans that they stood on the brink of Armageddon. Tensions eased in the wake of the Cuban crisis, and the two rivals signed a treaty banning atmospheric tests of nuclear weapons in 1963. Nevertheless, fear of nuclear war weighed on Americans. As the 1964 election approached, a whopping 54% of those queried by a Gallup Poll identified "war: nuclear war: living in fear of war: devastation from war's consequences" as their greatest fear "for the future of our country."[5]

While the test ban treaty represented a step toward improved U.S.–Soviet relations, the Cold War remained a source of concern. Indeed, the People's Republic of China, or Red China as Americans called it, propelled the conflict in new, confusing directions. Tensions between the Soviet Union and China, which became front-page news when the Soviets withdrew technical advisors from China in 1960, escalated as the decade progressed. Americans were heartened that they no longer faced a united front between the two Communist giants, but the break made the world a more complicated and no less dangerous place.

---

3 Lyndon Baines Johnson, *The Vantage Point: Perspectives of the Presidency, 1963–1969* (New York, 1971), 26.
4 Knight, 77.
5 October 1, 1964. Gallup/Potomac Poll # 1964-637POS: National Survey of Attitudes, Hopes, and Fears [Roper #31092367].

The People's Republic remained a looming threat. It supported Communist insurgents seeking to topple U.S. allies in Southeast Asia and became a member of the nuclear club in October 1964 when it detonated its first nuclear bomb.

Many Americans were anxious. The world continued to be a scary place with peace hanging in the balance and nuclear war a real threat. Ironically, Vietnam did little to contribute to this sense of alarm in 1964. When Communist rebels led by Ho Chi Minh defeated the French in 1954, a peace settlement divided Vietnam and stipulated that elections for leaders of a united Vietnam would be held in 1956. Fearing a Communist victory, the U.S. blocked elections, supported creation of a separate South Vietnamese government, and lent its support when Viet Cong insurgents backed by North Vietnam launched a guerilla campaign. U.S. officials viewed Vietnam as a test of U.S. resolve to resist Communist-supported "wars of national liberation," contain Communist expansion, and maintain credibility with allies and enemies alike. By the end of 1963, the U.S. was providing significant military assistance to South Vietnam, including over 15,000 military "advisers" who trained and supported the South Vietnamese army, flew air missions to support their attacks on Viet Cong rebels, and often fought alongside South Vietnamese forces. Despite this assistance, things weren't going well when Johnson became president. The Viet Cong controlled much of the countryside; the South Vietnamese army was ineffective; and South Vietnam's government was corrupt and lacked popular support.

Facing an election, Johnson, like his predecessor, declined to make the inevitable choice between escalating U.S. involvement and withdrawing. He maintained that Vietnam was vital to U.S. interests, modestly increased U.S. support for South Vietnam, and reassured Americans that victory was possible without expanding U.S. involvement. "We seek no wider war," he reassured Americans.[6] In August 1964, when Johnson received reports that North Vietnamese patrol boats had attacked U.S. destroyers off the coast of North Vietnam, he asked Congress to authorize him to take "all necessary measures to repel any armed attacks against the forces of the United States and to prevent further aggression."[7] Congress quickly assented, with only two dissenting votes in the Senate and none in the House. Having shown his resolve, LBJ chose not to escalate. By coupling firmness with restraint, he ensured that Vietnam did

---

6 *New York Times*, August 6, 1964 https://www.nytimes.com/1964/08/06/archives/wider-war.html.

7 "Joint Resolution to promote the maintenance of international peace and security in Southeast Asia," August 7, 1964 https://www.archives.gov/milestone-documents/tonkin-gulf-resolution#transcript.

not become top-of-mind for most Americans in 1964. In fact, when asked in late August if they had "given any attention to the happenings in South Vietnam," 31% of respondents to a Gallup Poll responded "very little" and 20% said "no."[8]

Americans worried more about racial conflict at home than a guerilla war on the other side of the world. Since the nation's founding, slavery, segregation, lynching, and disfranchisement of African Americans had made a mockery of its promise of liberty, equality, and opportunity. When Lyndon Johnson assumed the presidency, the gap between promise and reality remained wide, an embarrassment to a nation that claimed to be the leader of the Free World in the battle against Communism. In the South, segregation and disfranchisement were under assault but Whites were as determined to preserve them as their Confederate forebears had been to defend Richmond in 1865. Whether they lived on farms and plantations or in towns and cities, the vast majority of southern Blacks were desperately poor, had no voice in government, were vulnerable to violence at the hands of law enforcement officials and White citizens alike, and were relegated to the most menial jobs and inferior educational opportunities.

Since the beginning of the century, African Americans had fled the South's crumbling agricultural economy for northern cities and the promise of jobs and a better life. Between 1900 and 1940, almost 2 million southern Blacks made the trek, followed by another 3.6 million in the ensuing three decades.[9] While the North offered Black migrants greater economic opportunity, more personal freedom and security, and the right to vote, racism knew no geographical boundaries. Many northern employers balked at hiring Blacks, and when they did, typically offered them menial, low-paying positions. Realtors, bankers, and the Federal Housing Administration adopted practices that kept most Blacks, irrespective of their income, from leaving the ghetto. The few who defied the odds and moved into White neighborhoods often encountered hostility and even violence, as graphically portrayed by Lorraine Hansberry's 1959 Broadway hit, *A Raisin in the Sun*.[10] The vast majority of African Americans who lived in hypersegregated neighborhoods like Brooklyn's Bedford-Stuyvesant, Chicago's Lawndale, or Los Angeles' Watts, regularly encountered White police

---

8 Gallup Poll # 697, Question 11, USGALLUP.64-697.R08A, Gallup Organization (Cornell University, Ithaca, NY: Roper Center for Public Opinion Research, 1964).
9 James Gregory, "The Great Migration (African American)" https://depts.washington.edu/moving1/black_migration.shtml.
10 Lorraine Hansberry, *A Raisin in the Sun* (New York, 1959).

officers—only 6% of police officers in the nation's 300 largest cities were Black in the 1960s[11]—who acted like members of an occupying army.

Whether they lived in Mississippi or Harlem, Blacks were second-class citizens. They struggled to find work; throughout the 1950s and 1960s, Black unemployment was twice the rate of White.[12] While the median household income of Black families grew by 40% during the 1950s, it remained little more than half that of Whites in 1960—the same as it had been a decade before.[13] The poverty rate among Blacks fell by 10 points between 1959 and 1964, but 45% of Blacks still lived in poverty, compared to about 15% of Whites.[14] Because poverty and state policy limited access to education, only about 22% of Blacks were high-school graduates in 1960, compared to 45% of Whites,[15] further limiting opportunities to land better jobs.

Since the earliest years of the Republic, Blacks had fought to force the nation to keep promises made in its founding documents. In the years following World War II, their demands became more insistent. Groups like the National Association for the Advancement of Colored People (NAACP) and the Congress of Racial Equality (CORE) stepped up their campaign against segregation. Jackie Robinson broke the color line in major league baseball in 1947, President Harry Truman ordered integration of the armed forces a year later, and the U.S. Supreme Court proclaimed segregation in public education unconstitutional in its 1954 *Brown* decision. Grassroots protest also shook the foundations of Jim Crow. In December 1955, Rosa Parks, the secretary of the Montgomery, Alabama NAACP chapter, triggered a year-long boycott of the city's buses when she was arrested for flouting laws requiring segregation in public conveyances.

---

11 David Alan Slansky, "Not Your Father's Police Department: Making Sense of the New Demographics of Law Enforcement," *Journal of Criminal Law and Criminology*, 96 (Spring 2006), 1213.
12 Pew Research Center, "Black Unemployment rate is consistently twice that of whites" https://www.pewresearch.org/fact-tank/2013/08/21/through-good-times-and-bad-black-unemployment-is-consistently-double-that-of-whites/.
13 National Center for Education Statistics, "Median Family Income by Race and Ethnicity: 1950–1993" https://nces.ed.gov/pubs98/yi/y9616c.asp (accessed October 30, 2021).
14 U.S. Census Bureau, "Poverty in the U.S. 2000" https://www.census.gov/library/publications/2001/demo/p60-214.html (accessed October 30, 2021).
15 U.S. Census Bureau, "A Half Century of Learning: Historical Census Statistics on Educational Attainment in the United States, 1940–2000" https://www.census.gov/data/tables/time-series/demo/educational-attainment/educational-attainment-1940-2000.html (accessed October 30, 2021).

The campaign's success demonstrated the power of nonviolent civil disobedience and catapulted Martin Luther King, Jr., the charismatic 26-year-old Baptist minister who framed Gandhian nonviolence in the language of Christianity, to national prominence.

The success of nonviolent protest in Montgomery didn't immediately prompt others to follow suit. That changed in February 1960, when four Black students at North Carolina A & T College staged a sit-in at a segregated Woolworth's lunch counter in Greensboro, North Carolina. They never got the cup of coffee they ordered, but their bold act prompted dozens and then hundreds of other students and community members to join them in the ensuing days and weeks and sparked a wave of sit-ins that swept the South. Ella Baker, an NAACP veteran who had helped King organize the Southern Christian Leadership Conference (SCLC), was impressed by the passion and idealism of the young people who led the sit-ins. She attempted to put lightning in a jar by helping the students form the Student Nonviolent Coordinating Committee (SNCC). Older organizations like SCLC and CORE scrambled to keep up with the youthful militants, embracing nonviolent protest and launching new campaigns of their own. Philosophically committed to nonviolent protest, to meeting hate with love, soldiers in the movement endured insults and blows from White toughs and police and witnessed the cause by going to jail. Some lost their lives. Their goal was to shine a light on the daily indignities, gross injustice, and brutality woven into the nation's racial caste system, organize and empower common people to challenge it, and force the nation's reluctant political leaders to act.

Easier said than done. Presidents didn't want to offend White voters in a region where Democrats had long enjoyed unquestioning support but Republicans were making gains. The protests escalated, however, as did White Southerners' violent response. After three years of growing turmoil, massive protests in Birmingham, Alabama, led by King prompted a response from local officials that made the U.S. look more like Nazi Germany than the leader of the free world. They arrested hundreds of schoolchildren who joined the protest, turned high-pressure water hoses on activists, and unleashed snarling dogs on peaceful protesters. Embarrassed on the world stage and fearing a conflagration, President Kennedy made a dramatic appearance on national television in June 1963, announcing his support for sweeping civil rights legislation. Two months later, the leading civil rights organizations joined with organized labor to sponsor a March on Washington that brought a quarter million supporters to the Lincoln Memorial to demand change. King moved the country with his soaring message of racial reconciliation. Behind the scenes, however, older civil rights leaders struggled to modulate the more militant message that SNCC leaders wanted to send. Raw from the brutality he and his colleagues had endured, SNCC chairman John Lewis drafted a speech calling Kennedy's civil rights bill "too little, too late" and threatening "to march through the South like Sherman did" if things didn't change promptly. King and others prevailed on Lewis to tone down his remarks, but generational tensions within the movement were palpable and wouldn't be long contained.

Kennedy didn't live to see his civil rights bill enacted, but his successor made it his top priority. In July, Congress passed the Civil Rights Act of 1964, banning segregation in public accommodations and providing powerful remedies against employment discrimination and school segregation. However, racial conflict showed no signs of abating. "Freedom Summer," a SNCC initiative sent hundreds of northern (mostly White) college students to Mississippi to encourage African Americans to register to vote. It was met with a torrent of White violence. Black churches were burned, and civil rights workers were beaten and murdered. Just as racism wasn't limited to the South, neither was racial conflict. In July and August 1964, violence erupted in Philadelphia, Jersey City, Rochester, and New York City's Harlem. The uprisings typically began with altercations between White police officers and residents of Black neighborhoods. Frustrated by decades of police harassment, poor housing and city services, unemployment, and poverty, angry Blacks attacked police and burned and looted stores and other buildings.[16]

This conflict, chaos, and violence was unsettling to many Americans. A Gallup Poll conducted in late May 1964 revealed that 74% of respondents believed "mass demonstrations by Negroes" were more likely to hurt than help "the Negro's cause for racial equality."[17] The urban uprisings of July and August didn't improve matters. A Harris Poll conducted in August found that 87% of those queried believed that "the riots by Negroes in New York, Rochester and Jersey City" hurt Blacks' cause,[18] and an October Gallup Poll found that "the problem of maintaining law and order" was a concern for 86% of respondents.[19]

---

16 Thomas J. Sugrue, *Sweet Land of Liberty: The Forgotten Struggle for Civil Rights in the North* (New York, 2008), 325.
17 Gallup Poll, May 22–27, 1964. Gallup Poll # 691 [Roper #31087675].
18 Harris Poll, August 1964. Louis Harris & Associates Poll: August 1964 [Roper #31103185].
19 Gallup Poll, October 1964. Gallup/Potomac Poll # 1964-637POS: National Survey of Attitudes, Hopes, and Fears [Roper #31092367].

Northern Whites' uneasiness with Black protest offered the South's most famous demagogue, Alabama's George Wallace, an irresistible opportunity to get in the face of smug northern liberals. In April and May 1964, the flamboyant Wallace entered Democratic presidential primaries in two midwestern states— Wisconsin and Indiana—and one border state, Maryland. On the stump, he avoided the kind of overtly racist vitriol he dispensed back home. Instead, he appealed to Whites' racial resentments and fears indirectly. He attacked the civil rights bill as a violation of states' rights, a threat to property owners and union seniority systems, and a tool that federal bureaucrats would use to establish hiring quotas. With President Johnson not on the ballot,[20] Wallace shocked observers by winning about 30% of the vote in Wisconsin and Indiana and a whopping 46% in Maryland. Clearly, many northern Whites were threatened by Black demands, and many observers warned of a simmering White backlash that might upend the entire nation's politics and civic life.[21]

Many Americans also worried about the country's moral fiber. Asked in October about "the state of morals in the country at the present time," 41% of respondents to a poll conducted by the National Opinion Research Corporation indicated they were "pretty bad and getting worse."[22] Americans found many reasons for concern. Violent crime surged, increasing by a whopping 126% during the 1960s.[23] Many believed that public indifference to a fraying social fabric made matters worse. The fatal stabbing of Kitty Genovese, a 28-year-old bar manager, in Queens, New York, in March 1964, seemed to prove that Americans had lost their moral compass. *The New York Times* gave her murder front-page coverage, reporting that 38 eyewitnesses stood by while she was attacked and killed. Although the allegations later proved to be wildly

---

20 Primaries played a minor role in nominating presidential candidates before the 1970s. There were very few of them. Typically, the party's top office holders, rather than a sitting president, appeared on primary ballots, won, and surrendered the delegates pledged to them at the national convention.
21 Dan T. Carter, *The Politics of Rage: George C. Wallace, the Origins of the New Conservatism, and the Transformation of American Politics*, 2nd ed. (Baton Rouge, LA, 2000), 202–15.
22 National Opinion Research Corporation Poll, October 1–31, 1964. National Opinion Research Corp. Miscellaneous Poll # 1964-ANTISEM: Anti-Semitism in the United States [Roper #31094098] October 1964.
23 Brennan Center for Justice, "Americans' Faulty Perception of Crime Rates," March 16, 2015 https://www.brennancenter.org/our-work/analysis-opinion/americas-faulty-perception-crime-rates.

exaggerated, the murder became a *cause celebre*, evidence that Americans had become apathetic in the face of evil.[24]

U.S. Supreme Court decisions prohibiting prayer and Bible-reading in public schools and expanding First Amendment protection for pornography also produced considerable hand wringing. Reducing the influence of religion in schools while opening the floodgates of smut would only corrupt the nation's youth and hasten moral rot.[25] Groups like Citizens for Decent Literature protested the explosion of sexually explicit material—ads for "Strippers School Book," "Scanty Panties," or "Vibra Finger"—sent through the mail, prompting Congress to conduct hearings in 1963. The proliferation of sexually explicit movies brought sustained demands for state and local measures to classify movies and required theater owners to bar children from "adult" films.[26] But smut peddlers continued to flourish.

Women had many reasons to be angry, and some were. The post–World War II ideal, featured in TV favorites like "Leave it to Beaver" and the "Donna Reed Show," assumed that a woman's place was in the home, and that women found fulfillment in caring for their children and husbands. That assumption was at odds with the material needs and aspirations of a growing number of women. Between 1950 and 1964, women's workforce participation climbed steadily, from 34% to 40%, with the percentage of women with children under 6 working outside the home climbing even faster, from 12% to almost 30%.[27] Women who entered the workforce took positions as nurses, elementary and high-school teachers, social workers, clerks, bookkeepers, waitresses, and domestic workers. They were largely excluded from law, medicine, and the professoriate as well as jobs as executives, managers, police officers, firefighters, and construction and assembly line workers—positions that provided the highest pay in the booming

---

24 Nicholas Lemann, "A Call for Help: What the Kitty Genovese Story Really Means," *The New Yorker*, March 2, 2014 https://www.newyorker.com/magazine/2014/03/10/a-call-for-help.
25 National Opinion Research Corporation Poll, October 1–31, 1964. National Opinion Research Corp. Miscellaneous Poll # 1964-ANTISEM: Anti-Semitism in the United States [Roper #31094098].
26 Leigh Ann Wheeler, *How Sex Became a Civil Liberty* (New York, 2013), 68–92.
27 U.S. Bureau of Labor Statistics, "Women in the Workforce Before, During, and After the Great Recession" https://www.bls.gov/spotlight/2017/women-in-the-workforce-before-during-and-after-the-great-recession/pdf/women-in-the-workforce-before-during-and-after-the-great-recession.pdf (accessed October 30, 2021); PBS, "The First Measured Century" https://www.pbs.org/fmc/book/2work8.htm (accessed October 30, 2021).

postwar economy. Newspapers separated job postings into columns labeled "wanted—male help" and "wanted—female help," underscoring just how sex segregated the job market was. Not surprisingly, in 1960, women earned 60 cents on the dollar compared to men.[28]

Betty Friedan's 1963 manifesto, *The Feminine Mystique*, gave voice to the unhappiness of many women with the status quo. A Smith College graduate who joined the ranks of postwar suburban wives and mothers, Friedan challenged the very assumptions that supported prevailing gender norms, identifying "the problem that has no name."[29] It was the expectation that middle-class women should be satisfied with lives as mothers, wives, and consumers and not seek careers or fulfillment beyond home, family, and community organizations. Friedan's book received widespread attention and contributed to the emergence of second-wave feminism that prompted Congress to adopt the Equal Rights Amendment in 1972,[30] but it did not make women's issues central to the political conversation in 1964.

Adolescents were the fastest-growing segment of the population during the 1960s, and some had concerns of their own. As college enrollment exploded—more than doubling during the decade[31]—campuses became spaces where young people created their own world, free from the supervision of parents and the demands of employers. Most viewed college as an opportunity to make new friends, enjoy an independent social life, earn a degree that would guarantee a good job in an expanding economy, and find a suitable mate. For some, however, concern about the arms race, nuclear war, racism, and politicians who proclaimed support for freedom while assisting repressive anticommunist regimes sparked political engagement. Students at historically Black colleges like North Carolina A & T, Fisk, Spelman, Tougaloo, and others were in the vanguard, joining SNCC and other civil rights groups. A few students at predominantly White campuses like Ann Arbor, Berkeley, Harvard, Madison, and Oberlin also questioned the status quo. Students for a Democratic Society emerged in Ann Arbor in 1962 to challenge corporate domination of American society and demand participatory democracy. But by 1964, it claimed only a few

---

28 National Committee on Pay Equity, "The Wage Gap Over Time" https://www.pay-equity.org/info-time.html.
29 Betty Friedan, The *Feminine Mystique* (New York, 1963), 11.
30 Gail Collins, "The 'Feminine Mystique' at 50," *New York Times Magazine*, January 23, 2013 https://www.nytimes.com/2013/01/27/magazine/the-feminine-mystique-at-50.html.
31 U.S. Bureau of the Census, *Statistical Abstract of the United States 1980* (Washington, DC, 1980), 180.

thousand members, mainly on elite campuses. While SDS would never attract a large membership, the number of student activists grew a bit in the wake of SNCC's Freedom Summer. In the Fall of 1964, hundreds returned to their campuses from Mississippi imbued with the possibilities of grassroots organizing and willingness to challenge authority.

For some, that included questioning policies imposed by university administrators. In September 1964, administrators at the University of California at Berkeley informed students that a small space just off campus had been incorporated into the campus and was off limits to speakers who didn't receive approval from the University. A few days later, a CORE activist who had returned from Mississippi defied the ban. Campus police arrested him and placed him in the backseat of a squad car, only to find themselves surrounded, first by several hundred, then several thousand students. Speakers used the car's roof as a platform to denounce the University's restrictions on free speech. After 36 hours of pandemonium, university officials ended the standoff by signaling that they would withdraw charges against the CORE activist and review suspensions of students who had interfered with his arrest. While Berkeley students would make their campus a center of student activism in the coming months and years, the incident received little attention in the national media.[32] And because the restriction on campus political speech that triggered the event was unique to the University of California,[33] the Berkeley protest did not spread. Student activists found it difficult to distract their peers from fraternity and sorority rushes, football tailgating, papers and exams, and job interviews.

Americans were also concerned about poverty. When Michael Harrington published his blockbuster, *The Other America*, in 1962, many Americans were shocked to learn that nearly a quarter of their countrymen and women were poor. Indeed, there were more women than men in the ranks of the poor. If that came as a surprise, Harrington argued, it was because the poor were invisible, living in the nation's inner cities, separated from their more prosperous fellow citizens, millions of whom had fled cities for rapidly growing suburbs.[34] Harrington's book sold 70,000 copies in 1962[35] and captured the attention of

---

32 *New York Times*, October 3, 1964.
33 https://oac.cdlib.org/view?docId=hb6c6006vs;NAAN=13030&doc.view=frames&chunk.id=div00001&toc.depth=1&toc.id=div00001&brand=oac4 (accessed November 1, 2021).
34 Michael Harrington, *The Other America: Poverty in the United States* (New York, 1962), 4.
35 *New York Times*, June 19, 2009 https://www.nytimes.com/2009/06/21/books/review/Isserman-t.html (accessed October 31, 2021).

citizens as well as policymakers. How could such a rich nation allow so many people, children included, to suffer from inadequate nutrition, housing, health care, and education? Wouldn't the Communists use America's dirty secret to demonstrate that capitalism was an exploitative system after all? Wouldn't that undermine America's claim to offer a better model for developing countries in Asia and Africa? Many were disturbed by the paradox of poverty in a land of plenty and supported bold action. In October 1964, 70% of respondents to a Gallup Poll agreed that the "Federal Government has a responsibility to do away with poverty in this country."[36]

## A Time of Confidence

There was a lot to worry about. Nevertheless, Americans approached the future with optimism. Having pulled themselves out of the Great Depression, defeated fascism, and rebuilt Europe and Japan, Americans had, to borrow the phrase of historian James Patterson, grand expectations.[37] Despite deep concern about conflict with the Communist world, the U.S. had forced the Soviet Union to remove missiles from Cuba and had brokered a limited test ban treaty, reducing the threat of nuclear war at least a bit. At home, conflict over race didn't produce the backlash among northern Whites that many feared and some hoped for. An August Harris Poll that showed that most Americans believed the recent urban riots hurt Blacks' cause also revealed strong faith in continued progress in race relations. Asked if the country was "making more progress or less progress solving our racial problems" than the previous summer, only 29% said "less progress."[38] In October, 58% of respondents to a Gallup Poll said they approved Congress's passage of the Civil Rights Act of 1964 while only 31% disapproved.[39] Poverty was a problem, but the President had declared war on it and forceful action was underway, as Johnson's TV ads suggested.

Many took comfort in a sense of national unity that emerged during World War II and became a fixture of the 1950s. Radio and television, newspapers

---

36 Gallup Poll, October 1964 "Gallup/Potomac Poll # 1964-637POS: National Survey of Attitudes, Hopes, and Fears [Roper #31092367]."
37 James T. Patterson, *Grand Expectations: The United States, 1945–1971* (New York, 1996).
38 Harris Poll, August 1964. Louis Harris & Associates Poll: August 1964 [Roper #31103185].
39 Gallup Poll, October 1964. Gallup/Potomac Poll # 1964-637POS: National Survey of Attitudes, Hopes, and Fears [Roper #31092367].

and magazines, and schools and civic organizations relentlessly reminded Americans that they had transcended the divisions of the past and forged a national consensus. The messaging was so unremitting, many actually believed it. The Advertising Council—an association representing the nation's largest marketing firms—collaborated with groups like the National Conference of Christians and Jews, political leaders, and even representatives of organized labor to produce public service ads extolling Americans' shared beliefs. Worried about a postwar resurgence of the economic, ethnic, and religious conflict that had raged in the 1920s and 1930s, the ads extolled tolerance, condemned bigotry as un-American, and praised the Judeo-Christian values that suffused American life. The election of the nation's first Catholic president in 1960—albeit after a campaign inflected with vicious anti-Catholicism—confirmed the new-found sense of harmony. The new Era of Good Feelings even extended to relations between business and unions. According to the narrative, postwar American capitalism rested on collaboration between business leaders and unions and rewarded investors with strong profits, workers with steadily increasing wages and benefits, and consumers with goods that made their lives easier and more exciting.[40] All was well.

Indeed, consumers had much to celebrate. Technology promised a better future, as those who strolled through the exhibits at the 1964 World's Fair in Queens discovered: IBM demonstrated its Selectric typewriter, AT&T showed its Touchtone phone (in white or a variety of pastel colors), RCA displayed color televisions, and Ford debuted the Mustang, which brought the sports car within the reach of the middle class.[41] Popular culture reflected and contributed to the upbeat mood. Hit television shows like "The Donna Reed Show," "The Andy Griffith Show," "The Beverly Hillbillies," and "Bonanza" portrayed happy (if sometimes wacky), functional (White) families who always seemed to solve the problems that came their way in the span of 30 minutes—actually about 25 when time for commercials was removed.[42] If some adolescents were alienated, the music they listened to didn't suggest the number was large. Granted, Bob Dylan warned that "The Times They Are a Changin'." But his now-classic anthem peaked at 20 on the April 17th *Billboard* chart and didn't even appear

---

40 Wendy Wall, *Inventing the "American Way": The Politics of Consensus from the New Deal to the Civil Rights Movement* (New York, 2008), 163–200.
41 Rick Perlstein, *Before the Storm: Barry Goldwater and the Unmaking of the American Consensus* (New York, 2001), 327-28.
42 "Top 40 Programs from First Nielsen's of the First 1963–1964 Season" https://www.tvobscurities.com/2009/11/top-40-programs-from-first-nielsens-of-the-1963-1964-season/

on its "Year End Hot 100." It was chock-full of songs about young love, surfing, and cars.[43] Teens may not have been captivated by Dylan, but they were wild about the Beatles, who took the country by storm with must-see appearances on the "Ed Sullivan Show" and a headline-grabbing national tour featuring hits like "I Want to Hold Your Hand," "She Loves You," and "Love Me Do."[44]

The economy was a big reason Americans were so upbeat. By 1964, unemployment had fallen to 5.2% (although it exceeded 10% for Blacks),[45] gross domestic product grew at a whopping 6.5%,[46] and inflation dropped under 2%.[47] Union membership remained strong—about a third of workers engaged in nonagricultural employment belonged to unions[48]—and they continued to deliver better wages and benefits to their members. Changes in the economy also meant more opportunities to escape manual labor and enter white-collar employment, a sure sign of middle-class status. By the mid-1950s, more Americans worked in white collar than in blue-collar jobs.[49] The benefits of a booming economy were more equitably distributed with the share of national income claimed by the top 10% declining from 45% in 1940 to 35% in 1964.[50] Income was not only more evenly distributed, but Americans had more of it. Median household income, adjusted for inflation, grew by over 50% between 1950 and the mid-1960s,[51] putting new cars, homes in the suburbs, summer vacations, and a college education for the kids within the reach of more Americans. Asked what "fears and worries" they had about the country, an astonishing

---

43 https://www.billboard.com/music/bob-dylan/chart-history/billboard-200/3.
44 https://www.musicoutfitters.com/topsongs/1964.htm.
45 U.S. Bureau of Labor Statistics, Databases, Tables, and Calculators by Subject" https://data.bls.gov/timeseries/LNU04000000?years_option=all_years&periods_option=specific_periods&periods=Annual+Data.
46 Statista, "Annual Real Growth of GDP in the United States from 1930 to 2020" https://www.statista.com/statistics/996758/rea-gdp-growth-united-states-1930-2019/
47 Macrotrends, "U.S. Inflation Rate 1960–2021" https://www.macrotrends.net/countries/USA/united-states/inflation-rate-cpi.
48 Brantly Callaway and William J. Collins, "Unions, Workers, and Wages at the Peak of the American Labor Movement," National Bureau of Economic Research Working Paper 23516, June 2017 https://www.nber.org/system/files/working_papers/w23516/w23516.pdf (accessed November 1, 2021).
49 James T. Patterson, *Grand Expectations: The United States, 1945–1974* (New York, 1996), 323.
50 Income Inequality in the United States, 1910–2010 http://piketty.pse.ens.fr/files/capital21c/en/Piketty2014FiguresTables.pdf (accessed November 1, 2021).
51 "Median Family Income by Race/Ethnicity of Head of Household, 1950–1993" https://nces.ed.gov/pubs98/yi/yi16.pdf (accessed November 1, 2021).

68% of respondents to a Gallup Poll said, "Nothing."[52] Trust in government was also high, rising from 73% at the end of the Eisenhower administration to 77% on the eve of the 1964 election.[53] Most Americans were confident in their leaders and bullish on the country's future. That included African Americans who put even more faith in the federal government than Whites.[54]

Americans expected their political leaders to work together to solve the problems the country faced and keep the nation secure and the good times rolling. While the two major parties had differences, what is striking today is how narrow they were and how common bipartisan cooperation was. Both of the major parties had conservative and liberal wings. Conventional wisdom dictated that moving too far outside the political mainstream was dangerous, especially for Republicans. Throughout the 1950s and early 1960s, the percentage of potential voters who identified as Republicans declined from 33% in 1956, when Dwight Eisenhower won a second term, to 25% in 1964. To win, Republicans needed to attract independents, who constituted about 23% of the electorate in 1964, as well as make inroads among Democrats, as Eisenhower did in twice capturing the presidency. Democrats also worried about veering too far from the center. While the percentage of voting age Americans who identified as Democrats ranged from 43% in 1956 to 51% in 1964, party leaders knew that those impressive figures were inflated by southern Whites, most of whom identified as Democrats but often defected to the Republicans in presidential contests and did nothing to help it win closely contested states in the North.[55] In critical northern swing states, the parties were more closely divided, making prizes like New York, Illinois, Pennsylvania, and California competitive. Moreover, upper-income and college-educated voters—who were more likely to vote Republican—turned out at a much higher rate than groups—like labor union members—that tilted heavily Democratic.[56]

---

52 Potomac Associates, Gallup/Potomac Poll # 1964-637POS: National Survey of Attitudes, Hopes, and Fears, Question 5, USGALLUP.637POS.Q04B1, Gallup Organization (Cornell University, Ithaca, NY: Roper Center for Public Opinion Research, 1964).
53 Pew Research Center, "Public Trust in Government, 1958–2021" https://www.pewresearch.org/politics/2024/06/24/public-trust-in-government-1958-2024/.
54 Sugrue, *Sweet Land of Liberty*, 357.
55 Pew Research Center, "Trends in Party Identification, 1939–2014," April 7, 2015 https://www.pewresearch.org/politics/interactives/party-id-trend/.
56 Thomas Piketty, Brahmin Left vs Merchant Right: Rising Inequality & the Changing Structure of Political Conflict (Evidence from France, Britain, and the US, 1948–2017)" http://piketty.pse.ens.fr/files/Piketty2018.pdf (accessed November 2, 2021).

Dwight Eisenhower, the World War II hero whose landslide victory in 1952 ended 20 years of Democratic control of the presidency, moved the Republican party to the center. Conservative Republicans, who unsuccessfully backed Senator Robert Taft of Ohio for the 1952 nomination, were committed to rolling back the New Deal. They hoped to end or privatize Social Security, roll back agricultural subsidies, sell the Tennessee Valley Authority, and stop the use of monetary and fiscal policy to smooth the business cycle. Ike was a political and economic conservative who believed in free enterprise, limited government, and a balanced budget. But he was no fool. He understood that the public supported New Deal reforms like Social Security and expected the federal government to keep inflation and unemployment low and the economy booming. Trying to roll back the New Deal was a fool's errand, Eisenhower believed. Instead of refighting the political battles of the 1930s, which Republicans had lost and lost badly, the General embraced "Modern Republicanism." In the words of historians Elmo Richardson and Chester Patch, Ike insisted that "the party should take a middle ground, the only terrain for building consensus and reaching the vast majority of voters." Only by recognizing "the essential social responsibilities of the federal government," he believed, could Republicans "forestall efforts of liberal Democrats to enact more ambitious and expensive programs."[57]

As President, Eisenhower rejected conservative demands to shrink the role of the federal government. He persuaded Congress to expand Social Security coverage and increase benefits, make additional investments in public housing, support construction of the Interstate Highway System, and increase federal spending to combat recession. He reduced rather abandoned New Deal programs aimed at stabilizing the price of agricultural commodities.[58] A pragmatist, Eisenhower rejected the ideological purity of Republican conservatives who wished to turn back the clock to 1928, keenly aware that the New Deal had forever changed Americans' expectation of the federal government.

On other issues the differences between the two major parties were even narrower. The Cold War dominated discussion of foreign policy, and both parties supported robust military budgets and tough action to contain Communist

---

57 Chester Patch and Elmo Richardson, *The Presidency of Dwight Eisenhower* (Lawrence, KS, 1991).
58 Edward L. Schapsmeier and Frederick H. Schapsmeier, "Eisenhower and Agricultural Reform: Ike's Farm Policy Legacy Appraised," *The American Journal of Economics and Sociology*, 51 (April 1992), 147–59.

expansion while avoiding nuclear war. As the 1960 election approached, it was Democrats who warned of a dangerous "missile gap" between the U.S. and the Soviet Union and demanded increased defense spending while Eisenhower warned in his farewell address of a "military-industrial complex" that promoted excessive spending that was unnecessary and economically unsustainable.

Nor was there much light between the two parties on civil rights. Although most Blacks had shifted their loyalties away from the Party of Lincoln in the 1930s and 1940s, the Democratic Party's powerful southern wing continued to defend the caste system. It enjoyed an outsized influence in the party because southern Democrats chaired key congressional committees and delivered a big block of electoral votes to Democratic presidential candidates every four years. Eisenhower's status as a war hero, coupled with northern Democrats' attack on Jim Crow, allowed him to do surprisingly well in Dixie, cracking the Solid South. Republicans hoped to build on his success and expand their path to the 266 electoral votes necessary to win the presidency. But they also continued to appeal to northern Blacks, who were critical to victory in large, hotly contested states like New York, Pennsylvania, Ohio, Illinois, Michigan, and California. If Democrats could appeal to Southern segregationists and Black northerners, Republicans asked, why couldn't they?

Like their rivals, Republicans sought to walk a fine line between doing too little and doing too much on civil rights. Eisenhower refrained from vigorous enforcement of the *Brown* decision, but he acted decisively when Arkansas Governor Orville Faubus defied a federal court order admitting nine Black children to Little Rock's lily white Central High School. The General, whose farm outside Gettysburg reminded him that the Civil War had settled such matters, dispatched troops to compel their admission and to protect them as they attended classes. Eisenhower and most Republicans in Congress also supported the Civil Rights Acts of 1957 and 1960. Albeit modest in scope, they were the first civil rights laws since Reconstruction and refurbished the party's claim to the Lincoln legacy.

As the parties headed into the election of 1960, their differences remained modest. Ike's vice president, Richard Nixon, was the presumptive Republican nominee. A man with little interest in domestic policy and few deeply held principles, Nixon's north star was winning the presidency. Unbound by ideology, his finger to the political winds, he accepted Eisenhower's "Modern Republicanism" as the path of least resistance and best chance of success. As the party assembled for its convention in Chicago, Senator Barry Goldwater of Arizona came to the Windy City as something of a conservative star. His recently published *Conscience of a Conservative* thrilled the heirs of Robert Taft and a new generation of conservatives alike. He demanded a platform that embraced rugged individualism, called for an end to expansion of federal power that began with the New Deal, and demanded a foreign policy that would not only contain Communism but roll back the gains it had made since the end of World War II. With moderates firmly in control and Nixon unwilling to alienate Rockefeller and the party's liberal wing, the convention adopted a platform that committed the party to support for civil rights and the federal social safety net.[59]

John Kennedy, two years into his second term as a U.S. Senator from Massachusetts, faced a more difficult path to his party's nomination. Only 43, suspect in the eyes of liberals, and a Catholic, many doubted his ability to win. However, Kennedy had a good ground game and systematically won support from state and local party leaders who played an outsized role in determining the loyalties of convention delegates. He ran on a platform that differed only modestly from the Republicans'. It demanded greater defense spending to close the so-called missile gap while criticizing Eisenhower and his vice president for two recessions and high unemployment, promising sustained economic growth, and calling for a balanced budget and deficit reduction. Although the platform supported greater federal largesse than the Republicans for agricultural programs, health care for seniors, and education, its approach to civil rights differed little from the opposition.

The election's outcome was even closer than the candidates' positions. Kennedy won a comfortable electoral vote majority, 303-219, with segregationist Harry Byrd of Virginia taking 15 electoral votes. However, Kennedy's popular vote margin was less than 120,000 votes out of 69,000,000 votes cast. That Nixon made it so close was perhaps the biggest surprise. The economy was mired in recession and unemployment was high, leading many voters to question the wisdom of supporting a Republican again—especially when Ike wasn't on the ticket. Kennedy's selection of Lyndon Johnson as his running mate brought several southern states, including Texas, back into the Democratic column, while his October phone call to Coretta Scott King, expressing concern for her husband, Martin, who was serving time in a Georgia penal facility, electrified African American voters. Then, too, there was Nixon. Tricky Dick. The man with the haggard face and bad makeup who came off poorly in comparison to the handsome, relaxed, energetic Kennedy in the country's first televised presidential debate. Defeat was hardly an indictment of Modern Republicanism.

---

59 John Andrew, "The Struggle for the Republican Party in 1960," *The Historian*, 59 (Spring 1997), 613–31; Perlstein, *Before the Storm*, 78–82.

## Extremism Rebuffed

Conservatives thought otherwise, and there were plenty of them among the party's grassroots activists. Republicans lost, they insisted, because they had abandoned their principles and failed to offer the country an alternative. They included people like the self-styled Illinois homemaker, Phyllis Schlafly. Schlafly held a master's from Harvard, served as president of the Illinois Republican Federation of Women, unsuccessfully ran for Congress in 1952, hosted a 15-minute radio show, "America, Wake Up!," and authored *A Choice Not an Echo*. The latter was a 1964 bestseller that exposed a purported conspiracy among Northeastern liberals to steal Republican presidential nominations from conservatives like Taft who represented the party's rank and file. There was also Fred Koch, the Wichita oil millionaire who mailed 2,500 copies of *Conscience of a Conservative* to Kansas libraries, newspapers, and party leaders in early 1960. Longtime activists like Schlafly and Koch were joined by a new generation of conservatives who mobilized in groups like the Young Republicans and Young Americans for Freedom and brought youthful passion to the cause. William F. Buckley's acerbic free market, anti-Communist *National Review* gave intellectual heft to the movement, while Goldwater's *Conscience of a Conservative* provided a clear, simple manifesto of conservative principles.

Goldwater was the conservatives' darling. His credo rested on an uncompromising belief in individual freedom and responsibility. "Every man," he wrote, "... is responsible for his own development" and "the choices that govern his life are choices he must make; they cannot be made by any other human being." Because the growth of government power had steadily eroded individual freedom, Goldwater demanded radical change. "I do not undertake to promote welfare for I propose to extend freedom," he wrote. "My aim is not to pass laws, but repeal them. It is not to inaugurate new programs, but to cancel old ones...." Goldwater also criticized conventional wisdom on foreign policy which assumed that the U.S. could contain Communism through peaceful coexistence. That was naïve and dangerous, Goldwater argued; the Communists were a powerful, disciplined adversary bent on world domination. While conceding that the U.S. should avoid war "if possible," he insisted that averting hostilities should not be "our chief objective." "If we do that—if we tell ourselves that it is more important to avoid shooting than to keep our freedom—we are committed to a course that has only one terminal point: surrender."[60]

---

60 Barry Goldwater, *The Conscience of a Conservative* (Shepherdsville, KY, 1960), 12, 23, 91.

A Draft Goldwater Committee, led by William Rusher, publisher of the *National Review*, prominent conservative businessmen like South Carolina textile baron Roger Milliken, and Clif White, a former Young Republican leader, orchestrated support. Goldwater played hard to get but ultimately succumbed to their entreaties. In January 1964, he formally announced his candidacy, reprising ideas that thrilled conservatives and led thousands of young converts to prepare to storm the ramparts of the Republican establishment. Reassuring his supporters that he would not "change my beliefs to win votes," he promised voters "a choice, not an echo." The choice was stark. "I believe we must now make a choice in this land," he asserted, "and not continue drifting endlessly toward a time when all of us, our lives, our property, our hopes and even our prayers will become cogs in a vast government machine." He challenged Americans to answer a simple question: "Why not victory, victory for sound constitutional principles in government? Why not a victory over the evils of communism?"[61]

Goldwater turned to his Arizona mafia—Denison Kitchel, Richard Kleindienst, Dean Burch, and William Rehnquist, the future chief justice—to run his campaign and provide advice. Clif White cultivated conservative grassroots support and secured victories in Republican state conventions across the South, Midwest, and West. By late spring, Goldwater claimed enough delegates to secure the nomination. But the party's moderates and liberals wouldn't give up, hoping that they could mount a challenge that would persuade delegates to abandon Goldwater at the convention. Rockefeller mounted a late primary challenge that fizzled when Goldwater narrowly defeated him in California. But Goldwater, who prided himself on standing by his principles no matter what the cost, created a firestorm within the party by opposing the Civil Rights Act in the Senate, a measure supported by most of his Republican colleagues. Although he insisted that he was "unalterably opposed to discrimination or segregation on the basis of race," he charged that the bill violated business owners' "God given right" to serve and hire whom they pleased and would "require the creation of a federal police force of mammoth proportions" to enforce. Moderate and liberal Republicans were aghast and made one last attempt to stop Goldwater. They rallied around William Scranton, the handsome young governor of Pennsylvania, and attempted to persuade delegates that he was the only alternative to certain defeat in November.

---

61 *New York Times*, January 4, 1964 https://www.nytimes.com/1964/01/04/archives/goldwater-says-hell-run-to-give-nation-a-choice-he-joins-gop.html.

But it was too late. The Goldwater delegates were true believers, convinced that he alone could save the party and the country from creeping socialism at home and Communist triumph abroad. The convention met at San Francisco's Cow Palace—a New Deal project designed for livestock shows and rodeos—in July. Delegates gave Goldwater a hero's welcome and menaced members of the "Eastern establishment press." ABC's mild-mannered David Brinkley and Chet Huntley recalled hearing Goldwater supporters who shared elevators with them comment, "these nighttime TV news shows sound to me like they're being broadcast from Moscow."[62]

If Goldwater's speech on the Civil Rights Act was a high-profile exercise in principled self-destruction, his tone-deaf acceptance speech took his act to prime-time television. With the nation's eyes riveted on him, he spoke to his conservative base, not to the electorate. It was like belching during a job interview. "The Good Lord raised up this mighty ... Republic," he began after the "Battle Hymn of the Republic" blared as his walk-up music, "to be a home for the brave and to flourish as the land of the free, not to stagnate in the swampland of collectivism, not to cringe before the bully of communism." He lambasted Democrats for allowing Communism to advance in Europe, Cuba, and Southeast Asia and for tolerating "violence in the streets, corruption in our highest offices, aimlessness among our youth, anxiety among our elderly, and ... virtual despair among the many who look beyond material success to the inner meaning of their lives." The country's decline was not the product of "mere political mistakes," it was "the result of a fundamentally and absolutely wrong view of man, his nature and destiny." A Republican victory in November would set things right, way right. It would reduce federal power, ensure "the sanctity of private property [as] the only durable foundation of constitutional government in a free society," encourage a "free and competitive economy" while "maintaining law and order," and "look beyond the defense of freedom today to its extension tomorrow." "[E]xtremism in the defense of liberty is no vice," he exhorted his frenzied audience, "moderation in the pursuit of justice is no virtue."[63] Although his advisors warned that voters would find those lines unsettling, he delivered them anyway, sending chills down the spines of many Republicans and most

---

62 Perlstein, *Before the Storm*, 378–79.
63 *New York Times*, July 17, 1964 https://www.nytimes.com/1964/07/17/archives/transcript-of-goldwaters-speech-accepting-republican-presidential.html.

Americans.[64] A month later, the Cow Palace hosted a more successful—if no less raucous act—the Beatles.

If Goldwater was Jeremiah, Lyndon Johnson was Pangloss. Portraying himself as the devoted steward of the martyr's vision, he persuaded Congress to pass a massive tax cut to juice the economy, bring John Kennedy's stalled civil rights bill across the finish line, and launch a war on poverty. Those accomplishments would have been enough for most presidents, but not Johnson. In May, speaking before a commencement audience of 85,000 at the University of Michigan's massive football stadium, he set his sights even higher.[65] America should not settle for achieving "the rich society and the powerful society," he urged, but reach for "the Great Society"—a place "that demands an end to poverty and ... racial injustice," a place "where men are more concerned with the quality of their goals than the quantity of their goods," a place with cities that are magnets "where future generations come, not just to live, but to live the good life," a place where "the food we eat, the very air we breathe" are not threatened by pollution, a place where "every young mind is set free to scan the farthest reaches of thoughts and imagination."[66]

Unlike Goldwater's screed at the Cow Palace, Johnson was upbeat, sketching the outline of a bright future when he accepted his party's nomination. He understood that the U.S. was a center-right nation and that only a small fraction of voters identified themselves as liberals. But he also knew that Americans were flush with the triumph of World War II, believed that their country was a beacon of freedom, and enjoyed unparalleled prosperity that was broadly distributed. They would embrace an ambitious agenda that would realize the nation's enormous potential to do good not just well and establish him as the equal of his hero, Franklin Roosevelt. Johnson reminded Americans that they were experiencing "the largest and longest period of peacetime prosperity in our history" and challenged them to use their bounty to meet the needs of those in need. While acknowledging that the nation's problems were "many and great," Johnson insisted that "our opportunities are even greater," including "man's

---

64 *New York Times*, July 19, 1964 https://www.nytimes.com/1964/07/19/archives/as-the-republican-party-enters-a-new-era-the-nominee-for-64-the-new.html; *New York Times*, July 23, 1964 https://www.nytimes.com/1964/07/23/archives/news-analysis-the-extremism-issue-aides-say-goldwater-sought-to.html.
65 *New York Times*, May 22, 1964 https://www.nytimes.com/1964/05/23/archives/president-urges-new-federalism-to-enrich-life-in-talk-to-michigan.html?searchResultPosition=1.
66 https://www.presidency.ucsb.edu/documents/remarks-the-university-michigan.

first chance to build the Great Society—a place where the meaning of man's life matches the marvels of man's labor." Achieving these ambitious goals at home required a strong defense to deter adversaries as well as willingness to pursue peace. "There is no place in the world for weakness," LBJ insisted. "But there is also no place ... for recklessness ... with the nuclear weapons that could destroy us," a thinly veiled reminder that his opponent was scary. He ended with a reminder of the stark choice Americans faced. "Our tomorrow is on the way," he concluded. "It can be a shape of darkness or it can be a thing of beauty."[67] Most Americans had no doubt about who represented the forces of darkness.

Between Labor Day and November 3, when voters went to the polls, Goldwater did little to pivot from the themes that endeared him to his conservative base. Aware that many Americans feared that his apparent recklessness might lead the country into war, he toned down some of his most bellicose statements about nuclear weapons and the imperative of rolling back Communist gains. Still, he continued to hammer Democrats for their willingness to negotiate with the Soviet Union—whom they naively believed had "mellowed" into "a newfound friend"—and promised to regard all Communist powers as enemies who couldn't be trusted and must be confronted.[68]

Richard Nixon tried to help ease public concern that Goldwater couldn't be trusted with nuclear weapons. In a television appearance with Goldwater on October 9, Nixon again tried to make the candidate's views seem more moderate and statesmanlike. However, his demand that LBJ apologize for labeling Goldwater "reckless and a warmonger" only reminded voters why they had such deep reservations about the Republican candidate.[69] It was a little like saying Goldwater really had stopped beating his dog.

As Goldwater tried to dial down his saber-rattling, his comments on domestic matters became even darker and more intemperate. Johnson's Great Society would make the U.S. more like its Communist enemies, he asserted, a country where there "would be no penalty for failure and no reward for success."[70] Democrats should change their name to the Socialist Party, he snarled, because

---

67 https://www.presidency.ucsb.edu/documents/remarks-before-the-national-convention-upon-accepting-the-nomination.
68 *New York Times*, October 7, 1964 https://www.nytimes.com/1964/10/07/archives/goldwater-maps-ideological-drive-he-plans-to-stress-general-issues.html.
69 *New York Times*, October 10, 1964 https://www.nytimes.com/1964/10/10/archives/goldwater-on-tv-assails-president.html.
70 *New York Times*, September 19, 1964 https://www.nytimes.com/1964/09/19/archives/goldwater-derides-antipoverty-drive-in-appalachiatalk.html.

"that's what they are."[71] Did any beyond a small band of true believers think that LBJ was a socialist? He also decried the breakdown of law and order and deterioration of morals. His campaign manager labeled the Black urban uprisings "disturbing and appalling" while assuring reporters "we are not going to make any effort at capitalizing" on the inevitable resentment they stirred among Whites.[72] Apparently, Goldwater didn't get the message. He continued to denounce "gang rapes in California" and thugs who "have gone into the streets to seek with violence what can only be found in understanding." And he linked them directly to Johnson's policies. "If it is entirely proper for government to take from some to give to others, then won't some be led to believe that they can rightfully take from anyone who has more than they," he asked a Minneapolis audience.[73]

As the campaign progressed, Goldwater broadened his attack, linking Johnson to an appalling decline in the nation's moral standards. The "deterioration of the home, the family and the community, of law and order, of good morals and manners" were shocking, he charged. They were examples of moral "rot and decay" and the bitter fruit of "the philosophy of modern 'liberalism'."[74] Unfortunately for Goldwater, several hundred prominent religious leaders—including many leaders of his own Episcopalian faith—publicly disagreed. They called him dangerous and questioned his authority to lecture the nation on values. Of course, Goldwater, being Goldwater, amplified their criticism by publicly lambasting "clerical leaders for now becoming loud advocates of Lyndon Johnson," a man who "represents much that is in opposition to the thinking of every church I know."[75]

With Goldwater digging his own political grave, Johnson was on a glide path to victory. If Goldwater dumped gasoline on every brushfire that flared around him, Johnson was Smokey the Bear. He refused to elevate Goldwater's stature by agreeing to debate him. He deflected scrutiny of controversial issues like

---

71 *New York Times*, October 9, 1964 https://www.nytimes.com/1964/10/09/archives/goldwater-asserts-johnsons-integrity-is-the-main-issue.html.
72 *New York Times*, September 1, 1964 https://www.nytimes.com/1964/09/01/archives/goldwater-aide-asks-race-talks-johnson-should-act-to-end-rioting.html.
73 *New York Times*, September 11, 1964 https://www.nytimes.com/1964/09/11/archives/goldwater-links-the-welfare-state-to-rise-in-crime.html.
74 *New York Times*, October 12, 1964 https://www.nytimes.com/1964/10/12/archives/goldwater-puts-stress-on-ethics-shuns-orthodox-campaign-to-call-for.html.
75 *New York Times*, October 29, 1964 https://www.nytimes.com/1964/10/29/archives/goldwater-calls-churches-remiss-bids-clerics-concentrate-on.html.

race and civil rights by avoiding new initiatives, limiting remarks on the subject to uncontroversial statements about expanding equality and opportunity, and appearing at ceremonial events like signing the Civil Rights Act of 1964, where he was surrounded by Republicans and Democrats, Blacks and Whites in a kumbaya moment. He grabbed media attention in ways only a president could, touting a third-quarter spike in GDP and making a prime-time television address after China detonated a nuclear weapon to demonstrate his sure knowledge of foreign affairs.

Believing that the best defense is a good offense, the campaign mounted slick television ads that reminded Americans that Goldwater was dangerous. Its most famous depicted a child counting as she picked petals from a daisy followed by a voice from mission control counting down from 10. As the camera zeroed in on the child's eye, an explosion and a mushroom cloud appeared while President Johnson reminded listeners, "These are the stakes. To make a world where all God's children can live. We must either love each other or we shall die." That ad ran only once. Democrats pulled it after Republicans complained that it was unfair and unbecoming a president. But it left an impression. As did the ad depicting a saw cutting the eastern seaboard off a wooden map of the U.S. while a voice reminded viewers of Goldwater's statement (made in the 1930s) that the country would be better off without the Northeast. Or the ad showing a fist crumpling a Social Security card while a menacing voice warned voters of Goldwater's opposition to the popular program. Johnson's strategy used Goldwater's own words to feed doubts about his temperament. Meanwhile, as *The New York Times* observed, LBJ remained "less firmly fixed in the public mind as representing a particular set of views than is his challenger."[76]

The Goldwater campaign unleashed lightening a week before election day, when Ronald Reagan delivered a riveting prime-time television testimonial for Goldwater and his ideas. His acting career in eclipse and role as a spokesman for General Electric over, the former New Deal Democrat made the case for Goldwater more effectively than Goldwater himself. Reagan had a rare ability to connect with audiences, honed by years on the screen and the lecture circuit. He alternated between good-natured humor and indignation while speaking to his audience as if he was engaging them in a conversation in their living room. How could anyone doubt that government was out of control, he asked, when it took 37 cents of every dollar earned by Americans and used it for such

---

[76] *New York Times*, September 19, 1964 https://www.nytimes.com/1964/09/19/archives/news-analysis-mood-of-the-electorate-goldwater-appears-to-be-they.html.

ridiculous things as foreign aid that allowed Kenyan leaders to buy extra wives? And why, Reagan wondered, was an honorable man like Barry Goldwater wrong for suggesting that there may be a better alternative to Social Security? After all, a person who invested his contributions to the system in the stock market would be able to retire 10 years earlier than if he remained in the government-run retirement system. And shouldn't we all be outraged when a woman could divorce a husband, who earned $250 per month and receive $330 per month from welfare? What about our children's future? "Will we preserve for our children this, the last best hope of man," Reagan asked, "or will we sentence them to take the last step into a thousand years of darkness?" There could be no doubt if Americans did the right thing and elected Goldwater—because he "has faith that you and I have the ability ... to make our own decisions."[77]

Reagan was a hit. While he may have been washed up as an actor, many thought he might have a future in politics. But no matter how spellbinding, Reagan could not save Barry Goldwater, who may have been his political soulmate but lacked his ability to connect with voters. A Democratic bumper sticker said it all. Parodying the Goldwater campaign's slogan, "In your heart, you know he's right," it proclaimed, "In your guts, you know he's nuts." When the dust settled and the votes were counted, Johnson achieved the historic landslide he coveted, winning 61.1% of the popular vote and a 486-52 electoral vote margin. Goldwater carried only five Deep South states and his native Arizona. Even his Southern Strategy was something of a bust; he performed worse in the South than Eisenhower and Nixon.[78] Johnson also had long coattails. Democrats picked up 37 seats in the House, expanding their majority to 295-140. In the Senate, the net gain was only two, but that provided an astonishing 68-32 majority.

For Johnson and the Democrats—indeed, for the country—the future looked bright. Granted, Goldwater was a terrible candidate. He sowed the wind and reaped the whirlwind. Would a more attractive candidate have fared better? Undoubtedly. While Republicans may have lost anyway, they may not have taken the historic drubbing they did. And if the results had been more in line with 1960, LBJ would have been denied the mandate he claimed and his position with Congress would have been weaker. Instead, he received the mandate he craved and the Congress he wanted. *The New York Times* summed up the meaning of the election. Voters had rejected Goldwater's angry, ideological conservatism

---

77 Perlstein, *Before the Storm*, 499–504.
78 https://www.270towin.com/1964_Election/

and his call for a return to the past. Happy with a prosperous economy and favoring continuity, they embraced Johnson's vision of a Great Society and of "unity—unity of the parties, of the regions, of the allies, of the continents."

That bright moment would be short-lived, however. The situation in Vietnam was deteriorating rapidly, and hard decisions that had been postponed during the campaign would soon have to be made. "I'm afraid of Vietnam," Johnson told his young aide, Bill Moyers on election night.[79] And while Democrats were relieved that the White backlash they feared didn't develop, they knew that Black activists would continue to challenge segregation, North and South, producing conflict that would be difficult to contain. Yet victory was sweet, voters had chosen hope over fear, and differences between the major parties would narrow once again with Goldwater out of the way. Any threats on the horizon could be managed by the political maestro who had run the U.S. Senate so effectively and had just won the greatest landslide since James Monroe's election 144 years earlier.

---

79 Perlstein, *Before the* Storm, 544.

CHAPTER 2

# THE LIBERAL CONSENSUS UNDER FIRE, 1965–1969

### I shall not seek and I will not accept [...]

The President looked tired and much older than his 59 years when he addressed the nation on Sunday evening, March 31, 1968. Vietnam was on his mind and the minds of most Americans. Since 1965, over 20,000 U.S. troops had died in the war,[1] and the light at the end of the tunnel generals promised seemed as far away as ever. In fact, just two months earlier, at the beginning of Tet, the holiday celebrating the lunar new year, the enemy had launched a massive offensive that reached every corner of South Vietnam. Viet Cong commandos had even breached the U.S. embassy compound in Saigon. Critics on the left and the right attacked a President who just a few years before had scored the largest election victory in modern U.S. history. Eugene McCarthy, a reserved, little-known U.S. Senator from Minnesota had recently captured an astonishing 43% of the vote in the 1968 New Hampshire primary.

Johnson began his address by reviewing the situation in Vietnam. He asserted that the Communist offensive had been unsuccessful and the enemy had suffered punishing losses, yet he acknowledged the mounting human costs of the war. The President announced that he was "prepared to move immediately toward peace through negotiations," an offer he had made the previous August but North Vietnam had rejected. He told the nation that he would halt bombing North Vietnam immediately and unconditionally and had designated two of America's most distinguished diplomats to negotiate a settlement of the conflict. They would travel to "any forum, at any time, to discuss the means of bringing

---

[1] https://www.archives.gov/research/military/vietnam-war/casualty-statistics (accessed November 29, 2021).

this ugly war to an end." The president's announcement was surprise enough for a Sunday night, but what followed left viewers in disbelief. "With America's sons in the field far away, with America's future under challenge right here at home," Johnson had decided that he should not "devote an hour or day of my time to any personal partisan causes." "Accordingly, I shall not seek, and I will not accept the nomination of my party for another term as your President."[2] Even those who made a living providing instant political commentary were speechless. Asked for his thoughts, CBS veteran Roger Mudd responded, "What I'd rather do is go home and come back tomorrow morning to talk about it."[3] And why not? A vain man who had been elected in a landslide and who loved power would not seek reelection to an office that he coveted.

## The Great Society Takes Shape

The moment was stunning not just because of Johnson's historic landslide victory in 1964. In the wake of that victory, he had bent Congress to his will, winning support from many Republicans as well as Democrats for building the Great Society. The historic legislative victories he had won in 1964—a sweeping Civil Rights Act, funding for a War on Poverty, a bold tax cut—were just the beginning. In 1965, he sent a raft of legislation to the Hill and pressed Congress relentlessly to secure passage. By year's end, he was winning accolades for securing a reform agenda that rivaled Franklin Roosevelt's first term. *Time* magazine applauded Johnson's "immense achievement," adding that "it is doubtful that Kennedy could have mustered the painstaking, patient but relentless manner in which Johnson cultivates, pressures or pleads with members of Congress to get what he wants."[4]

LBJ was a giant, and he had giant goals. He wanted to transform American society, to bring its bounty and promise of equality to every American. When Johnson stood before Congress in January 1965 to deliver the State of the Union Address (the first to be televised since 1947), he reminded Americans that they

---

2 https://voicesofdemocracy.umd.edu/lyndon-baines-johnson-withdrawal-speech-31-march-1968/ (accessed November 29, 2021).
3 Ron Elving, "Remembering 1968: LBJ Surprises Nation with Announcement He Won't Seek Re-election," March 25, 2018. https://www.npr.org/2018/03/25/596805375/president-johnson-made-a-bombshell-announcement-50-years-ago (accessed November 29, 2021).
4 *Time*, November 26, 1965 http://content.time.com/time/subscriber/article/0,33009,834704-1,00.html (accessed December 1, 2021).

were "in the greatest upward surge in well-being in the history of any nation." The nation was poised to create the Great Society, a place where "freedom from the wants of the body can help fulfill the needs of the spirit." The President buried Vietnam in the middle of his discussion of foreign policy, giving it scant attention. He explained that "we are there because a friendly nation has asked us for help against the Communist aggression." He and two of his predecessors had "pledged our help," and we "will not break it now."[5] He quickly moved on to a lengthy, impassioned discussion of what he really cared about—building the Great Society.

In the months that followed, Johnson enjoyed the most successful legislative session since FDR's first hundred days, the gold standard for presidential achievement. Democrats had fought to bring medical care into the social safety network since the 1930s, but doctors, insurance companies, and Republican conservatives had thwarted their efforts by raising the specter of "socialized medicine." Johnson made extending hospital care to the elderly through Social Security his top priority in 1965 but ended up getting more than his initial ask. To Johnson's request for payment of the hospital bills of those 65 and older, the House added insurance coverage for doctors' bills and surgery, with the premiums to be shared by the government and the beneficiary. While Medicare provided for the elderly, another program added by the House, Medicaid, would meet the needs of the poor. An extension of the nation's welfare program, Aid to Families with Dependent Children (AFDC), Medicaid would be a federal–state partnership. The federal government would contribute 50% of what a state allocated to defray the cost of medical services for the poor. This formula was extended to AFDC payments, raising the federal contribution from 33% to 50% of a state's contribution, instantly providing more generous cash payments to the poor. AFDC and Medicaid created a crazy quilt. States determined who was eligible, and in many, the income required to qualify was well below the federal poverty line. Because they provided the base support that was matched by the federal government, states also determined how generous benefits would be. Still, Medicare and Medicaid represented a landmark expansion of the nation's social welfare system.

Education was a talisman for Johnson. He believed the opportunity to earn a college degree at Southwest Texas State Teachers College helped him escape

---

5 Lyndon Johnson, Annual Message to Congress on the State of the Union, January 4, 1965 https://www.presidency.ucsb.edu/documents/annual-message-the-congress-the-state-the-union-26 (accessed December 4, 2021).

the economic hardships he had experienced growing up in the Texas Hill Country. His first job as a teacher in a segregated school that served poor Mexican children and his subsequent work as head of the New Deal's National Youth Administration in Texas helped him understand the barriers poor people faced and reinforced his belief that education was the key to lift them out of poverty. Although support for schools had long been a state and local responsibility, Johnson's Elementary and Secondary Education Act made the federal government a player, providing support aimed at reducing inequities between rich and poor districts. By the end of the decade, approximately 10% of K-12 funding came from the federal government.[6]

Because he understood that a college education was becoming a qualification for jobs that supported a middle-class lifestyle, Johnson demanded that Congress make higher education more accessible. The Higher Education Act of 1965 dramatically expanded federal support for programs that brought college within the grasp of low-income students. The law, which he signed at his alma mater, provided expanded federal funding for historically Black colleges, scholarship support (now known as Pell grants) for poor students, federally subsidized student loans, and more money for Federal Work–Study Programs that benefitted low-income students.

In response to Johnson's call to expand the War on Poverty, Congress doubled support for anti-poverty programs. A Legal Services Program supported legal clinics to provide the poor access to lawyers who could help them challenge actions by slumlords, local welfare agencies, public housing authorities, and others who took advantage of them. Other new initiatives were aimed at helping poor children. One was Head Start, which provided pre-kindergarten educational programming as well as free breakfasts and lunches to poor children. The other was Upward Bound, which helped disadvantaged high-school students prepare for college. Additional funding flowed into job training programs, including the Neighborhood Youth Corps, which provided job training and counseling to teens in danger of dropping out of school or joining gangs.

A truly great society was open to new people and ideas. Immigration laws adopted between the 1880s and 1920s that excluded immigrants from most of Europe and the rest of the world were "alien to the American Dream" and

---

6 Patrick McGuinn and Jack Van Der Slik, Elementary and Secondary Education Act of 1965, *Encyclopedia of Federalism* http://encyclopedia.federalism.org/index.php/Elementary_and_Secondary_Education_Act_of_1965 (accessed January 24, 2023).

must be replaced. The Immigration Act of 1965 would restore "decency and equity" by doubling the number of immigrants admitted annually and ending discriminatory quotas put in place in the 1920s. The new law gave priority to skills and family reunification while recognizing the President's authority to admit refugees. Legislation creating the National Endowment for the Arts and the National Endowment for the Humanities provided support for individual artists and scholars as well as programs at universities, libraries, and museums. They would cultivate the "wisdom and vision" necessary to sustain democracy and enhance America's prestige. America's world leadership "cannot rest solely upon superior power, wealth, and technology," the act creating the endowments asserted, but must be built on its "high quality as a leader in the realm of ideas and of the spirit."[7]

A polluted environment wasn't good for the soul or the body, so there was legislation to clean it up. Over the firm opposition of the Big Three automobile manufacturers, major amendments to the Clean Air Act of 1963 sought to reduce the volume of carbon monoxide and other pollutants spewed from the growing number of cars and trucks on the nation's expanding highway system. It authorized the Secretary of Health, Education, and Welfare (HEW) to establish emission standards that producers would have to meet by September 1, 1967. Like the air, the nation's water had been fouled by sewage and industrial waste. Johnson aimed to reclaim it as well. The Water Quality Act established an office within HEW dedicated to monitoring pollution and supporting remediation. It also established a grant program to fund promising state or municipal projects that would remedy pollution and required states to establish water quality standards for all rivers, streams, and watersheds that crossed state lines. If they declined to act, HEW would set the standards. Johnson recognized that the bill, like the Clean Air Act, "will not completely assure us of absolute success," but he celebrated the act as the first step to ensure that "water pollution is doomed in this century."[8]

Voting rights was not on Johnson's agenda when the Congress convened in January 1965. It was, however, the top priority for Southern Christian Leadership Conference (SCLC) and Student Nonviolent Coordinating Committee (SNCC) whose leaders were organizing a campaign in Selma,

---

7 Public Law 89–209, September 29, 1965 https://www.govinfo.gov/content/pkg/STATUTE-79/pdf/STATUTE-79-Pg845.pdf (accessed December 6, 2021).
8 Remarks at the Signing of the Water Quality Act of 1965, https://www.presidency.ucsb.edu/documents/remarks-the-signing-the-water-quality-act-1965 (accessed December 6, 2021).

Alabama, to highlight the need for federal action to end Black disfranchisement. Fewer than 5% of African Americans were registered, and Sheriff Jim Clark and his officers brutalized Blacks who approached the courthouse to register, putting more than 3,000 protesters in jail as the campaign developed. Tempers rose among activists in mid-February when police in nearby Marion shot and killed Jimmy Lee Jackson after they broke up a demonstration. As campaign organizers led some 500 protesters on a march from Selma to Montgomery, Clark moved against them. Panic-stricken demonstrators were trampled by horsemen, shocked with electric cattle prods, and beaten with clubs and chains. That evening, television networks interrupted programs—ABC was airing *Judgment at Nuremberg*—to show the attack. The next morning Selma occupied headlines in newspapers across the country and around the world. His hand forced by activists, LBJ seized the moment. He went before Congress in a nationally televised speech to demand speedy passage of voting rights legislation. "It is not just Negroes, but really it is all of us who must overcome the crippling legacy of bigotry and injustice," the President told legislators. After a brief pause, he concluded with the movement's own language: "And we shall overcome."[9] It was a stunning moment. Martin Luther King, Jr., watching from Selma, wept. Lawmakers quickly fell into line, completing action on landmark legislation in less than five months.

The Voting Rights Act of 1965 created powerful mechanisms to root out the subterfuges that had long kept southern Blacks from the polls. It eliminated the literacy test, which state and local officials had long manipulated to prevent even well-educated Blacks from voting and authorized federal intervention when state officials persisted in keeping Blacks from voting. Most importantly, it offered oversight to prevent new strategies Whites might adopt to prevent Blacks from voting or influencing the political process. States with a history of discrimination must get approval from the Justice Department or a three-judge district court in Washington, DC, for any changes they made to election laws or procedures.

The session was historic, a triumph for Johnson. He could congratulate himself on securing passage of a reform agenda that dwarfed the accomplishments of predecessors who had been recognized for greatness, even his hero, Franklin Roosevelt. "Johnson has […] done more than FDR did or ever thought

---

[9] President Johnson's Special Message to Congress, March 15, 1965 http://www.lbjlibrary.org/lyndon-baines-johnson/speeches-films/president-johnsons-special-message-to-the-congress-the-american-promise (accessed May 5, 2019).

of doing," Senate majority leader Mike Mansfield claimed.[10] Notably, he did it with significant bipartisan support. With many powerful southern Democrats opposed, Republican support was critical. Fortunately, there were moderate and liberal Republicans who were persuadable, and their numbers were growing. While they sometimes exacted changes to measures the White House sent to Capitol Hill, LBJ could count on their votes. Republicans not only eased passage but ensured broader public support.

Viewing LBJ's impressive legislative achievement as the triumph of liberalism, as many have done, is to oversimplify. Certainly, the Great Society was rooted in the mid-century liberal faith that national power should be mobilized to ensure greater equity, promote the common good, bring an end to racial discrimination and religious bigotry, and prevent the spread of Communist tyranny abroad. But it was much more than a liberal project; it embodied the optimism of a moment, a time when material prosperity was increasing and becoming more broadly shared, a growing pie encouraged generosity, and Cold War imperatives suggested that tolerating poverty and racial discrimination in a land of plenty fed Communist propaganda. Johnson understood that most Americans were moderates, not liberals. The month of his landslide victory, a Harris Poll revealed that only 20% identified themselves as liberal.[11] With his uncanny sense of public sentiment, LBJ grounded his lofty aspirations in traditional American values adapted to the triumphant spirit of the moment. "Johnson cautioned aides against including anything in the poverty program that could be seen as a 'dole' or an attempt at redistribution of wealth," observes historian Robert Dallek. "He wanted the program to be seen as a 'hand up' not a 'hand out'." Conservative commentator Walter Lippman's assessment suggested he succeeded. LBJ's War on Poverty didn't mean "taking money from the haves and turning it over to the have nots," he explained, because the country had discovered that "the size of the pie can be increased by [...] organized fiscal policy" so the "whole society, not just one part of it, will grow richer."[12] Everyone would be a winner.

---

10 Robert Dallek, *Flawed Giant: Lyndon Johnson and His Times, 1961–1973* (New York, 1998), 231.
11 Louis Harris & Associates. Louis Harris & Associates Poll: November 1964, Question 24. USHARRIS.112364.R2C. Louis Harris & Associates (Cornell University, Ithaca, NY: Roper Center for Public Opinion Research, 1964).
12 Dallek, *Flawed Giant*, 74–75.

## Challenges Abroad and at Home

While Johnson enjoyed dazzling success in Congress, he found progress in the war he inherited from John Kennedy elusive. No matter how hard he tried, how much he cajoled South Vietnamese leaders, or how much he punished North Vietnam, the best he could achieve was a stalemate whose cost in blood and treasure ultimately dismayed those on the left and the right and divided the country. To be sure, Vietnam wasn't the only problem Johnson would face. But the war's toxic effect on almost every aspect of American society, and the way Johnson chose to pursue it transformed a successful president into a modern-day Job and undermined the trust in political leaders that sustained reform.

Like Kennedy, Johnson believed that American "credibility" was on the line. The U.S. had committed itself to stop Communist expansion in Asia and support South Vietnam. If it wasn't true to its word, why should allies trust it? And if Johnson surrendered South Vietnam, wouldn't the right come after him much as it had attacked Harry Truman for "losing" China to the Communists? While determined to block a Communist victory, he wanted to avoid alarming the public. Johnson was committed to a historic domestic reform agenda that required massive investments in domestic programs. If the cost of the war appeared too high, Congress would put the brakes on the Great Society. Balancing competing goals and deflecting concerns required sleight of hand, escalating commitments to the war gradually and in an understated manner. Although tapes of his phone conversations show that he harbored doubts, the President would avoid leveling with the nation about the likely costs and duration of the war.[13] That was a mistake. Once Congress and the public understood they had been misled, Johnson's credibility was in tatters and his domestic policies at risk.

He would try to avoid paying the piper as long as possible. As he readied legislation to send to Capitol Hill in the months following the election, Johnson expanded U.S. commitments in Vietnam. He didn't act because the public, politicians, or allies demanded it. Indeed, Vietnam was an afterthought—or no thought at all—for most Americans in late 1964. The war was identified as the most important issue facing the country by only 6% of those polled by a Gallup Poll in mid-October 1964.[14] Johnson and most of his advisors, however,

---

13 Lyndon Johnson telephone conversation with Richard Russell, May 27, 1964, Miller Center, University of Virginia https://millercenter.org/the-presidency/educational-resources/lbj-and-richard-russell-on-vietnam.

14 Gallup Poll, October 8–13, 1964 [Roper #31087683].

feared that South Vietnam was on the verge of collapse. Its leaders were corrupt and lacked popular support, and its army was ineffective. Governments came and went, often toppled by coups and public unrest. South Vietnam's army, while large, often folded like a two-dollar suitcase in the face of a determined enemy. Freed from concerns about how escalation might affect the election, Johnson authorized air strikes against North Vietnam and enemy supply lines in neighboring Laos in early 1965. In March, two Marine battalions landed at Da Nang, a northern coastal city, to protect a U.S. airbase. Although small in number, they were the first U.S. combat troops committed to the war. But not the last. Later that spring, the President sent an additional 40,000 troops, drawing the country further into the war.[15]

The expanded commitment was insufficient. North Vietnam sent more troops into the South, the Viet Cong expanded its control of the countryside, the South Vietnamese government remained unstable, and morale plummeted and desertions rose in the South Vietnamese army. Sensing that its ally was on the verge of collapse, Johnson expanded U.S. commitments during the summer. By the end of 1965, 184,000 American troops were "in country"[16] and the U.S. expanded its bombing campaign.

As he made these fateful decisions, Johnson chose to announce them piecemeal to keep the public from fully appreciating the implications. Americans would have to connect the dots. Many of his advisors urged him to mobilize the reserves and the National Guard, ask Congress to increase taxes, and declare a state of national emergency to signal that the nation was at war and victory required sacrifice. Johnson rejected their advice. Instead, he insisted that there was no change in policy; the U.S. was merely continuing to support an ally. With his ambitious legislative agenda moving through Congress, he didn't want to give naysayers ammunition to halt it by arguing that the nation had to choose between guns and butter. It was a risky approach because a president who loses credibility finds it difficult to gain support for his policies. Americans would start to pay closer attention, and as they did, trust would wither and support for Johnson's domestic policies and his conduct of the war would shrink.

If Vietnam caused consternation, progress toward building the Great Society assured that all was well on the home front. Or so Johnson thought. That changed on August 11, five days after the President signed the Voting Rights Act, when

---

15 Jackie Wasil, "Vietnam War Project: Graphs and Statistics," The History Channel https://vietnamjwasil.weebly.com/graphs-and-statistics.html (accessed January 24, 2023).
16 Ibid.

Watts, a 20-square mile ghetto that was home to 90% of Los Angeles's Black residents, exploded. The rebellion began when two California Highway Patrol officers stopped a young Black man who was driving erratically. As a crowd gathered, the cops arrested him and shoved him into the back of a patrol car. The incident sparked anger among members of a community that endured high unemployment, slumlords, and merchants who exploited them, and white police who often acted as an occupying army. As the officers drove off, the crowd erupted, throwing rocks and bottles at passing cars and buses, accosting Whites who were unlucky enough to walk or drive through the neighborhood, and breaking windows, looting, and burning White businesses. As police responded in force, the crowd became larger and angrier. Cries of "Burn, baby, burn" and "Get Whitey" punctuated the sound of breaking glass, gunfire, and sirens. For the next five days, violence and destruction raged, leaving 34 dead, over 4,000 under arrest, $46 million of property destroyed, and over 700 buildings in ruins. Only the presence of hundreds of Los Angeles police and 14,000 National Guard troops restored a tense peace.[17]

The ferocity of the uprising shocked White Americans, many of whom congratulated themselves on the progress the country had made on civil rights. White journalists acknowledged the barriers poor Blacks faced but found the rebellion misguided and counterproductive. *Time* magazine chided the rioters for taking to the streets rather than taking advantage of the opportunities opened by the civil rights movement and Great Society reforms. "Opportunity is society's only obligation, and the Negro has to reach out and seize it," the editors insisted.[18] Optimism about how much progress had been made and a tendency to blame the victim informed the response of many who considered themselves allies. Those less favorable to the civil rights cause took a harder line. Frightened by images of Black rioters and stories describing their hostility to Whites, many suburban Whites rushed to buy guns and nodded approvingly when conservative politicians like Ronald Reagan demanded tough action to preserve law and order. Three months after Watts, when the Lou Harris Poll

---

17 Report of the National Advisory Commission on Civil Disorders (Washington, DC, 1967), 20 https://babel.hathitrust.org/cgi/pt?id=mdp.39015000225410&view=1up&seq=12 (accessed February 24, 2023); Doug Smith, Stunned by the Watts riots, the L.A. Times struggled to make sense of the violence, *Los Angeles Times*, August 12, 2015 https://graphics.latimes.com/watts-annotations/ (accessed February 24, 2023).

18 *Time*, August 27, 1965 http://content.time.com/time/subscriber/article/0,33009,828322-1,00.html (accessed December 7, 2021).

asked individuals whether they felt that "Negroes have tried to move too fast, too slow, or at about the right pace," only 32% said "about the right pace."[19]

A report written by an ambitious young academic serving as an assistant secretary in the Department of Labor fueled further debate over civil rights and race. Perhaps because of Watts, Daniel Patrick Moynihan's *The Negro Family: The Case for National Action* generated widespread attention from the press and the public when the Government Printing Office released an unheard of 70,000 copies in late August. Moynihan presented an avalanche of data showing that single-parent female-headed families and out-of-wedlock births had become the norm in Black communities. Moynihan acknowledged that this was the product of slavery, segregation, inferior housing and education, and high rates of unemployment. Nevertheless, his report suggested that Black family structure itself created a "tangle of pathology"[20] that made dysfunctional behavior—crime, drug use, joblessness, and dropping out of school—common in African American communities. Black family structure, he seemed to argue— and many who read it concluded—created a dysfunctional culture.

The "Moynihan Report," as it became known, generated intense discussion and sharp controversy. For many civil rights advocates, it was proof that the government must invest in a domestic Marshall Plan; the Urban League's Whitney Young put the size at $145 billion (which, it turned out, was less than the ultimate cost of the war in Vietnam). Many conservatives—and even more important, many working and middle-class Whites—concluded that Blacks were responsible for their situation; unless they made more responsible choices, nothing government did would help them. According to the *Wall Street Journal*, successful African Americans must "enlighten even the most down trodden Negroes to the middle-class outlook." Moynihan's critics on the left pushed back, arguing that he was blaming the victim. "The reason we are in the bag we are in isn't because of my mama," SNCC's Stokley Carmichael responded, "it's because of what they did to my mama."[21]

What Moynihan wanted the most was the attention of the occupant of 1600 Pennsylvania Avenue. And he got it—several months before his report

---

19 Louis Harris & Associates Poll, November 1965 [Roper #31103194].
20 Office of Policy Planning and Research, U.S. Department of Labor, "The Negro Family: The Case for National Action," March 1965 https://www.dol.gov/general/aboutdol/history/webid-moynihan (accessed January 24, 2023).
21 Daniel Geary, *Beyond Civil Rights: The Moynihan Report and Its Legacy* (Philadelphia, 2015), 87–88, 119.

was published. Moved by Moynihan's analysis of the persistent effects of slavery and racism, Johnson opened "the next and most profound stage of the battle for civil rights" in a June 4 commencement speech at Howard University. "Freedom is not enough," he proclaimed. The nation must provide "not just equality as a right and a theory but equality as a fact and as a result." "You do not take a person who, for years, has been hobbled by chains and liberate him," LBJ argued, "bring him up to the starting line of a race and then say, 'you are free to compete with all the others,' and still justly believe that you have been completely fair."[22] Additional federal action would be required to enable African Americans to compete.

Johnson's words were inspiring, and he meant them. But political and economic realities limited what was feasible. While war in Vietnam and racial conflict at home did not stop Johnson from pressing Congress to continue to build the Great Society, they limited what he could get from Congress. When he delivered the State of the Union address in January 1966, he insisted that the nation could afford guns and butter. "The nation is flourishing," he reminded Americans. In the past five years, individuals' after-tax income had grown by 33%, corporate profits by 65%, and farm income by 40%. The nation's Gross Domestic Prouct (GDP) had grown by over 6% the previous year, assuring sufficient revenue to invest in domestic programs, defend freedom in Southeast Asia, and have one of the smallest budget deficits "in many years." He asked Congress for legislation to ban discrimination in housing, expanded investments in the War on Poverty, significant funding for urban renewal programs designed to "rebuild entire sections and neighborhoods," support for local police forces "to overcome growing crime and lawlessness," a new federal highway safety program, legislation to protect the nation's rivers, and consolidation of some 35 federal agencies into a new Department of Transportation.

Johnson devoted at least half of his message to Vietnam, explaining why he believed the U.S. needed to stay the course there. Countries around the world depended on America's commitment; to abandon Vietnam would weaken their confidence in the U.S., "whet the appetite of aggression," and threaten freedom. The U.S. had reluctantly increased its presence in South Vietnam in the past year, the President insisted, because "swiftly increasing numbers of armed men from the North" entered South Vietnam, believing that they

---

22 "Commencement Address at Howard University: 'To Fulfill These Rights," June 4, 1965 https://www.presidency.ucsb.edu/documents/commencement-address-howard-university-fulfill-these-rights (accessed January 2, 2022).

would secure victory because Americans "lacked the will to continue." The U.S. had stood by its ally, blunting the offensive and ensuring that "the enemy is no longer close to victory" and "time is no longer on his side." While committed to defend South Vietnam, Johnson insisted, the U.S. had and would continue to pursue a negotiated settlement. Its only condition was "that the people of South Vietnam should be able to choose their own course." "The days may become months, and the months may become years," he added, "but we will stay as long as aggression commands us to battle."[23] It all made sense to Americans who believed that World War II had taught them that aggression, unchallenged, bred more aggression and that the U.S., as the leader of the "free world," had a responsibility to defend freedom.

The public responded positively. When the Gallup Poll asked Americans if they agreed that the nation should continue to support spending for ambitious domestic programs despite the cost of the war, 58% responded affirmatively.[24] That represented the triumph of optimism, not liberal ideology. Congress was another matter. Inflationary pressures were growing as a result of spending on the war and the Great Society, and the Federal Reserve had raised interest rates in December 1965. Facing mid-term elections, members of Congress took note. They were skeptical of Johnson's optimistic budget projections, and Democrats worried that Republican opponents would weaponize fears about inflation as well as the specter of lawlessness Watts created.

Johnson scored some successes, but they were modest. Congress created the Department of Transportation, set federal safety standards for motor vehicles, adopted consumer protection laws, and strengthened federal regulation of the nation's rivers and watersheds. However, legislators trimmed his request for $2.4 billion to remake the nation's inner cities to $900 million over two years to support planning grants. It spread too little money over too many cities to make a difference. His request for a civil rights bill banning discrimination in the sale and rental of housing and treating racially motivated violence as a federal crime fared worse. State open housing legislation had been controversial. In 1964, California voters had supported a referendum measure repealing a recently adopted state open housing law, and two years

---

23 State of the Union Address, January 12, 1966 https://millercenter.org/the-presidency/presidential-speeches/january-12-1966-state-union (accessed December 8, 2021).
24 Gallup Poll, January 21–26, 1966 [Roper #31087704] https://ropercenter-cornell-edu.proxy.binghamton.edu/ipoll/study/31087704/questions#939449b7-4aed-49ae-b9c1-c423cbded5da (accessed December 8, 2021).

later, Maryland Democrats selected an opponent of open housing as their gubernatorial candidate. LBJ's housing bill cleared the House, and a majority of senators supported it. However, even with the backing of 10 Republicans, Senate Democrats could not muster the 67 votes needed to end a filibuster led by southern diehards. The Republican leader, Everett Dirksen, whose support had been critical to the success of the Civil Rights Act of 1964 and the Voting Rights Act, refused to budge, arguing that the bill was a threat to the rights of property owners.

## Conflict over Means and Ends

Civil rights was losing some of its allure. Segregation and disfranchisement southern style, sustained by angry white mobs, the Ku Klux Klan, and snarling police dogs, had stirred outrage among many White northerners. However, when the movement turned its attention to the North's vast ghettoes, White support wavered. Watts underscored for King and other leaders that their hard-fought victories over legal discrimination in the South were just the start. The complex web of poverty, unemployment, residential segregation, inferior housing and schools, high drop-out rates, and harassment by police kept the opportunities opened by the victories of the past decade beyond the grasp of far too many Blacks. Those problems existed in the rural South, of course, but they were most pronounced in the great cities of the North, where over six million southern Blacks had migrated in the first seven decades of the century. For most of the migrants and their children and grandchildren, life in the North was better. But as the fury of the rebellion in Watts revealed, too many had little hope of escaping the grinding poverty that defined their lives and limited their children's opportunities.

During his speaking engagements in Chicago, King was impressed by local leaders who had begun fighting school segregation. By August 1965, King and the SCLC committed to "intensified work in the North, using Chicago as a pilot project."[25] SCLC staff worked throughout the fall with Black leaders in Chicago to plan and organize volunteers. In January 1966, King and his wife, Coretta, moved into a four-room apartment in a run-down building in the heart of the Lawndale ghetto on the city's west side. King described his campaign as a "war on the slums." It was designed to expose the North's blighted,

---

25 David J. Garrow, *Bearing the Cross: Martin Luther King, Jr. and the Southern Christian Leadership Conference* (New York, 1986), 443.

segregated neighborhoods that isolated hundreds of thousands of Blacks and ensured that they lacked access to jobs, decent housing and public services, good schools, and hope. King worked indefatigably with his staff and Chicago leaders to build mass support for demonstrations they planned to launch in the summer. They would force the city and the nation to confront the ugly realities, dismantle the slums, and open opportunities to their residents.

King had never worked in a city approaching the size and complexity of Chicago, and gaining the attention and commitment of its residents proved challenging. Many young inner-city Blacks assumed that fists, knives, and guns were necessary to survive and found the southern preacher's insistence on nonviolence absurd. King remained committed to nonviolent protest, believing that violence was antithetical to Christian teaching and would alienate Whites whose support was essential. As protests began in July, violence erupted in the city's west side ghetto when police arrested six Blacks who had opened a fire hydrant to cool neighborhood children on a sweltering night. Fearing another Watts, King and his allies walked the streets urging crowds of Black youth to disband and avoid violence. In an all-night session, he engaged the leaders of three gangs in a debate about means and ends, explaining his philosophy of nonviolence, patiently answering questions and challenges posed by the gang leaders, and, finally, winning their commitment to order their members to stand down.

As tensions subsided, King and movement leaders turned their attention to demonstrations designed to force the city to act. Chicago was a thoroughly segregated city. Actions by realtors, lenders, and White homeowners kept most Blacks, irrespective of their means, bottled up in ghettoes on the south and west sides. Housing segregation created the slums that the movement was targeting, so activists planned a series of marches into White working-class enclaves like Gage Park, Marquette Park, Chicago Lawn, and Belmont-Cragin. Whites responded angrily, hurling epithets, bottles, rocks, and bricks at protesters while police stood by. In early August, as King got out of a car to lead a march in Marquette Park, he dropped to one knee, dazed, as a rock struck his head. After a few moments, he rose to resume the march, but continued harassment resulted in 30 injuries and 41 arrests.

In mid-August, with more demonstrations planned, city officials and business and civic leaders offered to negotiate with King and movement leaders. After two weeks of testy discussions, the city agreed to more aggressive enforcement of its existing ordinance against housing discrimination, the Chicago Real Estate Board publicly endorsed nondiscriminatory open housing, the Chicago Housing Authority pledged to stop construction of high-rise public housing in the ghettos and develop smaller projects scattered throughout the city, and the county welfare department promised to end assignment of welfare recipients to public housing projects in ways that maintained residential segregation. While the city's concessions were a step in the right direction, they left individual homeowners, banks, and realtors plenty of latitude to perpetuate discriminatory practices. And, of course, they did nothing to open educational and economic opportunities that would help ghetto residents escape poverty and leave the slums. That would only happen through federal action. However, northern Whites' opposition to integration of their neighborhoods, highlighted by the events in Chicago, signified a new coolness to civil rights. It prompted some northern politicians like Illinois' Everett Dirksen to oppose Johnson's open housing law and, combined with concerns about inflation and the cost of the war, made expansion of the War on Poverty unlikely.

As the Chicago campaign unfolded, new militancy in the civil rights movement raised eyebrows among many Whites. SNCC had been at the forefront of the South's civil rights battles. By 1965, its members were tired, battered, and disillusioned. They had gone to jail and taken the blows while federal officials had failed to protect them, King had received the credit, and White politicians had temporized and compromised as they bled. In early 1966, Stokley Carmichael, a charismatic figure who questioned the organization's end—integration—and its means—nonviolence—was elected chair. He ousted John Lewis, a founding member, diehard proponent of nonviolence and cooperation with Whites, and admirer of King. While Lewis and other civil rights leaders had often clashed with Democratic Party leaders, they worked within the party to bend it toward civil rights. Not Carmichael. He believed that Blacks and poor people would only force the system to respond to their needs by forming a separate political party. "To ask Negroes to get in the Democratic party," he quipped, "is like asking the Jews to join the Nazi party."[26] That turned heads in the administration, the movement itself, and among the public at large. It was just what the flamboyant Carmichael intended.

The implications of SNCC's left turn became apparent in Mississippi in June 1966, just as Chicago was heating up. James Meredith, who had braved white violence to integrate the University of Mississippi in 1962, was shot shortly after he began a one-man "March Against Fear" from Memphis to Jackson. SCLC, SNCC, and the Congress of Racial Equality (CORE) took up Meredith's cause. King shuttled back and forth from Chicago to participate,

---

26 *New York Times*, May 22, 1966 https://timesmachine.nytimes.com/timesmachine/1966/05/22/82798161.pdf?pdf_redirect=true&ip=0 (accessed December 11, 2021).

and Carmichael and Floyd McKissick, CORE's militant leader, joined him. During the march, Carmichael and McKissick needled King about his naïve faith in nonviolence, integration, and cooperation with Whites. At evening rallies, Carmichael roused the faithful by exhorting them to demand Black Power. Power, he insisted, was the only thing Whites respected. The significance of his move was not lost on King who believed that Carmichael's rhetoric undermined racial reconciliation and alienated White supporters. He and his supporters countered with their own slogan, "Freedom Now." So as marchers held evening rallies on the road to Jackson, speakers would ask audiences what they wanted, prompting dueling responses of "Black Power" and "Freedom Now."

Many Whites were confused and apprehensive; just as Congress had passed landmark civil rights legislation ending segregation and disfranchisement, Black militants questioned their good faith and demanded to reset the agenda. "It is an angry movement, designed to shake the Negro into political action," the *New York Times* advised readers, "by telling him [...] that white society has failed him, that it is demeaning to ask the white man for anything [...] and that whatever the Negro wants he should take by drowning 'white paternalism' in a sea of black votes."[27] Many outside the rarified atmosphere of liberal journalism were even less charitable.

While King and Carmichael generated headlines, a nascent feminist movement called out sex discrimination as a system of laws, customs, and attitudes that kept women subordinate to men, every bit as effectively as Jim Crow, disfranchisement, and lynching had established white supremacy. They didn't generate as much attention, but they began a movement that would have an equally profound effect on American society and politics.

During the debate on the Civil Rights Act of 1964, Howard Smith, a segregationist Virginia congressman, introduced the word "sex" into Title VII of the bill, which banned employment discrimination. Although Smith hoped his amendment would undermine support for the measure, a handful of women in Congress, led by Martha Griffiths, a Michigan Democrat, rallied sufficient support to win acceptance of Smith's amendment. As a result, the final bill provided remedies against discrimination in employment on account of "race, sex, religion, or national origin." Most Americans considered discrimination against women in the workplace normal, rooted in essential

---

27 *New York Times*, June 28, 1966 https://timesmachine.nytimes.com/timesmachine/1966/06/28/82824211.pdf?pdf_redirect=true&ip=0 (accessed December 12, 2021).

differences between women and men. The men who sat on the body responsible for enforcing Title VII—the Equal Employment Opportunity Commission (EEOC)—shared those assumptions. EEOC's director described the inclusion of sex in the law "a fluke [...] conceived out of wedlock" and told the press that members of the commission "think that no man should be required to have a male secretary." Rather than express outrage that the Commission ignored Congress's clear intent, the media applauded. "Why should a mischievous joke perpetrated on the floor of the House of Representatives be treated by a responsible administrative body with this kind of seriousness," asked the staunchly liberal *New Republic*?[28] Perhaps because it was the law.

A small band of women who had fought hard, within the system, for equal treatment were outraged. They included civil servants and government attorneys who had not complained when men less competent than they received promotions and they did not; members of the state women's commissions created in the early 1960s; and pioneering feminists like Betty Friedan. In June 1966, during a conference of state women's commissioners in Washington, Friedan and a dozen or so other delegates laid the groundwork for the National Organization for Women (NOW). By October, NOW had 300 charter members, 30 of whom convened in Washington to hammer out a "Statement of Purpose" to guide the fledgling organization.

The delegates—middle-aged women, White and Black, and one man—weren't radicals. They were professionals committed to working within the system to achieve "true equality for all women [...] and a fully equal partnership of the sexes." In a society in which government, the professions, employment, religion, education, marriage, and the family rested on patriarchy, however, it was a truly radical goal. It necessitated bold action to "break through the silken curtain of prejudice and discrimination against women in government, industry, the professions, the churches, the political parties, the judiciary, the labor unions, in education, science, medicine, law, religion and every other field of importance in American society." That was a tall order, but it was just the beginning. To ensure that women need not "choose between marriage and motherhood, on the one hand, and serious participation in industry or the professions on the other," would require "a national network of child-care centers." Even more fundamentally, it would necessitate "a different concept of marriage," one based on "equitable sharing of the responsibilities of home and children and

---

28 Ruth Rosen, *The World Split Open: How the Modern Women's Movement Changed America* (New York, 2000), 70–81.

of the economic burdens of their support." Because "there is no civil rights movement to speak for women, as there has been for Negroes and other victims of discrimination," organizers noted, progress had been glacial. "The National Organization must therefore begin to speak."[29]

And speak it did, even though its membership was small and its budget meager. NOW focused much of its attention on the EEOC's persistent refusal to challenge even the most blatant sex discrimination. After years of demanding an end to sex-segregated "help wanted" columns in newspapers, the EEOC finally agreed. In 1965, President Johnson had issued an executive order requiring government contractors to take affirmative action to create equal employment opportunity for minorities—but not for women as a class.[30] After persistent lobbying, in 1967, NOW persuaded the administration to broaden the order to include women.[31]

Despite their radical agenda, the middle-aged professionals who led NOW were a bit staid in their appearance, language, and commitment to work for change through lobbying and litigation—much like the National Association for the Advancement of Colored People had worked to dismantle Jim Crow and disfranchisement. As NOW began its work, a diffuse group of young women—they could have been the daughters of NOW leaders—took a different approach. Their political consciousness and sensibilities were shaped by the civil rights and anti-war movements. While they shared NOW's understanding of the problem—a culture suffused with patriarchy—their style was markedly different. They dressed in jeans and sweatshirts, routinely lobbed the F-bomb, were much less likely to see sex tied to marriage, equated patriarchy with Western domination of Third World countries, and wanted to topple the establishment, not claim positions in it. At least for now.

Young women began their journey to women's liberation in radical organizations like SNCC and Students for a Democratic Society (SDS). In late 1964, two seasoned white SNCC staffers, Casey Hayden and Mary King, began

---

29 National Organization for Women, "Statement of Purpose," October 29, 1966 https://now.org/about/history/statement-of-purpose/ (accessed December 28, 2021).
30 Executive Order 11246—Equal Employment Opportunity, September 24, 1965 https://www.presidency.ucsb.edu/documents/executive-order-11246-equal-employment-opportunity (accessed January 24, 2023).
31 Executive Order 11375—Amending Executive Order 11246 Relating to Equal Employment Opportunity, October 13, 1967 https://www.presidency.ucsb.edu/documents/executive-order-11375-amending-executive-order-no-11246-relating-equal-employment (accessed January 24, 2023).

to ask why women played a subordinate role in an organization dedicated to equality and participatory democracy. In November 1965, they circulated what they called "A Kind of Memo" to 40 women in the civil rights, peace, and anti-poverty movements. Drawing on the "ways we have learned to see from the movement," they pointed out that sex—like race—functioned as a caste system that placed women "in a position of inequality to men in work and personal situations." In the movement, men were leaders and spokespersons while women cleaned the Freedom House. Yet subordination of women went unnoticed, even by "people who are very hip to the implications of the racial caste system." When women tried to talk about their position, men's "usual response is laughter" because the "whole idea is either beyond their comprehension or threatens to expose them." Hayden and King suggested that if women talked to one another about their individual experiences, they would be able to see patterns, understand that they were not alone, and build solidarity. Because the likelihood of starting a movement to challenge the sex–caste system "seems slim," they concluded that activists would continue to devote themselves to issues like race, war, and poverty while pursuing "efforts at dialog" about "the problems of women functioning in society as equal beings."[32]

Hayden, King, and other White women left SNCC as Black Power carried the day. They joined radical groups, like SDS, that sought to mobilize the poor or organize opposition to the war. But they found the men who controlled these groups were no more enlightened than their SNCC colleagues. Maybe less. Hayden and King published their memo in *Liberation*, a pacifist magazine, and they and other women demanded discussion of systemic sex discrimination. To no avail. Men continued to dominate, and women rose and fell in influence depending on their romantic relationships with male power brokers. When women raised the issue of sex, it was ignored or met with ridicule. At the SDS national convention in 1967, they presented a resolution insisting that the "liberation of women must be part of the larger fight for human freedom," Liberation required support for women's reproductive rights, access to child care, shared responsibility for domestic tasks with men, and programs to prepare women for leadership. *New Left Notes* published the resolution—accompanied by an illustration of a young girl in a polka dot miniskirt holding a sign with the slogan, "We Want Our Rights, and We Want Them Now."[33] It was the last straw for many women.

---

32 Casey Hayden and Mary King, A Kind f Memo, November 18, 1966 https://www.crmvet.org/docs/651118_kindof_memo.pdf (accessed December 29, 2021).
33 Rosen, *The World Split Open*, 110–27.

Many women abandoned SDS and joined women's organizations that proliferated in cities and on college campuses across the country. Building on Hayden's and King's fundamental insight about the importance of women talking to one another about their experiences and aspirations, they formed consciousness-raising groups that recruited new members and encouraged them to explore their personal frustrations, feelings of inadequacy, and anger. Their conversations led them to critique conventional gender norms and demand women's liberation.

## The Midcentury Consensus Challenged

As conflict over race and sex roiled the once placid American political scene, the Vietnam war sparked sharp debate over America's place in the world. Together they would divide the country, end the illusion of consensus, and erode the buoyant optimism of 1964. They would also challenge some Americans' faith in their country's commitment to justice and democracy. Johnson committed an additional 200,000 troops to Vietnam in 1966, bringing the number to 385,000 by year's end.[34] The steady escalation and uncertain progress of the U.S. effort sparked growing criticism. Anti-war protests began in the spring of 1965, with most occurring on college campuses. Faculty organized teach-ins at schools as diverse as Michigan, Harvard, Illinois, Marist, Carleton, and Flint Junior College, with 20,000 students participating in a 36-hour marathon teach-in at Berkeley. In April, 20,000 protesters gathered outside the White House, and in June, 17,000 attended a rally at Madison Square Garden where Senator Wayne Morse of Oregon, Coretta Scott King, and Dr. Benjamin Spock, America's favorite pediatrician, called for American withdrawal. The protests were small and scattered, and even on college campuses, many supported the President. A survey conducted in January 1966 at the University of Wisconsin revealed that almost three-quarters of the students at one of the nation's most liberal universities stood behind Johnson's actions.

Nevertheless, criticism continued to grow, even among members of Johnson's own party in Congress. William Fulbright, chair of the Senate Foreign Relations Committee, held hearings on the war in April 1966. They featured testimony by prominent critics of U.S. policy, including George F. Kennan, the father of containment. Other senators—Mike Mansfield, Wayne Morse,

---

34 Wasil, Vietnam War Project: Graphs and Statistics.

George McGovern, Eugene McCarthy, and Frank Church—and a number of House members joined Fulbright's critique.

Persistent racial conflict, a divided civil rights movement that targeted the North, questions about Vietnam, fears of inflation, concern about the President's credibility combined to create the perfect storm for Democrats in the 1966 mid-term elections. No one expected the Democrats to maintain the oversized congressional majorities they assembled in the 1964 landslide. After all, the President's party usually lost seats in the mid-terms. But Democratic losses were far larger than expected. Republicans picked up 47 seats in the House and three in the Senate. While conservatives took heart from Ronald Reagan's landslide victory in the California governor's race, liberal and moderate Republicans were the big winners.[35]

Voters sent no clear message. Republicans made inroads in Democratic support in the big cities of the North, perhaps buoyed by White concerns about Black unrest.[36] Clearly, Ronald Reagan, whose campaign focused like a laser on the breakdown of law and order, benefited from a White backlash in California. While admitting that appeals to racism prevailed in some states, however, King denied that Republicans won because of a white backlash. "Despite appeals to bigotry of an intensity and vulgarity never before witnessed in the North," he argued, "millions of white voters remain unshaken in their commitment to decency," citing the election of Massachusetts Republican Edward Brooke to the U.S. Senate, the first African American to serve in that body since Reconstruction.[37] Attractive moderate Republican candidates such as Brooke and Charles Percy, who took an Illinois Senate seat from 74-year-old liberal warhorse Paul Douglas, were undoubtedly a factor in Republican success. So, too, were growing doubts about Lyndon Johnson. On the eve of the election, when a Gallup Poll asked Americans whether they "approved or disapproved of the way Johnson is handling his job as President," only 44% approved.[38] It represented a fall from grace for a man who had won over 60% of the vote

---

35 *New York Times*, November 10, 1966 https://timesmachine.nytimes.com/timesmachine/1966/11/10/82948175.pdf?pdf_redirect=true&ip=0 (accessed December 12, 1966).

36 *New York Times*, November 10, 1966 https://timesmachine.nytimes.com/timesmachine/1966/11/10/82948439.pdf?pdf_redirect=true&ip=0 (accessed December 12, 2021).

37 *New York Times*, November 10, 1966 https://timesmachine.nytimes.com/timesmachine/1966/11/10/82948357.pdf?pdf_redirect=true&ip=0 (accessed December 12, 2021).

38 Gallup Poll, October 21–26, 1966 [Roper #31087717] https://ropercenter-cornell-edu.proxy.binghamton.edu/ipoll/study/31087717/questions#1f13782e-5ac2-4bd5-b708-8a4d4f06d8a0 (accessed December 12, 2022).

just two years before. Johnson's growing unpopularity probably damaged the chances for re-election of dozens of first-term Democrats who won election to the House in 1964 when Johnson's coattails were long and the party picked up 67 seats. While there was growing uneasiness, the Republican victory represented a return to equilibrium rather than an outright repudiation of LBJ.

The biggest threat to Johnson's domestic initiatives came not from Republican success but from the war. As the U.S. dispatched more troops and increased financial support to the government of South Vietnam, the war's price tag grew rapidly. A cost of $700 million in fiscal year 1965 climbed to $15 billion in 1966 and $22 billion in 1967.[39] By fiscal year 1968, it would rise another $4 billion. That was real money. Compared to less than $2 billion for the Office of Economic Opportunity, which ran the War on Poverty, and approximately $6 billion for AFDC, the nation's principal welfare program, the cost was staggering.[40] It also contributed to growing budget deficits, stoked inflation, and had led the Fed to tap the economic brakes by raising interest rates.

When he appeared before Congress in January 1967 for his State of the Union Address, Johnson put on his game face. He made the case for staying the course in Vietnam even though the effort would bring "more costs, more loss, and more agony" and he could not promise that victory "will come this year—or come next year."[41] Such candor was long overdue but came too late for critics. To prosecute the war and sustain Great Society programs while heading off budget deficits and inflation, Johnson called for a 6% income tax surtax—a tax on the federal income tax individuals paid. He also reminded legislators of the landmark legislation adopted in the previous three years and insisted that the cost of the war shouldn't dissuade Congress from continuing to build the Great Society. Many of his initiatives—the civil rights bill that a filibuster had stopped the previous year, consumer protection legislation, additional environmental regulations—would require little additional funding. His call to continue the War on Poverty and urban renewal came with a promise to review the programs to ensure greater efficiency. Rather than asking Congress

---

39 CQ Almanac Online, Vietnam Statistics—War Costs https://library.cqpress.com/cqalmanac/document.php?id=cqal75-1213988 (accessed December 12, 2021).
40 U.S. Department of Health and Human Services, Federal and State Expenditures for AFDC, https://aspe.hhs.gov/sites/default/files/private/pdf/167036/4spending.pdf (accessed December 12, 2022).
41 State of the Union Address, January 10, 1967 https://millercenter.org/the-presidency/presidential-speeches/january-10-1967-state-union-address (accessed December 12, 2021).

for significant increases in spending, he hoped to persuade it to provide support at current levels. His only big ask was funding for the Safe Streets and Crime Control Act, a measure calculated to respond to growing concern about crime without giving in to repressive measures demanded by conservatives.

Johnson's request for the surtax got nowhere. It was unpopular with the public. After all, who wanted to pay a tax on their tax bill? And Wilbur Mills of Arkansas, the conservative chair of the House Ways and Means Committee, wouldn't lend his support unless Johnson agreed to support significant cuts in domestic spending. In the wake of Johnson's landslide victory in 1964, Mills had swallowed his conservative principles and supported Johnson's ambitious domestic programs. But in the aftermath of Democratic losses in 1966 and the new economic realities, he knew he could stand firm because Johnson had far less support on the Hill and across the country. The result was a standoff. Johnson didn't get the tax increase, and Mills didn't get the spending cuts. Support for domestic programs didn't increase, but they enjoyed stable funding levels, even if inflation meant the money didn't go as far. The civil rights bill failed once again, and Congress blocked the Safe Streets Act. Nevertheless, Johnson remained optimistic that the 1967 session was but a bump in the road. When he told his secretary of HEW that his department's budget would be cut, he assured him that better days were ahead. "We're going to end this damned war," he confided, "and then you'll have all the money you want for education, and health, and everything else."[42]

Unfortunately, there was no end to "this damned war." Faced with a determined enemy and saddled with an unreliable ally, Johnson committed additional troops. By the end of 1967, nearly a half million U.S. troops were in Vietnam.[43] General William Westmoreland, the U.S. commander, deployed his forces against the enemy across the South Vietnam's countryside. Massive numbers of helicopters provided mobility, allowing U.S. forces to strike rural areas controlled by the Viet Cong and engage the enemy in punishing fire fights in which superior American firepower inflicted heavy losses. U.S. commanders waged a war of attrition, seeking to deplete enemy ranks and measuring success by "body count." The U.S. also stepped up its bombing campaign, intensifying strikes against enemy positions in South Vietnam, North Vietnamese supply routes through Laos and Cambodia, and North Vietnam itself. The air campaign inflicted suffering on North Vietnam, damaged war production,

---

42 Dallek, *Flawed Giant*, 402.
43 Wasil, Vietnam War Project: Graphs and Statistics.

slowed transportation of troops and war material to the South, and pummeled Viet Cong positions in the South. But it didn't break the enemy's will or turn the tide of the war. Combined with the massive build-up of U.S. troops and their effectiveness in taking the war to the countryside, the air war prevented the collapse of South Vietnam that had appeared imminent in early 1965. It also shrunk Viet Cong control of the countryside. These successes, however, produced stalemate, not victory.

As the war expanded, more Americans paid attention, and criticism of U.S. policy increased. It came from many directions. Some saw the war as misguided, arguing that Ho Chi Minh was a Vietnamese nationalist, not a puppet of Moscow or Beijing. North Vietnam didn't threaten America's vital interests, they insisted. Others argued that U.S. intervention was immoral. Under the guise of stopping Communism and defending democracy, the U.S. propped up a corrupt, repressive South Vietnamese regime—or series of regimes—that denied basic rights to citizens. American intervention, these critics argued, was part of an imperialist project, thwarted national self-determination, and reigned death and destruction on innocent civilians. Because college students could escape the draft, the war was waged disproportionately by working class and minority boys, reinforcing race and class disparities at home. Criticism also came from the right. Many Americans believed that stopping Communist expansion was vital and asked why Johnson wouldn't take the gloves off and take the war to the North. Johnson's inclination to do "enough but not too much" was too much for some but not enough for others, leaving him attacked from all sides.

Protest against the war had begun in 1965 and grew as U.S. involvement expanded during 1966 and 1967. In April 1967, 150,000 anti-war demonstrators descended on United Nations Plaza in New York. Six months later, in October, protesters organized a "Stop the Draft" week, and 100,000 anti-war activists came to Washington, DC. While they captured the nation's attention, these protests were nevertheless smaller than the 1963 March on Washington. Mass demonstrations were but a part of the story, however. Anti-war activists burned their draft cards, laid down on railroad tracks to block trains transporting conscripts, and rallied to protest the presence on their campuses of Reserve Officer Training Corps (ROTC) programs and recruiters for companies that profited from the war. As passions grew, the Viet Cong flag and chants of "Hey, hey, LBJ, how many boys did you kill today?" punctuated anti-war rallies.

Many young anti-war protesters adopted some of the styles and behaviors favored by members of what Americans were beginning to call the counterculture. Rejecting middle-class conventions they considered repressive, hypocritical, and unnatural, they dropped out of mainstream society. Men sported long hair and beards, and men and women alike often wore outlandish clothing, experimented with mind-expanding drugs like marijuana, lysergic acid diethylamide (LSD), and other substances, embraced free love, and often formed communes. Mostly children of economically comfortable families, the bounty of 1960s America allowed them to adopt a lifestyle that stood middle-class values on their head. While true hippies, as they came to be known, were small in number, they attracted considerable attention. In 1967, when rebels in San Francisco's Haight-Ashbury neighborhood proclaimed a "Summer of Love" that attracted young people from across the country, more Americans took notice, with responses ranging from disbelief and amusement to anger and fear.

While most youthful anti-war protesters were college students who, by definition, hadn't dropped out, many adopted aspects of the counterculture. Disgusted by a war that they considered immoral, contemptuous of a president who misled the public, annoyed by parents who expected conformity, eager to experiment with the taboo, and fearful that, if male, they might end up in Vietnam, many traded the neatly cropped hair, chinos, and skirts worn by most college students in the early 1960s for jeans, work shirts, long hair, mustaches, and beards. And they found pot, foul language ("Fuck the draft"), and premarital sex ways of expressing their contempt for America's conformist, repressive culture. "Make love, not war," they insisted. "Do your own thing."

The counterculture changed the music many young people listened to. Catchy but inane hits like the Turtles' "Happy Together" still populated the upper reaches of the pop charts in 1967, but the anti-war movement was making its mark. Folk singer Phil Ochs performed songs like "We Seek No Wider War" and "I'm Not Fighting Anymore" that laid bare LBJ's deceit and the hypocrisy of politicians who justified savagery in the name freedom. While popular on the folk scene and among activists, his biting lyrics never enjoyed the attention they deserved. The counterculture made a much bigger impact. Established folk-rock groups like the Byrds paid homage to experimentation with mind-altering substances in their hit, "Eight Miles High." Psychedelic rock exploded onto the pop scene with a cacophony of sounds and lyrics that reflected the new possibilities opened to musicians by mind-expanding drugs such as LSD. The Doors "Light My Fire" beckoned listeners to uninhibited sex while Jefferson Airplane's "White Rabbit" took listeners on a hallucinatory trip into the mad world of Alice in Wonderland. Rock's hottest band, the Beatles, released the year's top album, *Sgt. Pepper's Lonely Hearts Club Band*. It included songs that were whimsical, featured an Indian sitar and crescendoing orchestral music played backward, and offered a musical description of a mind-bending trip in "Lucy in the Sky with Diamonds," a not-too-subtle reference to LSD.

The youth rebellion—in politics, sex, drugs and rock 'n roll—puzzled and shocked parents who had survived the depression and World War II, believed that the U.S. was a force for good, worked hard to achieve solid middle-class comforts, and sent their kids to college so that they could have a better future, not protest and smoke pot.

More prominent political and moral leaders condemned the war. In March 1967, Senator Robert Kennedy, whose pedigree, charisma, and ambition threatened Johnson, joined the critics. He urged a unilateral bombing halt, a cease-fire, and elections in South Vietnam that would be open to all parties, including the Viet Cong. A month later, Dr. Martin Luther King, Jr. excoriated the war in a highly publicized speech at New York's Riverside Church. Denouncing "the madness of Vietnam," King charged that the U.S. was supporting a brutal dictatorship and terrorizing civilians in pursuit of its misguided anti-Communist crusade. The war was also "devastating the poor at home," "taking the black young men who had been crippled by our society and sending them eight thousand miles away to guarantee liberties in Southeast Asia which they had not found in southwest Georgia or East Harlem." The U.S. must "atone for our sins and errors in Vietnam," King demanded, by accepting a cease fire, opening peace talks, and setting a date by which it would remove all troops.[44]

Most of the criticism was directed at Johnson, and it became intensely personal. That should have come as no surprise. After all, LBJ had refused to level with the country about the sacrifices the war would require or ask Congress to share responsibility with him. The 1964 Tonkin Gulf resolution didn't count because it was adopted when American commitments were limited and Johnson insisted that the U.S. sought "no wider war." Incremental approvals of spending for the war didn't come close to a full-throated congressional endorsement of the war; members were simply giving their approval to "support our boys." Why a man who knew the ways of Congress so well chose not to seek full debate and unequivocal support is puzzling. He may have feared that discussion of the war's true costs would be an excuse to stop funding the Great Society. Without full debate and clear congressional approval, however, Johnson was alone when things went south and criticism mounted.

Not only did LBJ deny Congress the right to share ownership, he also made the war his own by the way he spoke about it. American troops were

---

44 Martin Luther King, Jr., Beyond Vietnam: A Time to Break the Silence, April 4, 1967 https://www.americanrhetoric.com/speeches/mlkatimetobreaksilence.htm (accessed December 2, 2021).

"my boys," the war was "my war," the planes delivering the bombs were "my planes." Just as he identified the war as his, so did his critics. "Don't refer to 'my troops' and 'my planes,'" journalist Drew Pearson warned LBJ in spring 1967. "It gives people the impression that it's your war and not theirs; and enough of your political enemies are already trying to make this point."[45] Johnson ignored the advice.

By personalizing the war, Johnson made critics his enemies, people who were out to destroy him and the country. The critics gave aid and comfort to the enemy, he repeatedly told advisors. Why would Hanoi enter negotiations if it believed that anti-war critics at home would force him to throw in the towel? By fall 1967, the President was certain that the anti-war movement had become a tool of the Communists. After the October anti-war protests in Washington, Johnson told his advisors that he wasn't "going to allow the Communists to take this government and they're doing it right now."[46] His fury and suspicion grew, foreclosed meaningful communication, and left him isolated.

For Johnson, 1967 wasn't the summer of love. Nor was love in the air in many U.S. cities as the nation experienced another long, hot summer. The racial violence that had exploded in 43 cities in 1966 was merely a warmup for the summer of 1967, when rioting erupted in 167 urban areas. As in Watts two years before, those who lived in Black enclaves in large and small cities were frustrated by the contradiction between the promise of the civil rights movement and the reality of their lives. Most uprisings were triggered by an altercation between cops and a community member. In some cases, angry crowds were egged on by militants advocating Black Power. But all were given oxygen by the anger Blacks felt toward a system that kept them poor and powerless. Rioting in Tampa, Cincinnati, Atlanta, Newark, and dozens of smaller cities was alarming, but the uprising in Detroit shook the nation. On July 23, angry Blacks threw rocks and bottles at police who raided a "blind pig"—an unlicensed drinking and gambling club—and arrested 82 patrons, several of whom had just returned from service in Vietnam. The violence grew in intensity over the following days, and when it subsided on July 28, 43 lay dead, 7,200 had been arrested, and $22 million worth of property had been destroyed. Almost 10,000 National Guard and Army troops occupied the city.[47]

---

45 Dallek, *Flawed Giant*, 453.
46 Ibid., 488.
47 https://www.ncjrs.gov/pdffiles1/Digitization/8073NCJRS.pdf, 19–61 (accessed April 29, 2024).

Johnson was shaken by the violence, but disagreed with conservatives who demanded harsh measures to restore law and order while ignoring the underlying causes. When he addressed the nation as the fires in Detroit were still burning, he condemned the rioters, insisting that they "must be dealt with forcefully, and swiftly, and certainly—under the law." But he asserted that "this is not a time for angry reaction," arguing that "it would be a tragedy [...] [to] settle for order imposed at the barrel of a gun." "The only genuine, long-range solution to what has happened lies in an attack [...] upon the conditions that breed despair and violence," he cautioned. Johnson appointed a National Commission on Civil Disorders—popularly known as the Kerner Commission after co-chair Illinois Governor Otto Kerner—"to investigate the causes of the violence and recommend what can be done to prevent it from happening again and again."[48]

Even before the commission gave its report, Johnson pressed Congress for action to address the underlying causes of urban unrest in his 1968 State of the Union Address. To attack unemployment, he asked for $2 billion to fund a new job training partnership with industry. To rebuild America's cities, he called for further investments in his Model Cities program. To ensure that low- and middle-income Americans had access to decent housing, he asked for public investments that would allow builders to construct six million new units of affordable housing in the next decade. To address shocking levels of infant mortality, he insisted on greater support for "health services from prenatal care of the mother through the child's first year." To address growing crime rates, he called on Congress to pass the Safe Streets Act—which it had rejected the previous year—to help cities and states provide better training for police and more sophisticated technology to aid law enforcement. To end housing segregation, he urged Congress to pass his open housing bill.[49]

It was Texas-sized agenda, but there was little chance Congress would adopt it. The cost of the war was already driving deficits higher. Combined with high levels of consumer spending, it was fueling inflation and increasing the trade deficit. These trends threatened the Bretton Woods agreement established in 1944 to ensure international financial stability. Breton Woods pegged the value of other currencies to the dollar, whose stability was guaranteed by making it redeemable in gold at $35 per ounce. As economies in Europe and

---

48 https://www.ncjrs.gov/pdffiles1/Digitization/8073NCJRS.pdf, 297 (accessed April 29, 2024).
49 State of the Union Address, January 17, 1968 https://millercenter.org/the-presidency/presidential-speeches/january-17-1968-state-union-address (accessed December 14, 2021).

Japan rebounded after World War II's destruction and cash-flush Americans purchased more goods from abroad, dollars flowed overseas. Governments, banks, and speculators responded by converting dollars to gold, rapidly drawing down U.S. gold reserves. By late 1967, many feared that U.S. gold reserves would soon be depleted, forcing the U.S. to stop redeeming dollars for gold and upending the international financial order. Johnson responded by asking Congress for a 10% surtax—higher than the request it had rejected the previous year—to slow spending and inflation and reduce the flow of dollars overseas.[50]

Scaling back the U.S. commitment in Vietnam wasn't on the table. Acknowledging that the nation "is challenged, at home and abroad," Johnson expressed optimism about the progress of the war. Democratic elections had been held in South Vietnam, "the enemy has been defeated in battle after battle," and "the number of South Vietnamese living under the protection of the government tonight has grown by one million since January of last year." While the President had convinced himself that his strategy was working, analyses by the Central Intelligence Agency (CIA) were inconsistent and inconclusive. They offered mixed reports on the effectiveness of U.S. bombing, progress against the Viet Cong, the combat-worthiness of the South Vietnamese army, and more. However, Westmoreland and Henry Cabot Lodge, the U.S. ambassador to South Vietnam, were unfailingly optimistic, insisting that the U.S. was winning. Johnson veered between pessimism and optimism but persuaded himself that success was within reach. "Wishful thinking had replaced rational assessment," historian Robert Dallek concluded.[51] Johnson and his aides remained upbeat in public statements; in a highly publicized speech at the National Press Club in November, Westmoreland assured his audience that "we have reached an important point where the end comes into view."[52]

## 1968: Things Fall Apart

Two weeks after Johnson's State of the Union Address, the North Vietnamese and Viet Cong punctured the illusion that victory was in sight. On January 31, 1968, the Viet Cong launched a massive offensive to coincide with the beginning of Tet, the Lunar New Year holiday. Enemy forces struck 36 of

---

50 Robert M. Collins, "The Economic Crisis of 1968 and the Waning of the America Century,'" *American Historical Review*, 101 (April 1996), 396–422.
51 Dallek, *Flawed Giant*, 485.
52 U.S. Department of State, *American Foreign Policy: Current Documents, 1967* (Washington, 1969), 1036.

44 provincial capitals from one end of the country to the other. Even though they were surprised, U.S. and South Vietnamese forces blunted the offensive and inflicted punishing casualties on the Viet Cong, who suffered as many as 40,000 battlefield deaths compared to 1,100 American and 2,300 South Vietnamese Army fatalities. Although the Viet Cong would never recover from the losses, the offensive shocked the American public. The administration's credibility gap was now as wide as the Mississippi River. Walter Cronkite, the avuncular CBS News anchor who was the country's most trusted journalist, proclaimed that the emperor had no clothes. "To say we are closer to victory today is to believe [...] the optimists who have been wrong in the past," he concluded. "To say that we are mired in a stalemate is the only reasonable, yet unsatisfactory conclusion." Cronkite's assessment reinforced the growing sentiment that the administration's predictions were erroneous and there was no end in sight. Approval of Johnson's conduct of the war fell to 26% during Tet; by March, 78% of Americans believed that the U.S. was not making progress toward victory.[53]

Johnson soon announced that he would not seek reelection, upending the approaching presidential election campaign. Robert Kennedy quickly entered, challenging McCarthy for the fealty of anti-war Democrats. Hubert Humphrey, Johnson's vice president, walked a tightrope, seeking to rally the party's Black, urban, blue-collar base while not separating himself from his boss on Vietnam. The Republican field was less volatile, but still cluttered. Richard Nixon, near-winner in 1960 and loyal campaigner for Republicans of all stripes in 1964 and 1966, was the clear front-runner. But he faced a challenge from George Romney, Nelson Rockefeller, and Ronald Reagan—governors, respectively, of Michigan, New York, and California. Nixon's staid, buttoned-down persona convinced many that, while he was boring and awkward, his expertise in foreign policy seemed to make him the candidate best qualified to clean up the mess in Vietnam. And his ability to straddle the moderate and conservative wings of the party led many to see him as the person who could bring unity to a party that had been left bitterly divided by Goldwater.

As if spirited battles in both major parties weren't enough, George Wallace entered the fray as the candidate of the American Independent Party. Wallace's candidacy offered additional evidence that the optimism and illusion of consensus that prevailed in 1964 were quickly evaporating. An acerbic populist conservative who lobbed zingers at government bureaucrats and appealed to

---

53 Herring, *America's Longest War* (New York, 2019) 233–49.

a growing White backlash with coded language, he scared the major parties. Democrats knew from his primary successes in 1964, he appealed to northern White working-class voters while Republicans feared that he would sweep the South, reversing the gains they had made there since 1952.

The man in the White House remained preoccupied with Vietnam. In early April, North Vietnam agreed to enter negotiations. Its demand for an unconditional bombing halt throughout Vietnam, however, assured that progress would be glacial. In the meantime, U.S. and South Vietnamese forces intensified the air campaign against Viet Cong positions in South Vietnam and North Vietnamese supply routes in Cambodia and Laos and launched a punishing ground offensive against Viet Cong positions.

At home, Johnson was at loggerheads with Congress over the 10% income tax surcharge he requested in his State of the Union Address. House Ways and Means Committee chairman Wilbur Mills insisted on a 10% discretionary domestic spending cut as the price for moving the tax forward. Johnson, reluctant to gut Great Society programs, resisted. But by June, Johnson swallowed the bitter pill Mills offered. Although the cuts turned out to be less deep than Mills had initially demanded, they marked an end to expansion of Great Society social programs at the very moment that the Kerner Commission recommended a Marshall Plan for the cities.

The President's battles with Congress took place against a background of violence that bitterly divided the nation and made many yearn for the consensus—or at least illusion of consensus—that had prevailed a few years before. In April 1968, while organizing a Poor People's Campaign that would bring thousands to Washington to demand greater investment in the War on Poverty, Martin Luther King, Jr. was gunned down in Memphis by James Earl Ray, an escaped convict, White supremacist, and Wallace supporter. King's murder sparked rage in African American communities across the nation. Uprisings erupted in 130 cities and resulted in property destruction estimated at $100 million, 20,000 arrests, and deployment of 130,000 troops. Two months later, after celebrating his victory in California's Democratic primary at Los Angeles's Ambassador Hotel, Robert Kennedy was shot to death by a Palestinian hotel employee who was outraged by Kennedy's support for Israel. With him died Democrats' hopes of a nominee who would make a clean break with Johnson's discredited Vietnam policy and unite an increasingly splintered Democratic Party.

The murders sent shock waves through the nation and moved Congress to act on several of Johnson's legislative priorities. In February, the Senate had passed Johnson's civil rights bill, which made it a federal offense to discriminate on the basis of race in selling or renting real estate. Six days after King's murder, the House gave its approval. Two months later, Congress passed Johnson's crime bill. Although conservatives extracted provisions that gave state officials broad wiretapping authority that Johnson found repugnant, the bill provided $400 million over two years for grants to support and professionalize state and local law enforcement. It also included gun control provisions Johnson had sought for several years, banning sale of handguns through the mail, prohibiting sale of handguns to the resident of another state, and licensing gun dealers. In October, Johnson persuaded Congress to expand coverage to rifles and shotguns.

Violence seemed to erupt almost everywhere, including the Democratic National Convention which convened in Chicago in July. Robert Kennedy's assassination left Eugene McCarthy, the enigmatic, cerebral Minnesota poet, professor, and U.S. Senator as the anti-war Democrats' standard bearer. Even though Kennedy had defeated him in California, McCarthy had done well enough in the other primaries to be a force at the convention. But primaries didn't determine the outcome because there were so few of them. Most delegates were selected by state conventions, where Humphrey's influence with party insiders like Chicago's mayor, Richard Daley, sent him to the convention with enough delegates to win the nomination. Thousands of anti-war activists, determined to make a statement against Johnson, Humphrey, and the war flocked to Chicago. Clashes between activists and Daley's police in Lincoln Park got convention week off to an exciting start. As the convention got underway, delegates engaged in a fierce debate over language in the platform endorsing Johnson's Vietnam policies. When anti-war delegates failed to defeat it, pandemonium broke out in the hall and also in Grant Park, where 10,000 protesters had gathered. Police prevented them from moving toward the convention hall several miles away, but several thousand moved on the Conrad Hilton Hotel, where Humphrey and other party dignitaries lodged. As voting began that would lead to Humphrey's nomination, police charged the surging crowd, lobbing tear gas, and beating demonstrators. Television crews alternated images of profanity-laced arguments on the convention floor with scenes of police clubbing protesters on the streets. Disgusted by the protesters, many viewers criticized the networks for biased coverage that made the police look bad. It began the narrative of liberal bias in the media that would become an article of faith among conservatives.

Discord in Chicago and charges of media bias suited George Wallace just fine. Wallace had exploited racial division to achieve undisputed power in Alabama, and he had discovered that it appealed to some White Democrats in the North when he entered the Wisconsin and Indiana primaries in 1964. That experience had given him a presidential itch he needed to scratch.

In 1967, he formed the American Independent Party and generated enough petition signatures—2.7 million in all—to place his name on the ballot in all but seven states and the District of Columbia. Avoiding the N word and defense of segregation, he instead vowed to "Stand Up for America." His supporters knew that meant standing up for White America—the people who paid taxes to support lazy (Black) welfare recipients, were threatened by (Black) civil disorder and (Black) criminals, saw (Black) criminals returned to the streets because liberals on the Supreme Court coddled criminals, and couldn't send their kids to (White) schools of their choice because federal judges and bureaucrats didn't believe in freedom (to discriminate). If anyone doubted that racism motivated his supporters, the Confederate flags and "White Power" signs they displayed at his rallies dispelled them.

On the campaign trail, Wallace's energy, barbed humor, and clever one-liners thrilled large, raucous audiences. His supporters believed that he shared their frustration with paying taxes to support welfare recipients, being told by Washington bureaucrats how their local schools should be run just so Blacks and Whites could attend school together, and watching scruffy, long-haired protesters burn Old Glory or wave the Viet Cong flag. "You people work hard, you save your money, you teach your children to respect the law," he told a blue-collar audience in California. Liberal judges and politicians, on the other hand, created a double standard, making excuses for disadvantaged youth who burned cities or murdered law-abiding citizens. These "'pseudo intellectuals' explain it away," Wallace smirked, "by saying the killer didn't get enough watermelon to eat when he was 10 years old." That would end when he was president. "We don't have riots in Alabama," Wallace told a raucous crowd at New York's Madison Square Garden. "They start a riot down there, the first one of 'em to pick up a brick gets a bullet in the brain, that's all."[54]

Wallace's raw, angry language and his contempt for elites who disdained white working people struck a chord in the North and the South. "You don't have to worry about where he stands," a steelworker in Youngstown, Ohio commented. "He tells it like it really is."[55] What he told anyone who listened was that liberals hated working people like them, were destroying their lives, and must be vanquished. He appealed to an almost primal anger that threatened to transform politics into a kind of blood sport, wiping out any sense that there

---

54 Dan T. Carter, *The Politics of Rage: George Wallace, the Origins of the New Conservatism, and the Transformation of American Politics* (New York, 1995), 335.
55 Ibid., 313, 367, 335.

might be common ground and room for compromise. The symbol of White southern resistance who now had a national following. Wallace was southernizing American politics, NBC News reporter Douglas Kiker observed: "They all hate black people [...]. They're all afraid of them. That's it! They're all Southern! The whole United States is Southern!"[56] It was a dramatic change from 1964, when a White Southerner committed to civil rights and fond of seeking consensus with the invitation, "Come, let us reason together," won the presidency in a landslide.

Richard Nixon understood the threat Wallace posed and pivoted to meet it. During the spring of 1968, his supporters worked the state Republican conventions and built a big lead in delegates to the Republican national convention. Romney's campaign fizzled in the New Hampshire primary, and he soon dropped out of the race. While Rockefeller continued to pursue the holy grail, he never gained momentum, winning only one primary while failing to capture even 20% of the vote in the seven others he contested. Reagan never formally declared his candidacy, but he crisscrossed the country giving speeches to Republican groups as if he had. He won the California primary in June because he was the state's governor and ran unopposed. After the primary, he began a charm offensive in the South, where he had established his conservative bona fides during the Goldwater campaign. His goal was to win over enough Nixon delegates to deny him the nomination on the first ballot, create an open convention, and persuade conservatives that he—not Nixon—was the one.

It didn't work. The South was already central to Nixon's strategy. He believed that Johnson's support for civil rights provided Republicans an opportunity to make further inroads in Dixie. Sunbelt suburbanites were mobilizing against the federal government and its insistence on school desegregation. Nixon was watching and grasped the opportunity their dissent presented. Looking ahead to the general election, Wallace's candidacy worried him, so he had already given considerable attention to courting southern Republicans. Wallace would be hard to beat in the Deep South, but Nixon had high hopes for places like Virginia, North Carolina, Arkansas, Tennessee, and Kentucky. His campaign crafted a message that appealed to white southerners. He focused on "law and order," criticizing liberals who sought to shift attention from the lawlessness of rioters to the conditions that produced violence, skewering the Supreme Court for being more concerned about the rights of criminals than their victims, and paying homage to "the silent center, the millions of people in the middle of

---

56 Carter, *Politics of Rage*, 344.

the American political spectrum who do not demonstrate, who do not picket or protest loudly."[57] It was a soft cover of Wallace's angry anthem. Nixon courted Strom Thurmond, the legendary South Carolina segregationist who had joined the Republican party in 1964. As the convention began, Thurmond stood beside Nixon as he met with members of the southern delegations and assured them that, as president, he would do as little as possible to support school desegregation orders. Nor would he feel obliged to "satisfy some professional civil-rights group."[58] Charming as he was, Reagan didn't have a chance; Nixon waltzed to a first ballot victory.

As the campaign kicked off, Nixon pursued his Southern strategy, figuring that it would help him make inroads with working-class White Democrats in the North and attract voters in the South. He denounced rioters, criminals, bleeding heart liberals, and the Supreme Court, and promised to restore law and order. To underscore his point, he reminded those who attended his rallies that while they listened to him there had been "one murder, two rapes, forty-five major crimes of violence, countless robberies and auto thefts,"[59] leaving those in his audiences to conjure up the faces of Black perpetrators. As federal courts tired of subterfuges and pushed school districts—North and South—to integrate by busing students to schools outside their neighborhoods, Nixon pushed back, defending parents' freedom of choice. He was against segregation, he insisted, but he also opposed court-mandated integration. Of course, in a society in which most Whites opposed integration, that meant supporting segregation.

There was more to Nixon's strategy than appeals to the South and White animosity toward Blacks. Awkward, restrained, and always in a business suit and white shirt, Nixon struck many as boring. The campaign made his charisma deficit an asset. It depicted him as a sober, experienced statesman who would bring reason, good judgment, and steadiness to the presidency. He would end the conflict, lawlessness, immorality, and war in Southeast Asia that were tearing the country apart. A television ad produced by Roger Ailes, a young media whiz, appealed to many Whites' animosity toward Blacks and anti-war protesters while sounding measured and reasonable. The ad flashed images of ragged protesters, angry Blacks, police firing cannisters of tear gas, troops in the streets, a body lying in a pool of blood, and buildings in flames

---

57 Stephen E. Ambrose, *Nixon: The Triumph of the Politician* (New York, 1989), 161.
58 Carter, *Politics of Rage*, 329.
59 Ambrose, *Triumph of the Politician*, 209.

as a voiceover from Nixon himself proclaimed, "in a system [...] that provides for peaceful change, there is no cause that justifies resort to violence." He went on, "The first civil right of every American is to be free of domestic violence."[60] In a country that was coming apart, Nixon seemed to take the high ground, acknowledging the right to protest peacefully while insisting that violence and lawlessness must not be tolerated. Nixon and George Wallace had a similar message, but Nixon's was delivered mostly without Wallace's snarling, angry histrionics.

Humphrey was sober enough and certainly experienced. He was the Happy Warrior, the embodiment of the politics of optimism that characterized the early 1960s. But as Johnson's vice president, he carried all the baggage of his unpopular boss. Those who believed the Great Society was a failed experiment that wasted taxpayers' hard-earned money to support the undeserving poor, disliked him because he was a liberal. Opponents of the war denounced him as an imperialist who lacked the imagination and will to end an immoral war that was tearing the country apart. If that weren't enough, Humphrey emerged from the Democrats' bloodbath in Chicago, the head of a party at war with itself. As the campaign began, he trailed Nixon 38% to 29% with 20% going to Wallace.[61] Nixon's biggest concern was that Wallace would carry the South, no candidate would win a majority in the Electoral College, and the Democratic-controlled House of Representatives would decide the outcome.

By October, however, Humphrey was surging and Wallace fading. Union leaders, alarmed by Wallace's appeal to their White members, reminded them that, as governor, he had supported anti-union policies that attracted jobs to the South, where wages were lower and unions weaker. But it was Wallace's selection of retired General Curtis LeMay as his running mate that let the air out of his balloon. Asked by a reporter whether it would be necessary to use nuclear weapons in Vietnam, LeMay said it wouldn't. Unable to leave well enough alone, however, he complained that Americans had "a phobia about nuclear weapons" and that "there may be times when it would be most efficient

---

60 Richard Nixon [Republican] 1968 Campaign Ad "Law and Order," Congressional Archives Carl Albert Center https://www.youtube.com/watch?v=lV_14O5wuDM (accessed January 24, 2023).
61 Gallup Organization, Gallup Poll # 1968-0767: 1968 Presidential Election/Vietnam, Question 5, USGALLUP.68-767.R05A, Gallup Organization (Cornell University, Ithaca, NY: Roper Center for Public Opinion Research, 1968).

to use" them.[62] By mid-October, polls showed that Wallace's support had dipped from 20% to 15%.[63]

While Nixon picked up some Wallace defectors in the North and even more in the border states, Humphrey surged in the polls. He benefitted from the unions' anti-Wallace campaign, from anti-Johnson Democrats who returned to the fold because they could not abide a Nixon victory, and from Johnson's apparent success in jump-starting negotiations with North Vietnam to end the war. In mid-October, Johnson informed all three candidates that North Vietnam would allow representatives of the South Vietnamese government to participate in the Paris peace talks if the U.S. stopped the bombing. No deal had been reached because Johnson also demanded that North Vietnam stop attacks across its border with the South and against cities in the South. Nevertheless, Johnson was optimistic about the prospects for peace, which made Nixon nervous. Talks would lead many to conclude that peace was at hand and reward LBJ's vice president with their votes.

Although Johnson's briefing was confidential, Nixon hinted publicly that Johnson might soon halt the bombing as a way to undermine his candidacy. Working through Anna Chenault, a supporter who had contacts at the highest levels of the South Vietnamese government, he encouraged South Vietnam's president, Nguyen Van Thieu, to blow up the deal by refusing to enter negotiations. On October 31, the North Vietnamese accepted Johnson's terms, LBJ announced that the U.S. would cease its air campaign, peace talks would begin immediately, and the Viet Cong and the South Vietnamese government were welcome to participate. Humphrey surged in the polls. On November 2, however, Thieu announced that his government wouldn't participate, dashing hopes for peace.

The election was close. Nixon won 43.4% of the popular vote to Humphrey's 42.7% while Wallace faded to 13.5%. But Nixon won a commanding electoral majority, taking 301 electoral votes to 191 for Humphrey and 45 for Wallace, who carried only four Deep South states and Arkansas. Nixon's Southern

---

62 Carter, *Politics of Rage*, 359.
63 Gallup Organization, Gallup Poll # 1968-0770: Presidential Election/Political Party, October 17–22, 1968, Question 5, USGALLUP.770.Q04A, Gallup Organization (Cornell University, Ithaca, NY: Roper Center for Public Opinion Research, 1968); Louis Harris & Associates, Louis Harris & Associates Poll: October 27–28, 1968, Question 1, USHARRIS.110168.R1, Louis Harris & Associates (Cornell University, Ithaca, NY: Roper Center for Public Opinion Research, 1968).

strategy had paid off, and he did well in the North, carrying New Jersey, Ohio, Illinois, and California. Given Nixon's razor thin victory, it was no surprise that the balance of power in Congress shifted very little. Republicans picked up only five seats in the House, leaving Democrats with a commanding 243–192 margin. Republicans did better in the Senate, where they were defending only 11 seats to the Democrats' 23. They won seven seats previously held by Democrats while Democrats picked off two Republican seats, giving the GOP a net gain of five seats and narrowing the Democrats' margin to 58–42. However, most of the newly elected members—Democrat and Republican—were moderate or liberal, leaving the chamber only slightly more conservative.

When Nixon addressed his cheering supporters at New York's Waldorf Astoria Hotel on November 6, he spoke of his aspirations as president. As he campaigned in a small Ohio town, he told his audience, he was struck by a young boy with a sign that read "Bring Us Together." "And that will be the great objective of this administration," he pledged, "to bring the American people together."[64] After four years of bitter division over the war and race, urban uprisings, assassinations, and mass protests, Nixon's words resonated with many, perhaps most, Americans. Many still believed that government must play an active role to ensure that all Americans had a shot at enjoying the nation's prosperity. A poll conducted by General Electric shortly after Nixon's inauguration in 1969 indicated that 44% of Americans thought the government should do more to help minorities and 34% said it should do the same; 41% wanted government to do more to support urban renewal while 35% said it should do the same; and 69% said it should do more to support education and 21% said it should do the same.[65] Small-government conservatives had failed to re-capture the Republican Party much less persuade most Americans that government was the enemy.

Despite the chaos of the preceding three years, the center held. Republicans had discovered that wedge issues like race and crime were useful in attracting support from key Democratic constituencies like White Southerners, suburbanites, and White working-class voters in the North. They were too tempting to abandon and threatened to perpetuate division and conflict. Yet differences between the parties were not as sharp as those that had divided Goldwater and Johnson in 1964. They differed over how ambitious government should be and which approaches were best suited to address problems of

---

64 Ambrose, *Triumph of the Politician*, 230.
65 General Electric Poll, January 31–February 9, 1969 [Roper #31092120].

race, poverty, the cities, education, and the environment. But just as they had in the 1950s, many Republicans and most Democrats agreed that government offered solutions to pressing problems and wasn't itself the problem.

Americans were bitterly divided, but those divisions did not define the two major parties or preclude compromises necessary for effective governing. The congressional delegations of each included conservatives, moderates, and liberals. Liberal Republican was not an oxymoron but a term that described a segment of the party, while Democrats like John Stennis of Mississippi were among the Senate's most conservative members. Diversity within the parties made cooperation between the parties on legislation not only possible but necessary if Congress was to legislate—as most legislators assumed their constituents expected them to do. Like divisions between the parties, the electorate also remained fluid. Some 28% of Americans identified as independent,[66] and ticket splitting was common. Indeed, 18 of the 34 senators elected in 1968 had a party affiliation different than that of the presidential candidate who carried their state. With so many voters up for grabs, politicians knew they had to reach beyond their party's base to be successful, and that meant not straying too far from the center. Divided government wouldn't produce gridlock.

Yet Americans' trust in their political leaders was strained. They were weary of the half-truths and dishonesty Johnson had used to lead the country into the morass of Vietnam. Most respected the presidency and didn't want to see another president fail. They wanted to trust their president and political leaders to help the country live up to its ideals and restore the place it had occupied for two decades after World War II as the leader of the Free World. The newly elected President's campaign told voters, "Nixon's the One!" They would soon find out he was, but not in the way they hoped.

---

66  Pew Research Center, *Trends in Party Identification*, 1939–2014, April 7, 2015 https://www.pewresearch.org/politics/interactives/party-id-trend/ (accessed April 23, 2023).

CHAPTER 3

# CONFLICT, CRISIS, AND CONTINUITY, 1969–1976

## Race and Realignment

Richard Nixon's promise to "bring us together" spoke to the hopes of most Americans. Nixon's advisors, however, regarded it as an obligatory platitude. It had to be said but wouldn't guide the President's political strategy. One member of the administration surely rolled his eyes. Kevin Phillips was a 28-year-old political junkie, intellectual, and writer who cut his teeth on the ethnic politics of the Bronx as a staffer for Republican congressman Paul Fino. He became a trusted advisor of Nixon's campaign manager and confidant, John Mitchell, and followed Mitchell to the Justice Department when Nixon named him attorney general. Phillips believed that the key to political success—Nixon's North Star—was exploiting conflict. "The whole secret of politics," he told Garry Wills in 1968, "is knowing who hates who."[1]

In June 1969, Phillips accomplished something quite rare. He published a dense 500-page analysis of contemporary American politics that became a bestseller. As its title suggested, *The Emerging Republican Majority*, argued that the nation was in the process of a tectonic shift, much like the realignment of 1932 that produced 36 years of Democratic hegemony. The driving forces were geography and, even more important, race. Power was shifting from the stodgy urban Northeast to the suburbs and the Sunbelt, a term Phillips coined to describe the vast, rapidly growing region stretching from Virginia to southern California. "[T]he Negro socioeconomic revolution and liberal Democratic inability to cope with it," Phillips wrote, was drawing many White Democrats to

---

[1] Gary Wills, "The Politics of Grievance," *The New York Review of Books*, July 19, 1990 https://www.nybooks.com/articles/1990/07/19/the-politics-of-grievance/ (accessed February 2, 2023).

the GOP. They were tired of their leaders' support for policies that transferred political power and resources to Blacks and were drawn to a Republican Party that stood for law and order, smaller government, and states' rights. Democrats, he asserted, "fell victim to the ideological impetus of a liberalism which had carried it beyond programs taxing the few for the benefit of the many (the New Deal) to programs taxing the many for the benefit of the few (the Great Society)."[2]

Even though parts of the manuscript had circulated among Nixon advisors, Phillips's analysis didn't inform campaign strategy in 1968. Certainly, Nixon appealed to White working- and middle-class fear of Blacks and revulsion against anti-war protesters with promises to restore "law and order." However, he cultivated an image as the sober, experienced statesman who could fix the mess in Vietnam and was wary of alienating his party's moderates and liberals. He was, therefore, determined to avoid being labeled an extremist. So, Nixon shrouded divisive appeals in carefully coded language and portrayed himself as a moderate who could bring the country together. In Phillips's words, he "steered between the Scylla of losing too many moderates to Humphrey and the Charybdis of leaving too many conservatives in the camp of George Wallace."[3] As with most things, Nixon was not driven by ideology, but by what he thought would help him win.

That approach prevailed after his inauguration. When Phillips's book appeared in mid-1969, it drew fire from many prominent Republicans. Hugh Scott, the Senate Republican leader, called it "baloney."[4] Nixon's top speechwriter, William Safire, was dismayed at the suggestion the party disregard the Northeast, worrying that a "tacit 'writing-off' any area is a big political mistake." Even Harry Dent, Nixon's chief southern operative, thought that overemphasizing the South and the Sunbelt would make Nixon look weak. "We should disavow the book," he told Nixon, "and assert that we are growing in strength nationally."[5] Exploiting opportunities was one thing, but single-mindedly pursuing a strategy of racial division risked alienating potential

---

2 Kevin Phillips, *The Emerging Republican Majority* (Princeton, NJ, 2015), 15.
3 Ibid., 12.
4 James Boyd, "Nixon's Southern Strategy 'It's All in the Charts,'" *New York Times*, May 17, 1970 https://www.nytimes.com/1970/05/17/archives/nixons-southern-strategy-its-all-in-the-charts.html (accessed February 2, 2023).
5 Dov Grohsgal and Kevin M. Kruse, "How the Republican Majority Emerged," *The Atlantic*, August 6, 2019 https://www.theatlantic.com/ideas/archive/2019/08/emerging-republican-majority/595504/ (accessed February 2, 2023).

allies inside and outside the party and sacrificing Nixon's hard-won reputation as a moderate. As he left the administration in May 1970, Phillips told a *New York Times* reporter that "the Nixon administration has not moved effectively to build the coalitions open to it."[6]

Nevertheless, Nixon understood the opportunity to expand his appeal in the South and bring disaffected Democrats in other regions into the Republican fold. He zigzagged, tacking from support for liberal policies to excoriating them, from showing solicitude for civil rights to playing the race card, from hardline anticommunism to détente. If his approach lacked consistency, it—combined with a Democratic Party in disarray—would allow him to win reelection in a landslide. Ultimately, his problem was not the preference for pragmatism over the single-minded approach Phillips urged. Rather, it was his utter lack of concern for ending discord, obsession with his enemies, and willingness to break the law to punish them that destroyed his presidency. By 1974, under siege, he found it necessary to assure the press, "I am not a crook!"[7] The result was another failed presidency, growing distrust of government, and bitter division over issues old and new.

## Peace with Honor

As he took the oath of office in January 1969, Nixon's chief concern was Vietnam. Like LBJ, he was in a bind. He knew that the U.S. could not win. "I've come to the conclusion we can't win the war," he told a speechwriter during the 1968 campaign. "But we can't say that, of course. In fact, we have to seem to say the opposite, just to keep some degree of bargaining leverage."[8] Like Johnson, he refused to cut and run. Doing so, he feared, would mark him as a loser, alienate his conservative base, and destroy U.S. credibility abroad. There were all sorts of problems with this analysis, of course. Because it was Johnson's war, he could have proclaimed it a colossal error on the part of the Democrats and moved on. Conservatives grumbled but stuck with Nixon when he pursued détente with

---

6 James Boyd, "Nixon's Southern Strategy 'It's All in the Charts,'" *New York Times*, May 17, 1970 https://www.nytimes.com/1970/05/17/archives/nixons-southern-strategy-its-all-in-the-charts.html (accessed February 2, 2023).

7 *Washington Post*, November 18, 1973 https://www.washingtonpost.com/politics/nixon-tells-editors-im-not-a-crook/2012/06/04/gJQA1RK6IV_story.html (accessed January 25, 2023).

8 Richard Whalen, *Catch the Falling Flag: A Republican's Challenge to His Party* (New York, 1972), 137–38.

the Soviet Union and opened relations with Red China. Most likely, they would have done the same had he cut the country's losses in Vietnam. As for the allies, most thought Vietnam was a mistake. But Nixon believed the only acceptable course was to win a negotiated settlement that swapped U.S. withdrawal for survival of its South Vietnamese ally—at least for a decent interval. To achieve this, he would make North Vietnam pay a high price if it refused to agree to a minimally acceptable settlement. He called it "peace with honor," an approach befitting the statesman he claimed to be.

Nixon's plan, such as it was, differed little from LBJ's and would have similar results, keeping the U.S. in Vietnam for four more years and feeding division at home. But there was a twist in Nixon's approach, Vietnamization. He knew that the draft and mounting U.S. combat deaths fueled the anti-war movement that had destroyed Johnson. So, he continued efforts begun by LBJ to make the South Vietnamese army more effective, continued to provide billions to support it, and shifted more and more responsibility for the fighting away from American soldiers. Between 1968 and 1971, the number of U.S. troops fell from 565,000 to 156,000. By 1972, when Nixon sought re-election, there were only 24,000 U.S. troops "in country."[9] Draft calls tapered off and fewer Americans died. Nixon may not have had a plan to end the war, but he had one to avoid LBJ's fate.

Nixon's pivot took time, so anti-war protest war actually grew. He ordered secret incursions, supported by massive bombing, against North Vietnamese installations and supply lines in Laos and Cambodia. During his first six months in office, 8,000 Americans died in heavy fighting, convincing anti-war activists that they needed to turn up the heat. Between January 1969 and April 1970, more than 7,000 activists were arrested for violent acts on college campuses alone, and mass protests continued. Moderate anti-war leaders established the Vietnam Moratorium Committee and coordinated peaceful vigils across the country in October 1969, when two million Americans joined protests in 200 cities.[10] A month later, on November 13–14, as many as a half million demonstrators descended on the Capital to demand peace.[11]

---

9 Ibid.

10 Todd Gitlin, "This isn't 1968. It's 1969," *Washington Post*, June 11, 2020 https://www.washingtonpost.com/outlook/antiwar-vietnam-protests-1969/2020/06/11/6a58d1cc-ab7a-11ea-9063-e69bd6520940_story.html (accessed January 25, 2023).

11 "November 15, 1969: Anti-Vietnam War Demonstration Held," *New York Times*, November 15, 2011 https://archive.nytimes.com/learning.blogs.nytimes.com/2011/11/15/nov-15-1969-anti-vietnam-war-demonstration-held/?module=ArrowsNav&contentCollection=undefined&action=keypress&region=FixedLeft&pgtype=Blogs (accessed January 25, 2023).

Nixon fought back, pitting what he called "the great Silent Majority" against the young, long-haired, often privileged college students who figured prominently in the protests. In a televised speech on November 3, 1969, he outlined his plan for Vietnamization, revealed that he had written directly to Ho Chi Minh in an effort to jump-start peace talks, and appealed to patriotic Americans to help him achieve "peace with honor." He was pleased with the public reaction to the speech and criticism of the massive demonstration in Washington. "We've got those liberal bastards on the run now," he gloated.[12]

Or so he thought. Nixon's strategy depended on North Vietnam's willingness to negotiate an agreement, but it refused to budge. The talks in Paris begun by LBJ went nowhere because the U.S. demanded a mutual withdrawal of forces from South Vietnam, and North Vietnam saw no reason to do so, given the drawdown of U.S. troops, continued anti-war protests, and growing anti-war sentiment on Capitol Hill. Frustrated by North Vietnamese recalcitrance, Nixon ordered U.S. and South Vietnamese troops into Cambodia to destroy enemy sanctuaries. When he announced the incursion in a televised speech on April 30, 1970, all hell broke loose. Angry students led demonstrations and strikes on over 800 college campuses and shut down some for the remainder of the academic year.[13] At Ohio's Kent State, where Governor James Rhodes called in the National Guard, rattled young Guardsmen opened fire, killing four students. Eleven days later, two students were killed and 11 wounded in an altercation at Jackson State University, a predominantly Black school in Mississippi. Crosby, Stills, Nash & Young expressed the anger and disbelief of most college students in their song "Ohio," and on May 9–10, 100,000 protesters—most of them students—descended on the Capital to demand peace. Nixon called them "bums" and took heart that there were fewer of them than the previous fall.

The Cambodian invasion destroyed vast amounts of enemy military equipment, but did not inflict significant losses on North Vietnamese forces. It did, however, help anti-war leaders in Congress win passage of a joint resolution demanding the withdrawal of all U.S. forces from Cambodia by June 30. Nixon hung tough, however. He knew he could count on support from his "Silent Majority," middle- and working-class Whites who were disgusted by

---

12 Melvin Small, *The Presidency of Richard Nixon* (Lawrence, KS, 1999), 75.
13 Amanda Miller, "May 1970 Student Antiwar Strikes," Mapping American Social Movements Project, University of Washington https://depts.washington.edu/moves/antiwar_may1970.shtml (accessed February 2, 2023).

campus disruptions. He was delighted when construction workers in New York City's lower Manhattan broke up a demonstration on May 8, bloodying some of the students. Twelve days later, 100,000 "hard hats" marched on City Hall to support his policies. Nixon was so pleased by his success in mobilizing White union members who traditionally voted Democratic against his critics that he hosted the march's leaders at the White House.

Nixon enjoyed greater success with the Soviets and the Chinese than with the North Vietnamese. Fancying himself a grand strategist who could realign great power relations to the advantage of the U.S., Nixon sought to ease conflict with the Soviets and the Chinese. His anti-communist bona fides gave him the cover to do it. In early 1969, he initiated discussions with the Soviet Union to limit nuclear weapons. He believed that the arms race was destabilizing and costly and damaged opportunities to expand economic relations with the Soviet Union. Nixon also hoped to use the carrot of improved relations to persuade the Soviets to pressure their North Vietnamese allies to be more forthcoming in Paris. In July 1971, Nixon announced that he would visit Moscow for a summit in 1972. He also had his eye on "Red" China, the emerging superpower the U.S. refused to recognize. Opening relations with China would be the ultimate coup. In addition to burnishing his reputation as a statesman, overtures to Beijing would alarm the Soviets. Of course, China might also be useful in convincing its North Vietnamese clients to be more tractable. Secret diplomatic exchanges began in 1970. National security advisor Henry Kissinger made a clandestine visit to China in July 1971, and a week later both sides announced that Nixon would visit Beijing in 1972.

Nixon and his sidekick Kissinger may have stunned the world, but success in Vietnam eluded them. The last large-scale protests occurred in April 1971, when 200,000 anti-war activists marched in Washington and 150,000 in San Francisco.[14] Publication of the *Pentagon Papers* by the *New York Times* in June 1971, however, assured that the war remained front-page news. The extensive study of the history of U.S. policy in Vietnam completed by the Rand Corporation in 1969 was classified as "top secret-sensitive" by the Defense Department. Not because the document contained much truly sensitive information, but because department officials had a penchant for secrecy and the report showed that U.S. leaders had consistently misled the public. Daniel Ellsberg, a Rand

---

14 *New York Times*, April 25, 1971 https://www.nytimes.com/1971/04/25/archives/200000-rally-in-capital-to-end-war-200000-rally-in-capital-to-end.html (accessed January 25, 2023).

staff member who had become a critic of the war, secretly delivered it to the *Times*. Nixon had little to lose by publication since the study covered events that occurred before his presidency began. But his commitment to defend presidential prerogatives, obsession with secrecy, and hatred for liberal reporters and critics moved him to action. The Justice Department sought an injunction to block publication but was rebuffed when the Supreme Court quickly ruled against the government. Nixon flew into a rage, as he often did when his enemies got the better of him. Determined to stop leaks, he ordered creation of the White House Special Investigations Unit (a.k.a. the Plumbers) to plug them. They would conduct wiretaps and break-ins to gather dirt on leakers and other enemies. Although their first assignment, a burglary of the office of Ellsberg's psychiatrist in Los Angeles, produced nothing of interest, other jobs awaited.

## I've always thought this country could run itself domestically without a President

If Nixon was frustrated by the North Vietnamese, he was bored by domestic policy. "I've always thought this country could run itself domestically without a President," he asserted. "All you need is a competent cabinet to run the country at home."[15] Unlike LBJ, a disciple of the New Deal, he didn't come to the White House with a vision for transforming American society. But as a moderate Republican, he wasn't intent on scrapping the social safety network created by the New Deal and the Great Society, either. He wouldn't swim against the prevailing current or devote the time and political capital necessary to win support for a new paradigm. Even if he had the inclination, success was unlikely because Democrats retained large majorities in both houses of Congress, and they could count on support from many liberal and moderate Republicans. So, his domestic initiatives were episodic, reactive, ideologically incoherent, and often simply tactical moves designed to hurt his enemies and strengthen him politically.

Like Vietnam, civil rights couldn't be ignored. In 1969, Southern schools remained almost completely segregated. Southern school districts employed all manner of subterfuge to escape more than token integration. Northern Whites admitted that their schools weren't integrated, but had a justification. They claimed that their segregation was *de facto*—a product of where people

---

15 Small, *Presidency of Richard Nixon*, 59.

chose to live. It differed from the South's *de jure* segregation because it wasn't the product of law or public policy. Since *Brown* prohibited segregation established by state action, northerners insisted, it provided no remedy for the unfortunate separation of the races that occurred in Northern schools.

In 1968, the Supreme Court ruled that states that had established segregation by law must, at long last, integrate their schools. It ordered federal courts to implement desegregation plans that ensured that schools reflected their community's racial composition. Northern schools didn't escape scrutiny, despite their insistence that racial imbalance occurred because of residential patterns. When plaintiffs proved that state and local officials had situated school buildings, drawn attendance zones, and manipulated transfer policies to create and maintain segregated schools, courts mandated integration. In cities that meant busing students to schools outside their neighborhoods to create schools with a racial balance similar to that of the community.

Most White parents objected—usually vehemently. Conservative politicians who had wholeheartedly supported segregation, now argued that the Constitution was color-blind. Courts violated the Fourteenth Amendment when they assigned kids to schools on the basis of race to achieve racial balance, they insisted. Southern districts claimed they needed more time to overcome significant logistical challenges inherent in dismantling their dual school systems. Fifteen years, apparently, was insufficient. In 1969, when Mississippi challenged court-ordered integration, Nixon ordered the Justice Department to support the state. It was payback for White Southerners' support and a down payment on their allegiance in 1972. To no one's surprise, the Court rejected Mississippi's request. In losing, however, Nixon won by showing White Southerners that he stood with them against the nasty liberal judges. So, too, with busing. As the courts developed desegregation plans that required busing students to schools outside their neighborhoods, Nixon expressed outrage. Clearly siding with busing opponents, he contended that neighborhood schools were sacred and insisted that children shouldn't be treated like guinea pigs in some social experiment. Once again, he lost but burnished his credentials with White voters, North and South.

With a few notable exceptions, there had been little controversy over Supreme Court nominees before the 1960s. However, the Warren Court's landmark decisions striking down segregation, expanding the rights of the criminally accused, and creating a wall of separation between church and state generated hostility from conservatives who looked to Nixon to end judicial activism. He made a promising start in 1969, when he named Warren Burger, a conservative Minnesota Republican, to replace liberal icon

Earl Warren as chief justice. Later that year, when Abe Fortas stepped down in the face of allegations of financial irregularities orchestrated by the White House, Nixon nominated Clement Haynsworth, a conservative federal judge from South Carolina. When organized labor and civil rights groups defeated the nomination, Nixon nominated another southerner, Harold Carswell. Not only was his judicial record undistinguished but he had made public statements supporting segregation in the late 1940s and early 1950s. Opposed by the American Bar Association and civil rights leaders, his nomination also failed. Nixon quickly pivoted, nominating Harry Blackmun, another Minnesota Republican, who easily won confirmation. Nixon snatched victory from the jaws of his nominees' defeat. "I understand the bitter feelings of millions of Americans who live in the South," he told the press after Carswell's defeat, "about the act of regional discrimination that took place in the Senate yesterday."[16] He hadn't delivered for them, but he understood their anger—and was happy to stoke it.

While supporting the White South was predictable, Nixon could surprise—as he did in his support for aggressive action against employment discrimination. For generations, African Americans were consigned to unskilled, low-paying, and menial jobs that kept them on the lowest rungs of the economic ladder. Title VII of the Civil Rights Act of 1964 opened opportunities by banning discrimination in hiring and giving the Equal Employment Opportunity Commission (EEOC) enforcement authority. The problem was that by the late 1960s, few employers were dumb enough to tell Blacks openly that they need not apply for openings. They did, however, use educational requirements and tests unrelated to job performance to screen out Blacks.

Civil rights advocates, including lawyers for the National Association for the Advancement of Colored People (NAACP) Legal Defense Fund, attacked these barriers. In *Griggs v. Duke Power*, a 1971 Supreme Court decision, they won a major victory against job qualifications that created greater barriers for Blacks than Whites. The Court held that qualifications that had a disparate impact on minorities and weren't clearly related to job performance were prohibited by the Civil Rights Act. The Labor Department joined the Court in attacking employment discrimination. In 1965, an executive order prohibited government contractors from discriminatory hiring and authorized the department to cancel contracts with companies that violated it. Department officials also began to develop policies that required contractors

---

16 Stephen E. Ambrose, *Nixon: The Triumph of a Politician, 1962–1972* (New York, 1989), 338.

to employ a workforce that reflected the racial composition of its local labor market. While the department piloted its policy in several cities and economic sectors, notably construction, it had not promulgated a general policy when Nixon became president.

George Schultz, Nixon's secretary of labor, picked up where the Johnson administration left off. He developed the Philadelphia Plan, which required construction firms doing business with the federal government in that city to establish goals and timelines to achieve equal employment, which it defined as a racially balanced workforce. It met sharp resistance from the trade unions that placed members—almost all of whom were White—on construction sites. Nixon supported the policy, in part as a slap at his enemies in organized labor who had helped torpedo Haynsworth's and Carswell's nominations. But he also wanted to root out persistent discrimination against Blacks. Indeed, he strongly supported the Philadelphia Plan and resisted efforts in Congress to block implementation. Subsequently, Labor Department officials issued regulations that extended the requirement for establishing goals and timelines to all government contractors. Ironically, Nixon was one of the architects of affirmative action.

In the early 1970s, Congress passed new laws targeting employment discrimination. It dramatically expanded the size of the EEOC staff and gave the agency authority to take offenders to court, a power the Civil Rights Act had withheld. In addition to initiating lawsuits against large employers, the Commission ruled that non-discriminatory hiring policies alone weren't sufficient to meet the requirements of Title VII. Employers must take affirmative action to break down barriers to employment of minorities and women, and their success would be judged by how effective they were in creating a workforce that reflected the racial composition of the community. Congress authorized federal courts to award attorney's fees as well as monetary damages to parties who prevailed in discrimination cases. That enticed private attorneys to represent clients who couldn't afford to pay a lawyer. The prospect of expensive lawsuits they might lose persuaded many employers to embrace affirmative action and create a more diverse workforce. Critics grumbled about "reverse discrimination" and the burdens of being a White man.

Congress also responded to a burgeoning women's movement. By 1970, politicians no longer dismissed feminists as a fringe group of angry man-haters who spent their time sharing their feelings in consciousness-raising groups. By the time Nixon entered the White House, a growing number of feminists were pursuing careers in business and the professions and becoming active in both major parties. In 1971, women engaged in mainstream Democratic and Republican politics gathered at Washington's tony Statler Hilton Hotel, three blocks from the White House, to create the National Women's Political Caucus. It worked to help women win office and soon made them a force in both parties.

By 1972, male politicians—Republican and Democrat—wanted to appear responsive to a movement that seemed to have half the electorate behind it. Congress mustered the two-thirds majorities necessary to pass the Equal Rights Amendment (ERA), which stipulated that equal rights "shall not be denied or abridged by the United States or any state on account of sex."[17] It also added Title IX to the 1972 amendments to the Education Act, barring discrimination in any education program supported by federal funds. In 1974, Congress struck at barriers women faced when seeking credit. The Equal Credit Opportunity Act prohibited financial institutions from denying loans and other forms of credit on the basis of race, color religion, national origin, sex, or marital status and gave anyone denied the right to know why.

The other two branches got in the act as well. In 1973, the Supreme Court struck a blow for women's reproductive rights in *Roe v. Wade*. With three of Nixon's four nominees in the majority, it ruled that a Texas law criminalizing abortion violated the Fourteenth Amendment's due process clause. Although Nixon opposed abortion, he generally positioned himself on the right side of the women's movement. When a reporter put him on the spot at a 1969 press conference by asking why there were so few women in his administration, Nixon got religion. By 1972, he had appointed hundreds of women to policy-making positions, mid-level federal jobs, and boards and commissions. *Newsweek* took note, asserting that "the person in Washington who has done the most for the women's movement may be Richard Nixon."[18] Although those in the know probably gagged, the President had shown that he was in step with the times and, more importantly, scored a public relations coup.

Nixon inherited anti-poverty programs and a national commitment to eradicate poverty from LBJ. It was shared by a majority in Congress, including Northern Democrats and many moderate and liberal Republicans. Aid to Families with Dependent Children (AFDC), along with Medicaid and Food Stamps, was centerpieces of the nation's welfare program. Few were

---

17 Joint Resolution of March 22, 1972, 86 STAT 1523, Proposing an Amendment to the Constitution of the United States Relative to Equal Rights for Men and Women https://catalog.archives.gov/id/7455549 (accessed January 25, 2023).
18 Spruill, *Divided We Stand*, 39.

happy with AFDC. Liberals argued that the program was fundamentally flawed. As a federal–state partnership, monthly benefits were determined by state contributions. That meant payments ranged from obscenely low in Mississippi, South Carolina, and a host of other states to woefully inadequate everywhere else.

Conservatives had their own complaints. They argued that the program encouraged unmarried women to have more children they couldn't support to increase their monthly benefits. They fumed that the program discouraged people from taking low-paying jobs because the wages were only marginally better than AFDC benefits, especially if they had to cover childcare costs. Conservatives also groused that the program was run by a raft of bureaucrats who processed applications and payments and social workers who counseled recipients. Not surprisingly, in an $8 billion program, some people found a way to cheat the system. Although few in number, many conservatives saw the cases that were reported as the tip of a very large iceberg. In 1970, Guy Drake, a White country singer, took aim at welfare fraud in "Welfare Cadillac." Narrated by a shiftless welfare recipient who gamed the system and always drove a new Cadillac, the song gave voice to conservatives' scorn. Drake's hit spoofed a White welfare cheat, but most conservatives racialized welfare fraud. AFDC, they charged, was a way for lazy Black people to avoid work at the expense of hard-working, over-taxed White folk. Never mind that far more Whites than Blacks received AFDC benefits.

Nixon's boldest domestic initiative, the Family Assistance Plan (FAP), aimed to transform the system. It was developed by Daniel Patrick Moynihan, the Harvard sociologist who had written the controversial report on Black families while a member of LBJ's administration and now served as a domestic policy advisor to Nixon. The FAP would replace the much-maligned AFDC program with a negative income tax. A family of four would receive $1,600 per year (approximately $13,600 in 2024 dollars), whether they resided in New York or Mississippi. The plan incentivized work and helped the working poor; the first $720 in employment income FAP recipients received would not reduce the $1600 base. When their earnings from employment exceeded $720, payments wouldn't stop but would be reduced by 50 cents for each dollar earned. That was far more generous than AFDC, which took away a dollar of benefits for each dollar earned. Not only did FAP offer an incentive to work, those who refused to enter a job training program or accept employment would see their base payment reduced.

Nixon loved the program. It was a bold stroke and would throw the liberals off balance. As Moynihan assured him, it was "a genuinely new, unmistakably

Nixon program [...] likely to reverberate through society for generations."[19] While adding many people to the welfare system, it would contain costs in the long run and encourage work. The plan would also shrink the federal bureaucracy, which Nixon believed was full of liberals who hated him. As excited as he was, Nixon wasn't committed to FAP. He declined to consult with congressional leaders and allies before announcing it in August 1969, even though his veteran congressional affairs advisor told him that snubbing Congress would doom the bill. The program stalled in the Senate after sailing through the House, a victim of crossfire between liberals who found it too meager and conservatives who believed it too generous. Nixon refused to work with the Senate to break the log jam, and the bill died. It was a missed opportunity that underscored just how disengaged Nixon was when it came to domestic policy. He had made a splash by announcing FAP, but refused to give it the attention necessary to make it a reality.

As he lost interest in welfare reform, Nixon derailed other ambitious efforts to expand the social safety net. In 1971, liberal Democrats Walter Mondale and John Brademas introduced legislation to offer federally supported childcare to all families, with fees established on a sliding scale based on income. In its first year, the program would provide $2 billion to support community childcare centers, with appropriations growing in subsequent years. The legislation was popular with working women, many of whom struggled to find affordable day care, and would eliminate a barrier that prevented women on welfare from entering the workforce. The bill cleared the Senate, 63–17, and the House by a 210–186 margin, with bipartisan support in both chambers.

Bombarded by letters and telegrams from evangelical and Catholic women who charged that the centers would undermine the family, Nixon sensed political advantage in a veto. He was encouraged by an outspoken young Catholic speechwriter, Pat Buchanan, who insisted that taking a hard line on an emerging cultural issue would strengthen Nixon's appeal to blue-collar, White ethnic voters, many of whom were Catholic. His veto emphasized that the bill undermined the family's role in child-rearing, charging that it diminished "parental authority and parental involvement with children" and committed "the vast moral authority of the National Government to the side of communal approaches to childrearing over against the family-centered approach."[20]

---

19 Ambrose, *Nixon: The Triumph of a Politician*, 291.
20 *New York Times*, December 10, 1971 https://www.nytimes.com/1971/12/10/archives/excerpts-from-nixons-veto-message.html?searchResultPosition=8 (accessed January 23, 2022).

Democrats and some Republicans criticized Nixon and voted to override, but they were unable to muster the two-thirds margins necessary.

The only Nixon initiative that came close to matching FAP in ambition was revenue sharing, or what Nixon called "the New Federalism." He announced the program in August 1969 along with his welfare reform proposal. It was designed to please conservative Republicans, who were hostile to federal power and, especially, to federal bureaucrats who, in their view, made life difficult for businesses as well as state and local governments. Democrats were skeptical, fearing that state and local officials would short-change the poor and people of color. So, Nixon's initiative floundered until 1972, when he renamed it the "New American Revolution." With the election approaching, Congress passed a modest revenue sharing bill that allocated around $6 billion per year for five years to state and local governments. Although Nixon claimed success, it was hardly the start of the revolution in federalism he promised.

The real revolution occurred in environmental policy and regulation, and it was led by environmentalists and Congress, not the White House. During the late 1960s, concerns about the world Americans would pass on to their children grew, culminating in Earth Day, April 22, 1970. As many as 20 million Americans participated in programs and demonstrations designed to raise awareness about the need for swift action to save the planet.[21] Nixon was no environmentalist. He called the environmental movement "overrated" and environmentalists "clowns," adding, "In a flat choice between smoke and jobs, we're for jobs."[22] But he was no fool, either. He understood that the movement had broad appeal among voters and on Capitol Hill. Standing against it was neither good politics nor calculated to make him look like a forward-looking statesman.

Congress initiated sweeping legislation to reverse the damage done, prevent further degradation, and extend controls to the environments in which Americans worked. It passed the National Environmental Policy Act in 1970, which required environmental impact studies before any federally funded construction project could begin. The same year it created the Environmental Protection Agency, which brought dozens of federal offices and programs together in one agency that was given authority to implement environmental

---

21 Adam Rome, "Earth Day 1970 was more than a protest. It built a movement," *Washington Post*, April 22, 2020 https://www.washingtonpost.com/outlook/2020/04/22/earth-day-1970-was-more-than-protest-it-built-movement/ (accessed January 25, 2023).
22 Small, *Presidency of Richard Nixon*, 197.

regulations. It also passed major amendments to the Clean Air Act that required automobile manufacturers to reduce emissions by 10% by 1975. Nixon battled Congress over amendments to the Clean Water Act that provided a whopping $24 billion to remediate fouled rivers, streams, and lakes. In 1972, however, Republicans joined Democrats in overriding his veto. Nor did the workplace escape the notice of reformers. In 1970, capping a banner legislative year, Congress created the Occupational Safety and Health Administration and tasked it with establishing health and safety regulations for the nation's factories, shops, shipyards, and other places of employment. Generally, with Nixon's assent, if not his leadership, bipartisan majorities in Congress mobilized the American regulatory state to expand environmental protection.

## The Economy, Vietnam, and Re-election

Nixon's attention often wandered from domestic issues. However, two domestic problems—inflation and unemployment—had the effect of a firing squad. They focused his mind. After all, they could mean political death, his greatest fear. During the last three years of LBJ's presidency, inflation had grown by 2.5%, from 1.9% in 1966 to 4.4% in 1969. Unemployment remained low in 1969, however, at 3.5%, a point lower than it had been in 1965. Spending on the war remained high, expenditures for programs like Social Security, Medicare, Medicaid, Food Stamps, and welfare climbed, and Congress approved new initiatives to protect the environment and expand EEOC. The budget deficit, which Johnson had tamed through a tax increase and spending cuts in 1968, ballooned to $23 billion in 1971. Inflation accelerated, climbing by another 2.5% to 6.1% in 1970 before receding to 5.3% in 1971. Not only did inflation remain high, but unemployment was on the rise, growing by 2.5% to almost 6% in 1971. Conventional wisdom held that unemployment and inflation moved in opposite directions. But they now both moved higher—a recipe for political disaster as the 1972 election loomed.[23]

What to do? A tax increase or budget cut was out of the question. They may have restrained inflation but would have been highly unpopular and increased unemployment. Raising interest rates may have helped curb inflation, but

---

23 "Historical Inflation Rates, 1914–2023," https://www.usinflationcalculator.com/inflation/historical-inflation-rates/ (accessed January 25, 2023); Kimberly Amadeo, "Historical US Unemployment Rate by Year," *The Balance*, December 6, 2022 https://www.thebalancemoney.com/unemployment-rate-by-year-3305506 (accessed January 25, 2023).

it would have slowed the economy and escalated unemployment. Johnson had taken bold action to curb the deficit, but Nixon didn't want to be a one-term president. His flexibility—some would say absence of principle—helped him develop a solution, or at least put a band-aid on the problem and help him win re-election. Without any advance warning, the President gave a televised address on August 15, 1971, a Sunday evening, announcing dramatic action to curb inflation. He told Americans he would issue an executive order prohibiting increases in the price of goods and services and also of wages, measures usually reserved for national emergencies like war. He also entered the arcane realm of international finance, announcing that the U.S. would no longer redeem dollars for gold at the rate of $35 an ounce. That brought an end to the Bretton Woods Agreement of 1944, which tied the dollar to gold and made it the basis of the international financial order. Henceforth, the dollar's value would float in relation to other currencies. The intended result was a devaluation of the dollar, which would make American exports cheaper, imports more expensive, the balance of trade deficit shrink, and ease inflationary pressure by shrinking the volume of dollars abroad. It was a band-aid, but it stopped the bleeding, at least temporarily.

The economic threat blunted, Nixon burnished his reputation for statesmanship by traveling to Beijing in February and to Moscow in May, where he signed the Strategic Arms Limitation Treaty (SALT). Vietnam was another matter, however. He had made no progress in fulfilling his promise to achieve "peace with honor," and the North Vietnamese showed no signs of negotiating a settlement. In May 1971, Nixon softened the U.S. position by informing the North Vietnamese that the mutual withdrawal of U.S. and North Vietnamese forces was no longer a condition for a settlement. But the North Vietnamese still refused to budge. Indeed, in February 1972, they launched a large-scale offensive against South Vietnamese forces. Only massive air strikes by U.S. bombers prevented a rout and allowed the South Vietnamese to regroup. Angered by North Vietnam's recalcitrance, Nixon mined Haiphong harbor in an effort to cut off Russian and Chinese aid to the North. He also authorized punishing bombing raids on North Vietnam and its manufacturing and transportation infrastructure. "The bastards have never been bombed like they're going to be bombed this time," he told advisors.[24]

By late summer, the North Vietnamese were ready to negotiate. The bombing hurt and their Russian and Chinese backers pressed them to be more

---

24 Small, *Presidency of Richard Nixon*, 89.

accommodating. In October, with the election only weeks away, it appeared that the U.S. and North Vietnam had reached an agreement. North Vietnamese forces would remain in place in the South, U.S. forces would be withdrawn, President Thieu would remain in office in South Vietnam, elections for a new government in the South would be held, and North Vietnam would return U.S. prisoners of war (POWs). South Vietnam now became Nixon's problem. Thieu refused to participate, and with polls showing that he would be re-elected, Nixon declined to force the issue. An almost identical agreement would be signed in January 1973, but only after Nixon ordered a massive Christmas bombing campaign.

Nixon cruised to re-election in a landslide. Part of the reason was cunning. His economic machinations tamed inflation, at least temporarily, without increasing unemployment. His visits to Moscow and Beijing were historic and perfectly choreographed for the reporters and TV cameras that followed him, making him appear presidential. There was no agreement with North Vietnam, but most Americans believed, as Kissinger said, that "peace is at hand." As if this weren't enough, George Wallace, the opponent Nixon most feared because of his appeal to White Southerners and blue-collar northern Whites, did not run. Left paralyzed by shots fired by a would-be assassin in May, he abandoned the race.

Nixon also had the good fortune to run against a weak opponent and a Democratic Party in disarray. After the 1968 election, when many complained of an undemocratic nominating process controlled by professional politicians, Democrats instituted reforms to give the rank and file a larger voice. More states selected their delegates in primaries and participatory caucuses, and the party required greater representation of women and minorities at its convention. The new system favored candidates who built strong grassroots organizations and could turn out the party's base. Primaries and caucuses attracted far fewer voters than a general election, so a candidate who mobilized a relatively small group of committed followers could win, even if they lacked broad appeal. In 1972, that candidate was Senator George McGovern, a man who understood the new process because he had chaired the party commission that created it. Strong support from the antiwar movement helped him assemble a strong organization and rally a highly engaged segment of the party.

The result was a strong showing in the primaries and caucuses that enabled him to control the party platform and win the nomination on the first ballot. Written by the party's left wing, the platform included such mainstream Democratic positions as support for ERA, protection of the environment, a more progressive tax system, and vigorous enforcement of civil rights. But it also demanded immediate and unconditional withdrawal from Vietnam, amnesty for those who left the country to avoid the draft, a guaranteed income, affirmative action for minorities and women, a national health insurance system, and "the right to be different, to maintain a cultural or ethnic heritage or lifestyle without being forced into a compelled homogeneity."[25] Many White working-class Democrats weren't exactly sure what that meant. But it sounded like party leaders were more concerned about supporting people whose lifestyle they abhorred than addressing pocketbook issues that were important to them.

The damage didn't stop with the platform. The appearance of many delegates telegraphed the influence of the counterculture, and the proceedings were chaotic. Debates went on interminably and the process of choosing McGovern's running mate became a circus. It seemed that anyone could make a nomination, so delegates considered a diverse group that included Benjamin Spock (the antiwar pediatrician), Cesar Chavez (the Chicano activist and head of the National Farm Workers Union), consumer activist Ralph Nader, SNCC organizer Julian Bond, and even Mao Zedong. McGovern might have been wise to choose one of them. Shortly after the convention ended, reporters revealed that his pick, Senator Thomas Eagleton, had received electroshock treatment for depression. At a time when mental illness was stigmatized, the revelation raised concern with many voters. But not as much as McGovern's response. After saying he stood behind Eagleton "1,000 percent," McGovern eased him off the ticket, leading many to doubt not only his judgment but his decisiveness. The election was over before it began.

On election day Nixon won in a landslide of almost Johnsonian dimensions, taking 60.8% of the popular vote and running up a 521–17 victory in the Electoral College. The margins probably said more about McGovern's weakness than Nixon's popularity, but it would be hard to claim that Nixon did not win the mandate he sought. He carried every southern and border state, but that was hardly a vindication of Kevin Phillips's projections. After all, he carried the Northeast, with the exception of Massachusetts, and every other region.

Nixon's coattails were short. Republicans scored a net gain of 12 seats in the House (with seven of those coming from southern and border states),

---

25 1972 Democratic Party Platform https://www.presidency.ucsb.edu/documents/1972-democratic-party-platform (accessed January 24, 2022).

but Democrats retained a 244–191 majority.[26] In the Senate, Democrats picked up two seats, giving them a 57–43 majority. That body was also likely to be more liberal because liberal Democrats took seats previously held by conservative Republicans in Colorado, Delaware, Iowa, Maine, and South Dakota.[27] So, when the dust settled, Nixon could claim the mandate he craved but the balance of power in Washington remained unchanged.

## Snatching Defeat from the Jaws of a Landslide Victory

Although Nixon basked in glow of his landslide win, the chickens would soon come home to roost. His insecurity, obsession with enemies, and willingness to break the law to destroy them would cause problems more intractable than even Vietnam. Despite his accomplishments—twice selected *Time* magazine "Man of the Year," election to the Senate, the vice presidency, and the presidency—Nixon was deeply insecure. He resented those (like the Kennedys) whose background, charm, and *savoir faire* he lacked. The powerful and well-placed had never taken him under their wing. After eight years of loyal service as Ike's vice president, the old man hadn't formally endorsed his presidential candidacy in 1960, claiming that, as president, he must stay above the fray. He was convinced that he never got the respect he deserved and was jealous of others. As Kissinger gained public acclaim, Nixon worried that his national security advisor was upstaging him and considered firing him. Certain the world was against him, he had many enemies—political foes, federal bureaucrats, publishers, reporters—and he itched to punish them.

Of course, Nixon didn't have to do the work himself. As president, he had lots of people on his staff and in federal departments who could help. It might mean fabricating a letter to embarrass an opponent, like the one Jane Muskie purportedly sent to the Manchester (NH) *Union Leader* in 1972. It included an ethnic slur denigrating French Canadians meant to embarrass her husband,

---

26  House: Republican Gain of 12, New Count 244–191 *Congressional Quarterly Almanac, 1972* https://library-cqpress-com.proxy.binghamton.edu/cqalmanac/document.php?id=cqal72-1249887&type=toc&num=10 (accessed February 3, 2023).

27  Senate: Increase of 2 Seats in Democratic Majority, *Congressional Quarterly Almanac, 1972* https://library-cqpress-com.proxy.binghamton.edu/cqalmanac/document.php?id=cqal72-1249825&type=toc&num=15 (accessed February 3, 2023).

Senator Ed Muskie, the leading candidate in the state's Democratic primary and the opponent Nixon most feared. Or it could mean establishing an espionage unit like the Plumbers to find dirt to discredit Daniel Ellsberg, who leaked the Pentagon Papers.

The Plumbers were disbanded as a White House unit, but key members found their way into Nixon's campaign organization. Nixon was obsessed with Larry O'Brien, the chairman of the Democratic National Committee (DNC). Not only was O'Brien privy to the opposition's strategy (such as it was), but he had once represented the reclusive billionaire, Howard Hughes. That meant he might have damaging information about financial largesse Nixon and his brother, Donald, had received from the old man. Whatever the reason, campaign operatives burglarized O'Brien's office in Washington's Watergate complex in May 1972 to search files and bug phones. Because one of the original bugs didn't work, they returned on June 17. Detected by a night watchman, they were arrested, arraigned for burglary, and scheduled for trial before Judge John Sirica in the U.S. District Court for the District of Columbia. Nixon was fortunate that the trial was scheduled for after the election, but not so lucky in the man who would preside. An Eisenhower appointee, Sirica was a no-nonsense judge whose iron control of his courtroom and stiff sentences earned him the nickname "Maximum John."

Nixon knew about the Plumbers and was aware that campaign staff engaged in clandestine activities against his opponents. He probably did not know, in advance, however, about the Watergate break-in. When he read about it in the newspaper, he thought it was stupid. When it became clear that the burglars were campaign employees, Nixon sought to learn more from White House staff and, within a week, began an elaborate effort to cover up links between the burglars, his campaign, and White House staff. He directed the CIA to pressure the FBI to back off its investigation. When that didn't work, Nixon used White House staff to get inside information from the Justice Department on the proceedings of the grand jury investigating the case. He also authorized hundreds of thousands of dollars of payments to the burglars to keep them quiet and indicated he was willing to offer clemency to any who were convicted. Nixon understood that this amounted to obstruction of justice, an offense as serious as initiating the burglary itself. But if he came clean, he feared, he would tarnish his campaign and reveal a pattern of illegal activities that might be traced back to the Ellsberg burglary. It might even reveal that the campaign had sent one of the Watergate defendants to Milwaukee in a failed effort to plant

McGovern literature in the apartment of Arthur Bremmer, the apolitical loner who shot Wallace.

Nixon's machinations failed. In January 1973, the burglars were convicted. A month later, the Senate created a special committee to investigate what was becoming known as Watergate, and in March, one of the burglars divulged shocking information to Judge Sirica. He claimed that senior members of the White House staff and campaign officials were deeply involved. By April, two of Nixon's closest advisors, John Ehrlichman and Robert Haldeman, resigned. Key members of the White House staff, seeking to save their skins, began to cooperate with the Senate committee, and reporters stepped up coverage. As the Senate committee began its hearings in May, Nixon succumbed to pressure from congressional Democrats and appointed Harvard law professor Archibald Cox as special prosecutor to lead an independent investigation. Working with Judge Sirica and his grand jury, Cox's team compiled evidence, and the Senate committee heard testimony from dozens of witnesses, including many from Nixon's own staff. The most critical was John Dean, who had orchestrated the cover-up for the White House, had a photographic memory as well as White House documents to share, and recounted in detail lengthy conversations about the cover-up with Nixon. A close second was Alexander Butterfield, a mid-level White House staffer, who revealed that Nixon had a voice-activated taping system in the Oval Office.

Dean's testimony was damning, and Butterfield's revelation led investigators to demand release of the tapes. Nixon declined, asserting executive privilege. The confidentiality of conversations a president had with advisors, he asserted, must be protected if the chief executive was to receive the candid advice necessary to fulfill his constitutional responsibilities. It was a new concept, but it just might work. Cox didn't agree that the conversations were privileged because they might contain evidence of criminal wrongdoing, and he refused to accept summaries of the tapes that Nixon offered. Oblivious to the optics, Nixon ordered Attorney General Elliott Richardson to fire Cox on Saturday, October 23, 1973. When he and his deputy, chose to resign rather than comply, Robert Bork, the third-ranking official at Justice, did the dirty work. The press quickly dubbed it the Saturday Night Massacre, and an outcry from the media and the public forced Nixon to hand over seven tapes to Sirica. He also reluctantly appointed a new special prosecutor, Leon Jaworski.

One step forward, three steps back. By November, the House Judiciary Committee, flush with evidence produced by the Senate Watergate committee and the special counsel, began an impeachment investigation. In March 1974,

Sirica's grand jury indicted eight White House officials and named an "unindicted co-conspirator" for his role in the cover-up. Widely assumed but unknown at the time, the unnamed party was the President. Jaworski believed he could not be prosecuted while he remained in office. Pressure to release all the tapes grew. Nixon produced over 1,200 pages of transcripts, but Jaworski insisted on the tapes themselves and took his case to the Supreme Court, which ruled in July that Nixon must produce them. By early August 1974, with the tapes available to prosecutors, the House Judiciary Committee approving articles of impeachment, and Republicans in Congress abandoning him, Nixon resigned. His vice president, Spiro Agnew, had resigned the previous October after he was charged with taking bribes while serving as a Maryland state official. Gerald Ford, whom Nixon had selected to replace Agnew, assumed the presidency. Many observers thought of the classic Abbot and Costello routine, "Who's on First?"

Watergate and Nixon's resignation shook the country. They tarnished the Republican brand and led to a Democratic rout in the 1974 elections. Democrats picked up four Senate seats, increasing their majority to a lopsided 61–39, and they gained 49 seats in the House for a 291–144 margin. It was reminiscent of the Democratic wave that accompanied LBJ's landslide 10 years earlier. Nixon's effort to establish a "New Majority," was in shambles. Kevin Phillips's Republican majority failed to emerge. Unfortunately for Democrats, it would be their Indian Summer.

## A Crisis of Confidence and Competence

If Democrats were the winners, the government and the nation's political culture—along with the Republican Party—were the losers. Eighteen months of intense investigations and thousands of stories by journalists revealed a governing process that was sordid, corrupt, self-serving, and nothing like what students learned in their history and civics classes. Even the edited versions of the tapes showed the President to be petty, vindictive, foul-mouthed, manipulative, and concerned principally with his own advancement or settling scores. Americans, who had returned him to office, not only had buyer's remorse, they felt deceived by Nixon and the system he came to represent. It was easy to assume, as his Republican defenders argued, that "they all do it." A torrent of self-congratulatory writing proclaimed that Watergate demonstrated that the system worked, but the scandal left Americans cynical and jaded about politics, government, and leadership. Polling done by the highly respected Pew Research Institute revealed that Americans' trust in government had fallen from a high of 77% in 1964 to 62% when LBJ left the White House. In the wake of Watergate, it plummeted to 36% and would continue fall.[28]

Vietnam and Watergate made heroes of a new generation of investigative journalists—Seymour Hersh, Daniel Schorr, Nina Totenberg, Bob Woodward, and Carl Bernstein. They and others found that the best path to a Pulitzer Prize or consistent bylines was reporting that exposed the machinations of the powerful. Their stories confirmed Americans' new-found cynicism about government and politicians. With the public suspicious of government and political leaders, it would be difficult to generate support for ambitious new initiatives designed to make things better. For too many, the government was becoming the problem rather than the solution.

Political leaders' response to new economic challenges only made matters worse. As the U.S. economy expanded in the 1960s and early 1970s, Americans developed an almost insatiable demand for gas-guzzling cars. That, in turn, led to greater reliance on imported petroleum, most of which came from the Middle East. In the early 1970s, as the dollar declined in value, the Organization of Petroleum Exporting Countries (OPEC), a consortium of oil producers, steadily increased oil prices, contributing to inflation. In October 1973, with Nixon distracted by Watergate, Egypt and Syria launched a massive attack on Israel. Surprised, the Israelis were initially pummeled and forced to pull back. However, massive deliveries of planes and munitions from the U.S. and the Israelis' superior military organization soon turned the tables. Arab members of OPEC came to the aid of their Egyptian and Syrian allies by embargoing oil shipments to the U.S. Prices rose fourfold by the time the U.S. persuaded OPEC to end the boycott in March 1974.

The embargo disrupted Americans' lives and sent shock waves through the economy. Gas prices soared—if it could be purchased at all. As the supply of oil shrunk, refineries produced less gasoline, and oil companies cut deliveries to filling stations. Motorists waited in lines, sometimes for hours, and some stations limited fill-ups to 10 gallons and cut back their hours. Saddled with gas guzzlers that drove only 14 miles on a gallon of gas,[29] Americans changed their driving habits, shunning family vacations, thinking twice about going to restaurants and the movies. They also started looking for smaller, more fuel-efficient cars,

---

28 Pew Research Center, "Public Trust in Government: 1958–2022," June 6, 2022 https://www.pewresearch.org/politics/2024/06/24/public-trust-in-government-1958-2024/ (accessed January 25, 2023).

29 Pew Charitable Trust, "Driving to 54.5 MPG: The History of Fuel Economy," April 20, 2011 https://www.pewtrusts.org/en/research-and-analysis/fact-sheets/2011/04/20/driving-to-545-mpg-the-history-of-fuel-economy (accessed January 26, 2023).

most of which were made abroad. The effect on hotels, motels, restaurants, theaters, and the automobile industry was devastating. To conserve gasoline, Congress lowered the speed limit from 70 mph on interstate roads to 55 mph. Perhaps the biggest impact of the oil shock was its effect on the confidence of Americans. People who assumed that resources—and possibilities—were boundless confronted a new reality, limits. In December 1973, the title of a *Time* magazine article surveying the wreckage captured Americans' unfathomable new world: "Shortages: Learning to Live with Less."[30]

The consequences of the oil crisis were felt across the economy. Spiking oil prices increased the cost of transporting goods and people, heating and cooling homes and businesses, food production, manufacturing, and more. Shortages and high prices forced many businesses to cut back, in some cases, lay off workers, and pass higher energy costs on to consumers. Inflation accelerated, rising from a worrisome 6% in 1973 to a shocking 11% in 1974 and 9% in 1975[31] and forcing consumers to scramble to make ends meet. Many turned to Hamburger Helper, a concoction of pasta and starches designed to stretch a pound of ground beef. Betty Crocker had introduced it in 1971 when an earlier wave of inflation sent meat prices soaring, and it enjoyed renewed popularity as another round of inflation made it harder to feed hungry families. Unemployment rose sharply, from 5% in 1973 to 8.2% in 1975.[32] That led many pundits to talk about the "misery index"—the combination of inflation and unemployment that measured the pain Americans felt. It was just one more sign that the government couldn't solve the problems Americans faced. It also eroded the optimism and spirit of generosity that sustained 1960s reforms.

The twin scourges of inflation and unemployment continued into the early 1980s, bedeviling Nixon's successors. Well-liked by Democrats and Republicans on Capitol Hill, Gerald Ford was amiable and good natured, but by no means flashy. As he told reporters, "I am a Ford, not a Lincoln."[33] After 18

---

30 *Time*, December 3, 1973 http://content.time.com/time/subscriber/article/0,33009,908218,00.html (accessed January 26, 2022).
31 "Historical Inflation Rates, 1914–2023," https://www.usinflationcalculator.com/inflation/historical-inflation-rates/ (accessed January 25, 2023); Kimberly Amadeo, "Historical US Unemployment Rate by Year," *The Balance*, December 6, 2022 https://www.thebalancemoney.com/unemployment-rate-by-year-3305506 (accessed January 25, 2023).
32 Ibid.
33 Associated Press, "Quotations: The Words of Gerald Ford," *New York Times*, December 27, 2006 https://www.nytimes.com/2006/12/27/washington/28fordquotescnd.html (accessed January 26, 2023).

months of drama, acrimony, and constitutional crisis, he believed that his job was to restore calm, heal the wounds inflicted by Watergate, and restore faith in the system. A month after Nixon resigned, Ford announced that he had pardoned his predecessor. While critics charged quid pro quo, Ford believed that he was turning the page from a painful and divisive chapter in American history.

Ford faced problems that seemed intractable, and his approach to them failed to restore faith in Washington. While inflation subsided a bit, it remained over 9% in 1975, unemployment stood at 8.2%,[34] oil prices rose, and the recession continued. To curb inflation, Ford called for a tax increase and spending cuts and urged Americans to curb energy consumption. His effort to encourage sacrifice through his "Whip Inflation Now" (WIN) campaign—complete with WIN buttons—inspired jokes not confidence. When Congress, controlled by Democrats who were alarmed by unemployment, demanded a tax cut and increased spending, political realities compelled Ford to acquiesce, opening him to charges of flip-flopping. Democrats continued to pass measures that increased spending, and he vetoed them. But his 66 vetoes[35]—12 of which were overridden—persuaded Americans that politicians would rather fight one another than solve their problems.

Ford had little more success with energy policy. Everyone agreed that U.S. dependence on oil from the Middle East made the nation economically and politically vulnerable, but Ford's proposed solution fueled political conflict rather than a timely response to the crisis. The only long-term answer to the nation's energy woes, he believed, was to end price controls on domestic oil, which constituted 65% of the oil Americans consumed.[36] He recognized that would lead to price increases, but he believed that they would stimulate exploration and production in the U.S. and persuade Americans to conserve energy. Predictably, Democrats on Capitol Hill pushed back, charging that Ford's plan would create a windfall for oil companies—which weren't winning any popularity contests

---

34 "Historical Inflation Rates, 1914–2023," https://www.usinflationcalculator.com/inflation/historical-inflation-rates/ (accessed January 25, 2023); Kimberly Amadeo, "Historical US Unemployment Rate by Year," *The Balance*, December 6, 2022 https://www.thebalancemoney.com/unemployment-rate-by-year-3305506 (accessed January 25, 2023).
35 U.S. Senate, "Vetoes, 1789–Present" https://www.senate.gov/legislative/vetoes/vetoCounts.htm (accessed January 26, 2023).
36 U.S. Energy Information Administration, "Oil and Petroleum Products Explained" https://www.eia.gov/energyexplained/oil-and-petroleum-products/imports-and-exports.php (accessed January 26, 2023).

in the mid-1970s—and increase gas prices. After wrangling with Congress for a year, the President concluded that "the time has come to end the long debate over national energy policy,"[37] and he signed a compromise bill. Many wondered why it took so long. The compromise retained price controls on domestic oil; extended for two years, the authority of the Federal Energy Administration to require power and other major fuel-consuming plants to replace oil with coal; set progressively higher fuel efficiency standards for new cars; authorized regulators to set efficiency standards for home appliances and the president to restrict exports of oil, gas, and coal.

As Ford prepared to run for election in his own right in 1976, he carried heavy baggage—and faced a charismatic challenger in his party's primaries. Ronald Reagan was the darling of the party's resurgent conservative wing. Insisting that government was the problem not the solution, he inspired conservative Republicans who had felt marginalized since the Goldwater debacle. Reagan's criticism of government resonated with the many Americans who were reeling from a decade of political blunders that had squandered the optimism, prosperity, and bipartisanship that supported what was supposed to be the American Century. The battle continued all the way to the convention in Kansas City, with Ford finally claiming a narrow victory and the right to face a little-known former governor of Georgia, Jimmy Carter, in the fall.

Many asked, "Jimmy who?" when Carter announced his candidacy. A graduate of the Naval Academy and an engineer, Carter left the Navy when his father died in the early 1950s to run the family peanut farm and brokerage in the tiny hamlet of Plains, Georgia. Elected to the state senate in 1962, he ran for governor as a political outsider, finally winning in 1970, after an unsuccessful campaign four years earlier. In a crowded field, Carter was a fresh face, an outsider who promised to restore integrity, decency, and competence to the presidency. Many within his own party saw him as a moderate who could restore the party's appeal to mainstream Democrats, including southerners and independents. Early success in the Iowa caucuses in January 1976 made Carter a media sensation, and victories in the New Hampshire and Florida primaries elevated him to frontrunner status. Building on that momentum, he moved methodically through the primaries and won a first-ballot victory at the convention.

---

37 Congressional Quarterly Almanac, "Ford Ends Stalemate, Signs Energy Bill" https://library.cqpress.com/cqalmanac/document.php?id=cqal75-1213681 (accessed January 31, 2022).

Carter was among a group of moderate Democratic southern governors—Dale Bumpers in Arkansas, Reuben Askew in Florida, Fritz Hollings in South Carolina—who came to office in the wake of the Civil Rights Movement. With the support of recently enfranchised Black voters, Carter returned the South to the Democratic fold, and he did well in the Northeast and parts of the industrial Midwest. Despite Ford's struggles as president, however, he made the election close by carrying key Midwestern states like Illinois and Michigan and sweeping the Great Plains, Southwest and West. When the dust settled, Carter won with 50.1% of the popular vote to Ford's 48% and an electoral majority of 297–240. Democrats also did well in congressional races. They added one seat to their lopsided House majority, which was something of a feat given that 79 new Democrats had come to Washington as part of the "Watergate" class of 1974. They also added one seat to their Senate majority, bringing it to 62–38.

Carter's victory had been close. But his sincerity, carefully cultivated image as an outsider, and promise to put an end to politics-as-usual persuaded many Americans that things would be different. He reinforced that hope on inauguration day, when he, Rosalynn, and their daughter Amy left the presidential limousine during the inaugural parade and walked down Pennsylvania Avenue amid cheering crowds. By March 1977, he enjoyed a 75% approval rating.[38]

It wouldn't last long. The Republican resurgence that Nixon's victories in 1968 and 1972 promised never materialized on Capitol Hill, leaving Nixon unable to dial back the reforms of the Great Society. In most respects, he never tried and swam with the liberal tide flowing from Capitol Hill. It was supported by Democrats, of course, but also by liberal and moderate Republicans. Although Nixon carried the border South in 1968 and swept the entire region in 1972, Republican gains in the region's congressional delegation were modest. Southern Democrats remained strong and served as a moderating force in the party. Watergate swept away most of the modest gains Republicans had made everywhere, leading to large Democratic majorities in Congress and election of a southern Democrat as president in 1976. Democrats could be forgiven for believing that their party had stemmed the Republican resurgence that the disruptions of the late 1960s

---

38 "Presidential Approval Ratings—Gallup Historical Statistics and Trends" https://news.gallup.com/poll/116677/Presidential-Approval-Ratings-Gallup-Historical-Statistics-Trends.aspx (accessed January 26, 2023).

threatened. However, they hadn't. The domestic economic problems that had bedeviled Nixon and Ford would overwhelm Carter. His unfamiliarity with the ways of Washington, combined with lack of discipline among congressional Democrats bred by overwhelming wins in 1974 and 1976, would take their toll. Intra-party conflict would make it harder to address intractable problems and erode public support. If that weren't enough, Republicans were about to get a new infusion of troops from a large group that had been politically quiescent.

CHAPTER 4

# A NEW RIGHT EMERGES, 1972–1980

## The Personal Becomes Political

Some 20,000 women (and a few men)—trailed by 1,500 curious reporters—traveled to Houston in November 1977 to participate in the National Women's Conference. It was the culmination of the International Women's Year, promoted by the United Nations. In the U.S., a presidential commission had encouraged meetings in every state to discuss issues women considered most important and adopt resolutions calling for action to address them. The state conventions selected 2,000 delegates to represent them in Houston. The delegates included Republicans and Democrats, Whites and Blacks, straight women and lesbians, celebrities like First Lady Rosalynn Carter, former First Ladies Betty Ford and Lady Bird Johnson, Coretta Scott King, and such feminist pioneers as Betty Friedan, Gloria Steinem, and Bella Abzug.

In many ways, it was the high-water mark of the women's rights movement. Feminism had moved to the mainstream as its ranks grew and garnered support from Republican and Democratic presidents. The movement had also achieved impressive legislative victories, including passage of the Equal Rights Amendment (ERA). It had sailed through Congress in 1972 and been endorsed by 35 of the 38 states needed for ratification when the Houston conference kicked off. Delegates bridged sharp differences—between radical and moderate feminists, straight women and lesbians, White women and women of color—to agree on a sweeping National Plan of Action. Its 26 planks demanded changes in areas ranging from employment to rape and violence against women, reproductive freedom, and welfare—to name a few. The conference was a smashing success. Participants left Houston exhilarated by the spirit of camaraderie that prevailed. Reflecting on the differences that had too often separated feminists, columnist Ellen Goodman commented wryly, "We have met the enemy, and for once, it isn't us."[1]

The enemy wasn't far away. It gathered in force across the sprawling city at Astro-Arena. As the National Women's Conference got underway, perhaps 20,000 conservative women (and several hundred conservative men) came from across the country, many in buses chartered by their churches, to attend a Pro-Life, Pro-Family Rally. The organizers were religious women who led groups that emerged in the early 1970s to challenge the feminist juggernaut. They opposed ratification of the ERA, abortion, and gay rights. The rally's organizers included STOP-ERA's Phyllis Schlafly, a Roman Catholic, anti-communist conservative Republican activist who had loomed large in the Goldwater campaign; Lottie Beth Hobbs, a fundamentalist Texan who led another anti-ERA group, Women Who Want to be Women (WWWW); and Nellie Gray, the Roman Catholic founder of the anti-abortion group, March for Life. Indeed, one of the gathering's greatest accomplishments was to bridge divides between conservative women who belonged to religious groups that hated one another.

Those who packed Astro-Arena were whipped into a frenzy by fiery speeches denouncing feminism as the work of the devil. A sign perched next to the podium said it all: "Women's Libbers ERA Lesbians REPENT Read the Bible While Your [sic] Alive." What feminists called "barriers," Hobbs insisted, were "safeguards" for women and the family that "wise men and women [...] have carefully built [...] into our system." Removing them "would surely plunge us into social and moral destruction." Nellie Gray lambasted "women's libbers" for trying to "dress up abortion" as choice. "No matter how you try to dress it up," she charged, "it comes down to killing a baby." Perhaps it was fitting that the rally ended with a speech by a man, Robert Dornan, a conservative California Republican congressman. Dornan charged that those who supported "sexual perversion" and the "murder of unborn babies" controlled Washington. He knew, however, that "the real majority are those who love and respect their God" and exhorted his audience to act. "Go to your Congressmen and Senators," Dornan urged. "Tell them what you think of their voting record [...] and how you expect them to vote in the future."[2]

---

1 Marjorie J. Spruill, *Divided We Stand: The Battle Over Women's Rights and Family Values that Polarized America* (New York, 2017), 231.
2 *Ibid.*, 254–65.

Matters that had been personal—marriage, family, sexuality, the uterus—were becoming political.

## Another Failed Presidency

Carter undoubtedly got a first-hand account of the conference from his wife, Roslyn, who participated. By late 1977, however, his focus was on economic problems and battles with a Congress controlled by his own party. The new president had many virtues, but they weren't the ones necessary for a president to navigate rough political waters. While few doubted his integrity, sincerity, and decency, he was an uninspiring speaker. He had an enormous capacity for work and the ability to master most subjects, no matter how complex. But his penchant for becoming immersed in details often kept him from seeing the big picture or presenting a compelling vision. Carter could also be rigid, too often assuming that he represented the common good while his opponents were prisoners of special interests. In Washington, however, success depended on forging compromises among diverse interest groups.

Speaker of the House Tip O'Neill desperately wanted Carter to succeed. With Democrats in control of the White House and Congress, he knew that the party would be judged on its success in solving problems—which were legion. When O'Neil met with Carter shortly after the election, however, he had a bad feeling about where things were headed. Campaign promises were one thing, O'Neil told Carter, passing legislation was another; the president would have to compromise with powerful members of Congress to succeed. Carter responded that when faced with similar situations as governor he had taken his case to the people and would do the same as president. O'Neil was appalled. Indeed, Carter's biggest strength in winning election—being an outsider—was a weakness once in office.

But it wasn't just Carter's naivete that compromised his success. Like Ford, the problems he faced seemed intractable, and he always felt like he was playing whack-a-mole. Disillusionment with government's ability to solve problems, combined with escalating budget deficits that fueled inflation, put transformative initiatives out of reach. The twin problems of inflation and unemployment also created a cruel dilemma because medicine for one seemed to worsen the other. Conflict in regions like the Middle East that Carter had little power to control further complicated matters. As if all of this weren't bad enough, the country was entering an age of limits, one far different than the era of boundless prosperity and seemingly endless possibilities that inspired the Great Society. Carter, like Ford, had to ask Americans to make difficult choices, to sacrifice, to adapt to an age of limits. It was a message neither politicians nor voters found palatable. Of course, there was a growing chorus on the right that welcomed the new realities, confident that they would inevitably require smaller government, lower taxes, and greater reliance on the private sector. With the pie seeming to shrink, many saw politics as a zero-sum game. Nowhere was that truer than in the civil rights arena. Blacks and women believed that there was unfinished business while many White men were certain that women and minorities had benefitted at their expense.

It wasn't the 1960s, and Carter had no desire to be Lyndon Johnson. But he did tackle major challenges with programs adapted to the realities of the 1970s. Energy was chief among them. Due to steadily rising prices and growing dependence on foreign oil, which now satisfied 50% of American demand, the nation faced an energy crisis.[3] Gone were the happy days of the 1960s, when filling stations waged "gas wars," dropping prices to attract customers. Carter's goal was to reduce demand, provide alternate energy sources, and do so in an equitable manner. The centerpiece of the bill he introduced in 1977 traded deregulation of domestic oil prices—which would raise prices, promote conservation, and encourage oil companies to explore new domestic sources—for a tax on producers that would prevent windfall profits and ease federal budget deficits. Carter's initiative raised the hackles of oil producers and legislators in energy-producing states, including Louisiana's Russell Long, the chair of the Senate Finance Committee. After almost two years, a weakened version of Carter's bill finally passed which created a more rational price structure for domestic natural gas, required newly constructed electric-generating and manufacturing plants to burn coal, and provided tax credits for energy conservation and development of alternatives to oil.

In 1979, the Iranian Revolution, followed by war between Iran and Iraq, led to new oil shortages and spiking prices. Only then did Congress grant Carter what he wanted most, a tax on deregulated domestic oil that would generate $290 billion by 1990. It also acceded to his request to create the Synthetic Fuel Corporation, which subsidized the development of alternative fuels, including gas produced by an environmentally unfriendly process known as fracking. By 1980, foreign oil made up 40% of the oil Americans consumed.[4]

---

3 U.S. Energy Information Administration, "Oil and Petroleum Products Explained" https://www.eia.gov/energyexplained/oil-and-petroleum-products/imports-and-exports.php (accessed January 26, 2023).
4 Ibid.

By the mid-1980s, domestic production had steadily increased and the price of energy had fallen. In the long run, Carter's policy was successful, but the fact that it took three years to secure passage made him appear inept. It also meant that the political benefits accrued to his successor.

As a candidate, Carter had endorsed comprehensive national health insurance, a priority for Democrats since the 1940s. It was also the top priority for Senator Edward Kennedy, a perennial presidential contender and favorite of the party's left. Carter's campaign promise met reality when he entered office. A government-run comprehensive program not only faced strong opposition from doctors, hospitals, and insurance companies, but its cost was prohibitive at a time of big deficits and high inflation. So, he decided to take an incremental approach. He proposed legislation that required employers to provide health insurance for their employees, set minimum levels of coverage for employer-provided plans, and created a government system of catastrophic insurance to cover expenses in excess of $2,500 incurred by families. It was a step in the right direction, but Kennedy opposed it and demanded universal care. While that was far too expensive to gain support in Congress, Kennedy and his allies ensured that Carter's approach died a quiet death. Sharply divided, Democrats failed to do what was possible, missing a golden opportunity to deliver a program that provided added protection for working families worried about the high cost of health care. Democrats lost the chance to deliver for White working-class voters who were attracted by the GOP's attacks on high taxes, big government, welfare, and affirmative action.

Welfare was another area where Carter overpromised and underdelivered. As a candidate, Carter called the nation's welfare system a disgrace and promised a thorough overhaul, although he provided no details. His approach was smart electioneering; almost everyone agreed that the patchwork of programs that made up the nation's welfare system was broken although they disagreed sharply about how to fix it. Liberals and welfare recipients disliked it because benefits were inequitable and inadequate. Conservatives complained that it was too expensive, discouraged work, and encouraged young unmarried women to have children they couldn't support. When he came to office, Carter directed Secretary of Health, Education and Welfare Joseph Califano to develop a comprehensive welfare reform proposal that was more equitable, pro-work, pro-family, and—here was kicker—cost no more than the current system.

Given the nation's economic quagmire and political resistance to spending more on a system many considered bloated, keeping the plan cost neutral was critical to Carter. As an engineer, he assumed that Califano could value-engineer the system, finding savings that would support necessary changes.

An engineer he was, but he had no appreciation for the intricacies of a system composed of multiple programs that involved state–federal partnerships. Califano made numerous presentations to the President, seeking to educate him about the complexities of welfare and the cost required to fix it. But Carter pushed back, insisting that reform be cost neutral. Ultimately, serious welfare reform eluded Carter. In 1979, when he submitted a modest proposal that merely tweaked the existing system, he aptly noted that no issue "had provided so much hopeful rhetoric and so much disappointment and frustration."[5] His frustration continued as Congress let even this modest proposal die, handing Republicans a potent issue.

Carter fared better in his effort to expand protection for the environment. Amendments to the Clean Air Act, passed in 1977, stiffened automobile emissions standards. The Clean Water Act of 1977 strengthened the Environmental Protection Agency, giving it authority to protect wetlands and directing it to require industry to adopt the best available technology to safeguard rivers, streams, and lakes. In 1980, Carter himself took the lead in mobilizing support to push the Alaska Lands Act through Congress, where it had been stalled for more than three years. A monument to preservation, it set aside over 100 million acres, protecting it from development (including oil and gas exploration), and established almost three dozen national parks, wildlife refuges, national monuments, and national forests. A week later, he persuaded Congress to allocate $1.6 billion for a federal superfund to clean up toxic waste sites that posed serious threats to public health.

While Carter enjoyed some wins, success on major issues like energy policy, health care, and welfare reform eluded him or came too late. The outsider who promised to restore integrity and competence to government seemed no match for problems that only got worse. By the mid-point of his presidency, his approval ratings fell to around 40%. To many, Carter was just another politician who over-promised and under-delivered while their lives got harder. Their disappointment further shook their faith in the political process and politicians.

Carter's last two years in office found him responding to a series of crises that made Job's trials look manageable. Inflation and unemployment whipsawed the economy and left Americans reeling. By mid-1979, inflation was spiking,

---

5 *Washington Post*, May 22, 1981 https://www.washingtonpost.com/archive/politics/1981/05/22/welfare-reform-a-dream-that-was-impossible/19924236-c5c3-4b79-8e4b-09a8e1cc4b77/ (accessed January 30, 2022).

and economists predicted that it would reach an unheard-of 14% in 1980. To make matters worse, Chrysler, one of the nation's Big Three automakers was on the brink, announcing that it would declare bankruptcy if it didn't receive a $1.5 loan from the federal government. Carter persuaded Congress to approve the loan and made fighting inflation his top priority. He asked for steep cuts in federal spending and appointed Paul Volker, a cigar chomping inflation hawk, chair of the Federal Reserve. Under Volker, the Fed put the brakes on credit. Interest rates climbed to almost 18% by March 1980.[6] Not surprisingly, unemployment rose as well, reaching almost 8% by mid-1980.[7] As the election approached, few remembered Carter's accomplishments, as Americans saw their purchasing power dip by 1.4% in February alone.[8]

Carter was also plagued by foreign policy crises that defied resolution. In November 1979, Iranian revolutionaries took 60 Americans hostage and held 53 of them throughout 1980. To add injury to insult, Iranian oil stopped flowing abroad, raising oil prices—and inflation—in the U.S. Then, in December 1979, the Soviet Union invaded Afghanistan, occupying Kabul and beginning a long—and ultimately unsuccessful—conflict with Muslim insurgents. Although Carter imposed economic sanctions and pulled the U.S. out of the Moscow Olympics, he could do nothing to force a Soviet withdrawal. The President looked as impotent abroad as at home, dealing yet another blow to Americans' confidence, optimism, and faith in government.

## Social Conservatives and Conflict over Values

If international crises and domestic economic catastrophes weren't enough, Americans were becoming increasingly divided over social and cultural issues—disagreements unlikely to be resolved by more or better data. Americans learned, if Vietnam hadn't already taught them, that the shared values trumpeted by 1950s promoters of the great American consensus were an illusion. They also discovered that debates over issues that turned on values could become nasty and impossible to resolve through compromise, bringing perpetual crisis and a sense of moral urgency to politics.

---

6 Macrotrends, "Federal Funds Rate—62 Year Historical Chart" https://www.macrotrends.net/2015/fed-funds-rate-historical-chart (accessed January 26, 2023).

7 U.S. Bureau of Labor Statistics, "Databases, Table & Calculators by Subject" https://data.bls.gov/timeseries/LNS14000000?years_option=all_years (accessed January 26, 2023).

8 Kaufman, *Presidency of James Earl Carter, Jr.*, 167.

That was certainly true of women's rights. As the 1970s began, many politicians assumed that women were largely united in support of the ERA. It proved about as accurate as the 100–1 odds Las Vegas gave New York's Amazin' Mets to win the 1969 World Series. The amendment had an auspicious start, passing Congress by overwhelming majorities in March 1972 and winning approval by 30 of the 38 states needed for ratification by the end of 1973. Keen observers noticed that sharp opposition had emerged in most southern states and a few in the Midwest and Southwest. There, conservative women, most of them Catholics, evangelicals, fundamentalists, and Mormons challenged the notion that the ERA represented progress for women. It was a stunning development. Many evangelicals and fundamentalists had eschewed politics, and they certainly hadn't encouraged women to enter the political thicket. When they did, however, it was a signal to men of all persuasions that standing up to feminist demands might be good politics.

The conservative women who opposed ERA believed that traditional roles assigned to women and men reflected essential differences between the two sexes rooted in God's design. Women's nature suited them to create a nurturing environment for their children and their husbands, while men's intellectual and physical qualities prepared them to succeed in the field, the factory, the office, the professions, politics, and war. Men had privileges that were denied to women, while women had the right to protection from men, custody of children, and alimony in the unfortunate event of divorce. If the ERA were passed, opponents contended, women would be drafted, unisex bathrooms mandated, and same-sex marriages permitted. Many opponents of the ERA insisted that the traditional division of labor, rights, and responsibility was essential. Strong families required men who provided support and women who ran the household, nurtured children, and offered men a place of refuge from the challenges they faced at work. Feminists ridiculed these ideas as antiquated and a product of false consciousness, infuriating conservative women and making them even more determined to push back and defeat the ERA.

One of them was Phyllis Schlafly, a conservative Catholic who had been active in conservative Republican politics since the 1950s. The mother of six, she presented herself as the embodiment of traditional womanhood, even beginning speeches by thanking her husband for allowing her to appear. In reality, Schlafly was a professional conservative activist who had twice run for Congress, hosted a syndicated radio show, and was a force in Republican politics.

Opposition to communism and support for a muscular foreign policy were her chief passions until early 1972, when she began to investigate the ERA.

In February, she published a lengthy article decrying the evils of the amendment in the *Phyllis Schlafly Report*, a newsletter that she mailed to thousands of conservatives whom she had encountered through her political work or the women's summer leadership conferences she hosted. "Of all the classes of people who have ever lived, the American woman is the most privileged," she told her readers. "We have the most rights and rewards, and the fewest duties."[9]

Schlafly's salvo produced immediate results. Ann Patterson, an Oklahoma subscriber, took note. "We didn't know anything about the amendment," Patterson recalled. "In fact, I thought it was a good thing until I read Phyllis's report."[10] Like Patterson, Schlafly's Oklahoma readers were alarmed. The state senate had passed the amendment the day after Congress had acted, and the Oklahoma house was poised to follow. Conservative women provided copies of Schlafly's case against the ERA to Republican legislators, testified against it before a house committee, and persuaded members to block it. Patterson then contacted conservative women in 28 states to inform them how she and her allies had blocked passage and urge them to take up the cause.

Patterson's call to arms was effective, although it paled in comparison to Schlafly's success. In July 1972, Schlafly convened a few activists in Chicago to launch a new organization, the National Committee to Stop ERA. In September, several hundred women gathered in St. Louis to launch a campaign against ERA in legislatures across the country. The new organization's logo, a red STOP sign emblazoned with STOP ERA, conveyed the message: stop taking our privileges. By early 1973, STOP ERA had organizations in 26 states, and it held annual fall conferences to prepare the troops for legislative combat. Schlafly became the face of the movement, speaking and appearing on television everywhere. Poised, focused, articulate, and sharp-witted, she was a formidable spokesperson and adversary.

Schlafly captured the spotlight, but she was by no means the only powerful force in the movement. Lottie Beth Hobbs organized Women Who Want to be Women (WWWW) to demand that Texas legislators reverse their vote to ratify. She didn't succeed but mobilized women from her own denomination,

---

9 Phyllis Schlafly, "What's Wrong with Equal Rights for Women," *The Phyllis Schlafly Report* (February 1972) https://eagleforum.org/publications/psr/feb1972.html (accessed February 1, 2022).
10 "A Tribute to How Phyllis Schlafly Changed Oklahoma," *Sooner Politics News*, September 5, 2016 https://www.soonerpolitics.org/editorial/a-feminists-tribute-to-how-phyllis-schlafly-changed-oklahoma (accessed January 31, 2022).

the Church of Christ, known for its patriarchal culture and insistence that women not speak in mixed gatherings. Church elders didn't object when their women spoke out to defend men's authority in family, church, and society. Soon membership spread across the South and beyond and attracted evangelical and fundamentalist women from conservative Presbyterian, Methodist, Baptist, and Church of Christ congregations. In 1976, the Mormon hierarchy made opposition to the ERA a matter of doctrine, marshalling tens of thousands of women and men, especially in the West, against ratification. By the late 1970s, a coalition of conservative Catholics, evangelical and fundamentalist Protestants, Mormons, and some Jews had stopped a feminist juggernaut. Although Congress extended the deadline for ratification by three years in 1979, no other states ratified, sealing ERA's fate. By politicizing thousands of women, the anti-ERA movement created an army eager to fight on behalf of what they called family values when summoned by conservative leaders.

Abortion became another flashpoint in the battle over gender, the family, and morality. Since the early twentieth century, states had banned abortion except when carrying a pregnancy to term threatened the life, or in a few states the health, of the mother. While some physicians conducted abortions in less dire circumstances, most women seeking to end a pregnancy turned to providers who lacked medical degrees. By the early 1960s, criticism of these so-called "back alley" abortions grew along with calls to liberalize state abortion laws. A popular 1963 film, *Love with a Proper Stranger*, starring A-list actors Natalie Wood and Steve McQueen included a scene in which Wood's character, pregnant after a one-night stand, seeks an abortion from an illegal provider who plied his trade in a dark warehouse. Wood's character fled, but in real life, many women didn't and suffered injuries or even death. Greater demands for sexual freedom, coupled with an emerging women's movement and criticism of restrictive laws by physicians and lawyers, spurred a movement for reform. By 1972, 13 states permitted abortions when the woman's life or health was at risk, the pregnancy was the result of rape or incest, or the baby would suffer from a severe mental or physical defect. Four states, including New York, repealed their abortion laws altogether.

Then, in 1973, the U.S. Supreme Court decided *Roe v. Wade*, holding that states could not restrict abortion during the first three months of pregnancy and could only impose regulations that protected maternal health in the second trimester. Liberalization sparked opposition. The National Right to Life Committee, organized by the American Catholic bishops in 1967, opposed loosening restrictions on abortion. It quickly transitioned to lay leadership, attracted support from Protestants, and spawned state anti-abortion groups.

*Roe* heightened the sense of urgency among opponents of abortion. New anti-abortion—or as the activists chose to label themselves, pro-life—groups emerged, including March for Life. Organized by Nellie Gray, a Texas native who worked as a Labor Department lawyer in Washington, DC, March organized a rally at the Supreme Court on January 22, 1974, the first anniversary of *Roe*. Capitol Police estimated that between 25,000 and 50,000 protesters marched; 100 buses brought protesters from New York and 23 busloads arrived from Pittsburgh. It would become an annual event and spark marches in cities across the country. *Roe* also got the attention of Congress. While there were opponents of legalizing abortion in both parties, conservative Republicans took the lead in introducing pro-life constitutional amendments. While they failed to advance, it was a sign of things to come.

Schlafly, Hobbs, and other opponents of ERA quickly linked feminism, ERA, and abortion. These evils, they argued, were a product of feminists' pursuit of their own rights and interests at the expense of the family and even life itself. As the ranks of ERA opponents swelled, the pro-life chorus grew louder.

Anti-abortion activism also grew among White evangelicals, who were the fastest-growing religious group in the country. Mainline Protestant denominations—Methodists, Presbyterians, Congregationalists, Lutherans, Episcopalians—were shrinking. Their members tended to be more affluent and mobile, less tied to the communities and congregations in which they grew up, and therefore less likely to be churchgoers. While White evangelical congregations included members from a variety of occupations and a range of incomes, they were more likely to include people who were less affluent, married earlier, had more children, and remained close to home and affiliated with their parents' church. White evangelicals could be found in all parts of the country, but their center of gravity was in the South and Southwest, a growing region with a deep vein of conservatism that was the product of longstanding suspicion of the federal government.

Although it appealed to evangelicals everywhere, the South's megachurches quickly became a hotbed of anti-abortion activity. Because these congregations were large and many broadcast their services across the region and beyond, they played a critical role in recruiting new members to the cause. Perhaps the most influential was the Thomas Road Baptist Church, which Jerry Falwell started in Lynchburg, Virginia in the 1950s. By the early 1970s, it claimed over 10,000 members, operated a K-12 school (begun as a refuge from desegregation for White families) and a fledgling college (the precursor of Liberty University), and employed 1,000 staff. Falwell's team also produced the *Old Time Gospel Hour*, a weekly program carried by several hundred TV stations across the country.

Falwell combined advice about how to live a Godly life while achieving material success. After all, he explained, success "is God's way of blessing those who put him first."[11] Well-ordered families built on a foundation of clearly defined sex roles, he insisted, were the glue of a Godly society. The husband and father must provide support, love, guidance, and discipline, while a wife was obligated to "submit to her husband's leadership and help him fulfill God's will for his life."[12] For Falwell, abortion was proof that the United States—once "a Christian nation"—had rejected God's word. Women who turned to the abortionist were "pregnant because of sin" or misguided feminists "caught up in the ERA movement" who wanted to "terminate their pregnancy because it limits their freedom and job opportunities."[13]

By the mid-1970s, Americans were divided on abortion, although most wanted greater access to abortion than pro-life activists were willing to accept. Polling done by Lou Harris & Associates in April 1975 told a complicated story. Respondents believed, by a 54%–38% margin, that women should have access to abortions during the first trimester of a pregnancy, but they opposed abortions in the second trimester (when *Roe* held that states might regulate but not criminalize abortions) by 68%–20%.[14] Americans were not only divided on abortion, with a majority favoring expanded access, majorities held divergent positions on different parts of *Roe*. That uncertainty might have led to interesting, nuanced discussions. Because there were such passionate feelings among sizeable groups on both sides, however, open discussion was rare and vilification of opponents the norm.

Conflict over abortion put political leaders in a difficult position. If they supported *Roe* or even a constitutional amendment overturning *Roe* and returning authority to the states, they risked the ire of those who were pro-life. If they opposed *Roe* and supported reversing or restricting it, they would invite the scorn of women's rights advocates as well as many who believed that abortion was a matter for the individual and not the state to decide. At a time when many Americans expected greater personal and sexual freedom, this was a large group. Taking a stand was a momentous decision because there were many who cared so deeply about the issue that it determined how they voted. While Democrats

---

11 Frances Fitzgerald, *The Evangelicals: The Struggle to Shape America* (New York, 2017), 281.
12 Fitzgerald, *The Evangelicals*, 280.
13 Daniel K. Williams, *God's Own Party: The Making of the Christian Right* (New York, 2010), 156.
14 Lou Harris & Associates Poll, April 16–18, 1975 [Roper # 31107845].

and Republicans came down on each side of the debate, Republicans tended to take a restrictive view while most Democrats supported women's right to choose.

For many Republicans, opposing abortion was especially tempting because it gave them the opportunity to win support from a historically Democratic constituency—Catholics—and also attract White Southerners. Consider the shifting position of Gerald Ford as the 1976 election approached. His wife, Betty, a strong supporter of the ERA and women's rights, was outspoken in her support for *Roe*. While Ford himself refused to be pinned down, most thought he supported a right to abortion in certain circumstances. Staying on the fence when his primary opponent, Ronald Reagan, appealed to pro-life voters by unequivocally opposing abortion, except in cases where a mother's life was threatened, was a risk. Ford dodged, saying that he opposed abortion on-demand and supported a constitutional amendment returning authority to the states. That wasn't good enough for leaders of March for Life, who charged that his "moderate position […] translates into killing just a 'moderate' amount of preborn human beings."[15] By the time the Republican convention met, Ford's running mate, Senator Bob Dole, capitulated to anti-abortion activists by accepting a provision in the platform that supported a constitutional amendment protecting the unborn. The strategy worked. The ticket won kind words from Cincinnati's Archbishop Joseph Bernardin and an endorsement by a number of prominent pro-life figures, including singer Pat Boone who recorded radio ads for Ford. While Ford lost, he brought many Catholics into the Republican fold and won a larger share of the White evangelical vote than Carter, a card-carrying born-again Christian. The lesson wasn't lost on Republicans, who made opposition to abortion central to their brand.

Gay rights sounded another alarm to defenders of traditional moral values. Homosexuality had long been stigmatized and criminalized. Most gays and lesbians hid their sexual orientation out of fear that their parents would disown them, their friends shun them, or their employers fire them. Beginning in the 1950s and 1960s, more gays and lesbians came out of the closet and asserted their right to love whom they chose. The sexual revolution, growing rights' consciousness, and admonition to "do your own thing" led to greater tolerance of lifestyles once considered taboo. Demands by gays and lesbians themselves led to dramatic changes in the 1970s. Twenty-two states repealed laws punishing sexual relations between consenting adults, 40 towns and cities banned discrimination on the basis of sexual orientation, and over 100

---

15 Williams, *God's Own Party*, 130.

corporations revoked policies discriminating against gays and lesbians. In 1979, a gay couple attended the senior prom in Sioux Falls, South Dakota—not known as a hot bed of liberalism.[16]

Christian conservatives and many others were alarmed by the growing acceptance of conduct they considered offensive to God and another blow to the family. Conservatives—and especially evangelicals—went on the offensive. Supporting gay rights sanctioned a perverted lifestyle that the Bible condemned and would invite the wrath God had unleashed on Sodom and Gomorrah. In Miami, where voters adopted an ordinance prohibiting discrimination against gays, including those seeking employment as teachers, Anita Bryant, a popular singer and devout evangelical Christian, sounded the alarm. She warned that the ordinance would enable gay men to recruit young boys to their "perverted, unnatural, and ungodly lifestyle" and take away her right as a mother to "teach my children and set examples." Bryant formed Save Our Children, a group dedicated to repeal, and traveled far and wide to raise money for the cause. Bryant's speaking tour of the South and fund-raising letters to conservative mailing lists netted $200,000, and she brought Falwell and 100 pastors to Miami for a "God and Decency" rally that attracted a crowd of 10,000. In June 1977, voters repealed the ordinance by a 2–1 margin, and Save Our Children spread its activities to other states. Although Bryant's campaign triggered an intense backlash, she became a hero to many. The *Good Housekeeping* poll identified her as the "Most Admired Woman" in 1978 and 1979.[17] The response was just another example of the potential cultural issues had to divide the country and invite politicians to exploit fear and resentment.

Race was another front in the emerging culture wars. Busing was one flash point. State and local government had been complicit in creating segregated schools in almost every U.S. city. In the South, segregation had been mandated by law, while in the North, it had been engineered by dozens of seemingly routine decisions—the location of school buildings, configuration of attendance zones, creation of transfer policies—not to mention the practices banks and realtors used to keep neighborhoods segregated. In the late 1960s and early 1970s, federal courts ruled that when government had acted to create segregation,

---

16 William N. Eskridge, Jr., *Dishonorable Passions: Sodomy Laws in America, 1861–2003* (New York, 2008), 201, 202, 279; Trevor J. Mitchell, "Sioux Falls' first gay prom couple wanted normalcy. Instead, they left a legacy," *Sioux Falls Argus Leader*, April 26, 2019 https://www.argusleader.com/story/news/2019/04/26/sioux-falls-prom-first-gay-couple-lgbt-history/3530310002/ (accessed February 25, 2023).
17 Ibid., 147–51.

busing children to schools outside their neighborhood to create racially balanced schools was an appropriate remedy. While some Black parents objected, most White parents were furious. Judges were taking away their kids' right to attend their neighborhood school, they fumed, ignoring the fact that many Blacks had been prevented from buying homes in those neighborhoods. Drawing on racist tropes of menacing, violent Black youth, many also argued that busing their children to schools in minority neighborhoods endangered them.

Richard Nixon had quickly learned that opposition to busing was a potent tool to attract White voters—North and South. It also put Democrats between a rock and hard place. If they supported busing they risked alienating long-time supporters, notably working-class Whites. But most concluded they had little choice if they hoped to retain Black support. So, Republicans hammered Democrats for threatening that sacred American tradition—the neighborhood school—and for assigning students to schools on the basis of race. Wasn't that what segregation had done? And weren't Whites now the victims of reverse discrimination, Republicans asked? Republicans put congressional Democrats on the spot by introducing legislation to prohibit the courts from ordering busing to dismantle segregation. In the early 1970s, these measures gained the support of most Republicans and also a significant number of Democrats who understood that their constituents hated busing. While a filibuster by Senate liberals prevented their adoption, a 1974 Supreme Court decision soon blunted the effectiveness of busing. It banned transporting students between urban and abutting suburban districts in the absence of proof that a suburban district was guilty of segregating its schools. That was unlikely, of course, because they were overwhelmingly White. The decision weakened busing as a remedy for segregation; it could do little to achieve integration of urban districts that had become heavily minority.

By the late 1970s, busing receded as a flashpoint, only to be replaced by affirmative action. Outlawing racial discrimination in higher education and employment was important, civil rights advocates acknowledged, but did not end it. Schools and employers screened out Black applicants, established criteria that were irrelevant to performance, or didn't make a good faith effort to recruit Blacks. Pretending race didn't—or shouldn't—matter ignored the realities of American life and promised to perpetuate racial disparities. Beginning in the mid-1960s, federal officials began to require businesses that held government contracts to take "affirmative action," that is to make extra efforts to recruit minorities and women. Ironically, it was Nixon who required government contractors to establish goals for hiring minorities and women and timelines to meet them. Federal policy put pressure on government contractors to be more aggressive in recruiting and hiring Blacks, and the EEOC subsequently weighed the results when considering complaints of discrimination. Very few employers or universities established hiring or admissions quotas (unless ordered to do so by courts to remedy actual discrimination), but critics argued that goals had become de facto quotas. Blacks received preferential treatment so employers and universities could meet their targets and avoid lawsuits, they argued, and Whites became victims of reverse discrimination. Admissions and hiring decisions should be color-blind insisted many who had once supported segregation.

White resentment was growing when the Supreme Court decided *Regents of the University of California v. Bakke* in 1978. To train more persons of color as physicians, the University of California at Davis set aside 16 of 100 seats in its first-year medical school class for minorities. Alan Bakke, 34-year-old Marine veteran and engineer, applied but was rejected even though his grades and test scores were higher than many minorities who were admitted. Bakke sued, claiming that the University had discriminated against him because he was White. According to *The New York Times*, he was driven by "an almost religious zeal to fight a system that he felt [...] treated whites less equitably than members of minority groups."[18] Even though the Court was splintered, it reached a Solomonic decision, thanks to Lewis Powell, the conservative Virginian who cast the deciding vote. Powell's opinion struck down the Davis admissions program because it was a race-based quota and violated the Civil Rights Act of 1964. However, he held that universities had an educational interest in achieving diversity and therefore endorsed admissions programs, like Harvard's, that used race as one criterion among many to achieve diversity, which he believed was a compelling interest for universities and justified affirmative action. The Court's decision—which *Newsweek* characterized as "No Quotas—But Race Can Count"[19]—resonated with many Americans who were ambivalent about the issue. Most conservatives, however, agreed with Robert Bork, the University of Chicago law professor who carried out Nixon's "Saturday Night Massacre." *Bakke*, he asserted, was a statement that "the 14th Amendment allows some,

---

18 Howard Ball, *The Bakke Case: Race, Education, and Affirmative Action* (Lawrence, KS, 2000), 47.
19 *Newsweek*, July 10, 1978 https://advance-lexis-com.proxy.binghamton.edu/document/?pdmfid=1516831&crid=6be720c1-2015-4cbd-9281-afee3d11b064&pddocfullpath=%2Fshared%2Fdocument%2Fnews%2Furn%3AcontentItem%3A3SJ4-F7H0-0008-X0RJ-00000-00&pdcontentcomponentid=5774&pdteaserkey=sr18&pditab=allpods&ecomp=zznyk&earg=sr18&prid=ee6e0415-6d90-4c57-b37e-8080a8e66cf0 (accessed February 25, 2023).

but not too much, reverse discrimination."[20] The bright side for conservatives, however, was that as long as affirmative action remained alive, it helped them energize White voters.

Welfare, a favorite conservative target, channeled White resentment even more effectively than affirmative action. Critics charged that the system undermined the family by supporting millions of women who had children out of wedlock, taxed hard-working Americans to support the idle, and flowed disproportionately to Blacks. When many Americans thought of welfare, they pictured a Black woman with three or four children who had never earned a paycheck and was probably scamming the system. Many conservative politicians used this trope, but none more effectively than Ronald Reagan. In 1976, when he challenged Gerald Ford for the Republican nomination, the welfare system was Exhibit A in his case against big government and wasteful spending. Using a story that he would ride to the White House, Reagan told audiences about a woman who would become known as "the welfare queen." "In Chicago, they found the woman who holds the record," he said, implying that her story was the tip of an iceberg. "She used 80 names, 30 addresses, 15 telephone numbers to collect food stamps, Social Security, veterans' benefits for four nonexistent deceased veteran husbands as well as welfare."[21] Reagan didn't make up the story; the woman's name was Linda Taylor and her success in defrauding the system was real. In 1974, authorities in Chicago prosecuted her, she spent two years in prison, and newspapers across the country told the story.

A seasoned speaker, Reagan knew the power of a memorable anecdote to make his point. Listeners didn't want to be bothered with statistics showing that welfare fraud was rare, officials prosecuted cheaters like Taylor, and most recipients struggled to make ends meet for themselves and their children. The "welfare queen" story was entertaining, and it confirmed the prejudices of many Whites about a system they didn't like. When asked in 1978 what percentage of welfare recipients "are 'chiselers', that is, are collecting money they are not entitled to," the median response of participants in a Gallup Poll was one-third.[22]

---

20 Robert H. Bork, "The Unpersuasive Bakke Decision," *Wall Street Journal*, July 21, 1978 https://www.wsj.com/articles/SB10001424127887324461604578189272139787196 (accessed February 3, 2022).

21 *Washington Post*, May 21, 2019 https://www.washingtonpost.com/history/2019/05/21/she-was-stereotyped-welfare-queen-truth-was-more-disturbing-new-book-says/

22 Gallup Poll, August 8–11, 1978 [Roper # 31087972].

## It took approximately 16 years to count the vote in the 1964 election

In 1964, Barry Goldwater's appeal to fear—of communism, government overreach, moral decline, and Blacks—failed. The economy was growing, real income was rising, Americans were optimistic, and lots of them believed that government should make society better and more equitable. By the 1970s, the country was reeling from a toxic mix of high unemployment and high inflation. After prolonged economic expansion in the 1960s, Americans suffered through recessions in 1970, 1973–1975, and 1980, and industries that formed the backbone of the U.S. economy shed jobs, market share, and profits. The steel industry, with its aging plants, found it difficult to compete with foreign producers. Plants closed and employment in an industry that had offered high wages to those with limited education fell by 25% between 1969 and 1980.[23] The impact on cities like Pittsburgh, Buffalo, Youngstown, Toledo, Gary, and East Chicago was devastating. Soaring gas prices encouraged Americans to buy more fuel-efficient European and Japanese cars, delivering a blow to America's Big Three automakers. While employment in the industry held steady across the decade, workers rode a rollercoaster. During the oil shock of 1973–1975, employment declined by almost 10% per year. Employment grew by 8.8% per year in the following three years, but a new spike in oil prices and a recession led to layoffs, with jobs evaporating at a rate of 6.5% a year between 1978 and 1983.[24] Employment in textile and shoe manufacturing declined by 25% and 49%, respectively, between the end of the 1960s and the early 1980s.[25] Little wonder that when Americans were asked by the Pew Research Corporation to rate the state of the nation, on a scale of 1–10, the mean was 6.5 in 1964 and 5.1 in 1981.

Disillusioned with government, worried about the future, and financially hard-pressed, many Americans grumbled about their taxes. As inflation raised property values, sometimes dramatically, home and business owners saw

---

23 David G. Tarr, "The Steel Crisis in the United States and the European Community: Causes and Adjustments," in Robert E. Baldwin, Carl B. Hamilton, and Andre Sapir, *Issues in US-EC Trade Relations* (Chicago, 1988), 171.

24 Christopher J. Singleton, "Auto Industry Jobs in the 1980s: A Decade of Transition," *Monthly Labor Review*, 115 (February 1992), 19–20.

25 U.S. Bureau of Labor Statistics, Employment, Hours, Earnings, United States, 1909–1990, 663, 968 https://fraser.stlouisfed.org/title/employment-earnings-united-states-189/employment-hours-earnings-united-states-1909-90-5435/content/pdf/emp_bmark_1909_1990_v1 (accessed February 26, 2023).

assessments and tax bills increase. While incomes rose, they didn't keep up with inflation, leaving most with less purchasing power but larger income tax bills because rising income pushed them into a higher tax bracket. A problem that government created—inflation—but couldn't control was forcing citizens to hand over a greater portion of their earnings to government—when everything was getting more expensive.

Howard Jarvis launched the anti-tax crusade in California with a line from a popular movie about a washed-up TV anchor who juices his ratings by becoming a ranting on-air populist. "I'm mad as hell—and I'm not going to take it anymore," growled Jarvis, a retired California chemical manufacturer and political gadfly.[26] Californians took note. Property values had risen sharply in the state due to population growth and inflation. As a result, tax bills increased every year. Jarvis founded the United Organization of Taxpayers (UOT) in the 1960s and subsequently became executive director of the Los Angeles Apartment Owners Association, a group deeply concerned about rising property taxes. The vehicle Jarvis chose to reduce taxes was the referendum, a venerable California tradition that allows individuals to place a proposed constitutional amendment—a proposition it was called—before the voters. All they needed to get a proposition on the ballot was signatures of 8% of the number of people who voted in the previous election for governor.

Jarvis tried but repeatedly failed to get enough signatures. However, in December 1977, with anti-tax sentiment growing, he secured 1.5 million signatures and put Proposition 13 on the ballot. It would slash rates to 1% of a property's assessed value—a 57% cut—and limit future increases to 2% a year. In June 1978, it passed by a 65–35 margin. Although Jarvis touted the outcome as the triumph of a grassroots insurgency, the campaign was hardly a spontaneous popular uprising. It had lavish financial support from apartment owners and businesses that allowed him to send targeted mailings encouraging likely supporters to vote and also write checks to support the cause. In all, UOT spent $2.2 million (almost $9 million in 2020 dollars) to persuade voters. Something more was at play than spontaneous outrage, although there was plenty of that.[27]

---

26 Benjamin Schneider, "Looking Back at Howard Jarvis and Prop 13," *SF Weekly*, October 8, 2020 https://www.sfweekly.com/film/looking-back-at-howard-jarvis-and-prop-13/article_50359baa-ed89-5978-9041-722b914d2b58.html (accessed February 26, 2023).
27 Daniel A. Smith, "Howard Jarvis, 'Populist' Entrepreneur: Re-evaluating the Cause of Proposition 13," *Social Science History*, 23 (Summer 1999), 173–210.

Voters spoke loudly, and the widespread belief that there had been a popular uprising in California spurred a nationwide campaign to lower taxes—property and income taxes, local, state, and federal levies. More than a dozen states considered measures to reduce property taxes or limit increases in state spending. In 1978, conservative Republicans Jack Kemp, a House member from New York, and William Roth, a senator from Delaware, introduced legislation that would slash federal taxes. Ronald Reagan, the leading contender for the party's 1980 nomination, promised to ignite a "prairie fire" of opposition to "costly, overpowering government."[28] Anti-taxers like Reagan, Kemp, and Roth were doing more than defending hard-pressed taxpayers. They were shifting the terms of discussion. Taxes, which transferred money from citizens to government to support projects designed to promote the common good, took money away from individuals and businesses who would use it in ways that benefitted individuals. Conservative economist Otto Eckstein understood that measures like Proposition 13 would result in "rapid growth in the private sector and a decline in the public sector."[29] Another conservative economist, Arthur Laffer, argued that lower taxes would ultimately produce more revenue because individuals would keep more of their earnings, have an incentive to work harder, invest more, produce more, hire more workers, and increase income and profits subject to taxation. An untested theory known as supply side economics, it quickly became conservatives' catnip.

Just as 1960s activists sought to mobilize supporters to challenge racism, sexism, militarism, and a host of other evils, conservatives in the 1970s organized to challenge big government and moral decay. They would no longer remain on the defensive but would take the initiative and demand change, just like Blacks, Chicanos, women, workers, and gays had done. Liberals would no longer have a monopoly on innovative ideas; conservatives would become the source of fresh thinking that challenged the status quo. The new conservatism would be bold, iconoclastic, and develop an appeal beyond the nation's country clubs. It would represent the values and aspirations of hard-working middle- and working-class Americans who believed in individual autonomy and feared the country was headed in the wrong direction.

---

28 *New York Times,* June 25, 1978 https://www.nytimes.com/1978/06/25/archives/reagan-urges-party-to-support-tax-cuts-calls-for-limited-government.html (accessed January 27, 2022).

29 *Time,* June 19, 1978 https://content.time.com/time/subscriber/article/0,33009,919742,00.html (accessed February 26, 2023).

It was a tall order, and it required a new approach to political mobilization. Politicians had long-maintained lists of supporters, people they could rely on to write checks and bring friends and neighbors to the cause. In the 1960s, access to computers—large mainframe devices—enabled political operatives to build electronic databases of supporters, add to them easily, and crank out communications to a large sympathetic audience quickly and cheaply. Organizers could also monetize their lists by renting them to others.

Richard Viguerie, a conservative Catholic Republican from Texas who cut his teeth in politics as a fundraiser for Young Americans for Freedom and a Goldwater supporter, developed his first mailing list in 1965. Federal election law required candidates to report all donations over $50 to the clerk of the U.S. House of Representatives. Viguerie marched into the clerk's office, requested access to the file, and copied some 12,500 names and addresses by hand. That file became the core of a mailing list that Viguerie augmented over the years, transferred to a computer database, rented, and deployed for causes near to his heart. For Viguerie, doing good—helping conservatives—allowed him to do well, very well. The Viguerie Company would become a multi-million-dollar enterprise that offered consulting services and mailing lists to conservative causes and candidates. Others entered the business, building databases for political, commercial, and charitable purposes and offering access to them to those willing to pay. Direct mail allowed politicians and political organizations to reach potential supporters with a narrative free of nuance and raise cash from a large base of small contributors who would then proselytize their friends and encourage them to vote. Highly charged cultural issues lent themselves to direct mail because they tapped primal feelings of fear and loathing that called voters to action.

Changes in campaign finance law complemented the direct mail revolution. Watergate sparked concern about the role of large donors in politics and led Congress to limit individual contributions to candidates to $1,000. However, it did not restrict small contributions generated by direct mail. The law also restricted expenditures by political action committees (PACs) that operated independent of candidates and their campaigns. However, a 1976 Supreme Court decision declared that these limits violated the First Amendment's guarantee of freedom of speech, leading to a proliferation of PACs on the left and right. They raised millions of dollars to influence voters and politicians on specific issues and advocated for and against individual candidates. Direct mail was a potent tool for PACs to raise money from a broad base, and social issues were a powerful way for them to motivate donors to write checks.

Aspiring candidates like Ronald Reagan formed PACs. But it was a small group of true believers who saw Goldwater's 1964 campaign as the beginning of a conservative insurgency that made PACs a vehicle for revolution. They were political operatives, and they had a grasp of what moved voters and won elections—and also which contests were competitive enough to merit their time and money. While they might sympathize with candidates who were ideological soulmates, their goal was to win elections. Spending their time and money on races that were within reach was the best way to accomplish that.

Paul Weyrich was one of these conservative revolutionaries. A working-class Midwesterner who had converted to the highly conservative Melkite Greek Catholic faith, he came to Washington as an aide to Colorado Senator Gordon Allott. He marveled at how liberal think-tanks like the Brookings Institution mobilized valuable data, analysis, and arguments to support policies he abhorred. Why couldn't conservatives do that, he wondered? So he left his staff position and developed organizations to support conservative insurgents. One was the Committee for the Survival of a Free Congress, a PAC Weyrich established in 1974. He wasn't alone. Howard Phillips, a Jewish convert to evangelical Christianity and Nixon insider, established the Conservative Caucus in 1974. A year later, Terry Dolan, a Young Republican leader who had worked on Nixon's 1972 campaign, joined two other Nixon loyalists, Charles Black and Roger Stone, to establish the National Conservative Political Action Committee.

Weyrich, Dolan, Phillips, and Viguerie prevailed on Jerry Falwell to form his own PAC. Falwell's appeal to evangelicals had the potential to expand conservative fundraising and recruit more activists to the cause. There was just one problem. Although Falwell was outspoken on moral issues, he believed that as a preacher, he should avoid partisan politics. In addition, politics necessitated building coalitions, and Falwell was reluctant to work with members of other religious groups, let alone unbelievers. "I believed that being yoked with 'unbelievers' for any cause was off limits," Falwell explained. "I didn't even get along very well with other kinds of Baptists, let alone Methodists, Presbyterians, or Catholics."[30] However, Falwell understood that only by entering the fray would he make a difference. He was also moved by the government's threat to remove his school's tax-exempt status. What got Falwell on board, Weyrich recalled, was "Carter's intervention against the Christian schools, trying to deny them tax-exempt status on the basis of so-called de facto segregation."[31]

---

30 Williams, *God's Own Party*, 173.
31 Fitzgerald, *The Evangelicals*, 394.

In 1979, Falwell agreed to create a new organization he called the Moral Majority—a name suggested by Weyrich. Falwell recruited members from evangelical churches, principally in the South. He and those who joined him encouraged evangelicals—an estimated 45% of whom were not registered to vote—to get involved. He also raised money and began to support conservative candidates, including Iowa congressman Charles Grassley who was then challenging John Culver, a Harvard classmate of Ted Kennedy, in a close Senate race. By fusing cultural conservatism with free market economics, the Moral Majority would bring fresh recruits to the conservative cause. Fear, loathing, and deeply held moral beliefs were more effective in raising money and mobilizing voters than abstract principles. "The shriller you are, the better it is to raise money," Dolan explained.[32] As American politics became increasingly shrill, room for compromise narrowed.

Of course, it wasn't only conservatives who were shrill. Voices on the left vilified opponents as a means of mobilizing supporters. The National Organization for Women's (NOW's) Eleanor Smeal called the right's agenda "a very serious threat that is not only anti-abortion, but really anti-woman,"[33] while George McGovern characterized "the 'family' issue raised by the right wing [...] a code word for putting women back in the kitchen."[34] Leaders of the American Civil Liberties Union were no less vehement. Ira Glasser labeled the Moral Majority's agenda "anti-bill of rights, for book censorship,"[35] and Dorothy Samuels charged that conservative groups "profoundly threaten traditional constitutional values."[36] Yale's president told freshmen that the religious right had "licensed a new meanness of spirit in our land [...] that manifests itself in racist and discriminatory postures, in threats of political retaliation, in injunctions to censorship, in acts of violence."[37] But it wasn't just leaders of

---

32 Williams, *God's Own Party*, 169.
33 *New York Times*, December 9, 1980 https://timesmachine.nytimes.com/timesmachine/1980/12/09/111323203.pdf?pdf_redirect=true&ip=0 (accessed February 12, 2022).
34 *New York Times*, November 7, 1980 https://timesmachine.nytimes.com/timesmachine/1980/11/07/112170219.pdf?pdf_redirect=true&ip=0 (accessed February 22, 2022).
35 *New York Times*, December 9, 1980 https://timesmachine.nytimes.com/timesmachine/1980/12/09/111323203.pdf?pdf_redirect=true&ip=0 (accessed February 12, 2022).
36 *New York Times*, November 23, 1980 https://timesmachine.nytimes.com/timesmachine/1980/11/23/114152084.pdf?pdf_redirect=true&ip=0 (accessed February 12, 2022).
37 *New York Times*, September 1, 1981 https://www.nytimes.com/1981/09/01/nyregion/head-of-yale-calls-moral-majority-peddlers-of-coercion-on-values.html (accessed February 12, 2022).

liberal organizations and academics who skewered conservative evangelicals. Many of their followers worked themselves into high dudgeon, alternating snide comments about their opponents' ignorant, benighted views with heated denunciations of the threat they posed. The "present danger emanates not only from the totalitarian but also from the totalitarian right at home," a letter to *The New York Times* exclaimed.[38]

While they raised millions from small donors, conservatives didn't neglect the super-rich. Big corporations might be reluctant to support far right causes, but conservative activists found like-minded spirits among in the ranks of wealthy men and women who controlled family foundations worth hundreds of millions of dollars. Conservative philanthropy would help an insurgent New Right establish institutions and forge an intellectually coherent case against liberalism. Their focus was on high taxes, the social safety net, and government regulation of private enterprise. They intended to make the Republican Party the party of ideas—even if those turned out to be little more than warmed-over anti-New Deal bromides dressed up in the language of academic social science. In 1973, Weyrich used his relationship with conservative beer heir, Joseph Coors, to secure a $250,000 donation to establish the Heritage Foundation. It supported research, conferences, policy papers, books, and articles that provided data, ideas, arguments, and spin to support conservative positions on a range of issues. It would be a worthy opponent of Brookings. Heritage quickly attracted other mega-donors, including Richard Mellon Scaife, heir to a vast Pittsburgh fortune amassed through banking, oil refining, and manufacturing. A libertarian rake who didn't give a hoot about the culture wars, Scaife was a devotee of limited (almost no) government who was attracted to conservatism as a young man and had flown Goldwater to the 1964 Republican convention in his private jet. Enthused by Heritage's anti-government stance, his support began in the 1970s. By 1984, he had contributed approximately $10 million, making Heritage a DC powerhouse.

Charles and David Koch, whose wealth came from their family's Wichita-based oil empire, imbibed uncompromising libertarian views from their father, an avid member of the John Birch Society and a Goldwater supporter. Charles's hostility to government was whetted by battles with federal agencies that charged his business with violating environmental regulations. "We need a movement,"

---

38 *New York Times*, November 23, 1980 https://timesmachine.nytimes.com/timesmachine/1980/11/23/114152079.pdf?pdf_redirect=true&ip=0 (accessed February 12, 2022).

A New Right Emerges, 1972–1980

he wrote in 1978, that would "destroy the prevalent statist paradigm."[39] After California financier Ed Crane failed in his quixotic 1976 Libertarian bid for the presidency, Charles persuaded Crane to join him in starting a libertarian think-tank. They named it the Cato Institute, and thanks to the $10–$20 million the Kochs donated, it became the best-supported and certainly the most uncompromising libertarian organization in the country. Cato supported writers, scholars, policy analysts, and advocates who shared Koch's belief that government's only purpose was to "serve as a night watchman to protect individuals and property [...]. That is the maximum."[40] Taxes to support welfare, Medicare, Medicaid, regulatory agencies, and even public schools transferred property from wealth creators to those who couldn't fend for themselves.

Conservative donors also trained their sights on universities, which they considered bastions of fuzzy-headed liberal thinking. By infiltrating universities— and especially elite universities—they hoped to influence the next generation of leaders while gaining legitimacy for their views. John Olin, a wealthy Cornell alumnus and member of the University's board of trustees, was horrified when armed Black students seized the Cornell student union in April 1969 and refused to leave until the administration agreed to establish a Black Studies program. It's hard to tell whether Olin was angrier at the students or Cornell's president. But the experience convinced him that universities needed more conservative voices, and he decided to use his Foundation to support them. The Olin Foundation took a special interest in legal education, providing $68 million to bring the "law and economics" movement to elite law schools. Grounded in faith in free markets, "law and economics" insisted that justice required courts to weigh economic considerations when applying the law. The movement took root in law schools across the country, including Harvard, Chicago, Columbia, Cornell, Yale, and Virginia, and encouraged thousands of students and perhaps hundreds of judges to temper justice with considerations of economic cost and efficiency. Leading figures in the movement such as Richard Posner and Frank Easterbrook became influential federal appellate judges.

Conservatives were energized as the 1980 election approached. Most Americans were distressed by the country's economic conditions, and many believed that gay rights, abortion, and feminism were rapidly destroying the country's moral fiber. The tables were turned from 1964, when LBJ

---

39 Jane Mayer, *Dark Money: The Hidden History of the Billionaires Behind the Rise of the Radical Right* (New York, 2016), 71.
40 Mayer, *Dark Money*, 107.

crushed Barry Goldwater. Discontent is the most potent force in politics, and conservatives were ready to make the most of it. They had built networks and institutions to mobilize dissatisfaction against Democrats. For most Republicans and many conservatives, Ronald Reagan seemed to be the perfect candidate to channel this popular restiveness. He had solid conservative credentials dating back to his much-heralded role in the Goldwater campaign and his narrow loss to an incumbent president in the 1976 Republican primaries. But his bona fides weren't good enough for some social conservatives, including Viguerie and Falwell. Initially, they supported Phillip Crane, a conservative firebrand and House member from Illinois, but fell in line behind Reagan as Crane quickly fizzled.

They exacted a price for their support—one Reagan was happy to pay. They pushed him to accept a platform that was anti-abortion, demanded appointment of pro-life judges, refused to endorse the ERA, opposed any action giving the government greater control over families, and promised to bar the IRS from denying tax exemptions for independent schools (even if they discriminated against Blacks). Conservative PACs provided millions of dollars to support Reagan's campaign, and his strong position on social issues strengthened his appeal to voters in the South and the rest of the Sunbelt. Shortly after winning the nomination, he appeared at a gathering in Dallas convened by conservative evangelical leaders and wowed the crowd by endorsing inclusion of the Biblical story of creation alongside evolution—which was only a theory, he asserted—in school curricula. "I know you can't endorse me," he told the ministers, "but [...] I want you to know that I endorse you and what you are doing."[41] He was one of them, at least when in their presence. Concerned about appearing too zealous, however, his team persuaded Falwell to tone down his public pronouncements on gay rights. Reagan wanted the votes of White evangelicals while avoiding being called a bigot.

While evangelical support buoyed spirits in the Reagan camp, it was but one reason to believe the campaign would overcome concerns about Reagan's age (he was 68) and his frequent gaffes (like his assertion that trees were responsible for 80% of air pollution). His opponent was the campaign's biggest reason for optimism. Carter's record in foreign policy was easy to attack, especially if you didn't have to provide solutions to the challenges he faced. As the campaign began, Iranian militants who seized the U.S. embassy in Teheran had held 53 Americans hostage for almost a year. A valiant but botched rescue effort

---

41 Fitzgerald, *The Evangelicals*, 314.

in April 1980 made the administration seem all the more impotent. A month after the hostage crisis began, Soviet troops rolled into Afghanistan, a move that many feared was the first step toward expanding Russian influence in the oil-rich Persian Gulf. Carter, who had been vigorously pursuing arms control negotiations and commercial relations with Moscow, appeared to have been hoodwinked.

Concern about the nation's international standing paled in comparison to economic angst. With plants closing, gas prices rising, inflation raging, and unemployment high, most voters were ready for a change. When Reagan met Carter for their lone debate, a week before the election, he dispelled doubts that casting a vote for him was risky. Appearing fit and nimble on his feet, he dispelled concerns about his age. Turning on his warm, folksy self-confidence, he seemed more likable than Carter, whose humorless demeanor and penchant for diving into the weeds turned off viewers. The clincher came in Reagan's closing statement, when he asked, "Are you better off than you were four years ago? [...] Is America as respected throughout the world as it was?"[42] For most Americans, the answers were painfully obvious.

Reagan cruised to victory. Because John Anderson, a Republican congressman turned Independent presidential candidate won almost 7% of the vote, Reagan received a bare majority of the popular vote, with Carter claiming 41%. Reagan crushed Carter where it counted most—the Electoral College. There he prevailed by a lopsided margin of 489–49. Carter won even fewer electoral votes than Herbert Hoover had claimed in the 1932 blowout. Turnout was its lowest since 1948, only 54%, which hurt Carter.[43] Reagan also cut into key Democratic constituencies, losing the vote of labor union families by only 8% and Jews by only 7%, while Anderson, running to Reagan's left drained more votes from Carter than his opponent, especially in the Northeast.[44] White evangelicals helped Reagan lock up the South and the Sunbelt. They were one of the few groups to vote in greater numbers than in 1976, and they supported Reagan by a 2–1 margin.[45] Reagan also had coattails, helping Republicans pick up 34 House seats—mostly in Democratic strongholds in the Northeast, Midwest, and California—and trim the Democratic majority to 242–191.

---

42 H.W. Brands, *Reagan: The Life* (New York, 2015), 229–30.
43 "Reagan Buries Carter in a Landslide," *Congressional Quarterly Almanac* (1980).
44 Ibid.
45 Clyde Haberman, "Religion and Right-Wing Politics: How Evangelicals Reshaped Elections," *New York Times*, October 28, 2018 https://www.nytimes.com/2018/10/28/us/religion-politics-evangelicals.html (accessed January 26, 2023).

In the Senate, Republicans gained a whopping 12 seats to take a 54–46 majority. Social conservatives claimed credit for taking down liberal lions like Birch Bayh (Indiana), Frank Church (Idaho), John Culver (Iowa), Warren Magnuson (Washington), and George McGovern (South Dakota), the Democratic standard bearer in 1972. The Senate would not only be less Democratic, it would be far more conservative.

Conservatives crowed about the results, seeing in them an epochal shift to the right. "It took approximately 16 years to count the vote in the '64 election," conservative pundit George Will quipped, "and Goldwater won."[46] Reagan's election certainly marked an end to the faith in active government that had dominated American politics in the 1960s and had survived into the 1970s. Carter, faced with intractable domestic challenges, had attempted to adjust Democratic commitments to workers, the poor, minorities, women, and the environment to new realities. Going forward, Democrats would have to trim their promises while addressing the needs of key constituencies. That would be a challenge because sharp conflict among key groups, notably Blacks, Northern working-class Whites, and Southern Whites, helped Republicans splinter the New Deal coalition. They had been trying since Nixon's 1968 campaign. But Reagan finally achieved what Nixon—and Wallace—had envisioned but failed to achieve.

Conservatives also changed the terms of political debate. Democrats would have to counter conservative arguments that government was the enemy, not the solution to the nation's problems. With public faith in government at an all-time low, that would be an even bigger challenge than winning elections. Democrats would have to regroup at a time when conflict was about ends as well as means and political rhetoric on both sides was becoming increasingly strident. The growing role of religious conservatives added a new, disturbing element to the nation's political discourse. As historian Frances Fitzgerald noted, figures like Jerry Falwell "introduced the fundamentalist sense of perpetual crisis, and of war between good and evil, into national politics, where the rhetoric has remained ever since."[47] It was a far cry from 1964 when the cult of consensus remained alive, voters rejected Goldwater as an extremist, and LBJ could expect support from Republicans for civil rights and expansion of the safety net.

---

46 *Washington Post*, February 24, 1981 https://www.washingtonpost.com/archive/politics/1981/02/24/trying-to-turn-a-collective-sentiment-into-a-government/45fc95f2-65e9-4359-acc9-6bf89eae0014/ (accessed February 6, 2022).
47 Fitzgerald, *The Evangelicals*, 318.

American politics had clearly shifted right. That, by itself, didn't necessarily mean the system was doomed to hyper-partisanship and gridlock. However, heated debates over race, gender, sexuality, the family, and abortion created a Manichean struggle between good and evil. Along with fundamental differences over the role of government, these conflicts brought deep, even vicious divisiveness to American politics. New technology—notably computer-driven direct mail—and wealthy donors stirred this toxic brew, demonizing the enemy, summoning supporters to the barricades, financing political warfare, and weaponizing ideas. Nevertheless, neither of the two major parties had become ideologically homogeneous. Moderates retained a strong voice in the Republican Party while pragmatic moderates and Blue Dog southerners were a force among Democrats. They would moderate their parties' positions and ensure the compromises necessary to make government function, even as the country took a right turn.

CHAPTER 5

# REAGAN: THE REVOLUTION THAT WASN'T—AND WAS, 1980–1988

### I Have a Dream

In the days after Martin Luther King's assassination in April 1968, as Washington, DC, and other American cities burned, a young congressman named John Conyers introduced legislation to make King's birthday a national holiday. Conyers, who represented Detroit's inner city, would enjoy many successes in his 52 years in Congress. But none gave him greater satisfaction than his long battle to recognize the role King and Black Americans had played in shaping the nation and its values by establishing a King holiday. Conyers' bill was controversial. King engaged in civil disobedience, condemned America's involvement in Vietnam, and criticized capitalism. A sanitized version of King as a man who preached love, operated within the system, and opposed Black militants had yet to emerge. To many conservatives, he was a radical, unworthy of becoming the first private citizen recognized with a national holiday.

Conyers persisted. The Congressional Black Caucus, which he cofounded in 1969, lent its support. So did President Jimmy Carter and pop music superstar Stevie Wonder, whose 1980 hit, "Happy Birthday," celebrated King's vision and advocated a holiday honoring it.[1] Conyers finally got a vote on his bill in the House in 1979, but it fell five votes short.[2] President Ronald Reagan

---

1 National Museum of African American History and Culture, "The 15 Year Battle for Martin Luther King, Jr. Day" https://nmaahc.si.edu/explore/stories/15-year-battle-martin-luther-king-jr-day (accessed May 1, 2023).
2 Don Wolfensberger, "The Martin Luther King, Jr. Holiday: The Long Struggle in Congress, An Introductory Essay," Woodrow Wilson International Center for Scholars, January 14, 2008 https://www.wilsoncenter.org/sites/default/files/media/documents/event/King%20Holiday-essay-drw.pdf (accessed May 1, 2023).

dismissed the idea. The country couldn't "afford all the holidays we'd have," he told reporters, if all the "revered figures in the history of many of the groups that make up our population here in America" were recognized.[3] In other words, King might be important to Blacks but he didn't have the stature of a Washington or Lincoln. Despite Reagan's opposition, Conyers finally succeeded in 1983, winning passage in the House by a lopsided majority. But the bill met resistance in the Senate. North Carolina's Jesse Helms, the body's most conservative Republican, mounted a filibuster to block passage, calling King a "proponent of action-oriented Marxism."[4] When questioned about whether he believed King was a communist, Reagan quipped, "We'll know in about 35 years, won't we?" (When King's FBI records were unsealed.) Reagan was out of step with a growing number of Republicans who now believed that opposition was damaging them politically. "I almost lost my dinner over that," David Gergen, Reagan's Communications Director, remarked.[5] The Senate passed the bill in October 1983, with even one-time Dixiecrat presidential candidate Strom Thurmond voting in favor.

Reagan signed the bill in a Rose Garden ceremony, extolling King as a man who "awakened something strong and true, a sense that true justice must be color blind."[6] One of his strengths as a politician was that he didn't tilt at windmills. When he lost a battle, he moved on, keeping his eye on winning the war. In the case of King, that meant using his memory and words to support conservative causes that King had opposed, like opposition to affirmative action. Reagan and his conservative allies—some of whom had been die-hard segregationists—insisted that the most important lesson of the civil rights movement was that treating people differently because of their race was immoral and violated the Constitution. They never tired quoting a line from King's most famous speech expressing hope that his children "will one day live in a nation where they will not be judged by the color of their skin but by the content of their character." Color-conscious remedies like busing and affirmative action, Reagan insisted, were at odds with King's beliefs because they harmed White men by giving special privileges to minorities and women. Far from opposing affirmative

---

[3] Denise M. Bostdorff and Steven R. Goldzwig, "History, Collective Memory, and the Appropriation of Martin Luther King, Jr.: Reagan's Rhetorical Legacy," *Presidential Studies Quarterly*, 35 (December 2005), 668.
[4] Ibid., 669.
[5] Ibid.
[6] Wolfensberger, "Martin Luther King, Jr. Holiday," 8.

action, of course, King had demanded that the nation "incorporate into its planning some compensatory consideration for the handicaps [...] [Blacks had] inherited from the past."[7]

Reagan even enlisted King in support his efforts to cut funding for Aid to Families with Dependent Children, food stamps, and Medicaid, key programs aimed at alleviating poverty. In 1981, as he persuaded Congress to slash funding for these programs while lowering taxes on the wealthy, Reagan asserted that his policies were consistent with the goals of King and the movement he led. Government programs had made the poor "government-dependent rather than independent," he told the annual meeting of the National Association for the Advancement of Colored People in 1981. They created "a new kind of bondage," he insisted. "Just as the Emancipation Proclamation freed black people [...] today we need to declare an economic emancipation." Cutting taxes and reducing government regulation, Reagan argued, would create jobs, open opportunity, lift the poor out of poverty, and end their demeaning dependence on government.[8]

Reagan's approach was as shrewd as it was disingenuous. He was aware that most Blacks—and many Whites—believed that conservatives lacked credibility on civil rights and saw their economic policies as an assault on the poor. The civil rights struggles of the 1950s and 1960s, led many Whites who didn't identify as liberals take a dim view of politicians tainted by racism. Reagan understood that portraying his policies as consistent with the principles espoused by King would blunt criticism and help him win support for his conservative agenda. His success was limited. He lost battles with civil rights advocates over affirmative action, voting rights, and tax exemptions for religious schools that practiced discrimination. But he and his allies shaped the terms of debate, increasing support for color-blind principles that, during the ensuing 40 years, would gain strength and undermine key victories of the civil rights movement. It was, in a sense, a microcosm of the Reagan Revolution.

## The Reagan "Revolution"

As he assumed the presidency, Reagan's message had changed little since 1964, when he gave the closing argument for Goldwater's candidacy. He believed

---

[7] Martin Luther King, Jr., *Why We Can't Wait* (New York, 1964), 146.
[8] Bostdorff and Goldzwig, "History, Collective Memory, and the Appropriation of Martin Luther King, Jr.," 677.

individual liberty made America great and good; federal power had eroded that liberty and must be curbed; taxes took wealth from those who created it, stunted growth, and must be reduced; America's struggle with communism must end in victory if liberty was to flourish. His message was consistent, and he delivered it in simple, sincere, and compelling language, mostly in a good-natured manner. As he sought the Republican nomination in 1976 and the presidency in 1980, Reagan added moral decline to the list of threats, eager to enlist the support of social conservatives who opposed abortion, gay rights, the ERA, affirmative action, and the Supreme Court's ban on prayer in public schools. His new-found interest in social issues was tactical, however, and never diverted him from his true priorities. Reducing the size and scope of government, lowering taxes, and defeating communism had been his north star for thirty years, and they guided his agenda when he entered the White House in 1981.

Like Franklin Roosevelt, his hero as a young man, an economic crisis smoothed Reagan's path to the presidency. Economic woes made the public and Congress sour on Keynesianism, the economic theory that guided the country's economic policy in the decades following World War II. Keynesians posited that policy makers could end recessions and maintain prosperity through a carefully calibrated combination of tax cuts and increased spending. They would fuel demand which would, in turn, stimulate employment, production, profits, and prosperity. Unfortunately, Keynesianism met its match in stagflation—the combination of high inflation and unemployment—that whipsawed the American economy during the 1970s. Keynesianism lost its allure, and many Americans were drawn to a surging anti-tax movement. Supply side economics, a theory touted by the *Wall Street Journal*, the American Enterprise Institute, and economists such as Paul Craig Roberts and Arthur Laffer lent a patina of academic respectability to the anti-tax crusade. Supply siders argued that lowering taxes while reducing spending was the answer. Steep tax cuts would encourage high earners to work harder, be more creative, invest more, produce more, and hire more employees. That would unleash economic growth, increase productivity, put people back to work, shake the economy out of the doldrums without fueling inflation, and increase government revenues in the long run.

These ideas had natural appeal to Reagan. As a successful actor in the 1940s, he had railed against a top marginal income tax rate of 90% that discouraged him and many of his Hollywood friends from accepting extra work. Not only would sharp cuts be fair to taxpayers—letting them keep more of their income—and boost the economy, they would accomplish another of his goals. Cutting taxes would force government to reduce spending and shrink its activities.

Reagan's team immediately got behind the Kemp-Roth tax cut bill, which had gained support from anti-tax crusaders in the late 1970s. Although Democrats who controlled the House offered stiff resistance, the Reaganites made steady progress during the administration's first months. An assassination attempt on March 30 that nearly took Reagan's life increased support for the popular president. Support swelled when Reagan appeared before Congress in late April to urge adoption of his economic program. Ultimately, more than 40 House Democrats, most of them from the South, bucked party leadership to support a popular president whose anti-tax, anti-government message resonated with their constituents. By July, Reagan could declare victory as Congress adopted a massive tax cut that reduced rates for each tax bracket by 5% in 1982 and 10% each year for the following two years. The bill also indexed tax brackets to inflation beginning in 1985, reduced the top rate on investment income from 70% to 50%, and cut the capital gains tax from 28% to 20%. There was something for low- and middle-income tax payers, but a lot more for the rich. "In order to make this palatable as a political matter, you had to bring down all the brackets," Reagan's budget director David Stockman later wrote. "But, I mean, Kemp-Roth was always a Trojan Horse to bring down the top rates."[9]

Some supply siders argued that the cuts would ultimately increase tax revenues once the economy took off. A few even believed it. However, Reagan and members of Congress knew that budget cuts must accompany tax relief lest the deficit balloon, fueling inflation and driving up interest rates. For Republicans—and especially Reagan—that was good news because cutting the budget would reduce the size of government. The only problem from their perspective was that too much of the budget was spared the knife. Committed to fighting Communism, Reagan insisted on increased defense spending, which was almost one-fourth of the federal budget in 1980. On the campaign trail he promised to raise defense spending 5% per year through 1986, but soon upped the ante, requesting a 7% annual increase. The price tag grew further when Stockman erroneously calculated the increase on base defense spending in the projected 1982 budget rather than the 1980 budget, which had been Reagan's target; the 1982 budget was $80 billion larger, significantly increasing the dollar value of the annual increases. As a result, defense spending grew by an astonishing 10% annually between 1980 and 1986.

---

9 Doug Rossinow, *The Reagan Era: A History of the 1980s* (New York, 2015), 61.

The military was not the only sacred cow. Medicare and Social Security were popular programs that were the third rail of American politics—touch it and you were fried. Reagan hated Social Security and had advocated privatization. However, politically savvy advisors like James Baker, his chief of staff, ultimately pulled him back to political reality. When the budget hawks floated a sharp cut in benefits to workers who chose early retirement—62 rather than 65—shrieks from Republicans as well as Democrats reached the White House. Carol Campbell, a conservative South Carolina Republican "lit into me like a junk yard dog," Stockman recalled. "I've got thousands of sixty-year-old textile workers who think it's the end of the world," Campbell vented. Democrats pounced. "I'm talking about decency," commented House Speaker Tip O'Neil. "It's a rotten thing to do."[10] And bad politics as well. Many early retirees were factory workers whose aging bodies found assembly line work punishing, and some were "Reagan Democrats." So, the President quickly disavowed knowledge of the proposal, taking Social Security and Medicare—about 25% of federal spending—off the table.

When interest payments on the debt were added—another 10% of expenditures—even less was in play, ensuring cuts in targeted areas were deep. Ultimately, the sharpest reductions came in programs that benefited the poor, which Reagan argued were rife with corruption and made recipients dependent on government. Among Republicans and some Democrats sympathy for the poor had declined sharply as the generosity created by the prosperity and optimism of the 1960s shrunk. In the House, where they held a majority, Democrats were, according to Speaker Tip O'Neil, "demoralized, discredited, and broke" and "there would be hell to pay in the mid-term elections" if Democrats appeared obstructionist.[11] With Democratic resistance weakened, Reagan pushed through punishing cuts. Aid to Families with Dependent Children took a 16% hit, and funding for food stamps fell by almost 19%.[12] School lunch programs were slashed; milk servings went from six ounces to four, and schools began to count ketchup and pickle relish as vegetables when calculating the nutritional value of

---

10 Martha Derthick and Steven Teles, "Riding the Third Rail: Social Security Reform," in W. Elliot Brownlee and Hugh Davis Graham, ed., *The Reagan Presidency: Pragmatic Conservatism and Its Legacies* (Lawrence, KS, 2003), 194.
11 Thomas P. O'Neil, *Man of the House* (London, 1987), 338, 344.
12 Sheldon Danziger and Robert Haveman, "The Reagan administration's budget cuts: Their impact on the poor," 15 https://www.irp.wisc.edu/publications/focus/pdfs/foc52b.pdf (accessed January 27, 2023).

meals.¹³ Agencies whose intrusiveness on behalf of workers or the environment drew conservatives' ire also saw sharp cuts.

Deep as they were, the cuts to the most vulnerable and a few regulatory agencies didn't come close to off-setting increased defense spending and decreased tax revenues. The administration took well over half of the budget off the table, and many areas where cuts were possible had defenders more powerful than the poor, so budget deficits swelled, growing from $74 billion in 1980 to $208 billion in 1983.

Eager to shrink government's reach—defense excepted, of course—Reagan also championed deregulation, promising to remove the "red tape" that increased the cost of doing business. Ford and Carter had taken aim at federal regulation in the trucking and airline industries. In those sectors, business—and in the case of trucking, labor—had captured the regulatory agencies and created rules that reduced service and kept prices artificially high. So, deregulation brought benefits to consumers. It also strengthened the conservative narrative that free markets produced the best outcomes and government intervention made things worse. Reagan and his lieutenants didn't need to be convinced. They quickly persuaded Congress to lift regulations that limited interest rates banks and savings and loan institutions (S&Ls) could pay on deposits to help them compete for funds as inflation raged. They also ended rules that prevented S&Ls—established to invest customers' deposits in home mortgages—from financing commercial real estate.

Aside from banking, Reagan didn't target specific industries for deregulation. Instead, he used his control of the federal agencies to reduce the regulatory burden. Most federal regulations aren't established by Congress. Rather, Congress typically legislates broad objectives and delegates authority to administrative agencies like the EPA to create detailed rules necessary to achieve them. Once established, regulations are subject to review, change, and repeal in light of changing circumstances—or a new president. Reagan acted decisively, reversing many regulations businesses found objectionable. He also used the 1980 Paperwork Reduction Act—which tasked the Office of Management and Budget (OMB) with ensuring that agencies did not require businesses to file unnecessary forms—to create a chokehold on new regulations. OMB defined those regulations whose costs outweighed their benefits as "unnecessary." It was a standard that his administration asserted could be

---

13 *New York Times*, September 26, 1981 https://www.nytimes.com/1981/09/26/politics/reagan-abandons-proposal-to-pare-school-nutrition.html (accessed January 27, 2023).

calculated objectively, although the assumptions that determined the result were subjective. Not surprisingly, businesses resisting new regulations found the cost-benefit requirement a godsend, allowing them to block new rules.

While Reagan used his muscle to advance his economic and defense agendas, social conservatives received moral support. Reagan backed measures championed by Senator Jesse Helms, a conservative North Carolina Republican, to reverse the Supreme Court's ban on prayer in public schools and support for abortion. Both failed, however, facing opposition from most Democrats and some Republicans. Beginning in 1985, Reagan addressed Washington's annual March for Life rally via telephone, demanding that *Roe v. Wade* be overturned. However, actions spoke louder than words. When he had his first opportunity to name a Supreme Court justice, in 1982, he appointed Sandra Day O'Connor, the Court's first woman. She was a supporter of the ERA who, as a conservative committed to precedent, was disinclined to overturn *Roe*. He followed a similar course on civil rights, denouncing affirmative action, opposing changes to the Voting Rights Act that made it easier for minorities to elect candidates of their choice, and supporting the right of private religious schools to retain tax-exempt status even when they discriminated. Here again, while his rhetoric reassured conservatives, Reagan failed to produce results. He signed legislation creating the King holiday and a more muscular Voting Rights Act that wouldn't expire until 2007. Indeed, the new version of the voting law included provisions supported by civil rights groups that required states and localities to create election districts that maximized Blacks' opportunity to elect candidates of their choice. Reagan was surprisingly candid about where social issues fell among his priorities. In 1982, when asked if they were "adornments [...] filigree so to speak," the President answered, "Yes."[14] Social issues continued to roil the waters and attract support from the Republican Party's right wing, but conservatives had limited success in advancing their social agenda. Failure had its benefits; issues that rallied the base remained weapons to brandish against Democrats, and Democrats could appeal to fear of the damage religious zealots on the right threatened.

Plagued by stagflation, the country entered the sharpest recession in 50 years in July 1981, just as the administration was celebrating its victory on taxes. Fed chair Paul Volker, determined to end inflation once and for all, gave Reagan a dose of the tight money treatment he had given Carter. Manufacturing and construction were hit hard, and unemployment spiked to almost 10% by

---

14 Rossinow, *The Reagan Era*, 31.

mid-1982, as the mid-term elections neared.[15] Misery spread across the country, and deep cuts to the social safety net made it worse. Reagan's own apparent lack of empathy hurt his standing. Frustrated by stories portraying the plight of individuals who lost their jobs, he peevishly asked a reporter, "Is it news that some fellow out in South Succotash someplace has just been laid off, that he should be interviewed nationwide?"[16] By late 1982, Reagan's approval rating dropped to around 40%,[17] and Republicans took a licking in the midterms, losing 26 seats in the House.

The recession reduced revenues further, producing staggering budget deficits that worried congressional leaders in both parties. Reagan recommended more budget cuts, principally to Medicaid and AFDC, but Democrats and even many Republicans pushed back. With Reagan weakened, House Democrats resisted steep cuts and demanded tax increases. Ultimately, Reagan swallowed the bitter pill and agreed to $100 billion in new taxes over the ensuing three years. The 1982 tax increase was the beginning of the end of the "Reagan Revolution," at least in domestic policy.

Insolvency loomed for Social Security. The system relied on taxes from current workers and their employers to pay benefits of retirees, with the surplus invested in a trust fund to pay benefits when baby boomers retired and the ratio of retirees to workers increased. By the early 1980s, however, the system was in trouble and could only be salvaged by an increase in payroll taxes or cuts in benefits. Reagan, never a fan of Social Security, preferred cuts, but realized that recommending them would further weaken him politically. So, he did what presidents faced with intractable problems often do—he appointed a bi-partisan commission to make recommendations. When the commission stalled, the administration, desperate to avoid holding the bag should the system collapse, engaged a small group of Democratic and Republican congressional leaders and cobbled together a compromise to save the system. The legislation achieved savings by deferring payment of cost-of-living increases from July 1983 to January 1984 (with all future increases taking effect in January). It also raised the age at which retirees could collect full benefits to 67 but not until 2027.

---

15  U.S. Bureau of Labor Statistics, "Monthly Unemployment Rate, 1948-Present," https://data.bls.gov/timeseries/LNS14000000?years_option=all_years (accessed January 27, 2023).
16  Rossinow, *The Reagan Era*, 93.
17  Gallup, "Presidential Approval Ratings—Gallup Historical Statistics and Trends" https://news.gallup.com/poll/116677/Presidential-Approval-Ratings-Gallup-Historical-Statistics-Trends.aspx (accessed January 27, 2023).

It increased revenue by accelerating payroll tax increases previously agreed to, taxing the Social Security benefits of high-income recipients, and including new federal employees in the system. While the outcome was a far cry from Reagan's vision when he entered the White House, his embrace of compromise was a testament to his pragmatism, his political foes' willingness to negotiate, and a critical mass of moderate Republicans in Congress.

Republicans' pragmatism also led to a bi-partisan overhaul of the tax system. The work began in 1984, driven by growing concern about the deficit and Democrats' success in identifying Reagan as a tool of the wealthy who sold out blue-collar voters who had supported him. Reagan's opponent in 1984 was Walter Mondale, Hubert Humphrey's protégé and an unapologetic defender of the Great Society. Mondale charged that Reagan took from working Americans to give to the rich, but he did not make tax equity a core issue of his campaign. Instead, he accepted the conservative narrative that high deficits were dangerous and positioned himself as a truth-teller. Promising to bring the deficit under control, Mondale painted the President as a shifty Washington insider. "It must be done[...]," he said, "Mr. Reagan will raise taxes, and so will I. He won't tell you. I just did."[18] It didn't work. The recession was over, inflation was under control, unemployment fell, and the Reagan campaign ran gauzy television ads showing the sun rising on happy Americans starting their day and proclaiming, "It's morning again in America." Reagan swept to victory with 59% of the popular vote and a crushing 525–13 electoral vote majority.

Yet Regan's advisors persuaded him to stay the course on tax reform. As his advisors refined a plan and negotiated with Republicans and Democrats on Capitol Hill, Reagan stumped the country. In places like Oshkosh, Wisconsin, a blue-collar Midwestern town, he articulated the goal, "a dramatic simplification that eliminates loopholes and makes the tax system straightforward, fair for all."[19] As the bill moved through the House, where Democrats held the majority, Republicans abandoned the President. Speaker Tip O'Neil demanded that Reagan deliver at least 50 Republican votes for the package, prompting Reagan's team to work the phones to meet O'Neil's demand. When it finally became law in 1986, the Tax Reform Act addressed concerns of liberals and conservatives. For the former, it increased the standard deduction and personal exemptions (including for children), which disproportionately benefitted low and middle-income Americans.

---

18 H.W. Brands, *Reagan: The Life* (New York, 2015), 453.
19 Brands, *Reagan*, 541.

The bill also increased the earned income tax credit, which put money back in the pockets of the working poor, and increased the capital gains tax rate for the wealthy. Equally important for liberals, it closed many tax loopholes and shelters. For conservatives, the law further reduced marginal tax rates, especially at the highest levels, and lowered corporate tax rates.

Immigration was another contested issue resolved through compromise. In the 1970s and '80s immigration spiked as the Immigration Act of 1965 raised the number who could enter the country each year. Because the vast majority of the new arrivals were Hispanic and Asian, the newcomers changed the nation's ethnic and cultural landscape. In the two decades after 1970, almost 12 million immigrants entered the U.S. legally,[20] and perhaps another 250,000 per year came illegally[21]. Hispanics, mostly Mexicans, dominated but large numbers also came from Vietnam, China, India, and other parts of Asia. Because the 1965 law privileged family reunification, those who were successful in entering often sponsored relatives. Most were unskilled, although many were well educated and possessed degrees in science, engineering, and medicine. Employers welcomed both groups. The unskilled took poorly paid jobs in agriculture, meatpacking, hotels and motels, restaurants, nursing homes, and hospitals that most Americans found unattractive. Those with skills took hard-to-fill positions in the growing high technology sector, hospitals, and universities. Many Americans applauded the new arrivals for opening restaurants that brought more exciting dining options to big cities and even small towns, where Chinese restaurants became common.

Not everyone was happy, however. With many Americans struggling to make ends meet in a bifurcated recovery, some saw the newcomers as competitors for jobs, or surplus labor that held down the wages of unskilled Americans. But the loudest cries came from those who feared that the new arrivals would undermine shared national values by bringing with them a proliferation of languages, cultural practices, and religions. Schools in communities with significant immigrant populations developed bilingual education programs to help immigrant children adapt, not to keep them from learning English. To a growing number of citizens, however, bilingualism was the first step toward a polyglot, disunited states. That included Democrats as well as Republicans.

---

20 Macrotrends, "U.S. Immigration Statistics, 1960–2023" https://www.macrotrends.net/countries/USA/united-states/immigration-statistics (accessed January 27, 2023).
21 "Why Immigrants Were Given Legal Status by Ronald Reagan," *Newsweek*, August 3, 1986 https://www.newsweek.com/reagan-immigration-reform-and-control-act-1986-641806 (accessed January 27, 2023).

Richard Lamm, Colorado's Democratic governor, insisted that English was the country's "social glue" and demanded policies that would ensure that the country was "a rainbow but not a cacophony."[22] In 1986, Californians approved, overwhelmingly, a ballot initiative recognizing English as the state's official language and requiring public officials to ensure its role as the state's common language. While the measure's text was vague and had few practical consequences, it signaled unease. Before the decade ended, 17 states followed California's lead.

In the face of growing discord, Senator Alan Simpson, a Wyoming Republican, and Representative Romano Mazzoli, a Kentucky Democrat, developed legislation that would provide illegals a path to citizenship while controlling the borders. Their bill strengthened border control and established penalties for employers who knowingly hired undocumented workers; it also offered amnesty to all who had been in the U.S. since 1982. Employers feared an additional layer of regulation and penalties for honest mistakes, and civil libertarians worried that the bill would open the way for national identity cards that might erode privacy. However, the law's weak enforcement provisions calmed employers, and Simpson and Mazzoli secured Reagan's backing. When it passed in 1986, Reagan hailed the law as "a bipartisan effort" that would "remove the incentives for illegal immigration by eliminating the jobs" which attracted illegals while improving "the lives of [...] individuals who now must hide in the shadows."[23] Republicans and Democrats disagreed sharply on many issues, but they could still get stuff done.

## Fighting Communism Abroad

If Reagan's approach to domestic policy could be flexible, he was unwavering in his determination to curb Soviet power. The President's visceral anti-communism and hatred of the Soviet Union grew from the same soil as his commitment to individual liberty, low taxes, and small government. As he assumed the presidency, he believed that the Soviets had gained the upper hand because of Nixon's détente policy, the nation's post-Vietnam bout of self-doubt, and Watergate-induced erosion of presidential authority.

---

22 *New York Times*, July 21, 1986 https://www.nytimes.com/1986/07/21/us/debates-growing-on-use-of-english.html?searchResultPosition=6 (accessed March 27, 2022).
23 Ronald Reagan, "Statement on Signing the Immigration Reform and Control Act of 1986," November 7, 1986 https://www.reaganlibrary.gov/archives/speech/statement-signing-immigration-reform-and-control-act-1986 (accessed March 27, 2022).

He was convinced—incorrectly—that the Soviets had gained superiority in nuclear weapons and saw their influence in terrorist activity in countries from Libya to Lebanon as well as in revolutionary movements closer to home in the Caribbean and Central America. To regain the upper hand, Reagan was determined to reclaim presidential authority over foreign policy, use it to restore U.S. supremacy, and take bold action against an adversary he labelled "the evil empire."[24]

In addition to a massive defense build-up, Reagan chose to flex U.S. muscle against the communist threat he perceived close to home. In El Salvador, a brutal right-wing dictatorship led by Roberto D'Aubuisson deployed death squads to gun down civilians suspected of supporting leftist rebels. Reagan's team brushed away criticism, arguing that D'Aubuisson was all that stood in the way of a communist takeover. The administration persuaded Congress to provide over $700 million in military aid to the regime between 1981 and 1983. Leftists were totalitarians who would never change their ways, Reaganites argued, while right wing dictators were merely authoritarians who would mellow with time, U.S. influence, and the defeat of their communist opponents. Critics saw it as a distinction without a difference.

Nicaragua's Samoza dictatorship, which the U.S. had supported for decades, showed no signs of mellowing. It had clung to power through violence and corruption until it was overthrown by leftist Sandinista rebels in 1979. Fearing that Nicaragua would become another Cuba, Reagan secured financial support from Congress for Contra rebels who operated against the new government from neighboring El Salvador and Honduras. When congressional Democrats restricted and, in 1984, barred U.S. funding for the rebels, the administration doubled down. It developed an elaborate plan to use money from an arms-for-American-hostages deal with Iran to supply the Contras. Reagan's willingness to violate the law, cut a deal with a prime sponsor of terrorism, and renege on a pledge never to bargain with hostage-takers underscored his anti-communist fervor.

Threats also lurked in the Middle East. The 1973 Yom Kippur War as well as the Iranian Revolution and Soviet invasion of Afghanistan in 1979 elevated the oil-rich region to the top of U.S. security concerns. Reagan's goal was to support Israel, Egypt, and Saudi Arabia, key allies, and

---

24 Andrew Glass, "Reagan brands Soviet Union 'evil empire,'" March 8, 1983," *Politico*, March 8, 2018 https://www.politico.com/story/2018/03/08/this-day-in-politics-march-8-1983-440258 (accessed January 27, 2023).

check Soviet clients like Syria and Libya. He and his advisors also wanted to contain terrorist groups intent on undermining U.S allies, destabilizing the region, and threatening the flow of oil. Tiny Lebanon produced no oil and was poor. Torn by civil war, it offered Hezbollah, a Syrian-backed terrorist group, a base of operations from which to attack Israel. Hezbollah's mayhem triggered Israeli incursions which, in turn, escalated violence, spread instability, and, in Reagan's eyes, served Soviet interests. The U.S., along with France, sent troops to Lebanon to restore stability. It was a fool's errand. In April 1983, a truck loaded with explosives drove into the U.S. embassy in Beirut where it exploded, killing 63 people. Five months later 241 Marines died when a truck bomb detonated near their barracks. Shaken by these events, Reagan quietly withdrew U.S. forces.

Anti-communist initiatives in the Caribbean and Middle East were secondary to Reagan's top concern—ending Soviet nuclear superiority. Convinced that the Russians had used arms limitation treaties to their advantage, he refused to seek Senate ratification of the arms control treaty Carter had negotiated or enter new talks. Instead, he relentlessly expanded the U.S. arsenal, revived production of the B-1 bomber, which Carter had halted, and deployed a new generation of intermediate range nuclear weapons in Europe. Fear of nuclear war among Americans reached levels not seen since the Cuban Missile Crisis. Support for a nuclear freeze swelled, bringing over a million demonstrators to New York City's Central Park in June 1982. Reagan pushed back, charging that freeze advocates were doing the Soviets' bidding. In March 1983, he announced a costly, futuristic new program called the Strategic Defense Initiative. SDI would deploy lasers and other high-tech weapons in space to create an impregnable defense that could destroy missiles launched by the Soviets before they could strike their targets. More science fiction than science, SDI drew jeers from critics who dubbed it Star Wars after the popular movie fantasy portraying a battle between good and evil in outer space. Nevertheless, in the high-stakes world of nuclear rivalry, SDI frightened the Soviets and was destabilizing. Wouldn't the Soviets deploy even more missiles to have a greater chance that at least some would get through? Fearing SDI's deployment, wouldn't they be more inclined to launch a pre-emptive attack?

Pursuit of an ill-conceived anti-missile shield didn't preclude negotiations with the Soviets to reduce or even eliminate nuclear weapons—although it did complicate them. Mutually Assured Destruction—the idea that large stockpiles of nuclear weapons prevented war by making its consequences unthinkable—had long dominated strategic thinking in the U.S. and Soviet

Union. But keeping the world on the brink of destruction made no sense to Reagan. The ultimate goal for the U.S., he believed, was not parity with the Soviets, but reduction and ultimately elimination of nuclear weapons. That could only happen safely if the U.S. were in the driver's seat. By 1984, Reagan believed that his defense build-up had restored U.S. superiority, creating a favorable environment for negotiations. There were also political considerations. As the election approached, he wished to shed his image as a warmonger. Reagan premiered his new role when he addressed the U.N. General Assembly in September 1984. Acknowledging that "there is no sane alternative to negotiations on arms control," he announced that the U.S. was "ready for constructive negotiations with the Soviet Union." The goal was "to reduce—and eventually eliminate—the threat and use of force in solving international disputes." The man who had denounced the Soviet Union as the "evil empire" now asked that the two nations "approach each other with ten-fold trust and thousand-fold affection."[25]

A historic change in Soviet leadership called Reagan—and raised him. Mikhail Gorbachev, a 54-year-old reformer focused on domestic issues, became general secretary of the Communist Party of the Soviet Union two months after Reagan's second term began in 1985. Aware that Soviet economic survival required deep cuts in defense spending, Gorbachev immediately pressed for a summit and announced a unilateral end to nuclear testing. Quickly, the two leaders became a kind of travelling show. They met in Geneva in late 1985 and in Iceland in October 1986 before appearing together in Washington in late 1987 and Moscow in May 1988. Despite the headlines, drama, and glimpses of the personal relationship that developed between the two men, the show tantalized but failed to deliver a dazzling finale. On several occasions the two leaders came close to agreement on sharp reductions or even a deal to eliminate ballistic missiles altogether. But Reagan's dogged refusal to yield on SDI brought progress to a halt. When Reagan left office in January 1989, the only thing he and Gorbachev had to show for their trouble was an agreement to eliminate all land-based, intermediate range missiles—the weapons the two sides had pointed at each other in Europe and Asia. It broke new ground by eliminating rather than limiting an entire class of weapons, but the bulk of the U.S. and Soviet arsenals were untouched.

---

25 Ronald Reagan, "Address by President Ronald Reagan to the U.N. General Assembly, September 24, 1984," https://2009-2017.state.gov/p/io/potusunga/207336.htm (accessed April 14, 2022).

## Winners and Losers

As tensions with the Soviets subsided, the economic divide in the U.S. grew. The Reagan economic boom brought great wealth to some but left many struggling. The great divide was apparent in once-prosperous industrial cities and towns where factories closed, small towns in the Midwest where many local businesses shuttered, and in Manhattan, Boston, Atlanta, Los Angeles, Palo Alto, Ann Arbor, Austin and many other cities and towns where prosperity reigned. If one drove from inner city Detroit or Flint where closed factories bred despair to prosperous suburbs like Bloomfield Hills, Royal Oak, and Grosse Pointe or a bustling university town like Ann Arbor, she could experience the divide in an afternoon.

As the nation climbed out of recession in 1983, the post-war shift from an industrial to an information economy accelerated. Manufacturing jobs declined from 18.2 million on the eve of Reagan's election to 17.4 million in 1990,[26] where they would remain until the 2000s, when they plunged more sharply. Automation played a role but so did competition from Japanese companies whose superior management, technology, and quality—combined with government policies that subsidized exports—allowed them to beat the pants off American firms in steel, autos, and consumer electronics. Workers lost union jobs that paid middle-class wages and young people graduating from high school found plans to follow their parents' footsteps dashed. Jobs that paid good wages to unskilled high school graduates were few and far between. Shuttered factories brought blight, declining populations, and shrinking tax bases to factory towns and cities. Between 1970 and 1990, Gary, Indiana's population fell from 178, 000 to 120,000, Milwaukee, Wisconsin from 717,000 to 628,000, Pittsburgh from 520,000 to 369,000, and Toledo, Ohio from 383,000 to 332,000.

Because union membership was concentrated in industry, the labor movement suffered. In the mid-1950s, unions represented 35% of private-sector workers in the U.S. That proportion declined steadily thereafter, but accelerated, falling from 20% in 1980 to 12% in 1990.[27] Public employees were the only group of workers who made significant strides in unionizing, but those gains were offset by losses in manufacturing and unions' failure to organize service

---

[26] FRED Economic Data, "All Employees, Manufacturing" https://fred.stlouisfed.org/series/MANEMP (accessed January 27, 2023).

[27] Lawrence Mishel, Lynn Rhinehart, and Lane Windham, "Explaining the erosion of private sector unions," November 18, 2020 https://www.epi.org/unequalpower/publications/private-sector-unions-corporate-legal-erosion/ (accessed January 27, 2023).

workers. Reagan's handling of the 1981 air traffic controllers strike also took a toll. When the controllers struck in a bid for raises that would keep pace with inflation, Reagan reminded them that federal law forbade them to strike and ordered them to return to work or lose their jobs. When they persisted, the President ordered replacements hired and refused to allow strikers rehired. "They made their bed and they can sleep in it," he commented.[28] Private sector employers took note and became much more aggressive in dealing with their workers.

The 1980s and '90s were hard on rural America as well. Agriculture was the backbone of rural communities that stretched across the Midwest, South, and Great Plains. Since the end of World War II, the number of farms had steadily declined while their average size grew. More sophisticated and expensive farm machinery as well as increased use of commercial fertilizers allowed farmers to increase the size of their operations and yields. Increasingly, they specialized in a few crops and were less likely to raise hogs, chickens, or cattle. That was being done at scale by producers who contracted with corporations like Tyson Foods to process chickens and distribute them to supermarkets. With fewer farms, farm population declining, and an expanded highway network making access to nearby cities easier, businesses in small towns floundered. Wal-Mart expanded, bringing cheap products to small towns across the South, Great Plains, and Midwest and forcing many small retailers to close. That left small towns with shuttered store-fronts where hardware, clothing, jewelry, and furniture stores once flourished. Young people with high school diplomas or less found jobs that would support a family elusive, and those with college degrees had no reason to return home.

As if the steady erosion of small-town America weren't bad enough, the economic tsunami of the early 1980s made matters worse. High interest rates made tractors, combines, and trucks even more expensive, and rising energy and fertilizer prices drove up production costs. At the same time, the price of agricultural commodities fell, thanks to a grain embargo Jimmy Carter imposed on Russia in the wake of its invasion of Afghanistan and Reagan kept in place. Farmers who mortgaged their land to finance equipment and expanded operations, struggled. Exposed themselves, banks foreclosed mortgages and in some cases were themselves forced into bankruptcy. The Farm Home Administration (FHA), which backed farm mortgages, foreclosed on almost 15,000 properties between 1988 and 1990. With their

---

28 Rossinow, *Reagan Era*, 86.

144    THE PATH TO PARALYSIS

customers suffering, small town car and farm machinery dealerships reeled, and many went bankrupt.

The new economy produced winners as well as losers. The demand for highly skilled workers, managers, executives, and innovators increased demand for higher education. American colleges and universities had experienced explosive growth in the 1960s, and they continued to expand, even as the baby boom tapered off. Between 1970 and the end of the century, the number of bachelors degrees awarded increased by about 50%,[29] while the number of graduate degrees grew even faster. Between 1970 and 2000, the number of masters and doctoral degrees conferred doubled.[30] Employment at colleges and universities grew apace. Between 1970 and 1990, faculty nearly doubled and professional staff grew slightly more rapidly.[31] University endowments—private and public—grew from $11 billion in 1970 to $68 billion in the ensuing twenty years.[32] Growing federal research funding also bolstered university budgets. The National Science Foundation (NSF) budget grew from a little more than a half billion dollars in 1970 to about $4 billion in 2000,[33] while the national Institutes of Health (NIH) rose from $1 billion in 1970 to $18 billion in 2000.[34]

---

29 National Center for Education Statistics, "Bachelor's degrees conferred by postsecondary institutions, by field of study: Selected years, 1970–71 through 2016–17" https://nces.ed.gov/programs/digest/d18/tables/dt18_322.10.asp (accessed January 27, 2023).
30 National Center for Education Statistics, "Master's degrees conferred by postsecondary institutions, by field of study: Selected years, 1970–71 through 2016–17" https://nces.ed.gov/programs/digest/d18/tables/dt18_323.10.asp (accessed January 27, 2023); National Center for Education Statistics, "Doctor's degrees conferred by postsecondary institutions, by field of study: Selected years, 1970–71 through 2016–17" https://nces.ed.gov/programs/digest/d18/tables/dt18_324.10.asp (accessed January 27, 2023).
31 National Center for Educational Statistics, "Number of faculty in degree-granting postsecondary institutions, by employment status, sex, control, and level of institution: Selected years, fall 1970 through fall 2017," https://nces.ed.gov/programs/digest/d18/tables/dt18_315.10.asp (accessed January 27, 2023).
32 National Center for Educational Statistics, *120 Years of American Education: A Statistical Portrait* (Washington, D.C., 1993), 92 https://nces.ed.gov/pubs93/93442.pdf (accessed January 27, 2023).
33 *Twentieth Annual Report of the National Science Foundation, 1970*, Appendix C (Financial Report for Fiscal Year 1970) https://www.nsf.gov/pubs/1970/annualreports/ar_1970_appendix_c.pdf (accessed January 27, 2023); National Science Foundation, *Accountability Report FY 2000*, "Financial Statements: Statements of Budgetary Resources" https://www.nsf.gov/pubs/2001/nsf0183/pages/budres.html (accessed January 27, 2023).
34 National Institutes of Health, *NIH Almanac: Appropriations* https://www.nih.gov/about-nih/what-we-do/nih-almanac/appropriations-section-2 (accessed January 27, 2023).

The envy of the world, American universities drew students from across the globe. Enrollment by international students grew by 76% between 1980 and 2000, bringing with it intellectual capital and, in many cases, tuition.[35]

University towns boomed, even in rural states. Between 1970 and 2000, Iowa City, Iowa grew by almost 30%, Manhattan, Kansas by 62%, Clemson, South Carolina by almost 80%, and Athens, Georgia by 126%. Universities also became economic drivers in cities like Boston, Columbus, Ohio, Raleigh-Durham, North Carolina, Austin, Texas, and Seattle, Washington. They were home to many relatively affluent young people, a large proportion of their employees were well-paid professionals, and businesses that relied on a highly skilled workforce often located in them. They not only supported student bars and eateries but upscale and chain restaurants, shopping malls, specialty shops, theaters, and middle and upper-middle-class housing. University towns in rural states were worlds apart—materially and culturally—from struggling farming communities close-by.

Health care also experienced explosive growth. During the post-war era, health insurance became a standard benefit in contracts private and public employers negotiated with their unions and extended to salaried white-collar and professional employees. In the 1960s, the federal government expanded medical coverage to the elderly and poor through Medicare and Medicaid. At the same time, private companies and the federal government made substantial investments in research and development that produced new drugs, more powerful diagnostic tools (e.g., CT Scanners, Magnetic Resonance Imaging machines, and ultrasound scanners), and innovative procedures that were expensive but extended and improved life. Between 1974 and 2010, U.S. patents for drugs, diagnostic tools, and surgical innovations increased six-fold.[36] Insurance paid for the new interventions and therapies, while encouraging companies and agencies like NIH to invest in additional research that developed yet more sophisticated (and expensive) tools and techniques. It was the medical

---

35 National Center for Education Statistics, "Foreign students enrolled in institutions of higher education in the United States, by continent, region, and selected countries of origin: Selected years, 1980–81 through 2017–18" https://nces.ed.gov/programs/digest/d18/tables/dt18_310.20.asp (accessed January 27, 2023).

36 Victor R. Fuchs, "Major Trends in the U.S. Health Economy since 1950," *New England Journal of Medicine*, March 15, 2012 https://www.nejm.org/doi/pdf/10.1056/NEJMp1200478?articleTools=true#:~:text=Major%20Trends%20in%20the%20U.S.%20Health%20Economy%20since,in%20health%20care%20expenditures%20fueled%20by%20private%20and (accessed February 26, 2023).

equivalent of the arms race, except, of course, that it saved rather than threatened lives. Not surprisingly, health care became one of the fastest growing areas of the economy, increasing from 5% of GDP in 1960 to 13.3% in 2000.[37] Manufacturing, by comparison, held steady at approximately 12% during these years.

The growth of health care created new opportunities. Pharmaceutical companies and firms that developed and manufactured medical equipment flourished. They also provided employment to scientists, engineers, executives, managers, marketing and sales staff, and skilled and unskilled workers. The ranks of medical professionals grew rapidly; the number of physicians increased by 91% and the number of nurses by 75% between 1980 and 1998.[38] The number of radiologists, phlebotomists, lab technicians, pharmacists, and physical and occupational therapists also grew rapidly, and hospitals and physicians' practices hired legions of accountants, clerical staff, cleaners, and food service workers. Medical centers became economic drivers in cities like Houston, Cleveland, New York City, Boston and Atlanta, and hospitals in smaller cities and towns were among their communities' largest employers.

The 1980s and '90s were the dawn of the "tech" revolution. During World War II, government and university researchers developed computers that processed and analyzed large amounts of data. In the decades after the war, companies like IBM expanded their power, and software engineers developed programs that enabled mainframe computers to process data that was the lifeblood of government, businesses, insurance, hospitals, engineering, and science. By the early 1980s, Apple, IBM, and dozens of small startups were putting "personal" computers on desks across the country, bringing word processing, graphic design, spreadsheets, and programs that calculated one's taxes to the masses. This explosion of computing fueled a demand for software engineers. Bill Gates's Micro-Soft became one of the country's most innovative and successful companies by offering software for a growing personal computer market, and computer services companies like Ross Perot's Electronic Data Services provided access to mainframes, programming, and data management expertise to government, manufacturing, health care, and insurance.

---

37 Statistia, "U.S. national health expenditure as percent of GDP from 1960 to 2021" https://www.statista.com/statistics/184968/us-health-expenditure-as-percent-of-gdp-since-1960/ (accessed January 27, 2023).

38 U.S. Census Bureau, *Statistical Abstract of the United States, 2000*, 122–23 https://www.census.gov/library/publications/2000/compendia/statab/120ed.html (accessed January 27, 2023).

Other high-tech innovations opened new opportunities for consumers, investors, and job seekers. Cable television expanded Americans' viewing options beyond three commercial networks and PBS, bringing sports, re-runs of movies and TV classics, niche entertainment, and the 24–7 news cycle to living rooms across the country. Content producers like CNN, ESPN, and many others hired creative, technical, and professional staff as well as armies of gophers while service providers in cities across the country employed technicians, clerical staff, accountants, and others to bring service into peoples' homes. Videocassette recorders (VCRs) freed consumers from the TV schedule and created a market for retailers like Blockbuster that rented movies for home-viewing. While most VCRs were manufactured abroad, they brought customers to electronics stores and video rental businesses in communities across the U.S. By the mid-1990s, cell phones were offering what seemed to be the ultimate in untethered communication and created demand for companies that manufactured phones, built transmission towers, and opened stores to serve eager consumers.

Finance produced the recovery's biggest winners. At the dawn of the '80s, the stock market continued a decade of sharp decline, and financial institutions were battered by inflation. With interest rates on deposits limited by law, banks found it hard to compete for capital with new investment tools like mutual funds. Large commercial banks also chafed under New Deal laws that barred them—as institutions whose depositors the government insured against loss—from the far riskier work of investment banks—underwriting corporate stocks, bonds, and other securities. S&Ls, which had their funds tied up in home mortgages that had been negotiated when interest rates were low, found themselves paying higher rates on deposits—which they needed to stay afloat—than the returns they received on loans. Many teetered on the brink of insolvency. Congress came to the rescue. In 1980, it increased insurance on deposits from $40,000 to $100,000 and lifted restrictions on interest rates banks and S&Ls could offer depositors. Two years later, it allowed S&Ls to make loans on commercial real estate. In 1987, the Fed permitted commercial banks to underwrite municipal bonds, commercial paper issued by corporations, and securities backed by mortgages. With the recovery accelerating in 1983, these changes enticed many financial institutions to make high risk, high reward investments that generated handsome profits.

Investment banks like Goldman Sachs, Drexel Burnham Lambert, and Merrill Lynch turned head-spinning profits. Corporate restructuring through mergers and acquisitions spiked during the mid-1980s and again after 1992. This whirlwind of activity generated handsome underwriting fees as well as profits from loans that financed the acquisitions. Those who orchestrated or financed the mergers claimed that they would make companies stronger through synergies among the firms brought together as well as more effective management. In many cases that was true, but too often corporate raiders financed the mergers with borrowed money, saddling the new firms with debt, siphoning off their cash reserves, plundering pension plans, selling off the most profitable parts of the company, and leaving closed factories and unemployed workers in their wake. But the rewards could be huge. Firms like Drexel Burnham Lambert logged staggering profits from junk bonds that carried high interest rates and facilitated risky deals. Drexel's junk bond master, Michael Milken, earned over $500 million in 1987 alone. When the market tanked in 1987, however, the firm was forced into bankruptcy and Milken went to jail for insider trading.

Before World War II, only the well-heeled invested in stocks, bonds, and other financial instruments. That changed in the post-war period. Union and public employee pension funds became big players; they were joined in the 1970s by millions of middle-class investors who made tax deductible contributions to Individual Retirement Accounts (IRAs) and turned to companies like Edward Jones that managed small investors' money. The financial industry developed a dizzying array of investment vehicles to reap solid returns for investors and handsome rewards for themselves. Mutual funds allowed investors to put their money in a diversified portfolio of stocks, bonds, and other securities managed by professionals who promised strong returns. Once the preserve of the wealthy, the number of funds and size of their holdings exploded in the 1970s and kept growing. By 1999, there were almost 8,000 mutual funds managing $6.8 trillion of assets.[39] Using computers and sophisticated modelling to forecast trends, investment firms generated eye-popping returns for themselves and their clients.

Credit cards, which grew in popularity in the 1970s, became a necessity for most Americans in the 1980s and 1990s. Banks marketed them by direct mail to adults and even to college students. Consumers could splurge on vacations, clothing, and other consumer goods, and if they couldn't pay their monthly balance, they could chip away at it over time. Of course, indulging desires came with a price tag; consumers paid interest rates approaching 20% per year on balances. As credit card debt climbed from $2 billion in 1968 to

---

39 Investment Company Institute, "U.S. Mutual Fund Developments in 1999" https://www.ici.org/system/files/attachments/2000_factbook.pdf (accessed January 27, 2023).

$620 billion in 2000,[40] banks and credit card clearing houses like Master Card and Visa reaped huge rewards.

Of course, there were downs as well as ups. Many S&Ls engaged in highly speculative commercial real estate loans that fed a bubble that burst in 1987, resulting in insolvency for hundreds of institutions. Depositors' accounts were insured by the Federal Savings and Loan Insurance Corporation, but losses far exceeded its assets, forcing Congress to provide $100 billion to resolve the mess in 1989. Many called it a classic case of moral hazard: institutions that made speculative investments were bailed out by taxpayers. It seemed like socialism for the rich, supported by politicians who received favors and campaign contributions from those who benefitted. The S&L crisis helped trigger a 22% plunge in the Stock market on October 22, 1987, the sharpest one-day drop in history. However, markets recovered and the good times continued to roll as the stock market resumed its surge in May 1988.

Many called it the New Gilded Age.[41] Those on top did very well. Between the 1940s and the early 1970s, real income doubled for those at the bottom, middle, and top of the country's income pyramid. Beginning in the late 1970s, the rich saw their incomes explode while most other groups experienced sluggish growth. Between 1980 and 2000, the income of the top 1% of households climbed by more than 200% while those in the next 19% rose by about 50% and those in the middle 60% grew by only 25%,[42] even though more families relied on two earners. Income also became more concentrated. Between 1930 and 1970, the share of income going to the top 10% fell from 45% to 34%, but by 2000 that had changed, with the top 10% claiming 48% of all income.[43]

The biggest winners were those in finance and corporate leadership, where the average pay of CEOs (adjusted for inflation) climbed from $1.2 million

---

40 Thomas A. Durkin, "Credit Cards: Use and Consumer Attitudes, 1970–2000," *Federal Reserve Bulletin* (September 2000), 623 https://www.federalreserve.gov/pubs/bulletin/2000/0900lead.pdf (accessed January 28, 2023).

41 Kevin Phillips, *The Politics of Rich and Poor: Wealth and the Electorate in the Reagan Aftermath* (New York, 1990).

42 Chad Stone, Danilo Trisi, Arloc Sherman, Jennifer Beltran, "A Guide to Statistics on Historical Trends in Income Inequality," Center on Budget and Policy Priorities, January 13, 2020 https://www.cbpp.org/research/poverty-and-inequality/a-guide-to-statistics-on-historical-trends-in-income-inequality (accessed January 28, 2023).

43 Thomas Piketty and Emanuel Saenz, "Inequality in the Long Run," *Science*, 344 (May 2014), 838.

in 1978 to $22.2 million in 2000.[44] Those who were college educated—especially those with advanced degrees in medicine, law, engineering, business, and computer science—also fared well. The earnings gap between high school and college graduates age 25–32 (adjusted for inflation) grew from $5,200 per year in 1965 to $11,500 in 1995,[45] and it widened when college graduates reached their prime earning years. While the percentage of Americans over 25 with a college degree grew from 17% to 26% between 1980 and 2000,[46] that left many on the wrong side of this earnings gap in an economy that had fewer high-paying, steady jobs for high school graduates.

America's long history of racism ensured that race as well as economic class defined those who got ahead and those left behind. In spite of Republicans' opposition, many of the tools created in the 1960s and 1970s to advance equality, like affirmative action, survived, helping African Americans make gains. By 2000, 14% of African Americans over 25 had earned a college degree—up from just 3% in 1960[47], and 27% held management or professional positions—compared with 11% in 1970.[48] Concomitantly, the percentage of Blacks living in poverty declined from over 40% in 1967 to 22% in 2000.[49] Popular culture celebrated the Black middle class in television sit-coms like *The Jeffersons* (1975–85), whose theme, "Movin' On Up," conveyed the sense of optimism many felt,

---

[44] Lawrence Mishel and Julia Wolfe, "CEO compensation has grown 940% since 1978," Economic Policy Institute, August 14, 2019 https://www.epi.org/publication/ceo-compensation-2018/ (accessed January 28, 2023).

[45] Pew Research Center, "The Rising Cost of Not Going to College. Chapter 1: Education and Economic Outcomes among the Young," February 11, 2014 https://www.pewresearch.org/social-trends/2014/02/11/chapter-1-education-and-economic-outcomes-among-the-young/ (accessed January 28, 2023).

[46] U.S. Census Bureau, A Half Century of Learning: Historical Statistics on Educational Attainment in the United States, 1940–2000," August 6, 2006 https://www.census.gov/data/tables/2000/dec/phc-t-41.html (accessed January 28, 2023).

[47] Ibid.

[48] U.S. Bureau of Labor Statistics, *Labor Force Characteristics by Race and Ethnicity, 2007* https://stats.bls.gov/opub/reports/race-and-ethnicity/archive/race_ethnicity_2007.pdf (accessed January 28, 2023); U.S. Bureau of Census, "Detailed Occupation of Employed Persons by Race and Sex for the United States: 1970," https://www2.census.gov/library/publications/decennial/1970/pc-s1-supplementary-reports/pc-s1-32.pdf (accessed January 28, 2023).

[49] U.S. Census Bureau, Poverty in the U.S.: 2000. Poverty Rates by Race and Hispanic Origins, 1959–2000. https://www2.census.gov/programs-surveys/demo/visualizations/p60/214/fig07.jpg (accessed January 28, 2023).

and *The Cosby Show* (1984–92), which featured the Huxtables, a happy, successful upper-middle-class Black family.

Their lives were far removed from the experience of millions of Blacks living near or below the poverty line. Good jobs—sometimes any jobs at all—were hard to come by, and unemployment rates were high in Black communities. From the 1970s through the mid-1990s, Black unemployment typically ranged from 10–15%—double White unemployment—and reached a high of 20% during the recession of the early 1980s.[50] Among Black youth, the unemployment rate exceeded 30% for most of the 1980s and 1990s, but rose to over 50% in the recession of the early 1980s.[51] While African American high school dropout rates declined from over 20% in 1972 to 14% in 2000,[52] far too many young African Americans lacked even the minimal education necessary to get a job. Despite a modest decline in residential segregation between 1970 and 2000, many African Americans lived in highly segregated neighborhoods in the urban core or older, inner suburbs like Ferguson, Missouri. Major metropolitan areas such as New York, Chicago, Detroit, Philadelphia, and Los Angeles remained heavily segregated. Cities and suburbs blocked construction of low-income housing in White neighborhoods; Whites fled when Blacks entered their neighborhoods; many realtors and lenders continued to discriminate against Black homebuyers and renters; and far too many African Americans lacked the financial resources to leave the ghetto. As a result, many remained trapped in neighborhoods where jobs were scarce, schools poor, crime common, and banks and supermarkets rare.

In the mid-1980s, as crack cocaine entered the nation's ghettos, life became even more fraught. Drug use defied the color line as *Saturday Night Live* icon John Belushi's death from a cocaine overdose, popular movies such as *Looking for Mr. Goodbar*, and Eric Clapton's 1977 hit song "Cocaine" suggested. Although Whites were just as likely to use drugs as Blacks, Whites—and the media that served them—had long associated drugs with African Americans. So, while growing cocaine use by Whites raised concern, when crack cocaine entered the nation's Black neighborhoods in the mid-1980s, it became an

---

50 U.S. Bureau of Labor Statistics, *Blacks in the Labor Force*, February 2018, 14 https://www.bls.gov/spotlight/2018/blacks-in-the-labor-force/pdf/blacks-in-the-labor-force.pdf (accessed January 28, 2023).
51 FRED Economic Data, "Unemployment Rate—16–19 Yrs., Black or African American" https://fred.stlouisfed.org/series/LNS14000018 (accessed January 28, 2023).
52 U.S. Bureau of Census, "88% of Blacks Have a High School Diploma, 26% a Bachelor's Degree," June 10, 2020 https://www.census.gov/library/stories/2020/06/black-high-school-attainment-nearly-on-par-with-national-average.html (accessed January 28, 2020).

"epidemic" and triggered a bi-partisan war on drugs that proved as devastating for African American communities as the drug itself.

Because a tenth of a gram of powder cocaine yielded a dose of crack, it was far cheaper than powder cocaine, selling for as little as $5-$10 per dose. While snorted powder cocaine remained popular in affluent communities, crack gained traction in poor communities. Inner city residents found that one hundred grams of powder cocaine could be used to produce a thousand rocks of crack that were cheap and would find a market among even young and poor residents in their neighborhoods. The number of producers and dealers grew dramatically in cities across the U.S., and crack was sold openly on the streets and from homes.

As dealers battled each other for turf, guns proliferated, including 9 mm semiautomatic handguns with magazines that held two dozen or more rounds that could be fired in a matter of seconds. Crack and semi-automatic weapons were a lethal combination. Dealers and their henchmen gunned down rivals and settled scores with customers unable to pay. After hitting a 15-year low of 7.9 murders per 100,000 population in 1984, the nation's murder rate climbed steadily, peaking at 9.5 in 1993 (after which it declined to 4.4 in 2014—its lowest in more than half a century).[53] Homicides tripled in Washington, DC, between 1985 and 1991, hitting a peak of almost 500 per year.[54] The victims were predominantly young African American men, age 15–24; the homicide rate for this group climbed from about 60 per 100,000 in 1980 to over 160 in 1993— approximately eight times the rate of young White men.[55]

In 1982, even before the crack epidemic struck fear in the public, President Reagan launched a war on drugs—just as a brutal recession struck and the President and his wife, Nancy, endured criticism for their lavish lifestyle. Whether coincidence or not, Nancy Reagan adopted as her cause a campaign against drugs in schools, and the president announced a war on drugs. "Drugs are bad and we're going after them," Reagan said sternly in his October 2, 1982 radio address.[56] The Administration's first "victory" was passage of

---

[53] Infoplease, Homicide Rate, 1950–2014 https://www.infoplease.com/us/crime/homicide-rate-1950-2014 (accessed January 28, 2023).

[54] District of Columbia Crime Rates, 1960–2019 https://www.disastercenter.com/crime/dccrime.htm (accessed January 28, 2023).

[55] Bureau of Justice, Homicide Trends in the United States: Homicide Victimization by Age, Gender, and Race, 1976–2005 https://bjs.ojp.gov/content/pub/pdf/htius.pdf (accessed January 28, 2023).

[56] *New York Times*, October 3, 1982 https://www.nytimes.com/1982/10/03/us/no-headline-194726.html (February 10, 2019).

the Comprehensive Crime Control Act of 1984. Drafted by the Justice Department, the bill ultimately received bipartisan support, as most Democrats did not wish to be on the wrong side of an issue that united the public in calls for action. The law created a mandatory minimum sentence for anyone who used a firearm in the commission of a violent federal crime and a mandatory sentence of fifteen years to life for anyone convicted of a third federal felony. It sharply limited federal judges' discretion by creating a commission that established sentencing guidelines. The law had a dramatic effect, significantly increasing the federal prison population within two years.[57] States followed suit, with similar results.

The public frenzy over drugs continued. In 1986, as the Crime Control Act began to take its toll, the media's obsession with illegal drugs and especially crack, peaked. *Newsweek* published cover stories on cocaine and crack on March 17 and June 20, 1986—"Kids and Cocaine" and "Crack and Crime"—and on Sunday, May 18, all three New York newspapers—including the *Times*—ran lengthy articles on crack and its consequences. Many African American leaders, whose communities were ravaged by crack, joined in demanding quick action against what many described as a plague that was destroying Black communities and Black youth. Civil rights icon Jesse Jackson told mourners at the funeral of Len Bias, the second pick in the NBA draft, "ropes never killed as many of our young people as the pushers of drugs,"[58] likening drug dealers to White lynch mobs.

Politicians responded quickly, with Democratic leaders in Congress—including most members of the Congressional Black Caucus—jumping on the issue. Smarting after twenty years of being portrayed by Republicans as "soft on crime" and deeply concerned about the consequences of crack in minority communities, they demanded that Congress pass comprehensive legislation before the 1986 mid-term elections. Republicans, worried that their opponents would steal the issue, quickly jumped on board. The result was speedy passage of the Anti-Drug Abuse Act of 1986.

The bill did nothing to address the underlying causes of the crack epidemic—poverty, unemployment, and failing schools—and provided minimal funding for drug education and treatment, which many believed the only hope of breaking the cycle of dependence. Lawmakers resorted

---

57 *Los Angeles Times*, January 9, 1986 https://www.latimes.com/archives/la-xpm-1986-01-09-mn-14186-story.html (accessed January 28, 2023).
58 *New York Times*, June 24, 1986.

to policing and prisons to address a public health crisis. Most funds were earmarked for state and local law enforcement agencies, allowing them to increase firepower and further militarize their operations; for hiring additional federal drug enforcement officials; and for building new prison cells. These would be sorely needed because the law created mandatory minimum sentences for trafficking and a sharp differential between dealers of cocaine and crack. Those selling five grams of crack would receive a mandatory minimum sentence of five years, the same penalty assigned to dealers caught with 500 g of cocaine. Proponents justified the difference by claiming that crack was more highly addictive than cocaine, although scientists disagreed. In 1988, Congress extended these mandatory minimums to cover possession as well as trafficking.

Patently discriminatory, the new federal drug laws, along with a spate of harsh laws passed by most states, devastated minority communities. Although many of the nation's largest cities had African American police chiefs and significant numbers of Black and Hispanic officers by the late 1980s, suspicion and mistrust between the police and minority communities persisted. Federal funding provided by the 1970s war on crime and augmented by new drug laws, allowed police departments to add firepower, including semiautomatic weapons, military assault rifles, tanks, airplanes, and helicopters. Facing a surge of violent crime and criminals armed with semiautomatic weapons, police deployed their new weaponry and resorted to aggressive tactics in encounters with young African Americans. When confronted by what they deemed suspicious behavior—often simply being young, Black, and hanging out on the street—officers questioned and searched young African Americans on the slightest pretense. Police also routinely stopped cars driven by African Americans, usually on the pretext of having defective tail lights or making a turn without signaling, and used the stop as an excuse for a search. Officers found evidence that justified arrests in a small percentage of searches, but the encounters intensified hostility to and suspicion of the police that had long existed in African American communities. All too often, when a suspect pitched attitude or resisted, police responded violently.

Equally serious were the new laws' harsh sentencing provisions. Emboldened by the mandate conferred by the war on drugs and armed with aggressive tactics, police arrested tens of thousands of African Americans. They charged them with dealing or using drugs, violent crimes connected to the drug culture, robbery or burglary committed to support a drug habit, and use of guns to commit a crime. Once arrested, they entered a criminal justice system—whether state or federal—that held them in overcrowded jails and methodically processed, convicted, and imprisoned them. Driven by a commitment to put away "bad guys" whom they believed were destroying communities, prosecutors resolved the vast majority of cases through plea bargains rather than trials. Armed with mandatory minimum sentencing laws that prescribed draconian penalties, they drove hard bargains to convince the accused to plead guilty to lesser charges and to provide evidence against others. As the U.S. Sentencing Commission noted in 1991, "the value of a mandatory minimum sentence lies [...] in its value as a bargaining chip to be given away in return for the resource-saving plea [...] a more leniently sanctioned charge."[59] Because most defendants were poor, they depended on overworked public defenders who lacked the time and resources to gather exculpatory evidence and typically advised clients to accept plea bargains that sent them to prison with reduced sentences.

The upshot was a dramatic and sustained growth in the number of African Americans incarcerated in federal and state penitentiaries. The U.S. prison population jumped from about 300,000 in 1980 to over one million in 1995 and peaked at 1.5 million in 2010.[60] The number of Americans enmeshed in the criminal justice system—in prison or jail, on probation or parole— was even larger, growing from about 1.8 million in 1980 to over seven million by 2010, more than 2% of the population.[61] Given urban police departments' focus on inner city neighborhoods, African American men were far more likely to be incarcerated than Whites. Between 1980 and 2000, the incarceration rate for Black men rose from under 1,000 per 100,000 (1%) to 3,500 per 100,000 (3.5%) while the rate for White men rose more modestly, from around 200 per 100,000 (.2%) to about 500 (.5%).[62]

---

59 United States Sentencing Commission, *Mandatory Minimum Penalties in the Federal Criminal Justice System* (August 1991), 15 https://www.ussc.gov/sites/default/files/pdf/news/congressional-testimony-and-reports/mandatory-minimum-penalties/1991_Mand_Min_Report.pdf (accessed July 2, 2018).
60 The Sentencing Project, Trends in U.S. Corrections: U.S. and Federal Prison Population, 1925–2019 https://www.sentencingproject.org/reports/mass-incarceration-trends/ (accessed January 28, 2023).
61 University at Albany School of Criminal Justice, Sourcebook of Criminal Justice Statistics Online. Table 6.1 2010. Adults on probation, in jail or prison, or on parole, 1980–2010 https://www.albany.edu/sourcebook/pdf/t612010.pdf (accessed January 28, 2023).
62 Katharina Buchholz, "Black Incarceration Rates are Dropping in the U.S.," Statista, February 19, 2021 https://www.statista.com/chart/18376/us-incarceration-rates-by-sex-and-race-ethnic-origin/ (accessed January 23, 2023).

The result of the war on crack was perhaps the most significant and sustained assault on the rights and well-being of African Americans in a century—what Michelle Alexander called "the new Jim Crow."[63] Millions of African Americans, most of them young men, lost years of their lives to prison. When they were released, their opportunities were even more limited than when they entered. Branded as felons many lost the right to vote. A 2013 study conducted by the NAACP and several other civil rights organizations found that almost 8% of adult African Americans were disfranchised because of a felony conviction—compared with fewer than 2% of non-African Americans.[64] Many employers also shied away from hiring felons. For young Black men who lacked a high school degree and had limited work experience, a felony conviction made prospects for employment even more remote. And without a job, ex-convicts were likely to return to crime and, before long, to prison, where they faced even harsher sentences as repeat offenders.

## The Twilight of the Reagan Presidency

While Reagan's call for a war on drugs generated bipartisan support, his magic wore thin during his last two years in office. Although his approval rating remained high in 1986, Democrats scored big wins in the November elections, picking up eight Senate seats to regain a 57–43 majority and control of both houses of Congress. The following year was even less kind to the President. As the Savings and Loan crisis deepened and the stock market tanked in October 1987, disenchantment grew. Stories of reckless speculation, insider trading, outright fraud—and the collateral damage they produced for individuals and communities across the country—filled the news. Perhaps the deregulation and faith in free markets that Reagan championed had their limits. Republicans might crow about the economic resurgence their policies generated, proclaiming, "It's morning again in America." But for too many it seemed like the morning of a cold, gray day. To be sure, stagflation was a memory, but the recovery revealed the unsavory side of capitalism.

---

63 Michelle Alexander, *The New Jim Crow: Mass Incarceration in the Age of Colorblindness* (New York, 2010).
64 Democracy Imprisoned: A Review of the Prevalence and Impact of Felony Disfranchisement Laws in the United States (September 2013), 2 http://civilrightsdocs.info/pdf/reports/ICCPR_Shadow_Report-Felony_Disenfranchisement.pdf (accessed January 23, 2023).

The benefits went principally to the top 10%, and those in the top 1% flaunted wealth reminiscent of the Gilded Age's robber barons. But many middle- and working-class Americans felt left behind. Even with two incomes, working families often struggled to make ends meet.

Equally damaging were revelations of what became known as the Iran-Contra scandal. Investigative journalists revealed that administration officials had sold arms to Iran in return for assistance in gaining the release of American hostages held by Islamic militants and used the proceeds to support the Nicaraguan Contras in defiance of the law. As is usual in these situations, details kept trickling out, culminating in televised hearings before congressional committees between May and July 1987. Those who planned and executed the complex scheme insisted that they had acted without Reagan's knowledge and involvement, but the affair badly damaged the President. In March 1987, just four months after assuring the Americans that his administration "did not, repeat, did not trade arms or anything for hostages,"[65] he was forced to recant. "A few months ago, I told the American people I did not trade arms for hostages," Reagan admitted. Swallowing hard, he added, while "my heart and best intentions still tell me that is true [...] the facts and evidence tell me it is not."[66] While Reagan ultimately dodged culpability, he appeared either to be lying or a figurehead who had lost control of his administration. His approval ratings remained below 50% throughout 1987, then crossed 50% and remained there throughout 1988. It was an indication of the affection many Americans felt for the genial conservative whom they credited with restoring the optimism that Vietnam, Watergate, and the stagflation of the 1970s had sapped.[67] But it was fondness for the man, not faith in his leadership.

Nevertheless, as Reagan's second term drew to an end, conservatives could take heart in their accomplishments. They had invested heavily in America's

---

65 *New York Times*, November 14, 1986 https://www.nytimes.com/1986/11/14/us/transcript-of-remarks-by-reagan-about-iran.html?searchResultPosition=8 (accessed April 16, 2022).

66 *New York Times*, November 5, 1987 https://www.nytimes.com/1987/03/04/world/transcript-of-reagan-statement-on-arms.html?searchResultPosition=4 (accessed April 16, 2022).

67 Gallup, Presidential Approval Ratings—Gallup Historical Statistics and Trends https://news.gallup.com/poll/116677/Presidential-Approval-Ratings-Gallup-Historical-Statistics-Trends.aspx (accessed January 28, 2023).

military, championed a muscular foreign policy, projected American power around the world, resumed negotiations with the Soviets from a position of strength, and re-asserted presidential primacy in foreign policy. They had notched important wins in domestic policy, cutting taxes and loosening a half-century of federal economic regulation. And they brought the voices of social conservatives into the corridors of power.

Yet the Reaganites' triumph was limited. Deep public support for entitlement programs and ballooning deficits created by the Reagan tax cuts helped Democrats force Reagan to shore up Social Security and Medicare and accept tax increases that compromised the Reagan Revolution. Nor did rhetorical support for social conservatives translate into action. The ERA died in 1983, but that owed more to the powerful movement orchestrated by Phyllis Schlafly than anything Reagan and his allies contributed. Affirmative action withstood constitutional challenges, and bi-partisan majorities in Congress strengthened the Voting Rights Act to help minorities elect candidates of their choice. *Roe v. Wade* remained the law of the land. Nor did Reagan bring about a political realignment, despite his success in winning the support of many erstwhile Democrats. The House remained a Democratic bastion, and the Republican majority in the Senate evaporated in 1986.

The real revolution Reagan wrought was in the country's political discourse. To Reagan, government was the problem and reducing its scope and authority the solution. He led a frontal assault on the assumptions that underlay half-a-century of American public policy. Government programs designed to help people, notably welfare, too often sapped their initiative and made them dependent. Demanding personal responsibility and fostering individual initiative would produce individual happiness, build stronger, more functional families, and generate innovation and prosperity. Taxes took from those whose success fueled the economy and supported ill-conceived programs that wasted money, limited freedom, and eroded personal responsibility. Government regulation substituted the designs of politicians and bureaucrats for the wisdom and efficiency of the market.

Among Democrats, liberals like Jesse Jackson, Howard Dean, and Ted Kennedy joined the battle with conservatives. Conservative prescriptions—and Reagan's policies, they charged, were warmed over Social Darwinism that promoted the interests of the rich at the expense of the poor, working- and middle-class Americans, and the environment. To most voters, however, their approach seemed anachronistic—a throwback to the 1960s and 70s, a period that many came to equate with excess, division, chaos, and national decline. Many Democrats, tired of quadrennial drubbings in the battle for the White House, adapted. Led by governors like Bill Clinton and members of Congress like Al Gore and Richard Gephardt who hailed from the Sunbelt and Midwest, they coalesced in the Democratic Leadership Conference and moved the party to the center. These so-called New Democrats admitted that market-based solutions were often superior to government programs, acknowledged the need for welfare reform, demanded tough responses to crime and drugs, conceded that the rights' consciousness of the 1960s compromised national unity, and insisted on the need for greater personal responsibility. They criticized Republicans for abandoning the middle class by supporting policies that benefitted business and the wealthy, and they maintained that government had an important role in creating opportunity, promoting equity, and ensuring that the nation could compete in a global economy. These New Democrats may not have abandoned the party's ends, but they adopted means they genuinely believed were better calculated to promote equity and that would allow them to compete on the playing field conservatives had reshaped.[68]

That was the Reagan Revolution. It moved the conversation to the right, in the process marginalizing progressive ideas and policies that had defined the Democratic Party for five decades. It was much like the GOP's pivot to Modern Republicanism in the 1950s. Rather than bringing the parties closer together ideologically, however, as had happened in the 1950s and early 1960s, it generated bitter conflict, made bipartisan cooperation difficult, and stoked hyper-partisanship. As Democrats abandoned positions that had made them easy targets, Republicans struggled with the inevitable baggage that accumulated during eight years in power. To make matters worse, Reagan exited public life and no one with his charisma emerged to take his place. His vice president and presumptive Republican nominee in 1988, George H.W. Bush, had a strong resume but he suffered from what *Newsweek* called "the wimp factor." While television "makes Ronald Reagan larger than life," the magazine asserted, it "diminishes George Bush" because "he does not project self-confidence, wit or warmth" and "comes across [...] as stiff or silly."[69]

---

68 Lily Geisner, *Left Behind: The Democrats' Failed Attempt to Solve Inequality* (New York, 2022).
69 Margaret Garrard Warner, "George H.W. Bush's Greatest Campaign Challenge: Revisit Newsweek's 1987 Cover Story, 'The Wimp Factor'." *Newsweek*, December 3, 2018 https://www.newsweek.com/newsweek-1987-cover-story-george-hw-bush-wimp-factor-1241611 (accessed April 30, 2023).

With differences between the parties narrowed, a historic thaw in the Cold War, and Reagan gone, Republicans turned to social issues. They were weapons the party had been sharpening since Goldwater's ill-fated campaign, and they promised to be as effective as the old tactics of denouncing Democrats as big government, tax and spend liberals who were soft on crime and Communism. Because they tapped into deeply held moral beliefs, cultural values, and identity, social and cultural issues promised to make arguments heated, encourage take-no-prisoner tactics, and limit room for compromise. It was a toxic mix that would make politics a blood sport and governing difficult.

CHAPTER 6

# CONSERVATIVES AT THE CROSSROADS, 1988–1992

## Willie Horton

George H. W. Bush had a presidential itch he needed to scratch. He had served Republican presidents since Nixon, including two terms as Reagan's loyal vice president. As Bush prepared to accept the Republican nomination in July 1988, it appeared that the prize he longed for might yet again elude him. His party had been damaged by the Savings and Loan (S&L) debacle, and most people assumed that, despite all the denials, Bush himself had been deeply involved in the deal with Iran to swap arms for hostages and use the proceeds to support anti-communist rebels in Nicaragua in clear violation of the law. Bush also lacked Reagan's charisma. As he prepared to accept the nomination, a Gallup Poll showed him trailing his Democratic opponent, Michael Dukakis, by a whopping 17 points. Dukakis was a nonideological technocrat, not a Great Society liberal. He touted his success as governor in making Massachusetts an economic powerhouse, making him harder to attack on economic issues than Carter and Mondale.

Outside Massachusetts, Dukakis was not well known, and the Bush campaign worked overtime to gather evidence to define him as just another out-of-touch liberal. Bush's campaign manager, Lee Atwater, licked his chops as he reviewed information detailing Dukakis's positions on such hot-button social issues as the death penalty and the Pledge of Allegiance. But Dukakis's vulnerability on race and crime was what caught Atwater's attention. Meeting with Bush's top aides in June, Atwater proposed a strategy that would "strip the bark off the little bastard."[1]

---

1 *New York Times*, January 13, 1991 https://www.nytimes.com/1991/01/13/us/gravely-ill-atwater-offers-apology.html.

William Horton, a Black man serving time in a Massachusetts prison for first-degree murder, had been convicted of stabbing to death a 17-year-old boy during a robbery and sentenced to life in prison. Like many states, Massachusetts had adopted a program that rewarded prisoners with furloughs for good behavior. In 1976, when the state supreme court ruled that all prisoners, including convicted murderers, were eligible for furloughs, the legislature defied the court. As governor, Dukakis vetoed the bill, not because he thought furloughs for convicted murderers was a good idea, but because the bill was a clear assault on the supreme court's authority. Horton received furloughs on 10 occasions. In 1988, he fled the state while on furlough, kidnapped a couple in Maryland, stabbed the man, and raped the woman. As Atwater reviewed information about Horton, he knew it was dynamite. With violent crime on the rise, Horton offered a way to use Whites' fear of Black men to destroy Dukakis. "If I can make Willie Horton a household name," Atwater predicted, "we'll win the election."[2]

So, William Horton became "Willie," a name Whites more readily associated with Blacks, and Bush began to use him to attack Dukakis' record on crime in stump speeches. Soon an independent political action committee (PAC) backing Bush released a TV ad entitled "Bush & Dukakis on Crime."[3] Produced by an independent PAC in consultation with Atwater's team, it became a classic of negative campaigning and the shape of things to come in American politics. The 30-second ad began with color pictures of Bush and Dukakis as the announcer proclaimed that Bush supported the death penalty. "Dukakis not only opposes the death penalty," the voiceover continued, "he allowed first-degree murderers to have weekend passes from prison." Enter Willie Horton, whose grainy, menacing mug shot appeared on the screen in black and white. "One was Willie Horton who murdered a boy in a robbery stabbing him 19 times," the announcer declared, and then received 10 "weekend passes from prison." As the screen revealed a black and white photo of Horton towering over a police officer, the announcer delivered the coup de grace: "Horton fled and kidnapped a young couple stabbing the man repeatedly and repeatedly raping his girlfriend." As the ad concluded, the words "Kidnapping, Stabbing, Raping" appeared on the screen followed by a picture of Dukakis, looking clueless.[4] While the campaign didn't run the ad itself, it released one

---

[2] *New York Times*, December 3, 2018 https://www.nytimes.com/2018/12/03/us/politics/bush-willie-horton.html (accessed April 28, 2023).

[3] Kathryn Cramer Brownell, *24/7 Politics: Cable Television and the Fragmenting of America from Watergate to Fox News* (Princeton, NJ, 2023), 256–60.

[4] https://www.youtube.com/watch?v=Io9KMSSEZ0Y (accessed April 28, 2023).

that didn't feature Horton—who had become a household name—but attacked the Dukakis furlough program. The campaign could deny responsibility for a blatantly racist ad while using White fear of Black men against their opponent.

## A Kinder, Gentler Presidency?

Exploiting Willie Horton was at odds with Bush's reputation for decency, but it was consistent with his fierce competitive streak. He was the man with the impeccable resume: World War II Navy combat pilot; successful Texas oil man; two-term member of the House; chair of the Republican National Committee; ambassador to China; director of the CIA; and Reagan's unfailingly loyal vice president. He cruised to the Republican nomination but had liabilities. He was an uninspiring speaker, he struggled to articulate a vision, and conservatives didn't trust him. They recalled that in the 1980 primaries he derided as "voodoo economics" Reagan's claim that tax cuts would generate economic growth and pay for themselves. (Of course, he had been correct.) Many conservatives wondered if he was a true Reaganite or supported Reaganomics as a way to achieve his political ambition. Given his New England upbringing and Yale education, they feared, he was a moderate who would compromise conservative principles.

As the 1988 election approached, there was no dominant candidate in the Democratic field as there had been in 1984 when liberal warhorse Walter Mondale won the nomination. But many considered that a good thing as it might produce a nominee who was better able to compete on the political landscape that Ronald Reagan had reshaped, a world in which big government was suspect and the free market a cure-all. Democrats had picked up eight Senate seats in 1986 by recruiting strong candidates who were fiscally responsible, promised lean, efficient government, and focused on local issues, like nuclear waste in Nevada and Washington or help for struggling farmers in North and South Dakota. They hoped that a similar nonideological approach would help them capture the presidency in 1988.

Pragmatists were not the only voices in the party. Unapologetic liberals were still a force, and they wanted a leader who would challenge policies that had benefited the rich and who was committed to the New Deal vision of government as a force for equity. They found their champion in Jesse Jackson, the charismatic civil rights activist who had been at Martin Luther King, Jr.'s side when he was assassinated and went on to became a successful community organizer in Chicago. Undeterred by those who said a Black man would never win, Jackson launched a campaign that energized the party's left. He advocated

New Deal-style programs to rebuild infrastructure and put the unemployed to work, an end to Reagan-era tax cuts for the top 10% of earners, reparations to the descendants of slaves, government support for small family-owned farms, free community college tuition, a nuclear freeze, ratification of the Equal Rights Amendment, and repeal of anti-union policies. Jackson's appeal to traditional Democratic values and policies appealed to a broad cross-section of the party—Blacks, many working-class Whites, college students, and feminists among others—making him a force to be reckoned with. He remained in the race to the end, won 13 primaries or caucuses, and went to the convention with over a thousand of the 2900 convention delegates pledged to him. It was a sign that progressives were still an important element of a party whose center was shifting right. Nevertheless, the pragmatists prevailed, rallying behind Michael Dukakis, the governor of Massachusetts who eschewed ideology and touted the technocratic skills that enabled him to transform his state into a heavyweight in the emerging knowledge economy.

Dukakis won the nomination, and polls gave him a substantial lead over Bush on the eve of the Republican convention. The Saving and Loan debacle, corruption on Wall Street, the stock market crash, the farm crisis, the decline of the manufacturing economy, income inequality, and, of course, Iran-Contra made many voters wonder whether four more years of Republican control was desirable. Seeking to deflect attention from the sea of problems engulfing the Reagan administration, Bush took the offensive, mobilizing social issues as the weapon. He changed the subject from the Reagan record by tying Dukakis to pornography, opposition to prayer in the schools, abortion, affirmative action, and support for criminals rather than their victims by repeatedly citing his opponent's membership in the American Civil Liberties Union (ACLU). "I am not a card-carrying member of the American Civil Liberties Union," Bush gloated. "I am for the people."[5] He repeatedly ripped Dukakis's veto of a bill requiring recitation of the pledge of allegiance in Massachusetts classrooms, visited a factory that made flags, wore a lapel-pin flag, and ostentatiously recited the pledge on every possible occasion. And, of course, Willie Horton helped him tie Dukakis to menacing Black men who threatened Whites.

If Bush betrayed his genteel upbringing to become the maestro of mudslinging, Dukakis looked like a punching bag. Rather than answer the negative ads,

---

5 *Washington Post*, September 22, 1988 https://www.washingtonpost.com/archive/opinions/1988/09/22/another-card-carrying-member-of-the-aclu/53953b45-414a-4988-b3fc-6c49d8d45e0c/ (accessed April 17, 2022).

he chose to take the high road and stay out of the gutter. It was a mistake. Bush defined Dukakis as an out-of-touch liberal who rejected mainstream values and couldn't identify with ordinary Americans while Dukakis failed to strike at Bush's greatest vulnerabilities. After all, the Vice President was the son of wealth and privilege, and it would have been easy to juxtapose images of Bush at his Kennebunkport, Maine estate with pictures of shuttered factories. But Dukakis refused to do so, instead emphasizing his knowledge, competence, and success in creating the "Massachusetts Miracle." Always the smartest boy in the room, he annoyed many voters. The outcome was predictable. Bush won 53% of the popular vote to 46% for Dukakis and tallied a 426–111 margin in the Electoral College. The only consolation for Democrats was that he had short coattails, and Democrats retained majorities in the House and Senate.

Bush was something of a paradox. A New England aristocrat who achieved success in the rough and tumble Texas oil business of the 1950s. A fiscally conservative Republican whose loyalty and ambition led him to support policies that produced huge budget deficits. A pro-choice Republican who supported ERA yet became a zealous advocate of causes championed by the religious right. A man with a reputation for unfailing graciousness who broke new ground in negative campaigning. So, perhaps it's not surprising that as president, he alternated between bipartisan problem-solving and the politics of division. Or that the compromises he made to demonstrate fealty to Reagan doomed him to be a one-term president. Reagan's charisma may not have rubbed off on Bush, but the consequences of his budget policies stuck to his successor like flypaper.

Delivering his inaugural address in January 1989, Bush consciously sought to separate himself from his predecessor. He didn't break with Reagan's vision of limited government or his belief that the market and community-based organizations provided the best solutions to social problems. However, he acknowledged the fiscal hangover that his predecessor's supply side binge bequeathed, reminding his audience, "our funds are low. We have a deficit to bring down." He also recognized that not everyone benefited from the Reagan recovery, calling attention to "the homeless, lost, and roaming [...] the children who have nothing, no love, no normalcy [...] those who cannot free themselves of enslavement [...] to drugs, welfare, the demoralization that rules the slums." He demanded "a new engagement in the lives of others, a new activism," through community organizations he described as "a thousand points of light." He pledged to "make kinder the face of the nation and gentler the face of the world." A kinder, gentler world began with politics. The man who benefited from the Willie Horton ad decried a political culture in which "our great political parties have too often been far apart and untrusting of each other" and promised "to rise above the merely partisan."[6]

In some respects, Bush was true to his word. Badly needed legislation to strengthen the Clean Air Act of 1970 had been stalled in Congress for more than a decade. Bush's team worked with the Democratic leader in the Senate, George Mitchell, to push legislation across the line. The result was the Clean Air Amendments of 1990—landmark legislation that placed stringent limits on tailpipe emissions and reduced discharges of pollutants from industrial sites and coal-burning power plants. It established a cap-and-trade program that allowed power companies whose emissions were below the limits assigned them to sell their unused capacity to pollute to companies that exceeded pollution limits and faced penalties. It was a creative approach championed by Democrat Al Gore to reward those who were environmentally friendly and make polluters pay. Bush also played a critical role in passage of the Americans with Disabilities Act, a measure with bipartisan support that faced stiff opposition from business groups.

Bipartisan compromise was becoming harder to achieve, however. A tectonic shift in American politics was underway. Both parties had always skewered their opponents for policies and personal indiscretions voters might find objectionable. They spun facts to make their opponents and the policies they advocated appear more outlandish than they were. And they routinely appealed to fear. But in the late 1980s and early 1990s, attacks became sharper and the battles more bruising, as the parties appealed to highly divisive social and cultural issues. The result was hard feelings and a desire to settle scores that made collaboration harder.

In 1987, Reagan nominated Robert Bork to succeed Lewis Powell as a Supreme Court justice. Powell was a conservative Virginian, appointed by Richard Nixon, but he had often compromised with his more liberal colleagues. Bork, however, was a doctrinaire conservative best known for firing Watergate special counsel Archibald Cox after the attorney general and his deputy resigned rather than doing Nixon's bidding. A scathing critic of the Warren and Burger Courts for their belief in a "living Constitution" that must be interpreted in light of contemporary circumstances, he insisted that the framers' intent govern the Court's decisions. His originalist approach led him to deny that the Constitution protected the right to privacy, the Equal Protection

---

[6] Inaugural Address of George Bush, January 20, 1989 https://avalon.law.yale.edu/20th_century/bush.asp (accessed April 18, 2022).

Clause guaranteed the rights of women, poll taxes and literacy tests were unconstitutional, and Congress had the authority to require private businesses to serve minorities. While the Senate had unanimously confirmed another staunch conservative, Antonin Scalia, a year earlier, Bork was a bridge too far. Democrats mobilized against his candidacy, stoking fear of the consequences of confirmation. "Robert Bork's America is a land where women would be forced into back-alley abortions, blacks would sit at segregated lunch counters, rogue police could break down citizens' doors in midnight raids, and schoolchildren could not be taught about evolution," Ted Kennedy warned.[7] After televised Judiciary Committee hearings in which Bork was candid about his views and appeared downright scary to most Americans, the Senate voted against confirmation by a 58–42 margin. While five Republican senators joined the majority, conservatives insisted that Bork had been the victim of a partisan smear campaign. Their outrage added a new term to the political lexicon: one subject to an unfair attack was "borked."

Civility and collegiality were becoming quaint relics of the past. While there was enough blame to go around, Republicans in the House of Representatives took give-no-quarter politics to a new level. A new generation of conservative Republican members chafed under the leadership of those like Bob Michel of Illinois, the genial minority leader who seemed comfortable with leading a loyal opposition and seeking to moderate policies advanced by the majority. By delegitimizing the Democrats, these young bomb throwers argued, Republicans could reclaim the majority they lost in 1954. The insurgents had new tools at their disposal: CSPAN brought angry speeches attacking Democrats (usually to an empty House chamber) into living rooms across the country; the 24–7 news cycle created by CNN meant that journalists needed stories to fill the air, ensuring that scandals took on a life of their own; and testosterone-rich talk radio hosts like Rush Limbaugh, who knew that insults and outrage attracted listeners fed the fire.

Newt Gingrich was an architect of this change, an agent provocateur who spewed venom, dispensed half-truths and outright lies, and sowed chaos in service of winning a Republican House majority. A boomer with an overweening ambition, like Bill Clinton, Gingrich earned a Ph.D. in Modern

---

7 Nina Totenberg, "Robert Bork's Supreme Court Nomination 'Changed Everything Maybe Forever,'" December 19, 2012 https://www.npr.org/sections/itsallpolitics/2012/12/19/167645600/robert-borks-supreme-court-nomination-changed-everything-maybe-forever (accessed May 23, 2022).

European History at Tulane University and went on to a faculty position at West Georgia College before winning election to the House in 1978 at age 35. A backbencher, he was known for adding intellectual gravitas to conservative advocacy, a penchant for capturing media attention, and an aversion to compromise. "We want to force a crisis," he proclaimed in 1982 while seeking to shut down the government if Congress refused to adopt a balanced budget amendment.[8]

Gingrich was willing to break institutional norms by unleashing vicious attacks on the opposition. "One of the great problems we have in the Republican Party is that we don't encourage you to be nasty," he told a group of Young Republicans in 1978. He inveighed against Democrats, using partisan invective that many colleagues found offensive. But he gained a following among young conservatives, and by the mid-1980s was sending cassette tapes and memos to Republican candidates across the country who wanted to "speak like Newt." When describing Democrats, he advised, they should use words like "sick, pathetic, lie, anti-flag, traitors, radical, corrupt," terms that he and other firebrand members regularly deployed.[9] Bush had taken the low road in 1988, but felt some shame when he went into the gutter. Gingrich and his allies, it seemed, had no remorse.

In the late 1980s, Gingrich attacked Democrats for corruption. Entering politics in the wake of Watergate, he knew that voters distrusted politicians. Their suspicion was fueled by a new breed of investigative journalists and liberal-leaning good government watchdog organizations like Common Cause that were eager to expose wrongdoing. Gingrich also understood that talk radio hosts and cable news had an insatiable appetite for scandal and that most citizens lacked the inclination to discover the facts. If voters saw smoke, they would assume there was fire.

The environment was perfect for Gingrich to attack Democratic corruption. Entrenched in the majority for 30 years, he argued, they used their power to promote the interests of powerful individuals who funded their campaigns and dealt them favors. As television became an essential tool in winning elections, members needed to raise even more money to stay in office. Constituents expected their representatives to bring home federal largesse for their districts,

---

8 Julian E. Zelizer, *Burning the House Down: Newt Gingrich, the Fall of a Speaker, and the Rise of a New Republican Party* (New York, 2020), 55.
9 McKay Coppins, "The Man who Broke Politics," *The Atlantic*, November 2018 https://www.theatlantic.com/magazine/archive/2018/11/newt-gingrich-says-youre-welcome/570832/ (accessed May 15, 2022).

whether new post offices, water projects, job training centers, agricultural subsidies, or urban redevelopment programs. Often the people who benefited most directly were real estate developers, business and labor leaders, and local politicians. Representatives developed close ties with them, and they often contributed to campaigns to ensure access. While this was the way politics had been practiced forever, these relationships gave the appearance of corruption. Incumbents of both parties played the game, but Democrats were easier targets because they controlled the House.

When Jim Wright became Speaker of the House in January 1987, Gingrich put a bull's eye on his back. Wright excelled at bringing federal pork to his district and used his mastery of House rules to steer legislation. As Speaker, he combined his sure knowledge of processes and personalities with an iron will to thwart Republican attempts to block the majority's priorities. Given Wright's seniority, connections with movers and shakers in his district and beyond, and success in raising money, stories alleging ethics violations dogged him. None were substantiated, but Gingrich understood that the appearance of impropriety was sufficient, especially when lots of allegations circulated. In late 1987, Gingrich's staff began assembling a binder with news stories scrutinizing Wright's fundraising and sweetheart deals with wealthy supporters. A master of innuendo and bombast, Gingrich used every opportunity to circulate the stories among House members and journalists, treating them as if they contained unimpeachable evidence of wrongdoing rather than unsubstantiated charges.

Gingrich's campaign gained momentum in early spring 1988 as public attention focused on the S&L crisis. Allegations that Wright had intervened with regulators to protect a wealthy associate whose reckless investments subsequently led to the collapse of a chain of Texas S&Ls rocked Washington. The accusations ultimately proved baseless, but many concluded that Wright had enabled a wealthy supporter to skirt rules established to protect depositors and the financial system, leaving taxpayers holding the bag. Fred Wertheimer, the director of Common Cause, was no fan of Gingrich. But the liberal good government advocate was outraged by what appeared to be blatant influence peddling. In May 1988, he asked the House Ethics Committee to investigate, adding a squeaky-clean nonpartisan voice to the formal request for an investigation signed by 72 of 177 Republican members and filed by Gingrich. Fearful that blocking an investigation would invite charges of a cover-up and damage them in the 1990 mid-term elections, Democrats fell in line. In June 1988, the Ethics Committee voted unanimously to begin an inquiry and to retain an independent counsel to investigate the charges, hoping to demonstrate that they wouldn't tolerate wrongdoing. It was a mistake.

The hearings played into the hands of Gingrich, who was more interested in creating chaos than governance.

Although he was a Democrat, Richard Phelan, the independent counsel, was Wright's worst nightmare. A Chicago attorney with political aspirations, Phelan sensed an opportunity to establish his reputation as a reform-minded independent. The report he submitted in March 1989 was, in the words of Julian Zelizer, "heavy handed with the evidence, twisting evidence in a negative fashion and inserting every charge into the document regardless of its veracity."[10]

While the committee rejected most of the charges in Phelan's tendentious report, it agreed that there was sufficient evidence to warrant a full public hearing. One target was royalties Wright received for his book, *Reflections of a Public Man*. Published by a political consultant who gave Wright an unheard-of 55% of sales as royalties, the book was sold in bulk to groups to whom Wright gave speeches, such as the National Association of Realtors. While there were no limits on royalties members could earn, House rules limited outside income. Wright's book sales appeared to be a thinly veiled way to bypass those limits. His relationship with George Mallick, a wealthy Texas real estate developer with whom he and his wife, Betty, created an investment company, raised additional concerns. Over the years, the Wrights had received benefits that Wright failed to report, as required by House rules, giving the impression that he was hiding something.

As Gingrich predicted, Wright's problems fed the insatiable appetite of the 24–7 news cycle. The media amplified these stories and breathlessly covered every new revelation and step in the investigation. Wright couldn't leave his office without being accosted by swarms of reporters asking him about the charges—and whether he believed he could survive. In May 1989, the Ethics Committee held public hearings, with Wright's attorney vigorously refuting the charges and the special counsel insisting that the Speaker had violated House rules and undermined the "integrity of this House." Wright's attorney made a strong technical argument, but most observers concluded that wealthy supporters enjoyed undue influence, and Wright had violated the spirit if not the letter of the rules. Democrats increasingly saw the Speaker as a liability, and many said publicly he wouldn't survive. Ultimately, Wright reached the same conclusion. On May 31, 1989, he addressed the House, defending his actions and denouncing the "mindless cannibalism" that was destroying the House's ability to take care of the people's business. But he couldn't ignore the realities.

---

10 Zelizer, *Burning Down the House*, 198.

Although the committee hadn't voted, he had lost in the court of public opinion and become an albatross for Democrats. Wright concluded by announcing he would resign, vindicating Gingrich's scorched earth approach.

Republicans took note, pleased that they had toppled the Speaker and defined Democrats as corrupt, self-serving insiders. In early 1989, even before Wright resigned, House Republicans rewarded Gingrich by electing him party whip, making him the second highest Republican in the House. Confronting and vilifying the majority proved more effective than criticizing its policies and seeking compromises that made legislation more palatable to conservatives. As a result, public trust in politicians and the political process declined further, governing became more difficult, and gridlock more intractable.

Bush got a taste of House Republicans' penchant for theatrics and confrontation when he had to make difficult decisions about the budget. Reagan's tax cuts and defense buildup had created huge deficits and prospects for ending them were dim. Economists feared that deficits would reignite inflation, compete with businesses for capital, lead to higher interest rates, and trigger recession. Any solution required a combination of spending cuts, unpopular with Democrats, and tax increases, which Republicans opposed. Never mind that conservatives' hero, Ronald Reagan, had agreed to several rounds of "revenue enhancements." To placate his party's right wing, Bush had taken the anti-tax pledge in his acceptance speech at the 1988 Republican convention. "Congress will push me to raise taxes [...]," he told the delegates in a line many of his advisors urged him to delete, "and I'll say to them, 'Read my lips: No new taxes'"[11] Bush should have known better. He was a fiscal conservative who understood that governing effectively required him to reduce the deficit.

House Republicans, who were more interested in scoring political points than governing, were his biggest obstacle. In July 1990, as word spread that Bush would support a tax increase as part of a deficit reduction deal, conservatives attacked. The July 5 headline in the *New York Post*, Gotham's shrill conservative tabloid, said it all: "Read My Lips: I Lied." By September, Bush and Democrats in Congress agreed to a $134 billion tax increase—half the amount Reagan had agreed to in the 1982 deficit reduction deal—and over $300 billion in spending cuts. Conservative Republicans in the House, led by Gingrich, revolted, joining House Democrats to torpedo the bill. The result was a three-day government

---

11 George H.W. Bush, "1988 Republican National Convention Acceptance Speech" https://www.americanrhetoric.com/speeches/georgehbush1988rnc.htm (accessed April 18, 2022).

shutdown that generated public outrage and brought negotiators back to the bargaining table. They negotiated a deal more to the liking of Democrats: it shifted cuts away from programs for the poor and targeted tax increases at the wealthy while reducing a regressive gasoline tax hike that had provided most of the additional revenue in the original bill. The bill passed with solid Democratic support, and Bush had no alternative but to sign it.

Bipartisanship was situational, as had always been the case. As he had shown in the 1988 campaign, Bush could wield the partisan hatchet with the best of them. Aware that reneging on his no-new-taxes pledge damaged his standing with conservatives, he looked for ways to mend fences. Plunging into the culture wars was the surest path to success, and Bush took it. When the U.S. Supreme Court struck down a Texas law punishing flag burning as a violation of the First Amendment in June 1989, Bush rallied behind those who demanded a constitutional amendment giving Congress authority to prohibit physical desecration of the flag. When the amendment failed to attract the necessary two-thirds majority, Bush signed into law a bill prohibiting flag burning. Everyone knew the bill violated the First Amendment, so when the Court struck it down, no one was surprised. But Bush had taken his stand, defending what he called "a unique national symbol."[12]

In his first year in office, Bush also established his bona fides with pro-life hardliners by vetoing a bill allowing public funding of abortions to end pregnancies that resulted from rape or incest. He acknowledged that "rape and incest are crimes of violence," but argued that the legislation "compound a violent act with the taking of an unborn life." If public funding for abortions weren't limited to cases in which a mother's life was at risk, "it would be difficult to limit to the few cases of actual rape or incest" and inevitably lead to "the taking of countless other lives of unborn children."[13]

With fear of crack surging, a strong stand against drugs was another way to show his conservative bona fides. Congress had created the Office of National Drug Control Policy in 1988, and Bush moved quickly to appoint William J. Bennett, Reagan's outspoken secretary of education to direct it. Bennet had a flair for the dramatic that had made him a favorite among conservatives. He immediately declared the District of Columbia as the first "high-intensity

---

12 *Los Angeles Times*, June 28, 1989 https://www.latimes.com/archives/la-xpm-1989-06-28-mn-4162-story.html (accessed April 18, 2022).

13 Letter to the Senate Appropriations Committee on Federal Funding for Abortion, October 17, 1989 https://bush41library.tamu.edu/archives/public-papers/1051 (accessed April 18, 2022).

drug-trafficking city" and mobilized resources for a crackdown. Not to be outdone, Bush himself engaged in a bit of theatrics. Federal agents lured a teenage drug dealer to Lafayette Park across from the White House where he sold them crack valued at almost $2,500. Four days later, in September 1989, Bush gave his first address from the Oval Office with the seized bag of crack on his desk. "This is crack cocaine seized a few days ago [...] in a park just across the street from the White House," he told his audience, aware that they would immediately assume that if the scourge of drugs was so close to the President's house, it could be in their neighborhood as well.[14] He then outlined an even more aggressive strategy to combat drugs than his predecessor had adopted. While Bush's drug initiative died in Congress, it assured the public that he was committed to the war on drugs—which many saw as a campaign to take control of Black neighborhoods in the nation's inner cities.

Defending "family values" was another sure way to appeal to conservatives. The Equal Rights Amendment was dead, and feminism on the defensive. Nevertheless, many social conservatives remained concerned that women were making gains at the expense of men and undermining the patriarchal family. In the wake of rioting in Los Angeles in 1991, occasioned by the brutal beating of Rodney King by police, Vice President Dan Quayle linked the violence to "a poverty of values" fostered by a popular TV sit-com, *Murphy Brown*. It featured a divorced TV anchor who becomes pregnant and decides to raise her child by herself. Quayle was troubled because the show portrayed "today's intelligent, highly paid professional woman [...] as mocking the importance of fathers, by bearing a child alone, and calling it just another 'life-style choice'."[15] Predictably, the issue became a kind of Rorschach test, with feminists and liberals pillorying Quayle and social conservatives applauding him for taking on the condescending East and West Coast snobs who mocked their commitment to traditional families. The President himself soon weighed in, telling reporters that he and his wife Barbara were dismayed that "broken families" were common and believed that having a father and mother present provided "the best environment [...] to give a kid the best shot at the American dream."[16]

---

14 Address to the Nation on the National Drug Control Strategy, September 5, 1989 https://bush41library.tamu.edu/archives/public-papers/863 (accessed April 18, 2022).
15 *Time*, June 1, 1992 https://content.time.com/time/subscriber/article/0,33009,975627,00.html (accessed April 18, 2022).
16 The President's News Conference with Prime Minister Brian Mulroney of Canada, May 20, 1992 https://bush41library.tamu.edu/archives/public-papers/4332 (accessed April 18, 2022).

Race was another contentious issue that offered an opportunity to show solidarity with conservatives. Bush understood that many White men resented affirmative action—or what many conservatives labeled quotas or reverse racism—making it a potent political tool. In 1989, the U.S. Supreme Court, handed down a series of decisions that weakened existing civil rights protections. Congress responded by passing the Civil Rights Restoration Act in 1990, clarifying and strengthening the provisions of foundational civil rights laws. Of special concern was a decision that weakened a landmark 1971 Supreme Court case, *Griggs v. Duke Power*. *Griggs* held that employment practices that had a disparate impact on Blacks or women, even if not adopted with discriminatory intent, violated the Civil Rights Act of 1964 unless the employer could prove that they were justified by business necessity. It made employers think twice about requirements that screened out Black or female job seekers. The Court's 1989 decision shifted the burden back to the plaintiff, requiring her to prove that the practice being challenged was not necessary. That made it much more difficult to challenge discriminatory practices and reduced pressure on employers to eliminate policies that resulted in hiring fewer Blacks and women. The 1990 bill shifted the burden of proof back to employers, requiring them to show that job qualifications that adversely affected minorities and women had a substantial relationship to job performance.

The bill had bipartisan support in Congress. Rather than signing it, however, Bush decided to play the race card, issuing a stinging veto. "When our efforts, no matter how well intentioned, result in quotas, equal opportunity is [...] thwarted," he insisted.[17] The civil rights movement's commitment to creating a color-blind society had run amok, he suggested, and Whites were now victims of discrimination. A year later, the bill's supporters, led by Missouri Senator John Danforth, passed the bill again. A moderate Republican, Danforth was deeply concerned about growing racial division symbolized by Ku Klux Klan leader David Duke's campaign for governor of Louisiana. Committed to "reconstituting a political consensus in this country that had been threatened,"[18] Danforth rallied enough Republican support to create a veto-proof majority in the Senate. Bush reluctantly signed the law in October 1991, but he had shown himself to be the avenger of White racial grievance.

---

17 Message to the Senate Returning Without Approval the Civil Rights Act of 1990, October 22, 1990 https://bush41library.tamu.edu/archives/public-papers/2345 (accessed April 18, 2022).

18 *New York Times*, October 31, 1991 https://www.nytimes.com/1991/10/31/us/senate-approves-civil-rights-bill-95-5.html?searchResultPosition=1 (accessed April 18, 2022).

Because of the pivotal role of the Supreme Court in hotly contested social issues, nominations to the high court were closely watched. With the Court closely divided, every nomination was an opportunity—or a threat—to tip the balance. Conservatives were disappointed by Bush's first nominee, David Souter, a moderate Republican whose judicial record on the New Hampshire Supreme Court provided little evidence of his fealty to conservative principles. When the legendary civil rights pioneer Thurgood Marshall retired in 1991, Bush thrilled conservatives by nominating one of their own, Clarence Thomas. He was the product of a Catholic education, a member of a charismatic Episcopal congregation, and a proud Black conservative who opposed affirmative action. He insisted that it was at odds with the Constitution, which was color-blind, and stigmatized its supposed beneficiaries by raising doubts about whether they had succeeded on their merits. While he drew fire from civil rights and women's groups, Bush knew Thomas would be a difficult target. He was an all-American success story who grew up dirt poor in rural Georgia, was raised by his grandfather, graduated from Holy Cross and Yale Law School, and served as chair of Reagan's Equal Employment Opportunity Commission (EEOC) and a judge on the prestigious U.S. Court of Appeals for the District of Columbia. He had worked on the staff of Senator John Danforth, who had become a mentor and whose support would make a difference in the clubby Senate.

There was one problem Bush hadn't anticipated. As hearings on his nomination proceeded, Senate staffers and reporters were contacted by individuals who alleged that Thomas had sexually harassed Anita Hill, when she served on his EEOC staff. At the time sexual harassment was not well-understood. Nevertheless, Hill's allegations were explosive, and she proved a composed and credible witness in seven hours of grilling by members of the Judiciary Committee. Thomas denied her charges, insisted that questions about his private life were off limits, and turned the tables on his critics by charging that they were conducting a "high tech lynching for uppity blacks."[19] Viewer surveys reported that 30% of American households tuned in to the televised hearings.[20] Bush stood by his besieged nominee, saying that he had

---

[19] Jane Mayer and Jill Abrahamson, *Strange Justice: The Selling of Clarence Thomas* (New York, 1995), 205.

[20] *New York Times*, October 13, 1991 https://www.nytimes.com/1991/10/13/us/thomas-nomination-hearing-captures-big-tv-audience-lp-television-audience-for.html?searchResultPosition=3 (accessed January 23, 2023).

"total confidence in his honor and integrity" and believed he was "telling the truth all out."[21] Ultimately, Thomas was confirmed by a 52–48 vote, with 11 Democrats voting aye and two Republicans nay. Of the 11 positive Democratic votes, seven came from southerners whose Black supporters strongly favored Thomas's confirmation.

### Bush: Triumph Abroad, Defeat at Home

Bush held his own in domestic political battles. But it was foreign policy that most engaged him and where he achieved his greatest success. Indeed, by early 1991, his diplomatic and military triumphs made it seem like he had a lock on reelection. As he entered the White House, Eastern Europe was in turmoil as popular opposition to the region's Soviet-backed communist governments escalated. The Soviet Union faced chronic food shortages and teetered on the brink of economic collapse. Its leader, Mikhail Gorbachev, committed to economic reform and greater political openness, wasn't willing to divert resources to prop up unpopular governments in Eastern Europe. As a result, one by one, beginning with Poland in February 1989 and spreading to Hungary, Czechoslovakia, Romania, and the Baltic states, popular uprisings toppled communist regimes. The Iron Curtin collapsed, nowhere more dramatically than in Berlin. In November, massive crowds took to the streets demanding that the communist government hold democratic elections and permit citizens to leave and reenter the country freely. On November 9, huge crowds stormed the wall dividing East and West Berlin. As hundreds climbed the wall, frightened guards opened the gates, allowing thousands to stream into West Berlin and others began to demolish the wall. The most iconic symbol of the Cold War and a divided Europe, the Berlin Wall, had fallen, signaling the end of an era.

Events took Bush by surprise. He believed that Reagan had moved too far, too fast in negotiations with Gorbachev. As he entered office, he declined Soviet requests to resume negotiations until his administration could conduct a review of U.S.–Soviet relations. But developments in Eastern Europe persuaded Bush to meet with Gorbachev. In June, he extended an invitation, and the two met in Malta in December 1989. While the Soviets were eager to discuss arms limitations, Bush focused on Germany, seeking to persuade Gorbachev

---

21 "Exchange with Reporters at Holly Hills Country Club," October 13, 1991 Public Papers of President George H.W. Bush https://bush41library.tamu.edu/archives/public-papers/3502 (accessed February 26, 2023).

that reunification was inevitable and a united Germany should be part of the North Atlantic Treaty Organization (NATO), if it chose. Gorbachev balked, fearing opposition from the Soviet military. To avoid embarrassing him, Bush agreed to say only that he believed reunification was a matter for Germans to decide. When the two met in Washington in June 1990, Gorbachev, eager to secure a trade deal with the U.S. and loans from Germany, agreed that NATO membership should be decided by the Germans themselves. By year's end, the two Germanies voted to unite and remain part of NATO.

Discussions with the Soviets soon broadened to include arms control. The arms race had defined the Cold War with the U.S. and the Soviets amassing huge nuclear stockpiles. For many, deterring war through a strategy of mutually assured destruction (MAD) was, well, mad. In July 1991, after intense negotiations between the two sides, Gorbachev and Bush signed a Strategic Arms Reduction Treaty that reduced each side's overall nuclear strength by 30%. Like the fall of the Berlin Wall and German reunification, it was a milestone.

But nothing signaled the end of the Cold War more dramatically than the demise of the Soviet Union. The spirit of rebellion spread from Eastern Europe to the republics that constituted the Soviet Union. From the small Baltic republics and Ukraine to states in Central and Southwest Asia, demands for independence from Moscow swelled. Dismayed by what they perceived as Gorbachev's weakness, a group of Soviet military leaders attempted to reverse course. In August 1991, they placed him under house arrest. The flamboyant (and often drunk) Boris Yeltsin, president of the Russian Federation, rallied opposition to the coup, which collapsed in a matter of days, and along with it the Soviet Union. By early September, the parliaments of eight republics voted to secede from the Soviet Union, and Russia's legislature disbanded the Communist Party. With only one of the principal adversaries standing, the Cold War was over. Bush could claim credit for skillfully ending a conflict that had shaped international politics and threatened nuclear Armageddon for almost 50 years. Republicans crowed about their success, even as they failed to appreciate how the Soviet Union's demise would deprive them of a favorite tool for mobilizing voters—fear of communism.

As the Cold War wound down, conflict in the Middle East escalated. Iran and Iraq had fought a bloody, expensive war that spanned the 1980s and ended inconclusively. Because of Iran's implacable hostility to the U.S., the Reagan administration had assisted Iraq and its brutal leader, Saddam Hussein. With his economy battered by eight years of war, Saddam felt little gratitude toward the U.S. and soon launched an invasion of tiny, oil-rich Kuwait, in August 1990. Within hours, Iraqi forces forced the badly outmanned Kuwaiti army to capitulate. A World War II veteran, Bush quickly drew parallels to Japanese and German aggression in the 1930s and insisted that failure to stand up to Saddam would encourage more aggression and ultimately plunge the world into war. Because Kuwait produced an astonishing 20% of the world's oil, bordered Saudi Arabia, and was situated at head of the Persian Gulf, the President also saw the invasion as a threat to world oil supplies.

Bush acted decisively. He won passage of United Nations resolutions condemning the invasion and calling for an embargo of Iraq and assembled an international coalition that contributed troops and financial support for a campaign to dislodge Saddam. By early November 1990, the U.S. had 230,000 troops on Saudi soil, and Bush announced that he would increase the number to more than half a million. In late November, the U.N. Security Council—with Soviet support—authorized coalition forces to use "all necessary means" to expel Saddam if he did not withdraw his forces by January 15, 1991. With antiwar sentiment growing in the U.S., Bush wanted to defuse potential opposition from Congress. In January 1991, as the UN deadline approached, he asked Congress for authorization to use force. After several days of intense debate, the Senate endorsed military action by a narrow vote of 52–47, with nine Democrats supporting the President; the House added its support by a 250–183 majority, with 86 Democrats voting aye.

The U.S. offensive began on January 17, 1991. In the ensuing five weeks, vastly superior U.S. air power established control of the skies and pummeled Iraqi forces. Then, in late February, coalition forces launched Desert Storm, a punishing ground offensive. In three days of combat, Iraqi forces suffered heavy losses and accepted a cease-fire dictated by the U.S. With Saddam out of Kuwait and his army battered, Bush decided against carrying the war to Baghdad and toppling Saddam. The potential cost—in loss of life and public support—were simply too great, and, besides, he had achieved what he set out to do. Bush had vanquished the ghosts of Vietnam. He had built an international coalition, gained congressional support, defined the mission clearly, and refused to broaden it. His approval ratings, which hit 70% in late 1989 when the Berlin Wall fell, climbed to 89% in March 1991.

Bush's surging popularity was truly astonishing, and it deterred most prominent Democrats—Mario Cuomo, Ted Kennedy, Jesse Jackson—from challenging him in 1992. But political popularity can be fleeting. As Saddam invaded Kuwait, the United States entered a recession that saw unemployment reach 8%, where it remained until mid-1992. Combined with conservatives' animosity toward Bush for reneging on his no-new-taxes pledge, the President's popularity fell below 50% as the 1992 primaries began and hit a low of 29% on Labor Day. Timing is everything in politics, and Bush's couldn't have been worse.

To compound his problem, Bush faced a formidable opponent in Bill Clinton, who, at 45, was the nation's longest-serving governor. Although Clinton's path to the nomination was nearly derailed by embarrassing revelations about his personal life, he proved remarkably resilient, bouncing back from every near-catastrophe. He supported the death penalty, called for more police to combat crime, and promised welfare reform. He also took on a Black rapper, Sister Souljah, who asked, "If black people kill black people every day, why not have a week and kill white people?"[22]

Even more important, Clinton attacked Bush where he was weakest, the economy. With a remarkable ability to convey empathy, he made Americans feel that he understood how the recession, unemployment, and declining real wages affected their lives. He tapped into disillusionment with an economy that rewarded the top 10% but left everyone ese working harder to keep their heads above water. "Middle class people are spending more time on the job, less time with their children and bringing home less money to pay more for health care and housing and education," Clinton asserted. Under Republicans, he charged, the middle class had experienced shrinking income and higher taxes while the wealthy made more and paid less. He would be a champion of working families, "preserving the American Dream, restoring the hopes of the forgotten middle class and reclaiming the future for our children."[23] It was a powerful message, and Clinton focused on it throughout the campaign. A banner at Clinton headquarters read, "It's the economy, stupid."[24]

As Clinton attacked Bush for being out of touch, Ross Perot, a pint-size Texas billionaire entered the race as an independent candidate. Politicians in both parties, he charged, were self-serving and ignored the needs of the people. What the country needed was a successful businessman like himself who could make data-driven decisions and stop spending money that the country didn't

---

22 *New York Times*, June 17, 1992 https://www.nytimes.com/1992/06/17/us/the-1992-campaign-racial-issues-rapper-chided-by-clinton-calls-him-a-hypocrite.html (accessed April 23, 2022).

23 *New York Times*, October 4, 1991 https://www.nytimes.com/1991/10/04/us/arkansas-clinton-enters-the-92-race-for-president.html (accessed April 23, 2022).

24 Julian Zelizer, "'It's the economy, stupid,' all over again," CNN, May 8, 2020 https://www.cnn.com/2020/05/08/opinions/economy-2020-election-trump-biden-zelizer/index.html (accessed January 23, 2023).

have on programs that didn't work. Perot benefitted from widespread alienation from politicians that had grown steadily since the 1960s, and his support surged during the summer of 1992. In late June, a Gallup Poll found that 28% of potential voters preferred him in a three-way contest with Bush and Clinton.[25] But Perot was eccentric. Toward the end of the summer, he dropped out of the race, only to reenter in October. His erratic behavior cost him support, and he was unable to rebuild the momentum he had developed during the summer.

When the votes were cast on November 3, Clinton was the winner. He captured 43% of the popular vote to 37% for Bush and a remarkable 19% for Perot. While Republicans believed that Perot cost Bush the race, exit polls indicated that equal numbers of Perot voters would have voted for Bush and Clinton while approximately a quarter of them would have stayed home. Clinton's strategy—focusing on the economy and showing empathy for working families paid off, making him the first Democrat to win the White House since 1976. However, he had no coattails. The Senate elections were a wash, with Democrats holding a 57–43 majority while Republicans picked up nine seats in the House to narrow the Democratic majority to 258–176.

Clinton wasn't the only "comeback kid" in 1992. The Democratic Party demonstrated its resilience by capturing the White House after losing five of the six previous presidential campaigns. After over two decades of futility in presidential politics, the Democratic Party's center of gravity had shifted right. There was still a strong progressive wing, and Democrats still gave shout-outs to the glory days of the New Deal and the Great Society. But the party occupied a far different place than in the days of FDR and LBJ. As labor unions hemorrhaged members, their influence declined. Although Blacks, college-educated women, and environmentalists remained a force, New Democrats like Clinton sought some separation from them. They took more conservative positions on issues ranging from crime and welfare to fiscal responsibility and the role of government in American life. They also directed their attention to addressing the economic challenges faced by middle- and working-class Americans.

Republicans had rung up smashing victories in presidential contests since 1968. They had mobilized White evangelicals and Catholics and strengthened their appeal to White working-class voters. They had also used fear of the Soviet

---

25 Gallup Organization, Gallup News Service Poll: June News Service Wave 2, Question 1, USGALLUP.322002.Q01, Gallup Organization, (Cornell University, Ithaca, NY: Roper Center for Public Opinion Research, 1992).

threat and support for a muscular anti-communist foreign policy to rally voters concerned about America's diminished role in the aftermath of Vietnam. But Republicans' success in presidential elections was not a precursor to political realignment. The GOP had not combined presidential victories with control of Congress. Support for policies that pleased social conservatives alienated many college-educated baby boomers who embraced libertarian values forged in the 1960s. The tried-and-true strategy of appealing to fear of the Soviet Union evaporated as the 1990s began, encouraging Republicans to double down on social issues. With the end of stagflation, the economy was an issue that could cut both ways. Republicans never completely shed their image as a party of corporate America, leaving many middle- and working-class Americans who felt left behind in the recovery of the 1980s skeptical of the Republican brand.

The nation was more closely divided politically than perhaps any time since the Gilded Age. It was an apt comparison since many critics labeled the late 1980s and 1990s, with its growing concentration of wealth, the New Gilded Age. The gap between Americans who identified as Democrats rather than Republicans narrowed from 41% to 27% in 1980 to 33%–28% in 1992. It remained there, with some fluctuation, the rest of the decade. A growing number of Americans—29% in 1980 and 36% in 1992—identified as independents.[26] The close division between the two major parties and the number of swing voters made it difficult for either party to achieve dominance. Leaders in both parties decided that the best way to navigate this landscape was to vilify the opposition, fire up the base, and rally skeptical independents against their opponents when they stumbled, which they usually did. Newt Gingrich's takedown of Jim Wright, the nation's most powerful Democrat, proved to many that bare-knuckle tactics were effective.

Gingrich's approach posed a threat. Members of each party's base might applaud their leaders when they stood their ground, hurled invective, and refused to compromise. But they were a fraction of a fraction—the roughly 60% of voters who identified with one of the two major parties. Most voters saw confrontation and polarization as signs that the system didn't work and that politicians weren't interested in doing their job. That was particularly disturbing at a time when wealth was becoming more concentrated and gains in real income among the bottom 80% of Americans were sluggish. Americans

---

26 Pew Research Center, "Trends in Party Identification, 1939–2014," April 7. 2015 https://www.pewresearch.org/politics/interactives/party-id-trend/ (accessed January 23, 2023).

who felt that they were putting in more hours on the job—or at two jobs—became increasingly alienated from politics and more distrustful of the system. Apathy and alienation grew. However, partisan warfare energized others who took joy in supporting their political "team" and relished sticking it to the enemy. Politics took on all the qualities of Yankees-Red Sox baseball weekends. In baseball, that's usually harmless, resulting in exchange of good-natured barbs, snarky, profanity-laced insults, or even a few minor fisticuffs. In politics, however, fear and loathing have more serious consequences. Winners wield power, and they can hurt their enemies, do damage to everyone, and erode political and legal institutions that are necessary to mediate conflict. "A house divided against itself cannot stand," Lincoln had cautioned Americans in the 1850s. More than a century later, sharp divisions—many morally and culturally grounded—had become woven into the fabric of American politics, posing as great a threat to the republic as slavery had for Lincoln's generation. As Democrats rejoiced in Clinton's victory, the division in the American house was about to become deeper. Ironically, it came at a time when the two major parties were growing closer ideologically.

CHAPTER 7

# IDEOLOGICAL CONVERGENCE AND POLITICAL POLARIZATION, 1992–2000

## Mobilizing Fear, Sewing Hate, Spreading Lies

Hillary Rodham understood the opportunities second-wave feminism opened as well as the powerful backlash it generated. It was the story of her life. She grew up in an upper-middle-class Republican family in suburban Chicago. A bright, highly motivated high school student, she excelled at Wellesley, where she was the president of her class, and in 1969, became the first student commencement speaker. She left Wellesley as a feminist committed to social justice and headed to Yale Law School to earn a J.D. that she hoped would equip her to use law as a tool of social change. At Yale, she fell in love with the irrepressible Bill Clinton who combined good looks with charisma and a like-minded commitment to make the world a better place. After graduation, he returned to Arkansas while she worked for Marian Wright Edelman's Children's Defense Fund and then on the staff of the House Judiciary Committee as it developed articles of impeachment against Richard Nixon. They remained romantically involved, and in 1974, she joined him in Arkansas, accepting a faculty position at the University of Arkansas Law School. Like many young women torn between love and career, she chose love, prompting her closest friend to demand, "Why on earth would you throw away your future?" "I chose to follow my heart, not my head," was Rodham's explanation.[1]

Life in the South wasn't easy for a professional woman who disdained makeup, often wore clothing purchased at thrift stores, had long straight hair, didn't change her name, and married an aspiring politician. Things didn't become easier when her husband became governor in 1978. She had resigned

---

1 Hillary Rodham Clinton, *Living History* (New York, 2003), 86.

her law school position, and they moved to Little Rock when he became attorney general in 1976. She made a dramatic career change, giving up the public interest law that her faculty position made possible to practice corporate law at The Rose Law Firm, the state's oldest and most prestigious. She became its first female associate and, subsequently, partner. As the governor's wife, however, she was under a microscope, and people asked why she dressed like a hippie and didn't change her name. After Bill lost his bid for re-election in 1980 and began planning a comeback, his advisors and supporters encouraged her to develop an image Arkansans expected of their First Lady. When Bill kicked off his 1982 campaign, she was introduced as Hillary Rodham Clinton.

Nine years later, as Bill announced that he was running for president, Hillary had balanced her life as a high-powered attorney, mother, and First Lady with aplomb. Arkansas had been hard to navigate, but she had won acceptance. The national political stage was much more treacherous. She entered a world in which gender was among the most highly charged, easily exploitable social issues, and politicians and talk radio hosts hadn't found a blow low enough to consider off limits. As the critical New Hampshire primary approached in early 1992, tabloids that everyone glanced at as they checked out at the supermarket told the steamy story of Bill's alleged 12-year affair with Gennifer Flowers, a Little Rock night club singer. With his candidacy on the line, Bill and Hillary agreed to appear on the popular CBS news show, *60 Minutes*—immediately after the Super Bowl, no less, which guaranteed an audience of 50 million viewers. The couple acknowledged marital problems, and Bill admitted "causing pain in my marriage." Offering a left-hand compliment, host Steve Kroft acknowledged "you've stayed together [...] and [...] you've seemed to reach some kind of understanding and arrangement." The implication that they saw their relationship as a means to achieve power was too much for Hillary. She shot back, "You know, I'm not sitting here—some little woman standing by my man like Tammy Wynette. I'm sitting here because I love him, and I respect him."[2]

The interview was a success—at least for Bill. Most observers credited it with resuscitating his candidacy when he finished a close second in New Hampshire and dubbed himself "the Comeback Kid." The blowback against Hillary, however, was fierce. She may have supported her husband, but did it in an assertive, take-charge manner that some found threatening. Tammy Wynette,

---

2 *Washington Post*, January 26, 1992 https://www.washingtonpost.com/wp-srv/politics/special/clinton/stories/flowers012792.htm (accessed September 5, 2022).

who, ironically, was on her fifth husband, led the attack. She wrote a public letter to Hillary, calling her out as a privileged yuppie who disdained working people who loved country music but didn't live the charmed life she and her friends did. "Mrs. Clinton," she chided, "you have offended every true country music fan and every person who has 'made it on their own' with no one to take them to a White House."[3]

Six weeks later, Hillary stepped on another landmine, although in truth there were so many, it was probably impossible for a self-respecting professional woman to avoid them. One of Bill's rivals for the Democratic nomination charged that Hillary had profited from state contracts directed to her firm by her husband, the governor. That infuriated Hillary, who had set up a firewall that prevented her from sharing any revenue her firm received from state work. Asked about the allegations on the campaign trail, she shot back, "I suppose I could have stayed home and baked cookies and had teas, but I decided to fulfill my profession, which I entered before my husband was in public life."[4] She added that she had worked "to assure that women can make the choices [...] whether it's full-time career, full-time motherhood, or some combination."[5] Reporters ignored the second part of her comment, making her sound like a condescending yuppie who had no empathy for women who chose not to work outside of the home.

Republicans and talk radio hosts pounced. Her insensitive remarks were proof, they charged, that she was a selfish, calculating professional woman who couldn't appreciate the limited options and difficult choices less-privileged women and families made. It was a great opportunity to stoke blue-collar voters' dislike for feminism. William Safire, Nixon's speechwriter turned *New York Times* columnist, spoke of "The Hillary Problem," charging that her "cookies and tea stereotype is elitism in action" and showed "contempt for women who work at home."[6] His old boss, the disgraced former president, piled on. "If the wife

---

3 Joe Edwards, "Tammy Wynette Want To Go 'Toe To Toe' With Mrs. Clinton With AM—Wynette Lyrics," AP News, January 28, 1992 https://apnews.com/article/15c018e 09e0bbdb0a20cd5609773d741 (accessed September 5, 2022).

4 Michael Kruse, "The TV Interview that Haunts Hillary Clinton," Politico, September 23, 2016 https://www.politico.com/magazine/story/2016/09/hillary-clinton-2016-60-minutes-1992-214275/ (accessed September 6, 2022).

5 *Time*, September 14, 1992 https://content.time.com/time/subscriber/article/0,33009,976448-7,00.html (accessed September 6, 2022).

6 *New York Times*, March 26, 1992 https://www.nytimes.com/1992/03/26/opinion/essay-the-hillary-problem.html (accessed September 6, 2022).

comes through as being too strong and too intelligent, it makes the husband look like a wimp," Richard Nixon commented.[7] Not only was she disdainful of everyday Americans, she was emasculating Bill.

If these sins weren't enough, critics charged that Hillary threatened the traditional family, the foundation of American values and social stability. Republicans, reported *Time* magazine, tried to "turn her into 'Willie Horton' for the '92 campaign, making her an emblem of all that is wrong with family values, working mothers and modern women in general."[8] The Bush campaign mischaracterized her earlier writings to claim that she had compared marriage to slavery and asserted that children should sue parents whom they believed mistreated them. Rich Bond, the chair of the Republican National Committee, expressed outrage for the Clintons' supposed contempt for traditional values. "We are America," he snorted. "These other people are not America."[9]

It was the beginning of a campaign of character assassination. With the Soviets vanquished, Democrats claiming the center on issues like crime and welfare, and the economy in recession, social issues offered Republicans a lifeline. They guaranteed that Hillary would continue to be an attractive target— the radical feminist bent on destroying the traditional family and determined to play the role of copresident. At the same time, they charged, she was greedy, using her influence to line her pockets. By 1994, there would be a Hillary Haters mailing list that Affinity Marketing Group sold to the Republican National Committee and assorted right-wing organizations. According to the company, "These good ol' boy types are pro-military, anti-gay, pro-gun, anti-welfare, pro-America, and anti-foreigner."[10] Nor were they high on feminists, a group talk radio host Rush Limbaugh derided as "feminazis."

## Here ruining people is considered a sport

The attacks on Hillary were part of Republicans' effort to mobilize divisive cultural issues against Democrats. The attacks would only become more venomous after Clinton assumed the presidency, fueling polarization that

---

7 Kruse, "The TV Interview that Haunts Hillary Clinton."

8 *Time*, September 14, 1992 https://content.time.com/time/subscriber/article/0,33009,976448-7,00.html (accessed September 6, 2022).

9 *New York Times*, February 2, 1993 https://www.nytimes.com/1993/02/02/opinion/rich-bond-right-but-late.html (accessed September 6, 2022).

10 *New York Times*, October 23, 1994 https://www.nytimes.com/1994/10/23/magazine/sunday-october-23-1994-enemies-lists.html (accessed January 29, 2023).

threatened to disrupt the difficult work of governing a closely divided nation. As the attacks on Hillary during the campaign presaged, polarization wasn't fueled by ideology or unbridgeable disagreements over public policy. The end of the Cold War had removed a longstanding subject of disagreement, and Clinton and his New Democrat supporters had moved closer to Republicans on domestic policy. He challenged the Republican narrative that Democrats were out of touch with the needs and values of middle- and working-class Americans and embraced market-oriented solutions while hewing to traditional Democratic themes of standing up for the little person. Clinton's success broke Republicans' apparent lock on the White House by blunting Republicans' most successful attack lines, making him a greater threat than Democrats like Ted Kennedy or Jesse Jackson with whom Republicans disagreed more sharply on policy.

As he assumed the presidency in January 1993, Clinton hewed to the themes he had honed as a New Democrat. In his inaugural address, he admitted that the country faced serious problems—global economic competition, "most people working harder for less," "the cost of health care that devastates our families and threatens to bankrupt our enterprises," a crime epidemic that "robs law abiding citizens of their freedom," and a growing national debt. Yet he expressed optimism reminiscent of Ronald Reagan. "There is nothing wrong with America that cannot be cured by what is right with America," he insisted. The new president demanded fiscal responsibility, pledging to "cut our massive debt" while finding ways to "invest more in our own people." He promised to "break the bad habit of expecting something for nothing from our Government or from each other" by offering "more opportunity for all" while demanding "more responsibility from all."[11] If Clinton's emphasis on personal responsibility and fiscal discipline sang from the Republican hymnal, he reassured Democrats by promising to level the playing field and restore opportunity to those whom Republican policies had left behind.

Clinton was true to his New Democrat self. As his team got down to business and developed their first budget, deficit reduction became his top priority. He desperately wanted to include new investments in transportation and education. They would not only fulfill his campaign promises, but would provide economic stimulus to jumpstart an economy slowly emerging from recession. However, his economic advisors, a conservative bunch led by Robert Rubin, the former head of Goldman Sachs who chaired the National Economic Council, insisted that deficit reduction take priority. And that precluded significant

---

11 William J. Clinton, Inaugural Address, January 20, 1993 https://www.presidency.ucsb.edu/documents/inaugural-address-51 (accessed July 21, 2022).

new investments. Thanks to the Reagan tax cuts and the Bush recession, the deficit had ballooned to $300 billion. If the president didn't take serious action, Fed chair Alan Greenspan and the bond market would increase interest rates, put the brakes on an already sluggish recovery, and ensure that he was a one-term president. Clinton bridled at their advice, raging "Do you mean to tell me that my program and my re-election hinges on the Federal Reserve and bunch of fucking bond traders?"[12] But he took it, trimming his investments and accepting budget cuts and tax increases that would halve the deficit in five years.

Predictably, the plan was whipsawed by opposition from left and right. Republicans proclaimed it dead on arrival because tax increases had become as appealing to them as castor oil. Besides, Clinton's centrism threatened them, and they were determined to deny him a win. Many Democrats wanted a bigger stimulus, although some who hailed from swing districts wanted to minimize tax increases and the size of any stimulus lest they be branded tax-and-spend liberals. Senators from oil-producing states—Democrats and Republicans—dug in their heels against the so-called British Thermal Unit (BTU) tax. By taxing fossil fuels based on their heat content, it promised to raise significant new revenue while encouraging energy conservation. In the end, the BTU tax was replaced by a hike in the regressive federal gasoline tax. A middle-class tax cut that candidate Clinton had championed was scrapped, and little remained of the infrastructure and education investments. Progressive features survived, including a significant boost in the earned income tax credit (a godsend to the working poor), increased spending for food stamps and childhood vaccinations, and an increase in the marginal tax rate on those with incomes of more than $100,000. When Clinton signed the bill in August 1993, its spending cuts of $255 billion matched $241 billion in tax increases, promising deficit reduction that the financial markets found credible. Combined with growing productivity, generated by heavy investments in technology during the previous decade, Clinton's policies helped spur dramatic growth. By 1999, GDP was rising by 4.8% annually, unemployment had been halved to 4%, inflation stood at 2.7%, and there was a $236 budget surplus.[13]

---

12 Steven M. Gillon, *The Pact: Bill Clinton, Newt Gingrich, and the Rivalry that Defined a Generation* (New York, 2008).
13 The World Bank, GDP Growth (annual %)—The United States https://data.worldbank.org/indicator/NY.GDP.MKTP.KD.ZG?end=2020&locations=US&start=1990 (accessed January 29, 2023); The Balance, Historical Unemployment Rate by Year https://www.thebalancemoney.com/unemployment-rate-by-year-3305506 (accessed January 29, 2023).

While Ike must have been smiling, his Republican descendants, led by the most un-Ike-like of them all, Newt Gingrich, refused Clinton's appeals to bipartisanship. Every GOP representative and senator voted against the package, a confirmation that they prized tax cuts more than fiscal responsibility. And because the package relied on tax increases, they charged that there was nothing really new about this Democratic president. He was just another tax-and-spend defender of big government.

Efforts at obstruction were situational and could evaporate when there were gains to be made. When Clinton threw his weight behind the North American Free Trade Agreement (NAFTA), which had been negotiated by his predecessor, Republicans quickly fell in line. Reflecting Republican commitment to free trade, the treaty with Canada and Mexico reduced or eliminated tariffs and other trade barriers, creating a free trade zone with two of the nation's most important trading partners. It was bitterly opposed by organized labor, historically a key Democratic constituency. Union leaders claimed it would accelerate job losses by encouraging companies to shift production to Mexico. But Clinton believed that by stimulating growth in Mexico and Canada, NAFTA would create stronger markets for U.S. goods, services, and investments. The jobs created would reduce Mexicans' desire to migrate to the U.S. and blunt the temptation of Mexico's leaders to consider overtures from countries hostile to the U.S. like Venezuela and Cuba. Many Democrats opposed the agreement while Republicans lined up behind the treaty. A majority of Republicans in the House and Senate were joined by a minority of Democrats to provide comfortable margins. The victory may have strengthened Clinton's reputation for working with the opposition but it came at a cost. Many blue-collar voters would come to see Democrats as more loyal to corporate leaders and investors than to people like themselves.

Declaring war on crime was perhaps better suited to outflanking Republicans while pleasing working and middle-class Americans. As governor and presidential candidate, Clinton had worked hard to take the crime issue away from Republicans. Although crime rates were actually falling in the early 1990s, polling suggested that most Americans still viewed crime as a major issue. So, it was no surprise that Clinton made it a priority. The crime bill he pushed through Congress provided funding to put 100,000 more cops on the streets and build more prisons, increased the number of federal crimes punishable by death to 60, and required federal judges to impose life sentences on those convicted of their third violent federal crime. Using a catchy phrase, "three strikes and you're out," signaled a tough approach championed by many conservatives.

There were progressive elements in Clinton's bill as well. It funded community policing initiatives designed to prevent crime by integrating police into the communities they served, banned 19 varieties of semiautomatic assault weapons, made investments in drug treatment programs, created a program to divert first-time nonviolent drug offenders from prison, and supported social programs (including night-time basketball leagues) designed to provide constructive options for inner city kids. It also included provisions to address violence against women by providing a federal civil rights remedy for victims of gender-based violence and grants to local governments to create programs to reduce domestic violence and child abuse.

While most Republicans ultimately backed the crime bill, Gingrich made a bipartisan victory as painful as possible. Conservative Republicans hammered the bill for its assault weapons ban, but their attack backfired when polls showed that most Americans supported it. As the bill neared passage in the summer of 1994, however, conservative talk radio hosts charged that the bill was laden with pork, including its support for misguided social programs like "midnight basketball leagues." These charges resonated, prompting many moderate Republicans to withdraw support. That proved catastrophic because Clinton needed them to overcome defections from Democrats, including those from conservative districts who opposed the assault weapons ban and members of the Congressional Black Caucus who objected to the bill's death penalty provisions. When it failed on a key procedural vote, Clinton was forced to negotiate with Republicans and trim support for social programs. That won over enough Republicans to ensure success, and Clinton signed the bill in September 1994, claiming a bipartisan triumph. However, Gingrich and many conservative Republicans continued to hammer the bill, creating the impression that Democrats hadn't really changed. They were still enamored of spending on soft-headed pork-laden projects meant to coddle inner city (aka, Black) constituents. "You know, this is like watching the President get into his Mustang and drive it into the ditch," Gingrich chortled.[14] The Mustang, of course, was a carefully chosen metaphor designed to tie Clinton to the alleged excesses of the 1960s.

Partisan battles over the budget and the crime bill were mild compared with attacks on Clinton's character. The President provided some of the ammunition himself. Candidate Clinton had pledged to appoint a cabinet that "looks like America." Once in office, he delivered. Applauding the selection of five women,

---

14 Peter J. Boyer, "Whip Cracker," *The New Yorker*, September 5, 1994, 38.

four Blacks, and two Hispanics to his 18-member cabinet, *The Washington Post* proclaimed that Clinton "has assembled the most diverse Cabinet in history."[15] Yet plaudits soon turned to criticism. In the late 1980s and early 1990s, both parties had honed their skills in "opposition research" (as it was called) to find dirt on opponents. Because Clinton had experienced this personally when his candidacy was nearly derailed by scandal, he should have paid greater attention to vetting nominees.

Two Justice Department nominations drew intense fire. Zoe Baird, Clinton's nominee as attorney general, made a splash with feminists. Only 40, Baird had an impeccable resume. Unfortunately, she and her husband had what became known as a "nanny problem." Like many upper-income, two-career couples, they had employed an undocumented immigrant to care for their child and had paid no Social Security taxes. News of Baird's transgression unleashed withering criticism, forcing her to withdraw. Her actions confirmed for many that members of the elite didn't have to play by the same rules as everyone else, something that candidate Clinton had promised would change when he was president. Lani Guinier, Clinton's nominee for assistant attorney general for civil rights set off an even louder alarm. An African American civil rights lawyer and law school classmate of Bill and Hillary, Guinier had published some dry-as-dust law review articles arguing that Black voting failed to translate into influence commensurate with their share of the population. Majoritarian politics denied Blacks a place at the table where decisions were made. As a remedy, Guinier suggested changes in voting procedures calculated to enhance Blacks' actual representation in the political system. Critics feasted on the articles, charging her with designs on creating proportional representation for minorities. In the words of a *Wall Street Journal* op ed, Guinier was the "quota queen."[16]

Clinton dropped her like a hot potato. He claimed he hadn't read her articles (which is undoubtedly true), but that when he did, he found them troubling (which he probably did not). To many Whites, Clinton's fulsome support for diversity was nothing more than a cynical effort to pay off key Democratic interest groups. For many White men, in particular, it was simply another example of women and minorities getting ahead at their expense. Clinton's hasty abandonment of his nominees fed criticism that he was untrustworthy and lacked the character to

---

15 *Washington Post*, January 20, 1993 https://www.washingtonpost.com/archive/politics/1993/01/20/clintons-cabinet/31310df4-2073-48c6-b5bf-1b47cfd7b135/ (accessed July 25, 2022).
16 Jim Naureckus and Bob Richie, "Lani Guinier: 'Quota Queen' or Misquoted Queen," FAIR, July 1, 1993 https://fair.org/home/elite-media-remember-lani-guinier-as-embattled-and-forget-how-they-battled-her/ (accessed January 29, 2023).

be president. It only reinforced the image that many already had of Clinton—the college student who had finagled his way out of the draft and the husband who had been unfaithful to his wife. Many concluded that Arkansas journalist Paul Greenberg nailed it when he gave Clinton the nickname "Slick Willie."

Several missteps early in his presidency fed the distrust and hostility. Having promised to repeal the ban on military service by gays and lesbians, Clinton was under intense pressure to act when he entered the White House. Unfortunately, the military, led by Colin Powell, the popular chair of the Joint Chiefs of Staff, pushed back, arguing that welcoming gays and lesbians would undermine unit cohesion and make U.S. forces less combat-ready. Clinton's first inclination—a familiar standby for politicians—was to create a commission to study the issue. But the issue wouldn't go away. Faced with opposition from the military and the prospect that Congress might write a ban on service by gays and lesbians into law, Clinton negotiated a compromise with the military and congressional critics. Under the new policy, known as "Don't Ask, Don't Tell, Don't Pursue," recruits could not be asked about their sexual orientation, and commanders could not harass or discriminate against those they suspected were gay or lesbian. Only if commanders had credible evidence of homosexual conduct could they initiate an investigation that might lead to dismissal.

Hoping to please everyone, Clinton ended up pleasing no one. The policy was confusing, encouraged deception, and left gays and lesbians living under the shadow of dismissal even as they served their country. While his options were limited, the policy did little to burnish his image as a strong leader. Gays and lesbians denounced it as a betrayal, while conservatives and members of the religious right charged that it proved what they had known all along—Clinton was an avatar of 1960s radicalism. For many others, it only confirmed the impression that Clinton was a wily politician who tried to have it all ways.

Health care, Clinton's signature initiative, became another debacle. Candidate Clinton had promised to reform welfare, an issue popular with conservatives, and provide all Americans with access to health care, a Democratic priority since Harry Truman's presidency. Having prioritized deficit reduction, a move that disappointed many in the Democratic base, Clinton backed off welfare reform, identified health care as a top priority, and appointed Hillary to head a task force to develop legislation. She certainly had the intellect and relevant experience, having successfully led initiatives in Arkansas to reform rural health care and improve education.

Health care, however, was as complex and politically fraught as any domestic policy issue. It was the nation's largest industry, provided services that were top of mind for most Americans, and was plagued by runaway costs.

Most Americans had coverage provided by their employer and were happy with the care they received; Medicare and Medicaid provided coverage for seniors and the poor. However, many Americans worked for employers who didn't provide coverage, and they often found purchasing insurance too expensive. Even those whose employers provided insurance feared losing their jobs and, with it, their health insurance. If they did and had a pre-existing condition, insurers would probably refuse coverage, even if they could pay for it. Many were happy with what they had, others had coverage but feared for the future, and some lacked insurance and worried what they would do if they or a spouse or child needed care.

Many liberals argued that the only way to provide equitable coverage and contain costs was a single-payer system. That meant the federal government would use tax revenues to defray the cost of health care for everyone—and set reimbursements for providers. Canada, the U.K., and most developed nations used that approach, as did Medicare and Medicaid. However, the U.S. had developed a system of private insurance during World War II and its aftermath, as unions had bargained with employers for robust healthcare packages. Talk of a single-payer system threatened powerful interests, namely, insurance companies and doctors, and faced political headwinds in a country that had soured on government's ability to deliver.

As a New Democrat who had worked hard to claim the political center, the single-payer solution was not an option for Clinton. The task force did impressive work to find an alternative. It drew on the expertise of hundreds of doctors, hospital administrators, and health policy experts to develop a comprehensive plan that avoided the single-payer solution. Hillary was a dedicated chair who worked Capitol Hill, paying visits to legislators—including many Republicans—to explain the task force's work and press the need for reliable, affordable health care. But developing a plan from scratch was complex and time-consuming. And as the plan emerged, it was so complicated that even well-informed citizens had trouble understanding it. Relying on the market, the plan proposed to create health insurance alliances, coordinated by the government. They would compete with one another to offer competitive healthcare plans from which consumers would choose. Who would pay? The plan included an employer mandate that required businesses to pay 80% of the cost with the balance picked up by the employee. For those with limited means, there would be government subsidies. It made sense on paper, but those who had steady jobs and good health insurance wondered if it would be as good as what they already had. Would they be able keep their current doctor or be forced to see someone else? To many it seemed like buying a pig in a poke.

Uncertainty provided the perfect opportunity for Republicans. So, too, did the time that it took to get a bill to Congress. Clinton had hoped to send a bill to Capitol Hill by mid-1993, but that proved unrealistic. Developing legislation on such a complicated matter took time, and delays over Clinton's budget put health care on the back burner. The delay provided opponents the opportunity to sow doubts. In September 1993, Clinton revived public support for reform with a mesmerizing nationally broadcast address to Congress. But opposition built again, with insurers and employers mobilizing a $300 million advertising blitz against the bill. Especially effective was an ad financed by the Health Insurance Association of America, featuring a couple, Harry and Louise, discussing the choices at their kitchen table. Contemplating a law that would "force us to pick from a few health care plans designed by government bureaucrats," Harry comments, "They choose," and Louise responds, "We lose."[17] The tires of the health reform bus quickly deflated.

As public support waned, Republicans moved in for the kill. In a Senate with a 57–43 Democratic majority, Democrats needed three Republican votes to get the 60 votes needed to break a filibuster. Sensing that the odds were against them, some Democrats expressed support for legislation introduced by moderate Republicans that removed the employer-mandate and provided government vouchers to the unemployed and tax breaks for everyone else. Even though Bob Dole, the Senate Republican leader, had been a sponsor of the compromise, he and other party leaders quickly pulled the plug on it. Giving Clinton a victory on health care was bad politics. In the words of Republican strategist William Kristol, it would allow Democrats to claim that they were the "protector of middle-class interests" and "strike a punishing blow against Republican claims to defend the middle class by restraining government."[18] Doing nothing was better than handing the enemy a victory that might establish its dominance for a generation. But Clinton, not Republicans, owned the defeat, leading many voters to conclude he was just another politician who promised to make things better but couldn't deliver.

Not all of Clinton's problems were of his own making. Despite—or perhaps because of—his aggressive efforts to claim the center, many on the right viewed him—and Hillary—as demons. Bill's centrism, they believed, was just an act designed to win votes. "The right's opposition to the Clintons was characterized

---

17 https://www.youtube.com/watch?v=Dt31nhleeCg.
18 Patrick J. Maney, *Bill Clinton: New Gilded Age President* (Lawrence, KS, 2016), 107.

by a level of malice that transcended normal partisan opposition," explained David Brock the right-wing scandal-monger who broke with conservatives in the late 1990s. "The Clintons were made into metaphors for all of the social changes of the past thirty years that the right-wing base in the country hated."[19] There were many Clinton haters, and some had the will, the connections, and the money to make his—and Hillary's—life miserable. In the process, they perfected the politics of personal destruction Gingrich had deployed against Jim Wright. Wild conspiracy theories, disregard for truth and evidence, a fixation on opponents' ethical lapses (especially those involving sex), and lacerating personal attacks that treated unsubstantiated rumors as fact crowded out serious debate over public policy. The viciousness made bipartisanship—always difficult—seem like a relic of the distant past and compromise—the essential lubricant of democratic politics—nearly impossible. Bringing politics into the gutter bred growing disgust for politics and politicians and fed political apathy as many voters concluded that politicians cared more about clinging to power that solving their problems.

Much of the fool's gold that made the anti-Clinton campaign glisten was in Arkansas, and the number of prospectors who beat a path there was reminiscent of the California Gold Rush. At the heart of the campaign was Whitewater, a real estate investment, the Clintons had entered with Jim McDougal, an Arkansas banker, and his wife Susan in the late 1970s. The plan was unremarkable: transform 230 acres of mountain land on the White River into lots for vacation homes. Like many such investments, it failed, a victim of the real estate bubble that burst in the 1980s. Subsequently, Jim McDougal was charged with banking fraud after several savings and loans he owned went belly-up. In March 1992, *the New York Times* ran a story about the failed investment. It did not accuse the Clintons of wrongdoing but fueled speculation that they had benefitted from McDougal's banking shenanigans and that Bill, as the governor, had pressured state regulators to overlook McDougal's fraudulent practices.

New developments fed speculation about wrongdoing after Clinton entered the White House. David Hale, a Little Rock municipal judge, was charged with channeling over $2 million in loans from the Small Business Administration into his personal accounts. Hale had ties to Jim McDougal, and, he alleged, to Clinton who pressured him to make an illegal $300,000 loan to McDougal

---

19 David Brock, *Blinded by the Right: The Conscience of an Ex-Conservative* (New York, 2002), 138–139.

that was somehow connected to the Whitewater project. Although years of investigations by congressional committees, reporters, and two special prosecutors failed to establish any wrongdoing by the Clintons, the fool's gold kept the reporters coming and their stories circulating.

A new, little understood force in politics made the onslaught especially fierce. It was the early days of the Internet—the World Wide Web as it was called then. The White House had only recently launched a website and only 10% of homes had access through dial up service. Staff in the White House Counsel's Office were bombarded by mainstream media with queries about wild conspiracy theories about the Clintons and wondered where they were coming from. When they probed the Internet, they uncovered, in the words of Chris Lehane, a staffer who went on to develop a successful political consulting firm, "an entire cottage industry devoted to conspiracy theories" about the Clintons. Their reports were picked up by highly partisan right-wing media outlets like *Human Events* and Richard Mellon Scaife's *Pittsburgh Tribune-Review*. Once there, they were mined by Republican-leaning mainstream outlets like the *New York Post* and the editorial page of the *Wall Street Journal*. That gave them more credibility and drew the attention of the mainstream media which often covered them, not as fact but as allegations. It also gave them oxygen and broader exposure.[20] A network of websites, chat rooms, and email lists fed readers half-truths and lies and shielded them from alternative perspectives and fact-checkers.

The wild conspiracies that Lehane and his colleagues investigated grew out of a tragedy that struck the White House in 1993. Vincent Foster, Hillary's partner in the Rose Law Firm and close friend of the Clintons, had come to Washington to serve as deputy counsel to the president. He worked closely with Hillary, managing leftover personal legal matters from Arkansas, fending off requests to make deliberations of the healthcare task force public, and providing advice on other matters. In July 1993, Foster's body was found in a suburban Virginia park near his home, where he had killed himself with a pistol. He suffered from depression and found life in Washington overwhelming. He was distraught by personal attacks, including a series of scathing editorials that appeared in the *Wall Street Journal* in June and July, directed at him and other alumni of the Rose Law Firm in the Clinton administration. "I was not meant

---

20 Chris Lehane, "Yeah, I Wrote the Vast Right-Wing Conspiracy Memo," *Politico*, April 27, 2014 https://www.politico.com/magazine/story/2014/04/chris-lehane-right-wing-conspiracy-memo-106059/ (accessed September 6, 2022).

for the job or the spotlight of public life in Washington," a note discovered in his briefcase lamented. "Here ruining people is considered sport."[21]

While years of investigations confirmed the contemporaneous verdict of suicide, White House actions complicated matters. Under pressure from Hillary, Foster's boss, White House counsel Bernard Nussbaum, kept Justice Department investigators from entering Foster's office for several days after the suicide and allowed a file labeled "Whitewater" to be taken to the family's private quarters. Not surprisingly, speculation about foul play began immediately and continued for years. Foster had been murdered on the orders of the Clintons to cover up what he knew about Whitewater and other corrupt activities, some charged. No, others insisted, he had been killed to cover up an affair with Hillary. By the following year, talk radio star Rush Limbaugh relayed to millions of listeners a story claiming that Foster had been murdered in an apartment owned by Hillary and his body taken to the Virginia park where he was found.

Richard Mellon Scaife, the billionaire heir to a Pittsburgh banking, petroleum, and manufacturing fortune, provided funds that fueled much of the campaign. A generous donor to conservative causes, Scaife hated Bill Clinton. In a 1998 interview, he accused Clinton of liquidating his enemies, insisting that "there must be 60 people—who have died mysteriously."[22] Scaife had long supported a conservative monthly, *The American Spectator*. In 1993, he began making large donations to the magazine for the Arkansas Project, a well-funded effort to dig up dirt on Clinton that would support impeachment. "We're going to get Clinton," he told a New York publisher in 1994. "And you'll be much happier because Al Gore will be president."[23] Eventually, Scaife would pour over $2 million into the project.

Not surprisingly, much of the work focused on sex. Few Americans believed that Bill Clinton was a choir boy, but charges of infidelity that surfaced during the primaries may have inoculated him against public outrage over his promiscuity. Moreover, the sexual revolution of the 1960s and 1970s was 30 years old, and most Americans believed that whom people chose to sleep with was a private matter. Nevertheless, much of the dirt that Clinton's Arkansas enemies wanted to dish was about sex. In mid-1993, *American Spectator* reporter David Brock, traveled to Arkansas at the behest of a Scaife ally to

---

21 John F. Harris, *The Survivor: Bill Clinton in the White House* (New York, 2005), 76.
22 *Washington Post*, May 2, 1999 https://www.washingtonpost.com/wp-srv/politics/special/clinton/stories/scaifemain050299.htm (accessed July 26, 2022).
23 Ibid.

explore charges that, as governor, Clinton had used state troopers to procure women for assignations. The stories, which Brock was ultimately unable to corroborate, depicted shouting matches between Bill and Hillary. As Brock later noted, they showed Bill as "a sexually voracious sociopath" and Hillary "as a foul-mouthed, castrating, power-mad harpy, joined together in a sham power marriage."[24] Brock's hit job appeared in January 1994, amping up anti-Clinton outrage.

The story had even more serious ramifications than Brock anticipated. His article included a story about "a woman named Paula"[25] whom state troopers had brought to a hotel room to have sex with Clinton. Paula, it turned out, was Paula Jones, who worked for the Arkansas Development Project, a state agency. She claimed that while working at an economic development conference, he had invited her to his hotel room where he propositioned her. In May 1994, only days before the statute of limitations would bar a lawsuit, she filed a sexual harassment claim in federal court in Little Rock. The lawsuit was more serious than the other stories because it alleged a violation of federal law and might constitute an impeachable offense. Jones's attorneys wanted to depose Clinton, but his attorneys fought back arguing that a sitting president could not be subpoenaed in a civil case because it would distract him from carrying out the duties of the office. The dispute, which would find its way to the U.S. Supreme Court (where Clinton lost) in 1997, kept the story in the news, adding to Clinton haters' outrage. But deposing Clinton was crucial to the endgame of well-placed, high-powered conservative attorneys like George Conway and Ted Olson who became involved in the litigation. By placing Clinton under oath and questioning him about his sex life, he would inevitably lie to protect himself. It was, as Brock wrote, "a deliberate perjury trap"[26] that could provide evidence to support impeachment.

By the end of Clinton's first year, charges of wrongdoing mounted. Most rested on flights of fancy and ridiculous conspiracy theories, but Republicans and their allies in the media succeeded in keeping the stories in the news. As he had done in his campaign to bring down Jim Wright, Gingrich succeeded in getting good government organizations to recommend an independent investigation. In January 1994, the *Washington Post*—no friend of conservatives—demanded the appointment of a special prosecutor. What was the harm in investigating?

---

24 Brock, *Blinded by the Right*, 165.
25 Ibid., 193.
26 Ibid., 201.

If the Clintons were innocent, they would be vindicated. That was naïve. "The investigation and the charges themselves," writes historian Steven Gillon, "would create the impression of impropriety, distract attention from the president's agenda, and erode his moral authority."[27] In early 1994, Attorney General Janet Reno appointed Robert Fiske, a respected Republican lawyer, as special counsel. By summer, he issued a report concluding that Vince Foster's death was, indeed, a suicide. It failed to silence the conspiracy theorists, however. When Congress acted to renew the independent counsel statute, the panel of judges authorized to name special counsels passed over Fiske and appointed Kenneth Starr, a hard-right partisan who had provided high-level legal advice to Paula Jones's attorneys.

## The "Comeback Kid" Rides Again

As Clinton approached the 1994 mid-terms, he was on the ropes. His signature healthcare initiative had failed, he was beset by attacks on his character, and a special prosecutor had declared open season on his private and public life. "If you believed everything you heard on the airwaves in 1994, you would conclude that your president was a communist, that the first lady was a murderess and that together they had hatched a plot to take away your guns and force you to give up your family doctor (if you had one) for a socialist health-care system," Hillary later wrote.[28] To make matters worse, the president's party usually loses congressional seats in mid-term elections. In 1994, Newt Gingrich was intent on breaking the Democratic majority in the House, and, as Jim Wright could testify, he wasn't to be taken lightly.

Clinton's woes were probably enough to sink the Democrats, but Gingrich left nothing to chance. He developed a strategy to ensure that all Republican candidates for the House were singing from the same hymnal. His "Contract with America" outlined what Republicans would do when they won the majority, offering something more than criticism of Clinton—which the media was doing a fine job of anyway. Standard Republican fare, it promised tax cuts, a balanced budget amendment, a "Personal Responsibility Act" that would impose a two-year limit on welfare benefits, congressional term limits, and a line-item veto. To avoid alienating moderates, the Contract avoided issues dear to the hearts of Christian conservatives like abortion, gay

---

27 Gillon, *The Pact*, 119.
28 Clinton, *Living History*, 245.

and lesbian rights, women's rights, and guns. Instead, it appealed to them by supporting a Family Reinforcement Act providing a tax credit of $5,000 to any couple who adopted a child and a $500 per child tax credit. It also promised to deny welfare benefits to unmarried mothers under 18 and end tax benefits for couples who lived together but weren't married. While hardly original, the Contract portrayed Republicans as a force for change, something voters disgusted with politicians and a gridlocked political system that Republicans had helped create welcomed.

The results were stunning. When the dust settled, Republicans gained 52 House seats, turning a 256–177 Democratic majority into a 230–204 Republican advantage. Republicans also won control of the Senate by flipping eight Democratic seats and picking up another the day after the election when a Democrat, Alabama Senator Richard Shelby, announced he was changing parties. That gave the GOP a 53–47 majority. Gingrich's Contract with America may have played a role, but the barrage of negative stories about the Clintons, the healthcare debacle, support for a trade bill that angered unions, and Clinton's declining approval ratings, which fell from 54% at the beginning of 1994 to the low 40s by mid-October were undoubtedly more important.[29]

The newly elected Republicans were, by and large, far more conservative than those they replaced. Their militant tone owed a great deal to Gingrich's bombastic style and take-no-prisoner tactics. The party's rightward shift was also a product of the large number of southerners, 19, in the freshman class. After 30 years of incremental gains in congressional elections in Dixie, Republicans finally broke through, securing a majority of House and Senate seats from the region. These men and women (almost all were men) were uncompromising conservatives who would drive the party to embrace a hard right agenda. Even though many new Republican senators—Rick Santorum in Pennsylvania, Jon Kyl in Arizona, Jim Inhofe in Oklahoma, Rod Grams in Minnesota, and Craig Thomas in Wyoming—weren't southerners, they were veterans of the House, where they had learned Gingrich's confrontational approach.[30] As Gingrich celebrated the historic victory that would make him

---

29 Gallup, Presidential Approval Ratings—Gallup Historical Statistics and Trends https://news.gallup.com/poll/116677/Presidential-Approval-Ratings-Gallup-Historical-Statistics-Trends.aspx (accessed January 29, 2023).

30 Sean Theriault, *The Gingrich Senators: The Roots of Partisan Warfare in Congress* (New York, 2013).

speaker, an aide offered a cautionary note. "Wait until you meet them," he said of the members of the freshman class. "You won't believe what a bunch of ideologues you are going to have to deal with."[31]

The warning was probably lost on Gingrich. The days and weeks following the election were exhilarating as he achieved rock star status. "It was as if a new king or new president had been elected," Clinton's friend and Secretary of Labor Robert Reich told an interviewer.[32] His smiling face may not have appeared on the cover of *Rolling Stone*, but it graced *Time* magazine's on January 9, 1995 along with the headline, "King of the Hill: How Newt Gingrich plans to pull off his revolution."[33] He stole the show from Clinton whom many predicted would become the next Jimmy Carter, a failed, one-term Democratic president. Clinton himself felt marginalized. At an April 18 press conference, a reporter asked if he worried "about making sure your voice is heard" in a political debate that Republicans appeared to dominate. Clinton shot back defensively, "The Constitution gives me relevance[...]." *New York Times* reporter Todd Purdum underscored his sense of desperation.[34] "President Clinton's paramount challenge these days," he observed, "is to persuade the public and a Republican Congress that he has a place in a political debate that risks passing him by."[35]

Tragedy quickly dispelled the doubts about Clinton's relevance. The day after the press conference a truck loaded with 5,000 pounds of ammonium nitrate fertilizer and diesel fuel detonated outside the Alfred P. Murrah Federal Building in Oklahoma City, killing 168 people, including 19 children and injuring 500. The bomber, Timothy McVeigh, was a decorated veteran of Operation Desert Storm who had become part of a network of highly decentralized but interconnected hate groups that had sprouted in the 1970s and spread during the 1980s and became increasingly radicalized in the early 1990s. They were populated with angry White men, many of whom had served in the military. Like so many working-class Americans, many members were alienated by declining economic prospects. Frustrated and angry, they were convinced

---

31 Gillon, *The Pact*, 129.
32 Ibid., 141.
33 http://content.time.com/time/magazine/0,9263,7601950109,00.html (accessed September 8, 2022).
34 The President's News Conference, April 18, 1995 https://www.govinfo.gov/content/pkg/PPP-1995-book1/pdf/PPP-1995-book1-doc-pg541-2.pdf (accessed September 8, 2022).
35 *New York Times*, April 20, 1995 https://www.nytimes.com/1995/04/20/us/undertones-of-relevance.html (accessed September 8, 2022).

that their country was being taken from them by Blacks, Jews, feminists, gays, and immigrants abetted by the U.S. government and its allies in international organizations like the United Nations. Together, these conspirators had created what White nationalists called the Zionist Occupational Government (ZOG) or the New World Order, a regime intent on displacing White people. Operating in small, decentralized cells, they staged armed robberies of banks and Brinks trucks and stole arms from military bases to support their war on the ZOG. By the late 1980s and early 1990s, they had spawned paramilitary groups in more than a dozen states.

Federal law enforcement officials responded with aggressive techniques common in inner-city neighborhoods, stoking militants' fear and anger. In August 1992, U.S. marshals travelled to Ruby Ridge, a remote location in Idaho, to arrest a White separatist named Randy Weaver who had been indicted on felony firearms charges. After one of the marshals and Weaver's son were killed in a firefight, hundreds of federal agents laid siege to Weaver's cabin. A shot aimed at Weaver by a sniper struck his wife, killing her as she held her baby in her arms. Weaver ultimately surrendered, but the heavy-handed response and brutal tactics made the Weavers martyrs and fueled outrage. A few months later, in April 1993, another violent confrontation showed that federal officials learned nothing from Ruby Ridge. Unable to serve a warrant for firearms violations on David Koresh, the leader of a religious cult called the Branch Davidians, federal and state officials laid siege to the group's sprawling compound near Waco, Texas. After almost two months, as law enforcement officers used tear gas to flush out the occupants, flames erupted, killing over 70 cult members including more than two dozen children. Ruby Ridge and Waco reinforced the belief already prevalent among White supremacists that the government was coming for them. McVeigh, who was on the scene when flames engulfed the Branch Davidian compound, "understood Waco as a massacre carried out by a rampant superstate and its corrupt agents."[36]

McVeigh was arrested shortly after the Oklahoma City bombing, pulled over by a state trooper because his getaway car didn't have a rear license plate and the officer who stopped him discovered he was carrying a concealed weapon. Investigators connected McVeigh to the rented truck that served as the bomb. Under questioning, he was remorseless and insisted that he acted alone. It soon became clear that he had at least two accomplices, Terry Nichols and Michael

---

36 Kathleen Belew, *Bring the War Home: The White Power Movement and Paramilitary America* (Cambridge, MA, 2018), 206.

Fortier, friends from the Army, who shared his White supremacist ideas and connections. Evidence produced at McVeigh's trial suggested that others were probably involved, although only McVeigh, Nichols, and Fortier were prosecuted. McVeigh was sentenced to death, Nichols to life in prison without parole, and Fortier to 12 years in prison. The enormity of the crime and what it revealed about a network of violent hate groups sent shock waves across the country as Americans learned about organizations like Aryan Nations, White Aryan Resistance (WAR), the White Patriot Party, Covenant, the Sword, and the Arm of God, the Michigan Militia, and many others.

In the midst of a national crisis, Clinton claimed center stage. He effectively coordinated the federal response, ensuring that the survivors of the bombing received prompt attention and the perpetrators were quickly arrested. He identified domestic terrorism as a serious problem and took the lead in developing legislation to check it. Congressional Republicans, who had a week before pressed for repeal of the assault weapon ban, were caught flat-footed. When they suggested that they wouldn't attach the repeal to an anti-terrorism bill if Clinton would accept an amendment limiting appeals in death penalty cases, the President pushed back effectively. "Don't make this into a political football," one of his aides chided. "Just get it done."[37]

Clinton struck the perfect balance between outrage and compassion. He called the bombing "an act of cowardice and [...] evil" and pledged that "justice will be certain, swift, and severe."[38] He also demonstrated deep empathy and the ability to connect with those who were shaken, grieving, and desperate to heal. He and Hillary traveled to Oklahoma City four days after the bombing where he spoke at a memorial service attended by an overflow crowd of 10,000 and viewed on closed circuit television at nearby sites by another 10,000. "Your pain is unimaginable," he remarked, "and we know we cannot undo it. That is God's work."[39] As the nation's mourner-in-chief, he dazzled, restoring the luster to his presidency.

---

37 *New York Times*, April 29, 1995 https://www.nytimes.com/1995/04/29/us/terror-oklahoma-president-clinton-warns-partisan-bickering-could-stall-efforts.html (accessed September 9, 2022).
38 *New York Times*, April 20, 1995 https://www.nytimes.com/1995/04/20/us/terror-oklahoma-city-official-response-statements-president-attorney-general.html (accessed September 9, 2022).
39 Remarks by President Bill Clinton, Time for Healing Ceremony, April 23, 1995 https://www.nytimes.com/1995/04/20/us/terror-oklahoma-city-official-response-statements-president-attorney-general.html (accessed September 8, 2022).

Clinton soon deftly linked Timothy McVeigh's hate with the venom and intolerance that suffused America's political discourse. In a speech in Minneapolis a day after the memorial service, he made the connection. There were "so many loud voices in America today whose sole goal seems to be to try to keep some people as paranoid as possible and the rest of us torn up and upset with each other," he observed. "They spread hate. They leave the impression [...] that violence is acceptable." Rush Limbaugh, the lord of talk-radio charged liberals with using the tragedy "for their own gain."[40] Newt Gingrich jumped into the fray as well, charging that it was "grotesque to jump from the legitimate dialogue of a free society to somebody setting a bomb off to kill Americans."[41]

Most Americans concluded that Clinton hadn't overstepped. *Time* magazine observed that vicious political diatribes were "in the air the moment the bomb went off." "In a nation that has entertained and appalled itself for years with hot talk on the radio and the campaign trail," its editors concluded, "the inflamed rhetoric of the '90s is suddenly an unindicted co-conspirator in the blast."[42] A *Los Angeles Times* poll conducted on April 26 and 27 found that respondents agreed by a 2–1 margin that Clinton's assessment hit the mark.[43] Clinton's handling of the crisis also received high marks. A *Time* magazine poll conducted on April 27 indicated that 84% of respondents approved of the way the President had handled the crisis.[44] His response to the tragedy boosted his overall approval from the mid-40s to over 50%.[45]

---

40 *New York Times*, 25, 1995 https://www.nytimes.com/1995/04/25/us/terror-oklahoma-president-shifting-debate-political-climate-clinton-condemns.html(accessed September 9, 2022).
41 *Time*, May 8, 1995 https://content.time.com/time/subscriber/article/0,33009,982898,00.html (accessed September 8, 2022).
42 Ibid.
43 Los Angeles Times, Los Angeles Times Poll # 1995-357: National Issues, Question 6, USLAT.042895.R08, Los Angeles Times, (Cornell University, Ithaca, NY: Roper Center for Public Opinion Research, 1995), Dataset, doi:10.25940/ROPER-31093047.
44 Time Magazine/Cable News Network (CNN), Yankelovich/Time Magazine/CNN Poll: Terrorism and Militia Groups, Question 28, USYANKP.050295.R26, Yankelovich Partners, Inc., (Cornell University, Ithaca, NY: Roper Center for Public Opinion Research, 1995), Dataset, doi:10.25940/ROPER-31099316.
45 Gallup, Presidential Approval Ratings—Gallup Historical Statistics and Trends https://news.gallup.com/poll/116677/Presidential-Approval-Ratings-Gallup-Historical-Statistics-Trends.aspx (accessed January 29, 2023).

Once again, he was the come-back kid. Gingrich, who had been riding high, was about to discover that being a celebrity invited scrutiny and popularity could be short-lived in Washington. As House Republicans developed legislation to fulfill promises made in the Contract with America, a balanced budget loomed large—and quickly brought confrontation with Clinton. Many of the President's advisors urged him to attack Republicans for gutting programs to support the elderly, children, the middle class, and the environment to pay for tax cuts to the rich. Clinton, however, took a more conciliatory approach, proclaiming his willingness to work with Republicans for the common good. At his April 18 news conference, he told reporters that he had "common goals" with Republicans on issues like the budget and welfare reform and pledged to "work with people of good faith in both parties [...] to do what is best for America."[46]

Convinced he had the upper-hand, Gingrich had little interest in a deal. His confidence buoyed by the election results, he knew that the zealous freshmen who swelled Republican ranks in the House didn't believe that their constituents sent them to Washington to compromise. The Republican budget combined tax cuts and steep reductions in federal programs that would shrink government and produce a balanced budget in six years. Clinton pushed back. He supported balancing the budget but over ten years rather than six and proposed smaller tax and budget cuts. As the debate intensified in the fall, Clinton went on the offensive. Democrats ran television ads attacking Republicans, who proposed substantial cuts in the *growth* of Medicare, as heartless ideologues who wanted to take away grandma's health care. They worked. Gingrich and company failed to understand that while many Americans wanted smaller government and lower taxes as an abstract matter, they valued programs like Medicare and Social Security.

With Clinton and congressional Republicans at an impasse and the government facing a shutdown, if no budget was approved by November 13, Republicans budged. They agreed to a continuing resolution to fund the government until a budget was approved. However, they added provisions mandating a balanced budget in six years and cutting a number of programs, including Medicare. Clinton didn't blink. To Gingrich's surprise, he vetoed the bill, precipitating a shutdown of most government departments. The veto made him look principled and decisive, producing a bump in his approval

---

46 *New York Times*, April 19, 1995 https://www.nytimes.com/1995/04/19/us/excerpts-from-the-news-conference-with-president-clinton.html.

ratings that would continue for the remainder of his presidency. Polls indicated that most Americans held Congress responsible for the impasse. Gingrich made the situation worse by grousing about how shabbily Clinton had treated him when he traveled with the President on Air Force One (at Clinton's invitation) to attend the funeral of Israeli Prime Minister Yitzak Rabin. How bad had it been? Clinton hadn't discussed the budget with him during the flight, and Gingrich, along with other congressional leaders (following standard protocol) exited the plane through the rear. A *Washington Post* story ran under the title "Underlying Gingrich Stance is His Pique About the President." The *New York Daily News*, no friend of Clinton, was more pointed, printing a caricature of Gingrich in a diaper with the words, "Cry Baby."[47]

Burned, Republicans quickly negotiated a continuing resolution with Clinton that kept the government operating for three weeks without conditions. With House conservatives unwilling to compromise, however, there was no agreement, and a second shutdown began on December 16 and continued for 27 days. Americans were disgusted by the petty partisanship, but most blamed Republicans. Senate Majority Leader Bob Dole, who had taken over negotiations with the White House after the first shutdown, moved to stop the bleeding. He was disgusted by Gingrich's ego and bombast and probably a little jealous of all the attention he had received. With his eyes on a presidential bid in 1996, Dole feared that a continued impasse damaged his reputation as a senior statesman who could make a creaky system work—his chief claim on the presidency. Republicans soon agreed to an open-ended continuing resolution without conditions.

The parties finally reached an agreement on a budget in April 1996, more than half-way through the fiscal year. The deal contained more modest cuts than the Republicans had demanded and left Medicare and other entitlements unscathed. Clinton also won about $5 billion in additional spending for "investments" in education, the environment, job-training programs, and hiring additional police. Republicans had caved, and many were not happy. "Most of these issues will be revisited in the coming weeks" as the 1997 budget was developed, the Republican chair of the House Appropriations Committee threatened. As Republicans sharpened their knives, Clinton rose above the fray and appeared, well, presidential. When congressional Republicans

---

47 *Washington Post*, November 16, 1995 https://www.washingtonpost.com/archive/politics/1995/11/16/underlying-gingrichs-stance-is-his-pique-about-president/cc78a470-7093-48ba-b2d0-386e0ede1372/; Gillon, *The Pact*, 160.

insist on "going it alone," he commented, "we get gridlock, stalemate, vetoes, Government shutdowns." However, the budget deal demonstrated that there was another way. "We can work together, and when we do, we can get good results for the American people," he insisted.[48] On the ropes after the mid-terms, he had taken a middle ground between Republicans and Democrats, played the Republicans' overreach like a Stradivarius, and emerged as someone more and more Americans regarded as a leader who could rise above the partisanship that made them hate politics.

Partisan warfare had become vicious, and the tactics nasty. Even so, brief truces led to major accomplishments—for good or ill. One of these was in telecommunications policy, where new technology was producing disruptive economic and cultural change. A 1934 law, adopted to address radio and telephone service, still governed the communications sector. Convinced that a free market would produce undesirable outcomes, legislators had established comprehensive government regulations and created the Federal Communications Commission (FCC) to administer them. Building a network of telephone lines that crossed the country and delivered service to individual homes was expensive and controlled by one entity—American Telephone and Telegraph and its regional subsidiaries. A free market did not exist, and fair prices and reasonable access could only be ensured by regulation. Radio and, subsequently, television posed a somewhat different challenge. A limited number of frequencies were available to deliver service so they needed to be allocated fairly, rationally, and in a manner that prevented a few broadcasters from controlling local and regional markets. So, the 1934 law also controlled access to the market, prices consumers paid, and allocation of scarce broadcast frequencies. It also required broadcasters to provide alternate points of view on controversial issues and to undergo periodic review and public comment to ensure they served the community. The FCC and Congress loosened regulations on cable TV in the 1970s and 1980s, but by the 1990s industry leaders were demanding additional changes. Many policymakers, captivated by the magic of the market, agreed that the system was ill-suited to emerging technology— satellite TV and radio, cell phones, and the internet.

As a candidate, Clinton had promised to build a bridge to the economy of the twenty-first century. He and his vice president, Al Gore, saw new

---

48 *New York Times*, April 26, 1995 https://www.nytimes.com/1996/04/26/us/the-budget-truce-the-overview-house-and-senate-vote-to-approve-96-spending-bill.html?searchResultPosition=1.

communications platforms as the foundation of that bridge. Gore spoke often of an "information superhighway" that was as critical to economic progress in the information age as Ike's interstate highway system had been to post-World War II America.[49] A White House task force he headed developed approaches better suited to emerging technology, and congressional leaders, with generous input from industry lobbyists, drafted legislation to adapt a 1930s law to the 1990s. The industry was intent on complete deregulation, claiming it would spur competition and provide consumers with better products and lower costs. As centrist Democrats who embraced market solutions, Clinton and Gore agreed with much—but not all—of industry executives' prescription for change.

The result was the Telecommunications Act of 1996, which marked a dramatic shift in communications law. Clinton fended off Republican efforts to abolish the FCC and won provisions to limit the concentration of ownership, restrict Internet pornography, require manufacturers to provide parents tools to control the content their children accessed, and guarantee that classrooms and libraries were wired. However, he embraced deregulation and signed a bill that dramatically reduced the FCC's authority, ended price controls on cable service, opened telephone markets to all comers, and promoted competition among service providers. Big telecom companies and the Wall Street investors who provided them capital were happy. Companies invested heavily, seeking to establish dominance in the markets they entered, prevent the competition they promised reform would deliver, and position themselves to keep prices high. Their goal, Clinton advisor and Nobel economics laureate Joseph Stiglitz observed, was "competition *for* the market, but not competition in the market."[50] The law may not have lowered prices for consumers, but it triggered a mad rush of investment to expand service that created a so-called dot-com bubble.

The law demonstrated that bipartisan compromise to address a complex problem was possible. All it took was support from powerful interests, failure of other groups to mobilize against it, and lack of attention by the media to an issue it considered arcane and less interesting than partisan food fights and wild conspiracy theories. Under these circumstances, politicians could work through disagreements, reach compromise, and pass important legislation. But for the most part, corporate America, not working people, were the beneficiaries. Unless you believed that what was good for Time Warner and Citicorp was good

---

[49] *New York Times*, November 10, 1992 https://www.nytimes.com/1992/11/10/science/clinton-to-promote-high-technology-with-gore-in-charge.html (accessed July 31, 2022.)
[50] Joseph E. Stiglitz, *The Roaring Nineties* (New York, 2003), 97.

for America. As time passed and the concentration of wealth continued, more and more Americans did not. Communications reform, like NAFTA and banking deregulation, convinced them that politicians could deliver for corporate America but not them.

Welfare was a more contentious issue. However, after bitter hand-to-hand combat, Democrats and Republicans ultimately agreed to the most systematic changes in welfare policy since the 1960s. Change was possible because virtually no one liked the existing system, and Republicans and Democrats stood to score points by fixing it. Many programs provided assistance to the poor, but when Americans spoke of welfare, Aid to Families with Dependent Children (AFDC) was what they meant. Few liked a program that they believed was antithetical to values they held dear, like hard work and self-reliance. Many regarded AFDC as "the dole," a program that provided cash payments to young, able-bodied people even when they refused to work. Most Whites pictured welfare recipients as young Black women—often teenage girls—who had children with a series of men they didn't marry. While Blacks were disproportionately represented among beneficiaries, the majority of recipients were White. Even so, many Whites believed AFDC was a program that used their taxes to enable indolent, promiscuous young Blacks to sustain a lifestyle that raised the middle finger to values they held dear.

Even many who were better informed and sympathetic to the poor disliked AFDC. Cash payments were woefully inadequate, they pointed out, even to residents of states like New York that provided the most generous benefits. While the percentage of Americans in poverty fell during the 1960s and early 1970s, it rose in the late 1970s and remained at elevated levels through the mid-1990s. The number of children living in poverty was also on the rise.[51] Between 1975 and 1995, the percentage of children who were poor grew by almost 5%. If AFDC was a weapon in the War on Poverty, many liberals concluded that it had misfired. Nor was increasing benefits the answer. Too many voters demanded a leaner government and wouldn't support the expansion of a program they believed helped people who wouldn't help themselves. Major

---

51 Center on Budget and Policy Priorities, "Official Poverty Table Masks Gains Made Over Past 50 Years," September 13, 2013 https://www.cbpp.org/research/official-poverty-measure-masks-gains-made-over-last-50-years (accessed January 29, 2023); Pew Research Center, "Who's Poor in America? 50 Years into the 'War on Poverty,' a Data Portrait," January 13, 2014 https://www.pewresearch.org/fact-tank/2014/01/13/whos-poor-in-america-50-years-into-the-war-on-poverty-a-data-portrait/ (accessed January 29, 2023).

books by prominent liberal scholars of poverty, including David Ellwood's *Poor Support* (1989) and Christopher Jencks's *Rethinking Social Policy* (1992), called for drastic changes.

Welfare was an issue that Republicans had long used as a cudgel to bash Democrats. They charged that Democrats clung to an expensive system that didn't work because they believed more government and higher taxes were the solution to every problem and they were beholden to Black welfare recipients. Variations of this argument were a staple in the Republican repertoire because they resonated with many voters. Charles Murray, a conservative policy analyst with a Ph.D. from M.I.T., lent academic respectability to the Republican attack in his influential 1984 book, *Losing Ground*. Murray charged that welfare hurt rather than helped the poor by preventing them from becoming self-supporting. Equally disturbing, the system encouraged illegitimacy, which destroyed the two-parent family, a vital institution essential to support children and prepare them to become self-sufficient adults. That grabbed the attention of the religious right, a key Republican constituency.

Eager to blunt Republican attacks, Clinton embraced welfare reform. As a presidential candidate, he had promised to "end welfare as we know it." "For too many years government has failed us," he charged in a TV ad, "and one of its worst failures in welfare." He would "break the cycle of welfare dependency" by providing education, job training, and child care, "but then those who are able must go to work either in the private sector or in public service."[52] Offering a third way between Democrats' penchant for handouts and Republicans' callousness, Clinton would help the poor help themselves—and make the offer too costly to turn down. He put the matter on the back burner after entering the White House. Combined with the austerity required by his deficit reduction plan, House Speaker Tom Foley warned, welfare reform would spark revolt among liberal Democrats on the Hill. Pursuing health reform made more sense.

Clinton finally sent legislation to Congress in June 1994—in time to claim that he was fulfilling a campaign promise but not soon enough that it would receive extended discussion before the mid-term elections. As *The New York Times* reported, at a January Cabinet meeting, Clinton asked advisors if he "could send up a bill that created the appearance of progress even while quietly urging

---

52 *Washington Post*, April 30, 2016 https://www.washingtonpost.com/video/politics/bill-clinton-in-1992-ad-a-plan-to-end-welfare-as-we-know-it/2016/08/30/9e6350f8-6ee0-11e6-993f-73c693a89820_video.html (accessed August 1, 2022).

Congress to defer action."[53] The bill established a two-year time limit for anyone born after 1971 to receive AFDC benefits. It also offered training programs to prepare welfare recipients for employment, funding for child care for mothers with young children, mechanisms to collect child support from absent fathers, and public service employment for anyone who couldn't find a private sector job. Those who didn't find a job but had made a good faith effort remained eligible for support.

Liberal Democrats were aghast. The two-year limit would leave hundreds of thousands of children without support, they argued, and funding provided for job training and child care was woefully inadequate. They also pointed out that the failure of health care reform ensured that many who left welfare for the workforce would lose health benefits. That, they charged, hardly rewarded work. Republicans had different concerns. They were contemptuous of the good faith exception, which they argued would become the rule. True reform required an inflexible time limit. They also charged that Clinton's proposal did nothing to address the crisis of illegitimacy, which was swelling the ranks of the poor, increasing welfare rolls, and fostering intergenerational poverty. Serious reform, many Republicans insisted, required tackling the scourge of illegitimacy by cutting off benefits to unmarried women under 21 who had babies and mothers who had additional children while on welfare.

As expected, Clinton's bill stalled in Congress. What Clinton didn't anticipate was the size of the Republican wave in the mid-terms that made his proposal irrelevant. "We got hit by a freight train, in part [...] because our own train moved too sluggishly," commented David Ellwood, the Harvard professor who helped design Clinton's bill.[54] Republicans seized the initiative and brought forward legislation that made Clinton's proposal seem like it had been written by bleeding heart liberals. Democrats and moderate Republicans in the Senate softened proposals coming from the House, and Clinton himself forced elimination of some especially mean-spirited provisions when he vetoed bills Congress sent him in December 1995 and January 1996. In August 1996, however, he signed a bill that he admitted had "serious flaws." Many of his advisors urged a veto, but the President knew Republicans would use it as a powerful weapon against

---

53 *New York Times*, July 15, 1994 https://www.nytimes.com/1994/07/15/us/pledge-plan-campaign-end-welfare-special-report-clinton-welfare-bill-long-stormy.html?searchResultPosition=7 (accessed August 2, 2022).

54 *New York Times*, August 2, 1996 https://www.nytimes.com/1996/08/02/us/clintons-welfare-shift-ends-tortuous-journey.html?searchResultPosition=20 (accessed August 2, 2022).

him in the fall, charging him with breaking his promise to "end welfare as we know it." Swallowing hard, Clinton explained that the bill "is the best chance we will have for a long, long time to complete the work of ending welfare as we know it, by moving people from welfare to work, demanding responsibility, and doing better by children."[55]

The Republican bill replaced AFDC with a new program largely controlled by the states called Temporary Assistance for Needy Families (TANF). The federal government would provide block grants to the states who would augment them with funding equal to at least 80% of their current contribution to AFDC. That was a concession to Democrats; the House bill had left states free to determine their contribution. But states remained free to decide how they would spend the money and also to define the level of cash benefits— an invitation to reduce already parsimonious monthly payments. Provisions ending payments to unmarried girls under 18 and denying additional payments to beneficiaries who had more children were eliminated. But states had discretionary authority to deny additional benefits to those who had more children. Immigrants who had resided in the U.S. legally for less than five years were ineligible to receive benefits. The bill also stipulated that no one could receive support for more than a total of five years. They could move on and off welfare, but when they had received benefits for a total of 60 months, they were done.

Many Democrats charged that the bill would create a Dickensian nightmare, increasing homelessness, taking food from the mouths of children, and forcing poor mothers to place their children in orphanages. By the end of the Clinton presidency, TANF had not produced the dire results critics predicted. The number of welfare recipients declined by 60% between 1994 and 2000, and the proportion of single mothers in the workforce grew from 58% to almost 75%.[56] The earnings of female-headed families increased through employment and the Earned Income Tax Credit, which Clinton had persuaded Congress to triple in 1993. The effects on Blacks were especially striking. The percentage of

---

55 *New York Times*, August 1, 1996 https://www.nytimes.com/1996/08/01/us/clinton-sign-welfare-bill-that-ends-us-aid-guarantee-gives-states-broad-power.html?searchResultPosition=25.

56 *Washington Post*, August 22, 2016 https://www.washingtonpost.com/news/wonk/wp/2016/08/22/the-enduring-legacy-of-welfare-reform-20-years-later/#:~:text=People%20receiving%20federal%20welfare%20payments%20fell%20by%20half,reached%20their%20apex%20of%2014.2%20million%20in%201994. (accessed January 29, 2023).

Black Americans living in poverty declined from almost 44% in 1994 to 31% in 2000[57]; the rate of poverty among children declined from 22% in 1994 to 16% in 2000[58]; and the proportion of female-headed families living in poverty fell from almost 40% in 1994 to 28% in 2000.[59] These were positive trends, but critics pointed out that a booming economy was largely responsible, far too many remained desperately poor, and the level of childhood poverty was a national disgrace.

Most who transitioned from welfare to work struggled to get by. As Barbara Ehrenreich showed in her 2004 bestseller, *Nickel and Dimed*, the minimum wage jobs available to those transitioning from welfare were physically demanding, often subjected workers to demeaning treatment, and in some cases provided irregular work and income. When the worst recession in 80 years struck in 2008, the ranks of the poor swelled, benefits available to those eligible for assistance had shrunk, and many poor people were no longer eligible for support.

Republicans believed that affirmative action, combined with welfare reform, would provide a one-two punch to take Clinton out. He outflanked them on welfare by supporting TANF and affirmative action by exploiting public ambivalence. With the 1996 election approaching, Republican presidential hopefuls were outdoing one another in demanding an end to affirmative action. As a Republican advisor explained, "the issue of […] racial preferences is very close to the top" of the party's priorities because it "is a no-lose proposition."[60]

Events in California seemed to confirm that assessment. Proposition 209, initiated by two White professors in the California State University system, barred the use of "race, sex, color, ethnicity, or national origin as a criterion for either discriminating against, or granting preferential treatment to,

---

57 Statistia, "Share of the population living in poverty by race and Hispanic origin in the United States, 1959–2019," https://www.statista.com/statistics/1225017/poverty-share-by-race-race-us/ (accessed January 29, 2019).

58 Statistia, "Child Poverty Rate in the U.S. 1990 to 2021," https://www.statista.com/statistics/200474/us-poverty-rate-among-children-under-18-since-1990/ (accessed January 29, 2023).

59 U.S. Census Bureau, "Poverty Rate for People in Female Householder Category Lowest on Record," September 10, 2019 https://www.census.gov/library/stories/2019/09/poverty-rate-for-people-in-female-householder-families-lowest-on-record.html (accessed January 29, 2023).

60 *New York Times*, February 2, 1995 https://www.nytimes.com/1995/02/07/us/backlash-against-affirmative-action-troubles-advocates.html (accessed February 23, 2023).

any individual or group in the operation of the State's system of public employment, public education, or public contracting." Governor Pete Wilson, a Republican presidential hopeful, had become a supporter. When the effort faltered, he enlisted his friend and longtime ally, African American businessman Ward Connerly, to help. Connerly assumed leadership of the campaign and succeeded in getting Proposition 209 before voters in November 1995. With Republicans on the attack and the election little more than a year away, Clinton chose to address the issue in a highly publicized speech in July 1995. While he admitted that affirmative action shouldn't continue forever and that some abused it, he embraced it as an essential tool in the struggle for equal rights. It reflected a commitment to equal opportunity, had been initiated with bipartisan support, and strengthened businesses, the military, government, and universities by infusing diversity in their ranks. It didn't mean quotas or hiring or admitting unqualified individuals, Clinton insisted, but it was necessary to battle historically rooted discrimination against women and minorities. Emphasizing that "the job of ending discrimination in this country is not over," he concluded that the best course was to "mend it, but don't end it."[61]

Clinton proved more persuasive than his Republican critics. Polls showed that while a majority of Americans opposed special treatment for minorities and women, an equally large majority favored affirmative action designed to help Blacks and women get better jobs and education. If affirmative action meant quotas, few supported it; if it meant creating opportunity, few opposed it. California's Proposition 209, which was framed as prohibiting preferential treatment, sailed to victory by a 54–46 percent margin. However, even before the 1996 campaign ended, opposition to affirmative action lost its allure for the GOP. Republican leaders in Congress abandoned their bill to eliminate federal affirmative action programs, and most candidates dropped the issue. "Heading into the final eight weeks of the election [...] the affirmative action issue has virtually fallen from view," the *Washington Post* exclaimed.[62] Americans' ambivalence, concern about alienating women, and Clinton's skillful reframing of the issue made affirmative action a less attractive target.

Clinton's defense of affirmative action played well with core Democratic constituencies and helped soften disappointment over welfare reform. Clinton

---

61 Bill Clinton, "Address on Affirmative Action, July 19, 1995," https://millercenter.org/the-presidency/presidential-speeches/july-19-1995-address-affirmative-action (accessed January 29, 2023).

62 *Washington Post*, September 18, 1996 https://www.washingtonpost.com/wp-srv/politics/special/affirm/stories/aa091896.htm (accessed January 23, 2023).

and Democratic leaders in Congress raised Democrats' spirits further by leveraging reluctant Republicans to support two measures dear to the party faithful. A minimum wage bill raised the rate from the existing $4.25 an hour to $4.75 in October and $5.15 the following year—a 21% hike. It was critical to the livelihood of many working people—including those transitioning into the workplace from welfare. It was also a do-or-die issue for organized labor, a key Democratic constituency Clinton had often disappointed. The second measure enacted a key piece of the comprehensive healthcare bill that went down to defeat in 1994. It required insurance companies to continue to offer coverage to workers who changed or lost their jobs and limited insurers' ability to jack up premiums.

Republicans fought both measures, and were especially determined to block a hike in the minimum wage, which was bitterly opposed by small business owners, one of the party's most loyal constituencies. But the measures had overwhelming support from voters according to the polls. GOP leaders smiled a crooked smile and claimed credit for both measures. However, they fell in line because, with the election fast approaching, they had little choice—and everyone knew it. Speaking of the minimum wage bill, a Republican aide in the Senate remarked, "We voted for it because it was killing us."[63]

Clinton succeeded in commanding the center and successfully cast Republicans as extremists who didn't understand working people, were a threat to Medicare and probably Social Security, and may have encouraged White supremacists. It was a tour de force that led to yet another comeback. He had neutralized Republican wedge issues like crime, welfare, and affirmative action, and his willingness to compromise made him appear moderate, pragmatic, and presidential. An economy that had shifted into high gear didn't hurt either. Nor did his opponent, the dour, acerbic 73-year-old Kansan, Bob Dole who emphasized issues that didn't inspire much enthusiasm—a balanced budget and more tax cuts—or were old news—Clinton's character. Clinton cruised to victory, winning 49.2% of the popular vote to 40.7% for Dole and 8.4% for Ross Perot, whose irascible personality and focus on the deficit inspired far fewer voters than four years earlier.

Both parties found reasons to be happy. Clinton was the first Democrat to win reelection since 1964, and he did so convincingly. He carried every age group, Catholics, those who described themselves as moderates, and half

---

63 *New York Times*, July 10, 1996 https://www.nytimes.com/1996/07/10/us/disregarding-pure-politics.html (accessed August 5, 2022).

of the male vote while securing a 20-point margin among women. Clinton also won back northern blue-collar Democrats. Nevertheless, the President's coattails were remarkably short. Republicans let out a sigh of relief because they held Congress, adding two seats to their Senate majority, bringing it to 55–45. They lost nine seats in the House, but retained a comfortable 227–208 majority. Republicans lost seats in the Northeast, Midwest, and West, but scored gains in the South. That pushed the party further right. The shift was most pronounced in the Senate, where most of the nine Republican freshmen were much more conservative than their predecessors. It was part of a troubling trend that was making the major parties more ideologically homogenous. Voter turn-out fell below 50% of the voting age population, the lowest since 1924.[64] That probably reflected the widespread assumption that a Clinton win was inevitable as well as a growing alienation from politics.

## Window of Opportunity Closed

Temperamentally drawn to the middle ground and compromise, Clinton believed that his success in commanding the center got him reelected. As he took the oath of office for a second time, he signaled that he would not veer from that path. "Government is not the problem, and Government is not the solution," he proclaimed, striking a balance between the liberals of his party and the conservatives who increasingly dominated the GOP. He reminded his audience that voters had "returned to office a President of one party and a Congress of another" and expected them to work together to solve problems and unleash the promise of the twenty-first century. Americans deplored "the politics of petty bickering and extreme partisanship," he insisted, and "call on us instead to be repairers of the breach and to move-on with America's mission."[65]

True to his word, Clinton reached out to his nemesis, Newt Gingrich, through his chief of staff Erskine Bowles, a North Carolina investment banker. The egotistical Gingrich had been taken down a notch or two by Clinton's resounding reelection, and he was smarting from a House vote to reprimand him for violating federal tax laws by diverting political contributions to

---

64 Congressional Quarterly Almanac, 1996, "Presidential Election: Voters Hand Clinton a Second Term" https://library-cqpress-com.proxy.binghamton.edu/cqalmanac/document.php?id=cqal96-841-24597-1091727&type=toc&num=6 (accessed January 23, 2023).
65 William J. Clinton, "Inaugural Address," January 20, 1997 https://avalon.law.yale.edu/20th_century/clinton2.asp (accessed August 7, 2022).

charitable foundations he controlled—and failing to report it to the House Ethics Committee. Convinced that continued confrontation and conflict might cost Republicans the House and him the speakership, he was open to Clinton's overture. During the spring and early summer of 1997, the parties reached a compromise on the budget that had something for each. "I made a very conscious decision that it was better for America and better for the Republican Party to prove we could govern," Gingrich told a reporter in 1997. "We decided that four years of incremental achievement in our direction are superior to four years of obstruction while we scream about values."[66] It was a jaw-dropping statement for a leader of the party that weaponized values-laden social issues to whip up hatred for the enemy and bring governing to a standstill. Perhaps grid lock would break.

In August, Clinton signed the budget bill as Gingrich, sounding a bit like the President, looked on and waxed poetic about the beauty of compromise: "we listened to the will of the American people [...] we reached beyond parties [...] we found ways to get things done."[67] Both sides could claim credit for balancing the budget, which Clinton's 1993 budget and growing tax revenues generated by stunning economic growth had brought within reach. The Republican faithful applauded tax cuts while Democrats were heartened by new spending on initiatives dear to their heart. Another piece of Clinton's healthcare initiative fell into place with $28 billion allocated to create the Children's Health Insurance Program. It extended Medicaid coverage to children in families of modest means who didn't have health insurance through their employers or weren't poor enough to qualify for Medicaid. The bill also expanded funding to states to hire more teachers, offered tax breaks to middle-class families for college tuition, increased support for mothers moving from welfare to work, and restored medical benefits to immigrants that the welfare reform bill had taken away. One liberal critic of welfare reform called the bill "a real win for the President [...] and a partial win for the poor."[68]

His success with the budget whetted Clinton's appetite for something bigger—Social Security and Medicare reform. They were the problems politicians had been trying to fix for more than 30 years without success. Social Security was the biggest challenge. Even the most vociferous opponents of big

---

66 Gillon, *The Pact*, 201.
67 Ibid.
68 *New York Times*, August 1, 1997 https://www.nytimes.com/1997/08/01/us/in-budget-bill-president-wins-welfare-battle.html?searchResultPosition=1 (accessed August 7, 2022).

government proclaimed their undying support for the program and were wary of suggesting any changes that appeared to reduce benefits. There was a structural problem, however. The system was funded by a payroll tax evenly divided between workers and employers. When the program began paying benefits in 1940 and for years thereafter, beneficiaries had paid little into the system, so their benefits were covered by payroll taxes on those currently employed. When these workers retired, their benefits wouldn't be fully paid by their contributions—most of which had gone to support a previous generation of retirees—but by current workers and their employers. That was sustainable as long as the ratio of workers to beneficiaries was high. Unfortunately, it declined from 5.2:1 in 1960 to about 3.4:1 in the mid-1990s, and it was projected to drop below 3:1 after 2010, when the first big wave of baby boomers began receiving payments. Payroll tax increases and other changes made by Congress over the years created a large reserve in the Social Security Trust Fund that was invested in Treasury notes. But with more boomers retiring and living longer actuaries projected that the trust fund would be empty in 2030. Then what? The easy fixes had been made, and most realized that raising the payroll tax above its current rate of 12.4% was a non-starter.

There were ideas about how to provide a permanent fix, but all of them required sacrifice or risk. The least controversial was to expand the number of workers in the system by extending the payroll tax to state and local government workers, bringing an infusion of cash without significant outlays for years to come. More controversial was increasing the age at which employees could claim full benefits. Changes in the 1980s increased the age at which beneficiaries would receive full benefits to 67, effective in 2027. With Americans living longer, however, some suggested indexing retirement age to life expectancy, pushing it past 67. Reducing benefits to surviving spouses was another possibility, as was requiring all beneficiaries to pay income tax on their monthly payments.

The proposal that generated the most heated opposition was investing a portion of employee contributions in the stock market. Proponents argued that stocks generated higher returns than Treasury notes, where current surpluses were invested. If a portion of the payroll tax each worker paid went into individual retirement accounts that they could use to support themselves in retirement, retirees would be better off and the burden on the Social Security system would be reduced. Those in the financial industry were enthusiastic backers. They admitted they would benefit from torrents of cash flooding the market, but insisted the country would benefit more. More money in the stock market would allow companies to grow, hire more workers, pay higher wages, and generate more tax revenue. Critics, however, focused on the risk. Privatization would shift the system from a defined benefit model providing a fixed monthly payment with a cost-of-living adjustment to a system in which retirees relied heavily on individual retirement accounts whose value would fluctuate with changes in the stock market. Privatization threatened to remove security from the program, forcing retirees to roll the dice in the Wall Street casino.

Medicare was also an expensive, highly popular sacred cow, and it faced the same problem as Social Security. Like Social Security, it was funded by a payroll tax; but monthly premiums paid by beneficiaries as well as appropriations from general revenues also supported the system. Current surpluses went into two trust funds that supported different components of the program. But Medicare, like Social Security, faced an uncertain future. The number of retirees entering the system was growing, and the cost of medical care was increasing far faster than inflation. Actuaries projected that the system would run in the red within 25 years. Fixing it would require higher payroll taxes, greater government support, higher retiree premiums and co-payments, a larger role for private insurers, or perhaps all the above. Available solutions for two troubled yet popular programs were bound to generate controversy and couldn't be adopted without bipartisan support.

Clinton believed the moment was right. Despite the vicious personal attacks on him, he had narrowed the ideological divide with Republicans. His success in the 1997 budget negotiations persuaded him that he could do business with Gingrich. Besides, with his last election behind him, he could afford to take risks and back initiatives that might be unpopular in the short term. Now history, not the electorate, would be his judge, and he believed that saving the nation's social safety net would establish him as one of the great presidents.

Like Clinton, Gingrich had an incentive to cut a deal. He didn't like Clinton, but recognized his intellect and political skill. After first misjudging Clinton, he understood that he was no pushover. After the government shutdown fiasco, when Republicans were roundly blamed for obstruction, Gingrich realized that while confrontation was good politics for those in the minority, it didn't work for those in power because voters expected them to get things done. Besides, he could take comfort from his success in changing the terms of the debate so that any compromise would be far more conservative and market oriented than most Democrats would have settled for a decade before.

During the fall of 1997, the outlines of a compromise took shape. Clinton knew it would draw fire from liberals in Congress, and Gingrich didn't doubt it would anger many conservative Republicans. After all, cooperation with Clinton was as appealing as the sound of nails on a chalkboard to conservatives. After serious discussions among their staff, Clinton and Gingrich met at the White House in late October 1997, where they agreed on the broad outlines of a deal. They would tackle Social Security first. Clinton would signal his commitment to support unspecified adjustments that would preserve the system without compromising the security it provided in his upcoming State of the Union Address. He would propose a year-long series of town hall meetings to get input from the public as well as experts. Then, after the mid-terms, he and Gingrich would announce a grand compromise that would include private retirement accounts. He pledged to take the heat from his party's left wing and the negative advertising that would inevitably follow. The two agreed to put Medicare reform on a slightly slower track. Clinton would appoint a commission to develop and submit recommendations by early 1999, and he and Gingrich would use these to craft reform legislation. In a decade when the politics of confrontation had threatened government's ability to function, two leaders who were bitter enemies committed themselves to support bipartisan compromise that would rely on moderates from each party to pass historic legislation to solidify the nation's social safety net. It was audacious and might restore public faith in politics and government.

Clinton's continued philandering and attempt to cover it up made a difficult task impossible. In November 1995, during the government shutdown, Clinton began a series of sexual encounters with a 22-year-old White House intern named Monica Lewinsky. The relationship ended in the spring of 1997, when Lewinsky was transferred to a job in the Defense Department. Advisors who feared that the relationship would become public heaved a sigh of relief, believing that Clinton had avoided another land mine. He hadn't. Lewinsky, crushed that Clinton had ended the relationship, was befriended by Linda Tripp, whom Clinton had previously transferred from the White House to the Pentagon. Lewinsky opened up about her relationship with Clinton, and Tripp secretly recorded some 20 hours of their conversations in which Lewinsky spoke in graphic detail about her relationship, even reporting that she had a blue dress stained with his semen.

Soon the information Tripp surreptitiously gathered from her young friend was weaponized against the President. The right-wing, Clinton-hating attorneys who represented Paula Jones in her sexual harassment suit learned about the relationship and subpoenaed Tripp and Lewinski. They also pulled the wire on a perjury trap set for Clinton by asking him about Lewinsky when they deposed him in January 1998. He denied everything, as did Lewinsky, whom he had counseled before she testified. Even before Clinton's deposition, Tripp turned over her tapes to Kenneth Starr. The special prosecutor had found no evidence to incriminate Clinton in Whitewater, but the tapes, the dress, and a confession obtained under duress from Lewinsky gave Starr's investigation new life and soon fed stories in the mainstream media.

In mid-January 1998, less than two weeks before Clinton's State of the Union Address, The *Washington Post* shocked the nation with a story alleging that Clinton had had an affair with an intern. Clinton denied it—to the public and also to those closest to him, including Hillary—setting off months of heated speculation that the White House dismissed as just the latest product of the Clinton-bashing machine. In July, however, when Starr compelled the President to testify before a grand jury, Clinton fessed up to Hillary and his advisors and made a televised apology. The fallout would continue for months and culminate in Clinton's impeachment. The moment the *Post* story appeared, however, the wind went out of the sails of the historic compromise with Gingrich. Nothing was said between the two men to end the deal they had struck the previous fall, and Clinton made Social Security reform the centerpiece of his State of the Union Address in January 1998. "Save Social Security first," he proclaimed, insisting that none of the budget surplus be spent until Congress had agreed on reforms that would make the system secure for generations to come.[69] He called for non-partisan forums to discuss the problem, and pledged to work with congressional leaders on bipartisan legislation.

The discussions and the conference would take place, but Clinton was either going through the motions or hoping that he could once again pull a rabbit out of the hat. But there was no rabbit. The natural forces of a political universe addicted to partisan recrimination years in the making took over. Republicans and their allies on cable TV and talk radio went for the jugular, reflexively mobilizing moral outrage against Clinton. Clinton understood that compromises necessary to win Republican support would alienate congressional Democrats whose support he needed to fend off Republicans calling for his head. The man whose presidency was defined by seeking the center had no choice but to appeal to partisan loyalties to save himself. He would propose a modest program of reform in early 1999, but it was not a fix. Besides, it lacked support from Republicans and many Democrats and died a quiet death.

Social Security reform ended with a whimper, but the Lewinsky scandal raged for months. And why not, it was even juicier than the 1989 film hit, *Sex, Lies, and Videotapes*. Starr's report, presented to Congress in September 1998, described in salacious detail Clinton's encounters with Lewinsky. There was also discussion of offenses like perjury, witness tampering, and obstruction of justice that might be grounds for impeachment. But these took a back seat to the lurid details of

---

69 Bill Clinton, "State of the Union Address," January 27, 1998 https://millercenter.org/the-presidency/presidential-speeches/january-27-1998-state-union-address (accessed August 10, 2022).

serial sexual encounters that Republicans believed would provide the silver bullet to bring down a wily opponent who had taken away their favorite attack lines and, since 1995 at least, had won every battle. Of course, they argued that they weren't concerned with a tawdry affair, but rather with preserving the rule of law. But they counted on the sex to fuel the public outrage that would force enough Democrats to turn on Clinton to allow Republicans to remove him from office.

Their strategy failed miserably. Most Americans believed that what Clinton had done was wrong. And they condemned him for it. But during a year when Americans were mesmerized by a new cable sit-com, *Sex in the City*, promiscuity seemed pretty mainstream. Most saw Clinton's relationship with Lewinsky as an extramarital affair between consenting adults, a private matter, a personal failing, not a violation of public trust that warranted impeachment. Sure, Clinton lied and coached Lewinsky and his secretary, Betty Currie, on how they should testify. But he didn't do it to cover up a conspiracy to undermine the constitutional order as Richard Nixon had done in Watergate. He did it, most Americans believed, to shield his personal life from public view, avoid humiliation, and, perhaps, save his marriage. Most people would have done the same thing. To Republicans' astonishment, Clinton remained popular. His approval rating never fell below 55%, and it soared to an astonishing 71% in the weeks after the charges surfaced.[70] Giddy over what appeared to be a gift, Republicans didn't appreciate that the value Americans placed on personal freedom and privacy, combined with changing sexual mores, would shape their view of Clinton's behavior. That was, perhaps, the most enduring legacy of the 1960s and most Americans embraced it. Instead of an ogre, he was a victim of partisanship and Starr and the Republicans were prudish zealots.

Incredulous at the public's support for Clinton, Republicans doubled down. Those on the extreme right—such as House Majority Whip Tom De Lay of Texas and Appropriations Committee Chair Bob Livingston of Louisiana—took the lead in demanding that Clinton resign or be removed from office. Their insistence drove House Republicans to authorize the Judiciary Committee to launch an impeachment investigation. And even after Democrats shocked them by gaining five seats in the 1998 mid-terms they persisted. With Gingrich replaced as speaker by conservative firebrand Bob Livingston in the wake of the mid-terms, the House voted to impeach Clinton in December 1998. The vote

---

[70] Pew Research Center, "Clinton's impeachment barely dented his public support, and it turned off many Americans," October 3, 2019 https://www.pewresearch.org/fact-tank/2019/10/03/clintons-impeachment-barely-dented-his-public-support-and-it-turned-off-many-americans/ (accessed January 29, 2023).

was almost exclusively along party lines, underscoring for most Americans that this was the partisan warfare they despised. Soon, even Republicans' moral outrage became the butt of jokes. Stories of Newt Gingrich's infidelities had circulated for years. Now reports emerged that Henry Hyde, the chair of the Judiciary Committee, had cheated on his wife 30 years earlier. And Bob Livingston announced that he would resign because he had an extramarital affair. When the Senate voted on two articles of impeachment in January 1999, the outcome was foreordained; neither article commanded a majority of senators, falling way short of the two-thirds majority the Constitution requires to remove a president.

Clinton survived, but the opportunity to accomplish big things, like Social Security and Medicare reform, did not. On the domestic front, there were a few successes, some of them dubious. He supported bi-partisan legislation that ended all restrictions on commercial banks' participation in investment and insurance activities and shielded complex, little understood investment vehicles—derivatives and credit-default swaps—from federal regulation. It allowed real estate development to proceed unchecked and, many would argue, inflated the bubble that would burst in 2008.

Seeking success where he had a freer hand, he turned to foreign policy. No problem had proven more elusive than the Israeli–Palestinian conflict that fueled much of the conflict that had wracked the geopolitically crucial Middle East for decades. Clinton brought Israeli and Palestinian leaders together, and when talks broke down, he sent a negotiating team to the Middle East to revive discussions. In the final two months of his presidency, he brought Israeli and Palestinian leaders to the White House for face-to-face talks. Ultimately, success eluded him, just as it had with Social Security reform. Yet he left the White House popular, if not beloved; according to the Gallup Poll, his approval rating stood at 66% the week he left office, higher than any post-World War II president.

Clinton was a survivor. He overcame his own impulsiveness as well as the slash-and-burn politics that conservatives unleashed against him. His centrist instincts, willingness to compromise, and poker player's skill in knowing when to hold 'em and when to fold 'em helped him achieve victories and lay the groundwork for a compromise resolving the two most intractable issues in American politics. Clinton's untamed libido quickly ended the prospects for a historic compromise. A hated Democratic president caught up in a sex scandal was a bonanza Republicans just couldn't pass up. They took the bait, launching an impeachment that reignited the bitter partisanship of the mid-1990s. That they lost—in the Senate and, perhaps more important, in the court of public opinion—cautioned politicians about the dangers of unrestrained partisanship.

Too many ignored the warning. Win-at-any-cost partisanship had become the crabgrass of American politics. It was impossible to eradicate because its roots were so well established, sown by Republicans dating back to Richard Nixon. Emphasis on highly divisive social issues mobilized both parties' core constituencies, and relentless attacks on the enemy remained the default strategy. Ironically, Democrats and Republicans had moved together ideologically, and no election in the 1960s, 1970s, 1980s, or 1990s had produced the kind of long-term realignment that had occurred in 1860, 1896, or 1932. Instead, control of the presidency and Congress shifted more frequently than at any time since the Gilded Age. The only rule seemed to be that swing voters—angry at politicians who ignored the erosion of the middle class, appeared beholden to economic and cultural elites, accomplished little, and fought a lot—quickly soured on the party in power. In this volatile atmosphere, politicians wanted to attract independents who shifted allegiance between the two parties, but they needed high turn-out among their most reliable, highly partisan supporters.

Bipartisan compromise to achieve imperfect solutions to difficult problems didn't excite the base. However, highly divisive red meat issues like abortion, race, gender, gay rights, moral decline, personal freedom, affirmative action, and, soon, immigration did. Direct mail and the emergence of cable news, talk radio, and the Internet enabled politicians to target their messaging. Growing segmentation of the media meant that more voters relied on sources of information that confirmed—and fed—their biases. Raising ever larger bundles of cash from the wealthy as well as from small donors fired up by talk radio and direct mail fueled the advertising—almost all of it negative—necessary to win close elections.

It was a witch's brew for hyper-partisanship that left most Americans disgusted with politics and politicians. As trust evaporated, politicians became ever more dependent on their base and less willing to compromise. The political ecosystem simply didn't sustain a culture that accepted politics as the art of the possible, even though that was necessary for any pluralistic democracy to survive. Clinton had fought that trend and won. His success wasn't lost on the candidates who faced off in the 2000 presidential election. Whether they could resist the pull of partisanship that had become so deeply rooted remained an open question.

CHAPTER 8

# THE LOST OPPORTUNITY, 2000–2008

*"I can hear you"*

Aside from the resplendent blue sky, September 11, 2001, was just another Tuesday morning in lower Manhattan. Thousands of commuters left their trains and hurried to offices in New York's financial district, the hub of the global economy. At 8.47 a.m., an American Airlines jet hit the North Tower of the World Trade Center, tearing a hole through several stories of the glistening steel structure and sending flames and black smoke billowing across the sky. Two minutes later, CNN interrupted its morning financial report with breaking news showing video of the burning tower as stunned anchors reported that a jetliner had struck the building around the 80th floor. A few minutes after 9 a.m., viewers looked on in disbelief as a second jetliner moved toward and then struck the South Tower. Within the hour, an American Airlines jet crashed into the west side of the Pentagon, just across the Potomac River from Washington, DC. Then a few minutes before 10 a.m., a fourth passenger jet went down in a remote field in central Pennsylvania before it could reach its intended target, the Capitol.

President George W. Bush, was in Florida promoting his education reform initiative. As he prepared to read *The Pet Goat* to a group of elementary school students, an aide advised him that the World Trade Center had been struck by a commercial jet. By the time Bush finished reading, about 9.15 a.m., he was informed that the second plane had struck and that terrorists were responsible. Before the third jetliner hit the Pentagon, Bush spoke to the nation for little more than a minute, informing the country that the incidents were "an apparent terrorist attack on our country," conveying sympathy for the victims, and vowing, "Terrorism against our country will not stand."[1]

In the days and months after September 11, a frightened, shocked, incredulous country demonstrated a spirit of unity that few thought possible. The 1990s had witnessed nasty partisan conflict, and a bitterly contested presidential election in 2000 only deepened divisions. As in 1941, however, a divided country came together when faced with an existential, external threat. While George W. Bush lacked FDR's eloquence, he reassured an uneasy public while fostering unity. When he visited the smoldering remains of the World Trade Center on September 14, Bush climbed atop a crumpled fire truck with a bullhorn to address the crowd. Responding to cries of "We can't hear you," the President rose to the moment. "I can hear you. The rest of the world hears you," he roared. "And the people who knocked these buildings down will hear all of us soon."[2] He mobilized his administration to identify the terrorists and their supporters, launch punishing attacks against their sanctuaries in Afghanistan, and prevent future attacks. Congress adopted a resolution authorizing the president to "use all necessary and appropriate force against those nations, organizations, or persons he determines planned [...] or aided the terrorist attacks."[3] The vote was 98–0 in the Senate and 420–1 in the House.

Predictably, some voices on the right cast blame on the Clinton administration and the American Civil Liberties Union or attributed the tragedy to God's displeasure with the nation's moral shortcomings. But Bush refused to identify an internal enemy. Aware of growing anti-Muslim sentiment, he spoke at Washington's Islamic Center on September 17. Asserting that "Islam is peace" and that the terrorists "violate the fundamental tenets" of one of the world's great religions, Bush reminded listeners that millions of American Muslims made "incredibly valuable contributions to our country." Addressing threats against Muslim women who wore the hijab, the President insisted that "moms who wear cover must not be intimidated [...]. That's not the America I know."[4]

---

1 "George W. Bush's Remarks from Emma Booker Elementary School on September 11, 2001," *Washington Post*, September 11, 2014 https://www.washingtonpost.com/video/politics/george-w-bushs-remarks-from-booker-elementary-on-sept-11-2001/2014/09/11/58e84c64-39cb-11e4-a023-1d61f7f31a05_video.html (accessed July 20, 2022).
2 John Robert Green, *The Presidency of George W. Bush* (Lawrence, KS, 2021), 148.
3 Green, *Presidency of George W. Bush*, 149.
4 Remarks by the President at Islamic Center of Washington, D.C., September 17, 2001 https://georgewbush-whitehouse.archives.gov/news/releases/2001/09/20010917-11.html (accessed July 21, 2022).

Bush's leadership and Democrats' eagerness to lend their support helped bring a fractured country together. Less than a month after the attacks, Gore called the man who had defeated him in the recent contested election "my commander in chief."[5] Bush's approval ratings soon jumped from a bare majority to an unheard-of 90%. Americans' trust in government rose from 30% to 64%, a throwback to the Ike Age. Nebraska Republican Chuck Hegel captured the spirit of the moment, asserting "We are forever changed."[6] Unfortunately, Hegel's crystal ball was cloudy. Within two years, partisanship had returned with a vengeance. In part, the short-lived unity was a victim of Bush's lack of transparency in leading the nation to war against Iraq. By 2006, Republican senator John McCain claimed that the country was "more divided and partisan than I've ever seen us."[7] The divisions were real and sharp, but not as great as McCain suggested. Nevertheless, the partisan demons that the 9–11 attacks quieted had not gone away.

## The Election that Wouldn't End

The return of the sharp partisan conflict McCain lamented came as a surprise to many. Not only because of Bush's role as uniter-in-chief in the wake of 9–11. But also because he won the presidency in a contest that seemed to accentuate the similarities rather than the differences between the two leading candidates. Perhaps as a reaction to a decade of bitter partisan conflict, the 2000 presidential election was among the tamest in recent memory—at least until vote counting started. Election year 2000 kicked off with a primary season that lacked much suspense. Al Gore, Clinton's vice president and fellow New Democrat, won his party's nomination without much of a contest. Republicans didn't see much of a fight either. Texas Governor George W. Bush, son of the 41st president, emerged as an early front-runner, and by March, he had locked up the nomination. Both Gore and Bush presented credible resumes—Bush as a successful, two-term governor of the nation's third most populous state and Gore as a Senate veteran and highly engaged two-term vice president. Neither had much charisma and both were uninspiring on the stump. But after the smooth-talking, empathic, inspirational, and undisciplined Clinton,

---

5 *Washington Post*, September 11, 2021 https://www.washingtonpost.com/politics/after-911-a-rush-of-national-unity-then-quickly-more-and-new-divisions/2021/09/11/8f6f7d8e-12a9-11ec-bc8a-8d9a5b534194_story.html (accessed July 21, 2022).

6 Ibid.

7 Ibid.

Americans were ready to trade excitement for a leader who didn't careen from crisis to crisis.

The Reform Party—one of five minor parties that fielded candidates—may have provided the campaign's most colorful characters. Its founder, Ross Perot, declined to run, opening the door to the likes of New York real estate developer and tabloid personality Donald Trump, John Hagelin, a theoretical physicist who taught at a small Iowa college established by Transcendental Meditation founder Maharishi Mahesh Yogi, and the eventual nominee, Patrick Buchanan, Richard Nixon's old speechwriter. Buchanan, who had challenged Bush senior from the right in 1992, brought a bombastic populism to the campaign. He promised to put "America first," "drain the swamp" in Washington, end America's role as the "world's policeman," dispatch troops to the southern border to stop the flood of illegal immigrants, pull the U.S. out of the United Nations, the International Monetary Fund, and the World Trade Organization, halt preferences for minorities and women, and stop the nation's moral rot by returning prayer and Bible-reading to schools.[8]

Buchanan offered the country red meat, but it had developed an appetite for something more heart-healthy. When the dust settled in November, he would claim less than 1% of the vote. "We used to have red meat conventions, but they frightened people away," Buchanan quoted an unnamed Republican governor as saying. "So, we're all vegetarians now."[9] Bush sensed that most Americans were tired of conflict. As a governor far removed from Washington, he claimed to have "no stake in the bitter arguments of the last few years" and promised to "change the tone [...] to one of civility and respect." Aware that many of the moderates and independents whose votes he needed associated conservatism with a mean-spirited disregard for the poor, Bush advocated "compassionate conservatism." Of course, he hit the notes that thrilled Republicans—across-the-board tax cuts, repeal of the estate tax (or "death tax" as he put it), and opposition to abortion. With so many problems, he insisted it was "not a time for third chances" by electing Clinton's vice president. Rather, it was "a time for new beginnings."[10]

---

8 Transcript of Pat Buchanan's Acceptance Speech, August 12, 2000 https://abcnews.go.com/Politics/story?id=123160&page=1 (accessed August 14, 2022).
9 Ibid.
10 George W. Bush, "Address Accepting the Presidential Nomination at the Republican National Convention in Philadelphia," August 3, 2000 https://www.presidency.ucsb.edu/documents/address-accepting-the-presidential-nomination-the-republican-national-convention-0 (accessed January 30, 2023).

Al Gore had the easier job. And the harder. He touted his role in an administration that "moved us out of recession and into the longest period of prosperity in American history." Not only were there budget surpluses, but the country enjoyed "the lowest inflation in a generation [and] [...] higher family incomes." He also took a page from the Democratic playbook, appealing to the public image of Republicans as the party of big business and the wealthy, promising to stand up for working families, and reminding voters that he had "taken on the powerful forces."[11] He would support a tax cut for the middle class, protect the environment, Social Security, and Medicare, double investment in medical research, add a prescription drug benefit to Medicare, raise the minimum wage, and more. The budget surpluses bequeathed by the Clinton–Gore team would underwrite all of it.

He had a lot going for him, but faced one big obstacle. He was joined at the hip to Bill Clinton. And while Americans gave Clinton high marks for job performance, they questioned his character, viewed him as personally untrustworthy, and were tired of the endless controversy that seemed to follow him. Clinton fatigue was a drag on Gore, perhaps as much as the candidate's penchant for diving into the details of policy rather than offering voters a crisp, inspiring vision of the future.

With the candidates uninspiring, the differences between them modest, and almost as many Americans identifying as independents as Republicans or Democrats, it's not surprising that the election was one of the closest in the nation's history. Gore won a half-million more votes than Bush, but Bush flipped 10 states that Clinton had carried in 1996. The big prize and—as it turned out—the big headache was Florida. Shortly after the polls had closed in the East on November 7, the networks called the state for Gore, giving him its 29 electoral votes and, the pundits projected, the election. Discovering that the exit polling they relied on for their projection was flawed, they soon retracted their prediction. By 2 a.m., with Bush ahead by 30,000 votes and 97% of all the state's precincts reporting, the networks called the state—and the election—for Bush. Gore called Bush to concede and then left his hotel for Nashville's War Memorial Plaza where his supporters were gathered. A funny thing happened on the way to the Plaza, however. Gore's advisors noticed

---

11 Address Accepting the Presidential Nomination at the Democratic Convention in Los Angeles, August 17, 2000 https://www.presidency.ucsb.edu/documents/address-accepting-the-presidential-nomination-the-democratic-national-convention-los (accessed August 14, 2022).

that Bush's lead was shrinking quickly. They persuaded Gore to return to his hotel, call Bush, and retract the concession. When the bleary-eyed candidates awoke the next morning, Bush's lead appeared to be about 1,700 votes.

The roller coaster ride was just beginning; it would be more than a month before the nation had a president-elect. Bush's whisker-thin margin in Florida meant that there would be a mandatory machine recount. That wasn't likely to change the outcome. However, election officials and observers began reporting significant irregularities in the vote counting. Not fraud but poorly maintained voting machines that had malfunctioned. Many precincts used old punch-card voting machines that required voters to punch a hole through the ballot next to the name of the candidate of their choice. In many counties, significant under-voting—ballots cast without a candidate selected—indicated that poorly maintained machines prevented some voters from punching through the ballot so that their choice could be recorded by the machines that tabulated the votes. Many of these ballots had an indentation, a partial perforation, or a "chad" hanging from, but not detached from, the ballot. In all of these cases, the voter probably intended to cast a vote that was not counted. The fact that most of the faulty machines appeared to be in low income, heavily minority precincts made the Gore camp confident that a hand recount would yield enough votes for him to carry the state.

Then there was Palm Beach County. Because there were 10 candidates on the ballot, in addition to a slot for a write-in candidate, election officials created a ballot with two columns of names with the dot to punch for each candidate in a column between them. However, the line with the candidate's name didn't perfectly align with the spot that voters had to punch to cast a vote for that candidate. So, many voters in the heavily Democratic county claimed that they had been confused and had probably cast their vote for the wrong candidate. The Gore camp argued that only a manual recount could provide a fair count and ensure that the true intentions of the voters prevailed.

Both candidates sent teams of lawyers to Florida, Gore to demand a manual recount, Bush to block it. Time was on Bush's side. Florida's Republican secretary of state, Katherine Harris, had sole authority to certify the vote, and she emphasized that she would not extend the November 14 deadline established by state law. But did she have the final say? Surely the courts would weigh in. Federal law required presidential electors to meet in their state capital to cast their votes on "the first Monday after the second Wednesday in December," or December 18, establishing the outer limit for a recount, which would be time-consuming and complicated. How would election officials determine what to do with a ballot that did not have a hole punched out completely but had an indentation or was partially punched out—those soon-to-become-famous "hanging chads." And what about those confusing butterfly ballots in Palm Beach County? How in the world would anyone determine whether a voter had cast their vote for someone other than their intended candidate? A 1975 decision by the Florida Supreme Court held that the "clear intention of the voter" should guide those counting votes. But doing so was easier said than done.

Gore's team decided against asking for hand recounts in all 67 Florida counties. That would be time consuming and the public might conclude that Gore was a sore loser who wanted a redo. The campaign selected four counties with clear irregularities and, not coincidentally, lots of Democrats. Secretary of State Harris threatened to short-circuit the recounts by insisting she would certify the vote on schedule and ignore counties that were conducting recounts and hadn't reported their final vote by November 14. Gore's lawyers asked the Florida Supreme Court to intervene. Its seven members, who had all been appointed by Democratic governors, supported the recounts and extended the deadline for counties to report results to Harris.

Bush's lawyers turned to the U.S. Supreme Court, with its five-member conservative majority, asking it to reverse the Florida court's decision. In early December, the Supremes voided the Florida court's order and sent the case back for further consideration. The decision stopped recounts while the clock ticked. When the Florida Supreme Court clarified its rationale and reaffirmed its support for the recounts, they resumed. But Bush's lawyers returned to Washington asking the high court to stop the recounts, once and for all. Gore's attorneys argued that interpreting Florida election law was a matter that should be left to the state courts, but their argument didn't fly. With five justices appointed by Reagan and Bush senior forming the majority, the high court ruled, 5–4, that the Florida court had violated the Fourteenth Amendment by allowing recounts in four counties. It had failed to establish uniform standards and procedures for county officials to follow in conducting recounts, so the process failed to guarantee "the rudimentary requirements of equal treatment and fundamental fairness" in violation of the equal protection and due process clauses of the Fourteenth Amendment.[12] Because there wasn't enough time to develop and implement them before Florida had to send its electoral vote to Congress, the recounts ended, Bush carried Florida by 537 votes, and became the 43rd President.

---

12 *Bush v. Gore*, 531 U.S. 109 (2000) https://supreme.justia.com/cases/federal/us/531/98/ (accessed August 16, 2022).

Gore had won the popular vote. Bush's victory hinged on Florida, and a conservative Supreme Court sealed his victory there. Democrats were angry. When asked by a TV news host whether Bush was the legitimate president, Richard Gephardt, the Democratic leader in the House, responded, "George W. Bush is the next president of the United States." When the host pressed his point, Gephardt simply repeated his statement. Fearing that he would be considered a spoilsport, Gephardt revised his assessment several days later, confirming that, yes, Bush was the legitimate president-elect.[13] Beginning with Al Gore, who promised to "honor the new president-elect and help him bring Americans together,"[14] most Democrats acknowledged the inevitable and made ritualistic comments about accepting the finality of the court's decision—and Bush's election—even though they disagreed with it. When Congress met on January 7, 2001, to certify the Electoral College vote, a small group of House Democrats attempted to block certification of Florida's vote but failed to persuade even a single Democratic senator to join them as required by law. As the disgruntled House members raised objections from the floor, Gore, presiding over the proceedings as vice president, slammed down his gavel, ruling them out of order.

Caryn James of the *New York Times* observed that only television news anchors and commentators, thrilled to have an ongoing story to fill the 24–7 news cycle, worked themselves into a lather. Many "maintained a relentlessly hysterical tone, an apocalyptic attitude," she wrote, but "nowhere (except in the street demonstrations carefully staged for the cameras in Florida) was there a sense of high anxiety."[15] As the controversy played out, Republicans worried that Democrats would succeed in reversing the outcome in Florida and snag the presidency. Once the contest was resolved, many Democrats were angry and some believed that a partisan Court had stolen the election for Bush. At no point, however, was there an effort to mobilize the party faithful to mass protest much less violence. Even after a decade of partisan bitterness, Americans still

---

13 *New York Times*, December 24, 2000 https://www.nytimes.com/2000/12/24/weekinreview/the-nation-bitterness-what-bitterness-smile-it-s-transition-time.html?searchResultPosition=15 (accessed August 16,2020).

14 *New York Times*, December 14, 2001 https://www.nytimes.com/2000/12/14/us/43rd-president-his-remarks-gore-says-he-will-help-bush-bring-american-together.html?searchResult Position=7 (accessed August 16, 2022).

15 *New York Times*, December 17, 2000 https://www.nytimes.com/2000/12/17/us/43rd-president-tv-coverage-critic-s-notebook-apocalyptic-attitude-gripped-tv.html?searchResult Position=39 (accessed August 16, 2022).

assumed that the peaceful transfer of power was the hallmark of American politics, a key element of the nation's exceptionalism.

Exit polls revealed that the electorate was just about as closely divided as Florida. Gore carried the popular vote but only by a half-percent. The two candidates evenly split the vote of a number of key demographics: those over 65, baby boomers, voters who came of age in the 1980s, independents, suburbanites, Westerners, Midwesterners, and Catholics. At the same time, there were some sharp differences. Gore had the significant edge with Blacks, Hispanics, women, gays and lesbians, union members, urban residents, and Easterners. Bush won by substantial margins among Southerners, men, White Protestants, and residents of small towns and by a somewhat smaller margin among White voters. After the brutal partisan battles of the 1990s, party lines had hardened, with nine of ten voters casting a ballot for their party's candidate. There was also a sharp geographical divide: the coasts were blue while the heartland—the South, Midwest, Great Plains, and Mountain West—was red, with a few small islands of blue. Looking at a map, commented Andrew Sullivan, "you would be forgiven for thinking that we live in essentially two nations," something akin to the map of pre-independence India with its vast expanses of Hindu-dominated areas with "a Muslim necklace in the regions that would shortly become Pakistan and Bangladesh." That was sobering because divisions on the sub-continent had led to violence and partition. The stereotypes produced by America's geographic divide—"'Wal-Mart versus Martha Stewart' or 'Family values versus a sense of entitlement'"—suggested that the partisan battles of the 1990s would flower again given the right circumstances.[16]

## Compassionate Conservatism

Bush was no Gingrich. He knew the country was divided but understood that most Americans professed disgust for the nasty partisanship of the past decade. So, he stressed his willingness to reach across the aisle, as he had done as governor, and his commitment to "compassionate conservatism." In his inaugural address, he revisited these themes, pledging "to build a single nation of justice and responsibility" and offering a "new commitment to live out our nation's promise through civility." Civility was essential to bridge divisions and reach compromise to solve the big problems the nation faced. "Civility

---

16 *New York Times*, November 8, 2000 https://www.nytimes.com/2000/11/26/magazine/the-way-we-live-now-11-26-00-two-nations-undivided.html (accessed August 15, 2022).

is not a tactic or a sentiment," he insisted. "It is the determined choice of trust over cynicism, of community over chaos."[17]

There were no overtures to bipartisanship in his cabinet picks. His team looked like a reunion of veterans from the Nixon, Reagan, and Bush senior administrations with some of his closest Texas advisors and Condoleezza Rice, the Stanford provost who had become his foreign policy mentor, thrown in for good measure. The only Democrat was Norman Mineta, a journeyman House member from California, who as Secretary of Transportation wasn't exactly part of the inner circle. Nevertheless, Bush steered clear of appealing to hot-button social issues. When confronted by rules developed by the Clinton administration to provide federal funding for research using stem cells taken from embryos, he took a middle course. Pro-life advocates wanted a ban on funding for any research using embryonic stem cells, but scientists argued that it was the clearest path to discovering cures for many life-threatening diseases. Bush announced that he would allow federal support for research on stem cell lines that had already been harvested but not for studies using new lines. Those on both sides were unhappy, but Bush had chosen not to use the issue to whip up support from the religious right.

He also courted Democratic support on the Hill for some of his policies. That was not only a measure of his desire to bring down the temperature, but a necessity given Democratic strength on the Hill. Bush had no coattails in November 2000. Republicans lost two seats in the House, narrowing their majority to 222–213. The Senate, where Republicans lost four seats, was deadlocked at 50–50. Republicans controlled the chamber with Vice President Dick Cheney breaking ties until Jim Jeffords of Vermont switched parties in mid-2001, giving Democrats a one-vote majority.

As Bush prepared his legislative agenda, he faced a recession. Its roots lay in the last year of Clinton's presidency when the so-called dot-com bubble burst. During the 1990s, the hottest area of a hot economy was communication. Cable providers expanded their operations, and cell phone providers raced to construct extensive networks that would attract customers. E-commerce exploded as entrepreneurs like Amazon's Jeff Bezos exploited the internet to give consumers what they wanted when they wanted it without operating costly, place-bound retail outlets. Software developers, hardware manufacturers, and service providers expanded rapidly to meet insatiable demand. Americans

---

17 George W. Bush, Inaugural Address, January 20, 2001 https://georgewbush-whitehouse.archives.gov/news/inaugural-address.html (accessed August 16, 2022).

not only fell in love with tech but used it to find love as the hit 1998 rom com, *You've Got Mail*, suggested. Investment bankers, hedge fund managers, private equity firms, pension funds, and individual investors, shared the love. Flush with profits from a bullish stock market and confident the good times would never end, they poured money into any start-up exploiting the brave new world of tech.

Some of the investments were sound, but many supported fledgling companies that offered flashy ideas based on pie-in-the-sky business plans. In mid-1999, the Fed began raising interest rates to cool an overheated economy and head off inflation. By taking away the punch bowl, it ended the party. Investors cut back the flow of cash, striking a fatal blow to many tech companies that had not begun to—and perhaps never would—generate a profit. As investors pulled back, many companies no longer had the cash necessary to continue operations and went belly up, leading to big losses for many banks, hedge funds, pension funds, and individual investors. NASDAQ, the tech-heavy stock exchange which had risen by 400% between 1995 and March 2000, plummeted, falling from a high of 7,915 in March 2000 to 3,093, finally hitting bottom at 1,918 in September 2002.[18]

Tech sector woes affected those who had inflated the bubble, including banks. By early 2001, other areas of the economy were suffering. With interest rates rising, home construction slowed significantly, as did automobile sales and production. A strong dollar caused declining sales of goods and services in the international market, and fears generated by the 9-11 terrorist attacks led to a sharp, if brief, decline in investor confidence and the stock market. The recession was brief, ending in November 2001, but it had longer-term effects on the job market. Unemployment rose from just over 4% at the beginning of 2001 to 5.5% in November and continued to grow, reaching 6.3% in mid-2003.[19]

The recession revealed a shocking level of rapaciousness among business leaders. In late 2001, Enron, a behemoth in the energy sector that *Fortune* dubbed "America's Most Innovative Company," declared bankruptcy. Information from a whistleblower soon revealed that the most innovative thing about Enron may have been its accounting, which shielded liabilities and made a company saddled with debt appear profitable to investors. Even sophisticated investors, who had

---

18 Macrotrends, NASDAQ Composite—45 Year Historical Chart https://www.macrotrends.net/1320/nasdaq-historical-chart (accessed January 30, 2023).

19 U.S. Unemployment Rate by Month, 1948-2022 https://www.thebalancemoney.com/unemployment-rate-by-year-3305506 (accessed January 30, 2023).

every reason to believe the company was sound, were left holding the bag. Revelations in early 2002 of similar schemes at WorldCom, a telecom giant, and Adelphia Communications, a major cable company, suggested that Enron was not an isolated case. The media feasted on the unfolding scandals, skewering corporate duplicity and greed. A hit movie, *Erin Brockovich*, told the story of a woman who exposed the corporate cover-up of environmental contamination that exposed residents of a small town to cancer. *Time* named whistleblowers at Enron and WorldCom its persons of the year in 2003 as public outrage over corporate malfeasance grew.

Congress, not known for its celerity, responded quickly. The Sarbanes-Oxley bill, which became law in July 2002, subjected executives who used a "scheme or artifice" to defraud investors to prison terms of 10 and 20 years, created a regulatory board to police the accounting industry, and protected whistleblowers.[20] President Bush, who had initially urged a more cautious approach, also got religion. By June, he fell in line with tough measures demanded by Senate Democrats, trumpeting his support for "greater corporate responsibility."[21] Despite politicians' almost ritualistic response, the takeaway for many Americans was that the system was tilted toward those at the top who reaped the benefits of a growing economy while they struggled to get by. With data showing that the share of wealth claimed by the top 1% continued to grow, who could blame them?

The dot-com debacle and the recession had an impact on the federal budget by reducing tax revenues. But that didn't deter Bush from pursuing his top priority, a large tax cut. Cutting taxes had been Republican orthodoxy since Reagan, and Bush had promised one as a candidate. Besides, reduced military spending occasioned by the end of the Cold War and Clinton's commitment to trimming budget deficits bequeathed Bush a surplus projected to be $4.2 trillion over 10 years. The recession only provided another reason to act; a tax cut would ensure a quick recovery and increase tax revenues. Democrats might salivate over ways to invest the surplus in programs to protect the environment, improve education, stabilize Social Security and Medicare, and more. But Republicans

---

20 *New York Times*, July 25, 2002 https://www.nytimes.com/2002/07/25/business/corporate-conduct-overview-negotiators-agree-broad-changes-business-laws.html (accessed August 31, 2022).
21 "President Bush Signs Corporate Responsibility Bill," July 30, 2002 https://georgewbush-whitehouse.archives.gov/news/releases/2002/07/20020730.html (accessed August 31, 2022).

believed that lower taxes would mean smaller government and more power in the hands of individuals and private enterprise. Bush viewed the surplus as the people's money and believed it should be returned to them. He succeeded in winning a $1.35 trillion cut over 10 years, somewhat less than he wanted, with Republicans united behind the bill and 29 Democrats in the House and 12 in the Senate joining them.

The largest tax cut since 1981, it reversed most of the increases Clinton had won as part of his 1993 deficit reduction plan, cutting the top tax bracket from 39.6% to 35%, most other brackets by 3%, and the lowest bracket by 5%. While Democrats charged that the largesse would go mainly to the wealthy, which was true, Republicans claimed that the working poor saw the sharpest reduction in their tax rate, which was also true. The child tax credit, especially important to low- and middle-income taxpayers, increased from $500 to $1,000. While the tax cut put more money in the hands of consumers, especially those who were well-off, there were opportunity costs. Investments that Democrats wanted to shore up entitlement programs and rebuild crumbling roads and bridges were not made even though they were badly needed. There was another problem. Tax cuts are easier to give than to take away. So, if military spending increased or a deep recession struck, projected budget surpluses—on which the cuts were premised—would turn into large deficits. With the economy in recession, Washington bean counters began warning the surpluses would soon be gone.

Bush's commitment to education reform drove much of the new spending that worried budget hawks. His support for reform came from his experience as governor, not the Republican playbook. Republicans and Democrats alike decried poor educational outcomes—especially among poor urban and rural children—that foreclosed opportunity, perpetuated intergenerational poverty, and denied employers a well-educated workforce. Although most Republicans believed fixing the problem was a matter for the states, Bush was convinced that his success in Texas provided a template that could improve education outcomes nationally. It would burnish his reputation as a problem solver, give him an early win, and demonstrate that compassionate conservatism was more than a slogan.

Bush reached out to Ted Kennedy, the liberal legend who chaired the Senate committee with authority over education. He became an ally and brought along with him strong Democratic support for Bush's "No Child Left Behind" initiative. As finally passed by Congress in December 2001, it mandated annual tests in reading and math to assess learning and required states to submit an annual "report card" on their schools' progress to ensure accountability. The bill also increased federal financial support for education by 20% and revised the formula for distributing it to benefit schools with large percentages of poor children. Supporters beat back efforts to provide vouchers for private school tuition, an initiative dear to the hearts of conservatives. It wasn't typical Republican fare and raised eyebrows in the GOP. But Bush warned the conservative Republican leadership in the House to stand down. While many parents and teachers would complain that it placed too much emphasis on standardized testing, the law nevertheless brought a major infusion of federal support for schools in poor communities.

Expanding Medicare to include coverage for prescription drugs was another issue that enjoyed bipartisan support, although the means to accomplish it didn't. As the pharmaceutical industry developed a cornucopia of medications to control acute and chronic conditions, prescription drugs became integral to health care. Companies developed them with an eye on the bottom line, so prices were high, placing a special burden on seniors, who were the largest consumers of prescription drugs. Discussion of how to provide drug coverage began shortly after Congress created Medicare in 1965, but adding to the scope of an expensive program whose cost grew faster than inflation was a non-starter.

In the late 1990s, circumstances changed. Drug prices escalated, Republicans had been burned politically by trying to cut Medicare spending as part of their deficit-reduction efforts, and budget surpluses left money in the till. Politicians were eager to use it to address a problem that affected a group that showed up at the polls. Republicans also believed they could use a prescription drug benefit to induce seniors to migrate from the traditional fee-for-service Medicare, in which beneficiaries chose their doctors and the government paid for services, to privately run managed-care plans, which received a flat fee to provide services. That would reduce government's role in health care, lower costs because private insurers would compete for seniors' business, and contain increases in one of the most expensive entitlement programs.

During the 2000 presidential campaign, both Bush and Gore promised seniors a Medicare prescription drug plan. Democrats and Republicans in Congress each developed legislation but were unable to reach consensus. After the 2002 mid-term elections, Republicans, who now controlled the White House and both houses of Congress, feared that should they fail to deliver a plan they would feel the wrath of seniors in 2004. Well over 80% of beneficiaries chose traditional fee-for-service Medicare that allowed them to choose their providers, and they liked it. "You couldn't move my mother out of [fee-for-service] Medicare with a bulldozer," quipped one conservative House Republican.[22] So, Bush's plan to tie prescription drug coverage to participation in private managed-care plans bit the dust. Benefits would extend to those who remained in fee-for-service Medicare.

Many conservatives had long argued that Medicare and Social Security should be means-tested. Why should wealthy seniors receive government support, they asked? However, seniors and their advocates, notably the American Association of Retired Persons (AARP), disagreed. If only low-income seniors qualified, the program would lose political support and become like Medicaid, the program for the poor that always seemed to get the knife when budgets were cut. So, Bush's initial proposal to offer a prescription drug benefit to low-income seniors, with coverage for other beneficiaries limited to expenses that exceeded $6,000 annually, died. As finally passed, the bill provided coverage to all beneficiaries, with those remaining in fee-for-service Medicare choosing a private prescription drug plan offered by private insurers. Medicare would pick up the tab, with beneficiaries paying a premium and the government subsidizing low-income beneficiaries.

Democrats and some Republicans criticized big pharma's obscene profits and wanted a mechanism to control prices. Some argued that the government should negotiate directly with drug companies to create a prescription drug plan that would compete with those offered by private insurers. Its power would allow it to leverage lower prices that would benefit seniors and save taxpayers billions. Many also urged ending the ban on the purchase of drugs from foreign countries, including Canada, where prices were far lower. Both ideas were nonstarters for the pharmaceutical industry which saw them as a threat to its bottom line. Lobbyists fought back and scuttled both ideas.

Initially, leading Democrats like Ted Kennedy were engaged in crafting the bill in the Senate. That changed as Republicans, flush with success in the mid-term elections, decided that collaboration wasn't necessary. They cut key Democrats out of the negotiations, drawing fire from Kennedy and other Democrats who charged that the benefits were too limited and that subsidies for the premiums of low-income beneficiaries were the first step toward means-testing and ultimately destroying Medicare. Calling the bill "a Trojan horse," Kennedy denounced it as "a program calculated to unravel Medicare, privatize

---

22 Thomas R. Oliver, Philip R. Lee, and Helene L. Lipton, "A Political History of Medicare and Prescription Drug Coverage," *Milbank Quarterly*, 82 (June 2004) https://www.ncbi.nlm.nih.gov/pmc/articles/PMC2690175/ (accessed August 22, 2022).

it and to force senior citizens into the cold hands of H. M. O.'s."[23] The bill garnered the support of AARP, however, and passed on narrow, mainly party-line votes, with only 16 Democrats in the House and 11 in the Senate voting in favor. The final product fulfilled Bush's campaign promise and, however imperfectly, expanded the nation's social safety net. While there were sharp differences between the two parties, they agreed that health care for seniors was a national responsibility.

Compassionate conservatism had an international dimension. Bush's national security advisor, Condoleezza Rice, put the scourge of AIDS in Africa on the President's radar. Rates of infection were astonishingly high and growing, and the number of children born with the disease was also increasing. Researchers predicted that 68 million Africans would die of AIDS by 2020. Working with scientists at NIH, the administration developed legislation that provided $15 billion over five years to provide new drugs that treated AIDS patients and reduced transmission from mother to child. It also created education programs, including some that promoted the use of condoms and others that advocated abstinence. The bill attracted strong bipartisan support that helped it prevail against the objections of those on the right who denounced the distribution of condoms and critics on the left who railed against abstinence education. Ultimately the program succeeded in reversing increases in transmission and death, winning kudos from public health experts.

Bush promised Social Security reform, but delivering it required bipartisan support, and he failed to develop it. He created a presidential commission chaired by a former Senate Democratic powerbroker, Daniel Patrick Moynihan, and Richard Parsons, CEO of AOL/Time Warner. Any reform, Bush insisted, must include private retirement accounts to supplement social security for younger workers who weren't close to retirement. Although he made a Democrat co-chair, he didn't build bridges to key Democrats in Congress as he had done on education reform. Not surprisingly, Democrats and retirees' organizations pushed back against "privatizing" the system by diverting part of younger workers' payroll taxes to accounts invested in the stock market. Doing so, they claimed, would starve the current system of funds and make younger workers vulnerable to the vagaries of the stock market. The principal beneficiaries, critics asserted, would be bankers, hedge fund managers, and corporate CEOs

---

23 *New York Times*, November 26, 2003 https://www.nytimes.com/2003/11/26/us/final-push-congress-overview-sweeping-medicare-change-wins-approval-congress.html (accessed August 22, 2022).

who would profit from a wave of new money entering the stock market. With critics mobilizing and allies in short supply, reform stalled.

Despite the Social Security debacle, partisanship and gridlock had eased during Bush's first term. There were differences between Republicans and Democrats, sometimes sharp, as there should have been. Bush won some and lost some, engaged in some partisan fights, and won Democratic support for some key initiatives. It seemed like a return to politics BG (before Gingrich), when governing mattered and compromise was possible. The hit TV series *West Wing* reflected a renewed sense of optimism about politics, portraying politicians as people who navigated a complex system, faced difficult choices, and achieved important, if imperfect, results.

## A War on Terror

The return to something resembling a normal political process would prove short-lived. Ironically, 9–11, the event that brought the country closer together, was responsible. What Bush called "the War on Terror" preoccupied him, and he made choices in waging it that generated conflict at home, chilled bipartisan collaboration, and ultimately undermined his popularity and authority. Winning the war meant punishing those responsible for planning, executing, and supporting the 9–11 attack and preventing future attacks. The first step was destroying Al-Qaida, the terrorist network headed by Usama Bin Laden. It had masterminded 9–11 and operated large training sites for jihadists hosted by Afghanistan's Taliban rulers. Bush launched the offensive in October 2001, sending U.S. troops into remote areas of the country, where they engaged in pitched combat with terrorists and their Taliban hosts. Facing a well-organized enemy ensconced in forbidding territory, Bush and his advisors were convinced that only extraordinary measures could ensure success. Impatient with normal constitutional and legal processes that he believed inadequate, Bush claimed broad powers as president to conduct the war abroad and protect Americans at home.

Key members of his administration encouraged and supported Bush's effort. Vice President Dick Cheney, his closest advisor, had long chafed at the measures Congress adopted in the wake of the Vietnam War to reign in the imperial presidency. They threatened national security, he believed, and violated authority the Constitution conferred on the executive branch. Lawyers in the Justice Department's Office of Legal Counsel (OLC) provided the theoretical justification as well as legal opinions to loosen and, in some cases, override restraints on the president. The theory of unitary executive authority, widely accepted in the administration, guided its work. The Constitution, Cheney and OLC asserted, lodged executive power in the president, giving him authority over officials in the executive branch that was not subject to limitation by Congress or the courts. It was a breathtaking claim of presidential power that ignored the principle of checks and balances that animated the Constitution.

Cheney had long found the Foreign Intelligence Surveillance Act especially offensive. Passed by Congress in 1978, in the wake of revelations of widespread wiretapping of citizens by the CIA, the law required officials to obtain a warrant for wiretaps from a special court whose members were appointed by the Chief Justice. Although the process allowed quick action, intelligence officials insisted that protecting the nation against terrorists required intelligence officials to enjoy the authority to engage in surveillance of all communications to or from parts of the world harboring terrorists without the delays inherent in obtaining approval.

A sympathetic OLC justified Operation Stellar Wind, a program that permitted warrantless interception of any electronic communications with individuals in Afghanistan or other suspect countries. Befitting a clandestine program, the OLC opinion justifying the program was—and remains—classified. Apparently, it argued that the joint resolution adopted by Congress on September 14, 2001, authorizing the president to use force against all parties involved in the 9-11 attacks, gave Bush implicit authority to order warrantless searches necessary to secure information to plan retaliatory action. As investigative reporter Jane Mayer put it, "while not a single member of Congress realized it [...] Congress had implicitly allowed the President to ignore the Foreign Intelligence Surveillance Act.[24]

Restrictions on the treatment of prisoners were another legal obstacle swept away by legal interpretation. As U.S. forces launched their campaign against terrorist sanctuaries in Afghanistan, they took hundreds of prisoners, including rank-and-file warriors and leaders. Reluctant to detain them in Afghan prisons, the administration divided them between a facility established on the U.S. naval base at Guantanamo Bay in Cuba and top-secret CIA detention centers throughout the Middle East known as "Black Sites." U.S. intelligence agents were eager to interrogate detainees, especially those who might have knowledge of Al-Qaida's organization, operations, and plans for future attacks. But they faced legal barriers. The first was the Geneva Convention Relative to Treatment of Prisoners of War, which had been ratified by the U.S. It provided

---

24 Jane Mayer, *The Dark Side* (New York, 2008), 67.

that prisoners-of-war could only be required to divulge their name, rank, serial number, and date of birth. If Al-Qaida prisoners were prisones of war (POWs), interrogations would be off-limits. Again, OLC rode to the rescue, ruling that the Geneva Convention was an agreement among nations and did not apply to non-state actors like Al-Qaida.

Al-Qaida operatives would be interrogated, then, but the United Nations Convention Against Torture set limits on the techniques. Most who studied interrogation believed that torture was ineffective as well as immoral. It typically produced false confessions and bogus information and invited retaliation against American prisoners. But Bush and his team insisted that it was essential. Of course, they didn't call their preferred methods torture. Rather, they labeled them "enhanced interrogation techniques"— facial slaps, cramped confinement, sleep deprivation, stress positions, mock burials, insects, and waterboarding, which simulated drowning. The UN Convention prohibited inflicting severe pain and mental suffering. However, OLC's interpretation of these categories was so narrow that the "enhanced techniques" cleared the bar. The administration got what it wanted from OLC, but the results would come back to haunt it when whistle-blowers and enterprising journalists made them public.

In the wake of 9–11, some in the administration trained their sights on Saddam Hussein, Iraq's brutal and bellicose leader who had been a thorn in the side of the U.S. for more than a decade. In 1998, he had expelled arms inspectors sent to Iraq to verify compliance with a U.N. resolution requiring it to destroy its weapons of mass destruction (WMD)—chemical and biological weapons that had been used against the Kurdish minority. Although Bush himself believed that his father should have toppled Saddam at the conclusion of the Gulf War, he refused to make Iraq a second front in the War on Terror after 9–11. Al-Qaida was headquartered in Afghanistan, and it had received support from that country's Taliban rulers, not Saddam. So, Bush understood that Afghanistan must be the immediate focus. Nevertheless, he believed that Saddam was a destabilizing force in the region and possessed WMD. What was the evidence? His use of chemical agents against the Kurds in the 1990s, refusal to submit to U.N. inspection, and intelligence from questionable sources. In fact, Iraq no longer had weapons of mass destruction; Saddam kept inspectors at bay because he believed he would deter his enemies if they thought he had them.

By early 2002, after driving Al-Qaida out of Afghanistan, Bush turned to Saddam. He began building a case for war, insisting that there was compelling evidence Iraq possessed WMD. In his State of the Union Address in

January 2002, Bush identified Iraq—along with Iran and North Korea—as an "axis of evil." They were regimes headed by ruthless dictators bent on developing or in possession of WMD, and they posed a serious threat to the U.S. "They could provide these arms to terrorists, giving them the means to match their hatred," Bush claimed.[25] In a June 2002 commencement speech at West Point, Bush warned that containing "unbalanced dictators with weapons of mass destruction" was not possible and insisted that the U.S. must "be ready for preemptive action."[26] In October, Bush spoke at the U.N. He denounced Saddam as a "grave and gathering danger" and demanded that the Security Council set a deadline for Iraq to identify and destroy its WMD.[27] The Council complied in early November, setting a deadline of December 7 for Iraq to disclose and destroy all WMD.

Bush also pressed Congress for a resolution authorizing him to use force against Iraq if circumstances warranted. Administration officials continued to marshal evidence that Iraq possessed WMD, even though they knew it rested on questionable sources. On October 10, 2002, with the mid-term elections approaching, Congress passed the resolution by large majorities, with more than a third of Democrats in each house going along. With the first election after 9–11 less than a month away, who wanted to be called soft on terrorism? Winning U.N. support was another matter. Even some NATO allies found evidence the U.S. presented unpersuasive. Aware that the Security Council would reject a resolution authorizing the use of force against Iraq, Bush withdrew it. Unlike his father, he would take the nation to war without the support of the UN. With Saddam refusing to give up WMD he didn't possess or to abandon power, Bush authorized U.S. forces and their allies to attack Iraq in March 2003. He labeled it Operation Iraqi Freedom, signaling his intention to remove Saddam and bring freedom to Iraq.

His chutzpah proved the adage father knows best. Bush senior, far more experienced in international affairs than his son, understood the risks involved in occupying Iraq. Secretary of State Colin Powell urged caution. In a private meeting in August 2002, he warned that the President had not given sufficient attention "either to non-military options or the aftermath of military conquest."

---

25 George W. Bush, State of the Union Address, January 29, 2002 https://georgewbush-whitehouse.archives.gov/news/releases/2002/01/20020129-11.html (accessed August 20, 2022).
26 John Robert Greene, *The Presidency of George W. Bush* (Lawrence, KS, 2021), 197–98.
27 Ibid., 203.

"If you break it, you own it," he cautioned.[28] Powell was quickly marginalized by more hawkish advisors who fed Bush's hubris, but his words were prophetic.

Events in the spring of 2003, as the war began, suggested that Powell was overly cautious. U.S. troops swept across Iraq, quickly defeating the Iraqi army and entering Baghdad less than a month after the war began. On May 1, Bush proclaimed victory in an address to sailors on the deck of the USS *Abraham Lincoln* that ran in endless loops on screens in the U.S. and around the world. He emphasized his goal of transforming a dictatorship into a democracy. "The transition [...] to democracy will take time," he acknowledged, but the U.S. and its allies "will stay until the work is done [...] and we will leave behind a free Iraq." Behind him, as he spoke a banner proclaimed, "Mission accomplished!" Those words would soon come back to haunt the President, who didn't appreciate that slogans wouldn't accomplish what many believed was mission impossible.

Even as Bush spoke on the *Abraham Lincoln*, the quick American victory was turning into a nightmare. Shi'a Muslim leaders who had opposed Saddam's ruling Baath party, which represented the country's Sunni Muslim minority, turned against the American occupiers. If that weren't enough, Abu Musab al-Zarqawi, a Jordanian who had led a force resisting the Soviets in Afghanistan in the 1980s and subsequently fought against American invaders after 9-11, turned his attention to Iraq. With the support of Usama Bin Laden, he formed a terrorist network that offered fierce resistance. For the next six years, Americans would engage in fierce fighting with Muslim guerillas who were committed to driving infidels from their country. Weary of nation-building, the administration transferred authority to Iraqis, appointing an interim prime minister in June 2004 and conducting parliamentary elections six months later.

Bush's success in rallying the nation after 9-11 and taking the war to Al-Qaida helped the Republicans beat the odds in the 2002 mid-terms. They increased their majority in the House by eight seats, and picked up two seats in the Senate to give them a slim majority in the upper chamber. As the 2004 presidential election approached, the war had become a liability for Bush. His "mission accomplished" speech offered growing opposition evidence that he was unrealistic and out of touch. Almost 150,000 U.S. troops remained in Iraq, and an average of 75 Americans died every month.[29]

---

28 Ibid., 202.
29 U.S. Casualties in Iraq https://www.globalsecurity.org/military/ops/iraq_casualties.htm (accessed February 26, 2023).

Evidence that Iraq possessed WMD proved elusive, further damaging the administration's credibility. It sought to buttress its case by claiming to have proof that Niger had supplied Saddam with uranium to develop a nuclear weapon. In mid-2003, however, the *New York Times* reported that a former U.S. diplomat had investigated and determined that documents supporting the claim had been forged. The administration stuck to its story, suggesting to many that it lacked evidence—and couldn't find any even after the U.S. occupied Iraq. *Saturday Night Live* signaled that the emperor had no clothes, airing a skit in which Bush displayed a measuring cup, rubber gloves, and a spatula discovered in Baghdad and assured Americans that his team had finally found the smoking gun.

Matters went from bad to worse. Vice President Cheney's chief of staff, Scooter Libby, attempted to undermine the anonymous diplomat's credibility by leaking information that his wife was an undercover CIA agent. That was not only illegal but made the administration's penchant for invoking national security to withhold information appear self-serving. The story stayed alive through 2007, when Libby was found guilty of perjury and obstruction of justice for trying to cover-up the leak. It would be a reminder that Bush misled the country.

As the election approached, the administration also reeled from revelations about its enhanced interrogation methods. U.S. troops detained captured Iraqi insurgents at the Abu Ghraib prison near Baghdad, where they engaged in downright sadistic treatment of the inmates. In April 2004, CBS's popular newsmagazine, *60 Minutes*, aired videos showing detainees naked, with hoods over their heads and electric wires attached to their bodies, being punched by guards, and even being forced to masturbate in front of female guards. It enraged many Americans, who found using torture to support Operation Iraqi Freedom farcical.

As Bush entered the campaign, his job approval ratings had fallen—from a phenomenal 90% after 9–11 and 75% in May 2003—to about 45% when the Republican convention met in August 2004.[30] A worried president who had won the election in 2000 by promising to return civility to American politics now played the cards a polarized political culture dealt him. He pivoted to highly charged social issues, hoping to energize his base. In 2003, the Supreme

---

30 Gallup, Presidential Approval Ratings—Gallup Historical Statistics and Trends https://news.gallup.com/poll/116677/Presidential-Approval-Ratings-Gallup-Historical-Statistics-Trends.aspx (accessed January 30, 2023).

Court reversed its 1986 decision upholding a Texas law criminalizing sodomy. Outraged, Christian conservatives predicted that recognition of same-sex marriage was next. Later that year, the Massachusetts high court held that the state constitution protected same-sex marriage. Bush quickly announced support for a constitutional amendment defining marriage as a contract between a man and a woman. His campaign hammered the opposition for bowing to pressure from gays and lesbians rather than defending traditional values.

He also shored up his support among pro-life voters. Dilation and extraction, a procedure developed by physicians in the 1990s, made late-term abortions safer. Most were performed because the mother's health was in danger or severe abnormalities were detected in the fetus late in the pregnancy. Anti-abortion activists called the procedure "partial birth abortion." The number of these procedures was relatively small, and most were done to protect women's health. But they offered opponents of abortion a powerful image of a fetus—they would say a baby—ripped from its mother's womb and destroyed. Republicans had passed two bills banning the procedure in the 1990s, and Clinton had vetoed both. When they passed another ban in 2003, Bush quickly signed it to the huzzahs of Christian conservatives.

Marriage and abortion weren't the only wedges Bush used to rally the base and pry voters away from the Democrats. The War on Terror filled a void in the Republican arsenal left by the end of the Cold War. Nixon, Reagan, and Bush senior never tired of attacking Democrats for being soft on Communism. Now Bush would appeal to the fear of terrorism triggered by 9–11. Achieving victory in Iraq might be slower than anticipated, he argued, but continuing the fight was necessary to prevent another attack on the homeland. Bush warned that if the U.S. showed "uncertainty or weakness, the world will drift to tragedy," quickly adding, "This isn't going to happen on my watch."[31] Democrats were either weak or interested in scoring political points at the expense of national security. Either way, their criticism of the Iraq war and eagerness to cut and run would leave the country vulnerable. A Bush TV ad showed wolves on the prowl as a voice warned, "Weakness attracts those who were waiting to do American harm."[32] A direct mail appeal showing images of smoke billowing from

---

31 *New York Times*, August 19, 2004 https://www.nytimes.com/2004/08/19/us/political-memo-a-war-president-reinforces-his-military-positions.html (accessed August 28, 2022).
32 *New York Times*, October 25, 2004 https://www.nytimes.com/2004/10/25/opinion/for-bush-bad-news-is-bad-news.html (accessed August 28, 2022).

the World Trade Center asked, "How can John Kerry lead America in a time of war?"[33]

John Kerry wasn't the adversary Bush wanted. He preferred to run against Howard Dean, the former Vermont governor. Dean developed a strong appeal to young voters with his vocal opposition to the Iraq war and plan to mitigate student loan debt. He also championed universal health care, a repeal of the Bush tax cuts, and an increase of taxes on the wealthy. He recruited an army of young idealistic volunteers who deftly used the Internet to mobilize volunteers and spread the campaign's message It was a marriage of high tech and politics that would revolutionize campaigning, but it didn't win the nomination for Dean. Faltering in Iowa, he never recovered.

Senator John Kerry of Massachusetts was the opponent Bush got. He was a decorated Vietnam veteran who had seen combat as a swift boat commander and won three Purple Hearts and a Bronze Star. Returning home convinced that the war was a mistake, he became a leader in Vietnam Veterans Against the War. His courage and patriotism seemed to position him to call Bush to account for the Iraq fiasco without appearing un-American. But in a highly partisan world no one was safe from character assassination. Kerry's Vietnam record came under attack before Labor Day by a group of veterans who never forgave him for his opposition to the war. With the support of a few wealthy Texas Republicans, the group—known as Swift Boat Veterans for Truth—raised several million dollars to produce four TV ads that falsely claimed that Kerry lied about his record and attacked him for betraying his comrades by criticizing the war.

Twenty years later, no evidence has surfaced to show that the group received financial support from or coordinated its activities directly with the Bush campaign, although several of the funders who were wealthy Texans had supported Bush. They acted independently, although they knew the ads would help Bush. Bush denounced the ads—but only after they were no longer running. Like other ostensibly independent groups that could spend unlimited amounts for negative campaign advertising, the Swift Boat Veterans' activities complemented Bush's efforts to sew doubts about Kerry. Probably fewer people saw them than heard about them in news stories that flooded cable and network news or read about the allegations in *Unfit for Command: Swift Boat Veterans Speak*

---

33 *New York Times*, October 31, 2004 https://www.nytimes.com/2004/10/31/politics/campaign/in-final-days-attacks-are-in-the-mail-and-below-the-radar.html (accessed August 28, 2022).

*Out Against John Kerry*, written by conservative hatchet men Jerome Corsi and John O'Neill. It's hard to gauge the campaign's effect. But at a time when politicians were suspect, many voters undoubtedly assumed that where there was smoke there was fire. Even more damaging was Kerry's patrician aloofness and his failure to articulate a compelling vision.

Bush won in another closely contested race. This time, he received three million more popular votes than his opponent and scored a 286–251 margin in the Electoral College. He narrowed the gender gap, perhaps owing to his concern for children, education, the poor, and the elderly; carried the Catholic vote, perhaps because of his forceful position on abortion; won a slight majority of voters 60 and older, perhaps because of his support for Medicare expansion; and polled far better among Hispanics than he did four years before, perhaps because of his support for a pathway to citizenship for undocumented immigrants.[34] He scored his biggest gains with evangelicals, who were enthusiastic about his own faith and his position on gays, marriage, and abortion. They showed up at the polls at a rate 9% higher than in 2000 and almost 80% of them voted for Bush. In Ohio, a closely contested state that Bush needed to win, 25% of those who voted identified as evangelical Christians, providing him with his margin of victory.[35] The pivot to social issues worked for a president whose job approval rating had fallen below 50%.

It was important but only one element of Bush's winning strategy. Like Clinton, his effort to occupy the middle—while wielding the social issues hatchet when necessary—probably paid dividends. In his first term, he had pushed tax cuts, championed smaller government, promoted strong defense, insisted that the U.S. remain a leader in world affairs, and defended the sanctity of life. It wasn't exactly Eisenhower Republicanism, but neither was it the slash and burn approach of Newt Gingrich and zealous conservatives who came to Congress after the 1994 mid-terms. Bush was aware that most Americans were tired of partisan warfare and ideological extremism and that many independents and moderates were turned off by Republicans' hostility to the disadvantaged. So, he pursued a strategy of triangulation that in some ways mirrored Clinton's. He pushed a major tax cut, advocated privatizing parts of Social Security, and ultimately took stands on abortion and marriage that won the plaudits

---

34 *New York Times*, November 7, 2004 https://www.nytimes.com/2004/11/07/weekinreview/how-americans-voted-a-political-portrait.html (accessed January 30, 2023).

35 Pew Research Center, Religion and the Presidential Vote, December 6, 2004 https://www.pewresearch.org/politics/2004/12/06/religion-and-the-presidential-vote/ (accessed January 30, 2023).

of conservative Christians. But he also expanded the federal role in education and health care to improve educational outcomes for poor children and provide seniors with critical services that Medicare ignored. His three million vote majority and growing appeal to women, Hispanics, and independents suggested that the strategy was working.

But Bush and his advisors couldn't be sure that their efforts to claim the center would be sufficient. His approval ratings had fallen, and the Iraq war was increasingly unpopular. So, he moved to excite the base by accentuating divisive social issues like abortion and marriage and suggesting that Democrats were soft on terrorism. But he did so in a modulated way to avoid appearing vicious, mean-spirited, or intolerant. That risked alienating moderates, whom he had worked so hard to attract. He wanted to have it both ways and largely succeeded, holding the center while motivating the base to turn out at a higher rate than in 2000.

The geographical divide between the parties widened a bit further in 2004. Bush added Iowa and New Mexico to the Republican stranglehold on the interior, and Kerry recouped New Hampshire for the Democrats. A look at the electoral map showed the coasts blue while the Midwest, South, Great Plains, and Mountain West were red, except for Michigan, Illinois, Minnesota, and Wisconsin. Some Democrats worried that voters in the heartland identified the party as coastal snobs who were contemptuous of them and their values. Democrats, *New York Times* columnist Nicholas Kristof observed, risk "being defined by [...] bicoastal, tree-hugging, gun-banning, French-speaking, Bordeau-sipping, Times-toting liberals."[36] That played into Republicans' hands, he warned, because it "means turning off swing voters." "You can't write off everything from Atlanta to California," observed Governor Janet Napolitano of Arizona, a state Clinton had carried but Gore and Kerry had lost.[37]

So, even though 2004 didn't see a return of the political bloodletting of the 1990s, sharp differences remained. Disagreement over policy had narrowed but not vanished. The biggest fault lines were race, region, religion, and gender, divisions that lent themselves to stereotypes and turned debate emotional. These divisions were baked into the parties, and party leaders reflexively

---

36 *New York Times*, November 6, 2004 2004 https://www.nytimes.com/2004/11/06/opinion/time-to-get-religion.html?searchResultPosition=18 (accessed August 20, 2022).

37 *New York Times*, November 7, 2004 https://www.nytimes.com/2004/11/07/weekinreview/how-americans-voted-a-political-portrait.html?searchResultPosition=2 (accessed August 20, 2022).

appealed to them when the going got tough. When they were the focus, conflict was nastier, bipartisanship more elusive, and gridlock tighter. Bush had invoked them but hadn't mobilized them in an all-out assault on Democrats. Nevertheless, the ease with which he turned to divisive "values" issues suggested that there was a shaky truce, not a peace treaty.

## A Sea of Troubles

Bush won, but his woes grew in the wake of his victory. Bashing Democrats who criticized the Iraq invasion for being soft on terrorism didn't have the same effect as charging opponents with being soft on Communism at the height of the Cold War. Unlike the Soviet Union, Iraq was not a world power. So, Bush's charges soon lost their effectiveness. There was no light at the end of the tunnel in Iraq, where the insurgency continued, the new Iraqi government floundered, and American troops continued to die at the rate of 850 per year.[38] The March 2003 claim—"Mission accomplished!"— continued to haunt Bush. So did ongoing reminders that the administration's justification for going to war was a sham. In November 2005, Scooter Libby was indicted for leaking classified information to undermine the credibility of Ambassador Joseph Wilson, who had leaked information suggesting that the administration relied on bogus intelligence in making its case for war—and did so knowingly. The story would remain in the news for the next two years until Libby was convicted, fanning charges that Bush had misled Congress and the public to win support for a war that Americans had tired of. By the end of 2005, almost half of Americans believed that going to war had been a mistake—a figure that would grow during the next three years. [39]

Many Americans also disliked the measures Bush employed to prosecute the war. A few days after the Libby indictment, the *Washington Post* published a story describing the CIA's "Black Sites," where U.S. officials used "enhanced interrogation techniques"—most people called it torture—to extract information from captured enemy combatants. It wasn't only Democrats who

---

[38] Statistia, Number of U.S. soldiers killed in the Iraq war from 2003 to 2020 https://www.statista.com/statistics/263798/american-soldiers-killed-in-iraq/ (accessed January 30, 2023).

[39] Pew Research Center, Public Attitudes Toward the War in Iraq: 2003–2008 https://www.pewresearch.org/2008/03/19/public-attitudes-toward-the-war-in-iraq-20032008/ (accessed January 30, 2023).

lambasted the administration's actions as immoral and illegal. In the Senate, two Republican hawks, John McCain of Arizona and Lindsey Graham of South Carolina, introduced legislation outlawing torture by U.S. personnel. It passed with a veto-proof majority.

As revelations about the war eroded support, a devastating Gulf Coast hurricane dealt Bush a blow from which he wouldn't recover. Katrina struck the Gulf Coast in late August 2005, bringing death and devastation from the Florida Panhandle to Louisiana. When the storm subsided, almost 2,000 had died and an estimated $150 billion worth of property had been destroyed. New Orleans took the worst hit with a storm surge of 30 feet in some places that left 80% of the city underwater. Several hundred thousand residents fled the city, and many of those who remained found shelter in the city's Superdome where food and water were in short supply. African American neighborhoods were hardest hit and slowest to get help.[40]

On vacation at his Texas ranch, Bush traveled to Arizona to attend a birthday party for Senator John McCain and then to San Diego to speak at an event commemorating the end of World War II in the Pacific. He only returned to Washington after New Orleans had been hit and the tragedy along the Gulf Coast had saturated the news for several days. Many Americans concluded that Bush didn't understand the magnitude of the disaster or didn't care. A photograph of Bush looking out the window of Air Force One as it flew over New Orleans on the trip back to the Capital captured what many thought: the President was floating above a disaster that destroyed the lives of hundreds of thousands. When Bush finally visited the region five days after Katrina hit New Orleans, he did little to restore public confidence. Criticism of FEMA's response was growing, but Bush publicly praised its director Mike Brown. "Brownie, you're doing a heck of a good job," he enthused, confirming for many that he was clueless.[41]

Bush's response to Katrina, combined with news from Iraq, put Bush's job approval ratings in the same place as New Orleans—underwater. By mid-September 2005, it had sunk to 40% and never recovered. It would reach a low point of 29% in mid-2007.[42] While comedians had long feasted on his penchant for mangling the English language, the parodies became more acerbic. The dog on the *Family Guy* animated TV comedy bragged to Lois, "I was the one

---

40 Ben Casselman, "Katrina Washed Away New Orleans's Black Middle Class," August 24, 2015 https://fivethirtyeight.com/features/katrina-washed-away-new-orleanss-black-middle-class/ (accessed January 30, 2023).
41 Greene, *Presidency of George W. Bush*, 271.
42 Gallup, Presidential Approval Ratings—Gallup Historical Statistics and Trends.

who found Bush after Hurricane Katrina." The story then shifted to the dog shouting at a tree house, "Uh, Mr. President, are you up there?" When Bush's head appeared in the window, the dog told him there had been a disaster in New Orleans, and the President responded, "Go away. I'm reading Super Fudge[…]. Don't make me do stuff."[43] Rapper Kanye West was even more biting, releasing a song called "George Bush Don't Care About Black People."

As Bush's popularity tanked, his ambitious domestic agenda ground to a halt. In his 2005 State of the Union Address, he warned that Social Security "is headed toward bankruptcy" and urged dramatic changes.[44] While no one 55 or older would see changes in the existing system, modifications affecting younger workers were essential for the program to survive. Bush laid out several, including increasing the retirement age, reducing benefits for wealthy Americans, and further lowering payments to those who retired early. One change was essential, he insisted—investing a portion of the payroll taxes paid by younger workers in the stock market. Critics called it privatization and charged that it was dangerous.

Bush had done nothing to bring Democrats into a conversation about private accounts, even though he knew it would be a tough sell. He appeared to count on using his bully pulpit to build public support and pick off the five Democratic senators he needed to join the 55 Republicans to break the filibuster and pass his bill. Democrats united in opposition, and they had a much better read on the sentiment of voters. They came out against privatization with guns blazing, charging that it would leave younger workers vulnerable to swings in the stock market and drain funds from the system, threatening the benefits of current retirees. The only beneficiaries would be stockbrokers. When members of Congress went home to their districts they got an earful, especially from older voters who turned out in large numbers in off-year elections. Bush stumped the country to defend his proposal, but it was dead on arrival.

Even the opportunity to fill a Supreme Court vacancy created problems. In late 2004, Chief Justice William Rehnquist announced that he was being treated for thyroid cancer. Believing he would retire, Bush began vetting successors and settled on John Roberts, a judge on the Court of Appeals for the District of Columbia.

---

43 https://www.binghamton.edu/news/story/3159/the-trailblazer-jean-quataert-transformed-the-field-of-history (accessed August 23, 2022) https://news.gallup.com/poll/116677/Presidential-Approval-Ratings-Gallup-Historical-Statistics-Trends.aspx (accessed January 30, 2023).

44 George W. Bush, "State of the Union," February 2, 2005 https://georgewbush-whitehouse.archives.gov/stateoftheunion/2005/ (accessed November 11, 2005).

In May 2005, with Rehnquist still on the bench, Justice Sandra Day surprised the White House by announcing her retirement. She was a critical swing vote who often sided with liberals on issues like abortion and affirmative action, so replacing her afforded an opportunity to shift the Court rightward. Bush quickly nominated Roberts, but then pivoted when Rehnquist died, announcing that he would nominate Roberts to the chief justiceship.

But whom to appoint to fill O'Connor's seat? The President went off his list and nominated Harriet Miers, a Dallas corporate lawyer then serving as White House Counsel. Bush trusted her, and she would allow him to appoint a woman to succeed O'Connor. But Miers raised a red flag for those on the left and the right. She had never served as a judge, had no judicial philosophy, was unfamiliar with basic constitutional issues, and appeared to conservatives unreliable on issues like abortion and gay rights. Facing withering criticism from the right, Bush withdrew the nomination and named Samuel Alito, a judge on the Court of Appeals for the Third Circuit. He was a no-doubter for conservatives. Both Roberts and Alito were confirmed, but the process alienated many conservatives. After the Miers nomination "a lot of conservatives filed for divorce from this administration," wrote the editor of the *National Review*.[45]

With the war going badly, Democrats itching to avenge their losses, and many conservatives angry, Republicans took a drubbing in the 2006 mid-terms. Democrats secured a net gain of 31 seats in the House, ending a dozen years of Republican control. They also won a 51–49 majority in the Senate. In races for both houses, Democrats not only flipped seats in states where the party was strong but also in red and purple states. The lesson for conservative Republicans—a term that was quickly becoming an oxymoron—was that a moderate like Bush gave away too much to the Democrats and eroded the enthusiasm of the base.

Bush's deteriorating political position didn't stop him from urging Congress to pass comprehensive immigration reform legislation. Disruptions in the Mexican economy and political upheaval in Central America produced a spike in illegal immigration to the U.S. from those areas between 1990 and 2005. The number in the U.S. illegally grew from 3.5 million in 1990 to over 10 million 15 years later.[46] Groups with clout in Washington, ranging from

---

45 Alex Markels, "Why Harriet Miers withdrew as Supreme Court Nominee," National Public Radio, October 27, 2005 https://www.npr.org/2005/10/27/4976787/why-miers-withdrew-as-supreme-court-nominee (accessed August 29, 2022).
46 USA Facts, Immigration and Border Security, "Unauthorized Immigrants," Data updated December 12, 2022 https://usafacts.org/topics/immigration-border-security (accessed February 26, 2023).

the Catholic Church, the U.S. Chamber of Commerce, and La Raza, pressed for reform that would swap citizenship for the undocumented for more effective sanctions on employers who hired illegal immigrants. They had support among Republicans, keen to please employers and eager to build on gains they had made among Hispanic voters in 2004. Democrats, intent on strengthening their standing with Hispanic voters and happy to please business lobbyists who contributed to their campaigns, also fell in line. In the Senate, Ted Kennedy and John McCain joined to sponsor reform legislation and won Bush's backing.

It seemed to be a revival of the situational bipartisanship that characterized the early years of Bush's presidency. But there was dissent in both parties, especially among House Republicans who were attuned to growing anti-immigrant sentiment in their districts. Employer sanctions included in the 1986 immigration legislation had been ineffective, they warned. Bush and reformers in the Senate were listening to business and civil rights groups and ignoring the surging anti-immigrant sentiment, they insisted. As House Republicans developed legislation, they agreed with Senate colleagues on one thing: creation of a nationwide, mandatory electronic employment verification system to prevent undocumented immigrants from getting jobs. Beyond that, their bill contained no provision for a path to citizenship for illegals but plenty of provisions designed to keep them out, including construction of "at least two layers of reinforced fencing" and "physical barriers, roads, lighting, cameras and sensors" along some 700 miles of the southern border.[47]

The stand-off would play out over the next two years. As the 2006 midterms approached, the Senate passed the Kennedy–McCain bill, giving undocumented immigrants who had been in the U.S. at least two years a path to citizenship and creating a program admitting several hundred thousand guest workers annually. The bill required the creation of an electronic verification system to ensure all employees were legally qualified to work in the U.S. and acquiesced in the House's demand for heavier border enforcement (although not a wall). However, with the two houses far apart, the debate carried over to the 110th Congress in 2007. In the intervening months, grassroots anti-immigrant sentiment created a firestorm that killed reform in the Senate. Organizations like Numbers USA and grassfire.com, used the internet to spread their message and mobilize citizens across the country. Talk radio hosts jumped on board, warning millions of their listeners that the Senate bill would

---

47 *New York Times*, May 25, 2006 https://www.nytimes.com/2006/05/25/washington/25IMMIGRATIONBILLS_GRAPHIC.html (accessed August 29, 2022).

increase the tide of immigration and take jobs from Americans, lower wages, and overwhelm schools and social services.

Opponents of reform on Capitol Hill welcomed the public outrage. Senators attempted to pass the bill "before Rush Limbaugh could tell the American people what was in it," chuckled Alabama Republican Senator Jeff Sessions, a staunch opponent. Limbaugh, other talk radio hosts, and restrictionist organizations tapped a growing fear among many White Americans that they were losing their country. Gays and lesbians were demanding same-sex marriage, the Census Bureau projected that Whites would be a minority by 2050, and Spanish-speaking immigrants were flooding their communities. A suburban Detroit resident, Monique Thibodeaux, spoke for many, complaining that immigrants took jobs from Americans and used public services supported by taxpayers. "What happened to taking care of our people first," she asked?[48] Although Bush worked the phones to hold Republican senators in line, the bill mustered only 46 votes. Republicans bolted *en masse*, with only 12 of 49, supporting the bill. What began as bipartisan immigration reform fueled a grass roots revolt that made immigration as divisive as abortion and created a new wedge issue for Republicans to exploit.

Bush didn't know it at the time, but things were about to get even worse. Much worse. Although most of the country remained oblivious, many in the know began to see signs of an economic tsunami on the horizon during the summer of 2007. The reason for their concern was the housing market. In response to the 2001 recession, the Fed had reduced interest rates, unleashing strong growth in consumer spending. Most sectors of the economy benefited, but none more than housing. As demand for homes grew, prices increased and construction companies built new houses and condominiums to meet consumer demand for new and, in many cases, bigger homes with more amenities. Lenders were eager to finance mortgages because they assured easy profits—on transaction fees as well as interest payments. With home prices rising steadily, the loans seemed to be low risk; if a borrower was unable to pay, the lender would own a property that had appreciated in value and could readily be sold in a brisk market. Many lenders provided mortgages to individuals who made minimal or even no down payments and were dubious credit risks. Indeed, some lenders offered so-called sub-prime mortgages to high-risk borrowers ("sub-prime" because of their income, assets, or credit history). They signed on to adjustable-rate mortgages

---

[48] *New York Times*, June 28, 2007 https://www.nytimes.com/2007/06/28/washington/28cnd-immig.html (accessed August 29, 2022).

that carried interest rates that might be low at the outset but grew with the life of the mortgage. Buyers most likely to default had mortgage payments that they could barely afford but that would increase over time. To make matters worse, many homeowners took out second mortgages that were available because the market value of their home had increased—not because they had made large down payments or had made principal payments for many years. Refinancing provided cash to pay off credit card debt, make home improvements, buy furniture, cars, and boats, take vacations, and send their kids to college.

Lenders were able to keep the party going by selling the mortgages they generated and bringing money back to their coffers to support additional loans. Two private entities with close ties to the federal government, Fannie Mae (the Federal National Mortgage Association) and Freddie Mac (the Federal Home Loan Mortgage Corporation), purchased mortgages, which they either held or bundled into packages (so-called mortgage-backed securities) that could be sold to banks, insurance companies, and other investors. The returns were good, especially if transactions were done at scale, and the products were secured by homes that were appreciating in value. Big profits in a hot economy, not to mention greater freedom as a result of deregulation, encouraged bankers to increase their investments by borrowing—often from one another. With interest rates low and returns high, why not? As investors purchased trillions of dollars of these new financial products, they also developed another form of investment to secure them, credit default swaps. These were complex instruments that indemnified purchasers of risky securities in the event of default. They were so complex that even many Wall Street CEOs didn't fully understand them, although they were sure they could make money on them.

By the summer of 2007, as the immigration bill blew up in Bush's face, there were indications that the real estate bubble might burst. The boom produced a housing glut that brought prices down. Foreclosures increased as those who couldn't afford mortgage payments defaulted, adding to the glut. As prices fell further, many borrowers were stuck with homes that were worth less—in some cases far less—than they owed the lender, who most likely held the loan through a mortgage-backed security. These borrowers had no choice but to walk away from their mortgage—and their home—worsening the housing glut. As housing prices declined, homeowners were unable—or unwilling, if they were smart— to obtain second mortgages. That reduced consumer spending and increased credit card debt, putting additional stress on individuals and the economy.

The housing crisis had a devastating effect on mortgage lenders. Fannie Mae and Freddie Mac were strictly regulated and couldn't purchase subprime mortgages. Those were sold on the secondary market to buyers willing to take greater risk in return for higher fees and interest. In August 2007, the secondary market crashed leaving lenders who relied on it with nowhere to turn. Several dozen, including a major player, American Home Mortgage, declared bankruptcy. Countrywide Finance, which financed 20% of all mortgages in the U.S. in 2006, stood on the brink. By January 2008, Bank of America purchased Countrywide for about a sixth of its 2006 market value. Shareholders took a beating.

The reverberations of the sub-prime mortgage debacle soon spread to the biggest players in American banking and finance. It was a crisis that wasn't limited to a few reckless firms. Two decades of deregulation allowed financial institutions to take greater risks, and a bull market that seemed a sure bet to guarantee ever greater returns encouraged them to continue to roll the dice. All the players were interconnected, so trouble at one firm set off shock waves that rocked others. Because so many big players "owned slices of [...] new-fangled financial instruments" like mortgage-backed securities," *New York Times* financial reporter Andrew Ross Sorkin wrote, "every firm was dependent on the others [...]. If one fell, it could become a series of falling dominoes."[49]

It wasn't long before the dominoes started to quiver. Bear Stearns, the smallest of Wall Street's Big Five investment banks, had bet heavily on investments in the sub-prime market. When it collapsed, Bear saw $1.6 billion wiped away. By March 2008, with investors pulling their money and traders refusing to do business with it, the bank was on the verge of collapse. Fearing disaster, Timothy Geithner, chair of the New York Federal Reserve Bank, Secretary of the Treasury Henry Paulson, and Jamie Dimon, CEO of JP Morgan, acted decisively to head off disaster. Geithner and Paulson persuaded Dimon to buy Bear at the almost-nominal price of $2 per share, contingent on the New York Fed buying $29 billion of Bear's debt. Critics in both political parties and many in the media called it a bailout. They slammed an administration already on the ropes politically for protecting wealthy bankers and their stockholders from the consequences of their arrogance and greed while everyday citizens were losing their homes to foreclosure. Some charged that Paulson, who left Goldman Sachs less than two years before to join the Bush administration, was just helping his buddies. Most Americans didn't understand the intricacies of Wall Street, but the takeaway for many was that the system was set up to help the wealthy and protect them when they screwed up. Financial writers called it moral hazard; for many voters, it was simply cronyism.

---

49 Andrew Ross Sorkin, *Too Big to Fail* (New York, 2009), 5.

Any reassurance the Bear deal brought was short-lived. By August, Fannie Mae and Freddie Mac were teetering on the verge of bankruptcy. Hammered by losses from mortgages that were in default and underwater, their stock had plummeted by 90% since the start of the year. Paulson worried that their collapse would cripple mortgage lending, further damaging the housing market. He enlisted a team from Morgan Stanley, one of the now-Big Four investment banks, to do a thorough analysis of the loans Fannie and Freddie held. The result was as bad as Paulson feared, prompting him to recommend and Bush to approve a government takeover. The Treasury would purchase $1 billion of stock in each company and take 80% control. The Fed backstopped each company's debt up to $200 billion to keep them from going under. Their management would be replaced, and there would be no golden parachutes.

The dominoes still teetered. Lenders and investors had hammered Lehman Brothers, another of the Big Four investment banks, and it faced insolvency in September 2008. Unable to find a buyer, with Goldman Sachs and Morgan Stanley themselves wobbling, Paulson and Bush refused a bailout, still smarting from criticism of the Bear deal. As Lehman declared bankruptcy, American International Group (AIG), a massive and highly successful global insurance and investment firm with its tentacles in a variety of other industries, stood on the brink as a result of heavy investment in real estate and credit default swaps gone south. Their collapse might take everyone down. So, Geithner developed and Paulson persuaded Bush to authorize a plan that allowed the Fed to provide a credit line of $95 billion to AIG in return for 80% ownership of the company, whose stock had by then fallen to $2 a share.

It still wasn't enough. Something unimaginable appeared likely. Goldman Sachs, the legendary investment bank Paulson had guided as CEO, stood on the verge of collapse, and Morgan Stanley wasn't far behind. If they fell, the rest of the dominoes would follow, sending the country into an economic collapse many feared would make the Great Depression look mild. Paulson and Geithner believed they had to act quickly and the solution had to be clean and simple. Enter TARP, the Troubled Asset Relief Program. It would create a $700 billion fund that the Treasury could use surgically to purchase toxic assets held by firms, providing infusions of capital where most needed. Bush approved the plan and assembled congressional leaders as well as the two major parties' presidential hopefuls, John McCain and Barack Obama, to hear Paulson's pitch. Although the meeting ended with McCain equivocal and Republicans reluctant to support the plan, Paulson prevailed on House Speaker Nancy Pelosi to bring congressional leaders to the table again. With Paulson emphasizing the dire consequences of inaction, they tweaked and then reached agreement to support the plan. In early October, with more than two-thirds of House Republicans voting nay, the bill went down to defeat, triggering the biggest one-day decline in the stock market in history. It was the shock the bill's proponents needed; three days later, after the Senate gave its assent, enough House Republicans fell in line to send TARP to Bush's desk. Continued Republican opposition was troubling. If they invoked small-government rhetoric to oppose a plan developed by a president of their own party to avert disaster, how would they would respond to a Democratic president? Democratic support, while it prevented disaster, set the party up to take the blame for an unpopular program developed by a Republican president to solve a disaster on his watch.

While TARP stabilized the dominoes on Wall Street, matters only got worse for those on Main Street. Shocked by their near collapse and aware that they remained vulnerable, banks tightened lending. That made it harder for consumers and businesses to borrow, constricting economic activity. Foreclosures on homes continued to rise, tripling between 2006 and 2008. Gross domestic product shrank by a whopping 5% and unemployment climbed. By 2008, it was 7% and would exceed 10% in 2009.[50] By the end of the year, General Motors and Chrysler stood on the edge of bankruptcy and were seeking government support. Securities were in free-fall, with stocks losing 35% of their value from July to December 2008.[51] The crash was devastating to middle- and working-class Americans whose 401-K retirement nest eggs and pension funds shrank.

There was shock and fear, but also plenty of anger. The resolution of the crisis had been orchestrated by the very people who had caused it. Paulson and Geithner, Wall Street insiders, made the most critical decisions, relying on executives at the big investment banks to implement the plans they developed. It probably couldn't have been otherwise. The system was so complex that few understood its inner workings well enough to make informed decisions. It all made sense, but the optics fueled public outrage.

For many Americans, TARP was a giveaway to an industry whose grossly overpaid executives drove the nation to the brink. Now men like Paulson and Geithner were pulling their buddies' chestnuts out of the fire. How could you not be angry at a bailout of Goldman Sachs when its CEO took home an unbelievable $68 million in 2007? Commentators wasted no time in calling

---

50 U.S. Unemployment Rate by Month, 1948–2020 https://www.thebalancemoney.com/unemployment-rate-by-year-3305506 (accessed January 30, 2023).

51 Macrotrends, Dow-Jones—DJIA—100 Year Historical Chart https://www.macrotrends.net/1319/dow-jones-100-year-historical-chart (accessed January 30, 2023).

attention to the hypocrisy of those who preached the importance of personal responsibility but supported bailouts for corporations that acted recklessly. "What do we have here?" asked popular columnist Ellen Goodman, "Socialism for the rich?"[52] Most Americans answered yes. A *New York Times*/CBS poll taken a week after Congress adopted TARP found that 63% of respondents believed that it would benefit "mostly just a few big investors and people who work on Wall Street."[53] Nor did the anger subside quickly. The Oscar-winning documentary *Inside Job* exposed, in the words of one prominent critic, "how the American housing industry set out deliberately to defraud the ordinary American investor."[54] During the 2010 primaries, challengers in both parties attacked those in the House and Senate who had supported TARP. In Utah, three-term U.S. Senator Robert Bennet, a TARP supporter, lost his bid for renomination. Opponents dubbed him "Bailout Bob" and jeered him at the state Republican convention with chants of "TARP, TARP, TARP."[55]

When he sought the presidency, Bush had promised to restore civility to American politics. In the wake of 9–11, he delivered on that promise by uniting the country in ways that it hadn't been since, perhaps, 1964. But unity was fleeting. Bush's decision to pursue war against Saddam and regime change in Iraq, coupled with his lack of transparency in justifying his policies, destroyed his popularity. Convinced that his actions were necessary to avert another terrorist attack, he charged that his opponents cared more about scoring political points than defending the homeland. That brought a level of vituperation to debates over foreign policy not seen since the end of the Cold War. His approval ratings declining, he relied on stoking the Republican base by running for reelection on highly divisive social issues that were effective but threatened to revive the bare-knuckles brawling of the 1990s. He also doubled down on Iraq, but with victory nowhere in sight it, too, became an albatross. Like Vietnam, many Americans concluded, arrogant leadership had taken the country into a war that was not vital to its security, that it couldn't win, and that had devastating consequences

---

52 *New York Times*, September 26, 2008 https://www.nytimes.com/2008/09/26/opinion/26iht-edgoodman.4.16512893.html?searchResultPosition=4 (accessed September 2, 2022).

53 *New York Times*, October 17, 2008 https://www.nytimes.com/2008/10/18/business/18charts.html (accessed September 2, 2022).

54 Roger Ebert, "Crime on the Streets, Victims in the Streets," *Chicago Sun Times*, October 13, 2010 https://www.rogerebert.com/reviews/inside-job-2010 (accessed March 8, 2024).

55 *New York Times*, July 10, 2010 https://www.nytimes.com/2010/07/11/us/politics/11tarp.html (accessed September 2, 2022).

for the hundreds of thousands who served. *The Hurt Locker*, winner of six Academy Awards in 2008, reminded viewers of the costs paid by those who had been deployed on a fool's errand.

Rendered politically ineffective by his growing unpopularity, Bush had the bad fortune to preside over a meltdown of the nation's economy in his last year as president. Much as Democrats tried to place responsibility on Bush and Republicans, there was plenty of blame to go around. Democrats had joined Republicans in touting the wisdom of the market and supporting deregulation. Like Republicans, they had benefited from the campaign contributions of investors and business magnates who grew rich in the New Gilded Age. And they had to share the blame for the diminished regulations that invited speculation and helped bring the financial system to the brink of collapse and cost taxpayers billions to stabilize. Many Americans felt betrayed by political leaders who appeared to act much more quickly to save the rich than to assist people like them. It was the second time in 20 years—going back to the savings and loan meltdown of the late 1980s—taxpayers had footed the bill for bad decisions made by greedy speculators. Many considered it proof that the system was rigged to help the wealthy.

As John McCain and Barack Obama battled to succeed Bush, they competed for a prize that would carry responsibility to lead recovery from an economic collapse second in severity only to the Great Depression. The extent of the economic disaster would make that challenging. But perhaps not as difficult as the rekindled polarization that Bush and the Great Recession bequeathed his successor. Democrats and some Republicans in Congress had come together to pass TARP, but only because they feared economic collapse. Even then, a mix of partisan opportunism and commitment to conservative free market, small-government principles led a majority of House Republicans to dig in their heels and vote against a bill advanced by a Republican president. The animosities that grew during Bush's second term as well as the blame showered on Republicans, as the party in power, for the economic catastrophe made additional collaboration to repair the damage unlikely. Indeed, as Democrats reveled in blaming Republicans for the country's woes, Republicans were disinclined to support programs they developed. After all, if Democrats were successful, they would tighten their grip on Washington. Most Republicans in Congress had come to Capitol Hill during the Gingrich revolution, and they itched for a bare-knuckle brawl.

It wasn't just the political players and climate in Washington that promised to make the next president's honeymoon short. Many Americans were angry, alienated, and worried about their future. The economic revival of the previous

25 years meant that they lived in a prosperous society whose popular culture flashed the opulence capitalism made available. To some at least. Prosperity had been very unevenly distributed as income and wealth was concentrated at the top in a way not seen since the 1920s. Those in the top 1% lived like robber barons and those in the top 10%–15% enjoyed the good life. But most Americans struggled to make ends meet. The Great Recession made their lives even harder, in some cases desperately so. They were angry that government always seemed to protect the elite, as it had during the financial crisis, while it ignored their problems. Anger lent itself to appeals to fear and to finding scapegoats.

The fallout of the financial crisis loomed large. But it wasn't the only source of disagreement and recrimination. Anti-immigrant sentiment was spreading as many White Americans directed their frustration and fear at immigrants and demanded protection from alien invaders. Race, gender, abortion, guns, and a host of other hot-button cultural issues continued to fuel sharp disagreements. Like immigration, they made many people's blood boil, and there were politicians eager to use them to rally voters against their opponents—especially if they wanted to change the subject. A changed political landscape also encouraged partisan conflict. The parties had become more ideologically homogeneous—especially Republicans who saw a once-strong contingent of moderates evaporate. They had also become realigned by region, with Democrats dominating the coasts and Republicans the South, the Midwest, and Mountain West. These changes made it easier to view the opposition as a culturally alien "other," making compromise more difficult.

It was a moment that would challenge any new president. Voters who were fearful and angry, didn't trust government, and disdained politicians. Politics was again becoming dangerously polarized, and political leaders, especially in the Republican Party, had mastered the art of using social divisions to their advantage. The most promising divisions to exploit were class, gender, religion, nationality, region, and, of course, the deepest of them all, race. It would be the fate of the first Black president to lead the nation out of economic catastrophe in this perilous political climate. Those who proclaimed his election a sign that America had entered a post-racial age would be sorely disappointed.

CHAPTER 9

# THE TIPPING POINT, 2008–2012

## Hope and Change Meets the Politics of Division

Barack Obama believed he could bridge differences. His confidence grew naturally from his own experience. He was born in 1961 in Hawaii, America's newest state, and long a cultural bridge between East and West. He was mixed race, the son of a White mother and a Muslim international student from Kenya. When his parents divorced in 1964, his mother married an Indonesian student and took young Barack to Jakarta, where he attended elementary school for four years before returning to Hawaii. There he was raised by maternal grandparents, who came of age in Kansas during the Great Depression. Two years after graduating from Columbia University in 1983, he took a job as a community organizer in a heavily Black neighborhood on Chicago's South Side, where he encountered a world far removed from his middle-class upbringing and Ivy League education. When he left Chicago for Harvard Law School in 1988, he found himself in the midst of sharp conflict between progressive and conservative students. Although his views were left of center, he won the election as the first Black president of the *Harvard Law Review* by winning support from conservative editors who believed that he listened and was fair minded.

After graduating, he returned to Chicago where he plunged into politics, confident that he could bridge differences, build coalitions, mitigate partisanship, and effect change. He won election to the Illinois Senate in 1996 and the U.S. Senate eight years later. Although his political base was in Black Chicago, he spent many hours in rural and suburban communities across his sprawling, diverse state, talking to farmers, small business owners, factory workers, teachers, nurses, and everyone he came in contact with. Ever the optimist, always the bridge builder, he concluded that they shared the "same values," had the "same hopes and dreams." He questioned the "reigning political assumptions about how divided we were" and embraced "a politics that bridged America's racial, ethnic, and religious divides, as well as the many strands of my own life."[1]

A fresh face and a commanding speaker with a compelling story, John Kerry selected Obama to deliver the keynote at the 2004 Democratic convention. Embracing the "politics of hope," he exhorted Americans to find common ground and bring about badly needed change to ensure that anyone willing to work hard could create a better life for themselves and their children. "There is not a liberal America and a conservative America [...] not a Black America and a White America and Latino America and Asian America," he asserted, "there's the United States of America."[2] Three years later, when he announced his candidacy for president, he reprised these themes. Campaign posters with a stylized portrait of Obama looking to the horizon, some with the single word "Hope" and others "Change," graphically represented the sense of optimism and possibility that animated his campaign. So did one of the campaign's signature slogans, "Yes, we can!" It seemed so retro as if the optimism that fueled LBJ's 1964 campaign and his Great Society was making a comeback. But it worked, as an improbable candidate won the nomination and the presidency. Perhaps Obama wasn't a naïve optimist and Americans were ready to embrace hope, seek common ground, and work to change what ailed the nation. A young Broadway director and composer, Lin Manuel Miranda, captured the spirit in a new musical he began work on in 2009. The story of Alexander Hamilton with Black and Latino actors playing the founders and singing hip-hop tunes, suggested that the nation and its history belonged to all when it opened to critical acclaim and sold-out houses six years later.

*Hamilton's* upbeat message of inclusion didn't prevail in Washington. Conservative activists and Republican strategists didn't see Obama's candidacy or election as a kumbaya moment. Instead, they looked forward to the next round, convinced that if they used the tools a constitutional system built on checks and balances provided, they could block his policy initiatives and sour voters on him and his presidency. Conservatives had mastered the art of using hot-button social issues to stoke division and mobilize their base for the next battle. They believed they had the perfect foil in a Black man named Barack Hussein Obama. As much as pundits celebrated his success as evidence of

---

[1] Barack Obama, *A Promised Land* (New York, 2020), 41.
[2] Barack Obama, "Keynote Address at the 2004 Democratic National Convention," July 27, 2004 https://www.presidency.ucsb.edu/documents/keynote-address-the-2004-democratic-national-convention (accessed September 30, 2022).

the nation's strides toward overcoming racism, many Americans had a different view. Some saw him as uncomfortably different, a man they couldn't relate to and viewed with suspicion. Many others found the very idea of a Black president—especially one whose father was Muslim and who had spent part of his youth in Indonesia—appalling. It would be easy to rally them against Obama and ensure that partisan warfare continued.

The attacks began as soon as Obama stepped on the national stage. In 2004, when he ran for the U.S. Senate, Andy Martin, a conservative gadfly, conspiracy theorist, and self-styled internet journalist, posted an article on Out2.com charging that Obama was "a complete fraud […] a Muslim who has concealed his religion." Republished by FreeRepublic.com,[3] it spread through email and was posted on other conservative websites where it appeared under headlines like "Barack Hussein Obama: Once a Muslim, Always a Muslim."[4] When Obama launched his presidential campaign in January 2007, the story took a new turn. He had not been born in the U.S. and wasn't qualified to be president.

Recalling how John Kerry's campaign had been damaged by refusing to respond to spurious charges that he lied about his military record, the Obama campaign acted quickly, posting a copy of Obama's birth certificate on the web in June 2008. While that satisfied many on the right, the charge continued to spread in the nether world of conspiracy theorists, bloggers, and internet "journalists." Many on the right saw these sites and the stories they produced as more credible than the mainstream media, which they believed was beholden to the establishment. They weren't celebrating Obama as a harbinger of a post-racial nation but saw his success as evidence that they were losing their country—a trend that had begun with the civil rights movement, was fueled by immigration, and reached fulfillment in Obama's election. So, the stories kept coming and found a receptive audience, stoking fear and outrage. Even if mainstream Republicans refused to embrace them, they served their interests by firing up the base in an election year in which Republicans desperately wanted to talk about anything but the economy.

---

3 "Columnist Say Barack Obama 'Lied to the American People;' Asks Publisher to Withdraw Obama's Book," August 11, 2004 www.freerepublic.com/focus/f-news/1189687/posts (accessed October 1, 2022).
4 Debbie Schussel, "Barack Hussein Obama: Once a Muslim, Always a Muslim," December 18, 2006 http://www.debbieschlussel.com/2750/barack-hussein-obama-once-a-muslim-always-a-muslim/ (accessed October 1, 2022).

While the stories circulated on websites, talk radio shows, and email chains that most Americans regarded as part of the right-wing fringe, they didn't stay there. They entered the mainstream media which was hungry for content to fill the 24–7 news cycle created by cable giants like CNN, MSNBC, and Fox News. While many considered Fox News little more than an organ of the Republican party, it was the most-watched cable news channel in the summer of 2008.[5] In August, its popular morning opinion show *Fox & Friends* featured an interview with Jerome Corsi, who had played a prominent role in attacking John Kerry's military record and had just published *The Obama Nation*. During the course of the interview, Corsi charged that the birth certificate Obama posted on the web was a fake. "There's been a good analysis of it on the Internet," he said, "and it's been shown to have watermarks from Photoshop."[6] His source, it turned out, was an email from "Techdude" referenced on *Atlas Shrugs*, a website operated by Pamela Geller, a former publisher of the *New York Observer* and well-known Islamaphobe.[7]

That month, Fox's Sean Hannity featured none other than Andy Martin, the father of the Obama-as-closet-Muslim lies, in a brief "documentary" on his popular show, *Hannity's America*. Martin had moved on, now focusing on Obama's allegedly dangerous radicalism and ties to terrorists. The documentary introduced Martin as "a Chicago-based internet journalist," lending respectability to a man who peddled conspiracy theories and had once been denied admission to the bar after a psychiatrist diagnosed him with a "moderately severe character defect manifested by well-documented ideation with a paranoid flavor and a grandiose character."[8] Obama, Martin breathlessly reported, was the protégé of Bill Ayers, a University of Illinois–Chicago education professor who had been designated a domestic terrorist by the FBI for his role in bombings orchestrated by the radical anti-war Weathermen in the 1960s and early 1970s. The two lived in the same neighborhood and had only a passing acquaintance. Yet Martin claimed, without evidence, that Ayers had been instrumental in recruiting Obama to come to Chicago as a community organizer. Obama had impressed Ayers and his radical allies during this trial run, Martin asserted, and

---

5 Paul Gough, "Cable makes big headlines in 2008," Reuters, December 30, 2008 https://www.reuters.com/article/us-cable-idUSTRE4BU0BZ20081231 (accessed January 30, 2023).

6 Jeremy Peters, *Insurgency* (New York, 2022), 96.

7 Ibid., 62, 96.

8 *New York Times*, October 13, 2008 https://www.nytimes.com/2008/10/13/us/politics/13martin.html (accessed October 1, 2022).

they decided to bring him back to Chicago after he graduated law school to be part of their left-wing cabal.

The documentary took it from there, charging that from his days as a community organizer to his work as a state senator Obama "surrounded himself with the city's most radical elements." The proof? "One need look no further," the narrator asserted, "than his current neighborhood,"[9] as a reporter strolled down Obama's street, pointing out that Ayers and Nation of Islam leader Louis Farrakhan lived within a half mile. Although the story presented no evidence of even casual association, it confirmed for Obama haters that he was dangerous.

The cumulative effect of the campaign to vilify Obama was evident on the campaign trail. His opponent, John McCain, experienced it as he took questions at a rally in Minnesota. "I don't trust Obama," one participant said. "I have read about him. He's an Arab." "Frankly, we're scared [...] of an Obama presidency," another commented, adding that "he's someone who consorts with domestic terrorists." McCain had authorized a TV ad tying Obama to Ayers, but he was shocked by the venom. He called Obama "a decent family man, a citizen that I just happen to have disagreements with on fundamental issues."[10] The audience would have none of it, however, and booed their candidate. Energized by spurious allegations from the campaign, some Republicans turned on their own candidate when he tried to dial back the hatred.

As the encounter suggested, the "birther" lie refused to die because it motivated some voters. As Donald Trump flirted with another bid for the presidency, he quickly resurrected it. Speaking at the Conservative Political Action Conference in 2011, he received only polite applause when he lambasted Democrats for supporting abortion and gun control. But he lit up the room when he went after Obama's allegedly shady background. "Our current president came out of nowhere," Trump proclaimed to loud applause. He kept going, asserting that "the people he went to school with [...] never saw him.

---

9 Eric Hanonoki, "On Fox News, Hannity hosted Andy Martin—who has called judge a "crooked, slimy Jew," accused African-Americans in public office of corruption—in Obama smear-fest," October 7, 2008 https://www.mediamatters.org/sean-hannity/fox-news-hannity-hosted-andy-martin-who-has-called-judge-crooked-slimy-jew-accused (accessed October 1, 2022).

10 Matt Spetalnik, "Republican Anger Boils Up at McCain Rally," October 10, 2008 https://www.reuters.com/article/us-usa-politics-mccain-idUSTRE49A0P720081011 (accessed October 1, 2022).

They don't know who he is. Crazy." When he made the rounds of national TV talk shows, he amplified the charge. He claimed to have investigators in Hawaii looking into the birth certificate and teased, "They cannot believe what they are finding." Asked by Fox's Sean Hannity if he thought that efforts to conceal the real birth certificate had anything to do with religion, Trump took the cue. "Maybe it says he a Muslim," he suggested.[11] Baseless as it was, the charge had power. It was a measure of how polarized the country had become, and how more and more Americans occupied media bubbles that insulated them from perspectives that challenged their own and where evidence was optional.

## Hope and Change Ascendant

Despite the baseless attacks, Obama remained convinced that he could bridge differences and bring people together to achieve change. As the election approached and hopefuls began announcing their candidacies in 2007, things looked good for Democrats. The Iraq War was growing more unpopular by the day, as was its architect, George W. Bush, and his party. Hillary Clinton, who had won a U.S. Senate seat in New York the year her husband left the White House, was the odds-on favorite. As the primaries began, she faced an unexpectedly strong challenge from Obama. He used the Internet to fill his campaign coffers with donations from hundreds of thousands, then millions of small contributors, engaged young people in record numbers, and built a sophisticated, tech-savvy grassroots organization to turn out his voters. After winning the Iowa caucuses and finishing a strong second in New Hampshire in January 2008, he defeated Clinton in a closely fought and protracted primary campaign that ended only after the last primaries concluded in June.

Winning the Republican nomination proved easier—although less of a prize given the party's unpopularity—for John McCain. A Navy pilot who had been shot down by the North Vietnamese and who spent five years as a POW, McCain was in his fourth term in the Senate. He had cultivated a reputation as a maverick by challenging his party's position on gay rights, gun control, campaign finance reform, and immigration. His principal challengers were Rudolph Giuliani, the former New York City mayor, Mike Huckabee, the former Arkansas governor who was popular with evangelicals, and Mitt Romney, the former governor of Massachusetts. Giuliani was plagued by personal scandals, and Huckabee and Romney divided conservatives, giving

---

11 Peters, *Insurgency*, 127–29.

McCain a path to the nomination. It came with the baggage—association with a highly unpopular Republican president and the suspicion of many conservatives. "He is not the choice of conservatives, as opposed to the choice of the Republican establishment," Rush Limbaugh told the millions who regularly tuned into his daily radio show.[12]

Obama had star power. He was not only the first African American to win the nomination of a major party, but his youthful energy, eloquence, charisma, meteoric rise, and compelling story had drawn huge crowds to his rallies from the moment he announced his candidacy. McCain wasn't a star, but he created one by selecting Sarah Palin as his running mate. She was an unconventional choice that McCain believed would shake up a race that polls showed him losing. The daughter of teachers in Wasilla, Alaska, Palin had bounced around five colleges and finished third in the 1984 Miss Alaska contest before graduating with a degree in communications from the University of Idaho. She married her high school sweetheart, who worked in oil production on Alaska's North Slope, and the couple had five children. A self-styled hockey mom and unabashed evangelical Christian, she served one term on the Wasilla town council and two as mayor before defeating Frank Murkowski, the state's most powerful politician, in the 2006 Republican gubernatorial primary and cruising to victory in the general election. Palin won by attacking establishment Republicans for their cozy relationship with oil companies and mobilizing a passionate group of working people and evangelical Christians behind her candidacy. She was telegenic and had a quick wit, sharp tongue, and unpretentious demeanor that inspired many Alaskans. Supporters believed that she understood them, represented their values, and would fight for them. They were, in the words of *Anchorage Daily News* reporter Amanda Coyne, "the kind of people [Republican insiders] derided as 'Valley Trash,' the people who hold Palin signs high and chant 'Sa-rah, Sa-rah and sculpt funny Palin hats and adorn their cars and bicycles with Palin bumper stickers and who vote."[13]

McCain's announcement created a media tsunami as reporters scrambled to find out just who Sarah Palin was. While many questioned her lack of experience, Palin herself changed the subject with a dazzling speech at the Republican

---

12 E.J. Dionne, Jr., *Why the Right Went Wrong: Conservatism from Goldwater to Trump and Beyond* (New York, 2016), 281.

13 Amanda Coyne, "How Palin turned on her own party and became governor," *Anchorage Daily News*, August 27, 2006 (updated June 30, 2016) https://www.adn.com/politics/article/how-palin-turned-her-own-party-and-became-governor/2006/08/29/ (accessed October 4, 2022).

Convention in early September. According to the *New York Times*, McCain's nomination became "a sideshow to the evening's main spectacle, the speech by the little-known Palin, a 44-year-old mother of five."[14] She electrified delegates and a national TV audience. Describing herself as "just the average hockey mom," she ad-libbed, "Know the difference between a hockey mom and a pit bull? Lipstick!" The audience roared, sensing that this one was a real fighter. She attacked liberals and turned the tables on critics who called her inexperienced with zingers at Obama. "I guess a small-town mayor is sort of like a 'community organizer,'" she quipped, "except that they have actual responsibilities." Separating herself from the Republican establishment, which carried the baggage of the recession anyway, Palin boasted that she was not "a member in good standing of the Washington elite."[15] She reveled in tweaking their noses, winning the allegiance of people—especially those in small towns and rural America—who felt that well-educated members of the establishment—whether Republicans or Democrats—viewed them with contempt.

There was a downside to Palin's selection, however. Early interviews with ABC's Charles Gibson and CBS's Katie Couric demonstrated that she was embarrassingly uninformed. When Couric asked what newspapers and magazines she read, the best she could do was, "Um, all of them, any of them that have been in front of me over all these years."[16] She was a bonanza for *Saturday Night Live's* ratings, as Tina Fey's side-splitting, dead-on parodies became must-see TV. Although she turned off many college-educated suburban independents, she attracted huge crowds of enthusiastic, boisterous supporters whose loyalty grew the more the media criticized her. She was one of them, and the attacks on her reminded them of the condescension they felt from members of the elite. "She's intelligent, she's adorable and she has the audacity to speak her mind," a man from a small town in North Carolina told a reporter.[17]

---

14 *New York Times*, September 4, 2008 https://www.nytimes.com/2008/09/04/world/americas/04iht-04repubday.15886363.html (accessed October 4, 2022).

15 "Transcript: Governor Sarah Palin at the RNC," September 3, 2008," https://www.npr.org/2008/09/03/94258995/transcript-gov-sarah-palin-at-the-rnc (accessed October 4, 2022).

16 Laura McGann, "John McCain, Sarah Palin, and the rise of reality TV politics," *Vox*, December 1, 2018 https://www.vox.com/policy-and-politics/2018/8/25/17779128/sarah-palin-john-mccain-legacy-trump (accessed October 4, 2022).

17 *New York Times*, October 13, 2008 https://www.nytimes.com/2008/10/14/us/politics/14palin.html (accessed October 4, 2008).

She also appealed to the fear and hatred many felt for Democrats, Obama, and the media. At rallies in Florida, she linked Obama to Bill Ayers, the 1960s domestic terrorist, adding "This is not a man who sees America the way you and I see America." Her remarks not only brought loud boos but a cry of "Kill him." When she blamed CBS's Katie Couric for her "less-than-successful interview with the kind of mainstream media," she brought down the crowd's wrath on the press. Some "turned on reporters in the press area, waving thunder sticks and shouting abuse," while others "hurled obscenities at a camera crew." *Washington Post* reporter Dana Milbank captured the spirit with the title of his story: "Unleashed, Palin Makes a Pit Bull Look Tame."[18]

Palin delivered her slashing attacks with a populist folksiness that resonated with a Republican base that had become more rural and working class, less college-educated and country-clubby over the years. Ultimately, however, she damaged McCain. Many voters concluded that it was reckless for a 72-year-old candidate with a history of melanoma to select a running mate who was so woefully ignorant. Even some conservatives were livid. Peggy Noonan, Ronald Reagan's speechwriter, called Palin "a symptom and expression of a new vulgarization in American politics" that was "no good, not for conservatism and not for the country."[19] Yet most conservatives disagreed. "Conservatives have been looking for leadership," commented Yale-educated Brent Bozell, publisher of the *National Review*, "and she's proven that she can electrify the grassroots like few people have in the past 20 years." She was the sign of a party and movement embarrassed by an unpopular war and a recession, transformed by 40 years of appeals to evangelicals, social conservatives, and the White South and fixated on wedging White working-class voters away from the Democrats. It had created a party with a hold on small town and rural America, the White South, and non-college-educated White voters, guaranteeing bitter polarization grounded in identity.

Of course, Palin wasn't McCain's only problem. His strongest credentials were in defense and foreign policy, but he doggedly supported an unpopular war in Iraq, arguing that the troop surge Bush had initiated in 2007 was working. But most Americans had long ago tired of a war that many believed Bush had lied to win support for. What most concerned Americans as election day

---

18 *Washington Post*, October 7, 2008 http://voices.washingtonpost.com/roughsketch/2008/10/unleashed_palin_makes_a_pit_bu.html (accessed October 4, 2022).

19 *Wall Street Journal*, October 17, 2008 https://peggynoonan.com/473/?hilite=sarah+palin (accessed October 4, 2022).

approached was the economy. Economic policy wasn't McCain's forte or even an interest. Besides, however he might try to distance himself from Bush, he was a Republican and the collapse occurred on his party's watch. To make matters worse, he appeared uncertain in the face of crisis. "The fundamentals of our economy are strong," he told reporters following the collapse of Lehman Brothers in mid-September, only to reverse himself a few days later, asserting that they "are at great risk."[20] On September 24, he announced that he was suspending his campaign, withdrawing from the first debate scheduled two days later, and returning to Washington to deal with the crisis. Obama indicated that he was in close contact with Treasury officials and would do whatever was needed to help resolve the crisis but would not suspend his campaign. "Presidents are going to have to deal with more than one thing at a time," he pointedly observed.[21] McCain and Obama attended a meeting called by Bush to build support for what became TARP. The leaks that followed indicated that "McCain was largely silent, with nothing to offer while Obama had asked a series of sharp questions."[22] McCain changed his mind yet again, resuming his campaign, participating in the debate, and reinforcing the impression that he was impulsive.

Obama ran a strong campaign, using the Internet to raise money, recruit volunteers, coordinate their activities, target messaging, and put himself in position to benefit from his opponent's blunders. He appeared calm, articulate, and in control of the facts, and his no-drama-Obama façade was reassuring, refuting charges that he was too inexperienced. The result was a wave election. Turnout was the highest since 1968, with over 61% of eligible voters casting ballots—1.5% more than in 2004. Obama won 53% of the popular vote and crushed McCain, 365–173, in the Electoral College. He made inroads in the heartland, picking up Iowa and Indiana, in the South by adding Virginia, North Carolina, and Florida, and the Mountain West by carrying New Mexico, Colorado, and Nevada. His efforts significantly increased turnout among African Americans and voters 18–30, and he carried those groups with 95% and 66% of the vote, respectively. He won the votes of 66% of Hispanics, 56% of women, 54% of Catholics, 52% of independents, and 50% of suburbanites. He carried 60% of voters with incomes under $50,000 and 52% of those with

---

20 Dan Balz and Haynes Johnson, *The Battle for America: The Story of an Extraordinary Election* (New York, 2009), 347.
21 Obama, *The Promised Land*, 183.
22 Balz and Jonson, *Battle for America*, 349.

incomes greater than $200,000.[23] Democrats picked up 21 seats in the House for a 257–178 majority, and eight seats in the Senate, giving them a filibuster-proof 60-vote majority (including two independents who caucused with them).

Obama's victory was chilling for Republican leaders. Rebounding from defeats at the hands of Clinton, the GOP won control of the House in 1994 and made Bush a two-term president. His reelection in 2004 persuaded Republicans they had built a coalition that would remain dominant for decades, allowing them to complete the conservative revolution begun by Reagan. Wave elections in 2006 and, now, 2008, crushed that dream. It wasn't only the size of Obama's victory that shocked them, but the realization that they were facing a demographic disaster that might give Democrats a hold on power like the one they had enjoyed from 1932 to 1968. Minorities were on their way to becoming the majority. Demographers predicted that the population would be less than 50% White by 2050, and Republicans fared poorly among people of color. Voters under 30 were by definition the future, and Obama had turned them out in record numbers and won the votes of two-thirds of them. Even the South, which had been so critical to the Republican revival since Nixon's day, seemed at risk.

Licking their wounds and fearing the future, 15 House and Senate Republicans gathered on January 20, 2008, hours after Obama's inauguration at a tony Capitol Hill steakhouse to discuss strategy. House members Paul Ryan, Kevin McCarthy, and Eric Cantor, the minority leader, were joined by Senators Jim DeMint, Jon Kyl, Tom Coburn, and John Ensign. Other prominent conservatives participating were former speaker Newt Gingrich, Fred Barnes of the *Weekly Standard*, and Frank Luntz, a pollster and consultant, who called them together. Those attending were in the words of Robert Draper, "behaviorally speaking, Washingtonians" who "unlike ordinary Americans [...] lived by a biennial calendar, the rhythms of their lives propelled by the electoral cycle."[24] They had learned the ways of the capital and accrued power, which also translated into wealth. And they had more of each when they were in the majority. They were part of the elite Palin had derided, but they knew that by appealing to social issues and hostility to government and politicians they could fire up the party's increasingly populist base and perhaps regain power.

---

23 Pew Research Center, "Inside Obama's Sweeping Victory," November 5, 2008 https://www.pewresearch.org/2008/11/05/inside-obamas-sweeping-victory/ (accessed January 30, 2023).

24 Robert Draper, *When the Tea Party Came to Town* (New York, 2012).

It probably didn't occur to them that people like Palin could turn that base against them.

The question that January night was how to regain the majority. The group agreed on several things. Ensign observed that Republicans lost their way because "we got obsessed with governing, making sure the trains run on time." Compromising with Democrats only muddied the party's message. "The only way we succeed is if we're united," Paul Ryan insisted. If Republicans broke ranks and cut deals with the majority, Democrats would get credit for creating popular programs. "If you act like the minority, you'll stay in the minority," Kevin McCarthy insisted. "We've gotta challenge them on every single bill and every single campaign."[25] By the time the group disbanded, they agreed to resist the new administration at every turn, even though the country was in the midst of economic catastrophe. Their calculation was that blame for gridlock and inaction would fall on the party in power.

Senate Republican leader Mitch McConnell hadn't attended the dinner; he and Luntz hated one another. But the Kentuckian was on the same page as those who were there. A master of Senate procedure, he placed reclaiming the majority above all else. Several weeks into the Obama presidency, McConnell held a retreat for his caucus at the tony Greenbrier resort in West Virginia's Blue Ridge mountains. Acknowledging Obama's sky-high approval ratings, he cautioned that direct attacks on the President would alienate voters tired of partisan bickering. But that didn't mean Republicans should work with Obama and seek compromises that would move his policies in a more conservative direction—the traditional role of a loyal opposition. Rather, they should avoid cooperation, oppose his initiatives, and prevent him from succeeding. "We do not take him on frontally," Utah Republican Bob Bennet recalls McConnell advising. "We find issues where we can win, and we [...] take him down one issue at a time." The endgame? "We create an inventory of losses, so it's Obama lost on this, Obama lost on that," Bennet continued. "And we wait for the time the image has been damaged to the point where we can take him on."[26] Americans were suffering as unemployment continued to rise, but McConnell—and his Republican colleagues—were preoccupied with regaining power. And if that meant creating gridlock, so be it.

Obama had the responsibility to govern, and he, unlike McConnell, would be judged on how effective the federal government dealt with the dire situation.

---

25 Ibid.
26 Alec MacGillis, *The Cynic: The Political Education of Mitch McConnell* (New York, 2014), 97.

Highly disciplined, he went to work on the problem weeks before the inauguration. Since the financial meltdown in September, he had been in close contact with Henry Paulson, Bush's Treasury Secretary, and Tim Geithner, chair of the Federal Reserve Bank of New York, the key players in staving off a global depression. And he worked closely with President Bush to support TARP, the $700 billion plan Paulson and Geithner developed to prevent the big banks from going under and taking the rest of the economy with them. Impressed with his cool and intellect, Obama named Geithner Treasury secretary and began developing a financial stimulus package. The economy was in free fall. The financial collapse had frozen credit, which in turn led businesses to reduce investments and cut back their activities and consumers to reduce purchases, especially of big-ticket items like cars and houses. As economic activity shrank, businesses laid off workers, and state and local governments, seeing tax revenues plummet, contemplated firing teachers, police officers, firefighters, and other public employees. Monetary policy couldn't turn things around because the Fed had already lowered interest rates to zero. Fiscal stimulus—a massive program of government spending—was the only way out, even though it would create huge deficits on top of those that the Bush tax cuts, wars in Afghanistan and Iraq, and TARP had bequeathed.

There were two principal questions for those designing the stimulus—how much to spend and what to spend it on. The consensus among Obama's advisors was that a stimulus on the order of $1.8 trillion would be needed to restore pre-recession conditions by 2011, not, coincidentally, the eve of the next presidential election. That figure, on top of the $700 billion TARP package, sent advisors like Obama's chief of staff Rahm Emanuel into orbit. "There's no fucking way,"[27] Emanuel insisted because no Republicans would support it and congressional Democrats from conservative districts would balk. So, Obama settled on $800 billion, which meant that recovery would be slower, causing political difficulties for Democrats. But then a much larger package would have caused a different kind of problem.

The amount decided, Obama's team focused on what to include in the package known as the American Recovery and Reinvestment Act (ARRA). The highest priority was to pump money into the system as fast as possible to prevent collapse, mitigate suffering, stem unemployment, and revive growth. The New Deal had invested in infrastructure—bridges, roads, public buildings, parks, naval ships, and the like. Such projects take time to plan, however, and immediate action

---

27 Obama, *A Promised Land*, 237.

was necessary, so infrastructure was a relatively small portion of the plan. Some money went to shovel-ready road and bridge projects, green energy initiatives like wind and solar power, electric vehicles, and LED streetlights, expansion of high-speed internet in underserved communities, and flood control projects. But most of the money went directly into the hands of low and middle-income Americans who suffered most from the collapse. The package provided additional unemployment benefits for those whose eligibility had expired, cash transfers to states to enable them to avoid layoffs, tax cuts for middle- and low-income people, and tax credits for companies that accelerated investments in plants and equipment. The tax cuts would not only put money in the hands of consumers but might resonate with Republicans who never saw a tax cut they didn't like. That was wishful thinking.

Obama moved quickly. The package was largely drafted by January 1, 2009, and four days later he and Vice President Joe Biden met with congressional leaders to build support. It wouldn't be forthcoming from Republicans. When David Obey, chair of the House Appropriations Committee, asked Jerry Lewis, the ranking Republican, what changes were necessary to gain his party's support, Lewis laughed. True to the strategy Republicans had agreed upon, Lewis told Obey that he had orders from leadership not to play ball. With support from large Democratic majorities in both houses, however, the bill passed, and Obama signed it less than 30 days after his inauguration.

In the House, no Republican supported it, while in the Senate, three Republicans—Susan Collins and Olympia Snowe of Maine and Arlen Specter of Pennsylvania—voted aye. It was the high-water mark of bipartisanship. For Specter, his vote came with a cost. Under withering criticism from Republicans and a primary challenge from the right, he switched parties—a move that might have provided short-term relief but that brought defeat in the 2010 Democratic primary. Collins and Snowe fared better, largely because they hailed from Maine, a state that expected those it sent to Washington to be independent. In 2012, however, Snowe announced that she would not seek reelection to a fourth term. A moderate who prided herself on bipartisan deal-making, she told reporters that the "atmosphere of polarization and 'my way or the highway' ideologies" that gripped the Senate guaranteed that another term promised six years of frustration.[28]

---

[28] Lucy Madison, "Olympia Snowe will not seek reelection," February 28, 2012 https://www.cbsnews.com/news/olympia-snowe-will-not-seek-re-election/ (accessed October 8, 2022).

Counting on voters to have short memories, Republicans justified their opposition by appeals to fiscal responsibility. Never mind that during George W. Bush's presidency they had turned a $200 billion annual surplus inherited from Bill Clinton into annual deficits of several hundred billion even before the recession hit in 2008. Most House Republicans had refused to support TARP, even though it was developed by Bush's team. Now they charged that ARRA, on top of TARP, was financially irresponsible because it caused the debt to skyrocket and would burden future generations. Republicans, whose knee-jerk support for tax cuts and increased military spending, had created big deficits under Reagan and the Bushes now became full-throated champions of fiscal responsibility. After the President submitted his first budget in March 2009, Republican leaders spoke with one voice. Asked about the President's budget, Mitch McConnell, the Senate Minority Leader, John Boehner, the House Minority Leader, and Judd Gregg, the ranking Republican on the Senate Budget Committee each responded, "It spends too much. It taxes too much. And it borrows too much."[29]

If Republicans felt the stimulus plan went too far, Obama believed even more needed to be done. The crisis had begun with the collapse of the housing market, an implosion that continued as Obama took office. Lenders had begun foreclosure proceedings on about three million families by early 2009, and another eight million were at risk. These were devastating for mortgage holders and the housing market as well as for families who lost their homes and saw their equity wiped out. When mortgage holders foreclosed, they sold properties as quickly as possible to liquidate assets that were incurring costs while generating no income. With housing prices falling, that meant sale prices were often less than the outstanding balance on the loan. Not only did many lenders take a haircut when they foreclosed, but by adding to the glut of homes on the market, they drove down real estate prices further. Another systemic risk came from those who owed more to lenders than their home's market value. Sometimes far more. Especially for those who struggled to make payments, it was tempting to default and that meant more homes on the market, depressing prices further.

To stabilize the market, Obama announced in February that government would use TARP funds to provide relief to some—but by no means all—homeowners threatened with foreclosure. In March, the administration launched

---

29 *New York Times*, March 10, 2009 https://archive.nytimes.com/thecaucus.blogs.nytimes.com/2009/03/10/spend-tax-borrow-repeat/ (accessed October 5, 2022).

two foreclosure relief programs. One (the Home Affordable Refinance Program) loosened lending restrictions that prevented banks from refinancing mortgages when the value of the home was less than the amount the homeowner owed. This allowed some to refinance at lower interest rates, reduce their monthly payments, and avoid foreclosure—or the temptation to default. A second program aimed to reduce monthly payments of qualifying homeowners to one-third of their monthly income by providing subsidies to lenders to lower interest payments, extend the life of the mortgage (e.g., from 30 to 40 years), or reduce the principal owed. The program protected several million Americans from losing their homes and helped stabilize a cratering housing market.

The automobile industry posed another challenge that the stimulus didn't address. Since the 1970s, America's Big Three struggled to compete with Japanese companies. By the early 2000s, they had begun to turn things around but had too many model lines and were saddled with debt and high labor costs. Ford had restructured its debt before the recession and could weather the storm. But General Motors and Chrysler hadn't, and their costs far exceeded revenue as car sales tanked. They couldn't get additional loans to pay their bills and stood on the brink of bankruptcy. Bush had infused about $17 billion from TARP into the struggling companies, but they quickly burned through it and were on the verge of collapse when Obama took office. That threatened unemployment for millions across the industrial Midwest, including those employed by parts suppliers and the vast economic infrastructure that relied on the auto industry.

Obama assembled an Auto Task Force with experts like investment banker Steven Rattner to assess the situation and develop a plan. Based on its analysis, he concluded that the cost of letting GM and Chrysler go under was too great. The administration used the bankruptcy process and TARP funds to thoroughly restructure both companies. It infused over $50 billion into GM, taking a controlling interest in the firm—which wags promptly dubbed Government Motors. It took a much smaller interest in Chrysler, instead brokering a deal in which a new company was formed with Italy's Fiat Motors owning a one-third interest, the United Auto Workers 55%, and the U.S. and Canadian governments 10%. Both firms underwent massive restructuring with changes in management, elimination of some product lines, reductions in pension benefits for retirees, significant losses for shareholders and lenders, downsizing the workforce, and closing some plants. The process inflicted plenty of pain, but the two companies survived and became profitable as the economy recovered. Millions of workers and retirees kept their jobs and their pensions, and dozens of Midwestern communities were spared the consequences of losing their largest employer.

As the scope of the administration's recovery effort expanded, criticism from the right became shriller. On the campaign trail, an Ohioan who called himself Joe the Plumber had told Obama that he was planning to buy his boss's business but worried that Obama's tax plan would make it hard to succeed as a small business owner. Obama assured him his plan would only raise taxes on the top 2% of earners and that corresponding investments in education and infrastructure would help working people like him prosper. "When you spread the wealth around," he added, everyone benefits. The McCain campaign jumped on the comment, charging that Obama's response revealed that he was a socialist. The epithet gained traction and became a cudgel. South Carolina's Republican Senator Jim DeMint told the New York Times that ARRA forced the country to make a choice. "We have to decide if we want to be a free-market economy [...] or if we want to be a government-directed economy, which is where we're headed," he warned.[30] Newt Gingrich was more direct, calling for war on Obama's "European Socialism transplanted to Washington."[31] Rick Santelli, a CNBC commentator, dialed up the rhetoric in a broadcast from the floor of the Chicago Mercantile Exchange on February 19, only a month into Obama's presidency. Santelli was furious when Obama announced he would use TARP funds to stem the tide of foreclosures. "How about this, President and new administration," he asked, "why don't you put up a web site to have people vote [...] to see if we really want to subsidize the losers' mortgages." Turning to the traders on the floor behind him, he shouted, "This is America! How many of you people want to pay for your neighbors' mortgage that has an extra bathroom and can't pay their bills?" The response was a hearty, "No!"[32] He urged viewers to join him in Chicago in July for a Tea Party to protest the giveaways. His comments went viral. They circulated via email, blogs, websites, and Fox News, served as fodder for conservative talk radio hosts, and became the focus of mainstream TV's Sunday morning talk shows.

---

30 *New York Times*, February 1, 2009 https://www.nytimes.com/2009/02/01/world/americas/01iht-obama.4.19849221.html (accessed October 5, 2022).

31 *New York Times*, February 27, 2009 https://www.nytimes.com/2009/02/28/us/politics/28conservatives.html (accessed October 5, 2022).

32 "Santelli's tea party rant, February 19, 2009" https://video.search.yahoo.com/yhs/search?fr=yhs-pty-ext-ff_freetestnow&ei=UTF-8&hsimp=yhs-ext-ff_freetestnow&hspart=pty&param1=20220501&param2=00000000-0000-0000-0000-000000000000&param3=speedtest_%7EUS%7Eappfocus1%7E&param4=%7Efirefox%7E%7E&p=rick+santelli+cnbc+rant+2009+youtube&type=yhs-ext-ff_freetestnow_appfocus1_ff#id=1&vid=c2e72a90ac822f99f805b0b8ee8bb600&action=click (accessed October 8, 2022).

"In this kind of a situation, you want to be dishing out the populism if you're the president," NPR's Mara Liasson commented presciently. "You don't want to be on the receiving end."[33]

She must have had a crystal ball. Almost immediately, Tea Party groups began organizing in communities across the country, holding meetings and recruiting volunteers to protest runaway government spending and demand a return to the limited government envisioned by the Founders. They were urged on by talk radio hosts, Fox News, and email chains sharing tips about organizing, opposition strategies, and perspectives on just how vast was the conspiracy to overturn the founders' vision of limited government. According to Theda Skocpol and Vanessa Williams, who attended Tea Party meetings and interviewed members, participants were overwhelmingly White, over 45 (with most being in their 60s or older), and Republican. Those who identified as independents were typically people who felt the Republican Party had strayed too far to the left. Most Tea Party members were conservative on social issues like abortion and same-sex marriage, but their focus was on what participants saw as runaway government spending, the debt, and runaway federal power. Their outrage didn't extend to Social Security or Medicare, which Tea Party members believed were sacrosanct because recipients had earned the benefits. They also railed against undocumented immigrants. "I want my country back," one activist in Massachusetts explained. "This plaintive call is perhaps the most characteristic and persistent theme in grassroots Tea Party activism," wrote Skocpol and Williams.[34] At least subliminally, it also reflected unease with a Black president.

Opposition to Obama's recovery measures soured public opinion on the stimulus. When it passed Congress in February 2009, a CNN poll revealed the public supported the plan by a 54%-44% margin. Ten months later, the tables had turned. A CNN poll found the public opposed to the plan, 56%-42%. The same poll, however, revealed that the public supported key parts of the stimulus: 80% approved spending on roads and bridges; 70% approved the tax cuts; and 60% liked support for mass transit projects. Another part of the poll revealed the reason for the disconnect: 54% of respondents said it benefitted bankers and investors while only 25% believed it helped the middle

---

33 Phil Rosenthal, "Rant goes viral, raising profile of CNBC's Rick Santelli," *Chicago Tribune*, February 23, 2009 (accessed October 8, 2022).

34 Theda Skocpol and Vanessa Williams, *The Tea Party and the Remaking of Republican Conservatism* (New York, 2012), 7.

class. According to the CNN polling director, the discrepancy "is due to the public confusing the stimulus bill with the various bailout bills," namely TARP, that were wildly unpopular because they helped the fat cats who had caused the recession.[35] Democrats' support for a Republican program they disliked but believed was necessary to prevent a depression was coming back to haunt them. It underscored how a fickle public that had become cynical about politics and politicians would punish leaders for distasteful but necessary decisions.

Tea Party anger surged as Obama tackled healthcare reform. A large majority of Americans had health insurance through employers or government programs such as Medicare and Medicaid. Many of those who weren't covered purchased their own policies, although rapidly escalating premiums put them out of reach for a substantial number of working- and middle-class families. In 2009, over 40 million Americans were without coverage, and even those who had insurance were vulnerable. Most insurance plans placed lifetime caps on benefits, forcing some insured families who experienced catastrophic illnesses into bankruptcy. Insurance companies were in the business of managing risk, so they often refused coverage to individuals with pre-existing conditions, and they terminated coverage for clients who had a history of serious illness. The system not only had gaps but it was more costly and delivered worse patient outcomes than those in Canada, Japan, France, Germany, and the United Kingdom. The upshot was rising costs for companies, individuals, and the government. Increases in payments to providers for those covered by Medicare and Medicaid contributed significantly to ballooning federal deficits. Yet most Americans had health insurance, liked their doctor, and were generally happy with the system—until they lost coverage when they became unemployed, were unable to find coverage due to a preexisting condition, or reached the lifetime cap on benefits. So, while there were problems, mobilizing broad support for change was challenging.

Obama understood the challenges but believed that fixing a fraying patchwork system was vital. He knew that there was a short window of opportunity, so he must move quickly. By early 2010, Capitol Hill would be preoccupied with the mid-term elections, making it difficult to move major legislation. Less than two months after taking office, Obama convened a group

---

35 "Polls: Stimulus unpopular, but its uses have broad support," February 1, 2010 https://www.cnn.com/2010/POLITICS/01/29/stimulus.poll/index.html (accessed October 21, 2022).

of 150 stakeholders at the White House to launch his initiative. They included influential Democratic and Republican lawmakers, representatives from hospitals, the American Medical Association, the insurance industry, and big pharma. Participation by industry stakeholders was the first step in making them part of the process so that they didn't launch a public relations offensive to scuttle reform. Harry and Louise had sunk Bill Clinton's initiative, and Obama wanted them to remain in retirement.

Administration officials were deeply involved in shaping the new policy, but they deferred to the key committees in the House and Senate to write the legislation. If they took ownership, they would be more likely to do the heavy lifting necessary to get a bill to Obama's desk. Salivating over the prospect of 40 million new customers who would gain coverage through private insurance providers and Medicaid, insurance companies and hospitals made concessions that would generate savings of close to $400 billion for Medicare and Medicaid. Equally important, the pharmaceutical industry provided discounts on prescriptions to most Medicare recipients, bringing the American Association of Retired Persons (AARP) into full-throated support.

On Capitol Hill, committee chairs drafted legislation, but it was slow going. Obama was keen to win at least some Republican support so he could claim a bipartisan victory. In the Senate, Max Baucus the chair of the Finance Committee, was certain he could win support from his friend Chuck Grassley. The Iowa senator played along for months, but encouraged by Mitch McConnell and fearing the Tea Party, he continued to hold out. His biggest concern about supporting the bill, he recalled, "would've been in the state of Iowa whether I would have had Tea Party opposition"—and forfeited party support against a primary challenge.[36] In September, Obama called the question, asking, "Are there any changes—any at all—that would get your vote?" Grassley's answer—"I guess not, Mr. President"—only confirmed Obama's suspicion. Republicans hung together, their solidarity reinforced by fear of the growing Tea Party insurgency.[37] None voted for the bill.

Freed of the illusion of bipartisanship, House Speaker Nancy Pelosi pushed legislation through the House in November. With no Republican support and many conservative Democrats—especially those who had carried traditionally Republican districts in 2006 and 2008—worried about Tea Party opposition in the mid-terms, it wasn't easy. The vote was 220–215. When the bill went

---

36 MacGillis, *The Cynic*, 103.
37 Obama, *Promised Land*, 408.

to the Senate, Democrats had a 60-seat majority, just enough to overcome a Republican filibuster if everyone was on board. But they weren't. Joe Lieberman, an Independent who caucused with the Democrats, immediately announced his opposition unless the "public option"—a provision authorizing the government to offer its own insurance plan to compete with private carriers—was removed. That was near and dear to the hearts of many House progressives, who longed for a single-payer system. Unable to win passage without Lieberman, Senate Majority Leader Harry Reid removed the public option. The amended bill cleared the Senate on Christmas Eve 2009, with no Republicans voting in favor.

The saving grace for Pelosi and her troops was that there was still a chance for compromise. Each chamber's version of the bill would go to a conference committee where differences could be worked out. Then the earth shook. Ted Kennedy had died in August, necessitating a special election to fill the final two years of his term. Most Democrats assumed that a U.S. Senate race in deep blue Massachusetts to replace the legendary Kennedy would be a "gimme." Unfortunately, that included their candidate, Martha Coakley, who ran a lackluster campaign. Her opponent, an unknown state senator named Scott Brown tapped into the populist outrage stoked by the Tea Party. He portrayed himself as an outsider, an underdog who would fight for them, unlike the Washington insiders who put a priority on bailing out the bankers and investors. Brown's victory meant that Republicans now had 41 seats in the Senate and could block passage of any revised bill that might emerge from a conference committee. House Democrats would have to swallow hard and accept the Senate bill without revisions.

In mid-March 2010, the House passed the Affordable Care Act (ACA) and sent it to the White House. It relied on a market solution to expand coverage—one that, ironically, had been developed by the Heritage Foundation, championed by a number of Senate Republicans in the 1990s as an alternative to Clinton's plan, and implemented in Massachusetts under the leadership of a Republican governor, Mitt Romney, in 2006. Socialist it was not. The legislation created healthcare exchanges in every state—virtual sites where consumers could compare policies offered by private insurers and select one whose cost and coverage best met their needs. The exchanges would encourage competition among insurers, creating better value for consumers. There were four levels of coverage to accommodate purchasers' needs, income, preferences, and tolerance for out-of-pocket expenses. For individuals who couldn't afford coverage but made too much to qualify for Medicaid, the government would provide subsidies. They included all whose earnings were 250% of the poverty rate, with the subsidies declining as income rose.

To accommodate more of the nation's working poor, the legislation expanded Medicaid. The ACA created a uniform standard of eligibility—anyone earning less than 133% of the poverty rate would now qualify—with the federal government picking up 90% of the cost of individuals who were newly eligible. An individual mandate taxed those who didn't have coverage through an employer, Medicare, or Medicaid and refused to purchase insurance—a penalty designed to encourage participation. That pleased insurance companies because it meant that risk was shared broadly—among those most and least likely to require care. In return, insurance companies could no longer set lifetime caps on benefits or refuse coverage to individuals with preexisting conditions.

The act also aimed to improve the entire healthcare system—17% of the nation's economy—by incentivizing more effective care at lower costs. Because they were traditionally paid for services provided to their patients—examinations, tests, procedures, lab work, consultations—doctors and hospitals had incentives to order more of them, even in the absence of evidence that they provided better outcomes. The result was rapidly escalating costs for insurers and the government. The ACA incentivized those providing services to Medicare and Medicaid patients to pay doctors a fixed salary instead of a fee-for-service model. It also reduced payments to hospitals that had high levels of preventable readmissions—an indication of ineffective treatment—and rewarded doctors and hospitals that spent less per patient but delivered better results. These provisions would encourage system-wide change because providers who served Medicare and Medicaid patients also treated individuals covered by private insurance.

Expanding care was costly. In the summer of 2009, the Congressional Budget Office put the price tag at $1.6 trillion over ten years, although the estimates subsequently came down to a mere $1 trillion. That was music to Republicans' ears because it fit their narrative of Obama as an irresponsible big spender who was driving the country to fiscal ruin. However, the act was designed to be revenue neutral. Reduced payments to pharmaceutical companies, hospitals, and doctors for Medicare and Medicaid patients covered almost half the cost of the program, while new taxes on the wealthy, insurance companies, manufacturers of medical devices, and the most lavish employer-provided insurance policies made up the balance. Of course, many skeptics charged that the plan for financing the law was smoke and mirrors.

## Telling Lies, Deflating Hope, Blocking Change

The law was one of the great achievements of U.S. social policy, a fitting complement to Social Security, Medicare, and Medicaid. Like those programs, it was controversial. But unlike them, about half of all Americans disliked it—even though it cut the number of uninsured by 80%, reduced seniors' prescription drug bills, protected individuals and families from losing coverage because they might need expensive treatments, and contained costs, saving businesses billions. Part of the problem was that most provisions of the law didn't take effect for several years, leading many to wonder what all the fuss was about. With the economy in turmoil, many thought the ACA didn't address the country's most pressing need. Equally problematic was the law itself. It was detailed (over 2,000 pages) and highly technical, with provisions concerning individual coverage, financing, and hospital practices, to name a few. That was essential for legislation transforming an entire industry. But the complexity ensured that the ACA was hard to understand, easy for opponents to caricature, and didn't lend itself to a sound bite that captured how it would make life better for most Americans. According to *The Hill*, an influential website covering U.S. politics, an Associated Press poll showed that two years after the law was passed "just 14% of adults identified the law's specifics correctly and with confidence."[38]

Republicans went on the attack. They were eager to deny Obama credit for a major accomplishment that might lock in gains Democrats had made in the wave elections of 2006 and 2008. A highly complex law that carried a big price tag and attempted to reengineer the entire healthcare system provided an opening for Republicans to portray Obama as a socialist bent on extending the reach of government and oblivious to the consequences of out-of-control deficits. News media had been steadily transformed by the growth of cable, the Internet, talk radio, and, more recently, social media platforms like Facebook. They lent themselves to conveying information about the law in a way that privileged distortion and downright lies over accuracy. As news outlets multiplied, the recipe for financial success emphasized winning the loyalty of particular segments of the population rather than appealing to everyone. The result was that many news outlets—Fox News and Breitbart. com, for example—blurred news, opinion, and entertainment and became unofficial subsidiaries of the Republican Party. More and more Americans got

---

38 Elise Viebeck, "Poll: Four in 10 believe in Obama healthcare law 'death panels'," *The Hill*, September 26, 2012 https://thehill.com/policy/healthcare/130054-poll-four-in-10-believe-in-obama-healthcare-law-death-panels/ (accessed October 21, 2022).

their news—and often their views—from sources that agreed with their political convictions.

Even as the ACA was in gestation, the attacks began. In August 2009, Sarah Palin fired a salvo that set the tone. Eager to remain relevant and capitalize on the notoriety she had achieved as John McCain's diva running mate, she claimed in a Facebook post that went viral that the new law would allow government bureaucrats to ration care. The elderly and disabled would be denied care and sent to early graves. "The America I know and love is not one in which my parents or my baby with Down Syndrome will have to stand in front of Obama's 'death panel' so his bureaucrats can decide [...] whether they are worthy of health care," she wrote.[39] It was a preposterous charge, completely devoid of evidence, but in a media environment that was evidence-optional, the more outrageous the claim, the more it confirmed a prejudice, the faster and further it spread.

So, Palin's death panels became fact in some quarters and were mobilized as evidence of just how scary the healthcare bill was. The charge circulated like wildfire on the Internet and spread through talk radio hosts like Rush Limbaugh who applauded Palin, saying "She's dead right." The charge added fuel to the Tea Party brushfire that was burning across the country. As members of Congress returned home in late summer 2009 for town hall meetings, tea partiers unleashed their wrath, disrupting many a meeting and letting their representatives know they would hold them accountable at the ballot box. But it wasn't just Internet sites, polemical talk show hosts, and Tea Party zealots who took up Palin's charge. It found its way into mainstream Republican talking points. Chuck Grassley, the experienced and knowledgeable Iowa senator who was intimately familiar with the bill, spread the lie. "We should not have a government program that determines you're gonna pull the plug on grandma," he told an Iowa audience. Even though PolitiFact, the nonpartisan fact-checking organization, named death panels "lie of the year," an Associated Press poll conducted in August 2012 revealed that almost 40% of Americans still believed the ACA authorized death panels.[40]

Opposition to the law became an article of faith to Republicans. Indeed, many Republican governors fought Medicaid expansion even though it would

---

39 Milbank, *The Destructionists*, 153.
40 Don Gonyea, "From the start Obama struggled with fallout from a kind of fake news," National Public Radio, January 10, 2017 https://www.npr.org/2017/01/10/509164679/from-the-start-obama-struggled-with-fallout-from-a-kind-of-fake-news (accessed October 21, 2022).

extend coverage to many uninsured in their states with the federal government picking up 90% of the cost. It was like cutting off your nose, no, your constituents' noses to spite their faces. Conservative media stepped up its attacks and spawned more horror stories about the bill's devastating consequences. Tea Party activists were the shock troops of the opposition, harassing senators and representatives when they held town halls and using the bill to encourage voters to turn out for candidates the party endorsed. Hatred for the ACA worked them into a white-hot frenzy that revealed the racism that lay just beneath the surface—and sometimes bubbled over. On March 20, 2010, as the House neared its vote on the ACA, thousands of Tea Party faithful mobilized in protest on Capitol Hill. John Lewis, the Georgia congressman whose skull had been fractured by Alabama troopers in Selma 45 years before, was taunted with racist epithets as he walked from his office to the Capitol. Protestors hoisted signs reading "Impeach the Muslim Marxist," "Obama's Plan: White Slavery," "Obama bin Lyin'," "Obamanomics: Monkey see, monkey spend," and "I Want My Country Back!"[41] Policies they didn't like (and probably didn't understand) were far more frightening because they were initiated by a Black man who held the most powerful office in the world. Republican leaders refused to denounce the lies and the racism, hoping a fired-up base would help them reclaim control of Congress in 2010.

In the 2010 mid-terms, they demolished Democrats in House races, picking up 62 seats, the biggest gain since 1938. That turned a 255–179 Democratic majority into a 240–191 Republican advantage and made Ohio's John Boehner speaker. Republicans picked up six Senate seats, leaving Democrats with a 53–47 majority. The GOP made perhaps its most significant gains at the state level. It achieved a net gain of six governorships, giving it control of the executive branch in 29 states, and ran the table in legislative elections, gaining almost 700 legislative seats. That gave Republicans control of both houses in a whopping 26 states and control of at least one house in nine others, putting them in the driver's seat for drawing state and congressional district lines after the 2010 census was completed. "You never want to have a bad election," commented Charlie Cook, publisher of the highly respected *Cook Political Report*, "But if you're going to have one, you really don't want to have it in a year that ends in a zero."[42]

The stars aligned to produce the Republican wave—only four years after the 2006 wave that swept Democrats into the majority. Perhaps the most

---

41 Milbank, *The Destructionists*, 136–37.
42 "State Gains Foster Future GOP House Hopes," *CQ Almanac* (2010).

important—but often overlooked—factor was a political landscape that had been transformed in the last decade of the twentieth century. Elections were closely contested, the parties' fortunes rose and fell, and no party achieved dominance. Party identification and loyalty had atrophied, with more than 30% of voters identifying as independents. Many of these voters moved back and forth between the two parties. Public faith in government, which was 77% in 1964, dropped sharply in the 1970s and hovered between the low 20s and low 40s for most of the following 30 years. At the time of Obama's election, it stood at 31%—up from 17% less than a month before—while on the eve of the mid-terms, it had dipped to 22%.[43] The collapse of faith in government reflected widespread cynicism about politics and politicians that made voters—and especially independents—impatient with those who didn't deliver—or who supported imperfect policies in the face of limited options. Candidates promised to change the world, but once they were in office the combination of intractable problems and political gridlock made that difficult—and political recrimination inevitable. Independents were disenchanted when politicians didn't deliver what they (over)promised and seemed more interested in fighting one another than governing. So, they often quickly turned to challengers who claimed to be outsiders who would change Washington. Voters commented one political consultant, had "decided to put politicians on a choke chain and pull the leash."[44]

Republican strategy in 2010 worked perfectly against a candidate who had promised change and bipartisanship but was confronted by the worst economic catastrophe in 80 years and a political opposition determined to make him fail. During the first two years of Obama's presidency, the suffering caused by the recession became more acute, with unemployment hitting nearly 10% as the mid-terms approached. The stimulus package, enacted at warp speed, headed off even deeper pain, but its results wouldn't be evident until 2011 and beyond. Four in 10 voters told pollsters they were worse off than two years before and six in 10 believed that the country was on the wrong track. Pointing out that things would have been worse without the stimulus didn't cut it. Although voters were split down the middle on the ACA, Republicans scored points by arguing that Obama's focus on health care diverted attention from the economy.

---

43 Pew Research Center, "Public Trust in Government, 1958–2022," June 6, 2022 https://www.pewresearch.org/politics/2022/06/06/public-trust-in-government-1958-2022/ (accessed January 30, 2023).
44 *New York Times*, November 3, 2010 https://www.nytimes.com/2010/11/04/us/politics/04region.html (accessed October 22, 2022).

Voters were disgusted with the bank bailouts, and many conflated TARP with Obama's stimulus plan. Their disenchantment, coupled with a spiking deficit produced by declining tax revenues and public spending necessary to stave off depression, made them receptive to Republican claims that Democratic profligacy was driving the nation to the poorhouse. "What I hear across my state are three words, 'Enough is enough'," remarked Senator Kent Conrad, a North Dakota Democrat.[45]

The Tea Party put a strong wind at the backs of Republicans. It amplified the alarm sounded by Republicans about the deficit, government overreach, and the drift to socialism. Tea Party activists generated fear, loathing, and a sense of urgency among many older, White, middle-class folks who normally voted Republican, persuading them to open their wallets and go to the polls. That was critical because with the parties closely divided getting supporters to vote was critical. Overall turnout in 2010 was typical for a mid-term election, slightly below 42% of the voting-age population. However, voters under 30, who tilted heavily Democratic, made up only 11% of participants in 2010, down from 18% in 2008; Black voters made up 10% of the electorate, down from 13% in 2008; voters over 65—a prime Tea Party demographic—were 23% of the electorate in 2010, up from 16% two years earlier.[46] Those numbers told the story.

The results reflected a country that was deeply divided. They promised more of the partisan rancor that had ebbed and flowed during the previous three decades and were making gridlock the defining feature of government. Democrats suffered devastating losses in the Midwest. Outside of its cities and college towns, the region was deep red, creating a political map that showed Democrats "clinging to the coasts, lonely strips of blue on a very red horizon."[47] The geographical divide reflected cultural, ethnic, and religious differences as stark as those that divided North and South in the 1850s. As the middle of the country turned red, the political center was also shrinking. "This is the first time in the history of polling," noted New York Times columnist Charles Blow, "that moderates were not the largest ideological voting bloc. They were

---

45 Ibid.
46 "Record Wins Hand House to GOP," *Congressional Quarterly Almanac*, 2010 https://library-cqpress-com.proxy.binghamton.edu/cqalmanac/document.php?id=cqal10-1278-70365-2371730&type=toc&num=4 (accessed January 23, 2023).
47 *New York Times*, November 3, 2010 https://www.nytimes.com/2010/11/04/us/politics/04region.html (accessed October 23, 2022).

trumped by conservatives."⁴⁸ If that seemed to bode ill for compromise, a Pew Research Center poll left no doubt. It revealed that 15% of Independents, 19% of Democrats, and a whopping 40% of Republicans were *less likely* to vote for a candidate who would compromise with people they disagreed with.⁴⁹ Compromise—the essential lubricant of any democratic political system—was becoming a dirty word among a plurality of Republicans.

The Republican majority that would control the House in the 112th Congress (set to begin work in January 2011) embodied that sentiment. There were 85 Republican freshmen, most of them elected with Tea Party support and all aware of tea partiers' power at the ballot box. Over 30 of them had never held public office. Instead of apologizing for their lack of experience, they wore it like a badge of honor, proof that they—like Sarah Palin who had stumped for some of them—weren't part of the political establishment. Most of the new representatives were zealous conservatives, convinced that there were simple solutions to the problems that beset the country—taking on the socialist president, cutting government spending, and reducing the size and scope of the federal government. Certain that they had the right answers, they weren't of a mind to compromise. Freshman Bobby Schilling, the father of 10 who operated a pizza business in Moline, Illinois captured the views of many. "We're here to fight," he announced.⁵⁰ They would not only be a pain in Obama's backside but a handful for Republican leaders.

Not that Republican congressional leaders were holding out an olive branch. Mitch McConnell, even more sour than usual because Republicans hadn't won the Senate and made him majority leader, set the tone. If our "friends on the other side," he declared in a speech at the Heritage Foundation, "change course," Republicans would work with them. "If they don't, we'll have disagreements ahead." He was suggesting that Democrats surrender rather than compromise, and he knew that wasn't likely with Democrats in control

---

48 Charles Blow, "The Great American Cleaving," *New York Times*, November 5, 2010 https://www.nytimes.com/2010/11/06/opinion/06blow.html (accessed October 23, 2022).

49 Pew Research Center, "Willingness to compromise a plus in the mid-terms," May 24, 2010 https://www.pewresearch.org/politics/2010/05/24/willingness-to-compromise-a-plus-in-midterms/ (accessed October 23, 2022).

50 Jonathan Karl and Gregory Simmons, "Moving Day for Congress: Out with the Old, In with the New," January 3, 2011 https://abcnews.go.com/Politics/112_Congress/112th-congress-members-20-years-tea-party/story?id=12532080 (accessed October 23, 2022).

of the White House and the Senate.⁵¹ Speaking to a *National Journal* reporter 10 days before the election, he was blunt: "The single most important thing we want to achieve is for President Obama to be a one term president."⁵²

Obama, of course, had other ideas. He used the lame-duck session of Congress, which met in the final weeks of 2010, to win approval for several major initiatives. He secured Senate ratification of a treaty he negotiated with the Russians reducing each country's nuclear warheads by a third as well as congressional repeal of the Clinton-era Don't Ask Don't Tell policy, freeing gays and lesbians to serve openly in the military. The Bush-era tax cuts were set to expire in 2011. They were near and dear to the hearts of Republicans, and Obama used the deadline to cut a deal with Mitch McConnell. So sacred were the tax cuts, McConnell broke his no-deals-with-Obama rule to preserve them. Like most Republican tax cuts, the rich benefitted disproportionately but there were modest gains for middle- and working-class Americans. Obama's preference was to end cuts for those making over $250,000 per year and renew them for others. A certain Republican filibuster made that impossible, however. Letting cuts for everyone lapse would attract the ire of middle-income taxpayers and stall the recovery. So, Obama made the best of a bad situation, agreeing to extend the cuts for two years—until the 2012 election had passed—in return for a 99-week extension of payments to workers who had exhausted their unemployment benefits, a continuation of refundable tax credits to the working poor, and a payroll tax cut that disproportionately benefitted middle-class taxpayers. The deal provided "an additional $212 billion worth of economic stimulus specifically targeted to those Americans most in need," Obama recalled, "the kind of package we'd have no hope of passing through a Republican-controlled House as a stand-alone bill."⁵³ Some priorities failed. With the Tea Party sounding the alarm about illegal immigration, the DREAM Act—which offered a path to citizenship to undocumented immigrants whose parents had brought them to the U.S. before they were 18—died.

---

51 *New York Times*, November 4, 2010 https://www.nytimes.com/2010/11/05/us/politics/05cong.html (accessed October 23, 2022).
52 *Washington Post*, September 25, 2012 https://www.washingtonpost.com/blogs/fact-checker/post/when-did-mcconnell-say-he-wanted-to-make-obama-a-one-term-president/2012/09/24/79fd5cd8-0696-11e2-afff-d6c7f20a83bf_blog.html (accessed October 23, 2022).
53 Obama, *The Promised Land*, 606.

Once the new Congress was sworn in, Obama was on the defensive. Repeal of the ACA was a holy war for Tea Party loyalists, and Republicans regularly introduced bills and amendments to kill it before it could take effect. It was great theatre and allowed new members to establish their anti-Obama bona fides. However, Republican leaders knew that these measures would never make it through the Senate much less be signed by the President. So, they trained their fire on the deficit and government spending, making battles over the budget the main event in Washington in 2011. Tax cuts and increased spending during Bush's presidency had more than doubled the nation's debt, even before 2008 bank bailouts. Under Obama, as tax revenues cratered and the stimulus kicked in, the debt climbed from about $9 trillion to $13.5 trillion in 2010. The alternative to much of the spending that drove the debt upward—TARP and the stimulus package—was permitting the economy to collapse. But far too many Americans seemed incapable of thinking about the relationship and accepting a ballooning debt as the lesser of two evils. For Tea Party zealots, the debt was the most important issue facing the country. For conservatives who weren't part of the Tea Party but were happy to use it as a battering ram, focusing on the debt was a way to redirect the conversation, cut spending, and achieve the holy grail of Barry Goldwater, Ronald Reagan, the Koch Brothers, and Newt Gingrich—rolling back the size and scope of the federal government.

Anyone serious about deficit reduction knew that it would require compromise. Not a kumbaya moment but a painful give and take of the sort that Clinton and Gingrich had engaged in 15 years before. Such compromise had appeared possible in late 2009 when two senior members of the Senate Budget Committee—Democrat Kent Conrad of North Dakota and Republican Judd Gregg of New Hampshire—proposed creating a bipartisan 18-member commission to recommend cuts that would then be considered by Congress via an expedited process. McConnell supported the plan, but when Obama got on board, he and other Republican supporters pulled out the rug, voting against it and depriving it of the 60 votes needed to overcome a filibuster. Denying Obama credit for bipartisanship was more important than the issue Republicans purported to be their top priority.

The budget process was where battles over the debt and national priorities were fought. Focused on the mid-terms, Democrats had not passed a budget for the fiscal year that began in October 2010. Government agencies would be forced to shut down in early March 2011 if Congress didn't approve a new budget or provide short-term spending authority for agencies. Tea Party freshmen had pledged to cut non-defense federal spending by $100 billion during their first year in Washington. Because the fiscal year was nearly half over, cuts would come from half a year's budget, effectively doubling their bite. A Democratic Senate and president would also have to sign off on the cuts, and they were certain to demand a smaller number. If no agreement was reached, however, the government would shut down. That prospect frightened Republican leaders, who recalled how badly the Gingrich shutdowns had damaged the party in 1995. Tea Party freshmen didn't think shutting down the government was such a bad thing, however, and they pressed House Republican leaders for steep cuts. Ultimately, when House Speaker John Boehner cut a deal with Democrats for a $38.5 billion cut, 59 Republicans voted against it. It passed only because 35 Democrats lent their support.

If an uneasy compromise avoided a shutdown, it didn't create a budget for fiscal year 2012. That would be the next order of business, and it would be even more contentious. The House Budget Committee laid down the gauntlet with a plan that included deep spending cuts coupled with big tax cuts. The brainchild of Paul Ryan, the 41-year-old chair who was a libertarian policy wonk and devotee of Ayn Rand, the so-called Ryan Budget would cut $6 trillion from federal spending over the next decade, with especially heavy cuts in Medicaid and other programs that benefitted the poor. For good measure, it replaced Medicare for all those under 55 (at the time the budget passed) with vouchers that would help them buy private insurance. Parsimonious with the poor and elderly, the plan doled out $2 trillion in tax cuts, including a reduction in the top bracket from 35% to 25%. The Ryan Budget would shrink the federal government, take support away from the poor and elderly, and benefit the wealthy, who had seen their share of income climb steadily since the late 1970s. In the conservatives' Darwinian world, they were the wealth-makers who created prosperity and should be rewarded.

Obama went after Ryan Hammer and Tongs. He invited the Speaker to a speech at George Washington University in April where he eviscerated him and his plan in full view of the media. "There's nothing serious about a plan that claims to reduce the deficit by spending a trillion dollars on tax cuts for millionaires and billionaires," he asserted in a shame-on-you riposte to a trapped Ryan. "There's nothing courageous about asking for sacrifice from those who can least afford it and don't have any clout on Capitol Hill."[54] Obama unveiled a plan that would cut over $4 trillion from the budget over 12 years. That equaled the Ryan cuts because Obama's plan eliminated the

---

54 *New York Times*, April 13, 2011 https://www.nytimes.com/2011/04/14/us/politics/14obama.html?searchResultPosition=9 (accessed October 24, 2011).

$2 trillion in tax cuts Ryan proposed. Instead, the President would close almost half of the deficit by increasing taxes on the wealthy.

There was even greater urgency than usual to reach a budget agreement. The Treasury projected that the nation would reach its borrowing limit in early August; if it wasn't raised, the government would run out of money to pay bondholders, employees (including those in the armed forces), and social security and Medicare beneficiaries. Raising the limit had been routine and uncontroversial. Relying on a provision adopted in 1979 known as the Gephardt rule, the House could raise the limit without casting a direct vote to do so. Republicans repealed the rule, inviting partisan one-ups-man-ship. Many conservative Republicans were eager for a fight over the debt limit and willing to hold it hostage to force Democrats to accede to their demands. Republican leaders like Boehner and McConnell understood that default would be catastrophic. But they were happy to use hotheads whom Boehner would later describe as "political terrorists" to force concessions from Obama.[55]

Negotiations between the administration and Republican leaders began in May and continued for the next three months. Vice President Biden engaged congressional leaders from both parties in negotiations, while Boehner and Obama held separate discussions that envisioned a grand bargain that included spending cuts, tax increases, and changes in Social Security, Medicare, and Medicaid. Neither set of negotiations came to fruition. The talks between Obama and Boehner broke down on July 22 as the President demanded more tax increases than Boehner thought he could sell to his rowdy members. The Speaker developed his own plan which relied exclusively on cuts and also promised a vote on a balanced budget amendment. It narrowly cleared the House but failed in the Democratically controlled Senate with three days left before the country would default. Only an agreement between the Vice President and McConnell on July 31, two days ahead of the August 2 deadline, resolved the crisis.

The agreement tilted toward the Republicans. There were no new taxes, only cuts. In return for $1 trillion in cuts over the next decade, the debt ceiling would be raised immediately to a level that would allow borrowing necessary to pay the bills for the remainder of 2011. A bipartisan congressional panel

---

55 Chris Megerian, "Review: Belly up to the bar with John Boehner for nostalgic tales of government paralysis," *Los Angeles Times*, April 9, 2021 https://www.latimes.com/entertainment-arts/books/story/2021-04-09/john-boehner-nostalgic-bitter-memoir-on-the-house (accessed January 14, 2023).

would propose an additional $1.5 trillion in cuts to take effect over the next decade. If Congress failed to approve them, the cuts would be achieved through sequestration—across-the-board reductions to all programs. The debt ceiling would be raised by an equal amount which would get the country through the 2012 presidential election. Congress passed the Biden–McConnell deal with significant defections from both parties. Although many Democrats were angry because the cuts were so deep, one commentator believed that "it's a little better than it appears at first glance."[56] Few cuts would take effect before 2013, and they were tilted toward defense rather than domestic programs dear to the hearts of Democrats.

Disaster was averted, but the nation had flirted with default. The episode signaled that partisan conflict was eroding the ability of the world's most powerful democracy to govern itself. Foreign leaders who depended on the U.S. militarily and financially wondered how reliable it was, and credit rating agencies like Standard & Poor's dropped the nation's credit rating from AAA to AA+. Yet Republican leaders were pleased with what they had accomplished. After the dust settled, McConnell admitted that "some of our members may have thought the default issue was a hostage you might take a chance at shooting." "Most of us didn't think that," he chuckled. "What we did learn was this—it's a hostage that's worth ransoming."[57] That boded ill for the future. Indeed, as the party's presidential primaries approached, most Republican candidates, including front-runner Mitt Romney, criticized the deal for giving too much to Democrats, an indication brinksmanship would continue.

## Less Hope, More Fight: Obama Pushes Back

The winds were shifting even as the Republican House majority put a populist veneer on conservative policies. The bank bailouts and a deep recession fueled activism on the left as well as the right. If the right's moment had come in the Tea Party summer of 2009, the left's came in the Occupy Wall Street fall of 2011. The movement began with a Twitter post (#OccupyWallStreet) by *Adbusters*, a small-circulation progressive Canadian magazine. It called for 20,000 people to camp out in the belly of the beast—Manhattan's financial district—to protest concentrated wealth and the politicians that enabled

---

56 Nate Cohen, "The Fine Print on the Debt Deal," *New York Times*, August 1, 2011 https://fivethirtyeight.com/features/the-fine-print-on-the-debt-deal/ (accessed October 24, 2022).
57 MacGillis, *The Cynic*, 116.

it. On September 17, hundreds flocked to Zuccotti Park several blocks from Wall Street, and set up an encampment that inspired protesters in over one hundred cities across the U.S. and around the world to follow their lead. The encampments attracted attention and moved the conversation away from budget deficits and big government. The real problem, Occupy activists insisted, was a political system that served the wealthiest 1%.

Occupy challenged the Republican preoccupation with fiscal responsibility by insisting that the growing concentration of wealth and power was the biggest threat to the republic. It was a perspective compatible with Obama's progressive views as well as his political interests. He quickly moved to reframe the debate with Republicans in a feisty speech in Osawatomie, Kansas—where Theodore Roosevelt had kicked off his bid for the presidency on the Progressive Party ticket a century before. Like TR, Obama acknowledged that "the free market is the greatest force for economic progress in human history." But he cautioned that it "has never been a free license to take whatever you can from whomever you can." Obama reminded his listeners that Roosevelt had championed reforms to protect the public from unscrupulous business leaders. The vested interests responded by calling him a socialist, the President chuckled.

The parallels were clear. Since the 1980s, Obama pointed out, the average income of the top 1% had grown by 250% while most Americans experienced a 6% decline in the last decade. While the middle class struggled, Obama charged, Republicans simply asserted that "we are better off when everybody is left to fend for themselves and play by their own rules." He disagreed, insisting that "this country succeeds when everyone gets a fair shot when everyone does their fair share, when everyone plays by the same rules." That meant government must check corporate greed, invest in education to open the doors to the middle class, support scientific research to fuel innovation, rebuild the crumbling infrastructure necessary for businesses to flourish, and provide incentives to develop new technology like wind and solar energy that would create good jobs while saving the planet. The choice was between "the investments we need in [...] things that helped make us an economic superpower" and preserving "tax breaks for the wealthiest Americans."[58]

With the election less than a year away, Obama signaled that he was not going to engage on the issues chosen by the Republicans. Republicans gave

---

58 "Remarks by the President on the Economy in Osawatomie, Kansas," December 6, 2011 https://obamawhitehouse.archives.gov/the-press-office/2011/12/06/remarks-president-economy-osawatomie-kansas (accessed October 25, 2022).

him an opponent who would struggle to compete on the issue Obama chose—meeting the needs of the middle class. Mitt Romney was the son of a former Republican governor of Michigan and presidential contender. He was telegenic, articulate, squeaky clean, and had an impeccable record as a successful businessman, a public-spirited leader who had salvaged the Salt Lake City Winter Olympics in 2002, and a popular Republican governor of deep blue Massachusetts. However, Republican voters never warmed up to Romney. Perhaps he was a bit too smooth, or his efforts to occupy the right wing of the presidential field seemed at odds with a very moderate record as governor that included securing healthcare reform that looked just like Obama's. Some, especially evangelical Christian conservatives, didn't like him because he was a Mormon.

Romney won because the Republican establishment coalesced around him, and he faced a weak field. How weak? Charles Krauthammer, the conservative pundit, called them "bumbling clowns."[59] The Tea Party had unleashed a powerful wave of conservative populism, but none of the candidates succeeded in riding it to victory. Sarah Palin's charisma and knack for mobilizing angry anti-establishment conservatives made her a natural. But after flirting with a presidential bid for a year-and-a-half, she announced that she wouldn't run. Michele Bachmann, a hard-right Minnesota congresswoman and Tea Party darling, ran but quickly suspended her campaign after finishing well back in the pack in the Iowa caucuses. Many thought that Governor Rick Perry of Texas could use his anti-Washington rhetoric and populist style to mobilize Tea Party activists. But he fell flat early in the candidate debates when he promised to eliminate three cabinet-level departments but could only recall two of them. Newt Gingrich's slashing attacks on Obama, Democrats, and a bloated federal government might have won Tea Party support if his egotistical bloviating hadn't grated on so many for so many years. Pennsylvania senator Rick Santorum, an earnest Catholic from a working-class family, gave Romney his biggest scare, winning evangelicals and working-class Whites. But his campaign lacked the resources to mount a sustained challenge.

With the nomination in hand, Romney pursued a two-pronged strategy. First, blame Obama for a failed economy with high unemployment and depressed wages. Higher taxes on small businesses and government intrusiveness were throttling those who created jobs and brought prosperity to their communities,

---

59 E.J. Dionne, Jr., *Why the Right Went Wrong: Conservatism from Goldwater to Trump and Beyond* (New York, 2016), 342.

he charged. "Today the time has come to turn the page," he insisted, "[…] to put the disappointments of the last four years behind us." The second part of his strategy was to tout his own success as a businessman in creating jobs and building prosperous communities. Obama, he asserted, lacked "the basic qualification that most Americans have and one that was essential to his task. He had almost no experience working in a business." Romney, however, had built a business and created jobs. At 37, he had struck out on his own and joined a group of partners to create "a small company," Bain Capital. It struggled, but with hard work and persistence, he claimed, it grew from 10 employees "into a great American success story."[60] The message was clear. He would bring his business acumen to the White House and restore prosperity.

There were two problems with this strategy. First, Bain was a private equity firm, and its activities were part of the creative destruction that was integral to capitalism. It acquired companies in leveraged buyouts, sold off parts of them, closed plants that were deemed unproductive, and sometimes shifted production overseas to take advantage of lower costs. The company's record made Romney an easy mark, and the Obama campaign struck quickly, running a series of TV ads in May that featured workers whose jobs evaporated and whose communities suffered when Bain closed plants, laid off workers, and relocated production overseas. Even before Romney accepted the nomination, Obama defined him as an ally of the rich, one of the 1%—no, the .1%—who enriched themselves at the expense of working people.

The image was reinforced in September when a tape of Romney speaking to a group of donors in Boca Raton went viral. He asserted that 47% of voters would automatically go for Obama. They were people who pay no taxes, "are dependent on government […] believe that they are victims […] that government has a responsibility to take care of them […] that they are entitled to health care, to food, to housing, you name it." He would never win their support, he insisted, so "my job is not to worry about those people—I'll never convince them that they should take responsibility for their lives."[61] Admitting that he had no concern for half the population struck many as disqualifying.

Romney had another problem. Not only had unemployment begun to decrease, but voters didn't have such short memories that they forgot that Obama inherited an economic catastrophe. A CNN/ORC poll conducted

---

[60] "Transcript: Mitt Romney's Acceptance Speech, August 30, 2012," https://www.npr.org/2012/08/30/160357612/transcript-mitt-romneys-acceptance-speech (accessed October 26, 2022).

[61] Dionne, *Why the Right Went Wrong*, 374–75.

in early September 2012 asked likely voters whether they thought "the policies of Barack Obama and the Democrats or George W. Bush and the Republicans are more responsible for the country's current economic problems." Bush and the Republicans got the blame by a 54%-35% margin. The poll also revealed that people were less pessimistic than the Romney campaign assumed. When asked whether they expected "economic conditions in this country will be—very good, somewhat good, somewhat poor, or very poor," two-thirds of likely voters responded very good (11%) or somewhat good (57%).[62] Romney's decision to tout his experience in business backfired, and his bet that voters would hold Obama responsible for the economy was a bad one.

Obama won handily, although his victory was not as commanding as four years before. He won five million more votes than Romney, beating him by a 50%-48% margin. His 332–206 victory in the Electoral College was more comfortable, although not as commanding as in 2008. Obama benefitted from higher turnout by two groups of his strongest supporters. Voters 18–29 made up 19% of the electorate in 2012 compared with 18% in 2008, and they went for Obama by 60%-37%. Voters of color constituted 26% of the electorate in 2008 and 28% four years later, when 93% of Blacks, 73% of Asian Americans, and 71% of Hispanics gave Obama their vote. The President also won a majority among women, those with incomes under $50,000, residents of big and medium-sized cities, gays and lesbians, and those who identified as moderates. Romney increased his party's share among Whites, those over 65, Catholics, White working-class voters (although Obama carried that demographic in critical industrial states like Ohio, Michigan, and Pennsylvania), and small towns and suburbs.[63]

With the electorate so closely divided, getting the party's base to the polls was critical, as Obama's success with the young and minorities showed. Circumstances, like an economy that showed signs of revival, also mattered. But party allegiance had hardened since the 1990s, as voters had sorted themselves by region, religion, race, and cultural values. Party affiliation aligned closely with identity, intensifying partisan loyalty and making it highly unlikely that many voters would shift between parties or cast a vote for a presidential candidate of one party and a U.S. senator or governor of another. The number of swing states—and true swing voters—was shrinking as Democrats gained a lock on the coasts and Republicans controlled most of the South, the Mountain West, and the Midwest.

---

62 CNN/ORC Poll, September 13, 2012 http://i2.cdn.turner.com/cnn/2012/images/09/13/rel10c.pdf (accessed October 26, 2022).
63 Dionne, *Where the Right Went Wrong*, 379–80.

Many voters, whether they resided in red states or blue, struggled with stagnant incomes, settled for work that paid the minimum wage or slightly more, or couldn't find work at all. Many lived in areas where good jobs for those without a college degree had disappeared years ago. But they knew that the rich had gotten richer and those with college and especially graduate degrees were doing well, sometimes very well. In rural areas and small cities and towns, Republicans were able to lock in the lion's share of these alienated voters by appealing to their suspicion of big government, scrappy individualism, religious conservatism, or hostility to groups like women or minorities. Many White voters in blue states shared this outlook, but they were outweighed by college-educated urban and suburban professionals who had more cosmopolitan values and minorities who disliked Republicans who had long scapegoated them. Nevertheless, there were some swing voters left, and the message made a difference in winning their votes. Obama proved that attention to working- and middle-class economic needs and aspirations could move enough voters to make a difference.

Obama had coattails, although they were shorter than in 2008. Democrats picked up two seats in the Senate, largely because Tea Party candidates in Missouri and Indiana were so far outside the political mainstream, that they lost races that Republicans should have won handily. Both supported a ban on abortion with no exceptions and dug the hole it put them in deeper with nonsensical justifications. When asked why he wouldn't support an exception in cases of rape, Indiana's Richard Mourdock responded, "I think even when life begins in that horrible situation of rape, that's something God intended to happen."[64] In House races, Democrats gained just two seats, leaving them in a 234–201 minority, despite the fact that they outpolled Republican rivals by almost two million votes. Control of redistricting in a majority of states after the 2010 census allowed Republicans to draw election maps that maximized Republican success.

Obama won, Democrats kept a majority in the Senate but not large enough to break the filibuster, and Republicans maintained a comfortable majority in the House. Before the election, Obama had been optimistic that his victory would break the partisan fever that gripped the capital. Because it was his last race, Republicans would realize that "the goal of beating Obama doesn't make much sense" and "we can start getting some cooperation again."[65]

---

64 Dionne, *Why the Right Went Wrong*, 361.
65 Sam Stein, "Obama: Republican Fever Will Break During My Second Term," June 1, 2012 https://www.huffpost.com/entry/obama-republican-fever_n_1563539 (accessed October 27, 2022).

In the aftermath of the election, he believed he could work with Republicans to make progress on a few critical issues like the deficit and immigration. Of course, as the victor, he assumed he would do so from a position of strength. Progress would require Republican leaders on Capitol Hill to compromise, not simply expect Obama to accept their terms. That seemed unlikely after years of bitter conflict and the presence of a large contingent of Tea Party members who saw compromise as a betrayal of principle. Nevertheless, establishment Republicans, including the likes of Mitch McConnell and John Boehner, were sobered by Romney's defeat. They feared that the party's hard line on immigration, race, and women's issues threatened the party's viability in a nation that was becoming more diverse. As 2013 began, the party began a thorough review of what had gone wrong and what it needed to do to avoid permanent minority status. Perhaps that included cooperation with Obama on important issues like immigration. Steven Spielberg's popular biopic, *Lincoln*, suggested that even in the midst of the Civil War presidential leadership could create enough bipartisanship to achieve ambitious goals like abolition.

The Republican Party's shift to the center in 2000, following its partisan war on Clinton, certainly offered a precedent. But such a shift in 2013 was a long shot. The partisan fever still burned and there seemed to be no cure for the virus that fed it. The party had come to rely on a base of working- and struggling middle-class Whites—especially those in rural and small-town America—who were angry and alienated. They believed that Democrats looked down on them as ignorant bigots, Blacks and Hispanics were getting ahead through special privileges bestowed by Washington liberals, immigrants were taking their country away, liberal politicians had forced policies on the country that undermined Christian values and the family, and good jobs that supported a middle-class lifestyle for those without a college degree had vanished because corporate leaders and politicians had colluded to outsource manufacturing jobs to countries with cheap labor. They wanted their leaders to stand up to the enemy, not to compromise. When they did, voters lost patience and were likely to turn on them by supporting primary challengers who promised to fight the good fight. Because turnout in primaries was typically low, challengers who mobilized a relatively small number of angry, passionate voters could prevail. The Internet and social media enabled challengers to get their message out and raise money from small donors. They might also win support from a political action committee eager to take down an incumbent who had veered from ideological purity. Because the Tea Party had succeeded in toppling so many incumbents and PACs like the Koch-funded Americans for Prosperity stood ready to support insurgents, most Republicans feared that collaboration with a hated Democratic president opened them to being "primaried."

Talk of reappraising the party's approach, developing a broader appeal, obstructing less, and compromising more made sense as a general matter. But when congressional Republicans returned home to hold town hall meetings with constituents, they were reminded of the heat they would face if they moved toward the center. There were presidential hopefuls who believed that the party needed to moderate its positions and become more appealing to college-educated suburban women especially. But there were also those who understood that throwing red meat to the base would enable them to win primaries and caucuses, where the party's base loomed large. Breaking the fever of hyper-partisanship and its attendant gridlock, while desirable and theoretically possible, would be a long shot. For 40 years, Republicans had built their base by appealing to White resentment on issues of race, gender, region, and religion. They were now its prisoners.

CHAPTER 10

# REAPING THE WHIRLWIND, 2013–2016

### Wither the GOP?

The Republican National Committee and its young chair, Reince Priebus, took Romney's loss hard. Having drunk the anti-Obama Kool-Aid, they were incredulous and deeply concerned about the election's implications. Priebus combed data from exit polls and commissioned a survey of voters in four swing states to understand why Romney lost. The results were sobering. They suggested that Republicans were losing badly among college-educated White women and groups like young people and Hispanics who would have an even larger voice in future contests.

The reports were a dope slap, suggesting that the party needed a major course correction. Priebus named five party insiders to draft a report suggesting changes that would make the party more competitive. Led by Ari Fleischer, George W. Bush's press secretary, all five were establishment conservatives who believed that Tea Party crazies had tarnished the party's brand. In March 2013, Priebus unveiled *Growth and Opportunity Project* at a Washington press conference. Informally known as the autopsy, it called for tactical changes such as compressing the primary season and conducting fewer debates among primary contenders. More importantly, the report criticized the party for its narrowness, charging that Republicans had "become expert in providing ideological reinforcement to like-minded people" while losing "the ability to be persuasive with, or welcoming to, those who do not agree with us on every issue." It must become "a Party whose brand of conservatism invites and inspires new people to visit us."[1] Especially the young, minorities, and women. Although it recommended few

---

1 *Growth and Opportunity Project*, p. 7 https://www.documentcloud.org/documents/624293-republican-national-committees-growth-and.html (accessed November 30, 2022).

changes in the party's position on the issues, it urged support for comprehensive immigration reform.

Establishment Republicans welcomed the report. House Speaker John Boehner, who found dealing with Tea Party members of his caucus about as pleasant as a root canal gave it a hearty shout-out. "I've told [Priebus] he will have my full support as he moves forward," he emailed a *New York Times* reporter who sought his reaction.[2] Members of the Tea Party and social conservatives within the party were enraged. They saw the report as an effort to revive George W. Bush's compassionate conservatism and marginalize them. "Those in the Tea Party movement don't need an 'autopsy' report from R.N.C. to know they failed to promote our principles, and lost because of it," one prominent Tea Party leader observed. Rush Limbaugh, joined the attack, suggesting that the party was being "totally bamboozled."[3]

Predictably, hardline conservatives offered their own explanations for Romney's defeat. The American Principles Project, a new think tank that advocated for conservative social policies, produced its own post-mortem, *Building a Winning GOP Coalition: The Lessons of 2012*. Assisted by Kellyanne Conway, a well-known pollster and consultant closely linked with social conservatives, the authors laid down the gauntlet to the establishment. The *Growth and Opportunity Project* got it all wrong, they insisted, by blaming the party's embrace of "extremist social issues" for defeat. To be successful Conway and her allies at APP asserted, "party elites need to acknowledge the failure of the 'truce model' […] and adopt a confident, integrated conservatism that will form a party eager to make the case for the social issues in order to build a winning national coalition, attracting Latinos and other non-white and blue collar voters."[4] The autopsy came under fire from others as well, especially for its support for comprehensive immigration reform. In the Senate, Jeff Sessions of Alabama doubled down on his uncompromising anti-immigrant positions, assisted by his communications director Steven Miller. Miller used his close ties with conservative media outlets like *Breitbart* and radio talk show celebrities like Laura Ingraham to sound the alarm against a deal on immigration.

---

2 *New York Times,* March 18, 2013 https://www.nytimes.com/2013/03/19/us/politics/republicans-plan-overhaul-for-2016-primary-season.html?searchResultPosition=3 (accessed November 30, 2022).

3 Ibid.

4 Francis Cannon, Maggie, Gallagher, and Rich Danker, *Building a Winning GOP Coalition: The Lessons of 2012,* p. 4 https://americanprinciplesproject.org/wp-content/uploads/2018/09/BuildingAWinningGOPCoalition.pdf (accessed November 30, 2022).

## The Fever Doesn't Break

Few expected the autopsy to change much in Washington. The Republican Party was badly divided between the establishment figures who orchestrated the project and conservative populist firebrands who took a hard line on social issues and whose constituents expected them to fight rather than compromise. Republican leaders in the Senate and, especially, the House needed the votes of the most conservative members of their caucus and lacked the tools to force them into line. The 17 Republicans eyeing a run for the White House were even more independent. Turn-out in primaries was always light, with conservative true-believers over-represented. So, making a splash by taking a hard line on social issues and, especially, immigration was attractive. The autopsy was little more than food for thought, and it offered broccoli rather than ice cream, so the number of takers was limited.

On rare occasions Congress embraced the healthy option, at least when both parties had something to gain. It happened in Congress's lame-duck session following the election. On January 1, 2013, the Bush tax cuts would expire. To make matters worse, deep across-the-board cuts to every government agency and program would take effect because a divided Congress had failed to agree to reductions mandated by the 2011 budget bill. Obama wanted more tax revenue and additional federal support for those still struggling because of the slow recovery, while McConnell wanted the tax cuts made permanent. John Boehner, hounded by pesky Tea Party ideologues, just wanted another glass of merlot. Obama sought to increase taxes on those earning more than $200,000 per year in return for making the Bush tax cuts permanent for everyone else. Boehner, fearing he might be ousted as speaker by Tea Party bomb throwers, couldn't even sell an increase on those making $1 million. McConnell, however, was willing to raise the rate on those making more than $450,000 to get a deal. A bill raising taxes on that group, making the Bush tax cuts permanent for everyone else, extending unemployment benefits and tax credits for child care, college tuition, and the working poor, and postponing scheduled across-the-board cuts passed the Senate on December 31. Boehner swallowed hard and agreed to bring it to the House for a vote, where it passed two days later despite the opposition of almost two-thirds of his caucus.

It was the exception that proved the rule. Partisan fever was still raging and would continue to rise. The ACA, conservatives' favorite punching bag, remained a tempting target for those who wanted to show their constituents that they were protecting the country from a socialist president. In September 2013, Ted Cruz, who had won election to the Senate from Texas the previous year as a Tea Party favorite, took up the fight. With his finger to the winds that Sarah Palin and the Tea Party had unleashed, the Princeton and Harvard Law graduate used the ACA to establish his populist anti-Obama bona fides.

A standoff over a budget agreement and the need to raise the debt ceiling presented the perfect opportunity to kill the ACA—or at least convince voters Cruz was doing his best. As the start of a new fiscal year approached on October 1, 2013, Congress had not adopted a budget or a continuing resolution to keep the government open. To the consternation of Boehner, Cruz conspired with House conservatives to attach a provision eliminating the ACA to the continuing resolution that would keep the government open. That created a standoff with the Senate, which refused to adopt it. But Cruz and his allies were insistent, arguing it was now or never. The state insurance exchanges created by the law were about to open, and once they did people would "get hooked on Obamacare so that it can never be unwound."[5] The government shutdown once again, and the public blamed Republicans who quickly back-pedaled, approving a continuing resolution that ended the shutdown and also raised the debt ceiling. Cruz lost the battle but became a hero among the party's base, which was the point anyway.

Battles over the budget and debt ceiling produced less drama during the remainder of Obama's presidency. Republicans had learned that brinksmanship didn't move the President, and shutting down the government or playing chicken with the debt ceiling backfired. Immigration reform was another matter. The Republican establishment believed support for reform would help the party shed its reputation for hostility to Hispanics and make inroads with a growing group of voters. Besides, business owners, a key Republican constituency, had pressed for reform since legislation had failed in 2007 and once again in 2012. A "gang of eight" senators, evenly split between Democrats and Republicans, developed a bill that provided a path to citizenship for those in the country illegally. To ward off critics, who labeled it amnesty, the path was tortuous, taking 13 years to travel. The measure also dramatically increased funding for border enforcement, including a 700-mile fence. Senator Marco Rubio, a Cuban-American freshman who was widely expected to seek the Republican presidential nomination in 2016, became a leading supporter. 13 of his Republican colleagues and a solid phalanx of Democrats joined him to pass the bill by a 68–32 margin in June.

---

5  E.J. Dionne, Jr., *Why the Right Went Wrong: Conservatism from Goldwater to Trump and Beyond* (New York, 2016), 395.

Anyone who followed Washington had seen this movie before. The lopsided Senate majority was intended to impress House Republicans and persuade the speaker to bring the measure to the floor, where enough Republicans would join Democrats to pass it. However, John Boehner was more fearful of anti-immigrant Tea Party zealots than wowed by a show of bipartisanship in the Senate. With conservatives denouncing it as "a big government piece of legislation resembling Obamacare," Boehner held his ground, refusing to bring the Senate bill to the House floor for debate. "We're going to do our own bill," he snorted.[6] It didn't include a path to citizenship, of course, thereby torpedoing any hope that reform could pass.

Some Republicans thought that support for modest gun control measures would help soften the party's image. Most Americans were sickened and angered by mass shootings that all-too-regularly took the lives of 32, or five, or 14, or nine innocent men, women, and children who were simply in the wrong place when a deranged man opened fire, often with a semiautomatic weapon. Politicians' fear of the gun lobby, highlighted by Michael Moore's biting 2002 satire, *Bowling for Columbine*, appalled many voters. Horrific attacks in 2011 and 2012 only increased demands that politicians do something. In January 2011, Congresswoman Gabrielle Giffords was shot in the head at a constituent event in Tucson; she and 12 others were wounded and six were killed. In July 2012, a gunman killed 12 and injured 70 in an Aurora, Colorado movie theater. Later that year, 26 people, 20 of them 6- and 7-year-old children, were murdered when a man opened fire in Sandy Hook Elementary School in Newtown, Connecticut. Coming in the wake of more than a decade of carnage, the Newtown murders produced deafening calls for action.

The vast majority of Americans supported legislation designed to keep guns out of the hands of those with criminal records or a history of mental illness. They also favored restrictions on semiautomatic weapons with large capacity magazines that allowed a shooter to fire several dozen rounds in a matter of seconds. Although a 1994 law had banned these so-called assault weapons, the National Rifle Association (NRA) succeeded in blocking renewal when it expired in 2004. The NRA was a force like none other on Capitol Hill. Historically an organization representing hunters, it developed a radical libertarian stance in the 1970s, opposing virtually all restrictions on firearms. By the 1990s, it was an important part of a conservative phalanx

---

6 *New York Times*, June 27, 2013 https://www.nytimes.com/2013/06/28/us/politics/immigration-bill-clears-final-hurdle-to-senate-approval.html (accessed October 31, 2022).

that fought government's effort to limit personal liberty and impose greater control. Hunters' right to own shotguns and rifles, or a citizen's right to keep a firearm for protection against criminals were beside the point. Any restriction, the NRA argued, would be the first step down the slippery slope to gun registration, confiscation, and a disarmed citizenry that lacked the means to stand up to tyranny. The organization raised millions every year and used it to reward friends and punish opponents. NRA members voted and earned a reputation for focusing on candidates' positions on gun owners' rights to the exclusion of all else. That made them a force in general and primary elections, especially in the heartland where a critical mass of voters took gun rights seriously.

Like so many other public policy issues, gun control was part of the ideological and cultural battles that stoked the partisan recriminations that made American politics so ugly. While many urban dwellers valued the right to own a gun to protect themselves against criminals, gun rights became a religion in rural America. The cause appealed to fear of overbearing government and became another way to poke a stick in the eye of coastal elites who looked down on small town and rural folk. As a candidate in 2008, Obama had fed that resentment with comments he made at a fundraiser in—where else—San Francisco that were recorded and made public. Asked why so many White working-class Pennsylvanians voted for Republicans who supported policies that benefitted the rich, he referenced economic despair bred by the loss of good jobs and anger at politicians who ignored their plight. Then came the sentence he wished he'd never uttered: "So, it's not surprising then that they get bitter, they cling to guns or religion or antipathy to people who aren't like them or anti-immigrant sentiment or anti-trade sentiment as a way to explain their frustrations."[7] His dismissive remarks made gun-rights supporters even more adamant.

After the Newtown massacre, Obama decried the madness and sent Congress new gun-control legislation. It closed a loophole in current law that limited background checks to federally licensed gun dealers while waiving checks on sales by private individuals. It also revived the 1994 restrictions on assault weapons. Predictably, the bill failed to win enough votes to break a Senate filibuster as did a compromise sponsored by Joe Manchin, a conservative Democrat from West Virginia, and Pat Toomey, a moderate Republican from Pennsylvania. The Manchin-Toomey bill didn't require universal background checks but extended checks to sales at gun shows and over the Internet. Manchin and Toomey had established their bona fides on gun owners' rights. Even so, only

---

7 Obama, *A Promised Land*, 144.

four Republicans supported their measure, and with four Democrats from red states voting no, it died. The day the Senate voted, the NRA spent a half million dollars to run an add urging voters, "Tell your senator to listen to America's police rather than listening to Obama and Bloomberg."[8] That was Michael Bloomberg, the billionaire New York Republican who supported gun control. What better way to rally supporters than to remind gun owners that a Black president and a filthy-rich New Yorker were coming after their guns and their rights?

## Interesting Things Happen in the Fourth Quarter

With the autopsy rejected or ignored by most Republicans and partisan warfare raging, Obama braced for the 2014 mid-terms. They were almost always unkind to the president's party. To make matters worse, Democrats were defending 20 of the 36 Senate seats in play, and gridlock probably benefited Republicans because it fed dissatisfaction with politicians. Dysfunction also bred apathy that resulted in the lowest turnout—less than 36%—in any national election since 1942.[9] That also benefitted Republicans. Economic recovery continued at a slow pace with unemployment over 6%, more than two-thirds of voters believed the economy was "not so good" or "poor," and Obama's job approval rating remained below 50%. The ACA didn't help. It hadn't been fully implemented so working families hadn't seen the benefits. To make matters worse, the website where the uninsured could sign up had crashed the day it went online in October 2013, leading many to question the administration's ability to deliver on its promises.

Democrats suffered a devastating defeat. Republicans picked up nine Senate seats, giving them a 54–46 majority and making Obama's nemesis, Mitch McConnell, majority leader. The GOP gained 13 seats in the House for a 247–188 majority, its largest since Harry Truman's presidency. Republicans won by heavy margins among Whites (who constituted 75% of the electorate), voters over 40, working-class White men, Catholics, and middle-income ($50-$100,000) voters. They also made gains among women, Asian Americans, Hispanics, and self-identified moderates. Groups that Obama had rallied in 2008 and 2012, notably minorities and young people, may have been growing demographics, but they turned out at a much lower rate in the mid-terms. 2014 was no exception.[10]

---

8 *New York Times*, April 17, 2013 https://www.nytimes.com/2013/04/18/us/politics/senate-obama-gun-control.html (accessed October 31, 2022).

9 Dionne, *Why the Right Went Wrong*, 407.

10 Ibid., 407–8.

Geographically, Republicans erased inroads Obama had made in the Midwest and South. The election's outcome made his 2004 criticism of those who "like to slice and dice our country into Red States and Blue States" seem naïve.[11] Geography increasingly aligned with ideology. Most voters cast their ballots in House, Senate, gubernatorial, and state legislative races for candidates of the party that held their allegiance in presidential races. That sounded the alarm among Democrats. Most red states may have had small populations (Texas, Florida, and Georgia excepted), but there were more of them, giving Republicans an advantage in assembling Senate and Electoral College majorities.

There were many reasons for the Republican blowout. Voters who had soured on government and worried about a sluggish economy didn't help. Many analysts also believed that Democrats had failed to develop a coherent message to appeal to working class Whites. That was a pity because they had successfully championed policies like the ACA, extension of unemployment benefits, the GM and Chrysler rescue, and generous tax credits that benefited working- and middle-class voters. The party had also secured changes in the tax code that ensured the wealthy paid more. However, Democrats failed to build on the class-oriented message Obama had made in Osawatomie. Given his low approval ratings, Democrats, perhaps unwisely, chose to keep him off the stump during 2014.

Crushing as it was, the election seemed to liberate Obama. In his year-end press conference, he was unrepentant, quipping "my presidency is entering the fourth quarter" and "interesting stuff happens in the fourth quarter."[12] The day following the election he had promised to work with Republicans but warned, "what I'm not going to do is wait." "I've shown a lot of patience and tried to work on a bipartisan basis [...] and I'm going to continue to do so," he insisted. "But in the meantime, let's see what we can do lawfully through executive actions." While the humorless McConnell likened his comment to "waving a red flag in front of a bull,"[13] Obama would show that his promise

---

11 Obama, "Keynote Address at the 2004 Democratic National Convention," July 27, 2004 https://www.pbs.org/newshour/show/barack-obamas-keynote-address-at-the-2004-democratic-national-convention (accessed January 31, 2023).
12 "Remarks by the President in Year-End Press Conference," December 19, 2014 https://obamawhitehouse.archives.gov/the-press-office/2014/12/19/remarks-president-year-end-press-conference (accessed November 4, 2022).
13 *New York Times*, November 5, 2014 https://www.nytimes.com/2014/11/06/us/politics/midterm-democratic-losses-grow.html (accessed October 31, 2022).

was no bull. Republican recalcitrance would only deepen as Tea Party Republicans in the House formed the Freedom Caucus. Its purpose was to attack Democrats and keep their own party's leadership from compromising conservative principles. To complicate matters further, a score of Republican presidential aspirants was testing the waters in Iowa and New Hampshire, and many of them were brandishing far-right positions to capture the base. The climate was not conducive to compromise, but Obama played as if he were behind in the fourth quarter of a must-win game. With Republicans in control of Congress, he would do it by using executive authority. It wasn't an ideal solution. Executive actions could be overturned by a court or a successor in the White House and were, therefore, unstable. Under the circumstances, however, they were the only alternative to gridlock.

He turned to immigration first. It was among the most pressing issues facing the country, but gridlock, partisanship, and grandstanding had repeatedly killed efforts to fix a broken system. Democrats (and some Republicans) wanted comprehensive immigration reform, but failing that they were willing to attack the problem piecemeal. The starting point was addressing the plight of young people, undocumented immigrants brought to the U.S. by their parents as children who had grown up in the U.S. They were not culpable for breaking U.S. laws, considered themselves Americans, and would be like fish out of water if deported. Efforts to address the problem went back more than a decade. In 2001, Illinois Democrat Richard Durbin and Utah Republican Orrin Hatch introduced the so-called DREAM Act (Development, Relief, and Education for Alien Minors) in the Senate. It provided temporary legal residency, with permission to work and attend school, to all aliens who entered the U.S. illegally before they were 16, had resided in the U.S. for five years, had no criminal record, and were attending school, had graduated from high school, obtained a GED, or attended college. After six years, these so-called Dreamers would qualify for citizenship if they had attended college for two years or served in the military. The legislation failed to make much progress until 2010, when the Democratic majority in the House passed it, only to see it defeated by a Senate filibuster.

Obama acted during the summer of 2012. He directed the Department of Homeland Security (DHS) to order officials responsible for deportation proceedings against illegal aliens to exercise their prosecutorial discretion and defer action against undocumented aliens covered by the DREAM Act. The secretary issued a directive to department officials to defer deportation proceedings for two years and create a process whereby Dreamers could apply for authorization to work in the U.S. The DACA program (Deferred Action for Childhood Arrivals) would take these young people out of the shadows and free them to work and attend school without fear, although it didn't offer citizenship. Republicans attacked, falsely claiming that Obama was usurping congressional authority. However, he had simply issued a directive—not an executive order—instructing a cabinet official to create guidelines for prioritizing deportations. DHS could initiate proceedings against only a small portion of the 11 million undocumented aliens in the U.S. The order recognized that, prioritized proceedings against criminals, and deferred action against those who posed the least threat and had the greatest moral claim to remain in the U.S.

In 2014, Obama increased the number of undocumented aliens who qualified for deferred action. Once again, he chose to act through a directive to the DHS secretary rather than an executive order, instructing the secretary to defer deportation proceedings against any undocumented immigrants, regardless of age, who had a child who was a U.S. citizen or a legal resident. Like young people who qualified for the DACA program, these individuals would qualify for work permits. Almost 700,000 undocumented aliens had taken advantage of the DACA program, and almost 4 million would qualify for relief under the 2014 directive. Obama's actions did not substitute for comprehensive immigration reform, but they compensated for congressional inaction. However, the Supreme Court reversed the order in June 2016, when it refused to overturn a lower court order blocking the 2014 directive. It was a reminder of the limits of executive action.

Climate change was another issue that had become hostage to partisanship and congressional gridlock. Scientists had long worried about the devastating consequences of a warming climate caused by carbon emissions that had grown in the wake of the industrial revolution, accelerated dramatically after World War II, and continued to increase as economic development spread to more countries. In the early 1990s, there was bipartisan agreement that human-caused climate change posed a threat to the planet. George H.W. Bush signed the 1992 United Nations Framework Convention on Climate Change which created a process for negotiating agreements to halt warming. Bill Clinton was more aggressive, establishing a Climate Change Action Plan that established voluntary measures to roll back U.S. carbon emissions to 1990 levels by the end of the century. He also was active in negotiating the Kyoto Protocol, the first agreement under the U.N. convention. Its signatories pledged to reduce emissions to pre-1990 levels by 2012, seeking to reverse the growth of greenhouse gases before it was too late. However, both Clinton's action plan and the Kyoto agreement were voluntary, and Clinton refused to submit the later to the Senate because he couldn't muster the two-thirds majority required for ratification. Climate change was gaining wider attention, as two Oscar-winning documentaries—*March of the Penguins* (2005) and *An Inconvenient Truth* (2006) suggested. But it proved difficult to muster support for sacrifices necessary to solve a problem whose consequences lay in the future. That required bipartisan leadership to rally public support and refrain from exploiting the issue for partisan advantage. Given the fractured state of American politics, neither was likely.

Efforts to tackle climate change also generated pushback. Exxon, one of the world's largest oil companies, invested heavily to support groups that sowed doubts about the scientific evidence that global warming was caused by human activity. George W. Bush and his vice president, Dick Cheney, were both oilmen who feared that efforts to reduce carbon emissions would harm fossil fuel producers, who were reliable Republican supporters. Less than 100 days into his term, Bush announced that the U.S. would withdraw from the Kyoto Protocol, a move that Christine Todd Whitman, his EPA director, later described as "'flipping the bird' [...] to the rest of the world."[14] Even worse, the administration sought to muzzle government scientists. Researchers at NASA and EPA publicly charged that superiors tried prevent them from publicizing data that showed global warming was accelerating or discussing the relationship between climate change and an increase in catastrophic floods, wildfires, and storms. When an international panel of scientists reported in early 2007 that there was "unequivocal" evidence that Earth was warming and humans were responsible, Cheney rejected the findings. There wasn't sufficient evidence, he claimed, "to slap together some policy that's going to 'solve' the problem."[15]

Obama believed the scientists and pledged to tackle global warming in his 2009 inaugural address. With the economy on the ropes, many urged him to back away from his commitment, fearing that policies to reduce carbon emissions would draw fire from Republicans for prioritizing a problem that wasn't an immediate threat over economic recovery. Obama pushed ahead anyway. He quickly announced that the government would use its authority under the Energy Policy Conservation Act of 1975 to establish higher efficiency

---

14 Suzanne Goldenberg, "The worst of times: Bush's environmental legacy examined," *The Guardian*, January 16, 2009 https://www.theguardian.com/politics/2009/jan/16/greenpolitics-georgebush (accessed November 1, 2022).

15 Tim Dickinson, "The Secret Campaign of President Bush's Administration to Deny Global Warming," *Rolling Stone*, June 20, 2007 https://www.google.com/search?client=firefox-b-1-d&q=rolling+stone+george+w+bush+deny+global+warming.

standards for light bulbs and appliances. Then his team negotiated an agreement with automakers that required cars and light trucks to achieve an average of 35 miles per gallon by 2020—up from the existing 25 mpg. Even more ambitious was his effort to pass a cap-and-trade bill that used market forces to reduce greenhouse gases. It was an approach the Bush Sr. administration had employed with great success in the 1990s to reduce acid rain. The bill set limits on carbon emissions, fined companies that exceeded their limits, and gave those that stayed under their allocation credits they could sell to firms that faced penalties. The House passed it in June 2009, but a few Democrats from energy-producing states joined Republicans to block the measure in the Senate. Republicans labeled it "cap and tax"[16] and "the national energy tax,"[17] claiming that it would lead to higher energy costs and reduce oil and gas exploration.

Democratic losses in the 2010 mid-terms slowed efforts to tackle climate change, but as the 2012 election approached, Obama renewed the effort. He announced a new agreement with automakers to raise fuel efficiency standards, this time to an average of 54 mpg by 2025. The move was possible, in part, because ARRA had invested $90 billion in clean energy technology, including electric vehicles. A year later, he announced that the EPA would use its authority under the Clean Air Act to create standards for power plants, which were responsible for over one-third of the nation's carbon emissions. In 2015, the EPA announced its Clean Power Plan, which would reduce carbon emissions by 32% of 2005 levels by 2030.

Because the problem was global, Obama worked on the international stage as well. He played a critical role in forging the 2009 Copenhagen agreement, which was signed by 75 nations that produced 80% of greenhouse gases. Developed countries pledged to reduce emissions, developing countries agreed to slow increases, and wealthy nations established a $100 billion fund to assist developing nations with the transition. China claimed that committing to further reductions would put it at a disadvantage with countries with mature economies like the U.S. As the Paris climate meeting approached, Obama wanted China to join the U.S. in supporting more aggressive climate action. In late November 2014, he announced an agreement with China pledging the U.S. to

---

16 *New York Times*, September 30, 2010 https://archive.nytimes.com/www.nytimes.com/cwire/2010/09/30/30climatewire-how-republicans-managed-to-rebrand-cap-and-t-95204.html (accessed November 2, 2022).

17 Daniel J. Weis, "The GOP changes its tune on cap-and-trade," *Grist*, October 22, 2010 https://grist.org/article/2010-10-22-gop-changes-tune-on-cap-and-trade-reagan/ (accessed November 2, 2022).

cut emissions 28% below 2005 levels by 2025 and China to cap its output by 2030. That set the stage for the landmark Paris Agreement, which was finalized in late 2015. Signed by the U.S. and China on the same day, it provided that all parties would establish binding commitments to reduce emissions to levels that would prevent the Earth's temperature from rising more than 2 degrees Celsius during the twenty-first century. Although binding in international law, Obama negotiated it as an executive agreement that, like the Kyoto and Copenhagen pacts, did not need Senate approval.

Obama had established an impressive record on climate issues through executive action, largely ignoring Congress. Republicans were furious. They charged him with usurping the Senate's constitutionally prescribed role to provide advice and consent on treaties. Of course, the criticism ignored a long line of Supreme Court precedents upholding presidential authority to enter arrangements with other nations through executive action. Constitutional considerations aside, Republicans insisted, the agreements were bad for the country. China would cheat and gain advantage over the U.S. "This kind of unilateral disarmament in our economy is reckless and it is hurting the American dream," charged Florida Republican presidential contender Marco Rubio.[18] Twenty Republican state attorneys-general joined a legal challenge to the EPA's plan to limit power plant emissions. In 2016, the U.S. Supreme Court issued a stay while the case, *West Virginia v. EPA*, was litigated in the lower courts. In a landmark 2022 decision, it would rule that the agency lacked authority under the Clean Air Act to establish the regulations, underscoring the fragility of executive action.

Some Republicans admitted that the Earth was warming and agreed that human activity was the cause. They simply believed that the problem was less urgent than scientists claimed, so they opposed remediation that they feared would slow economic growth. Republican presidential hopeful John Kasich acknowledged that humans were changing the climate but "not enough for me to go out and cost somebody their job."[19] Many Republicans, however, denied climate change, calling it a hoax perpetrated by liberals bent on expanding government control. Not surprisingly, Sarah Palin was at the head of the pack.

---

18 Devin Henry, "Republicans grope for ways to kill paris climate agreement," *The Hill*, December 20, 2015 https://thehill.com/policy/energy-environment/263780-gop-gropes-for-way-to-kill-paris-climate-deal/ (accessed November 2, 2022).

19 Kate Sheppard, "Kasich on Climate Change: 'I Just Don't Know Enough About It,'" *Huffington Post*, October 2, 2015 https://www.huffpost.com/entry/john-kasich-climate-change_n_560ec77be4b076812701d590 (accessed November 2, 2022).

Climate scientists "have studied the data that they are erroneously delivering to the public," she charged at the opening of a 2016 climate change denial film, *Climate Hustle*. Their goal was "to make us think that we can somehow change the weather and how they do that is to grow government and allow the government to have more control over us." Others, notably Donald Trump, a leading Republican presidential contender, supported her views as did many among the party's base. They were suspicious of elites, in this case scientists, who looked down on less educated folk, claimed to know what was best for them, and wanted to control them. Their objections moved global warming from the realm of science and policy to a cultural issue nearly as contentious as abortion or affirmative action.

Global warming became contested, but it paled in comparison to race, the most polarizing issue in American politics since the founding of the republic. As a Black man, Obama knew that race was never far from the surface and that it easily bubbled over. He was more acutely aware of the problems confronting African Americans than anyone who had occupied the White House, and he was committed to addressing them. However, he shied away from framing his priorities in terms of race. He believed that to be successful, he must be viewed as the president who was Black, not the Black president. Many Whites viewed him with suspicion, he realized, and if he appeared solicitous of Blacks, they would see reverse discrimination. "If I go out there saying, 'blacks, black, black,' do you think that will help black people," he asked a group of Black writers who had criticized his reticence to talk about race?[20]

Experience reinforced his inclination. In July 2009, Obama responded to a question about Henry Louis Gates, a distinguished Black Harvard professor who had been arrested while trying to enter his house. He had fumbled with a jammed lock on the front door of his home, a White passer-by called 911, and Gates, understandably, pitched attitude when questioned by the responding officers who then took him into custody. The incident became national news. When Obama was asked to comment, he said he didn't have all the facts and couldn't say what role race played. But he added, the "police acted stupidly in arresting someone when there was already evidence that they were in their own home." He also suggested that there was a context. "What I think we know separate and apart from this incident is [...] there's a long history of African-Americans and Latinos being stopped by law enforcement disproportionately.

---

20 Claude A. Clegg, III, *The Black President: Hope and Fury in the Age of Obama* (Baltimore, 2021), 184.

That's just a fact." His comments sparked a furious backlash from Republicans who had become committed to the fiction that race no longer mattered and anyone who said it did was just seeking special treatment for Blacks. The Republican Senatorial Campaign Committee immediately placed ads on conservative web sites "asking people to vote on whether Obama's comments were presidential."[21] A Republican congressman from Michigan, outraged that "the president again has overused his power and acknowledged making decisions based on bias," threatened to introduce a resolution demanding an apology.[22] And so it went.

Obama appeared on ABC News's *Nightline* to do damage control, and, in a characteristic effort to bridge differences, he invited the arresting officer and Gates to the White House for conversation and a beer. But the episode cost him politically. Polling, he later wrote, revealed that it "caused a huge drop in my support among white voters, bigger than any single event during the eight years of my presidency."[23] Burned, he was reticent to talk about race and hewed to what the historian Claude Clegg III described as "a universalist, pragmatic, race-neutral approach" that would "pay disproportionately high dividends to individuals and groups, including African Americans, who were the most disadvantaged segments of American society."[24]

Avoiding the subject wasn't always possible. Race was a frequent flashpoint, and Black people—and many Whites—expected any president, but certainly a Black president, to acknowledge the elephant in the room. So, in 2012, pressure grew when a Black teenager named Trayvon Martin was shot-to-death by a private citizen while walking to the home of his father's fiancee in a gated community in Florida. The provocation? Wearing a sweatshirt with the hood covering his head on a cool, rainy night, having a bottle of iced tea and a bag of Skittles in his hand, and being Black. The killing gained national attention, becoming part of a growing conversation about race. Obama initially avoided comment on the tragedy, but the pressure became too great as media coverage spiked and public demonstrations spread. When Obama finally commented, he was cautious, praising law enforcement for its work on the case and refusing

---

21 Ibid.
22 Joseph Weber, "McCotter to introduce resolution for Obama apology," *Washington Times*, July 27, 2009 https://www.washingtontimes.com/news/2009/jul/27/mccotter-introduce-resolution-obama-apology/ (accessed November 3, 2022).
23 Obama, *A Promised Land*, 397.
24 Clegg, *The Black President*, 132.

to discuss a matter that was under investigation. After expressing sympathy for "what these parents are going through," he veered from his universalist approach, insisting that "we examine [...] the context for what happened, as well as the specifics of the incident." He left no doubt that the context was race. "If I had a son, he'd look like Trayvon," Obama observed pointedly.[25]

Predictably, conservatives pounced. Newt Gingrich called the comments "disgraceful," bizarrely suggesting that Obama was moved by Trayvon's death only because he was Black. Columnist Michelle Malkin charged that Obama was "all too willing to pour gas on the fire." Like many conservatives, she seemed to assume that American society had become color-blind and race no longer mattered, even as she used it to stoke criticism of the President. "What do Trayvon's race and looks have to do with anything," she asked?[26]

Everything, almost all Black people and many Whites responded. A succession of police killings in Obama's second term showed anyone who was paying attention that race was a life and death matter. They also sparked a racial reckoning that would grow as the decade went on. Technology played a critical role, as cell phone videos of shootings went viral, and social media spread information, fanned outrage, and brought people together at warp speed to protest. When Trayvon's killer was acquitted in July 2013, massive protests erupted across the country, and three Black women created a twitter handle #blacklivesmatter as well as a Facebook platform to share information about the persistent racism Blacks encountered daily. When a young Black man named Michael Brown was killed by a White police officer in Ferguson, Missouri, a predominantly Black St. Louis suburb, in August 2014, protests erupted. #blacklivesmater lit up, spreading outrage nation-wide and prompting over 500 activists from 18 cities across the country to travel to Ferguson to join the protest.

Highly publicized killings continued. In late 2014, a 12-year-old Black boy wielding a plastic gun was killed by Cleveland police; in April 2015, a Black man was shot in the back while fleeing police after a being stopped for

---

25 Sam Stein, "Obama on Trayvon Martin Case: 'If I Had a Son, He'd Look Like Trayvon,'" *Politico*, March 23, 2012 https://www.huffpost.com/entry/obama-trayvon-martin_n_1375083 (accessed November 3, 2022).

26 Aliyah Shahid, "Conservatives blast President Obama's comments on Trayvon Martin: He's race baiting," *New York Daily News*, March 24, 2012 https://www.nydailynews.com/news/politics/conservatives-blast-president-obama-remarks-trayvon-martin-race-baiting-article-1.1050298 (accessed November 3, 2022).

a malfunctioning taillight; three months later a Black woman was found dead in a Texas jail cell after being arrested for a traffic violation; shortly after her death, a Black Cincinnatian was shot-to-death when he pulled away from police who had stopped him for a missing license plate. The senseless killings underscored the peril of living in the U.S. as a Black person, and they would continue throughout 2016 and beyond. Black Lives Matter (BLM) groups popped up across the country, operating in 30 cities by 2016. They expressed the outrage felt by many Americans, organized mass protests, and engaged in civil disobedience to demand justice. During the 2014 and 2015 Christmas shopping seasons, local BLM organizations orchestrated protests—including die-ins in which hundreds of protesters lay on floors in public places—at malls and shopping districts in Minneapolis, Chicago, Boston, Memphis, Seattle, and Washington. At Minneapolis' Mall of America, where 3,000 protesters shut down a portion of the nation's largest shopping mall, activists chanted, "While you are on your shopping spree, black people cannot breathe."[27] That was a reference to Staten Island's Eric Garner who died the previous July after New York City police used a chokehold while arresting him for selling single cigarettes from packs without tax stamps.

Predictably, conservatives took aim at BLM, using it as a way to stoke White fear and resentment against Blacks and Democrats, who acknowledged the reality of police brutality and demanded remedies. It was a tactic that had worked for every Republican president and many presidential hopefuls since Nixon. So, it wasn't surprising that in a hyper-polarized atmosphere with both parties focused on identity issues and a presidential election approaching Republicans dusted off the playbook, adapting it to the party's commitment to color-blind policies. Didn't *all* lives matter conservatives asked, ignoring the many ways that the nation's deeply racist history meant that African Americans were often killed *because* of their race. Wasn't an emphasis on *Black* lives racist? Hadn't these young activists forgotten that the point of the civil rights movement was to create a color-blind society? Didn't failure to give police the benefit of the doubt risk undermining their authority and giving license to criminals?

Stung by criticism that they were racist, police also pushed back. Officers in New York City formed a Blue Lives Matter organization to emphasize that they put their lives on the line every day to protect Americans. By the end

---

27 *New York Times*, December 20, 2014 https://www.nytimes.com/2014/12/21/us/chanting-black-lives-matter-protesters-shut-down-part-of-mall-of-america.html (July 20, 2018).

of 2014, a Blue Lives Matter flag appeared—blue and white stripes, a blue field in the upper left corner with white stars. A light blue horizontal line ran through the middle representing the police—the thin blue line that separated law abiding citizens from the chaos of crime. It was flown by many who wanted to show solidarity with the police and push back against BLM. Fox News personality Bill O'Reilly labeled BLM a hate group, and many of his Republican guests agreed. "I have seen them marching down the street essentially calling death to police," Republican presidential candidate Donald Trump told O'Reilly during a July 2016 interview.[28]

Obama and his attorney general, Eric Holder, understood that the disillusionment and rage that inspired BLM were legitimate and believed that its demands should be taken seriously. When Trayvon Martin's killer was acquitted, Obama made a rare, unannounced visit to the White House briefing room to comment. "Trayvon Martin could have been me 35 years ago," he said, adding "it's important to understand that the African American community is looking at this issue through a set of experiences and a history that doesn't go away."[29] The administration did more than sympathize with victims and their families. The Justice Department's Civil Rights Division conducted extensive investigations of 20 police departments—including those in Chicago, Detroit, Los Angeles, and smaller cities like Ferguson and North Charleston—where high-profile cases of police abuse suggested systemic civil rights violations. When investigations revealed a pattern of abuse—which they often did—Justice Department attorneys negotiated consent agreements that required police departments to submit to federal monitoring; collect and report data on stops, arrests, and use of force by race and gender; track police encounters with the mentally ill; and initiate cultural competence and implicit bias training programs for officers. Obama also convened a high-profile President's Task Force on 21st Century Policing that developed extensive recommendations to improve the quality of policing and especially police interactions with minorities, women, the mentally ill, and youth.

Obama also used executive authority to mitigate the effect of laws passed as part of the War on Drugs that resulted in mass incarceration of Blacks.

---

28 Reena Flores, "Donald Trump: Black Lives Matter calls for killing police," July 29, 2016 https://www.cbsnews.com/news/donald-trump-black-lives-matter-calls-for-killing-police/ (July 25, 2018).

29 Text of Obama's Speech on Trayvon Martin, July 19, 2013 https://www.businessinsider.com/obama-trayvon-martin-race-speech-video-text-2013-7 (July 24, 2018).

Among the most egregious were harsh mandatory minimum sentences for drug offenders that resulted in long sentences for first-time offenders and those guilty of possession or selling drugs on a small scale. Unsuccessful in securing legislation to deal with the problem, Obama and Holder used executive authority. Holder directed U.S. attorneys to "decline to pursue charges triggering a mandatory minimum sentence" in drug cases when the crime did not involve violence and the defendant did not have ties to a large-scale drug trafficking organization or a significant criminal history.[30] He also worked closely with the U.S. Sentencing Commission to modify federal sentencing guidelines to reduce the number of sentencing points judges assigned to approximately 70 percent of drug trafficking offenses. That reduced average drug sentences by almost one year. When Congress let the changes stand, the Commission applied them retroactively, triggering the release of over 6,000 federal prisoners.

Obama even scored a couple of modest legislative victories. In 2010, he won passage of the Fair Sentencing Act which reduced—but didn't eliminate—the differential between penalties for crack and cocaine. He also signed legislation requiring law enforcement agencies to report the deaths of citizens who were in custody. It was critical to provide data necessary to understand the dimensions of police brutality. However, as Obama neared the end of his second term, he harbored no illusions about the enormity of the challenges and the limits of what his administration had achieved. "Change has been too slow and we have to have a greater sense of urgency about this," he said in remarks delivered from Poland in 2016, after two more Black men died at the hands of police. "This not just a black issue," Obama added. "This is an American issue we should all care about [...]. We are better than this."[31] Donald Trump, the Republican candidate for president, preferred to fan the flames of fear and resentment. "President Obama just had a news conference," he tweeted in response, "but he doesn't have a clue. Our country is a divided crime scene, and it will only get worse!"[32]

---

30 Memorandum to the United States Attorneys and Assistant Attorney General for the Criminal Division, August 12, 2013 https://www.justice.gov/sites/default/files/oip/legacy/2014/07/23/ag-memo-department-policypon-charging-mandatory-minimum-sentences-recidivist-enhancements-in-certain-drugcases.pdf (accessed November 5, 2022).
31 http://time.com/4397611/president-obama/ (accessed July 26, 2018).
32 "Donald Trump presidential ampaign, 2016/Crime and justice" https://ballotpedia.org/Donald_Trump_presidential_campaign,_2016/Crime_and_justice (accessed December 4, 2022).

## A Presidential Campaign Feeds the Fever

One of the reasons that Obama was intent on wielding executive authority to get things done was his realization that time was running out. By late 2014, the media was full of speculation about the Republican presidential aspirants. When the first of a dozen Republican debates occurred in July 2015, 17 candidates had thrown their hat in the ring. They included U.S. Senators (Ted Cruz, Marco Rubio, and Lindsey Graham), governors (Jeb Bush of Florida, John Kasich of Ohio, Rick Perry of Texas, Chris Christie of New Jersey, Bobby Jindal of Louisiana, and Scott Walker of Wisconsin), and political novices (neurosurgeon Ben Carson, former Hewlett Packard CEO Carly Fiorino), and real estate mogul and showman Donald Trump. As the son and brother of former presidents, Jeb Bush was the early front-runner. Fluent in Spanish, married to a Colombian woman, and a champion of immigration reform, he was the dream candidate of the establishment Republicans who conducted the autopsy. Name recognition helped him in early polls, but neither he nor any of the other candidates achieved a breakthrough that lasted. With so many candidates competing for attention, most who rose in the polls—and many had their moment—quickly faded. With a crowded field and the competition keen, national and state party leaders kept their powder dry, making very few early endorsements.[33]

The big surprise was Donald Trump. Decades of self-promotion as a successful businessman and a long run as the star of the popular TV reality show, *The Apprentice*, gave him universal recognition. But he had no experience in government and politics and had teased presidential runs in 1988, 2000, and 2012 only to pull back. His campaign persona was unorthodox—impulsive, undignified, bombastic, egotistical, juvenile, offensive, sexist, and racist. When he launched his campaign in June 2015 at Trump Tower, a New York landmark and monument to his ego, he made a grand entrance, riding down a gold-plated escalator to the atrium. It sent chills down the spine of Steve Bannon, the head of Breitbart, recalling the opening scene of *Triumph of the Will* in which Hitler descends by plane to Nuremberg and a massive Nazi rally. Trump's speech was an appropriate sequel. He rambled, went off script, and delivered a shocking screed against immigration and immigrants. "The U.S. has become a dumping ground for everybody else's problems," he warned. Then he zeroed in on Mexico, charging that it "beats us all the time" and that Mexicans were "laughing at us, at our stupidity." Mexico was "sending people that have lots of

---

[33] John Sides, Michael Tesler, Lynn Vavreck, *Identity Crisis: The 2016 Presidential Campaign and the Battle for the Meaning of America* (Princeton, NJ, 2018), 67–70.

problems," he charged. "They're bringing drugs. They're bringing crime. They're rapists. And some, I assume, are good people." He would stop the invasion. "I will build a great, great wall on the southern border," he promised. "And I will have Mexico pay for that wall."[34] He understood the anti-immigrant anger in the Republican base and signaled that he would whip it into a fury to generate support for his unorthodox candidacy.

It was just the start. He zeroed in on Muslims, claiming that he had seen them celebrating on the roof tops of buildings in New Jersey on 9-11 and suggesting a ban on Muslim immigrants. He ridiculed his opponents, calling Bush "low energy," Rubio "little Marco," and Cruz "lyin' Ted." At the first debate, Fox's Megyn Kelly asked him to explain why he had called women he didn't like "fat pigs, dogs, slobs and disgusting animals." After the debate, he tweeted that she had been overly emotional and "really bombed." "There was blood coming out of her eyes, blood coming out of her wherever," he charged.[35] He abandoned Republican orthodoxy, criticizing free trade agreements that benefitted corporations but cost jobs, eschewed any changes to Social Security, and promised to quit NATO if its members didn't increase their defense spending. His defense of workers, seniors, and taxpayers whom he claimed had been footing the bill for Europe's defense, combined with his politically incorrect language and appeal to angry White men, played well in a party whose base had become rural, White, evangelical, and lacked a college education.

Party leadership—not to mention most Americans—were appalled. But Trump kept it up, and it worked. He quickly rose to the top of the field and stayed there, confounding reporters, politicians, and the public. He was the best-known person in a crowded field, and his outrageous statements got media attention, keeping his candidacy front-of-mind for voters. Services that tracked cable coverage of the candidates reported that Trump was mentioned in 52% of all cable news stories about the candidates between May 1, 2015 and April 30, 2016. Controversy attracts viewers, and Trump provided a steady stream. One network president put it succinctly, "He may not be good for America, but he's damn good for CBS."[36] Much of the coverage was negative, but it stirred

---

34 CBS News, "Transcript: Donald Trump announces his presidential candidacy," June 16, 2015 https://www.cbsnews.com/news/transcript-donald-trump-announces-his-presidential-candidacy/ (accessed December 1, 2022).

35 Paola Chavez, Veronica Stracqualursi, Meghan Keneally, "A History of the Donald Trump-Megyn Kelly Feud," October 26, 2016 https://abcnews.go.com/Politics/history-donald-trump-megyn-kelly-feud/story?id=36526503 (accessed December 2, 2022).

36 Sides, Tesler, Vavreck, *Identity Crisis*, 74.

the juices of a big chunk of the Republican base. These were voters who had been drawn to the party by its opposition to abortion, gay marriage, immigration, and policies perceived to help minorities and women, not its support for the free market and fiscal responsibility. They weren't impressed with establishment Republicans like the Bushes who spoke in polite, politically correct language but were too close to corporate America, supported free trade agreements, wanted to privatize Social Security, and gave away too much to the Democrats. They saw Trump as authentic. He used barroom language, told it like it was, and stuck it to the liberals who looked down on them. He also promised to raise taxes on the rich, protect government programs they liked, namely Social Security and Medicare, dial back free trade, and spend money on infrastructure to fix roads and bridges and put people to work.

In a crowded field, he didn't need to win majorities in the primaries and caucuses. If he could capture 30%–40% of the votes, he would win, drive out competitors, and create a sense of inevitability. After finishing a close second in Iowa, he tweeted, "Ted Cruz didn't win Iowa, he stole it"[37] and complained that the media was giving too much attention to Rubio who finished third. In the next two weeks, however, he won commanding victories in New Hampshire, South Carolina, and Nevada, and took seven of the 11 states contested on Super Tuesday, March 1. By late March, his only competitors were Ted Cruz and John Kasich, an establishment conservative who stayed in the race, not because he had a chance, but because he found Trump an affront to decency. By early May, Cruz and Kasich dropped out, conceding the nomination to a man many considered a bad joke a year before.

The Democrats had their own surprise, a hotly contested primary. Hillary Clinton had battled Barack Obama to the wire in the 2008 primaries, and most thought she would waltz to the nomination in 2016 after being a good loser and winning plaudits as Obama's secretary of state. Bernie Sanders, a self-described democratic-socialist who represented Vermont in the U.S. Senate as an Independent and caucused with the Democrats, had other ideas. Seventy-five years old, disheveled, and a scourge of corporate America and the 1%, he promised a single-payer healthcare system, free college tuition, a carbon tax, steep cuts in defense spending, and paid leave for workers. He inspired young Democrats who saw him as an idealistic, truth-telling grandfather. Progressives

---

37 *New York Times*, February 3, 2016 https://archive.nytimes.com/www.nytimes.com/politics/first-draft/2016/02/03/donald-trump-says-ted-cruz-stole-victory-in-iowa-caucuses/ (accessed December 2, 2022).

were also captivated, viewing him as offering a return to the glory days of the New Deal and the Great Society. Beginning in the summer of 2015, after he announced his candidacy, his rallies attracted huge crowds, generating widespread media attention and establishing him as a serious contender. Sanders also developed a strong ground game, recruiting legions of idealistic young volunteers and raising mountains of cash from small donors.

Clinton had liabilities—perhaps mainly that she was a woman in a culture tainted with misogyny. Since her husband first ran for president in 1992, she had been the subject of scurrilous attacks by conservatives who portrayed her as a ruthless, untrustworthy, power-hungry harpy who would stop at nothing to gain power. While almost all the charges were false, they became concerns for many voters. As the first woman to make a serious bid for the White House, she faced the cruel dilemma all professional women experienced: if she was forceful, she would be considered aggressive and nasty, if she wasn't, she would be regarded as too weak for the job. Then there were the emails. In March 2015, the *New York Times* reported that Clinton had violated federal government policies by using a private server in her home for official and personal emails while serving secretary of state. Although Sanders never made an issue of it, others pounced, charging her with violating the law and placing national security at risk. While she turned over all of the official emails, she deleted over 30,000 personal emails. Reporters and many Democratic advisors believed she was too cagy in explaining why she used a private server. That kept the story alive and generated continued questions about her forthrightness. To compound her problems, those on the right charged that she and Bill used their influence to leverage large gifts from foreign governments to the Clinton Foundation, trading access and influence. In April 2016, Donald Trump began calling her "crooked Hillary."[38]

But Clinton also had significant advantages. She was a loyal Democrat while Sanders wasn't a member of the party. She had been a key part of a highly successful presidency that led the party out of the wilderness in 1992, a hard-working U.S. Senator from New York, and a high-profile member of Obama's team. She and Bill had lots of friends and plenty of IOUs to call in, while most establishment Democrats believed Sanders was too far to the left to win. Before the primaries kicked off, 83% of Democratic senators, representatives, and governors had endorsed a candidate, and 80% of them supported Hillary.[39]

---

38 Amber Jamieson, "Trump Calls Clinton 'Crooked Hillary'—should she ignore it or fight back," *The Guardian*, May 25, 2016 https://www.theguardian.com/us-news/2016/may/25/donald-trump-crooked-hillary-clinton-nickname-ignore-fight (accessed January 31, 2023).
39 Sides, Tesler, Vavreck, *Identity Crisis*, 145.

Because many of these individuals were among the 714 superdelegates who would vote at the convention along with 4,051 delegates selected in primaries and caucuses, she entered the primaries with the wind at her back. Her history of support for civil rights and her close association with Obama built a big reservoir of support among Blacks and Hispanics. She also won heavy majorities of older Democrats who were attracted by her deep experience and always turned out in big numbers in the primaries.

Sanders gave her a run for her money, but he didn't have the horses to prevail. She won 36 primaries and caucuses to 23 for Sanders, prevailed in the most delegate-rich states like New York, California, Pennsylvania, New Jersey, Illinois, Ohio, and Massachusetts, and racked up crushing majorities in the South, where Black voters stood behind her. The primary campaign was bruising, leaving a residue of hard feelings. Sanders endorsed Clinton, but he did not become a highly engaged surrogate, and many of his supporters carried hard feelings into the general election.

The general election campaign was like no other in American history. It pitted a highly competent woman against a misogynist with no experience in public affairs; a disciplined, focused, experienced candidate whose statements were measured against an impulsive, name-calling, truth-averse novice who hurled invective; a political outsider who denounced a rigged system against a woman who touted her experience and competence; a person committed to addressing sexism and structural racism against a man who used a megaphone rather than a dog-whistle to appeal to racism and sexism. The candidates sometimes addressed differences on policy, but devoted far more attention to attacking their opponent's character. Trump hammered away at "Crooked Hillary," repeatedly homing in on her emails, the Clinton Foundation, and her support for her husband's abusive treatment of women. Clinton called out Trump for his racism and sexism, lack of experience in government, impulsiveness, and complete absence of presidential temperament and judgment. They focused even more attention on identity issues such as race, gender, and immigration. It was a nasty campaign in which both candidates emphasized longstanding, highly charged differences calculated to stoke the primal rage of the base.

An unanticipated crisis in Washington raised the temperature—and the stakes—of a race already on fire. In February 2016, as the primaries moved into high gear, Justice Antonin Scalia died suddenly, putting control of the Supreme Court up for grabs. An Obama appointment to replace Scalia would create a solid liberal majority, affecting outcomes on hot-button issues such as abortion, affirmative action, gun rights, religious freedom, and more. Even though

Obama had 11 months remaining in office, Mitch McConnell, the Senate Majority Leader, quickly announced that the Senate would not consider a nominee until a new president took office. McConnell's decision to block consideration of a nominee until a new president took office, escalated already intense conflict over judicial nominations to a new level. His justification was as thin as his move was audacious. In 1992, Joe Biden, then chair of the Senate Judiciary Committee, opined that no Supreme Court nominees should be considered in a presidential election year. Even though Biden had been addressing a hypothetical situation, McConnell treated it as binding precedent.[40]

Obama nominated Merrick Garland, a highly respected moderate who sat on the Court of Appeals for the District of Columbia, the high court's Triple-A farm team. But it didn't matter. Republicans wouldn't give Garland a hearing. It was a moment McConnell lived for. "One of my proudest moments," he said in August 2016, "was when I looked Barack Obama in the eye and I said, 'Mr. President, you will not fill the Supreme Court vacancy.'"[41] With a Supreme Court nomination hanging in the balance, he upped the ante for an already bitterly contested election, providing added motivation for Republican voters to turn out. Usually impulsive, Trump made the most of the opportunity. He consulted knowledgeable conservative legal experts with ties to the Federalist Society and the Heritage Foundation to create a list of potential Supreme Court nominees, which he released in September 2016. The names were serious, experienced conservative judges, assuring the party's base that his nominee would be a fitting replacement for Scalia and would vote right on important social issues, especially abortion.

In addition to contending with a level of partisan vitriol not seen since perhaps 1860, both candidates grappled with scandals that reduced their already-low favorability ratings. As the primaries concluded, 57% of Americans polled had an unfavorable impression of Clinton and 62% of Trump.[42] Trump's

---

40 "Mitch McConnell Supreme Court Speech on Merrick Garland, Obama Nomination: 'Let the American People Decide' Transcript," March 29, 2016, *rev* https://www.rev.com/blog/transcripts/mitch-mcconnell-obama-supreme-court-speech-on-merrick-garland-let-the-american-people-decide-transcript (accessed November 3, 2022).

41 Katherine Fung, "What Happened with Merrick Garland? What McConnell, Trump, and Others Said and Did During Obama's Nomination," *Newsweek*, October 12, 2020 https://www.newsweek.com/what-happened-merrick-garland-what-mcconnell-trump-others-said-did-during-obamas-nomination-1537842 (accessed November 3, 2020).

42 Sides, Tesler, Vavreck, *Identity Crisis*, 185.

unfiltered mouth and Twitter feed guaranteed constant negative publicity: hurling invective at Muslim parents whose son had died in combat in Iraq because they had denounced Trump's anti-Muslim diatribes at the Democratic convention; suggesting that his supporters assassinate Clinton; and responding to charges that he had used racist and sexist language about a Latina Miss Universe contestant by saying that she "had gained a massive amount of weight and it was a real problem" for him as the pageant producer. But the piece d'resistance came on October 4 when the *Washington Post* released a 2005 recording of Trump explaining the prerogatives of stardom to the host of *Access Hollywood*, a popular TV show. "When you're a star, they let you do it. Whatever you want," Trump bragged. "Grab them by the pussy. You can do anything."[43]

For Clinton, it was the emails. In 2015, the FBI launched an investigation into Clinton's use of a private email server while secretary of state. In July 2016, James Comey, the agency's director, announced that Clinton's conduct did not warrant prosecution. However, he scolded her for extreme carelessness in handling sensitive documents. Trump continued to hammer away on the issue, using it as Exhibit A in his case against "Crooked Hillary." But the FBI's decision at least lifted threat of prosecution from Clinton's campaign. Then, on October 28, with 10 days left in the campaign, Comey announced that he was reopening his investigation because emails found on the laptop of a former congressman who was married to Clinton's top aide raised concerns. The FBI never made public announcements about investigations, but Comey believed that Clinton would win and wanted to make sure he wasn't criticized for assisting her by keeping the investigation under wraps. The media pounced, keeping the story in the news until two days before the election when the FBI announced that it had found nothing concerning. As it had throughout the campaign, the mainstream media bent over backward to cover negative stories about Clinton in an effort to persuade conservatives that, they were objective. The timing couldn't have been worse; Clinton's favorability ratings sunk by several points as voters prepared to cast their ballots.[44]

The scandals marked a fitting end to a tumultuous, undignified campaign. Both candidates ended it, as they began, with extraordinarily high unfavorability ratings. Some Republicans had been critical of Trump's antics,

---

43 Ibid., 197.
44 Ibid., 207.

and in the wake of the *Access Hollywood* scandal, some at the RNC explored options for removing him from the ticket. In an intensely partisan atmosphere, however, Republicans came home to Trump, preferring a flawed Republican to a hated Democrat. Democrats rallied around Clinton, although not enough to deliver a victory.

To the surprise of most—including Trump and his team—Trump won a razor-thin victory. Although Clinton received three million more popular votes—a 2% margin—Trump comfortably carried the Electoral College, 304–227. The outcome hinged on three states that were part of what Democrats called the Blue Wall—Pennsylvania, Michigan, and Wisconsin. Trump won those usually reliable Democratic states by a total of less than 80,000 votes—11,000 in Michigan, 44,000 in Pennsylvania, and 23,000 in Wisconsin.[45] There were many reasons Trump won. African Americans voted for Clinton and Obama at comparable rates, but African American turnout dropped by about 5 points nationally and by 12 points in Michigan, Pennsylvania, and Wisconsin. Gender also played a role. Clinton won the women's vote by 12 points, but that was the same margin women gave Obama. Weaker solidarity among women than among Blacks meant she didn't get the boost she needed. At the same time, men bailed in droves; Trump carried men by a 12-point margin, significantly greater than Romney's seven-point margin in 2012.[46]

But perhaps the greatest factors were race and education. Trump's victory over Clinton among White voters was four points greater than Romney's spread over Obama. Among White voters, education told the tale. Clinton did 10 points better than Obama among college-educated Whites, but 14 points worse among those without a college degree. Because only about half as many whites have college degrees as do not, the shift was devastating.[47] In a campaign in which the candidates had emphasized race and immigration, noncollege-educated Whites opted for the candidate whom they believed would defend them against Blacks who were getting ahead and immigrants who were taking jobs from them, depressing wages, and threatening their culture. Trump not only promised to give Whites their country back, his use of openly racist and sexist language made him even more attractive to the base. He was tweaking the coastal liberals who looked down on the likes of them.

---

45 Ibid., 216.
46 Ibid., 225–34.
47 Ibid., 227–28.

It was a sentiment that would keep Trump's base loyal; attacks on him became attacks on members of his base.

Trump's victory was a shock. It excited some, like Former Klan leader and avowed White supremacist David Duke who celebrated with tweet: "It's time to TAKE AMERICA BACK." It appalled others like the editorial board of the *New York Times*. "President Donald Trump," the editors wrote the day after the election. "Three words that were unthinkable to tens of millions of Americans—and much of the rest of the world—have now become the future of the United States."[48] Trump's improbable victory was rooted in developments in American politics and society that stretched back over 50 years. Republicans had played the race card since Barry Goldwater's 1964 campaign, gradually bringing the White South into the fold and peeling off many northern working-class Whites from their traditional home in the Democratic Party. Democrats had unwittingly helped them by championing free trade agreements that workers believed cost the country jobs. Republicans had also used issues like abortion, gender, "family values," and homosexuality to reel in White evangelicals. Republicans' longstanding country club image changed dramatically as did the rhetoric and priorities of its leaders. As political debate became aligned with highly charged issues such as race, gender, region, and religion, partisan fights became more bitter and compromise more difficult. To make matters worse, elections became more competitive and control of the presidency and Congress shifted frequently. With control hotly contested and the issues dividing the parties grounded in identity and values, bipartisanship became more difficult, fights nastier, and governing more difficult. With victory in reach but precarious, party leaders made their peace with whatever and whomever brought victory, even if it meant highlighting Willie Horton, embracing Newt Gingrich, or supporting a Sarah Palin or Donald Trump.

Most observers were certain that the partisan warfare that had flared in the 1990s couldn't become worse, but they were wrong. By the early twenty-first century, liberal Republicans were long extinct and Republican moderates were endangered. Liberals gained a tighter grip on the Democratic Party, although it continued to be home to a group of moderates who exercised real influence because the party couldn't spare them. So, the views of people like Joe Manchin of West Virginia, Michael Bennett of Colorado, or Maggie Hassan of New Hampshire mattered and tempered Democratic priorities.

---

48 *New York Times*, November 9, 2016 https://www.nytimes.com/2016/11/09/opinion/donald-trumps-revolt.html?searchResultPosition=1 (accessed December 3, 2022).

Both parties became more geographically, culturally, and ideologically homogeneous, as Democrats gained a lock on the coasts, with some outposts in the industrial Midwest and Mountain West. The South, Mountain West, and most of the Midwest and Great Plains were reliably Republican. With such sharply defined divisions, scorn and even hatred for the enemy came naturally. For many Democrats, Republicans were fundamentalist, bigoted, ignorant, gun-toting rubes while Republicans dismissed Democrats as over-educated elitists who supported intrusive government, open borders, abortion, gay marriage, feminism, and special privileges for minorities. With wages stagnant, working- and middle-class people struggling, and urban professionals, bankers, investors, and corporate leaders claiming an ever-larger share of the nation's wealth, conservatives were able to turn resentment into anger at a party that had become identified with coastal elites, free trade, and deregulation.

The Tea Party insurgency of 2009–2010 fed the anger and produced an even more uncompromising crop of Republican representatives and senators. By taking more extreme positions, they received more media attention, raised more money, and were more likely to gain support for a presidential bid. They were also far less likely to face a primary challenge. Sarah Palin and Ted Cruz were proof that Republican voters no longer looked for leadership to sober, experienced politicians who had deep knowledge of the issues and chose their words carefully. Establishment Republicans like Mitch McConnell, John Boehner, and Paul Ryan found their antics repulsive but tolerated them as the price of victory.

With the advent of the Internet, social media, talk radio, and cable news, journalism had become democratized. Anyone with a website or a social media presence could be a journalist and disseminate news and analysis to the masses. Traditional journalistic standards, respect for facts, and fact-checking were optional, fueling distortion, lies, and conspiracy theories. More Americans got their information from sources—whether newspapers, magazines, Internet sites, radio and television, or social media—that agreed with them and reinforced their prejudices. That made it easier for the most polarizing candidates and outrageous conspiracy theories to get traction. After all, they had the imprimatur of a trusted source—not the politically correct mainstream media controlled by the elite—and they confirmed the worst about the low-down people in the other party they hated. It was a toxic mix that produced conflict rather than compromise, over-simplified complex issues, pandered to fear and loathing, and made governing nearly impossible. That made many voters tune out or conclude that politicians were only interested in power, not solving their problems. It also offered a perfect opening for a demagogue who would stir the pot rather than calm the waters or appeal to Americans' better angels. Donald Trump—the con man who had entertained Americans on TV, sold them steaks and bottled water at inflated prices, lured them to enroll in Trump University, perpetuated the birther lie, and helped send five innocent Black men to prison for decades—exploited an opportunity that had been years in the making. Now there would be a reckoning, and few Americans could imagine how close it would come to destroying the republic.

CHAPTER 11

# AMERICAN CARNAGE, 2016–2020

### The Resistance Emerges

As election night melted into the wee hours of November 8, many Americans struggled to understand what had happened while others began to think about ways to blunt an existential threat. Their goal was not to overturn the election but to show that a majority of Americans considered Trump's views and behavior not just wrong but un-American. After all, he had lost the popular vote by almost two points, there was growing evidence that the Russians had assisted him, and the FBI had put its thumb on the scale with its public comments on Clinton's emails. While Trump won the election, it was imperative that people of good will challenge what he represented, fight his harmful policies, and begin to build a coalition to ensure that he was a one-term president.

The resistance that quickly emerged was organic and massive, ensuring that the partisan fever gripping the country would increase. Women, offended by Trump's outrageous, in-your-face misogyny took the lead. In Hawaii, Theresa Shook, a retired attorney and grandmother who said she "wasn't that political,"[1] left a post on the pro-Clinton "Pant Suit Nation" Facebook page on election night. It suggested that women should march. By the time she woke up the next morning, over 10,000 people responded they would join her. After others made similar posts that also attracted interest from thousands, three women with deep experience in movement organizing stepped in to plan a march in Washington on the Saturday after Trump's inauguration. Carmen Perez,

---

1 *Washington Post*, January 31, 2017 https://www.washingtonpost.com/news/local/wp/2017/01/31/the-woman-who-started-the-womens-march-with-a-facebook-post-reflects-it-was-mind-boggling/#:~:text=The%20woman%20who%20started%20the%20Women%E2%80%99s%20March%20with,21.%20%28Oliver%20Contreras%20for%20The%20Washington%20Post%29%20Article (accessed December 13, 2022).

Linda Sarsour, and Tamika Mallory would work feverishly to gain the necessary permits, recruit speakers, plan activities, and publicize the event.

On January 21, 2017, perhaps a half million women descended on Washington, DC, to express their undying opposition to Trump and what he represented. Many wore pink "pussy" knit caps, a reference to Trump's misogynist comments on the *Access Hollywood* tape. They heard from Gloria Steinem, a founder of second wave feminism; Angela Davis, the activist philosophy professor and former Black Panther; a-list actor Scarlett Johansson; pop singer Janelle Monae; Randi Weingarten, the labor organizer; and Democratic Senator Kamala Harris, among others. The March's demands were as broad as its attendance large. Speakers called for equal pay, immigrant rights, reproductive freedom, an end to mass incarceration and police violence against people of color, transgender rights, and more. Turnout was not only massive, but a diverse group of women exuded unity and a sense of common purpose. Protest extended beyond Washington. There were over 600 marches across the U.S., not to mention many in cities around the globe. Those with expertise in estimating crowd size calculated that between 3.2 and 5.2 million Americans participated, making it the largest day of protest in U.S. history.

Although the Women's March received the most attention, another, equally important part of the resistance quickly emerged. In late November, three Democratic House staff members developed a 26-page handbook that drew on Tea Party tactics to offer a guide for grassroots activists to express their opposition to Trump's policies. After edits and suggestions from over 20 of their colleagues on Capitol Hill, they posted it on the Internet as the "Indivisible Guide." Noting that Trump was a minority president, it boldly asserted that "if a small minority in the Tea Party could stop President Obama, then we the majority can stop a petty tyrant named Trump."[2] When the group formed a nonprofit known as Indivisible in January, 225,000 individuals registered on its website. By early February 2017, 6,200 local organizations had been formed. Only about 40% used the name Indivisible, and the issues they focused on ranged from protecting the ACA and challenging Trump's Muslim ban to demanding criminal justice reform. But all mobilized people in their communities to challenge congressional Republicans when they returned to their districts. With the President's Day holiday in February, the confrontations began. They continued to grow

---

[2] Elena Schor and Rachael Bade, "Inside the protest movement that has Republicans reeling," *Politico*, February 10, 2017 https://www.politico.com/story/2017/02/protest-movement-republicans-234863 (accessed December 13, 2022).

in the following months and years, turning up the heat on Republicans and letting them know Trump's agenda wasn't popular with voters.

The battle was on. Democrats and progressives signaled that they found Trump's agenda illegitimate, and some asserted that Trump himself lacked legitimacy. "I don't see this President-elect as a legitimate president," civil rights icon and congressman John Lewis told NBC. "I think the Russians participated in helping this man get elected. And they helped destroy the candidacy of Hillary Clinton."[3] Lewis and more than 50 other Democratic House members boycotted Trump's inauguration. In May, three months after the inauguration, a Harris Poll found that 65% of Democrats didn't believe Trump had won fairly and was a legitimate president.[4] Partisan fever, already near the breaking point, rose another couple of degrees, and many feared for the patient's survival.

## Anger, Grievance, Payback, and Chaos

If anyone believed that the emerging resistance would prompt Trump to recalibrate, he provided a wake-up call on day one of his presidency. His inaugural address was dark, painting the picture of a nation that was on the cusp of collapse. In Trump's telling, political insiders had advanced their own interests at the expense of the people. Bad trade agreements had benefitted other countries, factories and jobs had vanished, roads and bridges had crumbled, schools failed, and the nation's borders had become porous, leaving it awash in illegal immigrants. America, he warned, had become a land where "mothers and children [were] trapped in poverty in our inner cities; rusted-out factories [were] scattered like tombstones across the landscape of our nation […] and […] crime and gangs and drugs […] have stolen too many lives." The problems were overwhelming, but he would fix them. "This American carnage stops right here and stops right now," he asserted, promising to "make America great again."[5]

---

3 Theodore Schleifer, "John Lewis: Trump is not a 'legitimate' president," CNN, January 14, 2017 https://www.cnn.com/2017/01/13/politics/john-lewis-donald-trump-legitimate/index.html (accessed December 13, 2022).

4 Jonathan Easley, "Poll: Dems don't accept Trump as legitimate president," The Hill, May 24, 2017 https://thehill.com/homenews/administration/334972-poll-dems-dont-accept-trump-as-legitimate-president/ (accessed January 31, 2023).

5 "Remarks of President Donald J. Trump – As Prepared for Delivery. Inaugural Address," January 20, 2017 https://trumpwhitehouse.archives.gov/briefings-statements/the-inaugural-address/ (accessed December 7. 2022).

This mix of ego, bombast, grievance, impulsiveness, exaggeration, falsehoods, and grandiosity would be themes in Trump's new reality show, and Americans could tune in every day. Day two of his presidency offered a preview. Trump became upset when the media estimated that the crowd on the National Mall was only about one-third the size of Obama's first inauguration. Stories were illustrated with side-by-side aerial photographs comparing the crowds in 2017 and 2009. Trump became enraged, suggesting that the photos had been altered to deny him credit for a record-setting turnout. Rather than getting the facts or letting a matter of no consequence go, he ordered his press secretary Sean Spicer to hold an impromptu Saturday press conference. Spicer insisted—without evidence—that his boss was right: "This was the largest audience ever to witness an inauguration, both in person and around the globe." What a way for a new press secretary to begin his relationship with reporters—challenging the media on its veracity in reporting a matter of little consequence. On display was Trump's pettiness, hostility to the media, and disregard for facts and truth. "The Trump administration is creating a baseline expectation among its loyalists that they can't trust anything said by the media," *Vox's* Ezra Klein presciently observed.[6]

Trump's worst qualities surfaced again as he became consumed by the investigation of Russia's effort to defeat Hillary Clinton. It began during the campaign, after the FBI verified that Russia was seeking to influence the election in Trump's favor by spreading disinformation on social media and disseminating emails it obtained by hacking Democratic National Committee servers. Concern grew as intelligence revealed contacts between Trump campaign officials and Russian agents. The Bureau expanded its investigation and conducted court-ordered wiretaps of campaign operatives who had contacts with Russian agents. Several weeks before Trump's inauguration, the FBI and CIA directors briefed the President-elect. After the meeting, FBI director James Comey told Trump privately that there was a dossier circulating that had been assembled by a British spy who did opposition research for the Clinton campaign. It contained allegations that the Russians possessed highly compromising information about orgies with prostitutes when he visited Moscow. Trump wasn't under investigation and the dossier was suspect, but Comey thought he should know.

---

6 Ezra Klein, "Trump's real war isn't with the media. It's with the facts," *Vox*, January 21, 2017 https://www.vox.com/policy-and-politics/2017/1/21/14347952/trump-spicer-press-conference-crowd-size-inauguration (accessed December 7, 2022).

Trump was furious, but the story wouldn't go away. In early February, Michael Flynn, a retired general and early supporter whom Trump named his national security advisor, lied to FBI agents about contacts with the Russian ambassador and was forced to resign. His resignation embarrassed the administration and fed speculation about the campaign's ties to Russia. Trump believed that Democrats and the media were trying to keep the story alive to discredit his victory, and he suspected that Comey was using the investigation to get the upper hand. In private meetings with Comey in mid-February, he told the director he needed "loyalty" and, referring to the Flynn case, asked him to "let this go."[7] Comey demurred, deepening Trump's anger.

At the beginning of March, the plot thickened. The *Washington Post* reported that Jeff Sessions, Trump's attorney general, had conversations with the Russian ambassador after the election and had failed to disclose them during his confirmation hearings. The report not only fed speculation about the campaign's relationship with Russia, but prompted Sessions to recuse himself from the FBI investigation, placing Deputy Attorney General Rod Rosenstein in charge. Trump was furious with Sessions, whom he would publicly berate until he removed him in late 2018. Because the compromising information about Sessions and Flynn came from wiretaps, Trump soon lashed out at Obama, tweeting, erroneously, that he "had my 'wires tapped' in Trump Tower just before the victory" and "This is Nixon/Watergate."[8] In early May, he summarily fired Comey, justifying his action by reference to a memo Rosenstein prepared suggesting that Comey's investigation of Hillary Clinton's emails had damaged the Bureau's credibility. Comey's action had violated Bureau practice and damaged Clinton, not to mention the Bureau's reputation. But no one believed that was why Trump fired the director, and he only fanned suspicion when he told the Russian ambassador and foreign minister—of all people—that firing Comey had relieved "great pressure." He upped the ante when he told NBC's Lester Holt in a televised interview, "when I decided to do it, I said to myself […] You know, this Russia thing with Trump and Russia is a made-up story, it's an excuse by the Democrats for

---

7 Maggie Haberman, *Con Man: Donald Trump and the Breaking of America* (New York, 2022), 284.
8 Elliot Smilowitz, "Trump accuses Obama of wire-tapping Trump Tower," *The Hill*, March 4, 2017 https://thehill.com/homenews/administration/322337-trump-accuses-obama-of-wiretapping-trump-tower/ (accessed January 31, 2017).

having lost an election."⁹ It appeared that Trump all but admitted to dismissing Comey to get him off the case.

As a number of aides had warned, firing Comey made matters worse for Trump. Comey had documented his interactions with Trump in detailed notes he kept in his files. Soon after he was fired, the *New York Times* published a story revealing that they showed that Trump had pressured Comey to back off the Flynn investigation. Given Rosenstein's involvement in Comey's firing, he now recused himself and appointed a special counsel to investigate whether there was a conspiracy between the Trump campaign and Russia and whether Trump had attempted to obstruct justice by firing Comey. The man he appointed, Robert Mueller, was a former FBI director with a reputation as a highly disciplined, smart, dogged, by-the-book investigator. For the next two years, Mueller would be a thorn in Trump's side, conducting a thorough, leak-free investigation that resulted in indictments of members of Trump's campaign staff as well as Russian diplomatic and intelligence officials. At its conclusion in March 2019, Mueller reported that he uncovered meetings between campaign officials and Russian agents but no evidence of a conspiracy. Because Department of Justice policy barred indictment of a sitting president, Mueller wouldn't comment on whether Trump should be charged with obstructing justice. But neither did he clear him. "While this report does not conclude that the President committed a crime," it said, "it also does not exonerate him."¹⁰ The investigation kept speculation about Trump's ties to Russia in the news for two years, distracting him and fueling his anger at Democrats, the media, and bureaucrats who followed the rules rather than showing him loyalty.

It wasn't only the Russia investigation that caused Trump to lash out at his enemies. Late in the summer of 2017, he became consumed with fallout from tragic events in Charlottesville, Virginia. Debates over race and racism continued to grow in the wake of ongoing protests against police brutality, a vibrant Black Lives Matter movement, and Trump's blatant racism. Monuments to the Confederacy and Confederate heroes that dotted southern towns and cities became part of the conversation. Progressives argued that they glorified a cause devoted to the preservation of slavery and White Supremacy and should come down. Many Whites vehemently disagreed. In Charlottesville,

---

9 Haberman, *Con Man*, 288.
10 Rosalind S. Helderman and Matt Zapotosky, ed., *The Mueller Report. Presented with Related Materials by the Washington Post* (New York, 2019), 12.

home to Mr. Jefferson's university, debate raged over an equestrian statue of Robert E. Lee in Lee Park. In early 2017, the city council voted to remove the statue and rename the park Emancipation Park. Opponents sued the city, making the statue's status an unresolved point of controversy.

It was the perfect rallying point for White supremacists and neo-Nazis who scheduled demonstrations in Charlottesville in mid-August to demand the statue's preservation as an artifact of White history and identity. The night before the demonstration as many as 250 White supremacists, some wearing armbands with swastikas, marched through the University's campus carrying torches and chanting "You will not replace us" and "Jews will not replace us."[11] The next day, as the White supremacists gathered in the park, they were confronted by counterprotesters from groups such as Black Lives Matter, Democratic Socialists of America, and antifa (a loose network of people from organizations committed to direct—often physical—confrontation with fascists and White supremacists). Fighting erupted, overwhelming local and state law enforcement officials. Virginia's governor declared a state of emergency, and police moved to disperse the mobs. During the battle, over 30 demonstrators were injured and one killed. The fatality and 19 of the most serious injuries occurred when a 19-year-old White supremacist from Ohio rammed his car into a group of counter-protesters.

The mayhem in Charlottesville attracted intensive media coverage. Asked by the media to comment, Trump had a chance to bring a divided nation together. Instead, he stoked discord. He refused to condemn White supremacists. "We condemn in the strongest possible terms this egregious display of hatred, bigotry and violence, on many sides," he commented. And then, as if to emphasize that he wasn't singling out White supremacists, he repeated, "On many sides."[12] Even Republicans were aghast. "Mr. President—we must call evil by its name," tweeted Colorado Senator Cory Gardner.[13]

Many believed that Trump wouldn't backtrack because he feared alienating his base. Two days later, he was in New York to announce policies designed to facilitate the infrastructure initiative he had promised during the campaign.

---

11 *New York Times*, August 12, 2017 https://www.nytimes.com/2017/08/12/us/charlottesville-protest-white-nationalist.html (accessed December 8, 2022).

12 Chris Cillizza, "Donald Trump's incredibly unpresidential statement on Charlottesville," CNN, August 12, 2017 https://www.cnn.com/2017/08/12/politics/trump-charlottesville-statement/index.html (accessed December 8, 2022).

13 *New York Times*, August 12, 2017 https://www.nytimes.com/2017/08/12/us/trump-charlottesville-protest-nationalist-riot.html (accessed December 8, 2022).

But reporters had Charlottesville on their minds and began peppering him with questions immediately after his remarks. Trump doubled down. He claimed that many of the protesters came to protect southern heritage, and then he tried to shift attention to counterprotesters, charging that they were just as culpable as the White supremacists. Asked if he was creating a moral equivalence between racists and those who stood up to bigotry, he lost it. "Yes, I think there is blame on both sides," he insisted. Pressed further, he admitted that there were "some very bad people" among the demonstrators, but insisted "you also had people that were fine people on both sides."[14] The criticism was deafening, but Trump dug in. He lashed out at his Republican critics, including Senator Lindsey Graham. Graham was just seeking publicity and still angry he had been humiliated in the Republican primaries, Trump tweeted, adding, "The people of South Carolina will remember."[15] The message was a not-too-subtle reminder that if Graham didn't fall in line, he could expect a primary challenge.

The chaos Trump spread may have signaled to the base that he was with them, but it got in the way of business. Combined with his ignorance of how policy was made and his unwillingness to do the hard work necessary to develop coherent policies and win support for them, the chaos ensured that he would accomplish little. Infrastructure was the perfect example. Huge investments were essential, Trump argued during the campaign, to rebuild roads and bridges and create good jobs. He proposed a $1 trillion investment, double what Hillary Clinton supported. He was a builder, and in case anyone had forgotten, he was the world's most successful deal-maker—the author of *The Art of the Deal*. He would easily negotiate a bipartisan agreement between Republicans, traditionally reticent about spending, and Democrats who saw infrastructure as a critical investment. Trump's position was politically popular, with 69% of voters polled during the campaign saying that it was "very important."[16] Investing in infrastructure was a winner politically, one that promised to garner Democratic support and make Trump appear bipartisan rather than divisive.

---

14 "Full Transcript and Video: Trump's News Conference in New York," *New York Times*, August 15, 2017 https://www.nytimes.com/2017/08/15/us/politics/trump-press-conference-transcript.html (accessed December 8, 2022).

15 *New York Times*, August 17, 2017 https://www.nytimes.com/2017/08/17/us/politics/trump-charlottesville-confederate-statues.html (accessed December 8, 2022).

16 Jason Scott Smith, "The Rhetoric and Reality of Infrastructure during the Trump Presidency," in Julian Zelizer, ed., *The Presidency of Donald Trump: The First Historical Assessment* (Princeton, NJ, 2022), 164.

To build support for his infrastructure initiative, the administration periodically declared "Infrastructure Week." The goal was to use press conferences, announcements, and visits to crumbling bridges and roads to call attention to the need, highlight steps being taken to meet it, and generate support from the public and legislators. However, almost without fail, "Infrastructure Week" was eclipsed by a scandal or a fight between Trump and his enemies. In June 2017, Trump highjacked a Rose Garden event designed to tout infrastructure with a diatribe against James Comey whom he had recently fired and who was now accusing the President of having pressured him to back off the Russia investigation. Two months later, a press conference to unveil new policies to facilitate construction projects was overtaken by Trump's heated exchange with the press about Charlottesville. In early 2018, Trump announced a $1.5 trillion infrastructure plan in his State of the Union Address. Democrats and Republicans alike expressed skepticism about the details, and the plan fell off the radar as allegations that a member of Trump's staff had physically abused two former spouses and Trump's private attorney had paid a porn star $130,000 to keep mum about an affair with Trump.

Infrastructure was one campaign promise among many. Curbing immigration was Trump's signature issue, and banning Muslims from entering the country was one of his most controversial campaign promises. Because he believed a ban could be accomplished by executive order, he moved quickly, signaling to his base that he meant business. During his first week in office, he ordered a temporary ban on travel to the U.S. by citizens of seven predominantly Muslim countries. Implemented without warning, it created chaos at U.S. airports as hundreds of travelers from the targeted countries who departed before it took effect were detained upon arrival. The order also swept broadly, barring individuals who were permanent residents, held U.S. visas, or were relatives of U.S. citizens. Federal courts quickly blocked the order because it denied those who had green cards or active visas due process. The administration went back to the drawing board, issuing a new order in March that took Iraq off the list and excluded individuals who had valid documentation. But the courts enjoined enforcement again, finding it a potential violation of the First Amendment's establishment clause, which prohibited government from favoring (or disfavoring) any religion. The U.S. Court of Appeals for the Fourth Circuit chided the government for an order that "speaks with vague words of national security. But in context drips with religious intolerance, animus and discrimination."[17]

---

17 *New York Times*, May 25, 2017 https://www.nytimes.com/2017/05/25/us/politics/trump-travel-ban-blocked.html (accessed December 9, 2022).

Although the Supreme Court allowed most of the order to take effect pending a full hearing, the Trump team went back to the drawing board and developed yet another order—travel ban 3.0, if you will. It outlined a process and established non-religious criteria to identify countries to be covered, creating at least the appearance of neutral standards. The criteria included levels of terrorism in the country, policies and technical capabilities for screening travelers, and willingness to change practices to meet U.S. concerns. Based on these considerations, citizens of six Muslim countries and North Korea were banned from entry unless they held green cards or visas. A small group of government officials from Venezuela, a U.S. adversary, were also banned. Based on local circumstances, the order also established a different set of restrictions for each country covered. Critics charged that the order was neutral on its face but nevertheless targeted nations on the basis of religion and was therefore a violation of the First Amendment. Trump, they argued, had clearly telegraphed his true motives on the campaign trail. Nevertheless, in June 2018, the Supreme Court upheld the order, ending the administration's 16-month quest to fulfill a signature campaign promise. With Neil Gorsuch, a Trump appointee providing the fifth vote, the Court ruled 5–4 that the Constitution and federal law gave the President authority to bar groups from entering the country to protect the nation's security. The process developed by the administration relied on neutral criteria related to improving security, the majority concluded, and the Court could not use inferences drawn from statements the President made during the campaign to conclude that he intended to discriminate. Trump's base knew better and celebrated the victory.

The episode revealed a lot about the dynamics of conflict during the Trump presidency. Trump's base might have concluded that the protracted effort to implement a ban was evidence of ineptitude. Instead, it believed Trump was battling against the political and legal establishment to fulfill a campaign promise to them. Procedural errors in executive orders? Those were simply legal technicalities that liberal groups like the ACLU manipulated to protect people who were a threat to the homeland. So, the more Trump failed, attacked those blocking his effort, and fought on, the happier his base was with him.

Building a border wall—that Mexico would pay for—was another signature pledge that suffered from poor execution, even as Trump's faltering efforts to build it won plaudits from his supporters. Democrats ridiculed the idea as an ineffective, expensive waste of money that diverted attention from comprehensive immigration reform and systematic border protection. Trump achieved a modest breakthrough in March 2018, when Congress passed an appropriations bill that included a modest down payment of $1.6 billion.

When Senate Democrats blocked $5.6 billion in funding he requested for the wall in the 2019 budget, he vetoed it, precipitating a government shutdown that lasted 35 days.

Trump got $1.4 billion in the agreement that ended the shutdown, but he didn't get Mexico to pay for the wall, as he had boasted. Ultimately, however, he secured $15 billion for the project by declaring a national emergency at the border as a pretext to reallocate funds from the Defense Department. By the time Trump left office, the government had built 450 miles of new wall, with about 200 miles under construction. Between 18 and 30 feet high, constructed of steel, anchored in a concrete base six feet deep, it was a formidable structure. Trump wanted to make it even more forbidding by painting it black so that it would absorb heat and burn the hands of anyone trying to scale it. He also wanted to build a moat filled with alligators and snakes and authorize guards to shoot trespassers in the legs. While the moat proved too expensive (not to mention impractical) and shooting migrants was illegal, Trump got the paint job. He could have achieved greater border security through bipartisan negotiation, Andrew Selee, president of the nonpartisan Migration Policy Institute concluded as Trump left office. "But that was never the purpose," he added. "This was always about a larger symbolism about walling off America from outside dangers."[18]

Like his battles to win funding for the wall, Trump's zero-tolerance approach to those entering the country illegally suffered from poor planning but pleased the base. He was much more aggressive than his predecessors with the 11 million undocumented immigrants already in the U.S. There were far too many for Immigration and Customs Enforcement (ICE) officials to arrest, process, and deport. Besides most had lived in the U.S. for many years, held jobs, had children, and were members of churches and communities. Obama had dealt with these realities by focusing limited enforcement resources on the border and undocumented immigrants who engaged in criminal activity. Under Trump, ICE took a different approach, launching indiscriminate raids at workplaces, on buses, at schools, wherever the undocumented could be found. The number of arrests, which increased from about 65,000 in 2016 to 95,000 in 2018, made only a small dent in the number of those residing in the U.S. illegally. But they took a psychological toll on millions who had established roots

---

18 Sabrina Rodriguez, "Trump's partially built 'big, beautiful wall,'" *CNN*, January 21, 2021 https://www.politico.com/news/2021/01/12/trump-border-wall-partially-built-458255 (accessed December 8, 2022).

in the U.S. and now feared that agents might show up when they were picking a child up at school.

In 2018, as the mid-term elections approached, Trump created the illusion of crisis at the southern border to justify even more aggressive action. Immigration from Mexico had slowed but the number entering from Central America was growing. Most came as families with children fleeing gang violence and political repression, and they sought asylum in the U.S. Trump exaggerated the numbers and the threat, calling it a caravan and claiming that many were gang members and drug traffickers. To stem the tide, in April 2018, the Justice Department announced a zero-tolerance policy. All adults apprehended at the border would be detained and separated from their children, who would be treated as unaccompanied minors and placed in facilities operated by the Department of Health and Human Service's Office of Refugee Resettlement. "If you don't like that, then don't smuggle children over our border," Attorney General Jeff Sessions warned.[19]

Shocking images of crying children in holding areas that looked like cages dominated the news. However they felt about immigration, most Americans were appalled by the squalid detention facilities, and even some congressional Republicans took exception. Senator Orrin Hatch of Utah said the policy was "not American." His colleague Rob Portman of Ohio added, "This is counter to our values."[20] Numbers quickly outstripped space in the detention facilities and apparently no one on Trump's team had considered the optics. The American Civil Liberties Union (ACLU) quickly filed suit and in late June a federal judge issued an injunction. Because the government separated parents and children without affording due process, he also ordered families reunited. The blowback was so intense that Trump rescinded the order days before the judge's ruling. However, the policy had been so poorly designed and implemented that many parents' whereabouts were unknown and some had been deported, making reunification impossible. By the time Trump left office, over 600 children had not been reunited with their families.

Because it had been established by Obama and offered some stability and security to undocumented immigrants who came as children, the Deferred

---

19 Pete Williams, "Sessions: Parents, children entering the U.S. illegally will be separated," *NBC News*, May 7, 2018 https://www.nbcnews.com/politics/justice-department/sessions-parents-children-entering-us-illegally-will-be-separated-n872081 (accessed December 9, 2022).

20 *New York Times*, June 19, 2018 https://www.nytimes.com/2018/06/19/us/politics/trump-immigration-children-separated-families.html (accessed December 10, 2022).

Action for Childhood Arrivals program (DACA) became a target. Even many who opposed creating a path to citizenship for those who had entered the U.S. illegally viewed the program sympathetically. Its beneficiaries had been brought to the U.S. by their families, many as very young children, and the countries they had come from were as alien to them as they were to most Americans. DACA was never the target of Trump's fury. In fact, he teased Democrats with his willingness to write DACA and a path to citizenship for DREAMERs into law in exchange for additional resources for border enforcement, including the wall. Although there was significant support for a deal among Senate Republicans, Trump repeatedly backed away when hard-line conservatives in Congress and the media blasted him for supporting amnesty.

In September 2017, Trump's Acting Secretary of Homeland Security issued an order winding down DACA. Given the administration's random arrest and deportation of undocumented people who had lived in the U.S. for years and not run afoul of the law, the order created panic among DREAMERs and their supporters. Fortunately for them, the administration's campaign against DACA fell victim to sloppiness, poor planning, and amateur execution. Shortly after Homeland Security issued its order, groups brought lawsuits and won injunctions that required the department to renew grants of deferred enforcement to anyone already enrolled in the program. The department challenged the decisions but couldn't persuade a very conservative Supreme Court to support them. The Court held that the Administrative Procedure Act required the executive branch to offer reasoned justification for its orders; even when they were within the scope of presidential authority, they couldn't be arbitrary. The acting secretary's order failed to offer thorough consideration of the issues, an exploration of alternatives, and a compelling rationale, raising "doubts about whether the agency appreciated the scope of its discretion or exercised that discretion in a reasonable fashion."[21]

Even something as important to Trump and the Republicans as repealing the Affordable Care Act (ACA) fell victim to incompetence. Republicans had opposed the ACA, repeatedly attempted to repeal it, and in 2013, had shut down the government and taken the country to the brink of default to kill it. All to no avail. Now Republicans controlled all three branches of government, and they could kill Obama's signature accomplishment if they were united. As a candidate, Trump had promised to repeal the ACA and replace it with

---

21 *Department of Homeland Security v. Regents of the University of California*, 591 U.S. \_\_\_ (2020) https://supreme.justia.com/cases/federal/us/591/18-587/ (accessed December 10, 2022).

something better. As he told a *60 Minutes* interviewer, "everybody's got to be covered [...]. Everybody's going to be taken care of much better than they're taken care of now."[22] He had no clue how because he didn't understand healthcare policy, wouldn't learn, and hadn't thought about much less developed a plan to deliver better care to everyone for less money. Congressional Republicans were united on repeal, but were sharply divided on whether to replace the ACA and, if so, what a new policy would look like. Tom Price, a physician and Republican congressman from Georgia who would become Trump's Secretary of Health and Human Services had developed a plan. But it needed to be fleshed out to address thousands of details that would determine whether it would win support from stakeholders, the public, and Republican lawmakers. That hadn't happened, so Republicans entered the fray sharply divided, without a united approach. "There was an intellectual simplicity or an intellectual laziness that for Republicans passed for policy development," recalled a Senate Republican staff member. "I think that bit us in the ass when it came to repeal and replace."[23]

Paul Ryan, the speaker of the House, took the lead on repeal. Ryan was a policy wonk and devotee of Ayn Rand, the writer and philosopher who believed selfishness was a virtue because it encouraged individual achievement that elevated the entire society. It was an updated, philosophically more sophisticated version of Social Darwinism. In Ryan's view, the ACA, like most Democratic social and economic policy, was immoral because it took from the haves in the form of taxes to subsidize health care for those who couldn't afford it. He was perfectly happy to repeal without replacing, but if Republicans had to replace the ACA with a plan of their own, he wanted to pare down support for subsidies and reduce the number of people covered by Medicaid. That would help reduce federal spending and open the way for a large tax cut that provided the greatest benefits to the wealthy. That, in Ryan's view, was ethical because it let those who were most successful keep more of the wealth they had earned.

Unfortunately for Ryan, it wasn't that simple. His president wanted to replace the ACA with something better, although he hadn't a clue what. And many congressional Republicans agreed with him, especially as they began to hear from constituents who were worried about losing critical, often life-saving

---

22 Jonathan Cohen, *The Ten Year War: Obamacare and the Crusade for Universal Coverage* (New York, 2021), 285.

23 Cohen, *Ten Year War*, 282.

benefits the ACA afforded. Indeed, in 2017, as Congress debated repeal and replace, Republicans faced hostile audiences at town hall meetings in their districts, giving them a taste of what Democrats experienced at the hands of the Tea Party in 2009. Public hostility was fed by grassroots activists who were part of Indivisible and by Democratic leaders, including Obama, who went to work explaining the dire consequences of repeal. That upped the ante. The focus was no longer on the ACA's shortcomings but whether the Republican replacement plan was as good. Republicans struggled to make the case because their bill cut subsidies, permitted insurance companies greater freedom to determine the price and extent of coverage their plans offered, reduced the number of Medicaid beneficiaries, protected only those who maintained continuous coverage from being rejected by insurers, and allowed insurers to move those with preexisting conditions into high-risk pools where coverage was more expensive and benefits were limited.

As the bill's provisions emerged, Republicans' problems mounted and then got worse when the bill went to the Congressional Budget Office for evaluation. Much worse. The CBO projected that 24 million Americans would lose coverage under the Republican plan and that older people who could still afford insurance—a bloc of faithful voters who leaned Republican—would pay more while younger people paid less. That's the way the free market worked. The CBO's report stirred more opposition from constituents and also brought sharper critiques from key stakeholders including hospitals, the American Medical Association, and the American Association of Retired Persons. Late-night TV host Jimmy Kimmel raised the stakes even higher. He broke into tears when he told viewers that his newborn son survived only because he had good insurance that paid for expensive heart surgery. "Let's stop with the nonsense," he pleaded. "No parent should ever have to decide whether they can afford to save their child's life. It just shouldn't happen. Not here."[24]

The Republican bill narrowly passed in the House, but it faced an uphill battle in the Senate. Although Mitch McConnell softened some of the rough edges of the House bill, deep cuts to Medicaid remained and shook Republicans senators in states like Arkansas, Ohio, Pennsylvania, West Virginia, and Kentucky where big segments of the population depended on it. Because the bill was a finance measure that could be considered under a process known

---

24 Ed Mazza, "Tearful Jimmy Kimmel Breaks Down Revealing Newborn Son's Heart Surgery," Huff Post, May 2, 2017 https://www.huffpost.com/entry/jimmy-kimmel-baby-heart-surgery_n_59081 1f6e4b05c397681f094 (accessed December 11, 2022).

as budget reconciliation, it needed only 50 votes to pass. Vice President Mike Pence, who doubled as president of the Senate, could cast the deciding 51st vote. Republicans had a 52-seat majority so they could spare just two votes. When McConnell couldn't round up 50 votes, he introduced a version that became known as "skinny repeal." It stripped the ACA of two critical provisions: the individual mandate (requiring those without employer-provided or government health care to purchase insurance) and the employer mandate (requiring employers to provide employees coverage). If it passed, the bill would go to a conference committee that would decide whether there would be a replacement and, if so, what would be in it.

McConnell's sleight-of-hand got some wavering Republicans on board, but not enough. Senator Lisa Murkowski of Alaska was a moderate Republican who had won reelection in 2010 as a write-in candidate after a Tea Party challenger backed by Sarah Palin had defeated her in the Republican primary. McConnell had refused to support Murkowski, and now she turned the tables, indicating she was a no. Maine's Susan Collins, another independent-minded moderate, had more to fear from a Democratic challenger in the general election than a Republican primary opponent, so she also declined to support the bill. Then there was John McCain, the independent-minded Arizona senator whom Trump had repeatedly attacked on Twitter. Returning to the Senate after surgery to remove a brain tumor that was killing him, he flashed a thumbs down in a dramatic midnight vote in late July 2017. The Republicans' long quest to upend the ACA was over. Defeat was another marker of Trump's incompetence and Republicans' unwillingness to do the heavy lifting necessary to develop a constructive alternative.

When repeal was all that was required and legislating wasn't necessary, Republicans did better, although competent execution remained a problem. Trump came to office a climate change denier committed to expanding production of fossil fuels, including the dirtiest of the bunch, coal. "I'm going to put the miners to work," Trump boasted as a candidate. "Get ready because you're going to work your asses off."[25] As president, he appointed climate change deniers to key positions. They moved quickly to weaken environmental regulation through executive orders. On his second day in office, Trump rescinded Obama's order barring construction of the Keystone XL Pipeline,

---

[25] Matt Egan, "Donald Trump could help—but not save—coal country," *CNN Business*, July 12, 2016 https://money.cnn.com/2016/07/11/investing/donald-trump-save-coal/index.html (accessed December 11, 2022).

which would carry tar sands oil from Canada across environmentally sensitive areas of the Great Plains to refineries in Oklahoma and Texas. Of course, it would also strengthen the country's reliance on fossil fuels—in this case, a heavy oil that required enormous energy inputs to refine. Several days later, Trump repealed Obama's Clean Power Plan, a monumental initiative designed to slash carbon emissions from power plants, the major producers of greenhouse gases. In June, he withdrew the U.S. from the Paris Climate Agreement, weakening the international coalition Obama had helped forge to battle a problem that required a global solution.

The administration took aggressive action but once again stumbled in developing orders that could withstand challenge. In November 2018, a federal judge in Montana blocked the construction of Keystone, holding that the administration had failed to comply with the Administrative Procedure Act, which required the administration to provide a reasoned justification for its actions. In this case, the Obama administration had based its decision on exhaustive studies of the project's environmental impact. The judge found that Trump's order asserted that the "climate related impacts" of the pipeline "would prove inconsequential" while ignoring expert findings in the Obama order and offering no supporting evidence to rebut them.[26] The decision to overturn the Clean Power Plan met a similar fate. On Trump's last day in office, the U.S. Court of Appeals for the District of Columbia ruled that the EPA had erred in holding that it was required to replace the plan because it violated the Clean Air Act Amendments of 1990. Not only did the agency misread the statute but its new rules rolled back well-established regulations without providing a compelling justification. It "offered what is at best a radically incomplete explanation," providing "undeveloped reasons of administrative convenience […] even as it ignored the environmental and public health effects" of its substitute.[27]

---

26 *Washington Post*, November 29, 2018 https://www.washingtonpost.com/nation/2018/11/09/keystone-xl-pipeline-blocked-by-federal-judge-major-blow-trump-administration/ (accessed December 11, 2022).

27 *American Lung Association and American Public Health Association v. Environmental Protection Agency, Andrew Wheeler, Administrator*, U.S. Court of Appeals for the District of Columbia, No. 19–1140, January 19, 2021 https://blogs.edf.org/climate411/files/2021/01/2021.01.19-ACE-Opinion.pdf?_gl=1*1fqiwip*_ga*MjA4OTc2NzkwNS4xNjcwNzg2NDA5*_ga_2B3856 Y9QW*MTY3MDc4NjQwOC4xLjAuMTY3MDc4NjQxMS41Ny4wLjA.*_ga_Q5CT TQBJD8*MTY3MDc4NjQwOS4xLjAuMTY3MDc4NjQxMS41OC4wLjA. (accessed December 11, 2022).

The administration's incompetence neutralized some of the environmental mischief it attempted and left an opening for the Biden administration to restore environmentally friendly policies. Biden would put the final nail in the Keystone XL's coffin, begin work to refine the Clean Power Plan, and secure readmission of the U.S. to the Paris Agreement.

After struggling with immigration and failing to harpoon the great white whale—the ACA—Republicans had greater success at what they did best—cutting taxes. They were as united on taxes as they had been divided on health care. Asked the difference between the party's success on taxes and failure on the ACA, Senator John Cornyn of Texas offered that the "single biggest difference" was that his colleagues "wanted to get it [tax cuts] done."[28] Republicans began work on a tax bill in earnest in September 2017, and Trump helped by largely absenting himself from the discussions and avoiding Twitter tantrums. Adopted in December 2017, the final product slashed corporate tax rates from 35% to 21%; reduced individual tax rates modestly, with those in the top bracket receiving the greatest largesse; doubled the size of estates exempt from taxation from $11 million to $22 million; allowed owners of pass-through businesses (sole proprietorships, limited liability corporations, and real estate rental companies) to deduct 20% of their income; and eliminated the ACA's requirement that all individuals not covered by their employer, Medicare, or Medicaid must purchase insurance.

House Speaker Paul Ryan was elated. "This is a day I have been looking forward to for a long time," he told his colleagues after dropping the gavel to proclaim passage by the House. "Today, we are giving the people of this country their money back."[29] Most of that money, of course, would go to the wealthy, and that made Ryan especially happy. In his view, they were the people who drove innovation and growth and made things better for everyone else. He and his colleagues were so pleased, in fact, that they brushed away projections that the bill would add $1 trillion to the deficit over the next decade. Gone were the jeremiads about the dire consequences of deficits once hurled at Obama. Like Reagan and Bush Junior, Republicans used supply-side arguments to reassure critics that cutting tax rates would actually increase tax revenues and soon close the deficit. Bush Senior had once

---

28 *New York Times*, December 19, 2017 https://www.nytimes.com/2017/12/19/us/politics/tax-bill-vote-congress.html (accessed December 12, 2022).
29 *New York Times*, December 19, 2017 https://www.nytimes.com/2017/12/19/us/politics/republican-tax-bill.html (accessed December 12, 2022).

called that "voodoo economics," but the supply-side argument had become part of the Republican script.

## The Tide Turns as the Chaos Grows

Republicans patted themselves on the back for their success. They knew that polls showed the tax cut wasn't popular, but told themselves that would change once the law took effect. But it didn't. As the 2018 mid-terms approached, Democrats crafted a message that focused on Republicans' disregard for the needs of the middle class. Their unsuccessful effort to take away health care was Exhibit A and a tax bill that benefitted the wealthy became Exhibit B. Nancy Pelosi and Chuck Schumer, the Democratic leaders House and Senate, kept their troops in line, fighting against efforts to make Trump's racism, sexism, and war on the environment the issue. They didn't need to do that because Trump put his egotism, nastiness, and impetuosity on display daily in Tweets, public statements, and interactions with the media. Rather than focusing on a booming economy with the lowest jobless rates in recent memory, he railed constantly against the "caravan" of migrants from Central America threatening to overwhelm the southern border. When health care was the top concern of twice as many Americans as immigration, it wasn't a smart move—especially when Trump's immigration policy was equated with family separation, something even a plurality of Republicans disapproved.

Between Democrats staying on message, Trump being Trump, and Republicans unwilling to break with him, the election was a disaster for the GOP.[30] Democrats lost two seats in the Senate because they were defending seats in three states that had gone for Trump in 2016 by double digits. However, they picked up 41 seats in the House to claim a 235–199 majority and make Pelosi speaker once again. Democrats benefitted because 40 Republican incumbents retired, many of them moderates who had run afoul of Trump. While a bumper crop of open seats made Democrats' path to victory a bit easier, it moved House Republicans even further to the right by winnowing the number of moderates in the caucus. The result was to deepen the ideological division between the parties and reduce the number of Republicans who could serve as agents of bipartisan compromise. Democrats also scored big gains among White college-educated women in the suburbs whom Trump had alienated.

---

30 BBC, "U.S. mid-term election results: Maps, charts, and analysis," November 28, 2017 https://www.bbc.com/news/world-us-canada-46076389 (accessed December 12, 2022).

By increasing turnout from an abysmal 38% in 2014 to almost 50% in 2018, Democrats triumphed in many Republican-leaning districts.[31] Turnout among minorities and voters under 30—key Democratic constituencies—increased by four and two points, respectively, compared to 2014.[32] Voters in the suburbs, who had gone for Republicans by 12 points in 2014,[33] divided evenly, while Republicans saw their share of the White evangelical vote fall from 83% to 78%, a big blow from its most loyal constituency.[34]

The election furthered cultural polarization that had been deepening for decades. Republicans strengthened their grip on rural America and White voters without a college degree while Democrats saw gains in metropolitan areas, including the suburbs, and among the college-educated. Their victories extended beyond the coasts to metropolitan areas in states like Georgia, Texas, Oklahoma, Kansas, and Arizona. Between 2016 and 2018, Democrats increased their margin among the 250 counties with the most White female college graduates from 157–93 to 195–55. In counties where 100% of the residents were rural, 580 voted Republican and only 61 Democratic.[35] Democratic inroads in historically Republican communities in red states—Atlanta's suburban Cobb County, for example—threatened to put those states in play in 2020 and beyond. "We've been on a steady trend losing suburbanites, losing college-educated women, and it's time for the Republican Party to adopt a suburban agenda," commented former House whip Eric Cantor.[36] He knew

---

31 BBC, "U.S. mid-term election results: Maps, charts, and analysis," November 28, 2017 https://www.bbc.com/news/world-us-canada-46076389 (accessed December 12, 2022).
32 Gary Langer and Benjamin Siu, "Election 2018 exit poll analysis: Voter turnout soars, Democrats take back the House, ABC projects," ABC News, November 7, 2018 https://abcnews.go.com/Politics/election-2018-exit-poll-analysis-56-percent-country/story?id=59006586.
33 Chris Cillizza, "14 key political trends from the 2018 exit polls," CNN, November 14, 2018 https://edition.cnn.com/2018/11/13/politics/2018-exit-polls/index.html (accessed December 12, 2022).
34 Gary Langer and Benjamin Siu, "Election 2018 exit poll analysis: Voter turnout soars, Democrats take back the House, ABC projects," ABC News, November 7, 2018 https://abcnews.go.com/Politics/election-2018-exit-poll-analysis-56-percent-country/story?id=59006586 (accessed December 12, 2022).
35 "U.S. mid-term election results 2018: Maps, charts, and analysis," BBC News, November 28, 2018 https://www.bbc.com/news/world-us-canada-46076389 (accessed January 31, 2023).
36 *New York Times*, November 7, 2018 https://www.nytimes.com/2018/11/07/us/politics/elections-divided-nation.html (accessed December 12, 2022).

from experience. In 2014, he had lost the primary in his suburban Richmond, Virginia district to a Tea Party bomb-thrower who went on to lose the once-safe Republican seat to a moderate Democrat in 2018.

If anyone wondered how Trump would deal with the new political landscape, he provided a hint at a news conference the morning after the election. It had been "a big day [...] an incredible day," he began, focusing on the two seats Republicans picked up in the Senate while glossing over the tsunami that hit the House. He was uncharacteristically kind to the Democrats and even applauded Nancy Pelosi for her post-election comments "about bipartisanship and getting together and uniting," predicting that we can all work together next year to continue delivering for the American people." Was he turning the page, seeking to tamp down the acrimony, compromise with Democrats, and loosen gridlock? He quickly brought optimists back to reality. Pressed by CNN's Jim Acosta about why he had mischaracterized Central Americans traveling to the southern border as an invasion, Trump lost it. He became testy and when Acosta pivoted to ask him about the Russia investigation, Trump shot back, "That's enough. Put down the mic." When Acosta persisted, Trump went on the attack against the reporter and the media. "CNN should be ashamed of itself having you working for them," he snarled. "You are a rude, terrible person." He continued when NBC's Peter Alexander defended Acosta and asked Trump why he called the media "the enemy of the people." "I'm not a big fan of yours either," he told Alexander. "When you report fake news, which CNN does a lot, you are the enemy of the people."[37]

Hope for even a smidgen of bipartisan cooperation quickly vanished as Trump was quickly at loggerheads with congressional Democrats who assumed control of the House in the midst of a government shutdown triggered by Trump's veto of a budget bill that didn't include money for the wall. Pelosi characterized the veto as "a temper tantrum by the president," adding, "I'm a mother of five, grandmother of nine. I know a temper tantrum when I see one."[38] It was the perfect zinger that struck Trump where it hurt—his manhood. Twelve days later, Pelosi told the President that he couldn't come to the Capitol to deliver the State of the Union Address because the shutdown left too

---

37 "Transcript: Trump's contentious press conference about mid-term elections," *Chicago Sun Times*, November 8, 2018 https://chicago.suntimes.com/2018/11/8/18413257/transcript-trump-s-contentious-press-conference-about-midterm-elections (accessed December 13, 2022).

38 @kylegriffin1 Tweet, January 11, 2019 https://twitter.com/kylegriffin1/status/1083867454260932608 (accessed December 13, 2022).

few staff in place to manage the event. Trump threatened to come anyway but soon relented, agreeing to give the address after the government reopened. But he couldn't resist turning on Chuck Schumer, the Senate minority leader. Schumer, he charged, "is dominated by the radical left, and he's dominated by Nancy Pelosi […] if you can believe that,"[39] projecting the sting he felt in having been bested by a powerful woman.

So, Trump gave his State of the Union late, and House Democrats used their newly won control to investigate him. Committees investigated allegations that he slowed hurricane relief to Puerto Rico, his company illegally inflated its assets, his daughter and son-in-law cut corners to get security clearances, and more. But what really infuriated him was the investigation of his ties to Russia launched by the House Intelligence Committee. He called its chair, Adam Schiff, "little shifty Schiff,"[40] and denounced his effort as yet another witch hunt by sore losers. Wasn't it enough, he wondered, that Robert Mueller's investigation dragged on, fueling speculation that its findings would lead to impeachment?

Trump doubled down on claims that a "caravan" of migrants from Central America threatened an invasion at the southern border. In February, he declared a national emergency at the border and used it as a pretext to transfer funds from the Defense Department to begin construction of the wall. His move was supported by a Supreme Court that was even more conservative after the addition of Brett Kavanaugh, who succeeded Anthony Kennedy in October 2018. Kirstjen Nielsen, Trump's secretary of homeland security was negotiating with Central American governments to make changes that would reduce violence in their countries, the principal cause of increased migration. But an effort to get at root causes wasn't calculated to produce quick results or satisfy demands from his base for tough action. Nielsen instituted what became euphemistically known as the Migrant Protection Program, which turned back those seeking asylum and required them to remain in squalid camps in Mexico. Claimants waited months for hearings, which were held by videoconference; immigration judges in their chambers in the U.S. questioned asylum seekers who responded from tents in Mexico. When Nielsen resisted Trump's demand to close the border, arguing that she lacked the authority to do so, he fired her.

---

39 *New York Times*, January 24, 2019 https://www.nytimes.com/2019/01/24/us/politics/nancy-pelosi-donald-trump.html (accessed December 13, 2022).

40 Rachel Frazin, "Trump blasts 'little shifty Schiff' over probe into finances," *The Hill*, March 2. 2019 https://thehill.com/homenews/house/432326-trump-blasts-little-shifty-schiff-over-probe-into-finances/ (accessed December 13, 2022).

But the problem didn't go away with Nielsen. To dramatize the situation, Trump had ordered U.S. troops to the border the previous fall. In his State of the Union address in February, he announced that he would send an additional 3,750 troops to "prepare for this enormous onslaught."[41] By June, there were 3,000 U.S. troops and another 2,000 Texas National Guardsmen at various points on the border. Because federal law prohibited them from being deployed for law enforcement, they were there mainly for show. *Business Insider* reported that troops were painting the wall black, prompting a retort from Senator Dick Durbin, the Illinois Democrat, that "our military has more important work to do than making Trump's wall beautiful."[42]

If there could be no bipartisanship on immigration, perhaps infrastructure would be different. After all, as a candidate Trump had promised a trillion-dollar investment, and at his disastrous post-election press conference, he had highlighted infrastructure as the most promising area for a deal. He followed up in his State of the Union Address, urging Democrats and Republicans to join him in a "great rebuilding of America's crumbling infrastructure."[43] Two months later, Trump met with Pelosi and Schumer to outline a $2 trillion plan. However, when the Democratic leaders returned to the White House in late May to discuss funding, Trump attacked Pelosi for continuing to investigate his campaign's ties to Russia. He stormed out of the meeting after a three-minute diatribe to attend a press conference where he railed against the Democratic witch-hunt. "I walked into the room and I told Senator Schumer and Speaker Pelosi: 'I want to do infrastructure. I want to do it more than you want to do it. I'd be really good at that, that's what I do,'" he told the press. "'But you know what? You can't do it under these circumstances. So get these phony investigations over with.'" Schumer called it a pretext, pointing out that the press conference had been planned well in advance. Trump wasn't serious, Schumer charged: when

---

41 "Remarks by President Trump in the State of the Union Address," February 5, 2019 https://trumpwhitehouse.archives.gov/briefings-statements/remarks-president-trump-state-union-address-2/ (accessed December 13, 2022).

42 Ryan Pickrell, "Trump sent troops to the southern border for a 'national emergency.' They're about to spend the next month painting his wall," *Insider*, June 6, 2019 https://www.businessinsider.com/us-troops-to-spend-a-month-painting-trumps-border-wall-2019-6 (accessed December 13, 2022).

43 "Remarks by President Trump in State of the Union Address," February 5, 2019 https://trumpwhitehouse.archives.gov/briefings-statements/remarks-president-trump-state-union-address-2/ (accessed December 21, 2022).

"he was forced to actually say how he would pay for it, he had to run away. And he came up with this preplanned excuse."[44]

By mid-summer, partisan warfare escalated, killing even the illusion of agreement on much of anything. Some Democrats had called for impeachment as soon as Trump took the oath of office, and now that they had a majority in the House they grew more insistent. But Pelosi kept the left-leaning never-Trumpers in line. Unless there was clear evidence of abuse of power, she believed that impeachment would cost Democrats support, especially in many competitive districts they had carried in 2018. In early September 2019, however, information about a disturbing phone call changed her mind. A whistle-blower reported to the inspector general of the intelligence community credible evidence of the call between Trump and the new president of Ukraine, Volodymyr Zelensky, in late July. Trump had allegedly agreed to release $391 million of military aid to Ukraine then being withheld if Zelensky conducted a couple of investigations. First, he should look into allegations that Joe Biden used his authority as vice president to stop an investigation of his son's role as a highly paid board member of a corrupt Ukrainian energy company. Next, Zelensky should explore rumors that Ukraine rather than Russia had been behind foreign interference in the 2016 U.S. elections. Both stories had been thoroughly discredited. The purpose of the investigations was to find dirt on his likely 2020 opponent and destroy the Democratic narrative that his campaign relied on Russia to defeat Clinton.

Between late September and November, more information surfaced. The transcript of the call itself and testimony from a parade of officials who had direct knowledge of the President's dealings with Ukraine convinced even conservative Democrats that Trump had crossed the line. They were shocked that he used his office and funds appropriated by Congress to seek foreign intervention in the 2020 election. Using the power of the presidency to undermine the integrity of elections and subvert the democratic process was the behavior the framers intended to curb when they wrote the Constitution's impeachment provisions, Democrats believed.

Checks and balances were alien to Trump. As the long-time CEO of a successful family business, he did what he pleased and saw no reason why things should be different as president. As he had learned from his mentor Roy Cohn, rules exist to be broken, concede nothing to those who call you out for violating

---

[44] *New York Times*, May 22, 2019 https://www.nytimes.com/2019/05/22/us/politics/donald-trump-speech-pelosi-schumer.html (accessed December 8, 2022).

them, deny you did anything wrong, and always punch back harder than you were hit. So as the story broke in late September 2019, Trump said the call was "perfect," labeled it just "another Fake News story out there," and charged that enemies inside the government were spying on him. "An American spy in one of our intelligence agencies may have been spying on our own president," he tweeted.[45] As the Democrats prepared to begin an impeachment investigation in early October, Trump escalated his attacks. "What is taking place is not an impeachment, it is a COUP," he screeched, "intended to take away the Power of the People, their VOTE, their Freedoms, their Second Amendment, Religion, Military, Border Wall, and their God-given rights as a Citizen of The United States of America!"[46] He also lashed out again at Adam Schiff, the chair of one of the committees that would be investigating. "He should resign from office in disgrace, and frankly, they should look at him for treason," Trump asserted.[47]

Trump probably knew he wasn't in danger of being removed. Democrats had a narrow majority in the House, so they might impeach him. But with a Republican majority in the Senate, there was little chance that his enemies could muster the two-thirds majority necessary to convict. In 1974, when they realized Nixon had obstructed justice, Republicans had abandoned their president. Not only were there moderate and even liberal Republicans, but closely divided states and districts forced politicians to reach beyond their party's base. In 2019, however, with the nation in the grip of hyper-partisanship, few truly competitive districts, and the party dominated by uncompromising conservatives, Republicans stood by their man.

After he left office, Nixon blamed himself for turning a burglary he had no knowledge of into a scandal that brought down his presidency. "I gave them a sword," he famously remarked to journalist David Frost.[48] Trump

---

45 Allan Smith, "Trump admits to discussing Biden in scrutinized talk with Ukrainian leader," September 23, 2019 https://www.msn.com/en-us/news/politics/trump-triples-down-claims-no-quid-pro-quo-when-he-discussed-biden-during-call-with-ukrainian-president/ar-AAHG0dA (accessed December 6, 2022).

46 Jon Sharman and Andrew Buncombe, "Trump falsely calls impeachment probe 'a coup' designed to strip citizens of rights in wild Twitter tirade," *The Independent*, October 2, 2019 https://www.independent.co.uk/news/world/americas/us-politics/trump-impeachment-latest-coup-tweet-democrats-ukraine-call-a9128866.html (accessed December 6, 2022).

47 Stephen Collinson, "Trump lashes out at Democrats leading impeachment inquiry," *CNN*, October 2, 2019 https://www.cnn.com/2019/10/02/politics/president-donald-trump-impeachment-democrats-pompeo/index.html (accessed December 6, 2022).

48 David Frost, *"I Gave Them a Sword,"* (New York, 1978).

gave his enemies a sword, but an army of loyalists stepped to his defense and wrested it from the Democrats. Many Republicans in Congress were tired of Trump's antics, and a few even said that Trump's behavior was unseemly and a full inquiry was warranted. The vast majority of Republicans, however, either changed the subject when asked about the call, said impeachment was a distraction from more important issues, criticized Democrats for the way they handled the investigation, claimed that there really hadn't been a quid pro quo, or maintained that if there was, it wasn't a criminal act and therefore didn't constitute the "high crimes and misdemeanors" demanded by the Constitution for impeachment.

What motivated Republicans and therefore shaped the impeachment drama was fear of Trump. Experience taught that Trump expected complete loyalty, and anyone who dared criticize him would be the target of scathing tweets and a primary challenge. Republicans had held their noses and pledged loyalty to Trump for years. They had entered a Faustian bargain, accepting a flawed, frustrating, and embarrassing president to gain an ally in the White House. It was now too late to turn back, especially when there was more to fear from a fired-up pro-Trump base than from swing voters who were repulsed by a racist, sexist egotistical bully who had no respect for institutions and norms. Even though the evidence was clear that Trump had abused his powers by soliciting interference by a foreign government in the 2020 presidential election, not one Republican in the House voted to impeach. When the Senate trial concluded in February 2020, only one Republican, Mitt Romney of Utah, voted to convict. Hyper-partisanship had produced Trump, and no matter how far he crossed what were once clear lines, Republicans supported him. "I have the most loyal people," he had bragged to an audience in Iowa in January 2016. "I could stand in the middle of Fifth Avenue and shoot somebody, and I wouldn't lose any voters."[49] The Republican Party was his.

Moderate Republican Susan Collins, who voted to acquit, said she believed "the president has learned from this case" and hoped that he would apologize for actions that "were wrong, improper—that [...] showed very poor judgment."[50] Like the Bourbons, however, Trump neither learned nor forgot.

---

49 Reena Flores, "Donald Trump: I could 'shoot somebody and I wouldn't lose any voters," CBS News, January 23, 2016 https://www.cbsnews.com/news/donald-trump-i-could-shoot-somebody-and-i-wouldnt-lose-any-voters/ (accessed December 6, 202).

50 CBS Evening News, "Susan Collins explains her vote to acquit Trump," February 4, 2020 https://www.cbsnews.com/news/susan-collins-explains-her-vote-to-acquit-trump/ (accessed December 14, 2022).

And he certainly wasn't in the mood to apologize. The morning after the Senate vote, he spoke at the bipartisan National Prayer Breakfast which was attended by many prominent Republicans and Democrats, including Nancy Pelosi and Mitt Romney. The keynote speaker urged attendees to end the acrimony and "love your enemies," but his message passed over Trump's head. When he came to the podium to speak, Trump hoisted two newspapers with banner headlines that read "Acquitted" and "Trump Acquitted" and then lit into his enemies. "Our great country and your president have been put through a terrible ordeal by some very dishonest and corrupt people," he charged.[51] Later that day, in a White House news conference, his comments were even more lacerating. "It was evil. It was corrupt. It was dirty cops. It was leakers and liars," he ranted. Nancy Pelosi was "a horrible person," Mitt Romney "a Failed presidential candidate [...] who used religion as a crutch," and Adam Schiff, the House impeachment manager, "a corrupt politician."[52] Actions spoke louder than his intemperate words. He quickly fired two officials who had delivered damning testimony at impeachment hearings.

With Trump looking back and settling scores, a new threat emerged that would shake the entire country and challenge his erratic leadership. In early January 2020, the World Health Organization (WHO) announced that a pneumonia-like disease affecting patients in Wuhan, China was caused by a novel coronavirus. By mid-January, tests confirmed cases of what had become labeled COVID-19 in Thailand, Japan, and Korea, and on January 20, the Centers for Disease Control (CDC) reported the first U.S. diagnosis in Washington State. By early March, the CDC reported that COVID cases had been detected in a dozen states, and the WHO declared it a global pandemic. With responsibility for public health divided between the federal government and the states, any effective response would require close cooperation. The public was frightened, and trust in science and experts in general had eroded during the previous two decades. It would be tested further as scientists' and public health officials' understanding of the virus and recommendations for dealing with it changed in response to new data and clinical experience. Too many Americans expected science to provide clear answers, when in reality, it rested on testing hypotheses, drawing conclusions, and then changing them as new data dictated.

---

51 *New York Times*, February 6, 2020 https://www.nytimes.com/2020/02/06/us/politics/trump-prayer-impeachment.html (accessed December 14, 2022).
52 *New York Times*, February 6, 2020 https://www.nytimes.com/2020/02/06/us/politics/trump-impeachment.html?searchResultPosition=3 (accessed December 14, 2022).

Steady leadership and good judgment were essential to meet the challenge. Instead, the nation was stuck with a mercurial, impulsive president who had little respect for science and based decisions on what he thought was best for his image and reelection prospects. By late January, Trump received briefings that made it clear just how deadly the virus was. His national security advisor told him it was the greatest threat he would face as president. Worried that he would create panic if he leveled with the public, he chose to downplay it. "This is a flu," he said in February. "This is like a flu."[53] He clearly knew better. "It's more deadly than even your strenuous flu," he told reporter Bob Woodward about the same time. "This is deadly stuff."[54] In late February, a CDC official told the public that widespread community spread was inevitable and would require measures that would dramatically change Americans' lives. Trump was livid and continued to minimize the significance of the virus, although he elevated the coronavirus task force he had created by bringing it into the White House and placing Vice President Mike Pence in charge. Trump was warned that the nation's stockpile of personal protective equipment (PPE)—N-95 masks, eye shields, medical gowns—was low and that testing would be essential to identify infected individuals so they could be isolated. But he refused to invoke the Defense Production Act, which allowed the government to direct private industry to produce items essential for national security. As a result, when cases spiked, healthcare workers lacked adequate PPE, and testing lagged for months.

Trump was correct to worry about the impact of the pandemic on the economy. From January to April, the stock market fell by 13%.[55] Unemployment rose as travel came to a standstill, restaurants, theaters, salons, college and professional sports shuttered, schools began to close, and businesses began to lay off workers or direct them to work from home. By April, the jobless rate would reach almost 15%[56] and GDP had fallen by 16%.[57] In late March, as the country was shutting down, Democrats and Republicans

---

53 Maggie Haberman, *Con Man: The Making of Donald Trump and the Breaking of America* (New York, 2022), 417.

54 John Sides, Chris Tausanovitch, Lynn Vavreck, *The Bitter End: The 2020 Presidential Campaign and the Challenge to America* (Princeton, NJ, 2022), 134.

55 Macrotrends, Dow Jones—DJIA—100 Year Historical Chart https://www.macrotrends.net/1319/dow-jones-100-year-historical-chart (accessed January 31, 2023).

56 U.S. Unemployment Rate by Month, 1948–2022 https://www.thebalancemoney.com/unemployment-rate-by-year-3305506 (accessed January 31, 2023).

57 U.S. Monthly GDP https://ycharts.com/indicators/us_monthly_gdp (accessed January 31, 2023).

in Congress did the unthinkable, passing a bipartisan stimulus bill in a matter of weeks. It wasn't without conflict and some drama, of course. Republicans wanted to keep the size small and direct most of the money to businesses threatened by the economic tsunami while Democrats demanded that a larger share go to enhanced unemployment benefits, support hospitals and healthcare workers who were on the frontline of the pandemic, expand support for virus research, and help state governments fill holes in their budgets created by declining sales and income tax revenues. Trump helped by absenting himself from negotiations, and Democrats got most of what they wanted.

In late March, Trump signed the $2 trillion stimulus, by far the largest in the nation's history. Americans whose incomes were under $75,000 received checks for $1,200 and an additional $500 for each child. Unemployment benefits were extended for 13 weeks and increased by a flat amount of $600 per month per worker. States received $150 billion, hospitals $100 billion, and $1 billion was directed to research. Many of these provisions would put money directly in the hands of consumers, buoying demand for goods and services. Although that was a boon to businesses, they also benefitted directly. $500 billion was allocated to support faltering companies through loans and direct investments, and another $377 billion was made available for loans to small businesses that would be forgiven if they kept their workers on the payroll.

As the pandemic gripped the country in March, political leaders also agreed with public health experts that the best way to stop the spread was by keeping people at home, out of contact with others. Most states shut down non-essential businesses like restaurants, gyms, salons, movies, and they closed schools and embraced remote learning. Trump had been reluctant to recognize the gravity of the situation and certainly wasn't prepared to take the lead on restricting social and economic activity. However, as state and local governments acted, he became supportive, at least for 10 days. On March 16, he announced a new initiative, "15 Days to Stop the Spread," at a White House press briefing. He asked Americans to stay home when possible, avoid restaurants and gatherings with friends, and refrain from travel, giving his blessing to directives coming from most governors. "If everyone makes […] these sacrifices now […] we will defeat the virus," he urged.[58]

---

58 Will Feuer and Noah Higgins Dunn, "A year later, Trump's '15 days to slow the spread' campaign shows how little we knew about Covid," *CNBC News*, March 16, 2021, https://www.cnbc.com/2021/03/16/covid-a-year-later-trumps-15-days-to-slow-the-spread-pledge-shows-how-little-we-knew.html (accessed December 14, 2022).

Trump also supported an aggressive, risky plan to develop a vaccine. Known as Operation Warp Speed (OWS), it emerged from negotiations between federal health officials and pharmaceutical companies in March and April, and the President announced it in May. Since the 1980s, scientists have been studying how messenger-RNA could be used to make effective vaccines. By the 2010s, research had advanced sufficiently to make it an option for a coronavirus vaccine. OWS committed the government to buy a massive quantity of the product before it had proven effective and safe in clinical trials. It was a big risk; the government could have paid billions for a product that couldn't be used. But the deal meant that once a vaccine was approved—assuring Americans that it was safe—healthcare professionals could begin putting needles in arms in a matter of days. It would prove a stunning success when two vaccines won approval in December and vaccinations began almost immediately.

If Trump's gamble on OWS was a good bet, his eagerness to reopen the country quickly wasn't. Although in mid-March he had endorsed social and economic restrictions designed to stop the spread, within 10 days he pivoted, concerned that they would further slow the economy and hurt his chances for re-election. Speaking on Fox News on March 24, he proclaimed, "I would love to have the country opened up and raring to go by Easter." That was less than a month away. "This cure is worse than the problem," he added. That was at odds with what just about every public health expert believed. Dr. Anthony Fauci, a White House coronavirus advisor, must have choked. The nation's leading infectious disease doctor, Fauci was the man whose guidance most Americans had come to trust. Trying to walk back Trump's comments without incurring his ire, Fauci commented, "You can look at that date, but you've got to be very flexible on it literally on a day-by-day week-by-week basis."[59]

Trump continued to assert that the virus was under control and reopening should proceed, even though a large majority of Americans identified the virus as the most important issue facing the country. Fearful for themselves and their loved ones, most Democrats and Republicans alike supported restrictive measures that states had imposed to stop the spread. There were critics, however. In early April, armed militia groups led

---

[59] Shannon Pettypiece and Peter Alexander, "Trump says he wants country 'opened up' by Easter, despite caution from health experts," *NBC News*, March 24, 2020 https://www.nbcnews.com/politics/white-house/trump-says-he-wants-country-open-back-april-12-easter-n1167721 (accessed December 15, 2022).

demonstrations at the Michigan capitol to protest aggressive policies imposed by Democratic Governor Gretchen Whitmer. Demonstrators also protested at state capitols in Virginia and Minnesota. Trump lacked the legal authority to order governors to make, loosen, or abandon restrictions, but he saw the demonstrations as an opportunity. On April 17, he Tweeted, "LIBERATE MINNESOTA!" followed by "LIBERATE MICHIGAN!" and "LIBERATE VIRGINIA, and save your great 2$^{nd}$ Amendment. It's under siege."[60] Many governors—almost exclusively Republicans—began to end restrictions. Trump's exhortations may also have incited a plot by Michigan militia members to kidnap Whitmer and overthrow the state government. The FBI and state authorities foiled it and arrested the conspirators in June, but the shocking plan indicated that pandemic response, like almost everything else, had become polarized.

Red and blue states began to diverge in their approach to the pandemic. Most Republican governors began lifting restrictions in early May while their Democratic counterparts eased but did not end restrictions like mask mandates. Predictably, Republican states generally saw surges in cases during the summer while Democratic states like New York that had been hard hit at the beginning saw declining numbers. Republicans justified their shift by arguing that restrictive policies violated their commitment to individual freedom and the right of individuals to make choices about their own lives (unless the choice involved pregnancy). Citizens, they insisted, should be trusted to do what was right for themselves. The messages sent by Trump and red state governors had an effect on party rank and file. During the summer, support for things like wearing masks declined among Republicans while mask-wearing remained popular among Democrats.[61] The pandemic and individual responses to it had become polarized, contributing to far higher mortality rate in the U.S. than anywhere in the world.

Race soon joined the pandemic response in intensifying conflict. On May 25, four Minneapolis police officers arrested George Floyd after he purchased a pack of cigarettes at a convenience store with a counterfeit 20-dollar bill. They handcuffed him and forced him to lie on his stomach on the pavement as one of the officers held him down with

---

[60] *Washington Post*, April 17, 2020 https://www.washingtonpost.com/outlook/2020/04/17/liberate-michigan-trump-constitution/ (accessed December 15, 2022).

[61] John Sides, Chris Tausanovitch, and Lynn Vavreck, *The Bitter End: The 2020 Presidential Campaign and the Challenge to American Democracy* (Princeton, NJ, 2022), 156.

his knee on the back of Floyd's neck as he pleaded for his life, "I can't breathe." After almost nine minutes, Floyd died of asphyxiation. Captured on a video that quickly went viral, it horrified almost everyone who saw it, including Trump. The video reignited protests over police brutality that had become dormant during the pandemic. Protests erupted in Minneapolis and spread to hundreds of communities across the country. In the month after Floyd's murder, data scientists estimated that between 15 and 26 million Americans participated in a demonstration.[62]

Initially, criticism of the police was bipartisan. Describing Floyd's killing as "absolutely horrendous," Senate Majority Leader Mitch McConnell called it one of "the latest disturbing chapters in our long, unfinished American struggle to ensure that equal justice under law is not conditional on the color of one's skin."[63] Journalists described the moment as a racial reckoning as companies and state and local governments condemned racism and affirmed support for equality. NASCAR banned the display of the Confederate flag, universities and major corporations issued statements condemning racism, Quaker Oats announced that it would drop the Aunt Jemima brand on its syrup, the Virginia governor ordered the removal of a Robert E. Lee statue from the capitol grounds, and many governors made Juneteenth (the day Black Texans celebrated emancipation) a state holiday.

Unfortunately, unity evaporated even faster than it had over efforts to stop the virus. Protests were largely peaceful. In some cities, however, they led to looting, burning cars and buildings, and clashes between protesters and police. Relatively few demonstrations involved violence, and even when they did, few participants set fires or looted. Predictably, television coverage focused on those protests that were large and sparked violence. Faced with a pandemic he couldn't control and a weak economy, Trump exploited the violence to rally supporters around the issue that always seemed to work for him—race. On May 29, four days after Floyd's death, Trump denounced the protesters in Minneapolis as "thugs" and assured Minnesota's governor that he would send troops if necessary,

---

62 Larry Buchanan, Quoctrung Bui, and Jugai K. Patel, "Black Lives Matter May Be the Largest Movement in U.S. History," *New York Times* July 3, 2020 https://www.nytimes.com/interactive/2020/07/03/us/george-floyd-protests-crowd-size.html (accessed February 26, 2023).

63 Andrew Desiderio, "McConnell says officers involved in George Floyd's death look 'pretty darn guilty'," *Politico*, May 29, 2020 https://www.politico.com/news/2020/05/29/mitch-mcconnell-police-officers-guilty-george-floyd-288915 (accessed December 15, 2022).

adding, "when the looting starts, the shooting starts."[64] That night, protesters near the White House breached barricades around the Treasury building next door, and the Secret Service took Trump and his family to a bunker under the mansion. Trump was furious because he thought it made him look weak, and he became enraged when the *New York Times* reported the evacuation.

Eager to punch back, he told his advisors that he wanted troops deployed and asked, "Can't you just shoot them? Shoot them in the legs or something?" When they pushed back, he finally accepted a suggestion that he walk from the White House through Lafayette Park, the center of protest activities, to St. John's Church where demonstrators had burned a section of the basement. It would demonstrate that he was strong and remained in control. U.S. Park Police cleared the way, using tear gas, pepper balls, and physical force to drive peaceful protesters out of the park. Then Trump and a group of high-level officials walked to the church where he was photographed holding a Bible his daughter had brought as a prop. Critics were outraged that he would use force against peaceful demonstrators for a photo-op. Trump's first secretary of defense, General James Mattis, was livid, calling Trump "the first American president in my lifetime who [...] tries to divide us."[65]

Throughout the summer and into the fall, Trump continued to hammer his opponents for supporting lawlessness while portraying himself as a defender of law and order. Although protests all but evaporated in most parts of the country by late June, unrest, sometimes violent, continued in Portland, Oregon for more than 100 days. In late August, the small city of Kenosha, Wisconsin erupted after police shot Jacob Blake, a Black resident, in the back seven times. Some protesters set fires, and fighting erupted between the protesters and White militia who flooded the city to disperse them. A White supremacist shot and killed two protesters and seriously wounded a third. As Trump called for a forceful response to preserve law and order, many insisted that police brutality was the real problem and demanded greater accountability. Some advocated defunding the police, which usually meant diverting some funding from law enforcement to services that supported minority communities. Defunding was roundly rejected by most Democrats, including Joe Biden, the party's presidential nominee. They favored reforms such as repeal of laws

---

64 "'When the looting starts, the shooting starts:' Trump tweet flagged by Twitter as 'glorifying violence'," CBS News, May 29, 2020 https://www.cbsnews.com/news/trump-minneapolis-protesters-thugs-flagged-twitter/ (accessed December 15, 2022).

65 Haberman, *Con Man*, 451–57.

that gave police immunity from civil suits for acts done in the line of duty, a ban on chokeholds, and adoption of policies that required police to activate body cameras when they engaged citizens. Trump kept up his attack, continuing to use Portland and Kenosha to portray Black protesters as a menace. In early September, he travelled to Kenosha for a photo op, even though state and local officials asked him to stay away. He called protesters "anti-American" and accused them of "domestic terror" without mentioning Blake, who lay in a hospital paralyzed.[66]

### A Battle for the Soul of the Nation

In the spring of 2019—before the pandemic and George Floyd's murder—seven Democrats signed on to compete for the party's presidential nomination. The candidate who drew the most interest was Obama's vice president, Joe Biden. He was 76, had served six terms in the Senate, run for president twice before and been sidelined early, was warm and compassionate, put his foot in his mouth too often, and had declined to challenge Hillary Clinton in 2016. Biden announced his candidacy in April 2019 in a video posted on his web site. His case ignored policy and concentrated on the events in Charlottesville in 2017, which he called "a defining moment for this nation." He had decided to run because "we're in the battle for the soul of this nation" and he had to be part of it. "If we give Donald Trump eight years in the White House, he will forever and fundamentally alter the character of this nation—who we are—and I cannot stand by and watch that happen."[67]

The Democratic hopefuls were sharply divided on policy—replacing the ACA with a single-payer system, free college for all, the best way to halt climate change, and more—but they agreed that defeating Donald Trump was the top priority. And many believed that Biden was best suited to do it because he was experienced, had close ties to Obama, and was someone whom voters wouldn't perceive as too far to the left. After stumbling badly

---

66 Jason Calvi and Bill Miston, "In Kenosha, President Trump calls violence 'domestic terror,' 'un-American,'" *Fox6 News* (Kenosha, WI), September 1, 2020 https://www.fox6now.com/news/in-kenosha-president-trump-calls-violence-domestic-terror-anti-american (accessed December 15, 2022).
67 Alexander Burns, "Joe Biden's Campaign Announcement Video, Annotated," *New York Times*, April 25, 2019 https://www.nytimes.com/2019/04/25/us/politics/biden-campaign-video-announcement.html?searchResultPosition=4 (accessed December 15, 2022).

in the early going he revived his candidacy in the South Carolina primary. With an endorsement from Jim Clyburn, the South Carolina congressman and dean of the Congressional Black caucus, and overwhelming support from Black voters, he crushed the field. Two rivals, Pete Buttigieg and Amy Klobuchar, dropped out and threw their support to him. The following week he carried 10 of 15 primaries on Super Tuesday, positioning him to waltz to the nomination as the nation shut down in the face of COVID-19.

The general election campaign played out against the background of the pandemic. COVID did little to change the importance of advertising on television and social media. Both campaigns spent freely, although Biden ran twice as many television ads in the final two months because he raised significantly more money than Trump. Television advertising aside, the pandemic turned things upside down. Biden's respect for public health guidelines meant that he staged fewer in-person rallies than Trump, and they were smaller because the campaign observed social distancing guidelines. Many were done drive-in style, with families in cars facing a stage with windows rolled down. Concerned about spreading the virus, Biden's team also waited until October to deploy door-to-door canvassers to encourage party faithful to vote. Trump rarely wore a mask and often attended large crowded in-person events where most guests weren't masked. Not surprisingly, his campaign held over 100 large in-person rallies—even where state and local officials banned them—and his volunteers knocked on doors throughout the campaign. But he couldn't control how states conducted elections. Because many voters were reluctant to visit a crowded polling place, most states made it easier to vote by mail. Trump railed against mail voting, claiming it lent itself to fraud (which it didn't). But voters of both parties embraced it; only 57% of voters cast ballots in person—down from 77% four years before.[68]

Biden continued to hammer away at Trump's assault on core American values, but increasingly he focused on the pandemic and the economy. Biden's working-class roots and tragic personal losses, his ads argued, enabled him to relate to average Americans and their struggles. He promised to protect Social Security, Medicare, and access to health care and to reverse high rates of unemployment that were devastating American families and communities. He also called Trump out for his irresponsible, erratic handling of the pandemic, which, he insisted, led

---

68 Christina A. Cassidy, "Report shows big spike in mail ballots during 2020 election," *AP News*, August 16, 2021 https://apnews.com/article/health-elections-coronavirus-pandemic-election-2020-campaign-2016-f6b627a5576014a55a7252e542e46508 (accessed January 23, 2022).

to unnecessary deaths. He assured Americans that he would follow the lead of scientists and public health experts to implement policies that would save lives, end the suffering, and restore normalcy. Viewed far more positively in personal terms than Trump by voters, Biden deployed far fewer attack ads and focused on his own compassion, concern for working Americans, and competence.[69]

Trump was, well, Trump. Faced with a struggling economy, he attempted to distract from an unemployment rate that was double what it had been when he took office. Biden, he insisted, was a tool of the radical socialists who controlled the Democratic Party and would support policies that would stall recovery. Faced with a surge of coronavirus cases and deaths in the summer and warnings about a resurgence in the winter months, he denied reality, insisting that the pandemic had almost run its course. However, he hurt his case when he tested positive in early October—after attending numerous crowded events where few wore masks. Seriously ill, he had to be taken by helicopter to Walter Reed Hospital. He continued to hammer away at the identity issues that animated his base. Biden would extend amnesty to 11 million undocumented immigrants, he charged, who would take jobs Americans desperately needed. He also claimed that Biden was a prisoner of Black activists and would support measures to defund the police—a policy Biden unequivocally rejected. Biden and the Democrats, he insisted, would stand by while rioters destroyed cities and encourage the construction of low-income housing in the suburbs, destroying the value of White homeowners' property.

Turnout increased dramatically, jumping from 60% in 2016 to almost 67% in 2020.[70] Undoubtedly, the convenience of mail voting, combined with the perceived stakes, were responsible. Polarization ensured that the outcome was close. The parties were deeply divided by race, geography, education, religion, and culture. Most voters had already chosen sides, and few were budging. One indication was how similar voting patterns were between 2016 and 2020: counties shifted, on average, only 1.9% in party allegiance in presidential voting.[71] There were few swing voters, but they probably moved in ways that had been forecast by the 2018 mid-terms when Republicans lost heavily among suburban college-educated White women. Trump's actions since then angered

---

69 Sides, Tausanovitch, Vavrek, *The Bitter End*, 197.

70 U.S. Census Bureau, "Record High Turnout in 2020 General Election," April 29, 2021 https://www.census.gov/library/stories/2021/04/record-high-turnout-in-2020-general-election.html (accessed January 31, 2023).

71 Sides, Tausanovitch, Vavreck, *The Bitter End*, 222–23.

many. His strategy may have solidified his base, but it didn't help him reach beyond it. That was devastating; his approval rating stood at only 46% when 2020 began and fell by about six points during the late spring and summer in response to his handling of the pandemic and demands for racial justice. Moreover, he wasn't facing Hillary Clinton, whose favorability rating in 2016 was almost as bad as his own. Voters viewed Joe Biden much more positively than Trump, making him a far stronger opponent.[72]

Biden scored a commanding victory in the popular vote, winning 51.3% to Trump's 46.9%, a seven-million-vote margin. He carried the Electoral College by a comfortable 306–232 margin by winning Georgia and Arizona—states that hadn't voted Democratic since 1976 and 1996, respectively—and Michigan, Pennsylvania, and Wisconsin, traditionally Democratic states Clinton had lost. But his margins in Arizona, Georgia, and Wisconsin were thin—between 10,000 and 20,000 votes. Biden did better than Clinton with Whites, women, college-educated White women, college graduates of both sexes, self-described moderates, suburban voters, and even White evangelical Christians. Remarkably, he did a bit worse with Blacks and Hispanics.[73] Political scientists John Sides, Chris Tausanovitch, and Lynn Vavreck attribute the shift to ideological sorting; with Trump's hard-right views even more pronounced than in 2016, minority voters who were hard-core conservatives moved to Trump.[74]

Biden won a decisive victory, but it took several days to come into focus. Almost half the ballots were cast by mail, and some states mandated that election officials couldn't count them before election day. When the networks finally called the contest for Biden late Saturday morning, November 7, celebrations erupted in cities across the U.S. A reporter described the scene in Chicago: "People shouting from their windows, ringing cowbells on their porches and blaring car horns in the streets […]. hundreds poured onto Clark Street, waving American flags, cheering and hugging." "I thought the Cubs won the World Series for a second," one resident laughed.[75] In Washington, Philadelphia, Los Angeles,

---

72 Ibid., 209.
73 Chris Alcantrara, Leslie Shapiro, Emily Guskin, Scott Clement, Brittany Renee Mayes, "How Independent Voters, Latinos, and Catholics shifted from 2016 and swung states for Biden and Trump," *Washington Post*, November 12, 2020 https://www.washingtonpost.com/graphics/2020/elections/exit-polls-changes-2016-2020/ (accessed January 31, 2023).
74 John Sides, Chris Tausanovitch, and Lynn Vavreck, *The Bitter End: The 2020 Presidential Campaign and the Challenge to American Democracy* (Princeton, NJ, 2022), 230.
75 *New York Times*, November 7, 2020 https://www.nytimes.com/2020/11/07/us/election-biden-reaction.html?searchResultPosition=1 (accessed December 20, 2022).

New York, and many other large and small cities, crowds filled the streets. When Senator Chuck Schumer called Biden from his home in Brooklyn to congratulate him, he held his phone aloft so that the President-elect could hear the roars in the streets outside.

Most of those celebrating hoped the election would end the chaos and nastiness and perhaps even ease partisanship. However, Trump soon signaled that he didn't consider the election over. Two days before the networks called it for Biden, he charged that Democrats were "trying to steal an election." After Biden was declared the winner, Trump asserted that "this election is far from over," tweeting, "MILLIONS OF MAIL-IN BALLOTS WERE SENT TO PEOPLE WHO NEVER ASKED FOR THEM!"[76] Trump's base wasn't celebrating and rallied to his claim that Democrats were trying to steal the presidency. In Harrisburg, Pennsylvania, a city Biden had easily carried, his celebrating supporters were confronted by hundreds of Trump loyalists who chanted, "Stop the steal!" A member of the Proud Boys, a right-wing group with a reputation for violence, carried a sign proclaiming, "Standing Back, Standing By, Mr. President."[77]

Partisan fever hadn't broken. It had risen for years and reached the point that many feared it would kill the republic. Trump approached his loss the way he dealt with other challenges he faced in business and politics. He attacked those who stood in his way, lied and doubled down on his lies when challenged, and intensified his attacks. It was calculated to appeal to and mobilize his base—the people who had stood by him in the face of conduct and scandals that would have taken down anyone else. The question was whether Republican leaders would countenance a president who challenged the peaceful transfer of power. If they failed to stand up to Trump, a coup or a civil war were distinct possibilities. What was once unthinkable now seemed possible. Trump's improbable victory in 2016 had brought the nation four years of chaos, and the worst was yet to come.

---

76 *New York Times*, November 7, 2020 https://www.nytimes.com/2020/11/07/us/politics/trump-white-house-biden.html (accessed December 16, 2020).
77 Ibid.

CHAPTER 12

# "A REPUBLIC, IF YOU CAN KEEP IT"

## Antrim County

Located 250 miles northwest of Detroit on Michigan's Lower Peninsula, Antrim County was known principally for its cherry orchards and beautiful vistas of Lake Michigan. At least before 2020, when the rural county that 23,400 Michiganders called home became the Gettysburg of Donald Trump's campaign to overturn the results of the election. The kerfuffle in Antrim grew out of a scheme to prevent the peaceful transfer of power—just the sort of thing that may have been on Benjamin Franklin's mind in August 1787 when he was asked whether he and the Constitution's other framers had given the country a monarchy or a republic. Aware that republics were vulnerable to demagogues, Franklin humorously but pointedly responded, "a republic, if you can keep it."[1] Franklin's observation was frequently quoted by politicians and political commentators during the chaos that followed the 2020 election. When partisan acrimony, wild conspiracy theories, and a defeated president who had no respect for constitutional norms created a witches' brew that threatened the survival of constitutional government in the United States.

One of the many conspiracies Trump pushed in the weeks following the election had its roots in an innocent error by Sheryl Guy, the Republican county clerk and life-long resident of Antrim County. In October, when the county added a candidate for village trustee to the ballot, Guy neglected to update the code in the Dominion voting machines that would scan ballots,

---

1 Gillian Brockell, "'A republic if you can keep it': Did Ben Franklin really say Impeachment Day's favorite quote?" *Washington Post*, December 18, 2019 https://www.washingtonpost.com/history/2019/12/18/republic-if-you-can-keep-it-did-ben-franklin-really-say-impeachment-days-favorite-quote/ (accessed December 22, 2022).

then feed data to tapes that showed all the votes, precinct by precinct, and record them on memory cards that were used to transfer the numbers to a computer in Guy's office that tabulated the county-wide vote. Unfortunately, Guy's programming error meant that votes ended up in the wrong columns on the tabulation sheet, giving Biden an improbable 7,700–4,500-vote victory over Trump. Something was amiss, and Guy knew it right away. Antrim County had voted solidly Republican since the 1880s, so she was peppered with calls and emails questioning the preliminary result. By November 6—a day before the networks called the election for Biden—Guy and her team had discovered the error and corrected it, giving the county to Trump by a margin of 3,800 votes.

What should have been the happy ending to a couple of stressful days turned into a nightmare for Guy. Convinced that the Democrats had stolen the election, Trump charged his personal attorney, former New York City Mayor Rudolph Giuliani, with leading a team to ferret out fraud, initiate lawsuits, secure judicial remedies, impugn the integrity of the election, and keep Trump in office. However, evidence of systematic fraud didn't exist, so Giuliani's team resorted to hearsay, wild stories, unreliable witnesses, and conspiracy theories. The most outrageous of them involved Dominion, the company that provided the voting machines used in Antrim, several dozen other Michigan counties, and thousands of counties around the U.S. Without a shred of proof, Giuliani alleged that the system had ties to Hugo Chavez's Venezuela and was programed to allow election officials to shift votes cast for Trump to Biden. Shifting had been widespread, he insisted, but he had no evidence to back up his claim. Then he got word of the Antrim County mess.

In early December, an Antrim County real estate agent filed a lawsuit demanding access to voting machines in several precincts. Represented by Matthew De Parno, an attorney and Trump loyalist from southwest Michigan, the plaintiff claimed that irregularities produced by the Dominion machines deprived him of his constitutional right to have his vote counted. De Parno and his client were coordinating with Giuliani's team. When the judge granted De Parno's client access to the system, Giuliani tweeted that a court had ordered "a forensic examination of 22 Dominion voting machines" in a county where "the untrustworthy Dominion machine [sic] flipped 6,000 votes from Trump to Biden." "Spiking of votes by Dominion happenned [sic] all over

---

2 Mark Bowden and Matthew Teague, *The Steal: The Attempt to Overturn the 2020 Election and the People who Stopped it* (New York, 2022), 157.

the state," he added.² Soon a team led by one of Giuliani's associates arrived by private jet. They appeared in Guy's office, accompanied by representatives of a Dallas computer security consulting firm, to examine the machines and the memory cards that recorded the votes. On December 13, the consultants issued a report concluding that Dominion machines were "intentionally and purposefully designed with inherent errors to create systemic fraud."³ The charges were bogus, but Giuliani breathlessly claimed that they were proof of systematic fraud—not only in Antrim County but in hundreds of other counties in Michigan and across the country that used Dominion machines.

A full investigation and manual recount of the Antrim County ballots on December 17 showed that the initial miscount had been the result of human error. The recount should have ended the recrimination that was tearing the county apart, but it didn't. Sheryl Guy, who had worked in the county clerk's office for 31 years before becoming clerk in 2012, was now a pariah to many of her neighbors who believed charges made by Washington political operatives and Dallas consultants that she was part of a conspiracy to steal the election. One local went so far as to say Guy "should be put in front of a firing squad." Even though she was a loyal Republican who had voted for Trump, a group of Antrim County Trump supporters held a prayer vigil outside her office. One of the participants asked what door she usually left by. The abuse and threats were so disturbing that Guy started avoiding community members. "You feel like you can't get air," she told Mark Bowden and Matthew Teague. "I drank a little more, I ate a little more."⁴ And decided she wouldn't seek re-election when her term ended in 2024.

Back in Washington, Giuliani kept up the attack on Dominion. In the face of irrefutable evidence to the contrary, members of his team insisted that the evidence from Antrim justified a presidential order authorizing the seizure of all voting machines in the country to conduct a full forensic analysis that would show that the election had been stolen. Two orders were drafted, but Ken Cuccinelli, the officer-in-charge at the Department of Homeland Security, and White House Counsel Pat Cipollone strenuously objected, so the orders were never issued. Nevertheless, Giuliani and Trump continued to spout the Dominion conspiracy theory in his campaign to persuade Republican legislators in Michigan to substitute Trump electors for Biden's.

---

3 Ibid.
4 Ibid., 160.

## The Big Lie and the Campaign against Democracy

Charges of election fraud in Antrim County were part of a campaign Trump and a group of his advisors waged to overturn the results of the election. As he met defeat, Trump refused to give up, adopting new strategies to remain in office. Many of Trump's closest advisors believed that he had lost and should take the high road, ensure a smooth transition, and preserve his legacy. They included his daughter, Ivanka, and her husband Jared Kushner, William Barr, the pugnacious attorney general, Pat Cipollone, the White House Counsel, Bill Stepien, Trump's reelection campaign manager, and Justin Clark, Stepien's deputy. Some, like Barr, were pointed and public in expressing their opinion and left the administration.

The realists didn't have Trump's ear. He tasked Rudy Giuliani, his personal attorney and the former mayor of New York, to find evidence of fraud and use it to derail Biden. Giuliani's team included attorneys better known for peddling conspiracy theories than for their legal acumen. Several other attorneys collaborated with Giuliani, including John Eastman, a former law clerk for Justice Clarence Thomas and dean of a small, private conservative law school in Orange County, California. Most of Trump's White House staff and cabinet had little respect for the group. In early December, before he resigned, Barr told Trump he had assembled "a clown show of lawyers."[5] But they had Trump's confidence because they believed the big lie and knew no bounds in pushing it, even when they lacked evidence.

Giuliani's team initiated a blizzard of lawsuits. Ultimately, he and other attorneys associated with Trump filed 62 lawsuits alleging election fraud between November 4, 2020, and January 6, 2021. They succeeded in only one, winning a ruling from a Pennsylvania court that election officials could not extend a November 9 deadline for voters to perfect provisional ballots they had cast. No allegations of fraud were involved, and the case affected only a few thousand votes, probably cast by as many Republicans as Democrats. The other cases were long on claims, many of them outlandish, but short on evidence. In almost half, judges issued summary judgments, tossing the cases without hearing evidence. A Michigan judge rejected a suit claiming "massive election fraud"

---

[5] Geoff Earle and Nikki Schwab, "Former AG Bill Barr says he DOES think Trump was 'responsible' for January 6 saying he wanted to 'intimidate Congress' and slams the 'clown show' of lawyers the ex-president hired to try and overturn the election," *Daily Mail*, March 4, 2022 https://www.dailymail.co.uk/news/article-10577865/Former-AG-Bill-Barr-slams-clown-lawyers-Trump-hired.html (accessed December 23, 2022).

because it rested on "nothing but speculation and conjecture." In Pennsylvania, a federal judge dismissed a suit against the state's chief election officer, chastising the plaintiffs for "strained legal arguments without merit and speculative accusations [...] unsubstantiated by evidence." His ruling was upheld by the U.S. Court of Appeals for the Third Circuit with a tart comment. "Charges require specific allegations and then proof," the court wrote. "We have neither here."[6] Trump remained undeterred, claiming that the problem was the judges, not the cases. "No judge, including the Supreme Court of the United States, has had the courage to allow it [the evidence] to be heard," he grumbled to a Fox News interviewer on December 13.[7]

The Department of Justice was as unimpressed by his claims of fraud as the courts. Attorney General William Barr had shown fierce loyalty to Trump during his two years in office, but supporting the outrageous claims coming from Giuliani's operation was a bridge too far. Two days after Biden was declared the winner, Barr authorized department personnel and the FBI to "pursue substantial allegations of voting and vote tabulating irregularities."[8] As he suspected, they found no evidence of significant fraud that would affect the outcome. On November 23, Barr met with Trump and told him as much. He zeroed in on the conspiracy theories Giuliani's team broadcast about Dominion voting machines. They were "crazy stuff," he said, adding that there was "absolutely zero basis for the allegations."[9] When Trump pushed back and criticized the department for being "missing in action," Barr had had enough. On December 1, he went public, telling a reporter "we have not seen fraud on a scale that could have affected a different outcome in the election."[10] Trump was furious and upbraided Barr, who resigned on December 14, the day the Electoral College met.

As lawsuits fizzled, Trump's team brought pressure on governors, election officials, and legislators in several of the most closely contested states.

---

6 *Final Report. Select Committee to Investigate the January 6th Attack on the United States Capitol*, 211–212 https://www.nytimes.com/interactive/2022/12/23/us/january-6-committee-final-report.html (accessed December 23, 2022).
7 Mark Moore, "Trump, 'disappointed' in SCOTUS, says election challenge 'not over'," *New York Post*, December 13, 2020 https://nypost.com/2020/12/13/trump-says-election-fight-is-not-over-on-fox-friends/ (accessed February 1, 2023).
8 *Final Report, Select Committee*, 902.
9 Ibid., 904.
10 Ibid., 907.

Arizona and Georgia had Republican governors and Republican majorities in their legislatures; in Michigan, Pennsylvania, and Wisconsin, Republicans controlled both houses of the legislature, although the governors were Democrats. Before the election, the campaign developed a plan to have pro-Trump electors in Republican-controlled states meet to cast their votes on December 14, even if Biden had carried their states. If state officials could be persuaded that Biden's victory was fraudulent, they could call their legislatures into session, decertify the results, and send the Trump slate of electors to Congress. In a highly partisan political culture, Republican governors and legislators would presumably leap at the opportunity to derail Biden's victory. Trump's grip on the party was tight, and most Republicans understood that those who crossed him paid a price. Surely if Trump turned up the pressure, Republican leaders would give him what he wanted.

The pressure from Trump and Giuliani was enormous. Phone calls, invitations to meet the President at the White House, public hearings convened by rogue legislators, public attacks charging recalcitrant Republicans with cowardice and disloyalty. Most state GOP elected officials resisted and put their legal responsibilities ahead of partisan advantage. In Pennsylvania, Giuliani worked with Doug Mastriano, a state senator and Trump loyalist, to convene an unofficial hearing at a Gettysburg hotel that produced wild, unsubstantiated claims of fraud. Republican leaders in both houses of the legislature, however, refused to buckle, stating publicly that the General Assembly "lacks the authority […] to overturn the popular vote and appoint our own slate of electors."[11]

It was the same story in other states. In Arizona, Governor Doug Ducey, a Republican, certified Biden's victory, bringing a wave of nasty tweets from Trump. Adding insult to injury, Rusty Bowers, the Republican speaker of the Arizona house, refused Trump's request to call a special session of the legislature. Giuliani did little to help his case when he told Bowers "we've got lots of theories, we just don't have the evidence."[12] In Georgia, Republican Governor Brian Kemp refused to convene the legislature, pointing out that state law barred it from substituting its own electors for those chosen by the voters. After meeting with Trump at the White House, Michigan's senate majority leader and house speaker, both Republicans, left no doubt about where they stood. "We have not yet been made aware of any information that would change the outcome of the election in Michigan," they asserted, "and […] will follow

---

11 Ibid., 720.
12 Ibid., 723.

the law and [...] normal processes regarding Michigan's electors."[13] At a time of toxic partisanship, state officials' commitment to facts and the law offered hope that the republic might survive Trump's assault.

As the meeting of the Electoral College approached on December 14, attention shifted to Trump electors in several closely contested states Biden carried. Trump's lieutenants pressed them to meet on the 14th, cast their votes for Trump, and submit their ballots to the National Archives for transmission to Congress prior to the joint session on January 6 where the electoral votes would be counted. Trump was assisted by Republican National Committee Chair Ronna McDaniel, who prodded defeated Republican electors to go to their state capitols to vote and provided them forms to transmit their ballot to Washington.

It was a half-baked scheme that yielded transparently bogus results. Out of 84 electors in seven states where Trump and the RNC encouraged defeated Trump electors to vote, 14 declined to participate because they doubted the scheme's legality. In five of the seven states, electors signed ballots falsely claiming they were "the duly elected and qualified Electors" from their state.[14] However, none of the ballots submitted had the seal of the state or the signature of the governor as required by law. So, when they arrived in the Senate, the parliamentarian ruled them invalid. In what reminded many of a Marx brothers farce, Wisconsin Senator Ron Johnson and Pennsylvania Congressman Mike Kelly directed staff to hand-deliver ballots from their states to Vice President Mike Pence on January 6, the day he would preside over a joint session to count votes. Pence's staff curtly rebuffed the effort.

Trump never gave up looking for allies. On January 2, he had a long phone call with Georgia's chief election officer, Secretary of State Brad Raffensperger. Raffensperger had followed state law to the letter in conducting the election, looked into the many allegations of fraud, insisted that they were without merit, and conducted a hand recount that confirmed Biden's victory. Having lost the state to Biden by only 11,779 votes, Trump called Rafensperger on January 2 and demanded his help. "So look. All I want to do is this," he said. "I just want to find 11,780 votes, which is one more than we have." Trump asserted that he had evidence of election workers tampering with ballots in violation of federal and state law. That put the secretary of state in jeopardy, he warned, because "you know what they did and you're not reporting it."[15]

---

13 Ibid., 714.
14 Ibid., 857.
15 Ibid., 681–82.

Raffensperger refused to budge, another Republican official who chose duty over partisanship.

After Barr's resignation as attorney general on December 15, Trump attempted to enlist the Department of Justice in his effort to overturn the election. Jeffrey Rosen, the acting attorney general, and his deputy Richard Donoghue were no more accommodating than Barr. Frustrated with the department's new leadership, Trump became infatuated with Jeffrey Clark, the head of the environmental division. Introduced to the President by a member of the House from Pennsylvania, Clark captivated Trump by telling him he needed a more aggressive attorney general to press the case. On December 28, Clark drafted a letter to be sent over Rosen's signature to officials in Georgia and several other states asserting that the department had found evidence of fraud and urging them to convene a special session of the legislature to "deliberate on the matter consistent with its duties under the U.S. Constitution."[16] When Rosen refused to sign the letter, Clark persuaded Trump to appoint him acting attorney general in place of the recalcitrant Rosen. However, Rosen stood firm, forcing a meeting with Trump, Clark, Donoghue, and several other Justice and White House officials on January 3. When department officials assured Trump that Clark's appointment would trigger massive resignations, the President backed down. Once again, Republicans pushed back, stopping Trump from using the department to overturn the election.

With options running out, Trump focused on what he considered his last best hope, Mike Pence. As president of the Senate, he would preside over the joint session of Congress where the electoral votes would be counted. His role was ceremonial, taking ballots handed him by the clerks, announcing the vote, one state at a time in alphabetical order, and asking if there were objections. In November and early December, Kenneth Chesebro, an attorney working for the Trump campaign, drafted three memos explaining why it was critical that Republican electors in closely contested states Biden had carried meet on December 14 to vote for Trump. The rationale for encouraging defeated electors to vote evolved. Initially, it was as a contingency in case a court found fraud and threw out the Biden electors. When it became clear that courts would not find fraud, Chesebro argued that even without proof of fraud, Congress might replace Biden electors with Trump's. Or Pence could simply recognize the Trump electors. In the event of conflicting slates of electors, Chesebro asserted, the vice president had full authority to decide which were legitimate.

---

16 Ibid., 930.

Put simply, having Trump electors in the wings would give Pence the opportunity to invoke his constitutional authority and swing the election to Trump—and himself. Of course, Chesebro's claim that the vice president was the decider flew in the face of the Constitution's text, federal law governing the counting of electoral votes, precedent, and common sense.

As Trump's options narrowed, he put his faith in Pence. On December 23, two weeks before Congress was to count the electoral votes, John Eastman, the law school dean who was one of Trump's advisors, sketched Pence's options. The Vice President could simply refuse to count any votes from the seven states with competing slates. That would give Trump a 232–222 margin over Biden and a majority of the electoral votes counted. If Democrats insisted that a majority of all the electors—270 votes—was required for victory, neither candidate would have a majority. That meant that the House would determine the winner, with each state casting one vote. Because Republicans had a majority in 26 of the 50 state delegations, Trump would win. There was yet a third possibility. Congress might give the legislatures of the seven contested states—five of which were controlled by Republicans—the opportunity to choose their state's electors.

There were two problems with the Chesebro-Eastman analysis. First, Congress didn't receive competing slates from any states. Two of the states where Trump electors met and cast ballots (Wisconsin and Michigan) didn't submit them in time; the other five Trump slates had been rejected by the Senate parliamentarian. Pence was an even bigger obstacle. He had been unfailingly loyal to Trump for four years, but he knew his role in counting the electoral votes was purely ceremonial. Research conducted by his staff and consultation with former House Speaker Paul Ryan and Vice President Dan Quayle assured him that he did not have the power that Chesebro, Eastman, and Trump attributed to him.

Although Pence resisted, Trump believed his base would never let him down. Three-quarters of his voters believed claims that the election had been stolen—40% said Trump definitely won and another 36% said he probably did.[17] Given the intense partisan bitterness of the previous decade, many supporters were true believers—people who saw Trump as the man called to deliver the country from socialists, Black Lives Matter arsonists, Muslims,

---

17 Pew Research Center, "Biden Begins Presidency with Positive Ratings; Trump Departs with Lowest-Ever Job Marks," January 15, 2021 https://www.pewresearch.org/politics/2021/01/15/voters-reflections-on-the-2020-election/ (accessed December 28, 2022).

immigrants, and feminists. They had flocked to Trump's rallies, sent small (and sometimes sizeable) contributions to his campaign, and were now committed to stop the steal. Among them were violent, well-armed White nationalist groups like the Proud Boys, the Oath Keepers, and a host of militia organizations that viewed Trump as one of their own.

Mobilization to stop Biden from becoming president had begun the day after the election. Ali Alexander, a young Trump supporter with a knack for promoting right-wing causes and conspiracy theories on social media, incorporated "Stop the Steal" within days of the election. Alexander worked closely with a variety of Trump supporters, including Alex Jones, the host of *InfoWars*, a highly popular website that traded in lies and some of the most outrageous conspiracy theories in the right-wing ecosystem. They organized "Stop the Steal" protests in cities across the country. In mid-November, led by Jones, they laid siege to the Georgia capitol and the home of Governor Brian Kemp. They also sponsored large rallies in Washington on November 14 and December 12. The latter got Trump's attention. "Wow! Thousands of people forming in Washington (D.C.) for Stop the Steal," he tweeted. "Didn't know about this, but I'll be seeing them!"[18] Later that day, he boarded Marine One and thrilled protesters with a fly-over.

That may have been the inspiration for Trump's next move. A week after the December 12 rally, he invited his followers to Washington on January 6, the day Congress would count the electoral votes. "Big protest in D.C. on January 6th," he tweeted. "Be there, will be wild."[19] The tweet lit a fire that would bring tens of thousands of his supporters to Washington, many of them intent on violence to stop Congress from confirming Biden's victory. Staff at Twitter later testified that his message—"essentially staking a flag in the ground [...] for his supporters to come and rally"—unleashed a torrent of violent rhetoric.[20] An Oath Keepers leader commented on Facebook, "He called us to the Capitol and wants us to make it wild. Sir Yes Sir!!!"[21] Along with the Proud Boys and militia groups, the Oath Keepers developed elaborate plans to disrupt the joint session of Congress. Alex Jones immediately began pumping the event on *InfoWars*. "He's calling you, he needs your help," Jones urged. "We need 10 million people there [...] we need martial law and have to prevent the police

---

18 *Final Report. Select Committee to Investigate the January 6th Attack on the United States Capitol*, 1161.
19 Ibid., 1150.
20 Ibid., 1151.
21 Ibid., 1153.

state of foreigners from taking over. It's literally in our hands."[22] If anyone doubted that Congress was the target, Jones's colleague Matt Bracken set them straight. "We're only going to be saved by millions of Americans [...] occupying the entire area, if—if necessary, storming right into the Capitol."[23]

As January 6 approached and Pence rebuffed Trump's demands, the President saw the crowd as his only chance to remain in office. There were protests scheduled for the evening of January 5, and a major rally on the Ellipse, the park that abuts the south fence of the White House grounds, on January 6. Before leaving the White House at about 11:30 on January 6 to speak at the Ellipse rally, Trump spoke with Pence by phone for 20 minutes. He pushed his vice president to reject Biden electors in the disputed states. When Pence refused, Trump became visibly upset and "angry," according to those who overheard the conversation. As the President left for the Ellipse, he ordered his speechwriters to insert text critical of Pence into his remarks. "Today, we will see whether Republicans stand strong for the integrity of our elections," he told more than 50,000 supporters who gathered at the Ellipse. "And we will see whether Mike Pence enters history as a truly great and courageous leader."[24] As he concluded, he exhorted the crowd: "we're going to the Capitol, and [...] we're going to give our Republicans, the weak ones [...] the kind of pride and boldness they need to take back our country."[25]

Shortly after 1 p.m., the crowd moved up Pennsylvania Avenue toward the Capitol, where several thousand Trump supporters had gathered. Trump insisted on accompanying them, but the Secret Service returned him to the White House after heated exchanges. When Trump entered the West Wing, angry that his protectors wouldn't take him to join the protestors, an employee told him that there was rioting at the Capitol. He moved quickly to the dining room off the Oval Office where he remained for the next three hours, watching mayhem unfold on television.

At 1 p.m., as Trump headed back to the White House under protest, Vice President Pence opened the joint session of Congress and began announcing the electoral votes cast by the states. When he reached the third state, Arizona, he announced that its 11 votes went to Biden. However, one of the state's representatives challenged the vote and presented a written statement from

---

22 Ibid., 1163.
23 Ibid.
24 Ibid., 1316.
25 Ibid., 1322–23.

Senator Ted Cruz of Texas supporting his objection. Under the Electoral Count Act, which governed the proceedings, that sent the two houses to their respective chambers where they had two hours to debate and vote on the objection. As the joint session progressed, several hundred members of the Proud Boys breached the fencing on the west side of the Capitol, allowing hundreds of protesters to surge onto the West Plaza, where a stage and stands for Biden's inauguration were being constructed. The mob grew in size as thousands arrived from the Ellipse. U.S. Capitol Police struggled to keep them from the Capitol itself, even as reinforcements arrived from the D.C. Metropolitan Police Department. Mobs also pressed against the police line protecting the plaza on the east side of the Capitol.

Shortly after 2, as senators and representatives debated the Arizona vote, a group of protesters led by the Proud Boys smashed a window on the west side of the building, entered the Senate wing, opened a nearby door, and allowed the mob to surge in. Soon, a group of Proud Boys and Oath Keepers, moving in a military stack, forced their way through the doors on the east side and into the rotunda. Police focused on moving members of Congress to safety. As they did, Trump took to Twitter to attack his vice president. "Mike Pence didn't have the courage to do what should have been done to protect our Country and our Constitution," he tweeted.[26] His message further inflamed the mob, which began chanting, "Hang Mike Pence." As Pence's Secret Service detail took him to a secure location, he came within 40 feet of angry rioters. Police evacuated Senate and House members to secure locations, where they remained for the next several hours. As protesters broke through a barricade at the main entrance to the House chamber, Ashli Babbit, one of the protesters was shot in the chest and died soon after.

As the mayhem unfolded, Trump watched on television, refusing to call his supporters off. White House Counsel Pat Cipollone demanded that Mark Meadows, Trump's chief of staff, join him to persuade Trump to urge the mob to disperse. But Meadows refused to intercede. "He doesn't want to do anything, Pat," he commented matter-of-factly.[27] House Republican leader Kevin McCarthy reached Trump by phone, pleading, "you've got to call these people off." Trump's response was unsympathetic: "Well, Kevin, I guess they're just more upset about election theft than you are."[28] Fox's Sean Hannity and

---

26 Ibid., 1340.
27 Ibid.
28 Ibid., 1345.

Brian Kilmeade, former chiefs of staff Reince Priebus and Mick Mulvaney, and Trump's eldest son sent desperate texts to Meadows. "We need an Oval address," texted Donald, Jr. "He has to lead now. It's gone too far."[29]

By 3 p.m., with senators and representatives out of danger, the police began to turn the tide. During the next three hours, they cleared rioters out of the building and pushed them off the East and West Plazas. Pence contacted officials at the Department of Defense, demanding that they send troops from the D.C. National Guard to help. Decision-makers at the Pentagon disagreed over who had the authority to call out the Guard, so no order came until after 5 p.m. The Guard didn't reach the Capitol until around 6 p.m. By the time they arrived, the police had done the heavy lifting, sustaining approximately 150 injuries in a pitched battle with the mob. Shortly after 4 p.m., Trump agreed to shoot a video, asking the rioters to leave the Capitol. It was pure Trump, doubling down on the big lie, blaming the Democrats, and praising his violent supporters. "It was a landslide election," he claimed, "and everyone knows it, especially the other side." "But we can't play into the hands of these people [i.e., the Democrats]," he concluded. "We have to go in peace. So go home, we love you. You're very special."[30] Between the efforts of the police to regain control and Trump's video, which was released at 4:17 p.m., the mob began to disperse, and senators and representatives returned to a battered, filthy Capitol.

Pence called the joint session to order at 8 p.m. Trump and Giuliani contacted congressional allies, urging them to postpone the count, still hopeful that they could buy time for state legislatures to meet and endorse Trump electors. But Pence and majorities in both chambers were determined to send a message to Trump, the mob, and the country that the rule of law had prevailed—if just barely. The Senate and the House returned to deliberations over the results in Arizona, rejecting the challenge to Biden's win, 93–6 and 303–121. When the joint session resumed Republicans challenged the vote of only one other state, Pennsylvania. It failed in the wee hours of the morning by margins of 92–7 and 282–138. Shortly before 4 a.m. on January 7, Pence declared Biden the winner with 306 electoral votes to Trump's 232. Although many Republicans held Trump responsible for inciting the mob to violence, his grip on the party was clear in the votes on Arizona and Pennsylvania, as two-thirds of Republican House members voted to reject the states' duly certified vote.

---

29 Ibid., 1355–56.
30 Ibid., 1358.

Despite ongoing support for the big lie among a majority of House Republicans, there were indications in the days following the insurrection that many Republicans saw Trump as a liability. Mitch McConnell and Kevin McCarthy, the party's leaders in the Senate and House, publicly stated that Trump was responsible for inciting the insurrection. Lindsey Graham, the South Carolina Republican senator who had gone from Trump critic to obsequious supporter, broke sharply with him, indicating that he was willing to consider invoking the 25th Amendment to remove him. "All I can say, is count me out," Graham told reporters. "Enough is enough."[31] Two cabinet officers and seven lower-level administration officials resigned in protest. The *Wall Street Journal* editorial page, once a reliable ally, demanded Trump's resignation.

Criticism wasn't sufficient, Democrats insisted. Trump's actions threatened the very foundations of the republic, and impeachment was the only way to hold him accountable. Trump had incited insurrection, and impeachment and conviction by the Senate would prevent him from ever again holding office. A week after the mob stormed the Capitol, the House adopted a single article of impeachment. By inciting the mob that stormed the Capitol, it charged, Trump had "threatened the integrity of the democratic system, interfered with the peaceful transition of power [...] imperiled a coequal branch of government [and] betrayed his trust as President."[32] The vote was 232–197 with only 10 Republicans joining a united Democratic front.

The Senate trial began on February 9, three weeks after Biden's inauguration, and lasted four days. Although seven Republican senators—14% of the Republican caucus—supported impeachment, the 57–43 vote fell 10 short of the two-thirds majority required to convict. Many of those who voted to acquit denounced Trump's conduct. Typical was Mitch McConnell, the Republican leader, who criticized Trump for his "disgraceful dereliction of duty" and held him "practically and morally responsible for provoking" the insurrection.[33] However, as guilty as Trump was, McConnell argued that he couldn't be impeached because he was no longer president. Other

---

31 *New York Times*, January 9, 2021 https://www.nytimes.com/2021/01/09/us/politics/republicans-trump-capitol.html (accessed December 28, 2022).
32 *Washington Post*, January 13, 2021 https://www.washingtonpost.com/context/read-article-of-impeachment-against-president-trump/204dd4b4-e431-47c2-ae4c-900dc70d2811/ (accessed December 30, 2022).
33 *New York Times*, February 13, 2021 https://www.nytimes.com/2021/02/13/us/politics/trump-impeachment.html?searchResultPosition=9 (accessed December 30, 2022).

Republicans grasped this fig leaf or claimed that it was time to move on and heal the nation's divisions. Of course, what really motivated Republicans was fear of Trump. "Their overriding political calculation was clear," a *New York Times* reporter explained. "After party leaders briefly entertained using the process to purge Mr. Trump from their ranks, Republicans doubled down on a bet made five years ago: that it was better not to stoke another open confrontation with a man millions of their voters still singularly embrace."[34] Indeed, in the days immediately following the insurrection, senators and representatives who had voiced criticism of Trump were mobbed by crowds demanding that they stand by the President. It became clear that challenging Trump and supporting fundamental constitutional principles was too risky for most Republicans. Even when he incited an insurrection watched by millions in real time, it was Trump's party. And that meant partisan fever would continue to burn.

## A Step Back from the Abyss?

Trump made his graceless departure for Mar-a-Lago, his Florida estate, on January 20, as Air Force One took off from Joint Base Andrews with Frank Sinatra's "My Way" blaring over loudspeakers. Doing the presidency his way had produced four years of constant chaos, escalated partisan acrimony, and nearly destroyed republican government. Boorish to the end, he declined to attend Biden's inauguration, the first President to absent himself since the disgraced Andrew Johnson snubbed Ulysses Grant in 1869. His absence brought the kind of relief a wedding planner might feel when the outdoor ceremony she had planned dodged a tornado. Trump was gone and few in Washington—even Republicans—were sorry. But he retained the unswerving loyalty of a big chunk of the Republican base and cast a long shadow over his party and American politics.

Joe Biden was Trump's polar opposite. He had deep respect for the institutions and processes of American government, aware of their limitations but convinced they permitted slow, if imperfect, progress. He promised to reclaim the values that sustained a pluralistic democracy, restore competence to government, respect expertise and facts, reestablish at least a modicum of trust between the parties, and repair relations with key allies around the world. He had his work cut out. When he took the oath of office on January 20, Biden presided over a nation that had narrowly escaped a coup, was bitterly divided, in the midst of

---

34 Ibid.

a pandemic that had already taken a half-million lives, and beset by economic woes the pandemic unleashed. At 78, he had won the office that had eluded him for decades and faced a range of seemingly intractable problems that would challenge the stamina of a person half his age. His opponents age-shamed him, claiming that he lacked energy and had lost whatever intellectual acuity he once possessed. But his 36 years in the Senate and eight as vice president had taught him how Washington worked and his party held a slim majority in the House and 50 seats in the Senate, which gave it an effective majority because Vice President Kamala Harris would cast the decisive vote when the parties split evenly.

Although Biden hoped that Trump would be forgotten as quickly as a bad dream, the former president became instead a recurring nightmare. Efforts to come to grips with the insurrection were an indication that the impeachment fiasco wouldn't be the only sign of Trump's grip on his party. In the days and weeks after January 6, Democrats and Republicans agreed that a full bipartisan investigation would help the nation learn from the tragedy and ensure that it never happened again. House Speaker Nancy Pelosi and minority leader Kevin McCarthy agreed to legislation establishing a National Commission to Investigate the January 6 Attack on the United States Capitol. Membership would include five Republicans and five Democrats led by a Democratic chair and Republican vice chair, each with equal power to issue subpoenas. The consensus quickly evaporated, however. In mid-May, just before the House voted on the commission, McCarthy withdrew his support. The bill passed the House, 253–175, but with the support of only 35 Republicans. When it moved the Senate, where 60 votes were needed to break a filibuster, it attracted only six Republicans and died.

Partisan considerations led Republicans to bail. McConnell claimed that the commission wasn't likely to "uncover crucial new facts or promote healing" and charged that it was a "purely political exercise" designed to damage Republicans. Senator John Thune, the Republican whip, made his party's motives crystal clear. "A lot of our members want to be moving forward," he explained, adding "anything that gets us rehashing the 2020 election is [...] a day lost."[35] Not to mention a reminder of the insurrection incited by a Republican president to whom most Republicans paid fealty. Trump

---

[35] Brian Naylor, "Senate Republicans Block Plan for An Independent Commission on Jan. 6 Capitol Riot," NPR, May 28, 2021 https://www.npr.org/2021/05/28/1000524897/senate-republicans-block-plan-for-independent-commission-on-jan-6-capitol-riot (accessed December 31, 2022).

also influenced Republican thinking. The day the House passed its January 6 Commission bill, Trump blasted it as a "Democrat trap" that promised "more partisan unfairness." "Hopefully, Mitch McConnell and Kevin McCarthy are listening," he added.[36] They were—and were reluctant to invite his wrath by cooperating with Democrats.

With the Senate paralyzed by the filibuster, the House voted to establish the Select Committee to Investigate the January 6 Attack on the United States Capitol, with just two Republicans joining 220 Democrats. Pelosi named eight members of the committee, including Liz Cheney, a conservative Republican who had voted to establish the committee and was the daughter of former Vice President Dick Cheney. Pelosi rejected three of the five Republicans McCarthy named because they had played a role in the attack or indicated that they would not approach the investigation with an open mind. The minority leader then withdrew his nominations altogether and refused to make new ones. In the end, Pelosi appointed all of the members, including Cheyney, who served as vice chair, and Adam Kinzinger, an Illinois Republican who had voted for Trump's impeachment. So, Republicans were represented, and they played an active and forceful role in the committee's deliberations. But they were persona non grata with their party, leaving most Republicans damning the committee as a partisan weapon even though its measured, evidence-based approach captivated much of the public and established credibility.

Like January 6, COVID continued to be a source of partisan division. Trump bequeathed Biden effective vaccines that promised to protect Americans and allow life to return to normal. Nevertheless, Biden faced logistical challenges inherent in delivering a two-dose vaccine quickly to over 300 million Americans. Effective collaboration with state public health officials brought steady progress. By June 1, 2021, over half of Americans had received at least one dose, and by year's end over 70% had received the vaccine.[37] Deaths fell dramatically, from over 21,000 per week when Biden was inaugurated to 3,700 during the first week of June. New variants caused a spike in infections during the summer of 2021 and the winter of 2022, leading to a resurgence of deaths. During the first week

---

36 Thomas Colson, "Trump says the January 6 commission is a 'Democrat trap' and tells Republicans to refuse to comply with it," *Yahoo News*, May 19, 2021 https://www.yahoo.com/news/trump-says-january-6-commission-104833650.html?fr=yhssrp_catchall (accessed December 31, 2022).

37 USA Facts, U.S. Coronavirus vaccine tracker https://usafacts.org/visualizations/covid-vaccine-tracker-states (accessed December 30, 2022).

in February 2022, 17,000 Americans succumbed to COVID. However, as more people received the vaccine and a booster that was released in April 2022, fatalities declined, dipping to 2,500 during the last week of 2022.[38]

The vaccines were safe and effective, but they quickly became engulfed in partisan conflict. Republicans, who had resisted pandemic-related restrictions such as mask mandates, were much more reluctant to get vaccinated than Democrats. A much higher percentage of Republicans questioned their safety, and many resisted efforts by public schools, universities, hospitals, and government to require individuals to be vaccinated.[39] In the fall of 2021, Biden ordered all companies doing business with the federal government to require that their employees be vaccinated or tested weekly. A group of Republican attorneys general won an injunction against the order in late 2021, which the U.S. Court of Appeals for the Fifth Circuit upheld in December 2022.[40] As medicine and public health fell victim to politics, so did mortality. A study of COVID deaths in Ohio and Florida found that deaths were 76% higher for Republicans than Democrats.[41]

Trump's signature issue, immigration, was another flashpoint. Even though Trump was gone, congressional Republicans understood that collaborating with Democrats to reform a broken immigration system would invoke the ire of Trump and invite a primary challenge. Besides, why resolve an issue that would be a potent weapon to use against Democrats in 2022 and beyond. Biden quickly dismantled Trump policies that Democrats considered barbaric and introduced legislation to reform a broken system that included a path to citizenship for those in the country illegally as well as new approaches to border security. Predictably, Senate Republicans closed ranks against it, and Democrats didn't have the votes to break a filibuster. Republican state attorneys general brought lawsuits to block

---

38 U.S. Center for Disease Control, COVID Data Tracker https://covid.cdc.gov/covid-data-tracker/#trends_weeklydeaths_select_00 (accessed December 30, 2022).

39 Gallup, "Partisanship and Vaccine Uptake Strategies," December 18, 2020 https://news.gallup.com/opinion/polling-matters/328034/partisanship-vaccine-uptake-strategies.aspx (accessed February 1, 2020).

40 Chris Pandolfo, "Court upholds injunction against Biden COVID-19 vaccine mandate for federal contractors in three states," *Fox News*, December 21, 2022 https://www.foxnews.com/politics/court-upholds-injunction-against-biden-covid-19-vaccine-mandate-federal-contractors-three-states (accessed December 30, 2022).

41 Paul Goldsmith-Pinkham, "Once COVID Vaccines Were Introduced, More Republicans Died than Democrats," *Yale Insights*, November 15, 2022 https://insights.som.yale.edu/insights/once-covid-vaccines-were-introduced-more-republicans-died-than-democrats (accessed December 30, 2022).

many of Biden's executive orders. By shrewdly picking sympathetic federal district court judges, they enjoyed considerable success in thwarting the administration's effort to roll back Trump policies. Meanwhile, the number of migrants seeking admission at the southern border swelled. They came not just from Central America but from countries like Venezuela, Cuba, Brazil, and Russia, where political turmoil and repression made life intolerable. In the case of Venezuela, nearly seven million people fled a repressive regime. While not all of them attempted to emigrate to the U.S., many did, contributing to surging numbers at the border. As was usually the case, the crisis was a product of factors beyond the president's control. Nevertheless, the surge was a gift to Republicans who kept up a drumbeat of criticism that they intensified when the administration, reacting to Trump's excesses, failed to take strong action to stem the tide.

Predictably, conflict extended to pandemic relief. Working-class and minority communities experienced especially high rates of unemployment and death as the pandemic continued in early 2021. With enhanced unemployment benefits about to expire, Biden pushed for another large infusion of cash to help those hardest hit and keep consumer spending strong. With control of the presidency and Congress in their hands for the first time in a decade, Democrats saw a relief bill as a golden opportunity to enact a progressive agenda. Predictably, Republicans pushed back, charging that the measure spent too much, discouraged workers from returning to the workforce, and used the pandemic as a pretext for expanding government social programs they had been trying to trim for decades. With Republicans united in opposition, Democrats used the budget reconciliation process as the way around a Senate filibuster, winning passage of the American Rescue Plan in March, less than two months after Biden's inauguration. The $1.9 trillion measure provided a one-time payment of $1,400 to those earning less than $75,000 per year, extended supplemental unemployment benefits of $300 per week until Labor Day, increased the child tax credit and subsidies for child care, expanded food stamp benefits and rent support for the unemployed, and provided $350 billion to support state and local governments, $130 billion for elementary and secondary schools, and an additional $14 billion for distributing vaccines. The bill struck a major blow against childhood poverty. "Not since Social Security have we made that kind of commitment to cut poverty," Columbia University's Christopher Wimer remarked.[42] However, it also contributed to a growing deficit and rising inflation that would quickly draw the wrath of many.

---

42 *New York Times*, March 13, 2021 https://www.nytimes.com/2021/03/06/us/politics/biden-stimulus-plan.html (accessed January 1, 2023).

Pandemic relief was just the start for Democrats. The partisan wars that had intensified during the previous decade, as well as the racial reckoning created by Black Lives Matter and George Floyd's murder, had moved the party's center of gravity leftward. Biden was a moderate by disposition and experience, but his finely honed political instincts gave him a sure understanding of the moment. He worked with Congress to develop what Democrats called the Build Back Better bill, a package of investments in clean energy, the green economy, and an expanded social safety network. The price tag was a whopping $2 trillion, leading some Democrats to push back. With economic recovery underway, labor shortages, pandemic-induced supply chain disruptions, and rising energy prices sparked inflation. By mid-2021, prices were rising at the rate of more than 5% annually, and by year's end inflation hit 7%, the highest in forty years. Republicans used it as a cudgel against Democrats, charging that reckless spending fueled the inflation that made it harder for families to pay their bills. It sent Biden's approval rating plummeting and made many Democrats worried that the bill would fuel inflation and prompt voters to revolt, as they had done in the 1970s.

The Senate was evenly split, and Democrats could only achieve a majority if all their members were on board and Vice President Harris could step in to cast the deciding vote. Conservative Democrats who represented closely contested states or districts—or in the case of Joe Manchin, a crimson state—had a veto. And they used it to block Build Back Better for more than a year. Patience, persistent negotiation with Manchin and other skeptics, and recognition that half a loaf was better than going hungry yielded success in August 2022. With Republicans unanimous in their opposition, Congress passed a $500 billion spending bill that achieved many of progressives' goals. Called the Inflation Reduction Act, it included $140 billion in tax credits to promote clean energy production and the purchase of electric vehicles, another $19 billion to support renewable, carbon-neutral biofuels, and $70 billion to bring down the cost of health insurance purchased through the Affordable Care Act. Bowing to Democratic conservatives, the bill jettisoned a carbon tax, cut the child tax credit included as a temporary measure in the American Rescue Plan, and eliminated funding universal pre-kindergarten. Independent analysts projected that the Inflation Reduction Act would cut carbon emissions to 50% of 2005 levels by 2030, the goal established by the Paris Climate Accord. Tax increases and provisions allowing the government to negotiate lower drug prices for Medicare enrollees balanced increases in spending, ensuring that it would be revenue neutral and contain inflation.

Biden was less successful in expanding federal protection for voting rights. The Supreme Court had significantly weakened the Voting Rights Act in a 2013 case, *Shelby County v. Holder*. The decision struck down a key provision of the Voting Rights Act and allowed Republican legislatures to adopt restrictive voting laws, especially in the South. Following the 2020 election, Republican-controlled states adopted a spate of laws designed to reduce turn-out, especially among low income and minority voters. Democrats called the restrictions voter suppression. With majorities in both houses, Democrats responded by introducing two major voting bills. The John Lewis Voting Rights Advancement Act restored provisions of the Voting Rights Act struck down in the *Shelby County* case. A second bill, the Freedom to Vote Act, was far more sweeping, replacing the patchwork of state regulations that governed voting with more uniform national standards. It required at least two weeks of early voting, permitted all Americans to vote by mail, made election day a national holiday, restored voting rights to felons upon release from incarceration, required states to ensure that voters waited in line to vote no more than 30 minutes, banned partisan gerrymandering, required states to allow voters to register online and vote the same day, and regulated procedures states used to purge lists of registered voters. Republicans used the filibuster to kill both bills, prompting many Democrats to demand that all votes in the Senate be decided by simple majorities. But conservative Democrats balked, the filibuster stood, and voting reform died.

So, during the first two years of the Biden administration, American politics resembled the kind of partisan warfare that wracked Obama's presidency. Republicans dug in and opposed Democratic initiatives on pandemic relief, the social safety network, immigration, the environment, and voting rights, charging that their enemies were big-spending socialists responsible for the worst tax of all—inflation. Nevertheless, with Trump in exile at his Florida estate and banned from Twitter for his role in inciting the insurrection, the temperature came down a bit. With Biden in the White House the daily dose of tantrums and chaos evaporated. The news seemed almost boring. However, partisan warfare continued and bipartisan compromise necessary to govern remained elusive.

Elusive but not impossible. Familiar with the ways of the Senate and many of the men and women who served, Biden prided himself on his ability to forge compromise and understood how to achieve it. Infrastructure, he sensed, was an issue where agreement was likely. Democrats and Republicans alike realized that the nation's roads and bridges needed attention, antiquated ports were creating supply chain backlogs that slowed recovery and fueled inflation, and large sections of rural and urban America suffered from inadequate broadband service. Trump had talked a good game on infrastructure but utterly failed to deliver. So, there was pent up demand for action, and Biden had the know-how to get a bill across the finish line.

An agreement came together slowly, with negotiations stretching out over the first ten months of Biden's presidency. Biden and members of his administration worked closely with Senate Republicans, including McConnell. "Multiple senators said the president and his team spent hours with them in person on Capitol Hill and on the phone hashing out the details [...], including thorny disagreements over how to finance billions of dollars in new spending," noted a *New York Times* reporter.[43] The President also brought down the size of the package by more than half and agreed to spread out spending over five years to placate Republicans concerned about the impact on the budget and inflation. By November, when the bill passed, Biden had won the support of 18 Republican senators, achieving more than the token support that often passed for bipartisanship. The legislation pumped federal dollars into roads, bridges, railroads, mass transit, and ports, ensured that all Americans would have access to high-speed internet, funded the replacement of all lead water pipes, and provided support to build 500,000 charging stations for electric vehicles. It was a major step toward making the nation more economically competitive. "Researchers at the Brookings Institution estimate that the money will increase federal infrastructure spending as a share of the economy by half over the next five years," explained the *New York Times*, "putting it nearly on par with the infrastructure provisions of the New Deal."[44] Biden, it turned out, understood the art of the deal better than his predecessor and proved that even in a bitterly divided city, cooperation was possible.

The pandemic revealed another problem—the nation's weakness in semiconductor research and production. Everything, from cars and coffee makers to advanced technologies like quantum computing, advanced sensors, autonomous vehicles, fighter jets, and rockets depended on chips, some more sophisticated than others. Few chips were manufactured in the U.S., and as the pandemic shuttered production overseas, automobile manufacturers couldn't access the supply they needed to produce vehicles. Soon cars were in short supply, driving up the cost of new and used vehicles and contributing

---

43 *New York Times*, July 29, 2021 https://www.nytimes.com/2021/07/29/business/economy/biden-infrastructure-deal.html (accessed January 1, 2023).

44 *New York Times*, November 15, 2021 https://www.nytimes.com/2021/11/15/us/politics/biden-signs-infrastructure-bill.html (accessed January 1, 2023).

to inflation. U.S. innovation also lagged, leading to fears that the country would fall behind international competitors, including China. Republicans and Democrats realized that market forces had encouraged American companies to rely on foreign producers rather than domestic suppliers and that government intervention was necessary to solve the problem. The Chips and Science Act invested over $250 billion in government-industry-university partnerships to reestablish U.S. independence and preeminence in semiconductors. Congress passed it in August 2022 with 17 Republican senators and 24 Republican House members joining Democrats to send it to Biden's desk.

More surprising was Biden's success in securing the first federal gun control legislation in 30 years. Its passage was spurred by two more horrendous mass killings. In May 2022, a teenage White supremacist opened fire with an assault rifle in a grocery store in Buffalo, killing 10 African Americans. Five weeks later, tragedy struck in an elementary school in Uvalde, Texas, where a gunman wielding a semiautomatic rifle killed 19 children and two teachers. Biden channeled public outrage to win enough Republican support to pass a bill that included modest provisions designed to prevent future violence. Many states had red flag laws that allowed law enforcement officials to temporarily take guns from individuals deemed a threat to themselves or others, but many police and sheriff's departments lacked the training and resources to enforce them. The new legislation provided funding to law enforcement agencies to develop and implement protocols to get guns out of the hands of those experiencing mental health issues before they struck. The law also gave officials conducting background checks on gun buyers additional time to review juvenile and mental health records, closed a loophole in the ban on gun purchases by domestic abusers, and provided more federal funding for mental health services and school security. Biden relented on stiffer provisions—a ban on high-capacity magazines and sale of semiautomatic weapons to those under 21 to win critical Republican votes in the Senate. Nevertheless, most Republicans showed fealty to the NRA, which opposed the bill. "Today, they're coming after our Second Amendment liberties," the ranking Republican on the House Judiciary Committee warned, "and who knows what it'll be tomorrow."[45] Ultimately, however, 15 Republican senators supported the bill, breaking a filibuster.

---

45 *New York Times*, June 24, 2022 https://www.nytimes.com/2022/06/24/us/politics/gun-control-bill-congress.html (accessed January 2, 2023).

### Republicans—and the Republic—at the Crossroads?

As midterm elections approached, Biden and congressional Democrats could boast some significant accomplishments, including success in working with Republicans to tackle problems that partisan conflict had allowed to fester. Nevertheless, they had reason to worry. During the previous century, the president's party had lost an average of almost 30 seats in midterms, and Republicans believed the situation was ripe for big Democratic losses. Inflation continued unabated, with gas prices rising even faster than other goods as the economic recovery dramatically increased demand and sanctions imposed on Russia after its invasion of Ukraine in February 2022 slashed supply. Every trip to the gas station became a reminder of inflation's toll, and many blamed the party in power. In many parts of the country, rising crime rates added concern about physical security to economic woes, and voters remained dismayed by a surge of immigrants. If Biden's approval rating, which fell to the low 40s, was a barometer, Democrats could expect a storm of historic proportions.

It didn't happen. As the election approached, Democrats portrayed themselves as the party that could govern, citing the American Rescue Plan and the Inflation Reduction Act as well as bipartisan legislation to rebuild crumbling infrastructure, regain U.S. leadership in semiconductors, and reduce gun violence. They realized, however, that even an Inflation Reduction Act wouldn't make voters forget about high prices, so they made the rather audacious move of attacking the party out of power for what *it* had done—restricting women's reproductive rights. Trump had fulfilled his pledge to the party's base by appointing three hardline conservative Supreme Court justices who were committed to overturning *Roe v. Wade*. Less than five months before the midterms, the Court struck, handing down its landmark decision in *Dobbs v. Jackson Women's Health Organization*. It overturned *Roe*, empowered states to restrict or even outlaw abortion, and catapulted women's reproductive rights to the forefront of political debate. Voters in Kansas, a deeply conservative state, quickly showed that the decision Republicans had worked toward for 40 years would bite them in the butt. In August, they overwhelmingly defeated a measure conservatives placed on the ballot to repeal a provision in the state constitution that protected abortion rights. The result persuaded Democrats that *Dobbs* would be a game changer. If the decision lit a fire in ruby red Kansas, they believed, it could be a powerful weapon in more closely divided states like Pennsylvania or Nevada.

Then there was Donald Trump. He couldn't resist making the midterms all about himself, the election he claimed had been stolen from him, his control of the party, and his political comeback. He endorsed over 300 Republican candidates across the country and persuaded hand-picked candidates to enter key races. All were election questioners (sewing doubts by asserting that there were unanswered questions that merited investigation), and some promoted the big lie, flatly asserting that Democrats had stolen the election. Many also took extreme positions on abortion. Doug Mastriano, who won the Pennsylvania Republican gubernatorial primary with Trump's support, was a case in point. A state senator who played a key role in organizing Giuliani's "Stop the Steal" hearing in Gettysburg in November 2020, he chartered a bus to take supporters to the Capitol on January 6 and promised to outlaw abortion if elected. Some of those Trump recruited were just plain weak. Herschel Walker, the former football star who won the Republican primary for U.S. Senate in Georgia with Trump's backing, was a disaster. Not only was he clueless about the issues; day after day stories trickled out about his sordid history of abusing women, fathering children he wouldn't support, and putting pressure on wives and lovers to have abortions.

Trump remained immensely popular with the party's base. However, many independents and even some Republicans had tired of his egotism and the constant chaos he sowed. Biden may have been unpopular, but as the 2022 midterms approached, Trump was even more intensely disliked. So, injecting himself into the campaign helped Democrats by making the election a choice between Trump and Biden rather than a referendum on an unpopular President. Public testimony in the January 6 committee by Trump insiders made it clear that he had incited an insurrection and watched on television as mobs beat police officers, disrupted Congress's proceedings, and called for Mike Pence to be hanged. If that wasn't enough, the Trump Organization was on trial in New York for tax fraud, New York's Attorney General initiated a civil suit seeking $250 million in damages from the former president for fraudulent business practices, and the Justice Department named a special prosecutor to investigate potential criminal charges against Trump for stealing classified documents and inciting insurrection. He disgusted many voters, making his endorsement the kiss of death for many candidates in critical states.

Democrats played the cards the Supreme Court and the former president dealt them well. They used *Dobbs* to make abortion an issue in states like Pennsylvania and Michigan, where Republican candidates promised to adopt restrictive laws if they won, and in Nevada where the Republican candidate for Senate called *Roe* "a joke."[46] With Trump-backed candidates who embraced

---

46 Igor Bobic, "GOP Senate Candidate Adam Laxalt Says It's 'Sad' Nevada Protects Abortion Rights," *HuffPost*, July 1, 2022 https://www.huffpost.com/entry/abortion-roe-adam-laxalt-nevada_n_62bef54ee4b00a9334e746b5 (accessed February 1, 2023).

the big lie on the ballot in states like Arizona, Pennsylvania, Michigan, and Nevada, Democrats also made the election a referendum on democracy. Biden used his bully pulpit to amplify the charges as the election approached. Speaking at Washington's Union Station, a stone's throw from the Capitol, he reminded voters that "democracy is on the ballot," urging them to take a stand "to preserve our democracy" when they went to the polls.[47]

The Democratic strategy proved to be a firewall against disaster. Republicans gained control of the House, but they scored only a net gain of ten seats, far short of the 40–50 seats pundits had been predicting. Their victory gave them a narrow 222–213 majority and put Kevin McCarthy's bid for the speakership in jeopardy as a small group of hardline conservatives opposed his candidacy. The concessions he made to the right-wing bomb throwers led many to conclude that life in the narrowly divided House would be chaotic, making governance difficult. If Republicans underperformed in House races, Democrats overperformed in Senate contests. Incumbents held hotly contested seats in Arizona, Georgia, and Nevada, and the party picked up an open seat in Pennsylvania, giving it a 51–49 majority.

Democrats celebrated while Republicans debated whether their poor showing reflected badly on Trump and would loosen his grip on the party. Trump denied responsibility—as he always did—but he had clearly played a leading role in his party's debacle. Granted, most of his candidates won. But they prevailed in solidly Republican states and districts where Republican victories were a foregone conclusion. In competitive states, Trump-endorsed candidates flopped. Their extremist views on the 2020 election and abortion energized Democrats, prompted independents to break sharply for Democrats, and led some Republicans to pull the lever for a Democrat. According to one Republican consultant whose client lost a Michigan House district that leaned Republican, voters were alienated by candidates whom they considered extremists. "The Dobbs decision, you take the Jan. 6 stuff, you take the election denialism and wrap it all together," he said, "it's not a good look for us."[48] A Republican who conducted focus groups with Arizona voters agreed. She recounted asking participants who said they were dissatisfied with the direction of the country

---

47 Susan Milligan, "Biden: 'Make No Mistake: Democracy Is on the Ballot'," *U.S. News*, November 2, 2022 https://www.usnews.com/news/elections/articles/2022-11-02/biden-make-no-mistake-democracy-is-on-the-ballot (accessed January 3, 2023).
48 *New York Times*, November 14, 2022 https://www.nytimes.com/2022/11/14/us/politics/gop-far-right-election-voters.html (accessed January 4, 2023).

whether they planned to vote for Mark Kelly, the incumbent Democratic candidate for senator, or Blake Masters, the Republican challenger. "And they'd say, 'Oh, Blake Masters is insane,'" she chuckled.[49]

Many held their breath as the midterms approached, fearing that a Republican wave would threaten the survival of democracy. In all the competitive states, Republicans aligned with Trump ran far behind Republican candidates who distanced themselves from him. The outcome alleviated concerns about the threat to democracy and encouraged many to predict that the party would finally recognize that Trump was a liability. If so, perhaps Washington could return to a modicum of functionality. After all, Biden had cut deals with Senate Republicans on a number of issues, including one of the most contentious, gun control. With independents and even some Republicans in critical states telegraphing that they were tired of extremism, perhaps Republican congressional leaders would take note. They might be more inclined to negotiate with Democrats to win compromises on legislation that tempered liberal Democratic nostrums with conservative principles.

If some saw reason for hope, others believed they had seen this movie before and knew it had an unhappy ending. The *Access Hollywood* revelation, Trump's refusal to disavow White supremacists after Charlottesville, his role in inciting the attack on the Capitol were all moments when pundits predicted that Republicans would abandon him. But they never did. They kept slinking back to Trump, finding ways to support, justify, or ignore his outrageous statements and actions. Why should it be any different this time? Republicans had underperformed in the midterms, but they had won control of the House and were only two votes shy of a majority in the Senate. They were disappointed the red wave hadn't materialized, but they had not been routed, as the Democrats had been in the 1980, 1984, and 1988 presidential elections or the 1994, 2010, and 2014 midterms. There was little reason for party leaders to rethink their position in fundamental ways, as Democrats had done in the 1980s when the Democratic Leadership Council moved the party to the right and Bill Clinton won the party's presidential nomination in 1992.

There were many reasons to stay the course. Partisan division had taken on stark geographical dimensions, with Republicans dominating rural and small-town America and the South, Midwest, Great Plains, and parts of the Mountain West. Only a few states and House districts were truly competitive, so candidates could flourish by playing to the base. Republicans knew that if

---

49 Ibid.

they strayed too far from conservative orthodoxy or criticized Trump, they might invite a primary challenge from the right. That posed a far greater threat than being attacked as an extremist by a Democrat in the general election. In the 2022 midterms, around 180 Republicans elected to the House expressed doubts about the outcome of the 2020 election, and 30 of them said it had been stolen.[50] Republicans who represented safe districts had little incentive to tone down their views or seek compromise with Democrats. They were much more likely to be rewarded by their constituents if they stood up to the enemy than if they reached across the aisle. Bipartisan legislation had passed in 2021–2022, but it had won the support of a handful of House Republicans and only about a third of GOP senators. It represented progress, but hardly proof of a new era of bipartisan deal-making.

Some Republican leaders recognized that Trump's racism and misogyny along with the chaos and divisiveness he sowed hurt the party. It played well in rural areas and with base voters, but it turned off many independents and college-educated suburban voters, especially women. Those were voters with whom Republicans had traditionally fared well, and the party needed them if it was to build a dominant majority. George W. Bush's compassionate conservatism had attracted them and helped Republicans achieve success in the 2002 and 2004 elections—before the stalemate in Iraq, Katrina, and the economic meltdown caused Bush's popularity to tank. In 2013, the Republican Growth and Opportunity Project recognized that the party needed to broaden its appeal to achieve a permanent majority. But Trump's victory in 2016 took Republicans in a different direction and inertia made it hard to go back. Despite his defeat in 2020, Trump remained the party's most powerful leader, reinforcing the views of hardline conservatives who insisted on appealing to the base and drowning out those who advocated a more positive and inclusive approach. Soon congressional leaders like Kevin McCarthy were making the trip to Mar A Lago to kiss the ring.

Congressional leaders didn't have the tools to chart a new course, even if they believed the party was headed in the wrong direction. Mitch McConnell was an experienced, disciplined leader but he could do little to keep bomb throwers like Rand Paul, Ted Cruz, Rick Scott, or Josh Hawley in line. Far from providing help to a man he routinely scorned, Trump created chaos. McConnell understood that recruiting strong candidates whose appeal transcended the

---

50 *New York Times*, November 10, 2022 https://www.nytimes.com/interactive/2022/11/09/us/politics/election-misinformation-midterms-results.html (accessed January 5, 2023).

party's base was critical to regain a majority in the Senate, where there were more competitive races than in the House. Yet Trump backed a host of Senate candidates in competitive states—Don Bolduc in New Hampshire, Blake Masters in Arizona, Adam Laxalt in Nevada, Mehemet Oz in Pennsylvania, and Herschel Walker in Georgia—whose views placed them far outside the mainstream or who carried so much personal baggage that they stumbled to the finish line. McConnell voiced his frustration in September 2022, warning a Kentucky audience that the party was unlikely to retake the Senate. "Candidate quality has a lot to do with the outcome," he explained in a thinly veiled criticism of Trump and Rick Scott, the Florida senator who headed the National Republican Senatorial Committee.[51] The conflict simmered throughout the fall and burst into the open after the election when Scott challenged McConnell for minority leader. Although Scott lost, he picked up 10 votes from Trump-aligned senators, an indication of the limits of McConnell's power.

The situation in the House was even more chaotic. Hard-right, Trump-aligned members made up a large segment of the Republican caucus. They had driven two speakers—John Boehner and Paul Ryan—into retirement. Now they went after Kevin McCarthy, the minority leader who was poised to become speaker after Republicans won a nine-seat majority in the 2022 midterms. If anyone doubted that the anarchy that had frustrated Boehner and Ryan would continue, reality soon set in. A small group of representatives who deemed McCarthy too moderate set out to deny him the speakership, aware that he could lose no more than four Republican votes in the narrowly divided chamber. McCarthy prevailed but only after five days, 14 ballots, and two Republicans nearly came to blows on the House floor. Not since 1859, as the nation stood on the brink of civil war, had electing a speaker been so protracted.

McCarthy was no Nancy Pelosi, but as the fate of more estimable leaders like Boehner and Ryan suggested, leading the Republican caucus was a fool's errand. The hostility conservatives had to government seemed to translate into a kind of knee-jerk resistance to authority, including their own leaders. They were as likely to employ their burn-it-down approach against party leaders as government programs, and there was precious little to restrain them. Social media and hard-right television, radio, and Internet sites allowed them to communicate directly with voters. They also helped them raise money, freeing

---

51 Max Greenwood, "McConnell-Scott feud bursts out into the open," *The Hill*, September 1, 2022 https://thehill.com/homenews/campaign/3624417-mcconnell-scott-feud-bursts-out-into-the-open/ (accessed January 6, 2023).

them from dependence on party leaders and the money they raised. Fundraising success depended less on accomplishing things than putting on an entertaining show and stoking outrage. "There are far more members here who are engaged in performance art and [...] really have no interest in governing," commented a Democratic committee chair as he left Congress after eight terms.[52] Theatrics brought members notoriety, made them heroes to the base, and kept the money flowing.

The House Republicans' new show turned out to be a comedy. In May, when the nation reached its borrowing limit, McCarthy struck a deal with Democrats to raise the debt limit without getting deep budget cuts or a draconian immigration bill in return. That infuriated a dozen or so hard-right members associated with the Freedom Caucus. In September, when the Speaker agreed to a stop-gap budget bill to avoid a government shutdown, eight members voted with Democrats to oust him. The bone McCarthy tossed to his right-wing antagonists—authorizing an impeachment inquiry against President Biden—might have added a new plot line to the farce, but it didn't save his speakership. For most of October, House business came to a halt as Republicans struggled to settle on someone a handful of right-wing merry pranksters would accept. Senior members Steve Scalise and then Tom Emmer were nominated by the Republican caucus but withdrew when they fell short of the 217 votes necessary to be elected. Finally, three weeks after McCarthy's ouster, Mike Johnson of Louisiana, a rather junior member who wasn't a member of the Freedom Caucus but whose hard-right positions endeared him to its members, prevailed.

Johnson walked a tightrope, knowing that a handful of members could show him the door at any time. When he negotiated another stop-gap spending bill in mid-November, the far right grumbled but didn't move against him. Nevertheless, they had him on a short leash, ensuring that the House brought governance to a halt. With Ukraine running out of military supplies in its war against Russian invaders, Israel engaged in a war against Hamas after a brutal October terrorist attack took the lives of 1,200 Israelis, and Taiwan facing rising military pressure from China, the House blocked appropriations to support the three U.S. allies. Many Republicans—perhaps most—supported the aid, but Johnson was a prisoner of the extreme right wing of his party—and of Donald Trump who signaled his opposition. With immigration continuing

---

52 *New York Times*, January 1, 2023 https://www.nytimes.com/2023/01/01/us/politics/senate-house-retiring-burr-shelby.html?searchResultPosition=1 (accessed January 7, 2023).

to surge at the southern border, Johnson also blocked a breakthrough on immigration policy that emerged in the Senate. Senate Democrats understood that immigration, along with inflation, was a top issue for voters. Indeed, even Democratic voters were demanding tougher measures. Senate Democrats agreed to a bill that provided no path to citizenship for any immigrants who had entered the country illegally and established stricter criteria for immigrants to claim asylum, faster processing of those seeking it, more funding for border security, and a mandate that the president shut down the border when Border Patrol encounters with migrants hit 5,000 per day for a week. But it wasn't enough. Preferring to keep immigration alive as an issue in 2024, Johnson pronounced the bill dead on arrival and Trump urged Republicans to reject it.

As the comedy in the House played on, the Republican presidential nominating process got underway. It, too, turned out to be a comedy rather than a thriller, albeit one with a dark ending. A dozen or so candidates entered the race, but Florida's governor, Ron DeSantis, appeared to many the only candidate who had a chance of beating Trump. He had won re-election in 2022 in a landslide and branded himself as a younger, more competent, less chaotic version of Trump. DeSantis and most of the other contenders refrained from criticizing Trump, fearing they would unleash the wrath of his loyal base. With his opponents tip-toeing around his many vulnerabilities and failing to dent his support, Trump refused to participate in the candidate debates, instead appearing at televised events that distracted attention from his opponents. Once primary season kicked off, Trump's dominance became apparent. After the Iowa caucuses, Nikki Haley was the only candidate remaining to challenge Trump. She put up a good fight and finally began skewering him for his many weaknesses. But she did poorly in New Hampshire, her home state of South Carolina, Nevada, and Michigan; lost in 15 of 16 states in early March's Super Tuesday; and dropped out of the race. The Republican Party was Trump's. In exit polling conducted in six states on Super Tuesday, a majority of those who voted Republican in each state said they would vote for Trump even if he were convicted on one of the 91 felony counts against him in four separate cases. At least 50% in each state also indicated they didn't believe Biden had won the 2020 election.

Trump had often been counted out. When he announced for president in 2015, when he won the nomination in 2016, after the Capitol Insurrection in 2021. But he had staying power because the Republican Party's base—which had been transformed by growing distrust of government, shrinking optimism about the country's future, decades of culture wars, economic changes that hollowed out rural and small-town America, a revolution in communication,

Obama's presidency, the Tea Party revolt—stuck with him no matter what. Party leaders were afraid to cross him, and as a new generation of leaders emerged, more and more of them were his acolytes. Two things were clear. The polarization that had tightened since the first decade of the millennium showed no signs of abating, ensuring that governance would remain difficult. Second, no one should discount Trump's chance of regaining the White House as he rallied a fired-up base and faced an opponent most Americans believed was too old to serve effectively and whom many independents and some Democrats blamed for inflation, a crisis at the southern border, and support for an Israeli war against Hamas that had created a humanitarian crisis in Gaza. While no one could say exactly what a second coming would mean, most outside the Republican Party—and some within it—worried that it would be another stress test for the republic.

# CONCLUSION

"Fast Car" hit the top of the country charts in the summer of 2023, when country music headliner Luke Combs released his cover of Tracy Chapman's 1988 folk hit. It was a moment that bridged deep divides in American culture. A song written and originally performed by a Black lesbian revived by a White man with a fan base in Red America. There are many reasons for the song's appeal to different worlds. Its simple, yet powerful chords and lyrics that call to be belted out; the romance of the car, America's freedom machine more than a century after Henry Ford brought it to the masses. But there was more. The song's lyrics evoke feelings of despair, of being trapped by circumstances shared by many—Black and LGBTQ people as well as many Whites in rural America, where good jobs are scarce and addiction is common. Yet the song also appeals to hope for escape and the security, dignity, and freedom promised by the American dream.

Chapman and Combs performed "Fast Car" as a duet at the 2024 Grammy Awards, underscoring shared problems and aspirations that unite across differences of identity and history. For me, it recalled the sense of optimism and possibility reflected in the TV ad run by the Johnson campaign in 1964, summoning Americans to protect future generations of children from poverty. But we're not in 1964. As the two artists came together to perform, the country's political divisions seemed sharper than ever, optimism was long gone as politicians continued to pit groups against one another in a lead-up to a presidential election that promised to be even nastier than the last. If music broke down barriers, politics encouraged people to demonize those who were different, sharpen their knives, and prepare for a fight.

Scholars and political analysts said we were polarized. It was division that went beyond sharp disagreement and healthy rivalry between the two major parties. Democrats and Republicans were deeply divided not just by political ideology but by identity—religion, race, region, sex, and education. The division had become so deep that there was little hope for the compromises necessary to solve problems. Sometimes it was even hard to agree on what the problems were. Denying the opponent a win was more important than addressing voters' concerns if doing so meant compromising principles or sacrificing talking points that could be used to skewer the opposition. Polarization also meant that voters themselves were sharply divided and many had developed deep emotional ties to one side of the divide, even if they considered themselves independents. Voters rarely split their ticket in national and state elections and weren't forgiving when those they elected failed to stand firm against the enemy. They blamed politicians for negativity, but they bore some responsibility.

The roots of our predicament are deep, going back to the 1960s. Conflict over race and ethnicity, which had long vexed Americans, took on new dimensions, leaving many White people threatened and people of color believing that hard-won gains were chimerical or in jeopardy. The personal became political, as sharp conflict emerged over women's rights, reproductive freedom, marriage, the family, and sexuality. Religion, long a divisive element in American politics, emerged with new force in the 1970s, as evangelicals sought to use the state to check what they perceived as moral decay, and those who embraced the commitment to personal autonomy that blossomed in the 1960s pushed back. Race, women's rights, sexuality, and the family introduced highly charged moral issues that supercharged political discourse. There were also tectonic changes in the economy. As the nation moved from an industrial to an information economy, those without advanced education struggled, rural America and once-thriving industrial cities were hollowed out, and disparities in income and wealth reached levels not seen since the 1920s, leaving many disillusioned, alienated, and angry. The end of the Cold War brought a brief sense of triumph even as it unsettled American politics by removing a long-standing point of consensus and focused greater attention on divisive cultural issues.

These were monumental, unsettling changes, and they invited politicians to exploit them. No one should have expected anything different from those who sought to promote their principles and careers in a business that was competitive by design. But taking advantage of division needn't have led to polarization and gridlock. Choices made by political leaders took us there. Lyndon Johnson's decision to escalate U.S. commitments in Vietnam by stealth, Richard Nixon's obstruction of justice in Watergate, Bill Clinton's undisciplined approach to life and his presidency, George W. Bush's decision for war in Iraq—all eroded faith in leaders and confidence in government's ability to promote the common good. As Americans became cynical about politicians, politics, and government, their faith in government's ability to solve their problems—or politicians' genuine willingness to try—withered. Politicians who seemed intent on vilifying their opponents, more interested in keeping divisive issues alive than solving problems fed the cynicism. As respect for and trust in political leaders evaporated, character assassination and conspiracy theories gained traction, feeding the nasty politics most Americans claimed to hate but too often joined.

Some of these changes emerged in the late 1960s and helped make the 1968 election a polarizing affair. They roiled the system in the ensuing three decades, but they didn't consume it until the twenty-first century. Ronald Reagan moved American politics to the right, triggering sharp ideological conflict and exploiting cultural issues. Nevertheless, during his administration, Republicans and Democrats forged compromises on issues as diverse as economic policy, civil rights, and immigration. After pitched battles over cultural issues between the two parties in the 1980s and 1990s, Bill Clinton and George W. Bush tacked to the center and sought bipartisan solutions to issues like spending, welfare, education, immigration, and even health care.

The system was strained but didn't break. The tipping point—the point of no return—came with the election of the nation's first Black president and the economic collapse of 2008. Divisions over religion, region, gender, sexual orientation, class, education, and, especially, race that had whipsawed American politics for decades coalesced and hardened. More voters chose sides and identified enemies; the number of true swing voters shrunk; few states and congressional districts remained competitive; the two major parties became more monolithic in outlook, and appeals to their base drove strategy and what passed for policy. In short, we became polarized. It was an atmosphere ripe for populist demagogues, and they emerged, mainly on the right, as Republicans struggled to blunt Obama's success and the threat of long-term realignment promised by the elections of 2006 and 2008. Appeals to race, gender, religion, regionalism, economic grievance, ideology, and more offered a way to blunt the threat, restore equilibrium, and regain power. Politicians believed they could manipulate these issues to take down Obama, but they soon became prisoners of them. Newcomers like Sarah Palin, Ted Cruz, and Donald Trump brandished conservative populist outrage to elevate their brand and win power, transforming American politics into a Manichean struggle between good and evil, heroes and enemies that was nasty, divisive, and never ending. The point was to feed the fury that kept them relevant rather than developing policies that provided imperfect solutions to real problems. With the base constantly in a state of outrage, those who broke ranks or sought compromise—the sine qua non of democratic politics in a diverse nation—faced irrelevance or political death.

One need to look no further than Mitt Romney, the Republican presidential nominee in 2012, who was censured by Utah Republicans for voting to impeach Donald Trump and decided not to seek reelection to his Senate seat in 2024.

Fundamental changes in the nation's dominant ideology were *not* the source of this mindless, destructive polarization. The U.S. was a center-right polity in 1964, as it embarked on the most sweeping period of reform since the New Deal; despite wrenching social and economic changes in the past 60 years, it remains center-right. What changed and fed the toxicity and polarization that plagues us in 2024 wasn't sharp ideological conflict over policy. It was the systematic erosion of optimism, trust, and sense of possibility that prevailed in the mid-1960s. They evaporated quickly—certainly by the late 1970s—creating a climate conducive to sharp conflict over divisive moral and cultural issues. That conflict whipsawed American politics for decades, but it awaited the perfect storm of the Great Recession and Barack Obama's election to become so deeply embedded in our politics that it's hard to see a way out.

Our two major parties remain more evenly balanced than at any time since the Gilded Age, with control of the White House and Congress shifting between them and one party only rarely controlling both branches. (In this century, it has happened only four times—two for Republicans and two for Democrats, lasting only two years on each occasion.) Eager to retain power or to regain it after losing it, politicians were more inclined to emphasize differences than work to find the common ground necessary to govern. The advent of cable news, the 24-7 news cycle, the Internet, and social media turned politics into performance art, intensified conflict, and fed partisanship. The media made molehills mountains, stoked perpetual outrage, and allowed political adversaries to operate in separate bubbles with their own version of the nation's most pressing problems, their own facts, and powerful tools to mobilize allies, raise millions to support messaging (most of it negative), and demonize the opposition. The new media fed a political ecosystem in which demagogues and conflict flourished, relationships and communication collapsed, and little comity remained between the two major parties. Politicians focused on the next election and worried more about retribution from their own voters than governing. Compromise became a dirty word and gridlock became the norm.

Politicians live for power and its perks (including the ability to effect change). So, they did what they needed to do to win or at least live to fight another day. Many citizens reveled in the excitement generated by the perpetual conflict that their favorite cable network or website served up 24-7. Political junkies enjoyed the thrill of combat, loved hating the enemy, and took joy in vanquishing them. But many, if not most, Americans were disgusted, turned off by politics, and dismissive of politicians whom they regarded as self-serving, unprincipled, and dishonest. They may have disagreed about the solutions and in some cases even the problems. But they believed that politicians spent more time attacking one another, often over trivial matters, than working together to solve their problems. They were frustrated, certain that there must be a better way but convinced they could do little to make the system more functional.

They're probably right. Polarization and gridlock aren't likely to recede any time soon. If the past is a guide, the only way out of our predicament is political realignment—an election or series of elections that gives one party a commanding and enduring majority. The founders created a system of checks and balances designed to keep an individual or faction from achieving too much power. Their goal was to prevent tyranny, not create gridlock. They valued deliberation and debate and were confident the system would force opponents to compromise to resolve their differences. But the system didn't work very well when margins of victory were small, power shifted back and forth between the parties, and social, cultural, and economic conflict was intense, as had been the case in the 1850s and the 1890s. Or the 2000s. Perhaps it was also better designed for a time when government's role in American life was limited rather than integral to almost everything, as it had become by the twenty-first century. If we didn't count on government in the ways we do, gridlock wouldn't matter so much. In some respects, that was the point of hard-right conservatives. For them, the government does too much, and grinding it to a halt is a good thing. But even cynical Americans still expect government to do a lot for them. Even Tea Partiers' demands betrayed that they had expectations of government, as illustrated by a South Carolinian who spoke at a town hall meeting sponsored by a Republican member of the House in 2009: "Keep your government hands off my Medicare."[1]

With the stakes and emotions high, politics seems like a never-ending existential crisis. It's probably the way Americans felt at other times of long-standing, seemingly unresolvable conflict—except that our forebearers didn't have a 24–7 news cycle or smartphones with news feeds to magnify minor incidents or remind them of the chaos on an hourly basis. From the 1840s to the early 1860s, conflict over slavery created perpetual deadlock that made governance difficult. It flared into a Civil War that ended slavery and

---

1 Bob Cesca, "Keep Your Goddam Government Hands Off My Medicare," *Huffington Post*, September 5, 2009 https://www.huffpost.com/entry/get-your-goddamn-governme_b_252326 (accessed March 7, 2024).

realigned American politics, producing two decades of Republican hegemony. Industrialization and the agrarian crisis of the 1880s and 1890s sparked a revolt in rural America that inflamed American politics. It came to a head in the election of 1896, which broke almost two decades of political stasis and ushered in over 30 years of Republican rule. A third realignment came in 1932 after an extended period of one-party dominance. Triggered by the dislocation and personal suffering brought by the Great Depression, it forged a Democratic coalition that governed for the next 40 years, through depression, world war, Cold War, and prosperity. Only a fool would predict the event or crisis that will break the current impasse or when it might occur. But if the past is prologue, it may be the only way out of a cul-de-sac over 50 years in the making. We can only hope that it's more like the crisis of the 1890s than the cataclysm of the 1850s. Or that it's not effected by a strongman who ignores democratic norms and subverts the rule of law. Given the events of the past eight years, however, we can't be sure.

# BIBLIOGRAPHICAL ESSAY

*The Path to Paralysis* draws heavily on a large and rich literature on U.S. politics, law, culture, society, religion, business, finance, economics, and technology from the 1960s to the present. Because it is aimed at an educated lay audience rather than specialists, I have decided to keep footnotes to a minimum and avoid delving into historiographical disputes. I have footnoted sources from which I quote and rely on for data, for example, public opinion polls, economic and demographic trends, exit polls, and voter surveys. This bibliographical essay acknowledges my intellectual debt to historians, political scientists, sociologists, journalists, and others whose analyses, interpretations, and accounts I have relied on and also provides a guide for readers who wish to dig deeper.

Good historical overviews of recent U.S. history include two books by James Patterson, *Grand Expectations: The United States, 1945–1971* (New York, 1996) and *Restless Giant: The United States from Watergate to Bush v. Gore* (New York, 2005); Kevin M. Kruse and Julian E. Zelizer, *Fault Lines: A History of the United States Since 1974* (New York, 2019); William H. Chafe, *The Unfinished Journey: America Since World War II* (9th ed; New York, 2021); and Daniel T. Rodgers, *Age of Fracture* (Cambridge, MA, 2011). Brent Cebul, Lily Geisner, and Mason B. Williams, *Shaped by the State: Toward a New Political History of the Twentieth Century* (Chicago, IL, 2019); E. J. Dionne, Jr., *Why the Right Went Wrong: Conservatism from Goldwater to Trump and Beyond* (New York, 2016); Heather Cox Richardson, *To Make Men Free: A History of the Republican Party* (New York, 2014); Geoffrey Kabaservice, *Rule and Ruin: The Downfall of Moderation and the Destruction of the Republican Party, from Eisenhower to the Tea Party* (New York, 2012); Stephen Skowronek, *The Politics Presidents Make: Leadership from John Adams to George Bush* (Cambridge, MA, 1997); and Angie Maxwell and Todd Shields, *The Long Southern Strategy: How Chasing White Voters in the South Changed American Politics* (New York, 2019) provide insightful treatment of broad trends in recent American politics.

Analyses of polarization I found especially insightful include Ezra Klein, *Why We're Polarized* (New York, 2020); Doug McAdam and Karina Kloos, *Deeply Divided: Racial Politics and Social Movements in Postwar America* (New York, 2014); Alan Abramowitz, *The Great Alignment: Race, Party Transformation, and the Rise of Donald Trump* (New Haven, CT, 2018); Bill Bishop, *The Big Sort: Why the Clustering of Like-Minded America is Tearing Us Apart* (New York, 2008); and Dannagal Goldthwaite Young, *Wrong: How Media, Politics, and Identity Drive Our Appetite for Misinformation* (Baltimore, MD, 2023). Thomas Zimmer, "Reflections on the Challenges of Writing a (Pre-)History of the 'Polarized' Present," *Modern American History*, 20 November 2019 https://www.cambridge.org/core/journals/modern-american-history/article/reflections-on-the-challenges-of-writing-a-prehistory-of-the-polarized-present/E096EAD1482CF4680A9FB1DA9EBE2BB8 argues that the concept has been overused, employed without sufficient analytical rigor, and ignores broad consensus on important issues such as mass incarceration and the role of the state that have dominated political and social discourse since the late 1960s. Bruce Schulman, "Post-1968 U.S. History: Neo-Consensus for an Age of Polarization," *Reviews in American History*, 49 (September 2019), 479–99 shows how broad agreement on some important issues coexisted with polarization.

American politics and society in the late 1950s and 1960s are the point of departure for this book. My analysis of Dwight Eisenhower and Modern Republicanism has been informed by Chester Patch and Elmo Richardson, *The Presidency of Dwight Eisenhower* (Lawrence, KS, 1991); Stephen E. Ambrose, *Eisenhower the President* (New York, 1984); Fred I. Greenstein, *The Hidden Hand Presidency: Eisenhower as Leader* (Baltimore, MD, 1982); Gary A. Donaldson, *When America Liked Ike: How Moderates Won the 1952 Election and Reshaped American Politics* (Lanham, MD, 2017); and John Robert Greene, *I Like Ike: The Presidential Election of 1952* (Lawrence, KS, 2017). Irwin Gellman, *The Campaign of the Century: Kennedy, Nixon, and the Election of 1960* (New Haven, CT, 2021) is an insightful treatment of Kennedy's victory in 1960. Rick Perlstein, *Before the Storm: Barry Goldwater and the Unmaking of the American Consensus* (New York, 2002) is a fast-paced, entertaining, and insightful account of Goldwater's rise and fall. Nancy Beck Young, *Two Suns of the Southwest: Lyndon Johnson, Barry Goldwater, and the 1964 Battle between Liberalism and Conservatism* (Lawrence, KS, 2019) is also a valuable account of the 1964 election. Wendy Wall, *Inventing the American Way: The Politics of Consensus from the New Deal to the Civil Rights Movement* (New York, 2008); Elaine Tyler May, *Homeward Bound: American Families in the Cold War* (New York, 2000); Lizbeth Cohen, *A Consumers' Republic: The Politics of Mass Consumption in Postwar America* (New York, 2003); Kenneth Jackson, *Crabgrass Frontier: The Suburbanization of the United States* (New York, 1985); Lisa McGirr, *Suburban Warriors: The Origins of the New American Right* (Princeton, NJ, 2001); Thomas J. Sugrue, *The Origins of the Urban Crisis: Race and Inequality in Postwar Detroit* (Princeton, NJ, 1996); and Donald T. Critchlow, *Phyllis Schlafly and Grassroots Conservatism: A Woman's Crusade* (Princeton, NJ, 2005) are especially useful in understanding American society and culture in the 1950s and early 1960s.

Scholarship on the 1960s has long been a cottage industry. I have relied heavily on Robert Dallek, *Flawed Giant: Lyndon B. Johnson and His Times, 1961–1973* (New York, 1998); Robert A. Caro, *The Years of Lyndon Johnson: The Passage of Power* (New York, 2012); Doris Kearns, *Lyndon Johnson and the American Dream* (New York, 1976); Eric Goldman, *The Tragedy of Lyndon Johnson* (New York, 1969); and Lyndon Baines Johnson, *The Vantage Point, 1961–1969* (New York, 1971) to understand Johnson and his presidency. The war that destroyed Johnson's presidency continues to attract historians' attention. George Herring's classic study, now in its sixth edition, *America's Longest War: The United States and Vietnam, 1950–1975* (New York, 2019) is still the best one-volume treatment, although it can be supplemented with Stanley Karnow, *The Vietnam War: A History* (New York, 1997); Andrew Hunt, *Lyndon Johnson's War: America's Cold War Crusade in Vietnam* (New York, 1997); and Christian G. Appy, *Patriots: The Vietnam War Remembered from All Sides* (New York, 2003) and *American Reckoning: The Vietnam War and Our National Identity* (New York, 2015). On civil rights, see David Garrow, *Bearing the Cross: Martin Luther King, Jr. and the Southern Christian Leadership Conference* (New York, 1986), which is indispensable, and also Kevin Boyle, *The Shattering: America in the 1960s* (New York, 2021); Glenn T. Eskew, *But for Birmingham: The Local and National Movements in the Civil Rights Struggle* (Chapel Hill, NC, 1997); Hugh Davis Graham, *The Civil Rights Era: Origins and Development of National Policy, 1960–1972* (New York, 1990); Wesley Hogan, *One Heart, Many Minds: SNCC's Dream for a New America* (Chapel Hill, NC, 2007); Taylor Branch's trilogy on America in the King Years, *Parting the Waters* (New York, 1988), *Pillar of Fire* (New York, 1999), and *At Canaan's Edge* (New York, 2006); Daniel Geary, *Beyond Civil Rights: The Moynihan Report and Its Legacy* (Philadelphia, PA, 2015); and John Lewis and Michael D'Orso, *Walking with the Wind: A Civil Rights Memoir* (New York, 1998). Donald G. Nieman, *Promises to Keep: African Americans and the Constitutional Order, 1776–Present* (New York, 2020; 2nd ed.) and its extensive bibliography are also useful. The kaleidoscope of social changes during the pivotal decade of the 1960s is treated in Terry H. Anderson, *The Movement and the Sixties: Protest in America from Greensboro to Wounded Knee* (New York, 1995); Robert O. Self, *All in the Family: The Realignment of American Democracy in the 1960s* (New York, 2012); Ruth Rosen, *The World Split Open: How the Modern Women's Movement Changed America* (New York, 2000); David Farber, *Chicago '68* (Chicago, IL, 1988); Matthew D. Lassiter, *The Silent Majority: Suburban Politics in the Sunbelt South* (Princeton, NJ, 2006); and Dan T. Carter, *The Politics of Rage: George Wallace, The Origins of the New Conservatism, and the Transformation of American Politics* (New York, 1995).

Richard Nixon was a pivotal figure in postwar politics. I have relied heavily on Stephen E. Ambrose's magnificent three-volume biography, especially *Nixon: The Triumph of a Politician, 1962–1972* (New York, 1989) and *Nixon: Ruin and Recovery, 1973–1990* (New York, 1991). Melvin Small, *The Presidency of Richard Nixon* (Lawrence, KS, 1999); Jeffrey P. Kimball, *Nixon's Vietnam War* (Lawrence, KS, 1998); and Richard P. Nathan, *The Plot that Failed: Nixon and the Administrative Presidency* (New York, 1975) are well researched and insightful. Stanley I. Kutler, *The Wars of Watergate: Richard Nixon's Last Crisis* (New York, 1990) is the best treatment of Watergate, although Michael Dobbs, *King Richard* (New York, 2021) and Keith Olson, *Watergate* (Lawrence, KS, 2016) are also useful.

There is a growing literature on American politics and society in the 1970s. Douglas Brinkley, *Gerald Ford* (New York, 2007); Richard Norton Smith, *An Ordinary Man: The Surprising Life and Historic Presidency of Gerald Ford* (New York, 2023); Burton I. Kaufman and Scott Kaufman, *The Presidency of James Earl Carter, Jr.* (Lawrence, KS, 2006; 2nd ed., rev.); and Laura Kalman, *Right Star Rising: A New Politics, 1974–1980* (New York, 2010) provide important analyses of 1970s politics. The wrenching social and economic changes of the 1970s are explored in Bruce Schulman, *The Seventies: The Great Shift in American Culture, Society, and Politics* (New York, 2001); Judith Stein, *Pivotal Decade: How the United States Traded Factories for Finance in the Seventies* (New Haven, CT, 2010); Meg Jacobs, *Panic at the Pump: The Energy Crisis and the Transformation of American Politics in the 1970s* (New York, 2017); Jefferson Cowie, *Stayin' Alive: The 1970s and the Last Days of the Working Class* (New York, 2010). The emergence of politically engaged religious and social conservatives in the 1970s and the populist sense of moral outrage they injected into political discourse are a big part of the story of our polarized politics. Leigh Ann Wheeler, *How Sex Became a Civil Liberty* (New York, 2013) is a brilliant treatment of the creation of constitutional rights social conservatives found abhorrent. The new conservatism itself is the subject of Marjorie J. Spruill, *Divided We Stand: The Battle over Women's Rights and Family Values that Polarized American Politics* (New York, 2017); Frances Fitzgerald, *The Evangelicals* (New York, 2017); Daniel K. Williams, *God's Own Party: The Making of the Christian Right* (New York, 2010); William Martin,

*With God on Our Side: The Rise of the Religious Right in America* (New York, 1996); Dominic Sandbrook, *Mad as Hell: The Crisis of the 1970s and the Rise of the Populist Right* (New York, 2011); Matthew Frye Jacobson, *Roots Too: White Ethnic Revival in Post-Civil Rights America* (Cambridge, MA, 2006); Donald G. Mathews and Jane Sharon DeHart, *Sex, Gender, and the Politics of ERA: A State and the Nation* (New York, 1990); Thomas B. Edsall, *Chain Reaction: The Impact of Race, Rights, and Taxes on American Politics* (New York, 1992); Richard A. Viguerie and David Franke, *America's Right Turn: How Conservatives Used New and Alternative Media to Take Power* (Chicago, IL, 2004). For the role of private wealth and new conservative think tanks in the 1970s and beyond, see Jane Mayer, *Dark Money* (New York, 2016); Nancy MacLean, *Democracy in Chains: The Deep History of the Radical Right's Stealth Plan for America* (New York, 2017); Jason Stahl, *Right Moves: The Conservative Think Tank in American Political Culture* (Chapel Hill, NC, 2016); and Steven M. Teles, *The Rise of the Conservative Legal Movement* (Princeton, NJ, 2008).

Ronald Reagan's election in 1980 was an important turning point in American politics and has generated a growing body of scholarship. On Reagan's victory, see Craig Shirley, *Reagan Rising: The Decisive Years, 1976–1980* (New York, 2017); Kiron Skinner, Annelise Anderson, and Martin Anderson, *Reagan's Path to Victory: The Shaping of Ronald Reagan's Vision* (New York, 2004); and Andrew E. Busch, *Reagan's Victory: The Presidential Election of 1980 and the Rise of the Right* (Lawrence, KS, 2005). Good analyses of Reagan's presidency can be found in Doug Rossinow, *The Reagan Era: A History of the 1980s* (New York, 2015); H. W. Brands, *Reagan: The Life* (New York, 2015); James Mann, *The Rebellion of Ronald Reagan: A History of the End of the Cold War* (New York, 2009); Chris Matthews, *Tip and the Gipper: When Politics Worked* (New York, 2013); and W. Elliot Brownlee and Hugh Davis Graham, ed., *The Reagan Presidency: Pragmatic Conservatism and Its Legacy* (Lawrence, KS, 2003).

The U.S. experienced an economic transformation in the late twentieth century that had profound effects on Americans and upended the nation's politics. While that history has yet to be written, important sources of data include Thomas Piketty, "Brahmin Left versus Merchant Right: Rising Inequality and the Changing Structure of Political Conflict (Evidence from France, Britain, and the U.S., 1948–2017," WID.world Working Paper Series No. 2017/18 https://wid.world/document/brahmin-left-versus-merchant-right-changing-political-cleavages-in-21-western-democracies-1948-2020-world-inequality-lab-wp-2021-15/; Moritz Kuhn, Moritz Schularick, and Ulrike I. Steins, "Income and Wealth Inequality in America, 1949–2016," Opportunity & Inclusive Growth Institute, Federal Reserve Bank of Minneapolis, Institute Working Paper 9 (June 2018) https://www.minneapolisfed.org/

research/institute-working-papers/income-and-wealth-inequality-in-america-1949-2016; and Thomas Piketty and Emmanuel Saez, "Inequality in the Long Run," *Science*, 344 (23 May 2014), 838–43 https://www.jstor.org/stable/24743922. Important analyses of economic change and its consequences include Jacob Hacker, *The Great Risk Shift: The New Economic Insecurity and the Decline of the American Dream* (2nd ed; New York, 2019); Jacob Hacker and Paul Pierson, *Winner Take-All Politics: How Washington Made the Rich Richer and Turned Its Back on the Middle Class* (New York, 2010); Kevin Phillips, *The Politics of Rich and Poor: Wealth and the American Electorate in the Reagan Aftermath* (New York, 1989); Joseph E. Stiglitz, *The Roaring Nineties: A New History of the World's Most Prosperous Decade* (New York, 2003); Alfred E. Eckes, Jr. and Thomas W. Zeiler, *Globalization and the American Century* (Cambridge, UK, 2003); Nelson Lichtenstein, *The Retail Revolution: How Wal-Mart Created a Brave New World of Business* (New York, 2010); Carl Benedict Frey, *The Technology Trap: Capital, Labor, and Power in the Age of Automation* (Princeton, NJ, 2019); Robert Kuttner, *The Squandering of America: How the Failure of Our Politics Undermines Our Prosperity* ( New York, 2007); and Robert Zieger, *American Workers, American Unions: The 20th and Early 21st Centuries* (4th ed.; Baltimore, MD, 2014).

Since Richard Nixon's 1968 presidential campaign, White politicians have exploited the intertwined issues of crime and race. Matthew Lassiter, *The Suburban Crisis and the War on Drugs* (Princeton, NJ, 2023) and Elizabeth Hinton, *From the War on Poverty to the War on Crime: The Making of Mass Incarceration in America* (Cambridge, MA, 2016) illuminate the origins of the obsession with crime and its impact on politics and policy, although Hinton's effort to locate its origins in the Johnson administration is strained. The consequences of the wars on crime and drugs for African-Americans were devastating. A number of books explore them, including Michelle Alexander, *The New Jim Crow* (New York, 2010); Nieman, *Promises to Keep*, mentioned earlier; Ta-Nehisi Coates, *Between the World and Me* (New York, 2015); and Erwin Chemerinsky, *Presumed Guilty: How the Supreme Court Empowered the Police and Subverted Civil Rights* (New York, 2021). James Foreman, *Locking Up Our Own* (New York, 2017) is indispensable.

Political realignments, culture wars, economic change, and the end of the Cold War intensified partisan battles in Washington during the late 1980s and the 1990s. The way these changes played out in the 1988 presidential campaign is illuminated in John J. Pitney, Jr., *After Reagan: Bush, Dukakis, and the 1988 Election* (Lawrence, KS, 2020) and Robert L. Fleeger, *Brutal Campaign: How the 1988 Election Set the Stage for 21st Century American Politics* (Chapel Hill, NC, 2023). Other valuable treatments of the scorched-earth politics of the 1980s and 1990s include Julian Zelizer, *Burning Down the House: Newt Gingrich and the Rise of the New Republican Party* (New York, 2020); Ethan Bronner, *Battle for Justice: How the Bork Nomination Shook America* (New York, 1989); David Brock, *Blinded by the Right: The Conscience of an Ex-Conservative* (New York, 2002); Nicole Hemmer, *The Partisans: The Conservative Revolutionaries Who Remade American Politics in the 1990s* (New York, 2022); Andrew Hartman, *A War for the Soul of America: A History of the Culture Wars* (2nd ed.; Chicago, IL, 2019); and Sean M. Theriault, *The Gingrich Senators* (New York, 2013). Kathleen Belew, *Bring the War Home: The White Power Movement and Paramilitary America* (Cambridge, MA, 2018) is essential to understand the many groups that believed violent resistance to the state was necessary to preserve a White Christian nation.

A media environment that had changed dramatically drove heightened partisanship toward polarization. Books that tell this important story include Nicole Hemmer, *Messengers of the Right: Conservative Media and the Transformation of American Politics* (Philadelphia, PA, 2016); Kathryn Cramer Brownell, *24/7 Politics: Cable Television and Fragmenting of America from Watergate to Fox News* (Princeton, NJ, 2023); Gabriel Sherman, *The Loudest Voice in the Room: How the Brilliant, Bombastic Roger Ailes Built Fox News and Divided a Country* (New York, 2014); Markus Prior, *Post-Broadcast Democracy: How Media Choice Increases Inequality in Political Involvement and Polarizes Elections* (Cambridge, UK, 2007); and Brian Rosenwald, *Talk Radio's America: How an Industry Took Over a Political Party that Took Over the United States* (Cambridge, MA, 2019).

Bush and the man who defeated him in 1992, Bill Clinton, navigated these treacherous political waters. On Bush's presidency, see John Robert Greene, *The Presidency of George H.W. Bush* (2nd ed.; Lawrence, KS, 2015); Peter Baker and Susan Glasser, *The Man Who Ran Washington: The Life and Times of James A. Baker III* (New York, 2020); and Jeffrey A. Engel, *When the World Seemed New: George H.W. Bush and the End of the Cold War* (New York, 2017). As a New Democrat, Clinton tacked to the center, accepting a smaller role for government, embracing market solutions to problems, and emphasizing the need for greater personal responsibility. Al From, one of the founders of the Democratic Leadership Council, explores the origins of these changes in *The New Democrats and the Return to Power* (New York, 2014). Lily Geismer, *Don't Blame Us: Suburban Liberals and the Transformation of the Democratic Party* (Princeton, NJ, 2015) finds the roots of the shift in the growing influence of White suburban professionals in the party. On Clinton's elections and presidency, see Michael Nelson, *Clinton's Elections: 1992, 1996, and a New Era of Governance* (Lawrence, KS, 2020); Patrick J. Maney, *Bill Clinton: The New Gilded Age President* (Lawrence, KS, 2016); Lily Geismer, *Left Behind: The Democrats' Failed Attempt to Solve Inequality* (New York, 2022); Nelson

Lichtenstein and Judith Stein, *A Fabulous Failure: Bill Clinton and the Transformation of American Capitalism* (Princeton, NJ, 2023); Steven M. Gillon, *The Pact: Bill Clinton, Newt Gingrich, and the Rivalry that Defined a Generation* (New York, 2008); Ron Haskins, *Work over Welfare: The Inside Story of the 1996 Welfare Reform Law* (Washington, DC, 2006); John F. Harris, *The Survivor: Bill Clinton in the White House* (New York, 2005); and Bill Clinton, *My Life* (New York, 2004).

James W. Caesar and Andrew E. Busch, *The Perfect Tie: The True Story of the 2000 Election* (Lanham, MD, 2001) is a useful study of the 2000 presidential campaign. Charles L. Zelden, *Bush v. Gore: Exposing the Growing Crisis in American Democracy* (3rd ed.; Lawrence, KS, 2020) is the best among the many books written on the epic Supreme Court case that determined the outcome. For Bush's presidency, see John Robert Greene, *The Presidency of George W. Bush* (Lawrence, KS, 2021); Donald R. Kelly and Todd G. Shields, *Taking the Measure: The Presidency of George W. Bush* (College Station, TX, 2013); Julian Zelizer, ed., *The Presidency of George W. Bush: A First Historical Assessment* (Princeton, NJ, 2010); Stephen Griffin, *Long Wars and the Constitution* (Cambridge, MA, 2013); Jane Mayer, *The Dark Side: The Inside Story of How the War on Terror Turned into a War on America's Ideals* (New York, 2009); Chris Edelson, *Power without Constraint: The Post-9/11 Presidency and National Security* (Madison, WI, 2016); Melvin P. Leffler, *Confronting Saddam Hussein: George W. Bush and the Invasion of Iraq* (New York, 2023). Larry J. Sabato, *Divided States of America: The Slash and Burn Politics of the 2004 Presidential Election* (New York, 2006) and James W. Caesar and Andrew E. Busch, *Red over Blue: The 2004 Elections and American Politics* (Lanham, MD, 2005) are good first-impression accounts of Bush's successful bid for reelection. Sarah Coleman, *The Walls Within: The Politics of Immigration in Modern America* (Princeton, NJ, 2021); Adam Goodman, *The Deportation Machine: America's Long History of Expelling Immigrants* (Princeton, NJ, 2020); and Jerry Kammer, *Losing Control: How a Left-Right Coalition Blocked Immigration Reform and Provoked the Backlash that Elected Trump* (Washington, DC, 2020) provide important background on immigration policy and the political standoff over reforming immigration law. The best book on the financial crisis of 2008 and the administration's response is Andrew Ross Sorkin, *Too Big to Fail: The Inside Story of How Washington and Wall Street Fought to Save the Financial System and Themselves* (New York, 2009).

David Garrow's magisterial *Rising Star: The Making of Barack Obama* (New York, 2017) is essential to understand the man and his meteoric rise. The final chapter offers an astute analysis of his presidency. Essential, too, is Obama's memoir, *Promised Land* (New York, 2020), which covers his early years and his first term as president; Thomas Sugrue, *Not Even Past: Barack Obama and the Burden of Race* (Princeton, NJ, 2010); and Claude A. Clegg, III, *The Black President: Hope and Fury in the Age of Obama* (Baltimore, MD, 2021). Good early treatments of the 2008 election include Dan Balz and Haynes Johnson, *The Battle for America: The Story of an Extraordinary Election* (New York, 2010); Kate Kenski, Bruce W. Hardy, and Kathleen Hall Jamieson, *The Obama Victory: How Media, Money, and Message Shaped the 2008 Election* (New York, 2010); and John Heilemann and Mark Halperin, *Game Change: Obama and the Clintons, McCain and Palin, and the Race of a Lifetime* (New York, 2010). For Obama's presidency, see Burton I. Kaufman, *Barack Obama: Conservative, Pragmatist, Progressive* (Ithaca, NY, 2021); Julian E. Zelizer, ed., *The Presidency of Barack Obama: A First Historical Assessment* (Princeton, NJ, 2018); Alan S. Blinder, *When the Music Stopped: The Financial Crisis, the Response, and the Work Ahead* (New York, 2013); Staff of the Washington Post, *Landmark: The Inside Story of America's New Health-Care Law and What It Means for All of Us* (New York, 2010). The rise of the Tea Party is treated in Theda Skocpol and Vanessa Williamson, *The Tea Party and the Remaking of Republican Conservatism* (New York, 2012); Theda Skocpol and Caroline Tervo, eds., *Upending American Politics: Polarizing Parties, Ideological Elites, and Citizen Activists from the Tea Party to the Anti-Trump Resistance* (New York, 2020); and Christopher S. Parker and Matt A. Barreto, *Change They Can't Believe In: The Tea Party and Reactionary Politics in America* (Princeton, NJ, 2013). The role of gerrymandering in polarization is illuminated in David Daley, *RatF\*\*ked: Why Your Vote Doesn't Count* (New York, 2016) and Alex Keena, Michael Lattner, Anthony J. McGann, and Charles Anthony Smith, *Gerrymandering the States: Partisanship, Race, and the Transformation of American Federalism* (New York, 2018). The Republican campaign to block Obama's agenda is examined in Thomas E. Mann and Norman Ornstein, *It's Even Worse than It Looks: How the American Constitutional System Collided with the New Politics of Extremism* (New York, 2012); Robert Draper, *When the Tea Party Came to Town* (New York, 2012); and Alec MacGillis, *The Cynic: The Political Education of Mitch McConnell* (New York, 2014).

American politics had become polarized and bitterly divided by the time Donald Trump announced his campaign for the presidency in 2015. With a showman's instinct for what his audience wanted, he understood the grievances, exploited the divisions, won the presidency, and transformed the Republican Party and American politics. Alan Abramowitz, *The Great Alignment: Race, Party Transformation, and the Rise of Donald Trump* (New Haven, CT, 2018); Jeremy W. Peters, *Insurgency: How Republicans Lost Their Party and Got Everything They Wanted* (New York, 2022); Dana Milbank, *The Destructionists: The Twenty-five Year Crack-Up of the Republican Party* (New York, 2022); and Maggie Haberman, *Confidence Man: The Making of Donald Trump and the Unmaking of America* (New York, 2022) are essential to understanding Trump and the political culture that he exploited to become president. The best analysis of Trump's victory in 2016 is John Sides, Michael Tesler, and Lynn Vavreck, *Identity Crisis: The 2016 Presidential Election and the Battle for the Meaning of America* (Princeton, NJ, 2018). Also useful are Jonathan Allen and Amie Parnes, *Shattered: Inside Hillary Clinton's Doomed Campaign* (New York, 2017); Larry J. Sabato, Kyle Kondik, and Geoffrey Skelley, eds., *Trumped: The 2016 Election that Broke All the Rules* (Lanham, MD, 2017); and The Editors of the Washington Post, *The Mueller Report Presented with Related Materials by the Washington Post* (New York, 2019). For Trump's chaotic presidency, see Haberman, *Confidence Man*; Julian Zelizer, ed., *The Donald J. Trump Presidency: The First Historical Appraisal* (Princeton, NJ, 2022); Jonathan Cohn, *The Ten-Year War: Obamacare and the Unfinished Crusade for Universal Coverage* (New York, 2021).

The 2020 election and its aftermath have generated considerable attention. John Sides, Michael Tesler, and Lynn Vavreck, *The Bitter End: The 2020 Presidential Campaign and the Challenge to American Democracy* (Princeton, NJ, 2022) provides a good analysis of why Biden won. Larry Sabato et al., eds., *A Return to Normalcy: The 2020 Election that (Almost) Broke America* (Lanham, MD, 2021) and Michael C. Bender, *Frankly We Did Win This Election: The Inside Story of How Trump Lost* (New York, 2021) are also useful. The New York Times, *The January 6 Report: Findings from the Select Committee to Investigate the Attack on the U.S. Capitol with Reporting, Analysis, and Visuals* (New York, 2022) provides a treasure trove of information on the conspiracy to overturn the election. Among the many books written about the insurrection and Trump's role in it, Michael Wolff, *Landslide: The Final Days of the Trump Presidency* (New York, 2021); Robert Draper, *Weapons of Mass Delusion: When the Republican Party Lost Its Mind* (New York, 2022); Mark Bowden and Matthew Teague, *The Steal: The Attempt to Overturn the 2020 Election and the People Who Stopped It* (New York, 2022); and Bob Woodward and Robert Cos, *Peril* (New York, 2021) are valuable.

# INDEX

9–11 terrorist attack
   attack 225
   Congress authorizes use of force 226
   President Bush's response 225–27
   public response 226–27
*60 Minutes* 184

abortion
   *Dobbs v. Jackson Women's Health Organization*
      decided 396
      sparks political mobilization 396
   evangelical opposition to 107–8
   Kansas referendum (2022) 396
   National Right to Life Committee 106
   pro-life movement 106–9
   public opinion (1970s) 108
   *Roe v. Wade*
      decided 79, 106
      overturned 396
      state laws and 106
Acosta, Jim 355
affirmative action
   Clinton defends 212–13
   conservatives oppose 111–13
   Lyndon Johnson and 39–40
   *Regents of the University of California v. Bakke* 112
   Republicans oppose 212–13
   Reverse discrimination charged 113
   Richard Nixon and 77–78
   Proposition 209 213–14

Affordable Care Act 283–88, 307–8, 347–50
African Americans
   civil rights movement, 6–7
   crack epidemic and 151–52
   disfranchised for felony convictions 156
   economic status of 6, 150–51
   families 39–40
   Great Migration 5
   Growth of Black middle class 150–51
   mass incarceration 154–56
   Moynihan Report 39–40
   policing and 8, 38–39, 56–57, 60, 154, 318–23, 365–66
   segregation 5, 151
   Trump gains support among 371
   unemployment 6, 151
   urban uprisings 8, 38–39, 56–57, 60
Agnew, Spiro 90
Aid to Families with Dependent Children
   Clinton ends 209–13
   conservatives criticize 113, 209–10
   Great Society expands 31
   liberals criticize 209–10
   public opinion and 113
   replaced by Temporary Assistance to Needy Families 211–13
   Richard Nixon and 79–81
   welfare reform assessed 212–13
Ailes, Roger 64
Al Qaida 225, 241–43
Alaska Lands Act (1980) 102

## Index

Alexander, Peter 355
American Independent Party 59–60
American Principles Project 306
American Rescue and Recovery Plan 391
American Rescue and Reinvestment Act 276–79
*American Spectator* 197
Anderson, John 123
anti-communism
  Barry Goldwater and 20–25
  Dwight Eisenhower and 17–18
  JFK and 3–4
  LBJ and 4, 35–37, 56
  Richard Nixon and 71–74, 84–85
  Ronald Reagan and 130, 138–41
Anti-Drug Abuse Act (1986) 153–54
Antrim County, MI
  controversy over voting machines 374–75
  presidential election (2020) in 373–74
Atwater, Lee 161–62
Ayers, Bill 268

Baird, Zoe 191
Baker, James A., III 132
Barr, William 377
Bayh, Birch 124
Beatles, The 15, 23, 54–55
Bezos, Jeff 234
Biden, Joe
  American Rescue and Recovery Plan 391
  background 387–88
  bi-partisan success 393–95
  Build Back Better Act 392
  Chips and Science Act 394–95
  COVID-19 policies 389–90
  declares candidacy for president (2019) 368
  gun control legislation 395
  immigration policy 390–91
  infrastructure bill 393–94
  presidential campaign (2020) 369–72
  public approval 392
  role in budget compromise (2011) 296–97
  role in stimulus plan (2009) 278
  voting rights legislation fails 393
  wins Democratic nomination (2020) 368–69
Black Lives Matter 320–21
Blackmun, Harry 77
Blake, Jacob 367
Blue Lives Matter 321–22
Boehner, John 279, 289, 303, 306–7, 309, 333
Bolduc, Don 401
Bork, Robert 89, 112–13, 166–67
Bowers, Rusty 378
Bozell, Brent 273
Brademas, John 81
Bremmer, Arthur 89
Brock, David 195–96
Brooke, Edward 50
Brown, Michael 320
Brown, Scott 285
Bryant, Anita 110
Buchanan, Patrick 81, 228
Buckley, William 20
Build Back Better Act (2022) 392
Burger, Warren 76–77
Bush, George H.W.
  Americans with Disabilities Act 166
  background 163, 165
  Clean Air Act (1990) 166
  climate change 314
  cultural issues 161–64, 172–76
  Eastern Europe 176–77
  election of 1992 177–79
  end of Cold War 176–77
  inaugural address 165
  Iraq war 177–78
  public approval 178–79
  recession in 1991 178–79
  Soviet Union 177
  tax increase (1990) 171–72
  "Willie" Horton ad 161–63
Bush, George W.
  alienates Republican right 254
  asserts unitary executive authority 241–42
  authorizes torture 242–43

## Index

bi-partisanship 233–34, 237–40, 255–56
combats AIDS in Africa 240, 253
education reform 237–38
faces recession in 2001 234–35
Florida recount (2000) 230–31
Hurricane Katrina 252–53
inaugural address (2001) 233–34
Iraq War 243–46, 251–52
Medicare expansion 238–40
Operation Stellar Wind 242
presidency assessed 261–63
presidential candidate (2000) 227–31
public approval ratings 227, 246
re-elected (2004) 247–50
rejects climate change 315
response to 9-11 attack 225–27, 241–46
response to Great Recession 258–60
selects cabinet 234
Social Security reform fails 240–41, 253
supports Sarbanes-Oxley Act 236
Supreme Court appointments 253–54
tax cut (2001) 236–37
War on Terror 241–46
Bush, Jeb 324
*Bush v. Gore* 230
busing 76, 110–11
Buttigieg, Pete 369

Califano, Joseph 101
campaign finance 117
Campbell, Carol 132
Carmichael, Stokely 39, 44–45
Carson, Ben 324
Carswell, Harold 77
Carter, Jimmy
  anti-inflation policies 104–5
  early life 94
  elected president 94–95
  energy policy 99–100
  environmental policy 102
  healthcare policy 101
  Iranian hostage crisis 103
  loses presidency (1980) 122–24
  presidential style 99
  supports Martin Luther King, Jr. holiday 127
  welfare reform 101–2
Catholics
  divide evenly in 2000 election 230
  majority supports Bill Clinton 215
  majority supports Obama 274, 301
  opposition to abortion among 106–9
  opposition to Equal Rights Amendment among 104–6
  opposition to feminism 98, 104, 106
  Richard Nixon appeals to 81–82
Cato Institute 121
Chapman, Tracy 405
Charlottesville, VA demonstration 341–42
Cheney, Dick 241, 314
Cheney, Liz 389
Chesebro, Kenneth 380, 381
China
  immigration from 134
  Nixon and 72, 74
  nuclear capability 3, 26
  Paris Climate Agreement 316–17
Chips and Science Act (2022) 394–95
*Choice Not an Echo, A* 20
Christie, Chris 324
Church, Frank 124
Cipollone, Pat 375, 384
Civil Rights
  affirmative action 39–40, 77–78, 111–13, 174–75
  Birmingham protests 7
  Dwight Eisenhower and 18
  employment discrimination 77–78, 174–75
  Freedom to Vote Act (2022) 393
  George H.W. Bush and 174–76
  JFK and 7–8
  John Lewis Voting Rights Advancement Act (2022) 393
  LBJ and 8, 33–34, 39–42, 57, 60–61
  March on Washington 7–8
  Mississippi Freedom Summer, 11–12
  Montgomery bus boycott 6–7
  Richard Nixon and 75–78
  Ronald Reagan and 134

Civil Rights (*Continued*)
  school desegregation 75–76, 110–11
  sit-ins 7, 11
  Voting Rights Act 33–34, 134, 393
  White backlash to 8–9, 24, 50, 60
Civil Rights Act of 1964
  adopted 8
  Barry Goldwater and 21
  JFK and 7–8
  LBJ and 8
  protects women's rights 45–46
  Richard Nixon and 73–78
Civil Rights Act of 1968 42, 60–61
Clean Air Act of 1963
  amended in 1965 33, 83
  amended in 1977 102
  amended 1990 166
  basis for Clean Power Plan 316, 351
Clean Water Act
  adopted (1972) 83
  amended (1977) 102
climate change policy 314–18
*Climate Hustle* (movie) 318
Clinton, Bill
  affirmative action 212–13
  budget compromises 205–7, 216–17
  cabinet controversy 191–92
  candidate for president 179–80, 184–86
  centrism 179–80, 187
  Children's Health Insurance Program 217
  climate change 313–14
  communications policy 207–8
  crime policy 189–90
  Democratic Leadership Council 159
  earned income tax credit tripled 212
  fiscal policies 187–88, 205–6
  government shutdown 205–6
  guarantees access to health insurance 215
  healthcare policy fails 192–99
  impeachment, *see* Clinton impeachment
  Israeli-Palestinian negotiations 223
  minimum wage increase 215
  negotiates entitlement reform with Gingrich 216–20
  Oklahoma City bombing 201–5
  Paula Jones allegations 198
  personal attacks on 183–86, 193–99
  public approval 200, 204, 222, 223
  scandals 184, 194–99, 220–23
  special prosecutor investigations 198–99
Clinton, Hillary
  background 183–84
  chairs healthcare taskforce 195
  election of 1992 184–86
  email controversy 327, 330
  personal attacks on 183–86, 194–97
  presidential candidacy 328–32
  presidential primaries (2008) 270
  wins presidential nomination (2016) 326–28
Clinton impeachment
  background 220
  ends entitlement reform 221–22
  fuels polarization 221–23
  House impeaches 222
  Senate acquits 223
  Starr report 221–22
Clyburn, James 369
Coakley, Martha 285
Cold War, end of
  domestic political consequences 181
  in early 1960s 3–4
  George H.W. Bush and 176–77
  Ronald Reagan and 138–41
Cold War consensus 13–14
Collins, Susan 278, 350, 360
Combs, Luke 405
Comey, James 327, 330, 338–40
Common Cause 169
communication, political
  cable TV 147, 167
  changes encourage polarization xxi–xxii, 333–34, 408
  CSPAN 167
  direct mail 117
  Howard Dean 248
  internet 196, 248
  spreads conspiracy theories 196
  talk radio 167
Comprehensive Crime Control Act (1984) 153

Congress of Racial Equality (CORE) 6–7, 44–45
Congressional Black Caucus
   Clinton crime bill 191
   Martin Luther King, Jr. holiday 127
   war on drugs 153, 190
Connerly, Ward 213
*Conscience of a Conservative* 20
Conservatism
   1950s 17
   1960s 18–23
   anti-communism 138–41
   Barry Goldwater and, 20–25
   changes terms of political discussion (1980) 124–25
   evangelicals 103–19
   Freedom Caucus 313, 402
   political action committees 117–19
   populist turn 273
   privatization of Medicare and Social Security 239–40
   supply side economics 131–33
   support from foundations 120–21
   support from think-tanks 120–21
   supports anti-tax movement (1970s) 114–16
   supports deregulation 133–34
   Tea Party 281–83, 291–92, 306
Contras 139
Conway, George 199
Conway, Kellyanne 306
Conyers, John 127–29
Cornyn, John 352
*Cosby Show, The* 151
Couric, Katie 272, 273
COVID-19 pandemic
   Biden administration policies 389–90
   economic stimulus 362–63, 390
   impact 362, 365
   issue in 2020 election 369–70
   origins 361
   partisan conflict over 363–65
   Trump administration response 361–65
   vaccine development 364, 389–90
Cox, Archibald 89
Crane, Ed 121

Crime
   Clinton policies 189–90
   concern about 9
   Democrats adopt anti-crime stance 153–55, 189–90
   LBJ and 57, 60–61
   Richard Nixon and law and order 63–65
   Reagan policies 152–53
Cronkite, Walter 59
Cruz, Ted 307–8, 324–25
Cuban Missile Crisis 3
Cuccinelli, Ken 375
culture wars
   abortion 172, 247, 396–98
   affirmative action 174–75
   American Principles Project 306–7
   attacks on the Clintons 186
   climate change 314–18
   crime 189–90
   drugs 172–73
   evangelicals and 103–13
   "family values" 173
   flag burning 172
   George H.W. Bush and 161–65, 172–76
   George W. Bush and 246–48
   gun control 309–11
   homosexuality 109–10, 246–47
   Pledge of allegiance 162
   race and 318–23
   Richard Nixon and 63–65, 69–71, 75–77, 81–82
   Ronald Reagan and 122, 127–29, 134
   Trump exploits 331–32
Culver, John 119, 124

Daley, Richard J. 61
De Lay, Tom 222
De Parno, Matthew 374
Dean, Howard 248
debt ceiling debates 297–98, 307–8
DeMint, Jim 281
Democratic Leadership Conference, *see* New Democrats

Democratic Party
  abortion 108–9
  Convention (1968) 61
  early 1960s 16
  New Democrats 158–59, 179–80
  response to Ronald Reagan 158–59
  shifts right 158–59, 163–65, 179–80
  war on drugs 153
Dent, Harry 70
deregulation
  Gerald Ford and 133
  Jimmy Carter and 133
  Ronald Reagan and 133–34
DeSantis, Ron 403
Dimon, Jamie 258
Dirksen, Everett 44
*Dobbs v. Jackson Women's Health Organization* 396
Dolan, Terry 118–19
Dole, Robert 109, 194, 206
Doors, The 54
Dornan, Robert 98
DREAM Act (Development, Relief, and Education for Alien Minors), *see* immigration
drugs
  cocaine and crack epidemic 151–52
  Ronald Reagan declares war on 152–53
  war on 152–56
Ducey, Doug 378
Dukakis, Michael 161–65
Dylan, Bob 14

Eagleton, Thomas 86
Earth Day 82
Eastman, John 376, 381
economy, U.S.
  credit cards 148
  decline of manufacturing 114, 142
  dot-com bubble 234–35
  finance 147–48, 258–60
  Great Recession (2008)
    Bush response 258–60
    Economic consequences 260–61
    financial crisis 258–60
  housing bubble 256–58
  political fallout 260–61
  impact of digital technology 146–47
  impact of healthcare 147
  impact of higher education 144–45
  mergers and acquisitions 147–48
  post-industrial transformation 142–50
  post-World War II growth 13–16
  recession in 2001 234–35
  rural communities 143–44
  union membership 142–43
Ehrenreich, Barbara 213
Eisenhower, Dwight
  and civil rights 18
  domestic policies of 17–18
  foreign policy of 18
El Salvador 139
elections, mid-term
  1966 50–51
  1974 90
  1986 156
  1994 199–201
  2006 254
  2010 289–92
  2014 311–12
  2018 353–54
  2022 396–99
elections, presidential
  1960 18–19
  1964 1–2, 20–28
  1968 61–67
  1972 85–87
  1976 94–95
  1980 122–24
  1984 136
  1988 161–65
  1992 178–80
  1996 215–16
  2000 227–33
  2004 248–51
  2008 272–75
  2012 298–99
  2016 324–34
  2020 369–85
    Capitol insurrection 383–85
    Capitol Police attacked 384

Dominion voting machine conspiracy alleged 374–75
electoral vote counted 385
electoral votes challenged 383–85
"fake electors" scheme 379
Justice Department rejects fraud charges 377
lawsuits alleging fraud fail 376–77
Metropolitan Police 384
National Guard intervene 385
Rudolph Giuliani challenges results 374–78, 385
Trump calls supporters to Washington, D.C. 382
Trump pressures Mike Pence to reject Biden electors 380–81, 383
Trump pressures state officials 377–79
Trump speaks at January 6 rally 383
William Barr rejects fraud claims 377
elections, presidential primary
  1960 19
  1964 9, 21
  1968 29, 59
  1972 85
  1976 94
  1988 163–64
  1992 178–79
  2000 221, 227–28
  2004 248
  2008 270–71
  2012 299–303
  2016 324–28
  2020 368–69
  2024 403
Elementary and Secondary Education Act 32
Ellsberg, Daniel 75
Ellwood, David 210
Emanuel, Rahm 277
*Emerging Republican Majority, The* 69–71
Emmer, Tom 402
Energy Crisis (1970s)
  Ford administration response 93–94
  gasoline shortages 91–92
  OPEC oil embargo 91
  stagflation and 92
Enron scandal 235–36
environmental policy
  Biden administration 352, 392
  Carter administration 102
  Clean Air Act 83, 102
  Clean Water Act 83, 102
  Clinton administration 314–15
  Environmental Protection Agency Created 82–83
  George H.W. Bush administration 166, 314, 316
  George W. Bush administration 315
  Johnson administration 33
  National Environmental Policy Act (1970) 82
  Obama administration 315–17
  Richard Nixon and 82–83
  Trump administration 350–53
  Water Quality Act 33
Equal Credit Opportunity Act 79
Equal Employment Opportunity Commission 46, 47, 78
Equal Rights Amendment
  campaign against 104–6
  Congress adopts 79
  defeated 106
  ratification process 97
evangelicals
  oppose abortion 106–9
  oppose Equal Rights Amendment 104–6
  politicized 103–10
  Ronald Reagan and 122–23

Falwell, Jerry
  establishes Moral Majority 119
  opposes abortion 108, 110
  opposes homosexuality 110
  Thomas Road Baptist Church 107–8
  views on women and family 108
Family Assistance Program 80–81
Fannie Mae 257
"Fast Car" (song) 405
Fauci, Anthony 364

Federal Bureau of Investigation (FBI)
  investigates Hillary Clinton emails
    327, 330
  investigates Trump's relations with
    Russia 338–40
Federal Reserve
  anti-inflationary policies (1970s) 104–5;
    (1980s) 134–35
  raises interest rates (1965) 41
*Feminine Mystique, The* 11
feminism
  abortion 79
  childcare 81–82
  credit 79
  employment discrimination 46, 47, 78
  mobilizes against Trump 335–36
  National Women's Conference (1977)
    97–98
  opposition to 98–99
  politics 78–79
  second wave emerges 46–49
  supports Equal Rights Amendment 79
  supports Title IX 79
Fey, Tina 272
finance
  changes in 1970s and 1980s 147–48
  dot-com bubble 234–35
  role in Great Recession (2008) 256–60
Fiorino, Carly 324
Fiske, Robert 199
Fleischer, Ari 305
Flowers, Gennifer 184
Floyd, George
  murder of 365–66
  protests of murder 366
  racial reckoning 366
  Trump attacks protesters 366–67
Flynn, Michael 339
Ford, Gerald
  abortion 109
  appointed vice president 90
  becomes president 90, 92–93
  challenged by Ronald Reagan 94
  defeated in 1976 election 95
  energy crisis 93–94
  pardons Nixon 93

Fortier, Michael 202–3
Foster, Vince 196–97
Fox News 268, 281–82, 287, 322,
    364, 377
Freddie Mac 257
Free Speech Movement (Berkeley) 12
free trade
  Clinton supports 189
  North America Free Trade Agreement
    (NAFTA) 189
Freedom Caucus (House)
  established 313
  ousts McCarthy as speaker 402
Freedom to Vote Act 393
Friedan, Betty 11, 46, 97
Fulbright, J. William 49

Gardner, Cory 341
Garner, Eric 321
Gates, Bill 146
Gates, Henry Louis 318
Geithner, Timothy 258, 277
Genovese, Kitty 9–10
Gephardt, Richard 159, 232, 296
Gingrich, Newt
  attack on Jim Wright 169–71
  attacks Obama 281
  becomes speaker 199–201
  budget negotiations with Clinton
    205–6, 216–17
  Contract with America 199–200
  crime issue 190
  demands balanced budget 171–72,
    205–6
  ethics violations 216–17
  infrastructure policy 341–43
  leads government shutdown 172, 205–6
  named minority whip 171
  negotiates entitlement reform with
    Clinton 216–20
  opposes Bush tax increase 171–72
  partisanship of 167–69
Giuliani, Rudolph 270, 374–76, 378, 385
Goldwater, Barry
  1960 election 18–19
  1964 election 20–27

Gorbachev, Mikhail 141, 176–77
Gore, Al
   Democratic Leadership Conference 159
   Florida recount (2000) 229–31
   presidential candidate (2000) 227, 229
   telecommunications policy 207–8
government, trust in 16, 67, 90–91, 290
Graham, Lindsay 252, 324, 342, 386
grassfire.com 255
Grassley, Charles 119, 284, 288
Gray, Nellie 98, 107
Great Recession (2008), *see* economy, U.S.
Great Society
   announced 23
   programs adopted 30–35, 41–42
   Richard Nixon and 75
   stalled 57–58, 60
*Griggs v. Duke Power* 77–78, 174
Guinier, Lani 191–92
gun control
   assault weapon ban 189–90
   Biden legislation 395–96
   LBJ and 60
   legislation defeated (2013) 309–11
   National Rifle Association 309–10
   Obama proposals fail 310–11
Guy, Sheryl 373–75

Hagelin, John 228
Hale, David 195
Haley, Nikki 403
*Hamilton* (musical) 266
Hannity, Sean 268, 270, 385
Hansberry, Lorraine 5
Harrington, Michael 12
Harris, Kamala 388
Hatch, Orrin 313, 346
Hayden, Casey 47–48
Haynsworth, Clement 77
Head Start 32
healthcare industry
   expansion 1970s–2000s 145–46
   opposes Clinton plan 194
healthcare policy
   access to insurance protected 215
   Carter administration 101
   Children's Health Insurance Program 217
   Clinton administration 192–99
   Great Society 30–31
   Obama administration and 283–88
   Trump administration and 347–50
Helms, Jesse 128
Heritage Foundation 120
higher education
   effect on income inequality 150
   expansion in 1960s 15
   trends 1970s–2000 144–45
Higher Education Act (1965) 32
Hillary Haters 186
Hobbs, Lottie Beth 98, 105–7
Holder, Eric 322–23
Holt, Lester 339
homosexuality
   changing attitudes toward (1970s) 109–10
   "Don't Ask, Don't Tell"
      Clinton adopts 192
      Obama repeals 293
   evangelicals oppose 110
   military service 192, 293
   Miami, Florida referendum 110
Huckabee, Mike 270
Hughes, Howard 88
Humphrey, Hubert 61, 65–67
Hussein, Saddam 177–78

immigration
   anti-immigrant sentiment 137–38, 255–56
   changing nature of 137
   Deferred Action for Childhood Arrivals (DACA)
      Obama announces 313–14
      Supreme Court and 314, 347
      Trump repeals 347
   Development, Relief, and Education for Alien Minors Act (DREAM)
      Democrats introduce 313
      Obama implements 313–14
      Republicans reject 293
   Immigration Act of 1965 32–33

immigration (*Continued*)
  reform adopted (1986)137–38
  reform fails (2007) 254–56; (2013) 308–9
  scale of 254–55
  Trump's policies 343–47
  undocumented immigrants 254–55, 345, 347
Immigration Act of 1965 33
income, distribution of
  1960s 15
  in New Gilded Age 149–50
  role of higher education 150
*Inconvenient Truth, An* (movie) 315
Indivisible 336–37
inflation
  1964 15
  Gerald Ford and 93
  issue in 2022 mid-terns 396
  Jimmy Carter and 102–3
  post-pandemic 392
  Richard Nixon and 83
  Vietnam War and 41
*Info Wars* 382
investigative journalism 91
Iran-Contra Scandal 157
Iranian hostage crisis 103
Iraq wars
  first (1991) 177–78
  second (2003) 243–46, 251–52

Jackson, Jesse 163–64
Jackson State University 73
January 6 Insurrection
  description 382–85
  House Select Committee to Investigate 389
  Republicans reject investigation of 388–89
Jarvis, Howard 115
Jaworski, Leon 89–90
*Jeffersons, The* 150
Jeffords, Jim 234
Jencks, Christopher 210

Jindal, Bobby 324
John Lewis Voting Rights Advancement Act (2021) 393
Johnson, Lyndon B.
  in 1968 election 29–30
  affirmative action 40, 47
  antiwar movement 30–31, 49–51, 54–56
  appoints Kerner Commission 57
  appoints Warren Commission 2–3
  approval ratings 41, 59
  Bretton Woods 57
  civil rights 7
  election (1964) 23–28
  Great Society 23, 30–35, 41–42, 51–52, 57–58, 60
  Howard University speech 40
  liberalism xv
  State of the Union Address
    1965 30–31
    1966 40–41
    1967 51–52
    1968 57
  surtax
    adopted 59
    requested 51–52, 57
  Vietnam War
    commits combat troops 36–37
    expands bombing 52–53
    Gulf of Tonkin resolution 4
    personalizes the war 55–56
    rationale for escalation 36–37, 40–41
    seeks peace negotiations 29, 60, 66
    U.S. troop commitments 36–37
Johnson, Mike 402
Johnson, Ron 379
Jones, Alex 382
Jones, Paula 198

Kasich, John 324–25
Kavanaugh, Brett 356
Kelly, Mike 379
Kemp, Brian 378

Kemp-Roth Bill 116, 131
Kennedy, Edward 101, 237, 239, 255
Kennedy, John F.
  1960 election 19
  assassination 2–3
  civil rights 7
  Cuban Missile Crisis 3
  Vietnam 4
Kennedy, Robert F.
  assassinated 60
  candidate for president 59
  opposes Vietnam War 55
Kennedy-McCain Immigration Bill 255–56
Kenosha, WI 367
Kent State University, 73
Kerner, Otto 57
Kerner Commission 57
Kerry, John 248–51
Keynesianism 130
Keystone XL Pipeline 350–51
Kilmeade, Brian 385
Kimmel, Jimmy 349
King, Coretta Scott 43, 49
King, Martin Luther, Jr.
  assassinated 60
  Birmingham protests, 7
  Chicago campaign 42–44
  King holiday controversy 127–29
  March on Washington 7–8
  Meredith March 44–45
  Montgomery boycott 6–7
  opposes Vietnam War 55
  Poor People's Campaign 60
  voting rights 33–34
King, Mary 47–48
Kinzinger, Adam 389
Kitchel, Denison 21
Klobuchar, Amy 369
Koch, Charles 120–21
Koch Foundation 121
Koresh, David 202
Kristol, William 194
Kyoto Protocol 315

Laffer, Arthur 116, 130
Lamm, Richard 138
law and economics 121
Laxalt, Adam 401
Legal Services Program 32
Lehane, Chris 196
LeMay, Curtis 65
Lewinsky, Monica 220–21
Liberalism
  defined xv
  Great Society 23, 30–35
  healthcare policy 31, 101, 193
  opposition to evangelical conservatives 119
  routed in 1980 Senate elections 124
  tempered by New Democrats 159
Lieberman, Joe 285
Limbaugh, Rush xx, 167, 186, 197, 204, 256, 271, 288, 306
*Lincoln* (movie) 303
Lippman, Walter 35
Livingston, Bob 222
Long, Russell 100
*Losing Ground* 210

Magnuson, Warren 124
Manchin, Joe 309
Mansfield, Mike 34–35, 49
manufacturing
  decline of 114, 142
  shift from in 1950s 15
March for Life 107
*March of the Penguins, The* (movie) 315
Martin, Andy 267, 268
Martin, Trayvon 319
Martin Luther King, Jr. Holiday 127–29
mass incarceration 155–56
Masters, Blake 399, 401
Mastriano, Doug 378, 397
Mazzoli, Romano 138
McCain, John
  challenges "birthers" 269
  equivocates on TARP 259
  Sarah Palin as running mate 271–72

McCain, John (*Continued*)
  supports immigration reform 255–56
  wins Republican nomination (2008) 270–71
McCarthy, Eugene 29, 50, 61
McCarthy, Kevin
  Capitol riot 384
  condemns Trump 386
  conflict with Freedom Caucus 401–2
  opposes Obama agenda 275
  ousted as speaker 401
  reconciles with Trump 389, 399
  rejects investigation of January 6 Insurrection 388
  wins speakership 401
McConnell, Mitch
  becomes Senate majority leader 311
  blocks Garland nomination 329
  budget compromise (2010) 293; (2011) 294–95; (2012) 307
  challenged for Republican leader 401
  condemns Trump 386
  George Floyd murder 366
  opposes stimulus 279
  opposes Trump impeachment 386
  repeal of Affordable Care Act 349–50
  stonewalls Obama 276, 292–93
McDougal, Jim 195
McDougal, Susan 195
McGovern, George 50, 85–86, 124
McKissick, Floyd 45
McVeigh, Timothy 201–3
Meadows, Mark 384
Medicaid
  adopted 31
  Obama expands 284, 286
Medicare
  adopted 31
  Clinton-Gingrich negotiations 216–20
  financial problems 219
  prescription drug coverage 238–40
Meredith, James 44

Middle East
  Bill Clinton and 223
  George H.W. Bush and 177–77
  George W. Bush and 225–27, 241–46
  Iraq invasion 243–46
  Jimmy Carter and 100–1, 122–23
  oil boycott (1973) 91–92
  Ronald Reagan and 139–40
  War on Terror 241–46
militia movement 201–2, 364–65, 372, 382, 384
Milken, Michael 147
Milliken, Roger 21
Mills, Wilbur 52
Modern Republicanism 17
Mondale, Walter 81, 136
Moral Majority 119
Morse, Wayne 49
Moyers, Bill xvi, 28
Moynihan, Daniel P. 39–40, 80–81, 240
Moynihan Report 39–40
Mudd, Roger 30
Mueller, Robert 340
Mueller Investigation 340
Murkowski, Lisa 350
*Murphy Brown* 173
Murray, Charles 210
Muskie, Edmund 88

National Association for the Advancement of Colored People (NAACP) 6, 7, 77, 156
National Endowment for the Arts 33
National Endowment for the Humanities 33
National Organization for Women (NOW) 46–47
*National Review* 20
National Rifle Association 309–10
National Right to Life Committee 106
National Women's Conference (1977) 97–98
National Women's Political Caucus 79
Neighborhood Youth Corps 32

New Democrats
  form Democratic Leadership
    Conference 159
  response to Ronald Reagan 158–59
New Federalism 82
Nicaragua 139
Nichols, Terry 202
*Nickle and Dimed* 213
Nielsen, Kirstjen 356
Nixon, Donald 88
Nixon, Richard
  in 1960 election 18–19
  in 1968 election 63–68
  in 1972 election 85–87
  antiwar movement 72–73
  appoints Gerald Ford vice
    president 90
  China policy 74, 84
  Christmas Bombing 85
  civil rights 75–78
  criticizes Hillary Clinton 184–85
  dirty tricks 87–88
  economic policy 83–84
  Family Assistance Program 80–81
  feminism 79
  gold standard 84
  Goldwater campaign 24
  insecurity 87
  "law and order" 63–65, 73–74
  *Pentagon Papers* 74–75
  resignation 90
  Southern Strategy 63–65, 69–70, 75–77
  Strategic Arms Limitation Treaty 84
  Supreme Court nominations 76–77
  vetoes childcare policy 81–82
  Vietnam policy
    in 1968 election 66
    Cambodian incursions 72–73
    peace negotiations 84–85
    Vietnamization 71–72
  Watergate 87–90
    appoints special prosecutors 89
    break-in 88
    cover-up 88–89
    creates White House Special
      Investigations Unit (Plumbers) 75, 87–88
    impeachment inquiry 89–90
    presidential tape recordings 88–90
    Saturday Night Massacre 89
    Senate Watergate Committee 89
  welfare 79–80
No Child Left Behind 237–38
Noonan, Peggy 273
North American Free Trade Agreement
  (NAFTA), *see* free trade
Nuclear Freeze 140
Nuclear Test Ban Treaty (1963) 3
Nuclear war, fear of 3, 140
Numbers USA 255
Nussbaum, Bernard 197

Oath Keepers 382, 384
Obama, Barack
  Affordable Care Act 283–38
  announces presidential candidacy 266
  attacks on 266–70, 281–83, 289, 318–20
  automobile industry 280
  background 265–66
  budget policy
    attacks Ryan budget 295–96
    compromise with Republicans (2010) 295; (2011) 294–95; (2012) 307
    stimulus plan 297–98
  Bush tax cuts 293–94
  climate policy 314–18
  criminal justice reform 322–23
  criminal sentencing reform 322–24
  Deferred Action for Childhood Arrivals (DACA) 313–14
  "Don't Ask, Don't Tell" 293
  expanded unemployment benefits 293
  gun control 309–11
  housing foreclosures 279–80
  immigration 293, 308–9, 313–14
  Merrick Garland nomination 328–29
  mid-term defeat (2010) 289–90; (2014) 311–12

434 Index

Obama, Barack (*Continued*)
 Ossawatomie Speech (2011) 298–99
 policing reform 322
 public approval 282–83, 300–1, 311
 race issue 318–23
 re-elected (2012) 298–301
 seeks bi-partisan support 277–79, 302–3
 supports TARP 259
 Tea Party opposes 282–83
 uses executive authority 312–24
O'Brien, Larry 88
Occupy Wall Street 297–98
Ochs, Phil 54
"Ohio" (Crosby, Stills, Nash & Young) 73
Oklahoma City bombing 201–4
Olin, John 121
Olin Foundation 121
Olson, Ted 199
O'Neil, Tip 99, 132, 136
Operation Warp Speed 364
O'Reilly, Bill 322
*Other America, The* 12
Oz, Mehemet 401

Palin, Sarah
 background 271
 climate denialism 318
 death panels 288
 populist message 272–73
 vice presidential candidate 271–73
Paperwork Reduction Act (1980) 133–34
Paris Climate Agreement 316–17, 351
Parks, Rosa 6
Patterson, Ann 105
Paulson, Henry 258
Pell Grants 32
Pelosi, Nancy
 Affordable Care Act 284
 January 6 committee 388–89
 strategy in 2018 mid-terms 353
 supports TARP 259
 supports Trump impeachment 358–61
 Trump attacks 361

Pence, Mike
 counts electoral votes 383–85
 demands National Guard be sent to Capitol 385
 threatened by mob 385
 won't reject Biden electoral votes 380, 383
*Pentagon Papers* 74–75
Percy, Charles 50
Perot, Ross 146, 179–80, 216
Perry, Rick 324
Phelan, Richard 169
Phillips, Howard 118
Phillips, Kevin 69–71
polarization
 2008 election and 275–76
 2010 mid-terms deepen 291–92
 2012 election and 301–3
 2014 mid-terms and 311–12
 2016 election and 331–33
 2018 mid-terms and 355–56
 2022 mid-terms and 399–401
 Affordable Care Act and 287–89
 Black Lives Matter and 320–22
 causes of xiv–xxiii, 405–9
 climate change 314–18
 Clinton impeachment 220–23
 Clinton presidency fuels 224
 debt ceiling and 291–92, 307–8
 eases after 2000 233–41
 emergence in 1980s 180–82
 evangelicals and 103–10, 122–23, 125, 249–50
 George W. Bush reignites 247–50
 Great Recession deepens 259–63
 immigration deepens 254–56, 313–14, 343–47
 personal attacks on Clintons 183–86, 193–99
 race and 318–23
 regional division 233, 250, 312
 role of social issues 180–81

Tea Party promotes 281–83,
    291–92, 306
  tipping point 407
police brutality, *see* African Americans,
    Policing and
political action committees, *see* campaign
    finance
populism
  anti-tax movement 115
  contributes to polarization 303–4,
    333–34, 399–401, 407–8
  Sarah Palin embraces 271–73
  Tea Party 281–83, 292–93
  Ted Cruz 307–8
Portland, OR 367
Portman, Rob 346
poverty
  American Rescue and Recovery Plan
    (2021) 391
  discovery of 12–13
  earned income tax credit
    expanded 137
    tripled (1993) 212
  extent of 212–13
  LBJ and 1–2, 23, 30–36
  minimum wage raised 214–15
  *Other America, The* 12
  Richard Nixon and 79–81
  War on Poverty 30–36
Powell, Colin
  Iraq War 244–45
  opposes gays in military 192
presidential elections, *see* elections,
    presidential
presidential primaries, *see* elections,
    presidential primary
Priebus, Reince 305, 385
Pro-Family, Pro-Life Rally (1977) 98–99
Proposition 13 (1978) 115
Proposition 209 213–14
Proud Boys 372, 382, 384

Quayle, Dan 173, 381

Raffensperger, Brad 379–80
*Raisin in the Sun, A* 5

Reagan, Ronald
  abortion 109, 134
  accepts tax increases 135
  air traffic controllers' strike 143
  anti-communist policies 138–41
  approval rating 135
  arms control 140–41
  assassination attempt on 131
  California governor 50
  Central America 139
  challenges Gerald Ford (1976) 94
  declares war on drugs 152–53
  deregulation 133–34
  environmental policy 133–34
  evangelicals 122–23, 134, 158
  Goldwater campaign 26–27
  Iran-Contra Scandal 157
  legacy 157–59
  Martin Luther King, Jr. holiday 127–29
  Middle East 139–40
  re-elected (1984) 136
  Social Security 132, 135–36
  Soviet Union 140–41
  Strategic Defense Initiative (Star Wars)
    140–41
  supports anti-tax movement 116
  supports expanded defense
    spending 131
  supports Kemp-Roth tax bill 131
  tax reform 136–37
  voting rights 134
  Watts uprising 38
  welfare 113, 132
  worldview 129–31
reapportionment 289
Reform Party 228
Rehnquist, William 21, 253
Reid, Harry 285
Republican Party
  abortion 108–9
  affirmative action 213–14
  anti-communism 138–41
  Barry Goldwater and 18, 20–23
  climate change denialism 317–18
  conservative wing 18–19, 20–23, 94,
    281–83, 292–93, 303–4, 313, 402

Republican Party (*Continued*)
  Dwight Eisenhower and 16–18
  *Growth and Opportunity Project* (2013) 305–6
  gun control 189–90, 309–11
  House Freedom Caucus 313, 402
  impeach Bill Clinton 220–23
  labels Obama socialist 281
  leaders stonewall Obama 275–76, 290–91
  mobilizes cultural issues 161–65, 172–75, 180–82, 186
  moderates in 17–18, 21, 50, 67
  Modern Republicanism 17
  Newt Gingrich reorients 167–72, 199–201
  opposes Affordable Care Act 283–84, 287–89
  opposes American Rescue and Recovery Plan 391
  opposes raising debt ceiling 296–97
  opposes stimulus (2009) 278–79
  populist shift 273, 333–34
  primaries chill bi-partisanship 303–4
  Richard Nixon and 18–19, 63–90
  shifts right 199–201
  southern influence 63–65, 69–71, 200
  Tea Party influence 281–83, 292–93, 303–4
  Trump captures 324–26, 360, 399–401
Rice, Condoleeza 240
Richardson, Elliott 89
Roberts, John 253
Roberts, Paul Craig 130
Romney, Mitt
  healthcare policy as governor 285
  presidential campaign (2012) 299–301
  presidential contender (2008) 270
  supports Trump's impeachment 360
Rosenstein, Rod 339, 340
Rubin, Robert 187
Rubio, Marco 308
Ruby Ridge siege 202
Rusher, William 21
Ryan, Paul 293, 295, 348–49, 352

Safire, William 70, 185
Sanders, Bernie 326–28
Santelli, Rick 281
Sarbanes-Oxley Act 236
*Saturday Night Live*
  parodies George W. Bush 246
  parodies Sarah Palin 272
savings & loans (S&Ls)
  crisis of 1980s 147, 149, 156
  deregulated 133
Scaife, Richard Mellon 120, 195
Scalise, Steve 402
Schiff, Adam 356, 361
Schlafly, Phyllis
  Goldwater campaign 20
  leads STOP-ERA 98, 104–6
Schultz, George 78
Schumer, Charles 355, 357–58, 372
Scott, Hugh 70
Scott, Rick 401
segregation
  Chicago 42–44
  Civil Rights Act of 1964 and 8
  factor in urban uprisings 8, 37–38
  housing 5–6, 41–42
  schools 75–76, 110–11
Selma, Alabama 33–34
Sessions, Jeff 256, 306, 339, 346
*Sex and the City* 222
*Shelby County v. Holder* 393
Simpson, Alan 138
Sirica, John 88–90
Smith, Howard 45
Snowe, Olympia 278
social media, *see* communication, political
Social Security
  Clinton-Gingrich negotiations 216–20
  Dwight Eisenhower expands 17
  financial problems 135, 217–18

George W. Bush seeks privatization 24–41, 253
reform (1983) 135–34
Southern Christian Leadership Conference (SCLC) 6–7, 44–45
Specter, Arlen 278
Spock, Benjamin 49
Starr, Kenneth
  appointed special prosecutor 199
  Lewinsky investigation 220–22
  report to Congress 222
"Stop the Steal" 382
STOP-ERA 98
Strategic Defense Initiative (Star Wars) 140–41
Student Non-Violent Coordinating Committee (SNCC) 7, 44–45
Students for a Democratic Society 11–12, 47–49
supply side economics 116, 131–33
Supreme Court, U.S.
  appointments to 76–77, 134, 166–67, 175–76, 253–54, 328–29
  *Bush v. Gore* 230
  climate policy 317
  *Griggs v. Duke Power* 77–78
  *Pentagon Papers* case 75
  pornography and 10
  religion and 10
  school desegregation 110–11
  voting rights 393

taxes
  anti-tax movement of 1970s 114–16
  Bill Clinton raises 188
  George H.W. Bush raises, 171
  George W. Bush cuts 236–37
  LBJ raises 51–52, 58
  Reagan administration 131–37
  Trump administration 352
Taylor, Linda 113
Tea Party 281–83, 291–92, 306
Telecommunications Act (1996) 208–9
Thomas, Clarence 175–76

Thune, John 388
Title IX 79
Toomey, Pat 310
Tripp, Linda 220
Troubled Asset Relief Program (TARP)
  created 259–60
  Democrats blamed for 283
  issue in 2008 election 274
  Obama uses 279–80
Trump, Donald
  *Access Hollywood* tape 330
  announces presidential candidacy (2015) 324–25
  anti-immigrant rhetoric 324–25
  border wall 325, 344–45
  campaign for re-election (2020) 369–72
  condemns Black Lives Matter 322
  conflict with media 338, 355
  COVID response 361–65
  elected president 331–34
  environmental policy 350–52
  fails to repeal Affordable Care Act 347–50
  immigration policy 345–47, 356–57
  impeachment (2019) 358–61
  impeachment (2021) 386–87
  implements Muslim ban 343–44
  inaugural address 337–38
  infrastructure policy 342–43, 357–58
  Presidential campaign 328–34
  proposes Muslim ban 325
  Republican primaries (2016) 324–26
  retains grip on Republican Party 399–401
  seeks Reform Party nomination 228
  seeks to overturn 2020 election 373–85
  spreads "birther" conspiracy 269–70
  suffers defeat in 2018 mid-terms 353–54
  supports white supremacists 340–42
  wins Republican nomination (2024) 403
  withholds Ukraine aid 358
Trump, Donald Jr. 385

Ukraine
  Trump withholds aid 358
  Republicans block aid 402
unemployment
  in 1960s 15
  in 1970s 83, 92–93
  in 1981 recession 134
  African American 6
United Taxpayers Organization 115
Upward Bound 32

Vietnam Moratorium Committee 72
Vietnam War
  in 1964 election 4–5, 28
  in 1968 election 61–68
  anti-war movement 49–50, 53–54
  combat troops committed 36–37
  cost 51
  draft 53, 72
  economic impact of 51, 57–58
  Gulf of Tonkin Resolution 4–5
  LBJ's policy 36–37, 40–41
  origins 4
  Tet Offensive, 30–31, 58–59
  U.S. advisors 4
  U.S. troops committed 36–37, 49, 52, 72
Viguerie, Richard 117
Volker, Paul 103, 134
Voting Rights Act
  adopted 33–34
  amended 134
  John Lewis Voting Rights Advancement Act (2021) fails 393
  Supreme Court weakens 393

Waco siege 202
Walker, Herschel 397, 401
Walker, Scott 324
Wallace, George
  assassination attempt on 85
  presidential candidacy (1968) 59–63, 65–66
  presidential primaries (1964) 9; (1972) 85

War on Poverty
  1964 campaign ad 1–2
  legislation, 3, 23, 32
War on Terror
  Afghanistan 241
  "Black Sites" 242
  Congress authorizes 226
  legal rationale for 241–43
  George W. Bush launches 225–27
  Guantanamo 242
  Operation Stellar Wind 242
  torture 242–43, 246
Warren, Earl 2
Warren Commission 2–3
Water Quality Act of 1965 33
Watergate, *see* Nixon, Richard
Watts uprising 38–39
Weaver, Randy 202
Welfare, *see* Aid to Families with Dependent Children, replaced by Temporary Assistance to Needy Families
Wertheimer, Fred 169
*West Virginia v. EPA* 317
Westmoreland, William 52, 58
Weyrich, Paul 118–19
Whip Inflation Now (WIN) 93
White, Clif 21
White backlash
  and 1966 mid-term elections 50
  George Wallace and 9, 59–63
  Urban uprisings in 1964 and 8
  Watts uprising and 38
Whitewater scandal 195–96
Whitmer, Gretchen 365
Willie Horton ad 161–63
Wilson, Pete 212–13
Women Who Want to be Women (WWWW) 98
Women's March (2017) 335–36
Wonder, Stevie 127
World's Fair (1964) 14

Wright, Jim
　ethics allegations against 169–70
　House Ethics Committee hearings 170
　Resigns as speaker 170–71
Wynette, Tammy 184

youth culture
　counterculture 53–55
　music (1960s) 14–15, 54–55

Zelensky, Volodymyr 358

www.ingramcontent.com/pod-product-compliance
Lightning Source LLC
Chambersburg PA
CBHW022006300426
44117CB00005B/60